Introduction to Container Ship Operations and Onboard Safety

Introduction to Container Ship Operations and Onboard Safety is an introduction for students and professionals involved in the maritime industry.

It provides an overview of the merchant navy from its beginnings to the present day, entry and training requirements, shipboard hierarchy and roles and responsibilities, shipboard safety organisation, inductions and new crew member familiarisation, safe means of access to enclosed spaces, general housekeeping, risk assessment, and risk management. In addition, it examines specific hazardous activities such as cargo loading and unloading, drydocking, drills, and actions to take in the event of an emergency.

This textbook provides a concise overview of core concepts and practices in the maritime industry that is appropriate for the cadet, experienced seafarer, industry professional, and the general maritime enthusiast.

Alexander Arnfinn Olsen is a Senior Learning and Development Consultant for a leading UK maritime and defence consultancy and freelance writer.

The Routledge Companion to Modernity, Space and Gender

The Routledge Companion to Modernity, Space and Gender reframes the discussion of modernity, space and gender by examining how "modernity" has been defined in various cultural contexts of the twentieth and twenty-first centuries, how this definition has been expressed spatially and architecturally, and what effect this has had on women in their everyday lives. In doing so, this volume presents theories and methods for understanding space and gender as they relate to the development of cities, urban space and individual building types (such as housing, work spaces or commercial spaces) in both the creation of and resistance to social transformations and modern global capitalism. The book contains a diverse range of case studies from the US, Europe, the UK, and Asian countries such as China and India, which bring together a multiplicity of approaches to a continuing and common issue and reinforces the need for alternatives to the existing theoretical canon.

Alexandra Staub is an Associate Professor of Architecture and an Affiliate Faculty of the Rock Ethics Institute at the Pennsylvania State University. She has written extensively on how architecture is shaped by cultural demands, most recently in her book *Conflicted Identities: Housing and the Politics of Cultural Representation*, which examines how architecture and space can express divergent identities in any given cultural context. She received a B.A. from Barnard College in New York, her Dip.-Ing. (Arch.) from the University of the Arts in Berlin, Germany, and her Ph.D. from the Brandenburg Technical University in Cottbus, Germany.

The Routledge Companion to Modernity, Space and Gender

Edited by Alexandra Staub

NEW YORK AND LONDON

First published 2018
by Routledge
711 Third Avenue, New York, NY 10017

and by Routledge
2 Park Square, Milton Park, Abingdon, Oxon, OX14 4RN

Routledge is an imprint of the Taylor & Francis Group, an informa business

© 2018 Taylor & Francis

The right of Alexandra Staub to be identified as the author of the editorial material, and of the authors for their individual chapters, has been asserted in accordance with sections 77 and 78 of the Copyright, Designs and Patents Act 1988.

All rights reserved. No part of this book may be reprinted or reproduced or utilised in any form or by any electronic, mechanical, or other means, now known or hereafter invented, including photocopying and recording, or in any information storage or retrieval system, without permission in writing from the publishers.

Trademark notice: Product or corporate names may be trademarks or registered trademarks, and are used only for identification and explanation without intent to infringe.

Library of Congress Cataloging-in-Publication Data
Names: Staub, Alexandra, editor.
Title: The Routledge companion to modernity, space and gender/edited by Alexandra Staub.
Description: New York : Routledge, 2018. | Includes bibliographical references and index.
Identifiers: LCCN 2017049524 | ISBN 9781138746411 (hb : alk. paper) | ISBN 9781315180472 (ebook)
Subjects: LCSH: Architecture and women. | Space (Architecture)—Social aspects.
Classification: LCC NA2543.W65 R68 2018 | DDC 701/.8—dc23
LC record available at https://lccn.loc.gov/2017049524

ISBN: 978-1-138-74641-1 (hbk)
ISBN: 978-1-315-18047-2 (ebk)

Typeset in Bembo
by Apex CoVantage, LLC

 Printed in the United Kingdom by Henry Ling Limited

Contents

Contributors   *viii*

Introduction   1

PART 1
Social Welfare as a Modern State   **9**

1   In the Name of Progress: Gender and Social Housing in Post–World War II Vienna   11
Maria Mesner

2   Planning for Patriarchy? Gender Equality in the Swedish Modern Built Environment   26
Irene Molina

3   Modern Home, Environment, and Gender: Built, Planned, and Lived Spaces in Post-war Finland   41
Kirsi Saarikangas and Liisa Horelli

PART 2
Liberal and Neoliberal Values   **67**

4   The "Industrial Revolution" in the Home: Household Technology and Social Change in the Twentieth Century   69
Ruth Schwartz Cowan

5   Women in the Office: Clerical Work, Modernity, and Workplaces   86
Kim England

6   Selling Desire: Gender Constructs, Social Stratification, and the Commercialization of Modern Living   100
Alexandra Staub

Contents

7   Engendering Urban Design: An Unfinished Story   119
    Marion Roberts

8   Zaha Hadid's Penthouse: Gender, Creativity, and "Biopolitics" in the
    Neoliberal Workplace   131
    Igea Santina Troiani

PART 3
Socialism and Beyond   **151**

9   Communist Comfort: Socialist Modernism and the Making of Cozy
    Homes in the Khrushchev Era   153
    Susan E. Reid

10 Women as "Socialist" Dwellers: Everyday Lives in the German Democratic
    Republic   186
    Christine Hannemann

11 Reclaiming Space for Women: Negotiating Modernity in Feminist
    Restorations in Post-socialist Eastern Germany   202
    Katja M. Guenther

12 Kin-Related Elder Care in Russian Families: Challenges for Homemaking   217
    Olga Tkach

13 Space, Body and Subjectivity in Ágnes Kocsis's Film, *Fresh Air* (2006)   238
    Nóra Séllei

PART 4
Modernism vs. Traditional Values   **251**

14 Unveiled Middle-Class Housing in Tehran, 1945–1979   253
    Rana Habibi

15 Appropriating the Masculine Sacred: Islamism, Gender, and Mosque
    Architecture in Contemporary Turkey   270
    Bülent Batuman

16 The Emergent Gender of Rural Modernities in Turkey   288
    Eda Acara

Contents

PART 5
A Rapidly Globalizing World   303

17 Migration, Gender and Space in China   305
    C. Cindy Fan

18 Migrant Women Walking Down the Cheap Road: Modernization and
    Being Fashionable in Shanghai   320
    Penn Tsz Ting Ip

19 Space and Gender in the Chinese Workplace: Past and Present   338
    Duanfang Lu

20 The Bungalow in the Colonial and Post-colonial Twentieth Century:
    Modernity, Dwelling and Gender in the Cultural Landscape of Gujarat,
    India   350
    Madhavi Desai

21 Gendered Household Expectations: Neoliberal Policies, Graveyard Shifts,
    and Women's Responsibilities in Mumbai, India   367
    Aparna Parikh

22 Reinterpreting Gender in Globalizing India: Afghan Sikh Refugees in Delhi
    City's Built Environment   380
    Shelly Pandey

Index   *391*

vii

Contributors

Eda Acara is an Assistant Professor of Sociology at Başkent University and a Visiting Research Fellow in the Urban Policy Planning and Local Governments Institution at the Middle East Technical University in Ankara, Turkey. She is a feminist environmental geographer problematizing the effects of neoliberalization within the context of mobilities across the rural–urban nexus, including water pollution and food, and has served as a permanent member of *Fe-Journal* for many years. She received her B.A. in Sociology from the Middle East Technical University in Ankara Turkey, her M.A. in Gender and Women Studies from St. Mary's University and Mount Saint Vincent University in Nova Scotia, Canada, and her Ph.D. in Geography from Queen's University in Ontario, Canada.

Bülent Batuman is an Associate Professor in the Department of Urban Design and Landscape Architecture at Bilkent University in Ankara, Turkey. He has published numerous articles through his research on the urban environment and ecology of Turkey. His recent research focuses on the relationship between political Islam and the built environment, as reflected in his forthcoming book *New Islamist Architecture and Urbanism: Negotiating Nation and Islam through the Built Environment in Turkey* (Routledge). He received his professional degree in architecture and his Masters of Architecture from the Middle East Technical University in Turkey, and his Ph.D. in History and Theory of Art and Architecture from the State University of New York in Binghamton.

Ruth Schwartz Cowan is a Professor Emerita of the History and Sociology of Science at the University of Pennsylvania. She has published numerous books on gender and technology, including *Heredity and Hope: The Case for Genetic Screening* (2008); *A Social History of American Technology* (1997); *Our Parents' Lives: The Americanization of Eastern European Jews* (1989); *Sir Francis Galton and the Study of Heredity in the Nineteenth Century* (1985); and *More Work for Mother: The Ironies of Household Technology from the Open Hearth to the Microwave* (1983). She received her B.A. from Barnard College, her M.A. from the University of California, Berkeley, and her Ph.D. from Johns Hopkins University.

Madhavi Desai is an Adjunct Faculty at CEPT University, Ahmedabad, India, who has lectured and taught internationally. She is a founding member of the Women Architects Forum. She is the co-author of *Architecture and Independence: The Search for Identity, India 1880 to 1980*, (Oxford University Press, 1997); *Architectural Heritage of Gujarat: Interpretation, Appreciation, Values* (Gujarat Government, 2012); and *The Bungalow in Twentieth Century India: The Cultural Expression of Changing Ways of Life and Aspirations in the Domestic Architecture of Colonial and Post-colonial Society* (Ashgate, 2012). She is the editor of *Gender and the Built Environment in India* (Zubaan, 2007); the author of *Traditional Architecture: House Form of the Islamic Community of the Bohras in Gujarat* (Council of Architecture, 2007); and more recently, *Women Architects and Modernism in India: Narratives and Contemporary Practices* (Routledge, 2017). She received her B.Arch. from CEPT University in India and her M.Arch. from the University of Texas in Austin.

Kim England is a Professor of Geography and an Adjunct Professor of Gender, Women and Sexuality Studies at the University of Washington, Seattle. She is an urban social and feminist geographer who focuses on care work, critical social policy analysis, labor markets, economic restructuring and inequalities in urban North America. She received her B.A. from the University of Leicester and her M.A. and Ph.D. from Ohio State University.

C. Cindy Fan is a Professor of Geography and Vice Provost for International Studies and Global Engagement at the University of California, Los Angeles (UCLA). Her book, *China on the Move*, is a pioneering study of rural-urban migration in China, and her current research focuses on the split household and gender inequity. She is a recipient of the Distinguished Scholar Award from AAG's Asian Geography Specialty Group and the UCLA Distinguished Teaching Award. She has given keynotes around the world and is a frequent contributor to the *New York Times*. She received her B.A. from the University of Hong Kong, her M.Phil. from the Chinese University of Hong Kong and her Ph.D. from Ohio State University.

Katja M. Guenther is an Associate Professor in the Department of Gender and Sexuality Studies at the University of California, Riverside. She has published extensively on feminist organizing after socialism, including numerous journal articles and her book, *Making Their Place: Feminism after Socialism in Eastern Germany*. She received her B.A. in Sociology from Smith College in Northampton, Massachusetts; her M.A. in Sociology from the University of California, Davis; and her Ph.D. in Sociology from the University of Minnesota.

Rana Habibi is an Independent Researcher in the Architecture Department of the University of Leuven and an Urban Designer in the Institute of Sweco, based in Brussels. Her writing focuses on how contemporary architecture functions in Iranian society. She has received a European Master of Urbanism from IUAV, Venice, Italy; a Master of Urbanism and Strategic Planning from the University of Leuven; and a Ph.D. in Architecture from the University of Leuven.

Christine Hannemann is a Professor at the Department of Architecture and Urban Planning, Institute Housing and Design (IWE) in the Department of Sociology of Architecture and Housing at the University of Stuttgart. She has edited and published books, many journal articles and book chapters on her area of research, which focuses on urban development with respect to the dwelling. She received her Diploma of Sociology at the Humboldt-University in Berlin, her Ph.D. in philosophy from the Technical University in Berlin and her Habilitation in Sociology from the Humboldt-University in Berlin.

Liisa Horelli is Adjunct Professor in the Department of the Built Environment at the Aalto University in Helsinki, Finland. She has published widely on urban planning and spatial development issues from the gender perspective. Currently she is engaged with the European Network on Gender and Spatial Development, with a book with the same title slated to appear in 2018, published by Routledge. She received her M.A. from the University of Helsinki and her Ph.D. from the Helsinki University of Technology.

Penn Tsz Ting Ip is currently finishing her Ph.D. in the Amsterdam School for Cultural Analysis at the University of Amsterdam, Netherlands. She completed a B.A. in the Humanities Programme from Hong Kong Baptist University; an M.A. in Intercultural Studies from the Chinese University of Hong Kong; and a Research Master of Arts in Cultural Analysis from the University of Amsterdam.

Duanfang Lu is Professor of Architecture and Urbanism in the Sydney School of Architecture, Design and Planning at the University of Sydney. She has published widely on modern architectural

Contributors

and planning history, including *Remaking Chinese Urban Form* (2006, 2011) and *Third World Modernism* (2010). Through a series of articles she has developed a conceptual framework on entangled modernities that has been used by scholars and students across the world to investigate non-Western built environments. Her anthology *The Routledge Companion to Contemporary Architectural History* will be published in 2018. She has been an Australian Research Council Future Fellow and co-founder and vice president of the Society of Architectural and Urban Historians–Asia. She received her B.Arch. from Tsinghua University in Beijing and her Ph.D. in Architecture from the University of California, Berkeley.

Maria Mesner is a Senior Lecturer in the Institute for Contemporary History in the Gender Research Office at the University of Vienna. She has published several works on spaces, gender, and autonomy with respect to sexuality and reproduction in Vienna; the most recent of which is titled "Room of One's Own." She is a recipient of a Fulbright Research Grant and a Fulbright Lecturing and Research Grant. She received her M.A. in Philosophy, Ph.D. in Philosophy, and Univ.-Doz. from the University of Vienna.

Irene Molina is a Professor in Human Geography, Settlement, and the Built Environment at the Institute for Housing and Urban Research at Uppsala University. She has written extensively on Swedish and Latin American housing and migration. She is also the Research Director of the Centre for Multidisciplinary Studies on Racism at Uppsala University. Currently, she is the head of the "Gender and Housing from an Intersectional Perspective" project. She received her M.A. in Geography from Universidad Católica de Chile and her Ph.D. in Human Geography from the Department of Social and Economic Geography from Uppsala University.

Shelly Pandey is an Assistant Professor in Gender Studies at Ambedkar University, Delhi, where she uses an interdisciplinary approach to study gender, urban spaces, globalization, information and communications technology (ICT) and work. She has written extensively on these issues and in 2012 was the recipient of the M. N. Srinivas Memorial Prize awarded by the Indian Sociological Society. Her Ph.D. is from the Indian Institute of Technology (IIT) Delhi on gendered experiences of the globalized work world in India.

Aparna Parikh is a doctoral candidate in the Departments of Geography and Women's, Gender and Sexuality Studies at the Pennsylvania State University. Funded by the Society of Woman Geographers and Social Science Research Council, her current research examines gendered experiences of shifts accompanying proliferation of transnational call centers in Mumbai, India. She received her B.Arch. from Kamla Raheja Vidyanidhi Institute of Architecture, Mumbai, and her M.Arch. from the Pennsylvania State University.

Susan E. Reid is a Professor of Cultural History in the Department of Politics, History and International Relations at Loughborough University, UK. Her research addresses socialism and utopia with respect to the aesthetics and function of past and present Soviet housing. She has published numerous journal articles and book chapters including "Everyday Aesthetics in the Khrushchev-Era Standard Apartment" included in *Everyday Life in Russia Past and Present*. She received her B.A. Hons. in Modern Languages (German and Russian), and her M.A. and Ph.D. in the History of Art from the University of Pennsylvania.

Marion Roberts was Professor of Urban Design in the Faculty of Architecture and the Built Environment at the University of Westminster, London. She has had a long-standing research interest in gender issues and planning and has many publications on the subject, most recently co-editing *Fair*

Shared Cities: The Impact of Gender Planning in Europe. Her B.Sc. and Diploma in Architecture were awarded by the Bartlett School, University College London and her Ph.D. by Cardiff University.

Kirsi Saarikangas is a Professor of Art History in the Faculty of Arts at the University of Helsinki, Finland. She has several publications on the dwelling and belonging in modern society and the built environment and gender; most recently she published "Sandboxes and Heavenly Dwellings: Gender, Agency, and Modernity in Lived Suburban Spaces in the Helsinki Metropolitan Area in the 1950s and 1960s." She also serves as the director of the project "Nature in Arts, Culture, and History; Temporal Sedimentations of Landscape and the Diversity of Nature" at the Academy of Finland. She received her B.A., M.A., and Ph.D. from the University of Helsinki.

Nóra Séllei is a Professor in the Department of British Studies, Institute of English and American Studies at the University of Debrecen, Hungary, and also at the Department of English, Catholic University in Ruzomberok, Slovakia. Her research spans various topics in feminist literature, including the semiotics of cultural spaces. She has explored these themes in five monographs and more than a hundred journal articles and book chapters; additionally she has translated Virginia Woolf's *Three Guineas* and *Moments of Beings*, and Jean Rhys's *Smile Please*. She received her B.A. cum M.A. as a teacher of English Language and Literature and Hungarian Language and Literature, her Ph.D. and Habilitation from Kossuth Lajos University of Debrecen, Hungary, and her D.Sc. from the Hungarian Academy.

Alexandra Staub is an Associate Professor of Architecture and an Affiliate Faculty of the Rock Ethics Institute at the Pennsylvania State University. She has written extensively on how architecture is shaped by cultural demands, most recently in her book *Conflicted Identities: Housing and the Politics of Cultural Representation*, which examines how architecture and space can express divergent identities in any given cultural context. She received her B.A. from Barnard College, her Dip.-Ing. (Arch.) from the University of the Arts in Berlin, Germany, and her Ph.D. from the Brandenburg Technical University in Cottbus, Germany.

Olga Tkach is a Senior Researcher at the Centre for Independent Social Research (CISR) in St. Petersburg and Lecturer at the Department of Sociology of the Higher School of Economics (HSE, St. Petersburg Campus), Russia. She holds a Ph.D. in sociology and studies migration and mobility; au pair placement; home, domestic and care work; and various aspects of the everyday. Funded by the KONE Foundation (Finland), her current research has been focused on the newly built multistory neighborhoods and related neighborness in the Russian metropolitan city.

Igea Santina Troiani is an architect, feminist filmmaker and academic who teaches in the School of Architecture at Oxford Brookes University. Her current research is on the influence of neoliberalism on the social, political and economic production of architecture and its effect on the female and male architect. She uses a range of media to produce architectural scholarship as traditional textual publication, film and exhibition. She is author of *The Politics of Making* (2007) and founder and editor in chief of the award-winning interdisciplinary journal, *Architecture and Culture*. She is currently writing the manuscript *Work-Life Balance in Architecture* (Routledge London).

Introduction

This volume examines how modernity has been defined in various cultural contexts, how concepts of modernity have been interpreted spatially, and how this spatial interpretation has affected women in their everyday lives. These three models—modernity, space and gender—have been examined individually or in pairs, but never together, and certainly not as part of a multicultural and multidisciplinary cross section.

Most disciplines have a long history of defining "humans" as gender-neutral individuals, which generally means the male has been taken to represent the whole species. This is certainly true for disciplines that explore spatial constructs: analyses of spaces, along with their production, use and meaning, have traditionally described a user who is assumed to be male. In architecture, for example, theoretical treatises have historically either ignored the presence of women in the built environment, have limited their concerns to specific problems such as "safety"[1] or have usurped distinctively female experiences as somehow being within the realm of male knowledge and expertise.[2] One reason that this volume focuses exclusively on women's experiences and perspectives is to allow an unmitigated focus on women's interactions with the built environment, a perspective that is sorely missing in much conventional scholarship.

This volume starts with the premise that there is no gender-neutral perception. Gender, like race, ethnicity or class, helps define who we are; the mosaic of possible experiences based on these parameters enriches our understanding of spatial and social phenomena. Layering feminine experience into common readings of space and the cultural concepts they stand proxy for allows us a deeper perception of both modernity and the spaces it has created. This volume's central aim is to help develop awareness for such a layer of perception, a mission that must continually be renewed in order to more fully appreciate the causes and effects of our modern world.

Defining Modernity

"Modernity" has many nuances of meaning, many of which are specific to various disciplines. When the term is used to describe political and social structures, it often assumes an economic system based on trade and capital, as well as a political system based on individual liberties. This definition has a long history, encompassing transformations in Europe after the medieval era[3] and taking on new fervor in the nineteenth-century industrialization of Europe and North America as well as the colonization that sought necessary raw materials and other resources for the industrial campaign.[4]

In English language usage, the term "modern" as an adjective had negative connotations at first, yet took on positive overtones starting in the nineteenth century, a trend that was accelerated in the twentieth century.[5] Modernization, in the Western political and social context at least, has been fueled by a fear of being materially and economically left behind or, even worse, cannibalized for the benefit of others. Modernization is now seen as a desirable state of being, at least in a national context. Governments emphasize their modernity as a way of asserting their position in an international hierarchy.[6]

Introduction

Modernity is seen as using growth and change in a quest towards being competitive and up to date. Lack of modernity is considered backwardness and is seen as a stigma.[7]

Feminist writers have challenged the popular view of modernity as a fixed concept. Rita Felski, surveying definitions of modernity in scholarly texts, has found that "modernity" has been interpreted as stability, coherence and world mastery, as an experience of instability and discontinuity, as a culture of rupture, or as a rational autonomous subject with absolutist unitary conceptions of truth.[8] She summarizes:

> [I]t is possible to identify certain key factors which contribute to this bewildering diversity of definitions. For example, the different understandings of the modern across national cultures and traditions lead to potential difficulties of translation when texts circulate within a global intellectual economy.[9]

In these fractured perceptions of modernity, modernizing tendencies might be lauded by one group of individuals in a given society, while others feel harmed by the same efforts. In part, this can be ascribed to power imbalances in the decision-making process: modern societies, for example, require a cadre of technocratic elites in order to run the systems that control cities and nations; these elites retain power that is not readily measured.[10]

Several countries have at some point in their history pursued extensive, top-down modernization programs. The largest attempt to modernize a society through social disruption started with the Russian Revolution in the early twentieth century, a revolution that set off a series of economic and social experiments by communist regimes that represents a broad attempt at comprehensive social and technical reform. Emphasizing social revolution in addition to rapid industrialization, the Soviet Union over the course of 70 years continually sought a way to join the expression of both, with profound effects throughout all of Eastern Europe that continue to the present day, as can be seen in the chapters of Part 3 of this volume. By contrast, in Iran and Turkey, state-sponsored modernization attempts have led to multilayered forms of rebuttal, as the chapters in Part 4 of this volume discuss.

The Western, populist interpretation of modernity as up-to-dateness serves an agenda of competitive advantage, yet this advantage—expressed in terms of value hierarchies—can be highly problematic. As Felski points out, the agenda of advantage has the perhaps unintended side effect that "within the field of social and political theory [. . .] the equation of modernity with particular public and institutional structures governed by men has led to an almost total elision of the lives, concerns, and perspectives of women."[11] This elision has skewed popular understandings of women in cultural representation including areas as diverse as commodification and consumerism, the private/public distinction, female sexuality, the politics of avant-garde aesthetics and mass culture, the organizational power of historical narrative and the differentiation of political, religious and scientific vocabularies.[12]

Modernity Expressed Spatially

Modernity and urban space have been theoretically interlinked since at least the nineteenth century, while in architectural theory the concepts have been linked since the early twentieth century. The European modern movement of the 1920s presented an early, and for many radical, reflection on women's role in society and how architectural expression intersected with this role, although most architectural projects and treatises were authored by men, which meant that a masculine view prevailed.[13] In geography, another discipline that deals with spatial production and use, the role of women in society was approached much later. Gillian Rose, in the introduction to her 1993 book *Feminism and Geography*, notes that the discipline remained fairly hostile to women academics throughout the 1970s, and that the first systematic survey of geographical studies of women was only published in 1982. In the early 1990s, she continued, geography continued to be resistant to work that focused on women. This is certainly true for English-language texts, although one may assume that the situation is not much better in bodies of scholarly work written in other languages.

Modernity is a social phenomenon; expressed spatially it has often begun with material or technical innovations. In the early twentieth century, movements such as the Futurists combined a deterministic, and perhaps nihilistic, display of technology with views of what they saw as social progress. In 1914, almost a decade before Le Corbusier presented his ideas for modern high-rise cities, the Futurists' architectural spokesperson, Antonio Sant'Elia, sketched bold visions of fortress-like power stations with smokestacks piercing the sky, vast transit hubs with gridded facades, and raging apartment blocks with external elevators.[14] The built displays of technical prowess became a defining aspect of further movements in the early twentieth century, including the architectural avant-garde in Western Europe and the constructivists in Russia. Modernity in its built form was quickly associated with a world of high-rise office and apartment buildings; steel, glass and concrete as building materials; and technical infrastructure projects, especially those dealing with power grids or transportation.

Modernity in architecture has consistently highlighted new technologies, using formal expression to showcase them. In an urban sense, nations have expressed modernity as a sense of stability and mastery through rational structures—gridded and numbered streets, separation of urban functions, and circulation corridors designed for mechanized travel—or through prominent placement of technically ambitious structures, such as skyscrapers or buildings with large spans. It is this vision of modernity that we often find in the playbooks of rapidly developing nations, as the sections in this volume on modernization and traditional values, and a rapidly globalizing world point out. Yet modernity, based on technical novelty and up-to-dateness, also implies a destructive force, or, as Marshall Berman states, the quest of the modern has created a system in which the bourgeoisie lives to destroy and tear down things so that they can be built anew.[15] Technical novelty and the state of the art have thus been linked with casting off the old in order to seek material newness in a hierarchical process that has come under critique for reasons such as environmental destruction or the erasure of place-specific culture.

In a world in which modernity is often considered synonymous with up-to-dateness, the concept, taken to its extreme, creates the problem of what might come next. A break with building traditions, often using new forms as a metaphor for a new social order, and constant renewal of existing structures requires a great deal of capital. In the socialist countries of the Soviet Union and Eastern Europe, this capital was provided by the state as part of a top-down program to demonstrate superiority to Western systems that relied on private capital. In the West and in countries that are rapidly developing economically, the constant quest for renewal and the system of capital such renewal is based on have led to great social stresses, especially for women. Even where the quest for modernity has turned to programs that seek social equality, for example in the Western European social welfare programs discussed in Part 1 or the socialist housing ideals discussed in Part 3, male dominance of the planning process has led to a dissonance between socially expressed theory and built reality.

The tendency for nation-states to emphasize their modernity is not universal. Some countries, or dominant groups within them, react to the social changes that are often a secondary result of modernization by championing cultural traditions. Conservative groups in Iran or Turkey provide examples of such countercultures in ways that influence women's lives dramatically. Yet even Western societies that otherwise champion modernism of all kinds have not reacted uniformly to modernism's potential forces. David Gartman has analyzed why architecture's High Modern movement originated in post–World War I Europe, and not in the US with its early embrace of Fordism and rationalized production. His analysis points to the multiple ways in which technical and social forces interact in the production of modernity.[16]

Considering the links between spatial, architectural and social modernization, it comes as no surprise that even progressive societies are often suspicious of women who are "too modern" in their claim to space, especially when such claims seem to go hand in hand with campaigns for women's suffrage, sexual self-determination or advanced career opportunities. While modernity as a technical

Introduction

process implies an economically competitive advantage, as a social process it often questions traditional systems of hierarchy that national decision-makers rely on to maintain their perceived advantages. Even in countries that consider themselves thoroughly "modern," there is a complex relationship between the technical modernity that fosters material progress and economic dominance and the social modernity that purports to extend individual rights, in this case to women.

Modernity Through a Gender Lens

Despite the link between physical and social renewal, and despite venues and journals[17] that showcase feminist research, the study of how technological and spatial modernity affects women's everyday lives has not become as mainstream as could be expected. Feminist scholars have analyzed architectural and spatial modernity in primarily two ways: through analyzing modern architecture and through examining the conceptionalization of space. In her article "The Split Wall: Domestic Voyeurism," for example, Beatriz Colomina dissects symbolic power constructs of European high modernists in an analysis of how iconic villas built by Adolf Loos and Le Corbusier in the early twentieth century framed women and objectified them within the house.[18] A further path of research has examined women's involvement in the production of iconic modern architecture, and how such involvement has helped define the ensuing project. An excellent example is Alice T. Friedman's book *Women and the Making of the Modern House*, which investigates how women clients influenced innovation in domestic architecture designed by renowned architects.[19] Yet the modernism assumed in such texts is that of precedents representing specific aesthetic and social movements that have resonated throughout many parts of the world, but that remain rooted in the European avant-garde of the 1920s. It is thus important to differentiate between modernity and modernism; the former is more broadly focused than the latter, which is generally defined as a social and aesthetic movement. Although related, the conceptual underpinnings of each are quite distinct.

A second body of literature has looked at spatial production more generally. Often based in geography or philosophy, scholars have theorized spatial production, perception, and use in a variety of ways. While some texts have worked towards creating a mainstream feminist point of view,[20] several dominant scholars have pursued a class-based viewpoint instead.[21] Based on the political, economic and sociological theories of Karl Marx and Friedrich Engels (whose writings on the "woman question" made up but a fraction of their respective oeuvres), "gender-neutral" class inequality has often served to push aside gender-conscious critiques of spatial phenomena.[22] The use of class as a lens for understanding social phenomena has thus contributed to a process by which the (white) male experience continues to be seen as representative of all human experience, while female experience remains marginalized, in a process that the philosopher Michèle Le Doeuff has termed masculinist.[23]

Widely respected post-modern analyses of space, such as the writings of geographers David Harvey or Edward Soja, are not immune to this masculinist gaze. Harvey's and Soja's analyses of the social production of space are based on class, missing an opportunity to understand space as a gendered or otherwise fractured experience. Writers such as Doreen Massey, Gillian Rose and Rosalyn Deutsche have criticized this absence; Rose writes that

> both [Soja and Harvey] ignore feminist and post-colonial writers[. . . .] [G]eography was central to anti-colonial movements from the eighteenth century onwards, and [. . .] feminist projects too have been organized over geographical networks [. . .] and have struggled against the patriarchal spatial imagery of the public/private division[. . . .] However, Soja proceeds oblivious.[24]

What effect has a male-dominated discourse on space, the built environment, and relevant social constructs had? How have such constructs shaped power relationships in the construction of social and spatial paradigms? To understand possible answers to these questions, it is useful to reflect, even briefly, on how our understanding of space is shaped in the first place. The most famous protagonists of modern space, including Charles Baudelaire's and Walter Benjamin's famous flaneurs, were privileged, upper-class males who could own the city with their gaze. The flaneur leads to a more common conception: a gendered analysis of space that has produced a binary approach by which public space is ascribed to the male, while the private space of domesticity is the realm of females. Jane Rendell discusses the gender dichotomy of male public realm and female private realm, describing this approach as both patriarchal and capitalist: "[A]s an ideology, it does not describe the full range of lived experience of all urban dwellers. This is problematic for feminists because assumptions regarding sex, gender and space contained within this binary hierarchy are continually reproduced."[25] In a process of deconstruction based on Jacques Derrida's writings, feminist theorists have attempted to deconstruct the hierarchy implied in the public-private binary, either reversing it so that the less valued term is celebrated as the more positive, or by staging what Rendell calls an "intervention," in which a new term is created that breaks open the binary logic.[26]

A further binary exists where modernity has been contrasted with traditionalism. This dichotomy, too, has taken on implied aspects of gender, a result of theorists creating a hierarchy and accepting both modernity and the male experience associated with it as experientially superior. Marshall Berman, in his analysis of modernity, describes how Goethe's Faust seduces and then dismisses a young *village* girl (emphasis mine) as evidence of a "modern . . . cultur[al] hero,"[27] a point that Rita Felski describes as "[w]oman [. . .] aligned with the dead weight of tradition and conservatism that the active, newly autonomous, and self-defining subject must seek to transcend."[28] This view, of the modern male impeded by tradition that is female, is a staple of modernist lore. Although the European high modernist architects of the 1920s admiringly presented the "new woman" as enjoying fast cars and the recreational time afforded through being bestowed with modern appliances and easy-care houses, such flouting of gender conventions was only short-lived. When Ernst May, the architect responsible for much of Frankfurt's modern worker housing of the 1920s, returned to Germany in the 1950s gushing about new neighborhood units to be built as anchors and security for the "modern nomad," it was clear that this restless nomad would be male.[29]

The public-private binary, and with it male and female space, express among other things a power hierarchy. Modernity and its associated public space have been celebrated through the male gaze, and despite women's presence in both public and private space, women's perception of and interaction with public space remains within the realm of the "other" in a way that questions the very existence of such experience. (Why encouraging this fuller understanding of spatial experience seems to primarily fall to women is another question.) Feminist theorists have noted that the encounter of modernity in literature and art is described from a male vantage point, and that this has resulted in hierarchical gender binaries based on female "otherness."[30] The experience of modernity in space, both architectural and urban, follows similar patterns. Once more invoking the flaneur of Charles Baudelaire and later Walter Benjamin—the archetype of the modern, urban (European) male interacting with an urban space—these powerful images have clawed their way to the forefront and erased a more nuanced view; as the perspective of the flaneuse, where she is allowed to exist, remains invisible in mainstream chronicles.

A Widely Faceted View of Modernity, Space and Gender

This volume is divided into five parts that correspond roughly to political or socioeconomic systems found worldwide. The first includes states that have a strong tradition of modernization through social welfare programs; the second looks at countries where a market economy has driven approaches to modernity; the third examines the socialist experiment in modernity; the fourth examines tensions in countries where religion has imposed a traditionalist power structure that runs counter to a globalizing, westernized ideal of modernity; and the fifth examines countries that are pursuing modernization

Introduction

through rapid economic and social development. In exploring the various forms of modernity identified in these five sections, space and gender play fascinatingly different roles in the various cultural contexts presented.

In some cases, as in states with a strong social welfare tradition, modernity has been translated into social programs leading to better living standards for workers and the middle class. Maria Mesner, Irene Molina, and Kirsi Saarikangas and Liisa Horelli explore post–World War II, state-sponsored housing programs in Austria, Sweden, and Finland respectively, examining how housing choices created largely by a male cadre of planners both aided women and cemented their roles in a heteronormative society.

In chapters that explore aspects of technology and marketing within the context of highly capitalist or neoliberal economic systems, Ruth Schwartz Cowan and Kim England examine the industrial revolution in the household and the office respectively, and how technological changes affected the lives of the women who used those spaces. Alexandra Staub examines how images of modernity and traditionalism are used to market housing in the US; Marion Roberts reflects on the disconnect between legislated gender equality and contemporary city building in Great Britain; and Igea Santina Troiani explores the modernity of one of architecture's few female stars of the twentieth century, Zaha Hadid.

In looking at socialism and post-socialism, Susan E. Reid examines tensions inherent in redefining modern Soviet domestic spaces in the Khrushchev era of the 1960s; Christine Hannemann explores the role that state-sponsored housing played for gender equality in the German Democratic Republic (GDR); Katja M. Guenther chronicles how socialist-era environments in the GDR have been used to create new, women-friendly spaces in a post-socialist era; Olga Tkach highlights the lives of women performing elderly care in contemporary post-Soviet Russia; and Nóra Séllei examines the tension-laden but lyrical life of a mother and daughter in today's working-class Hungary.

In chapters that examine religious traditionalism and modernization, Rana Habibi discusses the symbolic "unveiling" of Tehran in the 1960s; Bülent Batuman examines two modern Turkish mosques whose interiors were designed by women; and Eda Acara explores how rural women in Turkey have become activists in order to counter industrial contamination of their water supply.

Modernity has frequently been exalted in countries that are undergoing rapid economic development as part of economic and social globalization. In more nuanced examinations of implications for women, Cindy Fan looks at how rural-urban migration in China affects family life; Penn Tsz Ting Ip examines young migrant women's lives in Shanghai; Duanfang Lu traces the living and working conditions of factory workers in China; Madhavi Desai examines the bungalow as a modern housing form in India; Aparna Parikh looks at the lives of female call-center workers in Mumbai; and Shelly Pandey traces the lives of Afghan refugee women in today's Delhi.

The diverse cultures presented in this volume are illuminated through methods of analysis culled from an equally diverse range of disciplines, including architecture, geography, history, literature, sociology and visual studies, among others. Presenting this volume as a network of sites and methods serves a deeper purpose: feminist thinking has done much to deconstruct both the male gaze and the male-defined hierarchical binaries that result through embracing the concept of fragmented realities and multiple perspectives of events and phenomena. This fragmented way of working lends itself well to a volume that explores multiple experiences of modernity in various national contexts, recognizing that this multiplicity must exist without hierarchy. In exploring different cultural contexts with cross-disciplinary methods, the contributors have been strengthened in uncovering women's contributions to, experiences with, and reactions to modernity in their specific spatial contexts. As Rosalyn Deutsche states in support of the fragmented view as a means of gaining deeper understanding:

> If representations are relationships, rather than embodiments of essential meanings, then the high ground of total knowledge can only be gained by a particular encounter with differences—the violent relegation of other subjectivities to positions of invisibility or, what amounts to the same thing, subordination.[31]

This volume does not attempt to offer a comprehensive feminist theory of modernity and space. In keeping with feminist thinking, it does not attempt to be comprehensive at all. Instead, this volume offers a multicultural cross-section and a starting point towards a new, or renewed, discipline-spanning dialog about spatial production and use, a discussion that does not fall into the trap of springing from a heteronormative viewpoint. As cultures seek modernity in various ways, and as spaces are created to accommodate this modernity, the importance of understanding this process and its effects on women specifically should not be underestimated.

In offering a cross section of examples that center on aspects of spatial use and perception missing in the traditional canon, this volume provides a broadly based yet focused analysis that spans diverse social and cultural contexts. The selections can be read individually or as a comparative group, and it is my hope that they inspire further work, especially in areas of the world that this volume does not cover.

Notes

1. Texts often portray women's safety in urban environments as a central concern, thus sidestepping the problem of violence in domestic environments.
2. See Agrest 2000 [1993].
3. Williams 1976, 155–6; Bennett, Grossberg, and Morris 2005.
4. Bennett, Grossberg, and Morris 2005; Blaut 2012.
5. Williams 1976, 156.
6. See Massey 1999.
7. Staub 2015, 77–81.
8. Felski 1995, 11.
9. Felski 1995, 11–12.
10. Winner 1988.
11. Felski 1995, 16.
12. Felski 1995, 209.
13. For example, in the classic anthology *Programs and Manifestoes on 20th Century Architecture* (Conrads 1971), none of the 68 texts is by a woman.
14. Meyer 1995.
15. Berman 1983, 99.
16. Gartman 2009.
17. For example the journal *Gender, Place and Culture* presents feminist research in geography and related areas.
18. Colomina 1992, 73ff.
19. Friedman 2006.
20. Among them, texts by Rosalyn Deutsche, Rita Felski, Doreen Massey (cf. Massey 1994), Linda McDowell (1999), Jane Rendell (especially Borden, Penner, and Rendell 1999), Gillian Rose, Daphne Spain (especially Spain 1993), Despina Stratigakos (2008), and many of the authors of this volume.
21. Rose 1993, 3.
22. Rose 1991.
23. Cited in Rose 1993, 4.
24. Rose 1991.
25. Rendell in Borden, Penner, and Rendell 1999, 103.
26. Rendell in Borden, Penner, and Rendell 1999, 103–4.
27. Berman 1983, 38.
28. Felski 2009, 2.
29. Quoted in *Der Spiegel* 19/1955, 37.
30. Wolff 1985; Pollock 1988; Deutsche 1996.
31. Deutsche 1996.

References

Agrest, Diana. 2000 [1993]. "Architecture From Without: Body, Logic and Sex." In *Gender Space Architecture*, edited by Jane Rendell, Barbara Penner, and Iain Borden, 358–370. London and New York: Routledge.

Bennett, Tony, Lawrence Grossberg, and Meaghan Morris, eds. 2005. *New Keywords: A Revised Vocabulary of Culture and Society*. Malden, MA: Wiley-Blackwell.

Introduction

Berman, Marshall. 1983. *All that Is Solid Melts into Air: The Experience of Modernity*. New York and London: Verso.

Blaut, James Morris. 2012. *The Colonizer's Model of the World: Geographical Diffusionism and Eurocentric History*. New York: Guilford Press.

Borden, Iain, Barbara Penner, and Jane Rendell, eds. 1999. *Gender Space Architecture: An Interdisciplinary Introduction*. London and New York: Routledge.

Colomina, Beatriz. 1992. "The Split Wall: Domestic Voyeurism." In *Sexuality & Space*, edited by Beatriz Colomina, 73–130. New York: Princeton Architectural Press.

Conrads, Ulrich, ed. 1971. *Programs and Manifestoes on 20th-Century Architecture*. Translated by Michael Bullock. Cambridge, MA: MIT Press.

Der Spiegel. 1955. "May: Der Plan-Athlet." 19(May 4): 30–37.

Deutsche, Rosalyn. 1996. *Evictions: Art and Spatial Politics*. Cambridge, MA: MIT Press.

Felski, Rita. 1995. *The Gender of Modernity*. Cambridge, MA: Harvard University Press.

Friedman, Alice T. 2006. *Women and the Making of the Modern House*. New Haven, CT: Yale University Press.

Gartman, David. 2009. *From Autos to Architecture: Fordism and Architectural Aesthetics in the Twentieth Century*. New York: Princeton Architectural Press.

Massey, Doreen. 1994. *Space, Place and Gender*. Cambridge: Polity Press.

Massey, Doreen. 1999. "Imagining Globalization: Power-Geometries of Time-Space." In *Global Futures: Explorations in Sociology*, edited by Avtar Brah, Mary J. Hickman, and Máirt n Mac an Ghaill, 27–44. London: Palgrave Macmillan.

McDowell, Linda. 1999. *Gender, Identity and Place: Understanding Feminist Geographies*. Cambridge: Polity Press.

Meyer, Esther da Costa. 1995. *The Work of Antonio Sant'Elia: Retreat into the Future*. New Haven, CT: Yale University Press.

Pollock, Griselda. 1988. *Vision and Difference: Femininity, Feminism and the Histories of Art*. London and New York: Routledge.

Rendell, Jane. 1999. "Introduction: 'Gender, Space.'" In *Gender Space Architecture: An Interdisciplinary Introduction*, edited by Borden, Iain, Barbara Penner, and Jane Rendell, 101–111. London: Routledge.

Rose, Gillian. 1991. "Review of Edward Soja, *Postmodern Geographies* and David Harvey, *The Condition of Postmodernity*." *Journal of Historical Geography* 17(1): 118–121.

Rose, Gillian. 1993. *Feminism and Geography: The Limits of Geographical Knowledge*. Minneapolis: University of Minnesota Press.

Spain, Daphne. 1993. *Gendered Spaces*. Chapel Hill: University of North Carolina Press.

Staub, Alexandra. 2015. *Conflicted Identities: Housing and the Politics of Cultural Representation*. London and New York: Routledge.

Stratigakos, Despina. 2008. *A Woman's Berlin: Building the Modern City*. Minneapolis: University of Minnesota Press.

Williams, Raymond. 1976. *Keywords: A Vocabulary of Culture and Society*. Oxford: Oxford University Press.

Winner, Langdon. 1988. *The Whale and the Reactor: A Search for Limits in an Age of High Technology*. Chicago: University of Chicago Press.

Wolff, Janet. 1985. "The Invisible *Flaneuse*: Women and the Literature of Modernity." *Theory, Culture and Society* 2(3): 37.

Part 1
Social Welfare as a Modern State

Introduction

The social welfare states of Central and Northern Europe aimed to establish socially based market economies in the post–World War II era. As in the socialist states of Eastern Europe (Part 3 of this volume), housing became key to providing for the citizenry and for guaranteeing the health and wellbeing of the workers needed for (in this case market-based) industries. In many cases, including the ones discussed in Part 1, this resulted in a series of large-scale housing programs based on the ideals of modernist urban planning as well as concepts of a "modern" nuclear family based on a stated principle of gender equality.

Maria Mesner examines how the city of Vienna took up its interwar tradition of constructing public worker housing, creating post-war housing estates that provided standardized housing types and thus contributed to the homogenization of private life and the cementing of women's domestic identities. Irene Molina follows with the example of the "Million Program," an ambitious Swedish housing program that put large housing estates on the outskirts of cities. This program was considered "woman-friendly" at the time, and Molina shows how gender bias created spaces that allowed a patriarchal definition of women's roles. Finally, Kirsi Saarikangas and Liisa Horelli examine the "People's Home" in Finland, a post-war housing ideal of modern housing set in pristine forest environments, as well as more recent examples of cohousing. Pointing to the problem of men planning for women, whose interests they do not fully understand in the first case, they contrast such housing with the more egalitarian concepts presented in the second part.

The three chapters in Part 1 make clear that despite planners' stated intentions to provide egalitarian housing for a post–World War II society, women's roles in those societies were still largely determined by men, leading to spatial concepts that catered to patriarchal domestic ideals rather than empowering women to determine their own domestic and urban environments.

1

In the Name of Progress

Gender and Social Housing in Post–World War II Vienna[1]

Maria Mesner

[In the home] the child has his or her first impressions, the family lives its life and draws new energy, the ageing man enjoys the security it offers.[2]

—Franz Jonas, Mayor of Vienna, 1956

Introduction

After World War I, Vienna, a fast growing metropolis until 1914, was faced by a devastating shortage of housing, among other major problems as a result of the war. The cause was a major influx of people from parts of the former Habsburg monarchy that had become independent, an influx that was not balanced by those who left the former capital towards their homelands. In an effort to meet the needs of Vienna's inhabitants and to prove it was capable of efficient social reform, the Viennese Social Democratic city government started a comprehensive construction program, under which close to 65,000 apartments were built between 1919 and 1933. They were known as "people's apartments" or *Volkswohnungen* in contemporary language. Due to the social unrest after World War I, the city authorities also aimed to integrate and appease various reform movements. This resulted in various concepts for housing that were absorbed into the city's building program, in particular those emerging from the women's and the settlers' movements—two informal, variegated social reform movements based on a number of smaller associations but without a formal organizational center. The resulting construction program included a wide-ranging selection of housing types: single-family houses, spaces for single working women or couples with both partners working, as well as apartment buildings and superblocks. Each reflected a different set of social norms and utopias.

Three decades later, World War II again resulted in a housing crisis, as more than 20% of all apartments in Vienna were seriously damaged or destroyed in the war.[3] Again, the city of Vienna reacted with an enormous effort to construct public housing, with the result that by 1970, 96,000 apartments had been erected. Several major differences can be found between the post–World War I and post–World War II building programs, particularly in terms of architectural design and the amenities in individual apartments as well as in the buildings. The change that this chapter focuses on, however, is the reduction in the types of housing due to the absence of social movements and their potential impact on the city's housing activities: neither a settlers' nor a women's movement existed in the post–World War II era. As a result, a stricter standardization of housing types is characteristic for post–World War II public housing designs. At the same time, the 1950s saw a major social transformation, namely, a historically unprecedented homogenization of private life. For the first time in modern history, the nuclear family became the all-encompassing model, standard and norm in post-war Austria. This chapter will ask if and how this secular transformation influenced the post–World War II building activities through examining two broad types of sources: the actual buildings, and textual and pictorial discourses.

In a first step, I will outline the most important types of housing in the post–World War I era and identify the social norms and concepts at the basis of the various modes of public construction. This will serve as the background for my examination of post–World War II gender policies. I will focus on gendered concepts of private life and will use the term "reproductive arrangement" in order to analyze the norms and models I am focusing on. The notion of "reproductive arrangement" points to a crucial aspect of gender relations: at least since early modern times, the reproductive functions of men and women provide the basis for concepts of the heterosexual couple, concepts that serve as the core paradigm of gendered societies of the Western world. Furthermore, the couple stands for a symbolic ordering replete with dualities such as nature-culture, private-public, or active-passive. In her analysis of present-day lifestyles of heterosexual couples, sociologist Birgit Pfau-Effinger[4] coined the term "gender arrangement" to stress the importance of negotiations that take place in everyday practice between gendered individuals, in order to establish their individual lifestyle. Therefore the notion of gender arrangement implies formal and informal rules, guidelines, laws and models, as well as the everyday practice of individuals, but also of institutions. The term of reproductive arrangement I will use for my analysis also bears meanings of the everyday lifestyles of individuals and groups, as well as institutional settings, state, and local policies, and formal and informal rules.

Interestingly, although there is a considerable amount of research on the housing policies of pre–World War II Vienna, as well as some deep-reaching investigations of post–World War II construction, all of this research barely takes into account gender questions. This is all the more unexpected considering that the private lives the public housing provided space for were full of highly gendered activities. References to gender are scarce, not only in the literature, but also in historic source material. This comes as a surprise, because after World War I as well as after World War II, Vienna was ruled by Social Democrats.[5] Since the founding of the party in 1888–9, equal rights for men and women were part of its manifesto and, with a certain degree of ambivalence, its policies, too. Therefore, it seems a worthwhile endeavor to trace notions of gender and related concepts in Vienna's housing policies during the twentieth century. In order to do so, I will use various sources to make the buildings "talk about" their inhabitants: official publications issued by Vienna's housing authorities as well as images and artworks that accompanied the buildings' construction.

Prequel: "From a Narrow Courtyard to Light, Air, and Sun"[6]—The Interwar Era

After the Social Democratic Workers' Party (SDAP) gained a clear majority in the 1920 elections, the party implemented a project of social and political reform that is now referred to as "Red Vienna" [red being the predominant party color—Ed.]. One of the main problems of the former imperial capital was the lack of affordable housing. This lack was due to the migration that followed the disintegration of the Habsburg monarchy, social transformations since the turn of the century and low activity in private construction. Housing construction was not attractive to private investors, as rents were relatively low and stable due to strict wartime rent regulations, while legislation protected tenants from eviction. Saddled onto a massive tax reform, Red Vienna policies reorganized the city's bureaucratic apparatus and introduced a public health program, a workers' culture initiative and—most importantly—a public-housing program.[7] The housing program included the construction of close to 60,000 apartments and more than 5,000 single-family houses by 1933.[8] "The *Gemeindebau* became the nexus of Red Vienna's institutions and the spatial embodiment of its communitarian and pedagogic ideals."[9] The housing program aimed at redistribution of wealth. Its goal was to provide good quality and healthy housing for urban inhabitants. While housing was created for huge numbers of those in need, and mostly shielded from market forces, the approach was clearly top down, lacking any elements of self-organization by the future residents. The principal goal was to provide better quality housing with more light by lowering building density, with plumbing and a toilet within the apartments.[10] The program included superblocks as well as single apartment buildings, and was preceded by a period when the city of Vienna tried to integrate housing concepts of social movements into its own endeavors: the settler's movement and the women's movement.

The settlers, a heterogeneous reform movement based on very different ideological beliefs ranging from religious transformation to anarchist and communist ideas, aimed at the construction of single-family houses that were often semidetached. Future residents organized in cooperatives and were involved in the construction process. Each of the lots, which were often situated at the fringes of the city, included land to grow fruits and vegetables and keep small livestock as a basis for a self-sufficient life. In terms of reproductive arrangements, this lifestyle called for a relatively high volume of household work: in addition to washing, cooking and so forth, produce had to be tended to and preserved through canning, pickling or drying. The settlers would finally own their land and follow a non-industrial, rural lifestyle, with the wife or both partners working in the house. Although apartment buildings in a more urban setting by far outnumbered single-family homes by the end of the 1920s, the city of Vienna incorporated the settlers' movement into its institutional framework. The official argument for the city's preference for multistory houses and superblocks was the more economical use of land they allowed for. The city's Social Democratic leadership also entertained a certain amount of distrust towards the cooperative mode of housing, however, not because of the reproductive arrangement it represented and fostered, but because of the suspicion that private ownership of land would support a more conservative political attitude and corrupt the socialist ethos.

The "single-kitchen building," a project the city of Vienna inherited from the women's movement, represented a very different model of housing, in which single and married women were to be relieved of reproductive chores like cooking and washing. The two buildings (with about 300 apartments total) included a central kitchen and a central laundry with employed staff. The tenants of the buildings paid for their service. Clearly, the project aimed at the emancipation of women through commodifying housework. Only single women and couples with both partners employed were eligible to be tenants. The scheme remained unique throughout the interwar era. The bulk of public housing was embedded in the rhetoric of eugenics: the buildings were seen as a "positive investment" in the future of society. They were to provide sun, air and better hygienic standards to the proletariat—who carried the promise for a just, socialist future—to enable them to bear and raise a new, and better, generation. For this reason, the blocks included childcare facilities, libraries and public pools, but also common baths and showers.[11] The worker couple was to be the reproductive arrangement for a bright socialist future.

The public housing built between 1919 and 1934 included central laundries but no employed staff. The laundries were shared by the inhabitants of the building. Oral history interviews show that only the wives, no matter if they were wage earning or housewives, took care of the laundry.[12] The shared facilities were to help them come to terms with the gendered division of work. Laundry facilities were not meant to challenge this division through commodifying housework or sharing it between spouses. In contrast to their attitudes in favor of the political emancipation of women, Social Democrats viewed the working-class couple at the center of the reproductive arrangement as an entity they wanted to support by providing high-quality housing. The power relations and the gendered division of labor within the couple were not at stake.

To sum up the period between 1919 and 1934, the public housing efforts of the city of Vienna aimed to provide affordable housing to working-class families. Although city authorities clearly preferred the construction of small apartments in multistory complexes, they also aimed to integrate social reform movements with very different family and housing concepts. The building program therefore included "single-kitchen-houses" and single-family homes, as well as semidetached and row houses. As a result, diverse reproductive arrangements, however dissimilar in scale and in the number of people affected, co-existed in different and separate spaces of public housing.

Public Housing Policies in Post–World War II Vienna

After World War II, the city of Vienna again faced a serious shortage of housing, but for a different reason: the massive destruction resulting from World War II. City authorities took up the inter-War tradition and again started to build a considerable amount of public housing. Up to 1970, 96,000 units were completed, outnumbering the 65,000 apartments built from 1918 to 1934. Most housing was built by the public sector; for example, in 1946 83% of all apartments were built by the city of Vienna. Although in the long run this figure dropped, the share of public housing among all newly built apartments in Vienna remained above 50% between 1945 and 1970.[13] As of this writing, 25% of the Viennese population lives in apartments owned by the city of Vienna.[14] As in the interwar era, the city erected single apartment blocks as well as extended complexes with several thousand apartments. These apartments were located in all Viennese districts, from the imperial city center to the hills of the Vienna Woods, and the hitherto undeveloped plain north of the Danube River.

While some buildings of the interwar era were influenced by the social reform efforts sketched out earlier, post–World War II public housing took a different approach in certain aspects. Still framing public housing as embodying progress, light and air, the Social Democrats, who were once more the municipal government's ruling party, now exclusively targeted the "modern" post-war family with a breadwinning man/father, a homemaking woman/mother who did not earn wages, and their children, along with the family's gendered activities and spaces. This coincided with a major social change, whereby the nuclear family, consisting of a married heterosexual couple with (usually) a low number of children, became the pervasively dominating family form in Austria. Ninety percent of the generation that came of age after World War II was married, 85% of all women had at least one child and 80% of the population lived in households made up of parents and their offspring. Fifty years earlier, about a third of the population had never married and had not been able to set up a household.[15] Nevertheless, it can be assumed that even in the interwar era, a major share of public housing inhabitants belonged to nuclear families. The spaces and functions had not been as properly gendered, however, as many wives from working-class families had to earn part of the family income because the wages of male breadwinners were often too small for a family with two or more children.

In the reconstruction period after World War I, different housing models had co-existed under the city of Vienna's umbrella; by contrast, Austrian fascism and National Socialism had destroyed social reform movements by the end of World War II. A few buildings still showed architectural features similar to interwar buildings inspired by reform ideals: one of the first apartment complexes built after 1945 resembled—with its three-story single-family row houses—the settlements of the interwar era. The complex lacked the basic concept of the interwar precedents, however, namely the idea of cooperation between the future occupants in the construction process.[16] The single-kitchen buildings from before World War II had changed fundamentally by 1945. The central facilities had been dismantled by order of the Austrofascist and National Socialist authorities and the apartments retrofitted with small individual kitchens. Other communal services had been shut down.

The buildings erected in the post–World War II era had plainer facades, due to the lack of construction material after the war and a different interior arrangement. While perimeter blocks with enclosed courtyards had dominated public housing construction during the interwar era, after World

War II slabs arranged in parallel rows with open green areas between them were popular, as they were thought to allow for a better circulation of air[17] and prevent the expansion of fires. Most were designed by a new generation of architects, most of whom were trained during National Socialism. For example, the head of the city's Department for Planning from 1958 to 1962, a former member of the National Socialist German Workers' Party (NSDAP), rejected all kinds of shared housing, even those with only two stories,[18] although he was not able to prevail with his urban vision of low-rise buildings.

In the newly built apartment complexes of the 1950s and 1960s, central facilities for reproductive work had a different emphasis. Laundries, for example, were reduced while public childcare facilities and schools in the larger residential sites[19] remained important. "In the interest of housewives,"[20] smaller laundries in every building had replaced the previous central laundries within larger complexes. The rationalization of the household was on its way: "In general, the housewives need to spend only half a day per washing cycle in the laundries,"[21] the authorities boasted. When washing machines moved into the apartments, these smaller laundries became obsolete. Instead of the shared baths that were sometimes found during the interwar era, individual bathrooms were included in each apartment.

In general, common facilities were less important after World War II. This was not an explicit gender policy, as it can be attributed to the rise in living standards. Nevertheless, it had a striking impact on the reproductive arrangement. Whereas there had been spaces shared by all homemakers in the earlier buildings, during the 1950s reproductive activities were shifted to the privacy of the apartments, where the homemaker accomplished them in isolation. The retreat and concentration of reproductive activities into the secluded homes that took place in the 1950s was a continuation of earlier developments. When public housing apartments were furnished with plumbing after World War I, the previous spaces to fetch fresh water, situated in the hallways of private working-class residential buildings, vanished. This not only made reproductive work easier (in the name of progress), but also reduced the spaces of communication usually frequented by homemakers. The *Bassenatratsch*, which can roughly be translated as "sink gossip" and often mentioned in popular literature and songs, lost its territory. It went without saying that these homemakers were all female. During the 1950s, additional shared spaces where reproductive work took place vanished, such as shared laundries. The individualization of female reproductive work thus progressed.

Without a question, reproductive work was ascribed to women. In order to scrutinize the reproductive arrangement I turned to *Aufbau*, a monthly journal published by the Vienna Municipal Building Authority.[22] *Aufbau* translates roughly as "construction," and was by no means a gender-neutral term. As Siegfried Mattl correctly states, the iconic image of the post–World War II era of *Aufbau* was male.[23]

In many public spaces, posters announcing popular exhibitions or as part of election campaigns, for example, presented superhuman working-class heroes as a modern version of Hercules (for examples, see Figures 1.1 and 1.2). Such figures piled bricks into modern post-war houses with seemingly minor effort, or swung enormous hammers to forge hot steel or destroy swastikas.

The title of the journal *Aufbau* is no coincidence, as hardly any female authors can be found during the first decades after its launch in 1946: post-war "construction" was clearly a male issue. At a first glance, the language of *Aufbau* was gender neutral, yet a closer inspection shows that males dominated, both as authors and as protagonists in the *Aufbau* articles. Throughout the city of Vienna's building efforts of the time, women were very rare, both as speakers as well as those spoken of. Sometimes women were spoken of as being "too numerous" (after two world wars), compared to the male part of the population. In 1951, when the first national census after World War II was conducted, the ratio of women to men in the age category 25 to 44 was 1,000 to 778,[24] yet this demographic fact is not mirrored in social housing of the time and its surrounding rhetoric. It was the heterosexual couple that was presented as the universal inhabitant of the *Gemeindewohnung*. Single mothers, widows or single women were not a point of reference.

Figure 1.1 Antifascist Exhibition 1945, Poster and Pamphlet
Source: Kreisky Archives 100/3.

In the Name of Progress

Figure 1.2 ERP-Fonds (1948) Poster
Source: Kreisky Archives 100/9.

When researching the reproductive arrangement envisioned by the city of Vienna's architects, the home is clearly "the realm of the women," "for the husband uses his home for the regeneration of his strength. The shared meal, playing with the children, social life in general, and his rest are his part in the home."[25] It comes as no surprise that "women" were most frequently mentioned in relation to the "kitchen." Indisputably the kitchen was *their* space. The architects' goal was to provide them with a space to accomplish their various reproductive tasks. Kitchens were advertised as being spacious enough to allow children to play there so their mother could watch them while performing household duties, and allowed the husband to talk to his wife after his work, while she continued to perform household chores. Another, smaller type of kitchen, the "working kitchen," was described as a space off-limits for children and the husband.[26] A few years later, the term "rational housekeeping" came up and showed that material standards had improved, and the "Economic Miracle" was on its way and had started to take over. In an effort to encourage and educate housewives for the new exigencies, one author in *Aufbau* suggested that women should buy containers, vessels and appliances that would help them to rationalize their work in the household. The new fitted kitchens were praised for keeping distances short for the housewife as she accomplished her various household activities.[27]

"Rationalization" of housework is a term significant for the reproductive arrangement of the *Aufbau* era: as workers' wages were kept relatively low by trade unions as well as employers in a joint show of support for reconstruction, women needed to make extra money, mostly with part-time jobs that would allow them to buy at least some of the gadgets the new Fordist consumerism offered, such as refrigerators, washing machines and electric mixers. The discourse around the construction of public housing is a telling example of the stunning ambivalence prevalent in the 1950s: while public images and rhetoric were full of happy housewives, the workforce participation of women did not drop significantly during this time. Thirty-five percent of women were employed and 44% of these employed women were married,[28] leading to the gainful employment of women becoming a widespread anathema during the 1950s.[29] Cracks soon emerged in the ostentatiously happy post-war picture, as contradictions and frictions were inevitable between the exigencies of employed and reproductive work. Working mothers had to deal with this growing problem. The rationalization and mechanization of households was supposed to support them in keeping their lives balanced, without challenging the hegemonic reproductive arrangement. Even the Socialist Party, the ruling party in Vienna as well as part of the governing coalition on the Austrian federal level, wrote in drafts of their 1958 party manifesto that the "mechanization of the household" was among the feminist demands of the day. The authors of *Aufbau* certainly had that arrangement in mind when they praised the public housing being built at that time.

While *Aufbau* was a special interest journal addressing professionals and other people with a thorough interest in construction and public housing, the city of Vienna's poster campaigns addressed a much broader audience, including potential voters, female as well as male, and the Viennese population, in order to inform them about all the achievements of the Socialist city administration. As a random but representative example for the widespread imagery, I picked a poster from 1955 (see Figure 1.3), placarded to mobilize for the first of May, a Socialist holiday celebrated with mass parades in Vienna's main streets.

Figure 1.3 SPÖ Wall Newspaper No. 85 (1955)
Source: Kreisky Archives 100/85.

The poster's[30] right half bears an enormous party logo on a red background. The left side shows a world split in two. In the center, muscular timber workers easily shift heavy beams to erect one of the new buildings. At the left margin, a woman with children is standing on her balcony, perhaps in one of the newly built houses, idly gazing in the direction of the reconstruction heroes. She is not an active participant in the endeavor of *Aufbau*, or construction, but exists as an onlooker, a beneficiary of the male effort.[31] The picture veils some major tensions straining the reconstruction society. After the end of World War II, the authorities obligated women to perform reconstruction work if they were between 16 and 40 years old. With more men coming back from prisoner-of-war (POW) camps, women were pushed out of the labor force, not only in construction but in many relatively well-paying, formerly male jobs.[32]

Women like the one in the poster had not taken on their passive role entirely by choice. After the destruction and ruptures of the National Socialism and wartime eras, the restoration of seemingly idyllic families through a feverish reconstruction effort became a high priority for a traumatized society seeking to erase the memory of crimes against humanity, as well as collective and individual guilt. Furthermore, the defeat in World War II damaged hegemonic masculinity and humiliated men, who as soldiers had been killed, mutilated, captured or turned into POWs.

The construction worker hero of the post–World War II era was an alternative type of hero, one free of all the negative impairment of Nazi crimes and war. This new hero was complete, active and healthy. The imagery around the reconstruction process thus demonstratively made use of icons of restored and resurrected manhood bearing no signs of military loss. The frequent citation of such manhood in public images can be interpreted as an attempt to demonstrate the reconstruction of the gender order, as well as of the material side of society. On a symbolic level, public housing was aimed at providing homes for families who embodied a restored but also improved gender order, and therefore new and modern. The reproductive arrangement related to this new gender order was based on a family consisting of a breadwinner and a homemaker with clear-cut gendered roles, functions, bodies and spaces.

A slightly different picture emerges when we look at another kind of representation. The public housing complexes of the post–World War II decades, like some of the interwar buildings, were adorned with various works of art that were commissioned by the city of Vienna. Such artwork consisted of murals as well as sculptures, and was single or in groups, situated either in the yards of the apartment buildings and thus addressing mainly the occupants, on external walls facing the street, or in a transitional zone between residential spaces and the general public. After a period of trial and procedural uncertainty, the city decided in 1950 to have a civil servant within the city Department for Cultural Affairs decide which artist was to be commissioned (or more rarely, whose artwork should be bought). Previously, Vienna's Association of Artists had suggested one of their members for a specific commission, with the final decision being made by the city administration, usually the Building Authority.[33] The works selected in this manner mirrored the attitudes of the artists' associations as well as of high-level officials in the city administration. Although the works of art were not part of a conscious educational effort, they represented and expressed ideals at the heart of the construction effort, and established supporting messages.

In her comprehensive research on these issues, Irene Nierhaus counted 1,205 objects in 525 buildings erected by the city of Vienna between 1949 and 1960.[34] She catalogued 3,171 single objects for the period between 1949 and 1984, most of which were "representations of nature" (31%) and "non-figural" (31.8%), with 169 of the objects (5.3%) showing "family and other private relationships."[35] Those are the representations I analyzed for information on family and gender models and icons during my search for idealized reproductive arrangements.

Even the "representations of nature" provide material relevant to a gender analysis: there are frequent images of female animals with their offspring, which are always only one or two young animals. I agree with Nierhaus's interpretation that the displays of small groups of two or three animals evoke an intimate symbiosis of "mother and child."[36] The fact that animals are chosen for representation naturalizes this relationship, takes it out of social contexts, and renders it eternal, out of time, immutable and therefore stable.

The vicinity to housing complexes designated as spaces for family life casts a specific light on the meaning of family embodied in the images. On the one hand, the mother-child animal groups are a metaphor for families as stable social groups, based on unchanging nature. They can be read as safe bulwarks in a society shaken and traumatized by two wars and several major political and social ruptures that had taken place during the previous three decades. They can be also interpreted as (probably unintentional) displays of a social reality that society in a reconstruction era buzzing with activity usually ignored: "incomplete" families, with a male figure missing due to captivity or death.

Turning to explicit representations of "private relations," I decided to choose two very different but nonetheless characteristic artworks: a mural on the external wall of a residential building completed in 1951 (see Figure 1.4) and a pair of sculptures guarding the portal of a housing complex finished in 1957 (see Figures 1.5 and 1.6).

Figure 1.4 Walter Harnisch, *The Era of Baroque and Present Time in Hetzendorf*, 1951, 1130 Vienna, Hetzendorferstraße 175–187
Source: © M. Mesner 2017.

Figure 1.5 Rudolf Schmidt, *Woman and Child* and *Male Figure*, 1957/59, 1030 Vienna, Zaunergasse/Marokkanergasse
Source: © M. Mesner 2017.

Figure 1.6 Details from Rudolf Schmidt, *Woman and Child* (left) and *Male Figure* (right), 1957/59
Source: © M. Mesner 2017.

The mural, created by the artist Walter Harnisch and titled *The Era of Baroque and Present Time in Hetzendorf* (Hetzendorf being an area in the southwest of Vienna), does not focus directly on family or gender, but speaks all the more of gender norms and related attitudes, values and virtues. The mural, which extends over three floors, praises the benefits of contemporary public building in contrast to the baroque subjugation of workers. In the upper half of the mural, an obviously male subject bent over in subservience pays his dues to his master and the master's consort, both clad in imperial finery and looking down at their vassal. In the lower half, the scene is very different: directly below the subservient taxpayer is a man offering the viewer something like a construction plan, his work coat showing that he is a construction engineer. To his right a group consisting of a man, a child and a woman symbolizes the family as the beneficiary of the engineer's efforts as well as those of a bricklayer building a wall behind them. The woman, who appears very static, stands looking at her male counterpart and holds the young boy in her arm. The boy is reaching out towards the male (presumably his father), kneeling before him and offering fruit in a basket.

Both women, the aristocratic consort in the upper image and the worker's wife below, are passive. Whereas the woman situated in the baroque image does not show any purpose, apart from maybe decoration, the woman in the post-war image related to progressive improvement is depicted as a mother. Her main and only action is to hold the child, whereas the three adult male figures in the picture are related to professions, namely bricklayer, engineer and either breadwinner in general or perhaps even farmer.

Whereas Harnisch's mural broaches the issues of temporality and history, even if it idealizes the contemporary reconstruction era, the second representation I selected for closer inspection is a seemingly timeless pair of sculptures by the artist Rudolf Schmidt, called *Woman and Child* and *Male Figure*.

The figures are integrated into a portal framing the passage through a residential building complex, as if guarding the passage. The woman, who is placed to the left, rests her right hand protectively on a small child standing at her side. The male figure, on the right side of the portal, is naked and holds a large hammer before him, embodying the reconstruction hero described above. The woman wears a plain, unadorned dress reaching to her ankles. Both (or actually all three) figures have little to do with the reality of the surrounding city: industrial sites were not peopled by nearly naked men wielding enormous hammers, and women in the streets of 1950s Vienna were not barefoot, nor did they wear long frocks. Nierhaus calls the effect "retarding" and "substantializing,"[37] the latter term pointing to the symbolic charge of such representations. By placing the image out of sync with its time, thus turning it into a seemingly timeless display or one related to some blurred and idealistic past, general notions of clearly contemporary social values and attitudes become generic, abstract and indisputable. This mode of representation is very similar to the visual language formalized by the National Socialists, in which idealized and iconic men and women without any signs of their historic contingency represented the *Volksgemeinschaft* (national community). This is not to imply that Vienna's city administration of the 1950s intended to create a society similar to the National Socialist *Volksgemeinschaft*, but points to the long-lasting consequences and traces of Nazi rule. During the interwar period, human figural representations displaying workers in a socio-critical naturalistic tradition[38] prevailed, often showing humans visibly proud of their class, or else anti-ideal, explicitly not beautiful, or even haggard as a result of life in capitalist misery. Post–World War II representations in Vienna's public buildings often spoke different languages. The proletarian, defined by class, had been replaced by the idealized and generic male or female citizen "without qualities."

Conclusion

Post–World War II public housing in Vienna, and the pictorial and rhetoric discourses it triggered, shows a multilayered and complex concept of family and reproductive arrangements, with the different layers generating indissoluble tensions between conflicting goals and exigencies. One conceptual layer encompasses the modern family of the 1950s, ideally formed through a breadwinning father, a homemaking mother and two children. This is a model clearly borrowed from eighteenth- and nineteenth-century upper-class ideals, although substantially transformed to make them contemporary and "modern" for the 1950s. While the upper-class model was socially exclusive and restricted to a small share of society, the "modern" family seemed within reach of the lower-middle and working classes most public housing tenants belonged to. While the woman whose sole job was to be a homemaker continued to serve as the ideal, reality took a different turn for various reasons. First, most families could not afford to live only on one wage, and wives had to earn additional income to provide for a decent lifestyle. Second, unlike past and contemporary upper-class households that relied on servants, the post-war "modern" family model was a nuclear family relying on a different reproductive arrangement. The "modern" family lived in apartments whose spaces were becoming more and more secluded, with one nuclear family per apartment. During the *Aufbau* era, the delineation between the inside and the outside of the apartment became more distinct, with reproductive functions increasingly drawn into the apartments themselves to become invisible for everybody apart from family members. In reality, of course, the line between the reproductive inside and productive outside remained blurred. The female part of the couple frequently had to earn money for the household, in addition to her defining function as a mother and wife. For many members of the middle class, this was the only means to meet post-war Fordist ideals of consumerism. The rationalization and mechanization of reproductive work was an important aspect of the *Aufbau* era's reproductive arrangement, as it allowed for the concealment of contradictions between the need for extra money and the ideal of the perfect mother who was a full-time housewife.

The inherent tensions of the post-war model threatened its acceptance. Gender roles had to be legitimized by anchoring them in an ahistoric and asocial nature or in placing them in some blurred, unspecific past. In spite of their oft-voiced emancipatory statements, the Viennese building authorities legitimized the modern *Aufbau* family through premodern images. Such images were familiar from the National Socialist period but seemed not to be tainted by its crimes. In the fast-changing social world of the mid-twentieth century, a Europe riddled by wars, fascism, genocide and expulsion resulting in mass migration, the "modern" family, paradoxically anchored in the stability of eternal nature, was the promise for a successful reconstruction of society, one that the public housing effort sought to support in a quest for modernity.

Notes

1. I am indebted to Matthias Trinkaus, Bruno Kreisky Archives Vienna, for his continuing support with archival research.
2. "[D]as Kind empfängt in ihr seine ersten Eindrücke, die Familie lebt in ihr und schöpft Kraft aus ihr, der alternde Mensch genießt die Geborgenheit, die sie ihm schenkt." Jonas 1956, n.p.
3. Eigner, Matis, and Resch 1999, 16p.
4. Pfau-Effinger 1993; Pfau-Effinger 1996.
5. The related party was called SDAP (Sozialdemokratische Arbeiterpartei / Socialdemocratic Workers' Party) from 1918 until its prohibition in 1934. When it was refounded in 1945, its name was Socialist Party of Austria (SPÖ: Sozialistische Partei Österreichs).
6. "Aus der Enge des Hinterhofes zu Licht, Luft und Sonne," headline in a pamphlet praising the social housing efforts of the city of Vienna. *Der soziale Wohnbau der Stadt Wien* 1956, n.p.
7. Baldauf, Mesner, and Verlič 2016.
8. Trinkaus 2013, 32.
9. Blau 1999, 45.
10. Marchart 1984, 22–3.
11. Maderthaner 2006, 383.
12. Sieder 1988.
13. Swoboda 1978, tables 75p.
14. Statistik Austria 2016, 22.

15. Fischer Kowalski 1981, 88.
16. Eigner, Matis, and Resch 1999, 17.
17. Denk 2007, 78p., footnote 523.
18. Baumann 2012, 62.
19. Bramhas 1987, 73.
20. "Im Interesse der Hausfrauen"; Luley 1960, 70.
21. "So daß die Hausfrauen im allgemeinen nur mehr einen halben Tag pro Waschperiode in den Waschküchen zubringen müssen." Luley 1960, 70.
22. "Stadtbauamt."
23. Mattl 1992.
24. Mesner 1998, 30.
25. "Das Reich der Frau"; "Ihm [der Vater] dient die Wohnung zur Regeneration seiner Kräfte. Das gemeinsame Essen, das Spielen mit den Kindern, die Geselligkeit überhaupt und der Schlaf stellen den größten Teil seines Wohnens dar." Dolesch 1958, 223.
26. Schuster 1946, 68.
27. Schuster 1950, 64.
28. See Gehmacher and Mesner 2007, 42.
29. Saurer 1985, 48.
30. Kreisky Archiv Wien, Plakatarchiv 100/85, Vienna: Vorwärts 1955.
31. Mesner 1997, 199.
32. Bandhauer-Schöffmann 1996, 222–4.
33. Niehaus 1993, 22.
34. Niehaus 1993, 35.
35. Niehaus 1993, 102.
36. Niehaus 1993, 107.
37. Niehaus 1993, 104.
38. Niehaus 1993, 137.

References

Baldauf, Anette, Maria Mesner, and Mara Verlič. 2016. "Always Forward. Hermann Neubacher and the Commons." In *Spaces of Commoning: Artistic Research and the Utopia of Everyday*, edited by Anette Baldauf, Stefan Gruber, Moira Hille, Annette Krauss, Vladimir Miller, Mara Verlič, Hong-Kai Wang, and Julia Wieger, 132–145. Berlin: Sternberg Press.

Bandhauer-Schöffmann, Irene. 1996. "Weibliche Aufbauszenarien." In *Inventur 45/55. Österreich im ersten Jahrzehnt der Zweiten Republik*, edited by Wolfgang Kos and Georg Rigele, 201–231. Vienna: Sonderzahl.

Baumann, Natalie. 2012. *Die Entwicklung der Wiener Gemeindebauten im Kontext ihrer Architektur.* M.A. Thesis, University of Vienna.

Blau, Eve. 1999. *The Architecture of Red Vienna 1919–1934.* Cambridge, MA: MIT Press.

Bramhas, Erich. 1987. *Der Wiener Gemeindebau: vom Karl-Marx-Hof zum Hundertwasserhaus.* Basel, Boston, and Stuttgart: Birkhäuser.

Denk, Marcus. 2007. *Zerstörung als Chance? Städtebauliche Konzepte, Leitlinien und Projekte in Wien 1945–58.* Dissertation, University of Vienna.

Der soziale Wohnbau der Stadt Wien. 1956. Edited by Stadtbauamt der Stadt Wien. Vienna: Verlag für Jugend und Volk (= Der Aufbau 32).

Der soziale Wohnbau der Stadt Wien. 1960². Edited by Stadtbauamt der Stadt Wien. Vienna: Verlag für Jugend und Volk (= Der Aufbau 39).

Dolesch, Armin. 1958. "Familiengerechtes Wohnen." *Der Aufbau* 1958(6): 223–225.

Eigner, Peter, Herbert Matis, and Andreas Resch. 1999. "Sozialer Wohnbau in Wien. Eine historische Bestandsaufnahme." *Jahrbuch des Vereins für die Geschichte der Stadt Wien* 1999: 49–100.

Fischer Kowalski, Marina. 1981. "Zur Modernisierung von Eltern-Kind-Verhältnissen." In *Kindergruppenkinder. Selbstorganisierte Alternativen zum Kindergarten*, edited by Marina Fischer-Kowalski, Roswitha Fitzka-Puchberger, and Julius Mende, 87–96. Vienna: Verlag für Gesellschaftskritik.

Gehmacher, Johanna, and Maria Mesner. 2007. *Land der Söhne. Geschlechterverhältnisse in der Zweiten Republik.* Innsbruck, Vienna, and Bozen: Studienverlag.

Jonas, Franz. 1956. "Wir bauen eine bessere Stadt." In *Der soziale Wohnbau der Stadt Wien*, edited by Stadtbauamt der Stadt Wien, n.p. Vienna: Verlag für Jugend und Volk.

Luley, Walter. 1960. "Die Ausgestaltung der Waschküchen in den Wiener Gemeindebauten." *Der Aufbau* 39: 70–72.

Maderthaner, Wolfgang. 2006. "Von der Zeit um 1860 bis zum Jahr 1945." In *Wien. Geschichte einer Stadt, vol 3: Von 1790 bis zur Gegenwart*, edited by Peter Csendes and Ferdinand Oppl, 175–544. Vienna, Cologne, and Weimar: Böhlau.

Marchart, Peter. 1984. *Wohnbau in Wien. 1923–1983.* Vienna: Compress.

Mattl, Siegfried. 1992. "'Aufbau'—eine männliche Chiffre der Nachkriegszeit." In *Wiederaufbau weiblich. Dokumentation der Tagung 'Frauen in der österreichischen und deutschen Nachkriegszeit,'* edited by Irene Bandhauer-Schöffmann and Ela Hornung, 15–23. Vienna and Salzburg: Edition Geyer.

Mesner, Maria. 1997. "Die Neugestaltung des Ehe- und Familienrechts. Re-Definitionspotentiale im Geschlechterverhältnis der Aufbau-Zeit." *Zeitgeschichte* 24(5–6): 186–210.

Mesner, Maria. 1998. "'Frauenüberschuß' und 'alleinstehende Frauen.' Zur Konstruktion einer Existenz des Mangels." In *Der ledige Un-Wille. Norma e contrarietà. Zur Geschichte lediger Frauen in der Neuzeit*, edited by Siglinde Clementi and Alessandra Spada, 27–45. Vienna and Bozen: Folio.

Niehaus, Irene. 1993. *Kunst-am-Bau im Wiener kommunalen Wohnbau der fünfziger Jahre.* Vienna, Cologne, and Weimar: Böhlau.

Pfau-Effinger, Birgit. 1993. "Macht des Patriarchats oder Geschlechterkontrakt? Arbeitsmarktintegration von Frauen im internationalen Vergleich." *Prokla, Zeitschrift für kritische Sozialwissenschaft* 1993(4): 633–663.

Pfau-Effinger, Birgit. 1996. "Analyse internationaler Differenzen in der Erwerbsbeteiligung von Frauen. Theoretischer Rahmen und empirische Ergebnisse." *Kölner Zeitschrift für Soziologie und Sozialpsychologie* 1996(3): 462–492.

Saurer, Edith. 1985. "Schweißblätter. Gedankenfetzen zur Frauengeschichte in den fünfziger Jahren." In *Die "wilden" fünfziger Jahre. Gesellschaft, Formen und Gefühle eines Jahrzehnts in Österreich*, edited by Gerhard Jagschitz and Klaus-Dieter Mulley, 42–52. St. Pölten and Vienna: Niederösterreichisches Pressehaus.

Schuster, Franz. 1946. "Wohnküche, Kochküche oder Eßküche." *Der Aufbau* 1946(8): 68–70.

Schuster, Franz. 1950. "Einfache Einbauküchen in Volkswohnungen." *Der Aufbau* 1950(2): 49–64.

Sieder, Reinhard. 1988. *Zur alltäglichen Praxis der Wiener Arbeiterschaft im ersten Drittel des 20. Jahrhunderts.* Phil., Habilschrift University of Vienna, Vienna.

Statistik Austria, ed. 2016. *Wohnen 2015 Zahlen, Daten und Indikatoren der Wohnstatistik.* Vienna: Kommissionsverlag.

Swoboda, Hannes. 1978. "Die gesellschaftspolitische Bedeutung des kommunalen Wohnbaues nach 1945." In *Kommunaler Wohnbau in Wien. Die Leistungen in der 2. Republik*, 75–78. Vienna: Presse- und Informationsdienst der Stadt Wien.

Trinkaus, Matthias. 2013. *Wohnbaupolitik in Wien: 1934–1938.* M.A. Thesis, University of Vienna.

2

Planning for Patriarchy?
Gender Equality in the Swedish
Modern Built Environment

Irene Molina

Introduction

Sweden is internationally renowned as a just welfare society in which gender equality permeates all spheres of life. International measurements have largely counted Sweden and the rest of the Scandinavian countries as the best places in the world for women to live.[1] But is this an unequivocal truth? Even if Sweden's rank has been declining, from being first until 2007 but falling to fourth in 2016, the answer should be "yes" with regard to many aspects of everyday life and civil rights. There are, however, some intriguing exceptions in several societal areas where gender equality is surprisingly not fully satisfactory. One of these areas is urban planning and housing production, that is, the very production of urban space. As will be explained, although fair in many senses, the urban planning model for post-war Sweden was a problematic project from a gender equality perspective, which remains to be fully examined by feminist scholars. Swedish welfare policies regarding family and housing have traditionally had far-reaching equality aims regarding gender. Nevertheless, one important critique has pointed out that the policies have focused on a nuclear family norm in the form of a heterosexual and monogamous couple, a norm that has remained fairly intact in housing provision in the Swedish system, in spite of the fact that the nuclear family formation nowadays is less common than other types of households.[2] In spite of what statistics make evident, in a country with one of the highest rates of gender equality, the nuclear family is still the dominant norm for the organization of all components of housing provision processes, from planning to financing and distribution. This chapter asserts that the foundation for this stubborn trend was laid and cemented during the golden years of Swedish modern urban planning. There are other normative aspects of Swedish planning ideologies during modernity that also deserve to be analyzed. The "Million Program" was built in a time of intense international migration to the country, which had consequences for the patterns of residential segregation and urban exclusion that followed, and which shape the racialized cities of today.[3] Consequently, the questions asked in this chapter are: What are the corollaries for current gender-race-class power relations derived from post–World War II urban planning in Sweden? Which presuppositions about gender-race-class relations were embedded in the construction of the modern Swedish city? Is it appropriate to understand this planning ideology as, using Rose's concept, "masculinist"?[4] Using a postcolonial feminist perspective, what can we learn from this specific example about the modern production of the built environment and its current exclusions and inclusions?

The chapter takes as its starting point the fact that the establishment of the modern welfare state—the Swedish *Folkhem*—implied the consolidation of differentiated gender roles in both labor and daily life, including housing.[5] Building on the emblematic case of modern Swedish urban transformations, this chapter attempts to make a contribution to the understanding of (1) the importance of place, space and planning for the configuration of equal gender relations through time and (2) the need for intersectional perspectives on power and oppression for the analysis of particular public policies launched for the promotion of gender equality in the built environment, but which paradoxically, in practice, can become an impediment for the very achievement of that goal.

The Emblematic Million Program

Similar to several of the examples in this volume, Sweden confronted the modern challenges of industrialization and urbanization processes by launching ambitious projects for the construction of large housing estates in the outskirts of cities (see the cases of Finland, the Soviet Union and the German Democratic Republic in this volume). Housing shortages were practically eliminated in the middle of the 1970s by the big housing production investment in the so-called Million Program. High housing standards and state housing subsidies made decent housing available for the majority of Sweden's population, and put Sweden at the top of international comparisons of good housing provision.[6] Moreover, using a comprehensive regulation system coupled with the conditions for a subsidy system, state authorities were able to plan and control much of the housing construction with respect to what should be built and where. In spite of its goal of equal access to the housing market, it is important to remark that the modern system of housing provision in Sweden did not aim to erase class structures, not even within the housing market. Almost to the contrary, even though the policies provided all segments of the population with high standards and fair housing, the policies reinforced social segregation, maintaining fundamental socioeconomic differences.[7] As a matter of fact, during the whole nineteenth century and still today, the Swedish state has been influencing the patterns of gender, social and racial residential segregation through housing policy.[8] I will start by discussing the gender dimensions of modern planning first, and will follow with class and race aspects later on.

The Built Environment: A Male View of Women's Place

Modern planning ideologies were wrought in the plenitude of modernity and first massively materialized during the ten years of the Million Program, becoming what I, perhaps a bit provocatively, aim to call patriarchal urban planning. The Million Program was the biggest housing and infrastructure investment in modern Swedish history, with the construction of roughly one million dwellings between 1965 and 1974 throughout the whole country and in a variety of housing types and forms of tenure (Figure 2.1). As has been established by research, processes of urbanization and urban growth have everywhere gone hand in hand with rural–urban migration. The same applies to the case of Sweden, where the Million Program areas became in part neighborhoods of transition for domestic migrants still coming to the labor markets located in urban areas. But principally, the program came to alleviate the situation of precariousness and overcrowding caused by the high demand for housing in urban industrialized areas, which was exacerbated in times of state austerity. After the end of World War II and in the years that followed, the economy of the country was flourishing and the accumulation of private capital had to be absorbed,[9] which occurred in big infrastructure projects driven by the private sector, with state-subsidized investments in housing and urbanization. Whereas the goals of bringing good and safe housing to all citizens were largely achieved and the housing shortage eliminated by the mid-1970s, some downsides of the planning ideologies behind modern housing policy are revealed as pitfalls for women's emancipation. In terms of gendered spatial patterns, one key aspect to bring to the analysis is the character of the dominant planning ideologies of the post-war building epoch, with its combination of suburbanization and the emblematic traffic separation principle,

Irene Molina

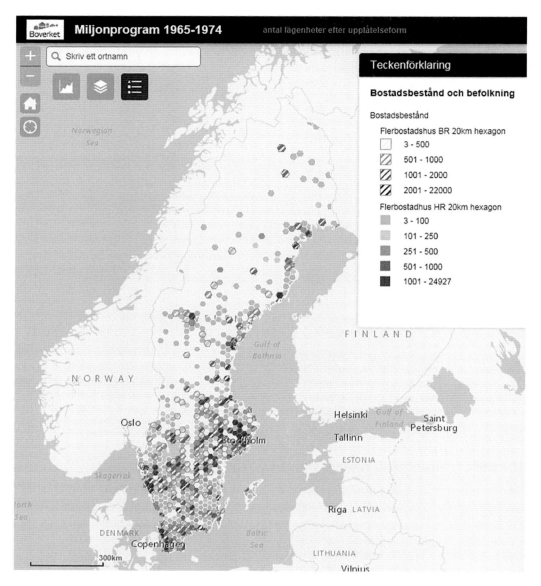

Figure 2.1 Distribution of the Housing Estates of the Million Program
Source: Swedish Housing Board—Boverket (adapted for this chapter).

attempting to bring safety to the population in the suburbs, "especially for mothers and children" who were the ones expected to spend most of their time in the neighborhood (Figure 2.2). Most of the housing estates of the Million Program were located on the outskirts of cities, and whereas an easily accessible infrastructure of routes for both private and public traffic was developed mainly for the use of the industrial (male) workers, the women, children and the elderly were supposed to stay within or close to the residential areas, where circulation was protected from traffic and a rich infrastructure of services was offered. Although the dominant planning ideology of the time was "family-friendly," it presupposed a special local labor market for women within childcare and elderly care services, local commerce, education, and part-time jobs. These social assumptions about women's labor might have

Figure 2.2 View Over Tensta Centrum
Source: MostPhotos.

contributed to creating the gender segregated structure of the labor market that still persists today, where almost 95% of all workers in health care and elderly care are women, and 97% of those in public childcare and 68% of all primary school teachers are women. Women are still overrepresented in part-time jobs and have a lower labor frequency than men; 78% of all women in labor craft (ages 15–65) have jobs, but 29% of them have part-time jobs, while 83% among the male labor craft works and only 11% of them work part time.[10] Given this gender divided labor force, a long journey to work with stops at the nursery or the school, for example, may have imposed and still imposes a major obstacle for accessing a distant workplace or working full time. This relationship between part-time work and jobs within the service sector, which still today characterizes the gender segregated labor market structure in Sweden, should come as no surprise. Patriarchal structures still lie behind patterns of gender inequality within the organization of labor. Similarly, the heritage from modern planning has left its mark on both labor and housing structures, and in spite of its high place in the international gender equality ranking, the gender divide is still reflected in the Swedish labor market and also in the gender division of domestic work.

Integrating gender perspectives into the understanding of social urban space has been a task adopted by feminist urban geographers. For contextualizing the gendered notion of the spatial, it is convenient to turn the gaze back to the recent development of human geography, which as late as the past four decades has become permeable to the feminist movement's progress within and outside academia. One possible explanation for geographers' slow interest in gender analyses and theory may be concerned with the scale that geographic research moves within. Geographers, unlike sociologists, have tended to exclude the micro scale from their analysis, including the levels of the home and the body. Similarly to the binary gender division between the male and the female, space has also been conceptualized in a binary way, as a space for either private or public. Within this binary spatial theory, the private/public dichotomy has been an influential foundation of gender and housing research. This dichotomy is part of the construction of the relationship between spaces that is only available for the subject (private/ women/feminine/reproduction) and spaces that are available for the general public (public/men/ masculine/production).[11] The division of private/public is part of a worldview where dichotomies such as feminine/masculine, inside/outside, residence/workplace, and consumption/production play a central role in the social construction of gender relations; this in its turn influences who has access to which spaces and who is excluded.[12] The dichotomous conceptualization of space also has a material imprint on physical spaces intended for reproduction (often the home) and spaces intended for production (public space).[13] For some women the division has reduced access to several of the city's spaces and has been one of the most limiting aspects of urban life. Women's experience of insecurity and safety in public space is, according to this theoretical approach, based on the difficulty of securing an indisputable right to occupy public space.[14]

Thus, the private sphere of everyday life, considered as the inner world happening indoors, at the home and in its vicinity, has been left outside of the geographical field of study, although of course the social organization of space includes the lines of gender (and race). But both the development of cultural geography and changes in the broader social structure, such as the massive entry of women into the sphere of working life, has meant that women have started to become more and more visible in the geographical landscape and to its scholars, often male. The complex and dynamic relationship between gender and the built environment has been gradually incorporated into Anglo-American geographical research beginning in the 1990s. An important starting point in the relationship between gender and place was the overall development of gender theory, bringing insights about gender as a socially constructed category to academic knowledge production. As many studies have argued, just as gender, sex is a social construction.[15] The female subject identity is the result of different expectations about gender roles and concrete opportunities for action. Gender is also performative and it works therefore affecting the expectations for women and the requirements put to them.[16] This idea relates closely to feminist geographer Gillian Rose's elaboration of paradoxical spaces, which are the spaces that are traditionally socially constructed for women to occupy, but which they can hardly internalize as their own spaces, because they have been created for the imagination of what women are, not for what women in fact are.[17] Similarly, Dagmar Reichert has referred to the figure of the imagined woman in masculine spaces as "Utopia"; because there is not and will never be a subject that is "a woman," the space of her body is per se a utopic place.[18] Anyway, the masculinist world of building, planning and managing the built environment puts obstacles or gives opportunities to individuals and groups in differentiated ways, depending among other things on the gender, class and race rules at stake. Consequently, the gendered division of space is a result of the ways in which society is structured; the resulting patterns of modern planning have been developed within an overarching patriarchal structure and cannot therefore be regarded as "something natural." Moreover, once produced, the built environment has lifelong duration, which means that the buildings and the urban infrastructure created continue to characterize the social space for a long time after they are built. The built environment that initially formed an all-male creation thus remains male dominated over generations. Referring to the role of patriarchy in the formation of western cities, Bondi and Rose declare:

> This "women and environments" literature began to make women visible as urban actors and to denounce the inherent sexism of the capitalist city. Particular emphasis was placed on the ways that urban land-use patterns and transportation systems created mobility barriers for women with young children, reinforced gendered inequities in access to employment, and, overall, helped to maintain traditional gender roles.[19]

Despite this important gender marking of urban space, space is still a neglected dimension in gender studies, and the field of urban studies suffers from a lack of gender theory. Besides a few but important works,[20] Swedish feminist research has not taken the roles played by the gendered division of space and patriarchy in the shaping of living spaces in modern cities seriously enough.

When it comes to the more symbolic significance of the male character of space, it is likely that buildings do not completely control our lives; however, insofar as they reflect different aspects of the society we live in, we are affected by them in various ways. Buildings reflect, for example, dominant male values, the prevailing political and architectural views of living, what people ask for, financial constraints, and more. Buildings affect us further in the sense that they contain ideas about women, about women's "own locations," about what is private and what is public, and about which things should be kept separate from each other and which should be put together. And just as language does, buildings incorporate and perpetuate some ideas about women in an indirect way. After all, we live our lives in these buildings created from the male perspective, although probably in ways other than how they were meant to be. Space can be used and has been used as instances of resistance and mobilization. Nevertheless, exploring the masculinist suburban space more thoroughly, we must acknowledge that urban space in general and housing in particular are intended neither for men nor for women. They are perhaps intended for what the men involved in the processes of production of the built environment believed to be women's needs and preferences, and probably in the belief that women in general indeed wanted to organize their daily lives around the home (if not within the home), and close to the children. In that sense, even if residential areas were planned to facilitate women's everyday movement, it is probable that in practice they had the opposite effect of constraining that mobility, and that the supposedly woman-friendly space turned into a trap for women, where they eventually saw their mobility limited outside the residential area and its immediate environment. A weak labor market position, combined with a continued vision of the home and its immediate surroundings as natural female environments and the tasks performed therein as natural female tasks, promotes the maintenance and reproduction of women's traditional place in the urban space as well as an essentialist view of gender differences. This means, for instance, that when the traditional binary gender perspective is applied to analyzing patterns of urban planning, it results often in problematic and essentialist understandings of women in space; history repeats itself. The placement of women in the domestic sphere may explain why there is an important amount of research regarding gender in everyday life and working life, as well as on childcare facilities.[21] City planning has also been analyzed from gender perspectives, but from the reductionist perspective of women as subjects of fear.[22] For example, following the trend to plan gender-equal residential areas, since the early 1990s some municipalities in Sweden have been drawing up checklists, using surveys that include questions about what might be women's specific criteria for quality in residential areas. Often these checklists start from the observed reality in the lives of women and men, seldom questioning structures of gender inequality. The consequence becomes circular reasoning with dead ends, such as in the following example:

> Research and statistics show that women generally work closer to the home than men do and thus use regional transportation on a daily basis to a lesser extent. On the other hand, women use local public transportation to a greater extent.[23]

Nonetheless, it is important to remark that gender and housing have been neglected by research, which is interestingly illustrated in one of the UN's final reports on gender equality, where housing was not included at all.[24]

A more truly gender-inspired perspective on planning would include aspects such as the need for a democratic planning process, opportunities for integration between different population groups, recreation opportunities, relationships between housing and work, physical security in the area and the facilities that should be available in the service areas. The premise of this proposal is that all planning should be an instrument for building a democratic, egalitarian and equal society.[25] Nonetheless, a remaining problem is that gender-based initiatives still start from presuppositions that reveal their (1) essentialism—women and men are assumed to want different things; (2) heteronormativity—there are only two binary gender identities, excluding LGBTQ sexual identities; (3) ethnocentrism—all women and all men are homogeneous categories without different experiences of racism, migration, culture and several forms of discrimination; and (4) elitism—there are no class-related differences in experiences of residence, or the only class experiences counted are those perceived by the gaze of middle-class white feminist planners. So unmistakably, if we want to design a real woman-friendly city, we face a major challenge when dealing with poverty, racism, sexism, patriarchy, heteronormativity and other oppressing systems.[26] Therefore, the proposal from this work consists of pointing out that what is really needed for a comprehensive democratization of urban planning and building processes is an intersectional perspective and a deliberative concept of planning, where individuals should be given the opportunity, as far as possible, to influence their own housing situations, starting from a perspective of diversity rather than homogeneity. We will come back to the question of intersectionality after having discussed in more depth the importance of race for the current urban condition, in particular for some of the Million Program areas produced in the 1960s and 1970s.

Racialization and Neoliberalization

The long-term effects of masculinist urban planning and its consequences for the cities of today must be analyzed in light of the overarching political and economic changes that have occurred in the country as a whole and in urban landscapes in particular. One of them is racialization, that is, the particular form of ethnic residential segregation that has been shaped in Swedish cities during modernity, in which clear racial hierarchies characterize housing distribution spatially.[27] An important social transformation that occurred in Sweden after World War II was increased international migration, first needed for the flourishing industrial sector and recruited from Finland and from Southern Europe, and later on (in the 1970s) arriving from all world regions as a result of a more generous refugee policy driven by Olof Palme's Social Democratic regime. Many of the Million Program neighborhoods housed this racially diverse migrant population. In the years to come, while ethnic Swedes started to move out or avoided moving into the Million Program areas through processes that some researchers have called white flight and white avoidance,[28] the migrant population of non-European origin has tended to stay in the Million Program neighborhoods. This, however, as we will see later on, has not changed the processes of stigmatization of the Million Program neighborhoods.

Besides racialization, during almost three decades, Sweden has been moving from its former Keynesian Social Democratic regime to a more neoliberal one. Whereas the Million Program was built during a time of economic wellbeing and welfare Keynesianism, the model being installed from the beginning of the 1990s has been labeled a "monstrous hybrid" due to the combination of deregulation and the remaining aspects of the old regulated housing policy.[29] The hybrid character of the new economic model can be observed in several sectors other than housing, including education, health care and elderly care. State subsidization of the private sector today guarantees capitalists chances to profit from welfare services without further charging the users. For the housing market and in particular for urban planning, the neoliberal turn with its drastic reforms has meant a definite backlash, not only in terms of gender equality goals and ambitions, but also for the very conception of housing as a human and civic right. The process of deregulation initiated at the beginning of the 1990s during the conservative administration of Carl Bildt (1991–1994) resulted in housing production diminishing dramatically in the ensuing 25 years. Housing shortages, homelessness and overcrowding consequently increased along with the strong setback in housing production. Consequently, scholars have begun to compare the current housing crises with the situation in the 1940s, which led to the construction of the Million Program.[30] To illustrate the critical current housing shortage, today's waiting time in the rental housing market for a flat produced during the

Million Program is on average ten years, a situation that primarily affects those who cannot afford the high prices in the increasingly privatized housing sector. Segregation and social polarization have constantly accelerated due to both the political legacy of post-war urban planning ideologies and the more recent neoliberal turn.[31] Although the million dwellings constructed during the Million Program were spatially spread out and consisted of different types of housing, the type of areas that are stigmatized today are those with a high migrant population located in the city suburbs. The stigmatization of the residential areas of the Million Program started at an early stage, as will be discussed in the coming section.

Socio-spatial Stigmatization

Slowly but consistently, the population of many of the Million Program areas changed, with the Swedish working class replaced by migrant labor craft. In 2008, in more than 50 of the Million Program areas, more than half of the population had a foreign background.[32] Socioeconomic and racial segregation in Swedish cities can be explained both in terms of their political and discursive or ideological dimensions.[33] Although considerable qualitative and quantitative research shows the crucial role of politics, stigmatizing media and other discourses, and racial discrimination, the most commonly accepted explanation in public debates is the one that blames the migrants for their own residential segregation, assuming that living in the segregated suburban neighborhoods is a matter of free choice; an explanation I have elsewhere called "cultural relativist."[34] In fact, the housing policy of the 1960s, in the form of the Million Program, established the grounds for a long-term pattern of social segregation, as planning separated the three basic segments of Swedish housing tenancy: public rental, cooperative, and privately owned housing. Additionally, these three housing segments consist of different types of housing, even today. Whereas rental and cooperative housing are primarily multifamily buildings, privately owned housing consists mostly of detached single-family houses. Each of these three segments came to represent its own class category. By the mid-1970s, social segregation was a visible feature of the urban landscape, not mainly in terms of the exposition of poverty and deprivation as it is elsewhere, but as the work of architectural design. Housing shortages were practically eliminated[35] and the standard of living drastically improved through the launching of the Million Program. But the spatial separation between social classes remained a fact.

As mentioned earlier, besides housing policy, migration policy has played its role in racial segregation, in particular because of its lack of strategies for avoiding such segregation. The new population of the early 1970s, consisting of asylum seekers from practically all over the world, was as one might expect directed to the empty flats of the newly produced public rental market in urban areas within or close to labor market regions. It is here, thus, that in the late 1970s social segregation met racial segregation. This merging started to shape the racialized patterns of Swedish cities that we find today. What took place during the following years was an intensified process of racialization, reinforced by the incapacity of authorities to launch anti-segregation housing policies, but also by an increased stigmatization of the areas where the migrant population was visibly concentrated.

From the very start, in the early 1960s, the media depicted public rental segments of the Million Program neighborhoods as problem areas. The first argument against the housing program held that the multifamily buildings, high population density, and the dominating presence of concrete blocks represented urban modernity. Probably influenced by the discourses against modernity and urbanization coming from the human ecological tradition of the Chicago school,[36] the Swedish critics of modernism accused politicians and architects of causing anonymity, social deviation, and mental disorders through the construction of the Million Program. In presenting those who moved into the housing as victims, reporters often approached women, and in particular young mothers, and asked how it felt to move to those areas. Pictures of women with their children in strollers trying to circulate through the areas under construction were used to illustrate how hard it was to live a

Irene Molina

Figure 2.3 Mothers and Children of the Million Program in the late 1960s
Source: MostPhotos.

"normal life" in these places (Figure 2.3). Although the answers were often very positive, the reporters represented their stories as those of dissatisfaction.[37] Paradoxically, both representations of the good and the dysfunctional neighborhood used the figure of the Swedish working-class mother. As a matter of fact, by the 1970s the racialization of the residents of the rental segments of the Million Program had not yet started, as everybody regardless of gender, national background or age were all considered victims of these unfriendly residential environments. In the 1980s, the presence of the migrant population was observed and some articles in newspapers mentioned the "risk of ghetto formation,"[38] but it was as late as the 1990s that the racialization of the Million Program came up more broadly in media stigmatization. The residents were no longer depicted as victims but rather as the very ones responsible for the whole phenomena of urban residential segregation; they were accused of gathering in "immigrant dense" suburbs as a way of rejecting integration. By this time, the processes of white flight had left some of the areas almost "free from" ethnic Swedes.[39] The racialized population of the stigmatized areas were ascribed gender and age, but as a part of "otherizing" them rather than as a means of normalizing their existence. Young men with migrant backgrounds were labeled "immigrant boys" and the young women "immigrant girls," whereas their parents were "immigrant fathers" and "immigrant mothers." All of them were ascribed problematic sexualities attached to Islamophobic and culturally racist generalizations such as honor killings and patriarchal control as well as the assumed inclination of the immigrant (Muslim) men to commit rape against white Swedish women.[40] This breaking point marked by the media's racialized stigmatization of the suburbs is crucial for understanding the new gendered roles that appeared in some of the representations of the suburbs of modernity. It is through this process of racialization that the rest of the Million Program suburbs (in fact the majority of them) become normalized as Swedish residential areas, integrated into the city, and their problematic character erased. The process of racializing the city washed away from the white Swedish areas the stigma inherited from the origins of the Million Program. In contrast to the 1970s, when all areas of the Million Program were depicted as dirty and dangerous, this description is applied today in large part only to the areas associated with a high concentration of immigrants.

Intersectionality Is Reality

Patterns of inequality in urban space are mediated by complex sets of historical and political processes and are crossed transversally by dominant ideologies; this makes the intersectional perspective for democratic planning proposed in this text necessary. In practice, when analyzing power asymmetries in urban residential patterns, it is often hard to find simple dichotomous divisions between women and men conceived of as homogenous categories without taking into consideration the role played by aspects such as sexuality, class, age, and race. The Swedish case shows that there is an intricate relationship between the national backgrounds of women and men, income distribution, skills, education, demographic variables, and the gendered patterns of residence.[41] The often genderless analysis of housing patterns might partly be explained by the legitimation of the heterosexual, monogamous couple and the normative nuclear family hidden in the innocent statistical term of "household." As feminists have shown, the nuclear family is functional to the economic capitalist system based on the household's consumption, which is facilitated by the incomes from two breadwinners.[42] It is also easier to navigate an expensive housing market as a couple than as an individual.[43] Feminist research has consequently criticized the focus that social sciences often put on couples' and households' incomes instead of individuals' incomes, for this focus does not show the individuals' actual ability to act, and their capacities in the event of separation or when individuals choose to stay in single-living patterns. The non-nuclear family, and for instance LGBTQ formations in which there can be more than one couple of parents, have simply been ignored by housing and planning research.[44] Regarding race, whereas Swedish-born single mothers show better positions in the housing market, their situation compared to Swedish-born men is worse; this trend was earlier observed by Lindén, who found the highest proportion of single parents in public (municipal) rental housing units.[45] Similarly, in situations of divorce and separation, highly skilled, high-income white men show a greater probability than women for staying at the couple's former home. At the same time, mothers tend to move out with their children, which explains an overrepresentation of single mothers after divorce or separation in more deprived areas. This situation is the opposite when looking at the patterns for the non-European, foreign-born population, where after separation women show better positions in the housing market than men.[46] Regarding age, elderly women owning their homes stay there after the death of the partner (men have a lower life expectancy rate than women), but their economic situation is worsened. These female widows can become seriously affected by current trends to "renoviction" (renovation with eviction), that is, when urban renewal leads to extreme gentrification, because they often cannot afford the higher rent levels after renovation and cannot return to the flat they rented before renovation.[47] Gentrification has consequently meant very different things for women belonging to different social, demographic and ethnic groups. Single women with good economic standing have the opportunity to choose a central location, which might also lead to an enhanced quality of life. For other women, especially poor elderly women, renoviction has meant deteriorating living conditions and reduced choices. Housing conditions are thus not only an expression of inequality, but they can also generate more inequality. By influencing such factors as health, access to schools and labor market accommodation, housing becomes a facilitator or sometimes a necessary condition for the access to other resources.[48]

Most likely due to the scarce literature on housing markets and discrimination in general, gender has only recently been included in the analysis of housing discrimination. In 2010 a major study on housing discrimination in Sweden was launched; it was a study based on the field experiment "situation testing."[49] Briefly, the study showed that discrimination occurred to a greater extent in the rental market (by both public and private landlords) than in the cooperative housing market. Discrimination occurred in large and middle-sized cities and in small towns, and it was shown to be stronger on the basis of ethnicity than other grounds for discrimination, although combinations of factors as gender and ethnicity or gender and religion became evident, leading to a need for more research. An earlier study had shown that women with a Swedish name seemed to have an advantage in the rental housing market.[50] This is consistent with the findings in Magnusson Turner's study on social exclusion and (risk of) homelessness, where women more easily got help from social services compared to men in the same situation.[51] Nevertheless, those results are partly contradicted by another study that suggests that young women without children fare worse in the housing market than young men, although the latter faced more suspicion and difficulties when renting rooms or sub-renting flats.[52] The general impression given by previous research in the field of genderized urban planning confirms the complexity of the matter; simple assumptions such as that women in general are discriminated against in the housing market, while men as a group are privileged must be nuanced and properly contextualized.

Analogous to findings of studies on the labor market,[53] a racial hierarchical structure or a structure of racialization has developed within the housing market as well.[54] Racialization has affected the structure of power relations in the country, connecting race, gender and class to each other in intricate intersectional ways. The gender-segregated residential patterns produced under the decade of the Million Program still persist today in the labor market, and one wonders how much the patterns found in the planning of Swedish suburbs have contributed to the crystallization of a gender and racially divided labor market. Those relations of today are racialized gender relations, and the women living in some of the Million Program areas of today are non-European immigrants with high levels of unemployment.[55]

Conclusions

In this chapter, I have presented a historical review of modern (post–World War II) housing policy and urban planning ideologies and practices from a gendered intersectional perspective including class and race relations in the Swedish city. Starting from the most influential housing project during modernity in Sweden, I analyze how this project was transformed during the deregulation and neoliberalization of the former Keynesian economy (including housing policies) and through an era of racialization. Moreover, I analyze the effects of the intensive process of urbanization that occurred after World War II that fixed gender roles to both the home and special segments of the labor market.[56] Large housing estates built in the cities' outskirts followed a planning logic of full access to local municipal and commercial services and traffic separation. This planning ideology was considered to be woman-friendly, but feminist researchers have asserted that it led to a "relegation" of the mothers to the sphere of the home.[57] While an easily accessible infrastructure of routes for both private and public traffic was developed mainly for male workers, it was assumed that women, children, and the elderly would stay within or close to the residential areas, where circulation was protected from traffic and a rich infrastructure of services was offered. This family-friendly planning ideology had consequences for gender roles and possibly even for Sweden's gender-segregated labor structure. An important social transformation occurred in Sweden after World War II with the increased influx of migrants, who were first recruited from Finland and Southern Europe for the flourishing industrial sector, and later on in the 1970s arrived from all world regions.

Gender-segregated patterns still persist today in both the housing and the labor markets, but a shift from white Swedish women to racialized migrant women has occurred in many of the Million Program neighborhoods. Research indicates that racialization processes of the workforce and racialization of the housing market have affected the country's structure of power relations, connecting race, gender and class to each other in intricate, intersectional ways.[58] Remarkably, the country is still internationally associated with its well-known model of welfare fairness in spite of the fact that since the 1990s Sweden has been moving from a long-term Keynesian Social Democratic regime to a neoliberal one.[59] Finally, the chapter critically analyzed the construction of public space as masculine and private space as feminine in a dichotomous conceptualization. Critics point to an underlying essentialist, ethnocentric and heteronormative conception, which applies mainly to white middle-class women and men but fails to include broader sectors of the population.

Finally, it is necessary to stress that Sweden is in urgent need of research on gender relations in housing patterns and housing policies.[60] Tenure-neutral housing allowances, child allowances, separate income taxation for couples, the right to paid parental leave, and the right to public day care are examples of the most important gender policies in Sweden. When it comes to gender and housing, there is surprisingly little research.

Notes

1. World Economic Forum (WEF) 2016.
2. Andersson 2011; see also Statistics Sweden 2014, showing that only 45% of the population in 2013 was cohabiting in couples with or without children. Forty-two percent were single households with or without children and 13% were other (unspecified) family formations.
3. Andersson and Molina 2003.
4. Rose 1993; Gillian Rose is influenced by the French philosopher Michèle Le Doeuff.
5. Hirdman 1993; Molina 1997.
6. Dickens, Duncan, Goodwin, and Gray 1985.
7. Dickens, Duncan, Goodwin, and Gray 1985; Andersson and Molina 2003.
8. Grundström and Molina 2016.
9. Harvey 1985; Holgersen 2014.
10. Statistics Sweden 2016.
11. McDowell 1999, 12.
12. McDowell 1999.
13. Domosh and Seager 2001; McDowell 1999.
14. Rose 1993.
15. Bordo 1993; Harding 1991.
16. Butler 1993.
17. Rose 1993.
18. Reichert 1994.
19. Bondi and Rose 2003, 231.
20. Hirdman 1993; Listerborn 2007; Sandberg and Rönnblom 2016.
21. Friberg 1990; Almqvist 2004; Bernhardt, Noack, and Lyngstad 2008.
22. Friberg and Larsson 2002; Larsson 2006; Larsson and Jalakas 2008; Listerborn 2002; Friberg, Listerborn, Andersson, and Scholten 2005.
23. Länsstyrelsen i Hallands län 2009, 13.
24. Gender Equality Commission 2013.
25. Petracci 2007.
26. Fainstein 2011; Brenner, Marcuse, and Mayer 2012; Roy 2002.
27. Molina 1997; Pred 2000; Andersson and Molina 2003; Smith 1989.
28. Bråmå 2006.

29. Christophers 2013.
30. Hedin et al. 2012; Baeten et al. 2017; Grundström and Molina 2016.
31. Andersson 2013.
32. Andersson 2013, 173.
33. Molina 1997; Andersson and Molina 2003; see Pred 2000.
34. Molina 1997.
35. Hedin et al. 2012.
36. Wirth 1938.
37. Ericsson et al. 2002.
38. Ericsson et al. 2002.
39. Bråmå 2006.
40. Ericsson et al. 2002.
41. In the ongoing research project "Gendering Housing—Intersectional Perspectives on Housing Provision and Urban Planning with Emphasis on Gender Relations in Sweden," funded by the Swedish Research Council, VR, the author together with a research group have worked on both qualitative and quantitative data for mapping housing conditions. Some preliminary results from the project are referred to in this chapter.
42. Munro and Smith 1989; Smith 1990; Gilroy and Woods 1994.
43. Sandlie 2008.
44. Ongoing research project "Gendering Housing."
45. Lindén 1989.
46. Ongoing research project "Gendering Housing."
47. Baeten et al. 2017.
48. Morris and Winn 1990; Kennett and Chan 2011. In Sweden, lacking a home address means that you cannot be registered as a citizen.
49. Molina 2015. The study covered discrimination on grounds of gender, ethnicity, religion or other belief, disability and sexual orientation. The rental market was investigated through almost 400 phone calls to 150 landlords at 90 different locations. The cooperative housing market was investigated by a total of 44 visits to apartments in Stockholm, Helsingborg and Lund.
50. Bengtsson, Iverman, and Hinnerich 2012.
51. Magnusson-Turner 2010.
52. Andersson, Johansson, Molina, and Solid 2007.
53. Mulinari and Neergaard 2004; de los Reyes 2001.
54. Molina 1997; Pred 2000.
55. According to Statistics Sweden 2014, while women born in Sweden ages 25–44 had an unemployment rate of only 4%, women born in African countries were 31% unemployed, and women born in Asian countries 21% unemployed. It should be noted that this is not directly related to educational levels or class affiliation before migration.
56. Molina 1997; Listerborn 2007; Molina and Grundström 2012.
57. Hirdman 1993; Molina 1997; Westin 2014.
58. Mulinari and Neergard 2004; de los Reyes 2001; Molina 1997; Pred 2000.
59. Christophers 2013.
60. Larsson and Jalakas 2008; Johansson and Molina 2002; Molina and Grundström 2012; Listerborn 2002; Sahlin 2011.

References

Almqvist, Annika. 2004. *Drömmen om det egna boendet. Från bostadsförsörjning till livsprojekt.* Dissertation, Department of Sociology, Erlanders Gotab, Stockholm.
Andersson, Catrin. 2011. *Hundra år av tvåsamhet: Äktenskapet i svenska statliga utredningar 1909–2009.* Dissertation. Arkiv, Lund.
Andersson, Roger. 2013. "Reproducing and Reshaping Ethnic Residential Segregation in Stockholm: The Role of Selective Migration Moves." *Geografiska Annaler: Series B, Human Geography* 952: 163–187.
Andersson, Roger, Sara Johansson, Irene Molina, and Dennis Solid. 2007. "Någonstans att bo: En kvalitativ studie av ungdomars erfarenhet av bostadsmarknaden i större städer." In *Måste man ha tur? Studier av yngre på bostadsmarknaden i svenska städer.* SOU 2007:14, s., rapport nr 2 från Boutredningen, edited by R. Andersson, 81–110. Stockholm: Fritzes.
Andersson, Roger, and Irene Molina. 2003. "Racialization and Migration in Urban Segregation Processes. Key Issues for Critical Geographers." In *Voices From the North—New Trends in Nordic Human Geography*, edited by Jan Öhman and Kirsten Simonsen, 261–282. London: Ashgate.

Bengtsson, Ragnar, Ellis Iverman, and Björn Tyrefors Hinnerich. 2012. "Gender and Ethnic Discrimination in the Rental Housing Market." *Applied Economics Letters* 19(1): 1–5.

Baeten, Guy, Sara Westin, Emil Pull and Irene Molina. 2017. "Pressure and violence: Housing renovation and displacement in Sweden". *Environment and Planning A* 49(3): 631–651.

Bernhardt, Eva, Turid Noack, and Torkild Hovde Lyngstad. 2008. "Shared Housework in Norway and Sweden: Advancing the Gender Revolution." *Journal of European Social Policy* 18(3): 275–288.

Bondi, Liz, and Damaris Rose. 2003. "Constructing Gender, Constructing the Urban: A Review of Anglo-American Feminist Urban Geography." *Gender, Place and Culture* 10(3): 229–245.

Bordo, Susan. 1993. *Unbearable Weight: Feminism, Western Culture, and the Body*. Berkeley: University of California Press.

Bråmå, Åsa. 2006. "'White Flight?' The Production and Reproduction of Immigrant Concentration Areas in Swedish Cities, 1990–2000." *Urban Studies* 43(7): 1127–1146.

Brenner, Neil, Peter Marcuse, and Margit Mayer. 2012. *Cities for People, Not for Profit: Critical Urban Theory and the Right to the City*. London and New York: Routledge.

Butler, Judith. 1993. *Bodies that Matter: On the Discursive Limits of "Sex."* New York: Routledge.

Christophers, Brett. 2013. "A Monstrous Hybrid: The Political Economy of Housing in Early Twenty-first Century Sweden." *New Political Economy* 18(6), 885–911.

de los Reyes, Paulina. 2001. *Mångfald och differentiering: diskurs, olikhet och normbildning inom svensk forskning och samhällsdebatt*. Stockholm: Arbetslivsinstitutet.

Dickens, Peter, Simon Duncan, Mark Goodwin, and Fred Gray. 1985. *Housing, States and Localities*. London and New York: Methuen.

Domosh, Mona and Joni Seager. 2001. *Putting Women in Place*. New York: Guilford Press.

Ericsson, Urban, Irene Molina and Per Markku Riistilami. 2002. *Miljonprogram och media – föreställningar om människor och förorter*. Stockholm: Integrationsverket och Riksantikvarieämbetet.

Fainstein, Susan S. 2011. *The Just City*. Ithaca, NY: Cornell University Press.

Friberg, Tora. 1990. *Kvinnors vardag: Om kvinnors arbete och liv: anpassningsstrategier i tid och rum*. Dissertation, Lund University Press, Lund.

Friberg, Tora, and Anita Larsson. 2002. *Steg framåt: Strategier och villkor för att förverkliga genusperspektivet i översiktlig planering*. Lund: Lund University.

Friberg, Tora, Carina Listerborn, Birgitta Andersson, and Christina Scholten (eds.). 2005. *Speglingar av rum. Om Könskodade platser och sammanhang*. Stockholm: Symposion.

Gilroy, Rose, and Roberta Woods. 1994. *Housing Women*. London: Routledge.

Grundström, Karin, and Irene Molina. 2016. "From Folkhem to Life-style Housing in Sweden: Segregation and Urban Form, 1930's–2010's." *International Journal for Housing Policy* 6(3): 313–336.

Harding, Sandra. 1991. *Whose Science? Whose Knowledge? Thinking From Women's Lives*. Ithaca, NY: Cornell University Press.

Harvey, David. 1985. *The Urbanization of Capital*. Oxford: Basil Blackwell.

Hedin, Karin, Eric Clark, Emma Lundholm and Gunnar Malmberg. 2012. "Neoliberalization of Housing in Sweden: Gentrification, Filtering, and Social Polarization." *Annals of the Association of American Geographers* 102(2): 443–463.

Hirdman, Yvonne. 1993. *Folkhemstanken och kvinnorna—historiens andra sida*. Stockholm: Utbildningsförlaget Brevskolan.

Holgersen, Ståle. 2014. "Economic Crisis, Creative Destruction and the Current Urban Condition." *Antipode* 473: 689–707.

Kennett, Patricia, and Kam-Waheds Chan. 2011. *Women and Housing: An International Analysis*. London: Routledge.

Johansson, Susanne and Irene Molina. 2002. "Kön och ras/etnicitet i rumsliga identiteters konstruktioner." In Paulina de los Reyes, Irene Molina and Diana Mulinari (Eds.), *Maktens (o)lika förklädnader. Kön, klass & etnicitet i det postkoloniala Sverige*, 263–284. Stockholm: ATLAS.

Larsson, Anita. 2006. "From Equal Opportunities to Gender Awareness in Strategic Spatial Planning: Reflections Based on Swedish Experiences." *Town Planning Review* 77(5): 507–530.

Larsson, Anita, and Anne Jalakas. 2008. *Jämställdhet nästa! Samhällsplanering ur ett genusperspektiv*. 1. uppl. Stockholm: SNS förlag.

Lindén, Anna-Lisa. 1989. *Bostadsmarknadens ägarstruktur och hushållens boendemönster. Förändring och utveckling 1975–1985*. Rapport från forskargruppen boende och bebyggelse, Sociologiska institutionen, Lunds universitet.

Listerborn, Carina. 2002. *Trygg stad: diskurser om kvinnors rädsla i forskning, policyutveckling och lokal praktik*. Göteborg: Chalmers tekniska högskola.

Listerborn, Carina, ed. 2007. "Arkitektur och boende." *Tidskrift för genusvetenskap* 3: 3–85.

Magnusson-Turner, Lena. 2010. *Study on Housing and Exclusion*. Country Report Sweden, SOCOHO Research Project.

McDowell, Linda. 1999. *Gender, Identity and Place: Understanding Feminist Geographies.* Cambridge: Polity.

Molina, Irene. 1997. *Stadens rasifiering—Etnisk boendesegregation i folkhemmet.* Doctoral Dissertation, Uppsala University.

Molina, Irene. 2015. "Kvalitativ praktikprövning och rasdiskriminering på bostadsmarknaden—metodologiska reflektioner." In *Mångfaldens dilemman. Bostadssegregation och områdespolitik*, edited by Roger Andersson, Gunnar Myrberg, and Bo Bengtsson, 159–181. Malmö: Gleerups.

Molina, Irene, and Karin Grundström. 2012. "Gender and Space." In *International Encyclopedia of Housing and Home*, Vol. 2, edited by Susan J. Smith, Marja Elsinga, Lorna Fox O'Mahony, Ong Seow Eng, Susan Wachter, and Montserrat Pareja Eastaway, 250–254. Oxford: Elsevier.

Morris, Jenny, and Martin Winn. 1990. *Housing and Social Inequality.* London: Hilary Shipman.

Mulinari, Diana & Anders Neergaard. 2004. *Den nya svenska arbetarklassen: rasifierade arbetares kamp inom facket.* Umeå: Borea.

Munro, Moira, and Susan J. Smith. 1989. "Gender and Housing: Broadening the Debate." *Housing Studies* 4(1): 3–17.

Petracci, M. 2007. *Mujeres en número: La opinión y la situación de las mujeres de la Ciudad de Buenos Aires.* Informe final preparado para la Dirección del Gobierno de la Ciudad de Buenos Aires.

Pred, Allan. 2000. *Even in Sweden. Racisms, Racialized Spaces, and the Popular Geographical Imagination.* Berkeley: University of California Press.

Reichert, Dagmar. 1994. "Woman as Utopia—Against relations of representation." *Gender, Place and Culture* 1(1): 91–102.

Rose, Gillian. 1993. *Feminism & geography: the limits of geographical knowledge.* Cambridge: Polity Press.

Roy, Ananya. 2002. *City Requiem, Calcutta: Gender and the Politics of Poverty.* Minneapolis and London: University of Minnesota Press.

Sahlin, Ingrid. 2011. "Women's Housing in Sweden." In *Women and Housing: An International Analysis*, edited by Patricia Kenneth and Kam Wah Chan, 96–115. London: Routledge.

Sandberg, Linda, and Malin Rönnblom. 2016. "Imagining the Ideal City, Planning the Gender-equal City in Umeå, Sweden." *Gender, Place and Culture* 23(12): 1750–1762.

Sandlie, H. C. 2008. *To må man være—om ungdoms boligetableringer på 1990-tallet.* NOVA Report 9/08, NOVA, Oslo.

Smith, J. Susan. 1989. *The Politics of 'Race' and Residence: Citizenship, Segregation and White Supremacy in Britain.* Oxford: Polity Press.

Smith, J. Susan. 1990. "Income, Housing Wealth and Gender Inequality." *Urban Studies* 27(1): 67–88.

Westin, Sara. 2014. *The Paradoxes of Planning: A Psycho-Analytical Perspective.* Farnham: Ashgate.

Wirth, Louis. 1938. "Urbanism as a Way of Life: The City and Contemporary Civilization." *American Journal of Sociology* 44: 1–24.

Other Sources

Gender Equality Commission. 2013. "The Current Situation of Gender Equality in Sweden—Country Profile." http://ec.europa.eu/justice/gender-equality/files/epo_campaign/131006_country-profile_sweden.pdf.

Länsstyrelsen i Hallands län. 2009. *Checklista för jämställd planering i Halland.* Meddelanden 2009:04.

Statistics Sweden. 2014. *Women and Men in Sweden. Facts and Figures.* Örebro: SCB-Tryck, 2014:06.

Statistics Sweden. 2016. *Women and men in Sweden 2016. Facts and figures.* Örebro: SCB-Tryck, 2016:06.

World Economic Forum (WEF). 2016. http://reports.weforum.org/global-gender-gap-report-2016.

3

Modern Home, Environment, and Gender

Built, Planned, and Lived Spaces in Post-war Finland

Kirsi Saarikangas and Liisa Horelli

"Look children, how wonderful! An apartment with running water, private toilet, and balcony!" We had just moved in. I remember how my ecstatic mother almost flew across the empty living room of our new home onto the sunny balcony holding my little sister in her arms.[1]

This is the way a man recalled his new childhood home of the early 1950s in the late 1990s, when more than 300 suburbanites recorded their written memories of suburban living in the Helsinki region from the 1950s to the 1970s.[2] Housing in Finland underwent a major change after World War II. New homes and their modern facilities revolutionized everyday life and held out optimistic promises of a better future.[3] The narrators repeatedly contrasted the luxuries of new spacious apartments with their previous inadequate dwellings. Modern conveniences such as piped water, indoor toilets, shining bathrooms, standardized kitchen fittings, and balconies symbolized the change and aroused feelings of joy and happiness.

Both landscape and people were on the move as hundreds of thousands of new dwellings were constructed, from remote rural settlements to urban centers, and hundreds of thousands of people relocated to new home districts. The war had exacerbated the already existing urban housing shortage, as the economic recession had stopped almost all housing construction in the mid-1930s. Karelian refugees, more than 400,000 people (one-eighth of the total Finnish population) from the territories ceded to the Soviet Union, had to be resettled, and ex-servicemen, numerous new families established after the war, and the growing urban population needed new homes.

The emergence of new kinds of domestic and urban spaces fundamentally changed the Finnish landscape, housing customs, and the details of daily life affecting the space, time, and bodies of inhabitants. Post-war housing construction led to the wholesale modernization of Finnish housing. The modernist principles of spatial differentiation and the urban middle-class ideals of habitation that had emerged since the late 1920s were applied both indoors and outdoors. The post-war (re)construction of housing had two solutions. The reconstruction began in the countryside. Throughout the 1940s and early 1950s, the one-and-a-half-story standardized wooden one-family houses, nicknamed "veterans' houses," provided the main solution for new homes both in rural areas and population centers. The volume of urban construction only caught up with rural levels in 1956.[4] Until the 1970s, the principal solution for urban habitation was the suburban apartment close to nature (Figure 3.1).

Figure 3.1   Moving Into a New Home in Pohjois-Haaga (Tolarintie 3), Helsinki
Photo: K-G. Roos, 1956–1959; courtesy of The Finnish Museum of Photography.

The post-war changes in housing coincided with the rapid industrialization, urbanization, and modernization of Finnish society. In a few decades, the ratio of people who lived in rural areas and cities was turned on its head. At the end of World War II, almost 70% of the population resided in the countryside and lived off the forest and land, but by 1980, 70% lived in the cities and their new suburbs, and only 13% were directly employed in agriculture and forestry. The period of most intense urbanization occurred between 1965 and 1975. During the so-called years of great migration, masses of people moved from the northern and eastern countrysides to new homes in the urban centers of southern Finland and abroad to Sweden. More decent and affordable housing had to be built fast.[5] The suburban locale—and its homogeneous dwelling type—rapidly became the new national landscape of modern Finland.

If not obvious at first sight, gender was a key issue in the formation of a new spatial order of housing, from the spatial rearrangements of dwellings and housing areas to urban space as a whole. The dwelling took on an increasing importance as an instrument for improving everyday life in the setting up of a modern welfare state, the People's Home, in Finland and other Nordic countries, most notably in Sweden. The post-war housing construction turned the new architectural aesthetics into a centrally managed ethical, hygienic, and social project. New dwellings and suburbs epitomized the ideal spatial organization of post-war gender relations. They were planned according to the principles of the unity of space and function and for the ideal average inhabitants, that is, the nuclear—and by definition heterosexual—family, with a mother, father, and children. The spatial organization of new homes both reflected and produced the ideal nuclear family mode of living and the concomitant gendered division of labor.[6] Home and society formed a continuum in which both genders had their tasks along the lines of the dichotomous citizenship: the wife working at home and the husband outside the home.[7] The domestic environment as a whole, from dwellings to suburbs, was identified as women's and children's spheres of activities, and was considered to have a direct influence on their lives. Therefore, whereas women's activities within domestic space were valued, and attention was paid to the areas that had previously received only little architectural attention, the spatial organization of the functionally differentiated dwelling and town spaces alike were based on strict and polarized views of genders.

This chapter offers a historical review of the relations, negotiations, and tensions between modern Finnish housing and gender. Its particular focus is on the interrelationships of built, planned, and lived spaces. The chapter concentrates on housing from the 1940s to the 1970s—the decades dominated by the modern housing ideal. It discusses briefly the development of new dwelling ideals during the 1920s and 1930s, and presents rare feminist alternatives to challenge modern housing and town planning ideals in the late twentieth century. What conceptions of genders did planning rely on and generate? What gendered habits did spatial arrangements support or interfere with? Gendered spatial habits are formed in the reciprocity of built space, inhabitants, cultural conceptions, and negotiations in embodied spatial practices and routines such as habitation and homemaking, "in performing basic activities of life."[8] As silent knowledge stratified in the body, gendered habits are available for people to use.[9]

Our discussion combines the analyses of built spaces, discourses of planning, and embodied inhabited spaces. Our aim is not to demonstrate that the viewpoints of either planners, housing discussions, or inhabitants are right or wrong. Rather, the combination of various and sometimes contradictory perspectives offer a more nuanced view of the gendered dimensions of domestic spaces in post-war Finland. Moreover, these positions are not innocent or homogeneous, but located and multi-faceted. Instead of the dichotomy between active planners as creators of the built environment, and passive users for whom the environment is planned, we suggest that the shaping of the environment and its meanings is a much more complex process.

Modernisms, Modernizations, and Modernities

The relationship between gender and modern domestic spaces is tense and ambiguous. Urban public spaces, and the modern metropolis in particular, have often been depicted as paradigmatic spaces of modernity, whereas domestic and suburban environments have been regarded as refuges from or antitheses of modernity, as Judy Giles has pointed out.[10] Our chapter suggests instead that whereas the planning of new domestic environments in Finland was based on limited views of gender and family, such environments were crucial spaces for the experiences of modern life and for the formation of modern Finnish society and its gender relations. Numerous feminists discussing domestic and suburban spaces have pointed out that the emphasis on ephemeral modernity has neglected the everyday and suburban life as repetitious, not modern, passive, and feminine. As Rita Felski states: "The vocabulary of modernity is a vocabulary of anti-home."[11] The bias against spaces and practices associated with women has resulted in making natural the tie between domesticity and women, and the undervaluation of home and the practices culturally coded as feminine.[12] However, home and domestic spaces have been very much the focus of modernist architects. Moreover, even if the agency of modernism has been gendered male, women's agency from planning to practices of housing has been crucial in the shaping of new housing environments.[13] Despite the pivotal position of housing in the modern architectural movement, research on relations of gender, space, and modern dwelling was curiously underdeveloped until the late twentieth century.[14]

Interrelationships between modernity, gender, and space entered feminist discussion in the 1980s. Attention was first focused on urban space and the polarization of public, urban spaces and private, domestic spaces in the processes of industrialization and modernization along the lines of cultural conceptions of masculinity and femininity, and the supposed exclusion of women from public, urban spaces and their representations.[15] Since the 1990s, however, feminist researchers have argued that the polarization of spheres "was articulated much more clearly at the level of ideology than it was on the ground."[16] The division of modern, masculine, public, urban space and not-modern, feminine, private, domestic space is oversimplified and far from rigid.[17] Elizabeth Wilson has argued that despite its disadvantages, urban life "emancipated women more than rural life or suburban domesticity"[18] but valued urban spaces over domestic or suburban spaces. Feminist studies on domestic violence have demonstrated that in the terms of sexual and/or physical violence, private homes are not safe havens, but are often more dangerous spaces for women than public urban spaces.[19] Instead of an unambiguous and enclosed private space, home is an open and dynamic process of social relations, constructed in the interaction with the world outside.[20] Further, since the early 2000s, feminist scholars have challenged pathologized views of suburbia by more multifaceted approaches to the suburbs as both physical, built spaces and embodied, lived spaces.[21]

The "spatial turn" in the humanities and social sciences since the 1980s has brought a spatial perspective to buildings, and notable changes in the understanding of built environments and their formation of meanings. Together with feminist approaches, it has broadened the scope of architectural research towards the emergence of meanings of built space, spatial practices, and built spaces as complex, dynamic, and multidimensional processes. Instead of two- or three-dimensional physical constructions and points of fixed meaning, built spaces are approached as produced, represented, and practiced spaces. Embodied, lived spaces are formed in the encounters between inhabitants, environment, cultural conventions, and social relations, in a constant cycle of production and reproduction of space and its meanings in use, allowing for heterogeneous spatial practices and the agency of inhabitants.[22]

"Modern," "modernity," "modernization," and "modernism" are slippery notions, and when compounded with local variations, each can take on more than one meaning. Here, we use them as descriptive terms referring to the historical epoch of discussions about the "new dwelling" and construction of new housing, while at the same time the changes in the then contemporary housing and habitation are the objects of our analyses. According to Marshall Berman, modernity refers to the experiential level, while modernization denotes the complex historical, geographical, social, and economic processes that started with industrialization and urbanization. This distinction has been deployed by Giles, Hilde Heynen, and others.[23] The socio-spatial processes of modernization manifested in the improvement and construction of housing and infrastructure (street lighting, water supply, sewage), new domestic technologies, transport, and green areas, are discussed by Eda Acara in this volume. The most intense period of modernization, which Maria Kaika has called "the heroic moment of modernity's Promethean project," took place in the Western world from the late nineteenth century through the first three quarters of the twentieth century, with local variations.[24] "Modernism" in turn designates the new artistic and architectural ideals and programmatic visions for social change and progress since the late nineteenth century, collectively referred to in architecture as the Modern Movement, and called "Functionalism" in the Nordic countries.[25] Finally, "modernity" refers to the cultural negotiations and the experiences of space and time. The sense of modernity as the sense of newness was expressed both in the planning discussions and inhabitants' accounts of post-war habitation. According to Berman, the conflict with tradition and the dichotomy of the "now" and "then" and the "sense of living in two worlds simultaneously"—the radically changed new world and preceding old world—characterizes the experiences of modernity.[26] Or, as Alan O'Shea states, the sense of modernity is "the practical negotiation of one's life and one's identity within a complex and fast-changing world."[27]

The pursuit of improving people's lives through the improvement of their living environments brought housing to the center of international architectural modernism, and was intrinsically connected with the architectural and social planning of post-war Finnish society. The self-conscious aim of Western architectural modernism was to leave behind the housing modes of the past and create a dwelling that suited both the transformed society and its new lifestyles—spatially differentiated minimal dwelling—and was universally applicable: up-to-date and timeless at once. Discussions advocating the "new dwelling" simultaneously both defined and created the idea of the new dwelling and its supposed residents. The expressions used to present new Functionalist dwelling ideals in Finland included "current," "new," "novel," "up-to-date," "practical," and "functional," and were more common in the period from the 1920s to the 1950s than the term "modern."[28] Enhanced by the growing international fame of Finnish architecture and design in the 1950s, the narrative of heroic modernism and modern idiom took on a national flavor.[29]

From the late nineteenth century to the mid-twentieth century, housing reformers underlined the connections between the qualities of the housing environment and the physical and psychological health and morals of the inhabitants, using environmental deterministic tones. The idea of the "curative dwelling" was linked with the idea of the "curable city." The efforts to maximize sunlight and fresh air indoors and greenery outdoors were manifested in the new kind of open urban structure that replaced the dense urban layout with houses sparsely arranged in the landscape.[30] With its emphasis on fresh air, greenery, and sunshine, the creation of the modern housing environment has been depicted as "a gigantic ventilation project" and sanitation of a "bacteriological city."[31] The late nineteenth and early twentieth century efforts to create a new healthy urban environment concentrated on bringing nature to the cities in the form of public greenery (parks, leafy boulevards) and open courtyard housing blocks. After World War II, urban habitation was increasingly and paradoxically relocated closer to nature outside the existing urban structure (garden cities, suburbs). In the form of electricity and piped water provided in the modern homes, elements of nature became tamed and controlled commodities, and gradually changed from being wonders to becoming self-evident in modern habitation.[32]

Setting the Scene: Practical and Hygienic Dwellings of the 1920s and 1930s

In the international exchange of ideas, the efficient and hygienic, spatially differentiated modern home was defined architecturally largely in the 1920s and 1930s. Due to the economic recession of that period, however, social housing reform in Finland was realized in actual housing construction only after World War II. In Finland's post-war era, a modern, uniform type of family apartment that was seen as classless, yet based on urban middle-class housing ideals, gradually replaced the previous variety of housing for different social strata, becoming an almost unquestionable dwelling-type for decades. According to the minimal standards defined at the second CIAM (International Congress of Modern Architecture) in Frankfurt (called the *Existenzminimum* or "minimum needed for existence") and the Functionalist ideals of the unity of space and function, the fundamental functions of a dwelling, regarded as biological needs, were defined as rest, household work, and family socializing. The dwelling was redefined as private space, in contrast with the previous functions of the bourgeois home as a semipublic space for household activities, representation, and work. The reproductive home was pared down to three carefully oriented rooms of different sizes (to maximize sunshine): a smallish bedroom for sleep and intimacy (sexuality was never directly mentioned), a small kitchen for cooking, and a larger living room for family life, replacing the more or less similar sized rooms of current dwellings. All other functions and non-familial social life were located outside privatized apartments. The new apartment was supposed to be a place of rest for the husband and a place of work for the wife.[33]

Middle-class professionals connected the changes in housing, middle-class households, and women's position with each other, showing more interest than before in practical, efficient homes and kitchens. The number of urban, middle-class women working for wages outside the home expanded, and simultaneously the growing middle class could no longer afford domestic servants. Architect Alvar Aalto wrote in 1930: "The emancipation of women from subordinated position to working companion both in work and home life sets new demands for housing planning."[34] A practical kitchen would help liberate women to work outside the home and allow time for recreation.

The rationalization of household work was expressed in two ways: collective organization outside private apartments and, as the main solution, the rearrangement of the kitchen within the apartment. Rare examples of collective housing included central-kitchen apartment buildings built in the late 1910s and 1920s in Finland's largest towns, particularly in the new middle-class housing district Töölö in Helsinki, largely by a single entrepreneur, master builder Leuto A. Pajunen. Such houses allowed residents to purchase prepared food to eat in the canteen, or to be delivered to one's flat via a dumbwaiter. The one-kitchen houses were designated as alternatives for modern, urban, middle-class families and young couples; some of the buildings were for women only. The aim was to make life easier for women with jobs.[35] After World War II, *Naisten Huoltosäätiö* (Support Foundation of Finnish Women) built *White Lady* (1951), a collective apartment complex for former members of the women's military auxiliary and their families, as well as single mothers. The complex included a common kitchen, dining hall, laundry, nursery, sauna, and swimming pool—and it featured the first restaurant women were allowed to enter without a male companion. Before the various cohousing solutions of the early twenty-first century, collective housing never gained the same popularity in Finland as it did in neighboring Sweden, where Alva Myrdal, together with the radical architect Sven Markelius, shaped solutions for collective apartment buildings in the 1930s.[36] The collective organization of housework and care transformed the relations between women of different social classes more than it transformed the gender relations within the family, by outsourcing parts of the housework (cooking, dishwashing, buying, and storing food) to paid employees who were usually female.

The practical and hygienic kitchen within the dwelling became the main answer to arranging household work. Several women architects, interior designers, domestic scientists, women's organizations, and women's magazines carried out systematic research on housework, disseminated new radical housekeeping ideals, and developed patterns for kitchen furniture along the ideals of international, mainly Swedish and German, housing modernizers. The aim of practical household feminists or material feminists, as Dolores Hayden characterizes them,[37] was to elevate the status of housework by professionalizing it, and to find labor-saving arrangements for domestic space and daily routines, "that would save the mother from becoming solely a household-mother," as expressed by architect Signe Lagerborg-Stenius at the 1921 Women's Housing Convention, where professionals outlined ideal housing solutions from women's perspectives.[38] Conceptually, the home, kitchen, and women were closely connected, beginning with the planning of the kitchen for its projected users and daily practices. Following the epoch's notion of a complementary, gendered division of labor, household feminists articulated two novel options of feminine identity for a new, modern generation of women: either a skillful, active housewife or a self-supporting, independent woman.[39] The efforts to professionalize housework demonstrated an ambivalence towards domestic labor by simultaneously valuing it and regarding it as repetitive, monotonous, and requiring little imagination.[40]

Kitchens rapidly underwent drastic changes, from their overall planning down to the details. New rationalized laboratory-kitchen designs—regarded not as "the caprice of fashion, but the demand of the era"[41]—were based on systematic time-and-motion studies and the placement of kitchen furniture to save steps and movement, akin to procedures developed for repetitive assembly line work. According to the demands of hygiene, cooking was separated from sleeping and other domestic activities.[42]

The concern for a practical and healthy living environment generated a new kind of interest in domestic space. Trained architects began to design small dwellings, which were previously outside the scope of architecture. Although women were particularly active in shaping the new kitchens, male architects also began to address problems around domestic space according to the international ideals of an up-to-date minimal dwelling. Detailed attention was paid to rooms that had previously received little architectural consideration: the kitchen, bedroom, nursery, bathroom, toilet, and balcony. The conception of architecture's domain expanded from considering the aesthetic organization of space to covering the wider physical environment and its effects on inhabitants' bodies and minds. As a source of physical and moral health, hygienic, practical dwellings were regarded as vehicles for the sanitary, social, and aesthetic education of citizens as well as presenting a precondition for a better future.[43] Public and private intersected in the modern dwelling. The creation of new dwellings was linked to the concern for the smallest details of everyday life, which turned the private realm of the home into a public issue. Dwellings became simultaneously both more private and objects of intense public discussion, guidance, and control.[44] The publicity of the private is indeed a distinguishing feature of the modern dwelling, as Beatriz Colomina has suggested.[45] Despite the increased privacy, and the rooms reserved solely for familial functions, the modern home was not an enclosed private space. The home extended beyond its physical borders. And vice versa, even when at home, inhabitants were constantly relating to the surrounding world and its normative strategies and cultural agreements that filtered into the dwelling.[46]

Rural Functionalism: Type-Planned Veterans' Houses of the 1940s and 1950s

The reconstruction process began in rural areas in the 1940s in the form of the so-called veterans' houses: one-and-a-half-story, wooden, standardized, one-family houses. Throughout the 1940s and early 1950s, most new housing in Finland (70%) was constructed in rural areas. Numerous single-family neighborhoods of "veterans' houses" were also built on the outskirts of towns. The post-war housing construction was largely regulated by the state and municipalities. State-subsidized loans and accompanying building regulations covered 70% of Finnish housing construction during the 1940s and 1950s, whereas privately financed housebuilding increased from the 1960s on. Based on the Land Acquisition Act of 1945, the state established about 100,000 new small holdings in the countryside and about 75,000 residential buildings were built.[47]

The design and construction of these houses represents a unique Finnish permutation of international modernism. It was a combination of national guidance, centralized planning, and self-help. The government's settlement policy regulated the entire process from housing plans to actual construction: the state provided loans and a plot of land, while the residents themselves built their homes using prefabricated materials and type-plans designed by architects. For residents crippled by the war, new homes held optimistic promises of the future.

The construction of houses led to the comprehensive rationalization of the Finnish construction industry and efficiently spread modern housing models to the Finnish countryside. It extended architectural planning to rural building that had previously been dominated by the tradition of self-help, separating planners from users. The plans, in the form of standardized models or type-plans designed by architects, were the prerequisite for state loans. Type-plans also included drawings for cowsheds, saunas, and other outdoor buildings. Most often, personal hygiene took place in saunas, as many houses built in remote rural areas lacked piped water until the 1970s. A number of organizations, and both female and male professionals, participated in the design and production of houses, from the Reconstruction Office of the Finnish Association of Architects (established in 1942) to prefabrication companies and public works departments in municipalities. Despite numerous planners, the homogeneous idiom of houses developed quickly. Houses played a crucial role in the development of construction standards, from the components and details of buildings to entire type-planned houses. The Building Information File—a continuously revised and expanded collection of construction norms and standards—was established in 1942. Along with the standardization of building components, they accelerated the reconstruction process and made the previously unattainable ideal of the one-family house available to the masses.[48]

Houses are curious hybrids that merge modern idiom, spatial organization, and construction techniques with traditions and materials of rural habitation—an example of critical regionalism as discussed by Kenneth Frampton.[49] Light colors, freely placed windows, modest appearance, and the renunciation of everything "superfluous," combined the practical and rational aims of international modernism with regional, rural traditions of wooden houses with a gable roof (Figure 3.2).

Figure 3.2 Veterans' Houses From the 1940s in Western Pakila, Helsinki
Photo: Sirkka Valanto, 1971. Courtesy of Helsinki City Museum.

The interiors of houses were divided into a separate kitchen, a bedroom, and a living room of almost equal size on the ground floor. Two more bedrooms were often added later in the attic, or attic rooms could be sublet to another household. The development of kitchen standards was an integral part of house planning, and such standards always included plans for practical kitchen fittings. Female architects (Märta Blomstedt, Elsi Borg, Eva Kuhlefelt-Ekelund) designed preliminary standards in 1942, and the Reconstruction Office collaborated with the new Department of Home Economics (1943) at the Work Efficiency Institute, and published the first standards for kitchen fittings (25 cards in the Building Information File) in 1945. They were based on the ergonomic studies of the measurements and placement of furniture in rural kitchens. The measurements for the standards were self-evidently based on the average bodily dimensions of Finnish women, who were thus represented as the chief actors in the kitchen.[50]

The "rural functionalism" of houses[51] was most clearly manifested in their particular combination of the Functionalist spatial differentiation of almost equal-sized rooms and largish, multipurpose kitchens. The practical kitchens of veterans' houses deviated from the Frankfurt-type laboratory kitchen ideal (developed by German architect Margarete Schütte-Lihotzky in the 1920s) and were always large enough to accommodate a dining table, recalling the rural traditions of a multipurpose room. Indeed, the small laboratory kitchen never gained popularity in Finland. Inhabitants resisted the new laboratory kitchens because the very separation of cooking and dining went against ingrained customs of habitation. They fitted the dining table into the tiny space of the kitchen, and they even took turns eating there. Domestic scientists and designers complained that the modern kitchen was "so small that you can hardly turn around in it."[52] While the new urban and suburban dwellings accentuated the kitchen–family room axis, the connection between the kitchen and bedroom was typical in the type-planned houses. The kitchen communicated with the bedroom but not with the living room. Planners argued that the location of the bedroom next to the kitchen would save daily steps for mothers while she could keep an eye on children sleeping or playing in the bedroom, and that mothers would thus more easily enjoy close relations with their children.[53] The largish multipurpose kitchen served as the place for daily family socializing and was large enough for small children to play in or to do schoolwork. However, children's activities mostly took place outdoors. The more separately located living room preserved the parlor-like semipublic features of a rarely used "better room"—a tradition of rural and urban working-class housing that had been strongly criticized by Finnish and European housing reformers since the early twentieth century. Special efforts were made to separate sleeping from cooking, whereas residents often preferred to conserve a room distinguished from the messiness of everyday life.[54]

Type-planned houses were planned with the ideal of the average nuclear family in mind. The spatial organization of houses was based on a gendered division of labor and emphasized the home as the realm of active, practical housewives. The focus of architectural planning shifted from aesthetics to practice, from the man's leisure to the woman's work, from family rooms to the kitchen. The kitchen—perceived as the housewife's working place—was presented as the most important room in the house: it was the hub around which the entire home revolved. For the husband, home was the place of rest: he had his place in constructing the house and clearing and cultivating the land (Figure 3.3).

The analysis of housing ideals stresses the context of planning. However, construction work often continued when residents moved in. Habitation extended beyond the walls of the house to the yards and surroundings. Over half of the houses were constructed on small holdings in rural areas, and outdoor farming activities were a crucial part of habitation. Women worked in the fields and participated in construction work. On the outskirts of towns, residential plots were quite large: subsistence agriculture, fruit trees, and berry bushes were important aspects of habitation, particularly after the war, and continued rural lifestyles in an urban context. Moreover, even if the planning of houses was based on the ideal nuclear family, many inhabitants lived in other arrangements, including war widows with their children. Often, two households lived on separate floors of veterans' houses. Large, almost even-sized rooms also allowed for flexible usage. In the practices of habitation, the living room might have served as another bedroom, with a multipurpose kitchen as a family room.[55]

Figure 3.3 Reconstruction After the Winter War, Spring 1940
Photo: Pekka Kyytinen. Courtesy of The National Board of Antiquities.

Healthy Living Close to Nature: Suburban Environments From the 1950s to the 1970s

The focus of housing construction shifted from rural to urban areas in the 1950s. From the 1950s to the 1970s, dwellings in new suburbs were the main solution for the construction of new homes, and the suburbs became homes for the vast majority of the Finnish population. In the post-war decades, housing construction was the most important public building project, complemented by schools and churches. It was speeded up and regulated by a new system of state-subsidized housing loans, the ARAVA system, introduced in 1949.[56] At the beginning of the twenty-first century, a quarter of the population lived in suburbs. Many, therefore, experienced the pleasures of modern housing in the suburbs rather than in the cities.

Modern Home, Environment, and Gender

The ideal of healthy living close to nature was a leitmotif of housing planning. It directed housing construction as a whole to the new suburbs and visibly affected the urban morphology. Built amid pristine natural settings, the new forest suburbs epitomized the aesthetic and social ideals of open space and healthy living close to nature. On the basis of functionality and orientation, the urban space as a whole was reorganized. The combination of different kinds of low- and middle-rise multifamily buildings that were freely arranged in the landscape replaced the dense urban layouts. The functions of urban life and space were differentiated into the zones of habitation, industry, and commerce, separated from each other by circulation and greenbelts. The construction of new housing areas went hand in hand with the construction of the entire infrastructure, including streets, lighting, and the sewage system (Figure 3.4).[57]

Suburbia included a plethora of spaces. Topographic town planning of the 1950s emphasized the intimate scale and harmony between buildings and the environment. With the 1960s, the scale of buildings and housing areas became larger, and the appearance more austere. The emphasis was on the contrast between buildings and the environment. Building companies, in close collaboration with banks, started to build entire housing areas. While the physical appearance of suburbs and buildings varied, the same functionalist dwelling type was repeated through the decades, with small variations. Only the number of bedrooms increased, from an average of one in the 1950s to two in the 1960s.[58]

The construction of suburbs aimed to provide affordable and decent housing for a large number of people. A great number of good-quality family homes were built relatively quickly: "modest modernism," as Katja Lindroos has called it.[59] The aim of the Finnish housing policy that was also realized was to produce 500,000 new dwellings averaging 70 m^2 (750 sq. ft.) between 1966 and

Figure 3.4 **Playground in Pohjois-Haaga, Helsinki**
Photo: Jorma Harju, 1961. Courtesy of Helsinki City Museum.

1975. The program was comparable with the simultaneous Swedish Million Program discussed by Irene Molina in this volume. Serial production of similar dwelling and housing types fitt both with the goal of efficient construction and the epoch's emphasis on equality. However, as the construction industry expanded, the distance between the opinions of planners and residents also grew. Homes became an industrially produced commodity.[60]

The nuclear family and the welfare of children—the future citizens—were the cornerstone principles for designing new housing areas. New architectural thinking was characteristically utopian, but in a curious way. It aimed at the creation of a better future through the creation of better housing, but this future vision was stagnant. New homes were planned for the eternally young family consisting of a mother, father, and children who would never grow old. Although presented as classless, the new family model was based on urban middle-class ideals of family and gender. Most of the residents of new socially mixed suburbs were young middle- and working-class families with children (Figure 3.5).[61] Indeed, the nuclear family—as an ideal and practice—was never so widespread as it was in the 1950s and early 1960s, as also Maria Mesner points out in this volume in the context of public urban housing in Vienna.

Figure 3.5 Rowing a Boat in Kaukajärvi Suburb, Tampere
Photo: Matti Selänne 1968–1970. Courtesy of Vapriikki Photo Archives.

Modern Home, Environment, and Gender

The planning of suburbs was based on the gendered idea of the organization of housing and society from indoors to outdoors, from the dwelling space to the zoning of urban space. Reproduction and recreation were articulated as the main functions of homes and suburbs alike, with the nuclear family and the husband-wife couple as its basic units. In the continuum of home and society, both genders had their complementary tasks according to the pre-war idea of dichotomous citizenship: the active housewife mother and the breadwinning father. Home and the nearby surroundings were defined as the spaces of women's and children's activities, and their planning was a shared concern of both female and male planners. The suburbs of the 1950s were planned with pedestrians in mind. The alliance of nature and physical activities—playing children and active residents of all ages—dictated the layout and scale of the early suburbs. The residents' mobility—particularly the distance between homes and schools and the separation of pedestrian and vehicular traffic—was a basis for planning. Habitation was ideally based on neighborhood units and their services, such as grocery stores, schools, kindergartens, libraries, churches, cinemas, playgrounds, sports fields, green areas, and public transport. Careful planning included plantings, common green areas, and the nearby environment, most notably in Tapiola Garden City.[62] From the 1960s on, services were often concentrated in larger suburban centers. Suburbanization and motorization accelerated each other. In the 1960s, both traffic and traffic separation became increasingly important factors of urban planning.[63]

Pleasures of Modern "Heavenly" Homes

Extensive suburban construction brought the pleasures of the modern home—the provision of piped water, electricity, standardized kitchens, and domestic technology—within the reach of the masses. Modern amenities had a radical impact on the organization of daily life. Despite the modest size of the new apartments, relocation often marked a leap forward in living standards. A woman who moved to the suburbs as a child in 1965 wrote: "By eating soup, father and mother saved for a state-subsidized Arava home in Kontula. The studio flat changed into a three-room apartment."[64] The ownership of a new suburban dwelling with a shiny kitchen and bathroom was experienced as an achievement requiring hard work and steady saving. Moving to an up-to-date apartment with "hot and cold running water" was recalled as being "a dream come true," and contrasted with the previous inadequate homes. Likewise, a housewife who moved to the suburb of Pihlajamäki in 1965 was one of many women who recalled the new facilities as daily miracles: "It was like arriving in heaven! We had our own apartment with two rooms and a kitchenette. We had a bathroom with hot water and our own balcony! And there was light and splendid views from the eighth floor."[65]

Suburban dwellings, like veterans' houses, adapted the pre-war Functionalist ideal of the unity of space and function. Residents were ideally located in separate rooms according to the functions of rooms and gendered tasks of family members. Despite similarities, there were small but significant differences between the two dwelling types in terms of spatial closeness and openness and connections between different rooms. Both stressed home as a space for a nuclear family with the mother as its key actor. Type-planned houses typically connected the kitchen (i.e., woman) with the bedroom (and children) and separated it from the living room (resting father), accentuating the woman's two roles as a household worker and a mother. In suburban dwellings, the emphasis was on open, fluid spaces and the spatial continuum of kitchen, dining corner and living room with small bedrooms clearly separate. The living room with an adjacent dining corner was the largest space in the home, a place for dining, reading, school work, family togetherness, and socializing with guests, and from the 1960s on, watching TV.[66] Children's play had entered suburban homes and housing discussions increasingly since the 1950s. However, both in rural type-houses and smallish suburban homes, play often took place outdoors. Arrangements of suburban homes stressed the mother-child-family relations, the visibility of household work, and with the more distant bedroom(s), the privacy of family members and the intimacy between couples. Space and time intertwined when the "functionally differentiated woman" changed roles and places from household worker to mother and spouse according to the time of day, moving from the kitchen to living room to bedroom, as illustrated in the floor plans and numerous manuals for virtuous habitation (Figure 3.6).[67] The husband, in turn, had his place resting in the living room armchair and implicitly in the bedroom of the married couple. Ideally there would have been separate bedrooms for the married couple and for children of different genders. This however, remained an unattainable ideal during the post-war decades. Small children were often located in a single bedroom, and living rooms used for sleeping.

Figure 3.6 Woman Opening a Can in Her Modern Suburban Kitchen
Photo: Unknown, 1950s. Courtesy of Helsinki City Museum.

Open suburban spaces embodied the mother-child relationship from the placement of rooms inside the dwelling—kitchen-dining-living room axis—to the carefully thought-out relationship between home, yard, and surrounding environment. The emphasis on open spaces both indoors and outdoors set different areas of home life side by side. Open kitchens brought housework previously done in isolation into the social atmosphere of the family's shared spaces, and emphasized the connections between mothers and children. The mother, working in the kitchen, had visual and aural contact with the dining space and living room, where children played or did their homework. Suburban playgrounds for small children were located in the immediate vicinity of homes and were visible from living room and kitchen windows, making homes and yards extensions of each other. Schools, kindergartens, and shopping centers were within walking—or stroller—distance, whereas the sports fields of older children were located farther away.[68] The arrangement of the suburban environment, with zones gradually being distanced from homes, hence reflects the gradual separation of mother and child.

Gendered Suburban Criticism

The passionate criticism of modernist town planning and suburban lifestyles began simultaneously with the most intense period of suburban construction in the mid-1960s. In the 1950s, the new suburban apartment represented success and was considered to be a means of change and liberation. By the late 1960s, suburbs were categorized as "dormitory towns" and sites of "mere residing"[69] and regarded more and more as the antitheses of freedom. Journalists, architects, and researchers criticized suburbs for their lack of social relationships and sense of community. They saw suburbanites and particularly women as prisoners of space and existing passively within their lives. As stated in the major Finnish newspaper *Helsingin Sanomat* in an article from November 1, 1975:

> The dullness of suburban life is visible in the idleness of afternoons. The green widow [a suburban housewife whose husband works in the city—Ed.] goes to the store with curlers in her hair and does the same thing the next day, the next week, and the next month. Endlessly, she feels.[70]

It appears that considerable—almost obsessive—expectations of an ideal neighborhood spirit were attached to the new suburbs. Compared with the central parts of the city, they were assumed to be places of a more communal nature conducive to closer social relations. Social networks did exist in the suburbs, but they were formed and transformed mainly by women and children. A woman who as a young mother in 1969 moved to Kontula, an eastern suburb of Helsinki, opposed the image of isolated and victimized suburbanites:

> Surprise, surprise. We enjoyed living in Kontula right from the start. I soon realized that neighborly people lived in our building. In due course, there emerged a kind of agreement of mutual friendship and assistance, which gave everyone pleasure and benefit. It never became a burden. This was indeed a miracle, because in the inner city, my husband and I didn't even know our neighbor on the same floor.[71]

The criticism failed to recognize the positive aspects of women's suburban socializing, and labeled it as just the "practice of gossiping" around the sandbox, regarding suburban social networks to be of lesser value than those of the traditional urban fabric.[72] For many women, semipublic suburban spaces outside the home were sites of informal daily encounters, neighborliness, and friendship (Figure 3.7). A mother who moved to Pihlajamäki in 1963 wrote:

> Mothers socialized with each other next to the sand boxes. There was a good spirit of mutual assistance among the mothers—one could take turns and leave one's children in someone else's care if there were things to do in the city.[73]

Figure 3.7 Shopping Center in Herttoniemi, Helsinki, Designed by Architect Eliel Muoniovaara (1956)
Photo: S. Salokangas, 1957. Courtesy of Helsinki City Museum.

It is apparent that the planning of the suburbs was based on a uniform housing model and a narrow view of domesticity and genders. The criticism of the suburbs, however, overlooked the agency of women, considering suburban women as "just housewives."[74] Suburbs were viewed from an outside perspective, often a male one, and were regarded as passive, reproductive, and feminine spaces of lesser value than active, productive, and masculine urban spaces. The criticism created parallel figures of the unhappy suburban housewife (the "green widow") and alienated man as an outsider (or visitor) in the suburban environment, both reinforcing the connection between women and the domestic space and generating the idea of men as victims of that connection.[75]

The housewife had been both an ideal figure of suburban habitation and the target of suburban criticism since the late 1960s. The spread of the suburbs in the 1960s and 1970s took place simultaneously with the rupture of the ideal feminine identity. At the beginning of the 1970s, women's magazines and newspapers moved away from the discourse of the active housewife. The tune of the discussion changed rapidly. The cultural identity of the active and practical housewife was replaced by the wage-earning mother, who skillfully and efficiently combined motherhood and housework with work outside the home.[76]

The image of the new suburbs as realms of the housewives who lived there was oversimplified. During the early years, much construction work took place in the suburbs, bringing people—mostly men—to work there. Moreover, not all the recollections were positive; some were ambivalent, and a few were overtly negative, expressing the sense of isolation in the suburban "penal colony."[77] There also existed a contradiction of praxis and ideals. Whereas the post-war decades were characterized by home culture and the housewife ideal, the institution of housewifery never held sway on a large scale in Finland, whose industrialization and urbanization occurred at a relatively late stage but very rapidly. The number of married urban women working outside the home was quite high after World War II; indeed it was the highest of all Western countries, and continued to increase after the war. During the war, 31% of women worked outside the home; by 1950, 34% of married women living in towns worked outside the home, increasing to 45% in 1960 and 57% in 1970. Differences with other Western countries diminished during the 1960s. While many suburban mothers of small children were housewives working at home, some worked outside the home. Moreover, many women worked from home on a part-time basis, for example in bookkeeping, cleaning, or childcare.[78] This work, however, is not reflected well in the statistics. Mothers often went back to work when their children started school, following the new ideal of consecutive roles and phases of married women's lives advocated by Swedes Alva Myrdal and Viola Klein that replaced the earlier ideal of the complementary couple.[79]

Women's reminiscences of suburban life also voiced confusion, as their lifestyle, only recently valued, came to be viewed as suspect. By pointing out the drawbacks of the lifestyle of suburban housewives, the criticism created tensions among women. These tensions also seem to have been class-based: educated working women criticized less educated women for staying at home. Married suburban women from all classes increasingly went to work outside the home during the 1960s, but more often, it was middle-class rather than working-class women working outside the home.[80]

In the written accounts, suburban women referred themselves as "home mothers" (*kotiäiti*), not "housewives" (*kotirouva*), emphasizing their tasks as active caregivers, as Lena Marander-Eklund also demonstrates in her ethnographic study of Finnish housewives of the 1950s. Terms frequently used in the post-war housing discussions were *perheenemäntä* (literally "family household manager"), with reference to rural traditions, and *perheenäiti* (family mother), with urban middle-class connotations. Post-war Finland was dominated by rural habitation and had a relatively small middle class. The division of labor in rural households was based more on a sliding scale of women's and men's tasks than a sharp opposition. Women, however, were more flexible in crossing borders than men.[81]

Despite the new modern conveniences, managing everyday life in the new suburban homes was a time-consuming task. Gendered daily habits dividing housework into men's and women's tasks changed slowly. Double burdens—furthered by a cultural appreciation of hardworking, strong women—was the daily experience of many working mothers. Gender equality, day care problems, division of household work within the family, and the critique of family-centered living entered into the social discourses of the late 1960s. The feminist Association 9 (*Yhdistys 9*) was established in 1966. However, the relationship between housing and gender was not directly discussed.

Much suburban criticism was written within a modernist framework that valued movement and the unfamiliar: meaningful life took place outside suburban domesticity. The shift of focus from the perspective of the planners and outside observers to the lived suburban spaces made room for inhabitants' multiple spatial practices. At the level of societal planning, women were located in the domestic suburban space, which they shaped and reshaped through their daily activities. When suburban criticism observed suburbia from a bird's-eye view, and the outside perspectives of criticism or planning concentrated on the built environment, life in the suburbs looked static and determined, with limited opportunities for residents' agency. The inhabitants' accounts, instead, approached suburbs through situational mundane experiences. In the narratives, the suburban environment opens up as a locus of activities. The suburban landscape, its topography, and architecture take shape through use and mobility. New dwellings were sources of pride and joy. Moreover, habitation extended to the surrounding environments, forests, and wastelands outside the scope of an all-encompassing planning, as discussed more thoroughly elsewhere. Residents compared themselves to settlers in the unfinished suburban surroundings. Natural environments formed the flip side of architecture, providing secret hiding places to make into one's own, and creating parallel spaces and aesthetic and experiential diversity to the suburban landscape.[82] Life in the suburbs was not just one, but was many things.

The New Everyday Life in the 1980s and 1990s

The criticism of modern universal housing and town planning principles as suitable for all individuals in all locations began in the US in the early 1960s. While intense discussions were also initiated in Finland—a model country of architectural modernism—modernist housing and town planning principles were persistent. Key targets of Finnish criticism were the demolition of old historical architecture and the depopulation of urban centers, and the supposedly passive and isolated lifestyle of housewives in suburban dormitory towns. As the scattered layout of forest suburbs of the 1950s was regarded as unsuitable for creating social relations, expectations were put on the new ideal of dense, "compact town suburbs."[83]

Finnish women were among the first to enter the architectural profession in the 1890s, and *Architecta*, the Finnish Association of Women Architects, was founded in 1942, furthering women's position and visibility in the architectural profession.[84] However, feminist and postmodern approaches entered Finnish architectural discussions relatively late in the 1980s. Feminist planners and activists focused a new kind of attention on the agency of inhabitants. They pointed out the distance between the modern town planning machinery and residents, challenged the uniform housing model as the basis of planning, underlined the importance of diverse housing solutions, and developed participatory planning practices. Their emphasis on the daily environment continued the viewpoints of practical material feminists as well as the implicit connections between women, children, and the housing environment.

The work of "The New Everyday Life" group, a decade-long transdisciplinary women's group active in the 1980s and 1990s, is an example of feminist perspectives for community planning. In the early 1980s, the Nordic "Housing and Building on Women's Terms" group started to criticize modern town planning and its spatial separation of housing from work and other activities. The movement, inspired by the Nordic interpretation of Robert Owen and Charles Fourier's social utopian tradition, material feminists, and Patrick Geddes, John Turner, and Margaret Kennedy, sought to create alternatives to industrial and market-oriented urban development.[85] In the spirit of US material feminists, the movement provided a critique of the difficult conditions in the balance of work and private life, a vision of a just society, and a model of action.[86]

The vision of the New Everyday Life group was a concrete utopia of a post-industrial, mosaic-like society consisting of varying self-governing units that would be responsible for the use of local resources. Important elements were work (paid and unpaid), care, and housing; instead of being separated, these three elements were to be integrated into the living environment. The central motives for action were the needs of children and women, as well as the social reproduction of people and nature, which would be enhanced by the so-called supportive infrastructure of everyday life.

The model of action proposed was based on the building of an "intermediary level," a mediating structure between individual households and the public and private sectors, which would enable the reorganization and integration of housing, work, and care in the neighborhoods. As a new structure in the neighborhoods, the intermediary level was also to include environmentally friendly housing, services, employment, and other activities, which would support the residents irrespective of age and gender.[87] The functional basis of the intermediary level would be created by bringing to the neighborhood some of the daily tasks normally located in other sectors and places. The care of domestic chores and children could be transferred from private homes to communal spaces, as in the examples of cohousing. Environmental planning and management, as well as the care of older people, would be provided in the neighborhood and not in the centralized institutions of the public sector. These transactions were to result in new activities, called the local housework, local care, local production, and local planning and management.[88]

As a geographical phenomenon, the intermediary level was to be a locally limited territorial whole, varying in size from a group of dwellings or a block, to a neighborhood, village, or part of a town. As a physical phenomenon, it was to include shared arenas and spaces of communication. Its architecture would support different modes of housing and the identity of the local culture. It could be regarded as a mixture of New Urbanism[89] and the Just City.[90]

The applications of The New Everyday Life approach can be structured according to the level of aspired communality and the degree of informal/formal economy. This has resulted in a range of examples, such as a well-functioning housing area with shared spaces. These include the neighborhood of Tinggaarden outside Copenhagen; cohousing communities or collective houses, especially in Denmark and Sweden; communes of different sizes, particularly among Nordic students; service house communities with both cohousing and an exchange of unpaid and paid services in all Nordic countries; and lastly, communities in which members work in the residence in which they live, such as Svaneholm in Denmark, kibbutzim in Israel, and the eco-village Findhorn in Scotland.

The movement in Finland founded a non-governmental organization (NGO) comprising some 50 women interested in housing and planning issues. In the 1990s, the network was supported by the Ministry of the Environment, which enabled the arrangement of regional events, such as the international Gender and Human Settlement Network, and a conference with 300 participants in Hämeenlinna. The core group was invited to write the Participation paragraph in the new Land Use and Building Act that was enacted in force in 2000. The focus was mostly on spatial development issues, such as the participatory processes in zoning, the content of the plans stressing the integration of care and work, mobility, safety, and short distances to services in housing areas. The New Everyday Life approach has been applied since the 1990s in a number of gender-aware neighborhood improvements in various European countries, including Malminkartano, Helsinki, in Finland.[91]

The turn of the millennium has also witnessed various solutions for housing cooperatives that deviate from the prevalent family-centered idea of habitation. The long tradition of self-built housing, as described in the veterans' houses of the 1950s, has continued in the form of experiments on collaborative self-planning projects. *Loppukiri* ("The Final Sprint," 2000–2003) for people aged over 50 and *Malta House* for mixed ages (2013) in Helsinki are examples of novel types of cohousing projects in which residents manage planning. In addition to individually planned apartments that are smaller than those in basic multifamily houses, houses have shared spaces (over 20%) for dining, hobbies, and saunas (Figure 3.8).[92] In the earlier collective housing solutions, paid staff provided services, whereas the new modes of cohousing rely on residents' participation and the exchange of unpaid services. While the co-construction of gender identities in dwelling takes place through action in time and space, it is, however, culturally dependent on who spends time, where, how, and why.[93] The participatory housing planning practices tend to increase the residential satisfaction and inhabitant-environment fit, but they also tend to reproduce the existing practices of habitation and gender. However, it seems that the collective organization of activities in the less private and more shared semipublic and public spaces of cohouses furthers the sharing of tasks and is more flexible, and more equal gender contracts expand gendered daily habits.[94]

Figure 3.8 Malta Cohousing Project Commissioned by Its Residents (ARK-house Architects), Jätkäsaari, Helsinki, 2013
Photo: Heljä Herranen, 2014.

Interrelationships of Gender, Modernities, and Housing

Gender, modernity, and housing have been interrelated at several levels in post-war Finland, from the ideals and practices of planning to the lived domestic spaces. The positive and negative effects of the environment on residents, and the welfare of women and children, have motivated the formation of modern housing environments since the late nineteenth century. Women professionals (architects, home economists, interior and garden designers) played an early and crucial role in the reshaping of dwelling spaces according to the new ideals of rationalized housework and functional spatial differentiation outlined in the 1920s and 1930s, and they shaped new housing environments alongside their male colleagues. The construction of type-planned veterans' houses and suburban neighborhoods after World War II efficiently disseminated the modern, urban, middle-class ideals of spatially differentiated, practical dwellings for the daily life of numerous Finns. Both indoors and outdoors, new domestic environments embodied the gendered spatial organization of daily life and society along the new ideals of the nuclear family and the complementary, gendered division of labor between practical, active housewives and breadwinning fathers. Whereas women's activities were valued, domestic environments were simultaneously identified as women's spheres of action. Modern dwellings had a radical impact on the residents' lives. For many residents, new spacious dwellings with their modern amenities symbolized achievements, and were praised by women in particular.

As the idealized efficient housewife and mother or as the "green widow"—the isolated, idle housewife—the housewife was a key figure both in the suburban ideology of the 1950s and in the suburban criticism starting in the mid-1960s. Although it pointed out the drawbacks of suburban life, the criticism deeply undervalued suburbs and suburbanites. It was often written from the perspective of middle-class, mostly male outside experts, and was both gender and class biased. The chain of the concepts of women, children, home, and suburbs were thus attached to each other, while the reproductive, domestic, and suburban spaces became detached from the more valuable productive, public, urban spaces. Suburbanites' recollections, however, point out women's agency in suburban life, both in the labor and affective "home work"[95] that were needed to produce the place called home, and in the suburban social relationships that critics failed to recognize.

Since the 1980s and 1990s, feminist planners and activists have outlined alternatives for persistent modernist dwelling and town planning ideals, such as various cohousing and participatory planning initiatives. Moreover, at the beginning of the twenty-first century, urbanites' various hands-on activities, pop-up events (restaurant day, cleaning day, sauna day), and novel types of urban agriculture, together with self-organized housing movements and neighborhood groups from suburbs to city center, have gained popularity in Finland as elsewhere, often facilitated by increasing use of information and communication technology. They stress urbanites' rights to use and shape cities, instead of relying on the predesigned and fixed activities of top-down planning. Women are particularly active in the new pop-up culture—often 70%–80% of the participants are women of varying ages.[96] However, the focus of interest no longer lies in the care of children and the balancing of domestic and work life, but rather on the varieties of urban "buzz."

The combination of various perspectives of planners, developers, journalists, activists, and inhabitants allows a more nuanced view of gender, housing environments, and modernity. Instead of the dichotomy between active planners as creators of the built environment and inhabitants as passive users, for whom the environment is planned, the shaping of the environment and its meanings is a much more complex process. Even if inhabitants learn to live with what they have, they too shape their environment and its meanings in conjunction with planners. Between the extremes of actively designing and passively consuming space, a range of ways exists to use and shape the environment and its meanings. Built spaces and their meanings are formed in the interplay of humans and their environment; in the reciprocity of planners, inhabitants, objects and things; past and present cultural conventions and practices, artificial and natural processes, and stable and moving human and nonhuman environmental elements.[97] Along with socially planned or unplanned features, the "naturally unplanned"[98] features, such as weather, seasons, and use, also mold the environment. Therefore, built spaces and their meanings are not static, completed constructions but are dynamic processes. The formation of built spaces continues after their planning and construction, which means that they change over time and are also open to the future. The relations between inhabitants and their environment are reciprocal. Even if spatial arrangements and cultural conceptions and agreements define the use of space, and support—or interfere with—gendered spatial habits and practices, they do not determine the activities of the inhabitants, who both shape their environment and are shaped by it.

Notes

1. Åström 1999, 105–6.
2. A large body of written personal recollections of suburban life in the Helsinki region from the 1950s to the 1970s was collected between 1995 and 2000. The largest collection of such memoirs, titled "Life in the Suburbs" (*Elämää lähiöissä*), was amassed by the newspaper *Helsingin Sanomat* from 1995–1996 (Helsinki City Archives). It contains over 200 stories from over 40 different suburbs. The competitions organized by the Folklore Archives of the Finnish Literature Society (SKS, 1999–2000) drew 82 entrants from the neighborhoods of Kontula and Siilitie, and the competition "Helsinki as a Living Environment" (*Helsinki elämänympäristönä*) arranged by ethnologist Anna-Maria Åström in 1995 drew 182 entrants, 34 of them about suburbs.
3. With the local Finnish variations, the development parallels state-sponsored housing programs after World War II in several other countries, among them Britain and the Federal Republic of Germany.
4. Juntto 1990, 228–9.
5. Finnish housing stock is indeed literally modern: over 90% was built after 1920, and in 1980 over 80% had been built from the 1940s to the 1970s. Juntto 1990, 408; Mäkiö 1994, 15.
6. Saarikangas 2014, 41–3.
7. Sulkunen 1987, 171–2; Hirdman 1989, 96.
8. Young 1997, 162.
9. Jokinen 2005, 50–1.

10. Giles 2004, 4.
11. Felski 2000, 26.
12. Susan E. Reid discusses modernism's gendered antipathy for domesticity in the context of "communist comfort" in this volume.
13. McLeod 1996, 20–4; Young 1997, 156–60; Ahmed, Castañeda, Fortier, and Sheller 2003, 1–19; Heynen 2005, 1–3; Johansson and Saarikangas 2009, 12–16; Fraiman 2017, 3.
14. Early examples include Wright 1981; Eleb-Vidal and Debarre-Blanchard 1989; Colomina 1992; Saarikangas 1993. The thorough discussion of the relationship of dwelling and modern architecture by Hilde Heynen (1999) skips gender.
15. Wolff 1985; Pollock 1988.
16. Domosh and Seager 2001, 5.
17. Saarikangas 2002, 158–64; Spain 2014, 583–4.
18. Wilson 1991, 10.
19. Ruckenstein 2009, 239–41; Domosh and Seager 2001, 34.
20. Saarikangas 1993, 43–8; Massey 1994, 167–71; Johansson and Saarikangas 2009.
21. Hartley 1997; Spigel 2001; Giles 2004; Hapgood 2005; Saarikangas 2014. See also Saegert 1980.
22. de Certeau 1980, 139–42, 173–4; Colomina 1992; Massey 2005; Saarikangas 2010; Saarikangas 2013, 31–2. The writings of Michel de Certeau, Michel Foucault, Maurice Merleau-Ponty, and Henri Lefebvre, among others, have been crucial for the rich field of inquiry.
23. Berman 1988, 16; Giles 2004, 4–6. In relation to modern architecture, terms are thoroughly discussed by Heynen 1999, 8–25.
24. Kaika 2005, 6.
25. Henket 2002, 9.
26. Berman 1988, 15–16.
27. O'Shea 1996, 11.
28. Saarikangas 1993, 142; Saarikangas 2002, 46–7; Heynen 2005, 15–20.
29. Kalha 2000.
30. Saarikangas 2002, 44–6; Mattila 2006, 133.
31. Nilsson 1994, 198; Gandy 2006, 14.
32. Gandy 2002, 5–7; Kaika 2005, 6.
33. Saarikangas 1993, 144–9; Heynen 1999, 43–50.
34. Aalto 1930, 188.
35. The industrial town Tampere had a local type of wooden, multifamily, worker housing in which one-room dwellings surrounded a shared kitchen; see Saarikangas 1993, 175.
36. Saarikangas 2002, 202–8.
37. Hayden 1981, 183–4.
38. Lagerborg-Stenius 1921, 25.
39. Saarikangas 2006, 161–2; Saarikangas 2009a, 289–94.
40. Fraiman 2017, 12.
41. Setälä 1931, 14.
42. Henderson 1996, 245–6; Saarikangas 2006, 163–5.
43. Saarikangas 2002, 49; Saarikangas 2009a, 286–91.
44. Saarikangas 1993, 341–53.
45. Colomina 1994, 9.
46. Saarikangas 1993, 43–8; Massey 1994, 164; Johansson and Saarikangas 2009.
47. Juntto 1990, 228–9, 408.
48. Saarikangas 1993, 84–9, 264–71; Saarikangas 2009a, 295–7; Palomäki 2011.
49. Frampton 1983.
50. Simberg 1945, 72–3; Saarikangas 1993, 358–9; Saarikangas 2009a, 295–301.
51. Stigell 1939, 49.
52. Harmaja 1939, 744.
53. Lappi-Seppälä 1945, 72–3.
54. Saarikangas 2009a, 293–4.
55. Heininen-Blomstedt 2013, 91.
56. Juntto 1990, 228–9. In the 1970s and 1980s, attention turned again to the urban centers. In addition to suburbs, new housing was constructed in single-family house neighborhoods, former industrial waterfronts, and intermediate areas, resulting a more continuous urban fabric.
57. Saarikangas 2014, 41–3.

58. In the 1950s, average suburban homes were 50 m² (540 sq. ft.), in the 1960s 60 m² (650 sq. ft.). Juntto 1990, 233; Mäkiö 1994, 14–15.
59. Lindroos 2013.
60. Juntto 1990, 275.
61. Saarikangas 2014, 44.
62. Hertzen 1946 and Meurman 1947 were the most important books disseminating suburban ideology. See Saarikangas 2014.
63. Herranen 1997, 491–3.
64. "Life in the Suburbs" 1995, 72.
65. "Life in the Suburbs" 1995, 45.
66. Saarikangas 2014, 47–8; Spain 1992, 13; Attfield 1999, 96.
67. For example Stigell 1945.
68. Meurman 1947, 78–9.
69. Roivainen 1999, 60.
70. *Helsingin Sanomat* November 1, 1975.
71. "Life in the Suburbs" 1995, 76.
72. Kortteinen 1982, 79–80; Jokinen 1996, 183.
73. "Life in the Suburbs" 1995, 39.
74. Matthews 1987, xiii.
75. Saarikangas 2014, 51–5.
76. Jokinen 2009, 361.
77. "Life in the Suburbs" 1995, 29.
78. Moreover, in Finland women did not give up their jobs after the war, as was the general trend in many countries. See Jallinoja 1985, 256; Saarikangas 1993, 361–2; Salmi 2009, 170–1; Marander-Eklund 2014, 58–65. Women were often employed in the growing public sector and public spaces of care.
79. Myrdal and Klein 1956.
80. Salmi 2009, 171.
81. Marander-Eklund 2014, 50–4. The Finnish *perheenemäntä* does not have an English equivalent. It refers to the active and productive aspects of home economics in the rural society; *emäntä* meant household manager. *Kotirouva* (housewife) became more common in the 1960s but had a critical tone, while *kotiäiti* (homemother) and perheenäiti (familymother) had more positive connotations for the women themselves.
82. Saarikangas 2013; Saarikangas 2014.
83. Saarikangas 2014, 38.
84. Suominen-Kokkonen 1992, 9–11.
85. Horelli and Vepsä 1994.
86. Hayden 1981.
87. Horelli and Vepsä 1994.
88. The Research Group for the New Everyday Life 1991; Gilroy and Booth 1999.
89. In the sense that it stressed community building with small-scale architectural means and participatory processes by women and men.
90. Fainstein 2010.
91. Sanchez de Madariaga and Roberts 2013.
92. Saarikangas 2009b.
93. Horelli 1995.
94. Horelli and Vepsä 1994; Vestbro and Horelli 2012.
95. Young 1997, 162.
96. Horelli, Saad-Suloinen, Wallin, and Botero 2015.
97. Latour 2007, 32–3.
98. von Bonsdorff 2005, 73–4.

References

Aalto, Alvar. 1930. "Asuntomme probleemina." *Domus*: 176–189.
Ahmed, Sara, Claudia Castañeda, Anne-Marie Fortier, and Mimi Sheller. 2003. "Introduction." In *Uprootings/Regroundings: Questions of Home and Migration*, edited by Sara Ahmed, Claudia Castañeda, Anne-Marie Fortier, and Mimi Sheller, 1–19. Oxford: Berg.

Åström, Anna-Maria. 1999. "Koti ja naapurusto." In *Koti kaupungin laidalla: Työväestön asumisen pitkä linja*, edited by Elina Katainen, 79–122. Helsinki: Työväen historian ja perinteentutkimuksen seura.

Attfield, Judy. 1999. "Bringing Modernity Home: Open Plan in the British Domestic Interior." In *At Home: An Anthropology of Domestic Space*, edited by Irene Cieraad, 73–82. Syracuse, NY: Syracuse University Press.

Berman, Marshall. 1988. *All that Is Solid Melts Into Air: The Experience of Modernity*. New York: Penguin Books.

Bonsdorff, Pauline von. 2005. "Building and the Naturally Unplanned." In *The Aesthetics of Everyday Life*, edited by Andrew Light and Jonathan Smith, 73–91. New York: Columbia University Press.

Certeau, Michel de. 1990/1980. *L'invention du quotidien 1. arts de faire*. Paris: Gallimard, folio essais.

Colomina, Beatriz, ed. 1992. *Sexuality and Space*. Princeton, NJ: Princeton Architectural Press.

Colomina, Beatriz. 1994. *Privacy and Publicity: Modern Architecture as Mass Media*. Cambridge, MA: MIT Press.

Domosh, Mona, and Joni Seager. 2001. *Putting Women in Place: Feminist Geographies Make Sense of the World*. New York: Guilford Press.

Eleb-Vidal, Monique, and Anne Debarre-Blanchard. 1989. *Architecture de la vie privée: Maison et mentalités XVII-XIX siècles*. Brussels: AAM.

Fainstein, Susan S. 2010. *The Just City*. Ithaca, NY: Cornell University Press.

Felski, Rita. 2000. "The Invention of Everyday Life." *New Formations* 39: 15–31.

Fraiman, Susan. 2017. *Extreme Domesticity: A View From the Margins*. New York: Columbia University Press.

Frampton, Kenneth. 1983. "Towards a Critical Regionalism: Six Points for an Architecture of Resistance." In *Anti-Aesthetic: Essays on Postmodern Culture*, edited by Hal Foster, 16–30. Seattle, WA: Bay Press.

Gandy, Matthew. 2002. *Concrete and Clay: Reworking Nature in New York City*. Cambridge, MA: MIT Press.

Gandy, Matthew. 2006. "The Bacteriological City and Its Discontents." *Historical Geography* 34: 14–25.

Giles, Judy. 2004. *The Parlour and the Suburb: Domestic Identities, Class, Femininity and Modernity*. Oxford: Berg.

Gilroy, Rose, and Chris Booth. 1999. "Building an Infrastructure for Everyday Lives." *European Planning Studies* 7: 307–324.

Hapgood, Lynne. 2005. *Margins of Desire: The Suburbs in Fiction and Culture 1880–1925*. Manchester: Manchester University Press.

Harmaja, Laura. 1939. "Kehittyykö asuntokysymys oikeaaan suuntaan?" *Kotiliesi*: 742–764.

Hartley, John. 1997. "The Sexualization of Suburbia: The Diffusion of Knowledge in the Postmodern Public Sphere." In *Visions of Suburbia*, edited by Roger Silverstone, 180–216. London and New York: Routledge.

Hayden, Dolores. 1981. *The Grand Domestic Revolution: A History of Feminist Design for American Homes, Neighborhoods and Cities*. Cambridge, MA: MIT Press.

Heininen-Blomstedt, Kirsi. 2013. *Jälleenrakennuskauden tyyppitaloalue: Paikan merkitykset ja täydennysrakentaminen*. E-Thesis, University of Helsinki. http://urn.fi/URN:ISBN:978-952-10-8693-9.

Henderson, Susan B. 1996. "A Revolution in the Woman's Sphere: Grete Lihotzky and the Frankfurt Kitchen." In *Architecture and Feminism*, edited by Debra Coleman, Elizabeth Danze, and Carol Henderson, 221–253. Princeton, NJ: Princeton Architectural Press.

Henket, Hubert-Jan. 2002. "Back from Utopia: The Challenge of the Modern Movement." In *Back From Utopia: The Challenge of the Modern Movement*, edited by Hubert-Jan Henket and Hilde Heynen, 9–17. Rotterdam: 010 Publishers.

Herranen, Timo. 1997. "Joukkoliikenne." In *Helsingin historia vuodesta 1945*, edited by Oiva Turpeinen, Timo Herranen, and Kai Hoffman, osa 1: 474–495. Helsinki: Helsingin kaupunki.

Hertzen, Heikki von. 1946. *Koti vaiko kasarmi lapsillemme*. Helsinki: WSOY.

Heynen, Hilde. 1999. *Architecture and Modernity: A Critique*. Cambridge, MA: MIT Press.

Heynen, Hilde. 2005. "Modernity and Domesticity: Tensions and Contradictions." In *Negotiating Domesticity: Spatial Productions of Gender in Architecture*, edited by Hilde Heynen and Gülsüm Baydar, 1–29. New York: Routledge.

Hirdman, Yvonne. 1989. *Att lägga livet till rätta: Studier i svensk folkhemspolitik*. Stockholm: Carlsson.

Horelli, Liisa. 1995. "Self-Planned Housing and the Reproduction of Gender and Identity." In *Gender and the Built Environment: Emancipation in Planning, Housing and Mobility in Europe*, edited by L. Ottes, E. Poventud, M. van Schendelen, and G. Segond von Banchet, 22–28. Assen: Van Gorcum.

Horelli, Liisa, Joanna Saad-Suloinen, Sirkku Wallin, and Andrea Botero. 2015. "When Self-Organization Intersects with Urban Planning: Two Cases From Helsinki." *Planning Practice and Research* 30: 286–302. doi:10.108 0/02697459.2015.105294. www.tandfonline.com/eprint/txkrUshBu3Gi2CeVzz5y/full.

Horelli, Liisa, and Kirsti Vepsä. 1994. "In Search of Supportive Structures for Everyday Life." In *Women and the Environment: Human Behavior and Environment*, Vol. 13, edited by Irwin Altman and Arza Churchman, 201–226. New York: Plenum. http://link.springer.com/book/10.1007%2F978-1-4899-104-7.

Jallinoja, Riitta. 1985. "Miehet ja naiset." In *Suomalaiset: Yhteiskunnan rakenne teollistumisen aikana*, edited by Tapani Valkonen, 243–270. Helsinki: WSOY.

Johansson, Hanna, and Kirsi Saarikangas. 2009. "Introduction: Ambivalent Home." In *Homes in Transformation: Dwelling, Moving, Belonging*, edited by Hanna Johansson and Kirsi Saarikangas, 9–35. Helsinki: SKS.

Jokinen, Eeva. 1996. *Väsynyt äiti: Äitiyden omaelämäkerrallisia esityksiä.* Helsinki: Gaudeamus.

Jokinen, Eeva. 2005. *Aikuisten arki.* Helsinki: Gaudeamus.

Jokinen, Eeva. 2009. "Home, Work and Affects in the Fourth Shift." In *Homes in Transformation: Dwelling, Moving, Belonging*, edited by Hanna Johansson and Kirsi Saarikangas, 358–375. Helsinki: SKS.

Juntto, Anneli. 1990. *Asuntokysymys Suomessa: Topeliuksesta Tulopolitiikkaan.* Helsinki: Asuntohallitus.

Kaika, Maria. 2005. *City of Flows: Modernity, Nature, and the City.* New York: Routledge.

Kalha, Harri. 2000. "Kaj Franck & Kilta: 'G Endering the (Aesth) Ethics of Modernism.'" *Scandinavian Journal of Design History* 10: 29–45.

Kortteinen, Matti. 1982. *Lähiö: Tutkimus elämäntapojen muutoksesta.* Helsinki: Otava.

Lagerborg-Stenius, Signe. 1921. "2–4 huoneen ja keittiön huoneistot." In *Naisten asuntopäivät Helsingissä 19.–21.5.1925*, 24–47. Porvoo: WSOY.

Lappi-Seppälä, Jussi. 1945. "Pula-ajan koti, joka tyydyttää perheenemäntää." *Kotiliesi* 1945: 72–73.

Latour, Bruno. 2007. *Reassembling the Social: An Introduction to Actor-Network-Theory.* Oxford: Oxford University Press.

Lindroos, Katja. 2013. *MOMO—Koti elementeissään.* Helsinki: Egnahem Media Oy & Siltala.

Mäkiö, Erkki. 1994. *Kerrostalot 1960–1975.* Helsinki: Rakennustietosäätiö.

Marander-Eklund, Lena. 2014. *Att vara hemmafru: En studie av kvinnligt liv i 1950-talets Finland.* Helsingfors: SLS.

Massey, Doreen B. 1994. *Space, Place, and Gender.* Cambridge: Polity Press.

Massey, Doreen B. 2005. *For Space.* London: Sage.

Matthews, Glenna. 1987. *"Just a Housewife": The Rise & Fall of Domesticity in America.* Oxford: Oxford University Press.

Mattila, Hanna. 2006. "Puutarhakaupunki utopiana: Esimerkkinä Tapiola." In *Paradokseja paratiissa: Näkökulmia urbaanin luonnon kysymyksiin*, edited by Arto Haapala and Mia Kunnaskari, 133–156. Lahti: Soveltavan estetiikan instituutti.

McLeod, Mary. 1996. "Everyday and Other Spaces." In *Architecture and Feminism*, edited by Debra Coleman, Elizabeth Danze, and Carol Henderson, 1–37. Princeton, NJ: Princeton Architectural Press.

Meurman, Otto-I. 1947. *Asemakaavaoppi.* Helsinki: Otava.

Myrdal, Alva, and Viola Klein. 1956. *Women's Two Roles: Home and Work.* London: Routledge & Paul.

Nilsson, Jan Olof. 1994. *Alva Myrdal—en virvel i den moderna strömmen.* Stockholm: Symposion.

Palomäki, Antti. 2011. *Juoksuhaudoista jälleenrakennukseen: Siirtoväen ja rintamamiesten asutus- ja asuntokysymyksen järjestäminen kaupungeissa 1940–1960 ja sen käänteentekevä vaikutus asuntopolitiikkaan ja kaupunkirakentamiseen.* Tampere: Tampere University Press.

O'Shea, Alan. 1996. "English Subjects of Modernity." In *Modern Times: Reflections on a Century of English Modernity*, edited by Mica Nava and Alan O'Shea, 7–37. London: Routledge.

Pollock, Griselda. 1998. *Vision and Difference: Femininity, Feminism and the Histories of Art.* London: Routledge.

The Research Group for the New Everyday Life. 1991. *The New Everyday Life: Ways and Means.* Copenhagen: Nord.

Roivainen, Irene. 1999. *Sokeripala metsän keskellä: Lähiö sanomalehden konstruktiona.* Helsinki: Helsingin kaupungin tietokeskus.

Ruckenstein, Minna. 2009. "Dynamic Domestic Space: Violence and the Art of Home-Making." In *Homes in Transformation: Dwelling, Moving, Belonging*, edited by Hanna Johansson and Kirsi Saarikangas, 239–258. Helsinki: SKS.

Saarikangas, Kirsi. 1993. *Model Houses for Model Families: Gender, Ideology and the Modern Dwelling. The Type-Planned Houses of the 1940s in Finland.* Helsinki: SHS.

Saarikangas, Kirsi. 2002. *Asunnon muodonmuutoksia: Puhtauden estetiikka ja sukupuoli modernissa arkkitehtuurissa.* Helsinki: SKS.

Saarikangas, Kirsi. 2006. "Displays of the Everyday: Relations Between Gender and the Visibility of Domestic Work in the Modern Finnish Kitchen from the 1930s to the 1950s." *Gender, Place and Culture* 13: 161–172.

Saarikangas, Kirsi. 2009a. "What's New? Women Pioneers and the Finnish State Meet the American Kitchen." In *Kitchen Politics in the Cold War: Americanization, Technology, and the European Users*, edited by Ruth Oldenziel and Karin Zachman, 285–311. Cambridge, MA: MIT Press.

Saarikangas, Kirsi. 2009b. "The House the Seniors Built." *Books From Finland*, November 2009. www.booksfromfinland.fi/2009/11/the-house-the-seniors-built/.

Saarikangas, Kirsi. 2010. "From Images to Lived Spaces: Feminist Approaches to the Analysis of Built Space." In *Contemporary Feminist Studies and its Relation to Art History and Visual Studies*, edited by Bia Mankel and Alexandra Reiff, 55–75. Göteborg Acta: Universitatis Gothoburgensis.

Saarikangas, Kirsi. 2013. "Multisensory Memories and the Spaces of Suburban Childhood in the Greater Helsinki Region in the 1950s and 1960s." In *Imagined Spaces and Places*, edited by Saija Isomaa, Pirjo Lyytikäinen, Kirsi Saarikangas, and Renja Suominen-Kokkonen, 27–54. Cambridge: Cambridge Scholars.

Saarikangas, Kirsi. 2014. "Sandboxes and Heavenly Dwellings: Gender, Agency, and Modernity in Lived Suburban Spaces in the Helsinki Metropolitan Area in the 1950s and 1960s." *Home Cultures* 11: 33–64.

Saegert, Susan. 1980. "Masculine Cities and Feminine Suburbs: Polarized Ideas, Contradictory Realities." *Signs* 5(3 suppl.): S96–S111.

Salmi, Minna. 2009. "Kuvia 60-luvun naisesta." In *Filmi-Kela: Suomi-filmistä sosiaalipolitiikkaan*, edited by Tuula Helne and Laura Kalliomaa-Puha, 166–174. Helsinki: Kelan tutkimusosasto.

Sanchez de Madariaga, Ines, and Marion Roberts, eds. 2013. *Fair Shared Cities: The Impact of Gender Planning*. London: Ashgate.

Setälä, Salme. 1931. *Keittiön sisustus*. Helsinki: Otava.

Simberg, Kurt. 1945. "Maalaisasunnon keittiön sisustuksia." *Arkkitehti* 1945: 72–73.

Spain, Daphne. 1992. *Gendered Spaces*. Chapel Hill: University of North Carolina Press.

Spain, Daphne. 2014. "Gender and Urban Space." *Annual Review of Sociology* 40: 581–598.

Spigel, Lynn. 2001. *Welcome to the Dreamhouse: Popular Media and PostWar Suburbs*. Durham, NC: Duke University Press.

Stigell, Anna-Liisa. 1939. "Maasueudn funktionalismi." *Asuntonäyttely* 1939: 49–55.

Stigell, Anna-Liisa. 1945. *Vi sätter bo*. Helsingfors: Svenska befolknings förbundet I Finland.

Sulkunen, Irma. 1987. "Naisten järjestäytyminen ja kaksijakoinen kansalaisuus." In *Kansa liikkeessä*, edited by Risto Alapuro, 157–175. Helsinki: Kirjayhtymä.

Suominen-Kokkonen, Renja. 1992. *The Fringe of a Profession: Women as Architects in Finland from the 1890s to the 1950s*. Helsinki: Suomen Muinaismuistoyhdistys.

Vestbro, Dick Urban, and Liisa Horelli. 2012. "Design for Gender Equality: The History of Cohousing Ideas and Realities." *Built Environment* 38: 315–335.

Wilson, Elizabeth. 1991. *The Sphinx in the City: Urban Life, the Control of Disorder, and Women*. Berkeley: University of California Press.

Wolff, Janet. 1985. "The Invisible Flâneuse: Women and the Literature of Modernity." *Theory, Culture and Society* 2: 37–46.

Wright, Gwendolyn. 1981. *Building the Dream: A Social History of Housing in America*. Cambridge, MA: MIT Press.

Young, Iris Marion. 1997. *Intersecting Voices: Dilemmas of Gender, Political Philosophy, and Policy*. Princeton, NJ: Princeton University Press.

Archives

Elämää lähiöissä (Life in the Suburbs), written memories in *Helsingin Sanomat* collection. Helsinki City Archives, Helsinki.

Kirsi Saarikangas's work on this chapter took place under the auspices of the Academy of Finland research project number 278008 at the University of Helsinki; ORCID ID: 0000-0003-3370-2941.

Part 2
Liberal and Neoliberal Values

Introduction

Modernity in nations that have followed a policy of economic liberalism or neoliberalism is strongly linked to capitalism, and the view that modern societies are based on a meritocracy of production, consumption, and expanding economic opportunities. While this view has been common among policymakers in liberal and neoliberal societies, the chapters in Part 2 offer a more finely nuanced view of how concepts of modernity in societies focused on the advantages of capitalism affect women and their economic and social opportunities, using examples taken from the US and Great Britain.

Ruth Schwartz Cowan's chapter, on the revolutionary introduction of new household technology in the US at the turn of the twentieth century, shows how a technical modernization of the household went hand in hand with a shift of women's positions in the middle-class household—from one of managing servants to one of performing the work that servants had once done. Kim England, in her chapter that parallels this shift in household technologies, discusses how working-class women in the early twentieth century entered the white-collar workplace, a space previously denied them. The "new woman" that emerged challenged common spatial constructs that had kept women from accessing much of the public domain. Questions of capitalism and access to public space underlie Alexandra Staub's chapter as well, as she examines how the housing industry in the US today continues to frame women as domestic consumers, with ever more luxurious amenities taking over functions that were once in the public realm, while requiring a new caste of workers to maintain upscale lifestyles.

In her chapter on modernist urban design, Marion Roberts examines the congruence between the ideals of the early modern movement in architecture and urbanism and the objectives of gender-sensitive planning, using as a case study an exemplar mixed-income sustainable community in England. Finally, Igea Troiani takes to task the neoliberalism of architectural practice in Margaret Thatcher's England, analyzing how Zaha Hadid's penthouse apartment space, the marketing of her creativity, and her designs, all serve as a wrapper for architecture's starchitect "biopolitic," tying the body of the architect to an incessant drive for increased marketization through the concept of *homo oeconomicus*.

The chapters in Part 2, taken together, question whether modernity expressed through liberal or neoliberal policies has done women justice. At the very least, they point to the need to adopt a critical gender lens in assessing the full impact of such ideals.

4

The "Industrial Revolution" in the Home

Household Technology and Social Change in the Twentieth Century

Ruth Schwartz Cowan

When we think about the interaction between technology and society, we tend to think in fairly grandiose terms: massive computers invading the workplace, railroad tracks cutting through vast wildernesses, armies of woman and children toiling in the mills. These grand visions have blinded us to an important and rather peculiar technological revolution that has been going on right under our noses: the technological revolution in the home. This revolution has transformed the conduct of our daily lives, but in somewhat unexpected ways. The industrialization of the home was a process very different from the industrialization of other means of production, and the impact of that process was neither what we have been led to believe it was nor what students of the other industrial revolutions would have been led to predict.

Some years ago sociologists of the functionalist school formulated an explanation of the impact of industrial technology on the modern family. Although that explanation was not empirically verified, it has become almost universally accepted.[1] Despite some differences in emphasis, the basic tenets of the traditional interpretation can be roughly summarized as follows.

Before industrialization, the family was the basic social unit. Most families were rural, large, and self-sustaining; they produced and processed almost everything that was needed for their own support and for trading in the marketplace, while at the same time performing a host of other functions ranging from mutual protection to entertainment. In these preindustrial families women (adult women, that is) had a lot to do, and their time was almost entirely absorbed by household tasks. Under industrialization, the family is much less important. The household is no longer the focus of production; production for the marketplace and production for sustenance have been removed to other locations. Families are smaller and they are urban rather than rural. The number of social functions they perform is much reduced, until almost all that remains is consumption, socialization of small children, and tension management. As their functions diminished, families became atomized; the social bonds that had held them together were loosened. In these postindustrial families women have very little to do, and the tasks with which they fill their time have lost the social utility that they once possessed. Modern women are in trouble, the analysis goes, because modern families are in trouble; and modern families are in trouble because industrial technology has either eliminated or eased almost all their former functions, but modern ideologies have not kept pace with the change. The results of this time lag are several: some women suffer from role anxiety, others land in the divorce courts, some enter the labor market, and others take to burning their brassieres and demanding liberation.

This sociological analysis is a cultural artifact of vast importance. Many Americans believe that it is true and act upon that belief in various ways: some hope to reestablish family solidarity by relearning lost productive crafts—baking bread, tending a vegetable garden—others dismiss the women's liberation movement [of the late 1960s and 1970s—Ed.] as "simply a bunch of affluent housewives who have nothing better to do with their time." As disparate as they may seem, these reactions have a common ideological source—the standard sociological analysis of the impact of technological change on family life.

As a theory this functionalist approach has much to recommend it, but at present we have very little evidence to back it up. Family history is an infant discipline, and what evidence it has produced in recent years does not lend credence to the standard view.[2] Phillippe Aries has shown, for example, that in France the ideal of the small nuclear family predates industrialization by more than a century.[3] Historical demographers working on data from English and French families have been surprised to find that most families were quite small and that several generations did not ordinarily reside together; the extended family, which is supposed to have been the rule in preindustrial societies, did not occur in colonial New England either.[4] Rural English families routinely employed domestic servants, and even very small English villages had their butchers and bakers and candlestick makers; all these persons must have eased some of the chores that would otherwise have been the housewife's burden.[5] Preindustrial housewives no doubt had much with which to occupy their time, but we may have reason to wonder whether there was quite as much pressure on them as sociological orthodoxy has led us to suppose. The large rural family that was sufficient unto itself back there on the prairies may have been limited to the prairies—or it may never have existed at all (except, that is, in the reveries of sociologists).

Even if all the empirical evidence were to mesh with the functionalist theory, the theory would still have problems, because its logical structure is rather weak. Comparing the average farm family in 1750 (assuming that you knew what that family was like) with the average urban family in 1950 in order to discover the significant social changes that had occurred is an exercise rather like comparing apples with oranges; the differences between the fruits may have nothing to do with the differences in their evolution. Transferring the analogy to the case at hand, what we really need to know is the difference, say, between an urban laboring family of 1750 and an urban laboring family 100 and then 200 years later, or the difference between the rural nonfarm middle classes in all three centuries, or the difference between the urban rich yesterday and today. Surely in each of these cases the analyses will look very different from what we have been led to expect. As a guess, we might find that for the urban laboring families the changes have been precisely the opposite of what the model predicted; that is, that their family structure is much firmer today than it was in centuries past. Similarly, for the rural nonfarm middle class the results might be equally surprising; we might find that married women of that class rarely did any housework at all in 1890 because they had farm girls as servants, whereas in 1950 they bore the full brunt of the work themselves. I could go on, but the point is, I hope, clear: in order to verify or falsify the functionalist theory, it will be necessary to know more than we presently do about the impact of industrialization on families of similar classes and geographical locations.

With this problem in mind I have, for the purposes of this initial study, deliberately limited myself to one kind of technological change affecting one aspect of family life in only one of the many social classes of families that might have been considered. What happened, I asked, to middle-class American women when the implements with which they did their everyday household work changed? Did the technological change in household appliances have any effect upon the structure of American households, or upon the ideologies that governed the behavior of American women, or upon the functions that families needed to perform? Middle-class American women were defined as actual or

The "Industrial Revolution" in the Home

potential readers of the better-quality women's magazines, such as the *Ladies' Home Journal, American Home, Parents' Magazine, Good Housekeeping*, and *McCall's*.[6] Nonfictional material (articles and advertisements) in those magazines was used as a partial indicator of some of the technological and social changes that were occurring.

The *Ladies' Home Journal* has been in continuous publication since 1886. A casual survey of the nonfiction in the *Journal* yields the immediate impression that that decade between the end of World War I and the beginning of the Depression witnessed the most drastic changes in patterns of household work. Statistical data bear out this impression. Before 1918, for example, illustrations of homes lit by gaslight could still be found in the *Journal*; by 1928 gaslight had disappeared. In 1917 only one-quarter (24.3%) of the dwellings in the US had been electrified, but by 1920 this figure had doubled (47.4%— for rural nonfarm and urban dwellings), and by 1930 it had risen to four-fifths).[7] If electrification had meant simply the change from gas or oil lamps to electric lights, the changes in the housewife's routines might not have been very great (except for eliminating the chore of cleaning and filling oil lamps); but changes in lighting were the least of the changes that electrification implied. Small electric appliances followed quickly on the heels of the electric light, and some of those augured much more profound changes in the housewife's routine.

Ironing, for example, had traditionally been one of the most dreadful household chores, especially in warm weather when the kitchen stove had to be kept hot for the better part of the day; irons were heavy and they had to be returned to the stove frequently to be reheated. Electric irons eased a good part of this burden.[8] They were relatively inexpensive and very quickly replaced their predecessors; advertisements for electric irons first began to appear in the ladies' magazines after the war, and by the end of the decade the old flatiron had disappeared; by 1929 a survey of 100 Ford employees revealed that 98 of them had the new electric irons in their homes.[9]

Data on the diffusion of electric washing machines are somewhat harder to come by, but it is clear from the advertisements in the magazines, particularly advertisements for laundry soap, that by the middle of the 1920s those machines could be found in a significant number of homes. The washing machine is depicted just about as frequently as the laundry tub by the middle of the 1920s; in 1929, 49 out of those 100 Ford workers had the machines in their homes. The washing machines did not drastically reduce the time that had to be spent on household laundry, as they did not go through their cycles automatically and did not spin dry; the housewife had to stand guard, stopping and starting the machine at appropriate times, adding soap, sometimes attaching the drain pipes, and putting the clothes through the wringer manually. The machines did, however, reduce a good part of the drudgery that once had been associated with washday, and this was a matter of no small consequence.[10] Soap powders appeared on the market in the early 1920s, thus eliminating the need to scrape and boil bars of laundry soap.[11] By the end of the 1920s Blue Monday must have been considerably less blue for some housewives—and probably considerably less "Monday," for with an electric iron, a washing machine, and a hot water heater, there was no reason to limit the washing to just one day of the week.

Like the routines of washing the laundry, the routines of personal hygiene must have been transformed for many households during the 1920s—the years of the bathroom mania.[12] More and more bathrooms were built in older homes, and new homes began to include them as a matter of course. Before the war, most bathroom fixtures (tubs, sinks, and toilets) were made out of porcelain by hand; each bathroom was custom-made for the house in which it was installed. After the war, industrialization descended upon the bathroom industry; cast-iron enamelware went into mass production and fittings were standardized. In 1921 the dollar value of the production of enameled sanitary fixtures was $2.4 million, the same as it had been in 1915. By 1923, just two years later, that figure had doubled to $4.8 million; it rose again to $5.1 million in 1925.[13] The first recessed, double-shell cast iron enameled bathtub was put on the market in the early 1920s. A decade later the standard American bathroom had achieved its standard American form: the recessed tub, plus tiled floors and walls, brass plumbing, a

71

single-unit toilet, an enameled sink, and a medicine chest, all set into a small room that was very often 5 feet square (2.3 m²).[14] The bathroom evolved more quickly than any other room of the house; its standardized form was accomplished in just over a decade.

Along with bathrooms came modernized systems for heating hot water: 61% of the homes in Zanesville, Ohio, had indoor plumbing with centrally heated water by 1926, and 83% of the homes valued over $2,000 in Muncie, Indiana, had hot and cold running water by 1935.[15] These figures may not be typical of small American cities (or even large American cities) at those times, but they do jibe with the impression that one gets from the magazines: after 1918 references to hot water heated on the kitchen range, either for laundering or for bathing, become increasingly difficult to find.

Similarly, during the 1920s many homes were outfitted with central heating; in Muncie most of the homes of the business class had basement heating in 1924; by 1935 Federal Emergency Relief Administration data for the city indicated that only 22.4% of the dwellings valued over $2,000 were still heated by a kitchen stove.[16] What all these changes meant in terms of new habits for the average housewife is somewhat hard to calculate; changes there must have been, but it is difficult to know whether those changes produced an overall saving of labor and/or time. Some chores were eliminated—hauling water, heating water on the stove, maintaining the kitchen fire—but other chores were added—most notably the chore of keeping yet another room scrupulously clean.

It is not, however, difficult to be certain about the changing habits that were associated with the new American kitchen—a kitchen from which the coal stove had disappeared. In Muncie in 1924, cooking with gas was done in two out of three homes; in 1935 only 5% of the homes valued over $2,000 still had coal or wood stoves for cooking.[17] After 1918 advertisements for coal and wood stoves disappeared from the *Ladies' Home Journal*; stove manufacturers purveyed only their gas, oil, or electric models. Articles giving advice to homemakers on how to deal with the trials and tribulations of starting, stoking, and maintaining a coal or a wood fire also disappeared. Thus it seems a safe assumption that most middle-class homes had switched to the new method of cooking by the time the Depression began. The change in routine that was predicated on the change from coal or wood to gas or oil was profound; aside from the elimination of such chores as loading the fuel and removing the ashes, the new stoves were much easier to light, maintain, and regulate (even when they did not have thermostats, as the earliest models did not).[18] Kitchens were, in addition, much easier to clean when they did not have coal dust regularly tracked through them; one writer in the *Ladies' Home Journal* estimated that kitchen cleaning was reduced by one-half when coal stoves were eliminated.[19]

Along with new stoves came new foodstuffs and new dietary habits. Canned foods had been on the market since the middle of the nineteenth century, but they did not become an appreciable part of the standard middle-class diet until the 1920s—if the recipes given in cookbooks and in women's magazines are a reliable guide. By 1918 the variety of foods available in cans had been considerably expanded from the peas, corn, and succotash of the nineteenth century; an American housewife with sufficient means could have purchased almost any fruit or vegetable and quite a surprising array of ready-made meals in a can—from Heinz's spaghetti in meat sauce to Purity Cross's lobster à la Newburg. By the middle of the 1920s, home canning was becoming a lost art. Canning recipes were relegated to the back pages of the women's magazines; the business-class wives of Muncie reported that, while their mothers had once spent the better part of the summer and fall canning, they themselves rarely put up anything, except an occasional jelly or batch of tomatoes.[20] In part this was also due to changes in the technology of marketing food; increased use of refrigerated railroad cars during this period meant that fresh fruits and vegetables were in the markets all year round at reasonable prices.[21] By the early 1920s convenience foods were also appearing on American tables: cold breakfast cereals, pancake mixes, bouillon cubes, and packaged desserts could be found. Wartime shortages accustomed Americans to eating much lighter

The "Industrial Revolution" in the Home

meals than they had previously been wont to do; and as fewer family members were taking all their meals at home (businessmen started to eat lunch in restaurants downtown, and factories and schools began installing cafeterias), there was simply less cooking to be done, and what there was of it was easier to do.[22]

Many of the changes just described—from hand power to electric power, from coal and wood to gas and oil as fuels for cooking, from one-room heating to central heating, from pumping water to running water—are enormous technological changes. Changes of a similar dimension, either in the fundamental technology of an industry, in the diffusion of that technology, or in the routines of workers, would have long since been labeled an "industrial revolution." The change from the laundry tub to the washing machine is no less profound than the change from the hand loom to the power loom; the change from pumping water to turning on a water faucet is no less destructive of traditional habits than the change from manual to electric calculating. It seems odd to speak of an "industrial revolution" connected with housework, odd because we are talking about the technology of such homely things, and odd because we are not accustomed to thinking of housewives as a labor force or of housework as an economic commodity—but despite this oddity, I think the term is altogether appropriate.

In this case other questions come immediately to mind, questions that we do not hesitate to ask, say, about textile workers in Britain in the early nineteenth century, but we have never thought to ask about housewives in America in the twentieth century. What happened to this particular workforce when the technology of its work was revolutionized? Did structural changes occur? Were new jobs created for which new skills were required? Can we discern new ideologies that influenced the behavior of the workers?

The answer to all of these questions, surprisingly enough, seems to be yes. There were marked structural changes in the workforce, changes that increased the workload and the job description of the workers that remained. New jobs were created for which new skills were required; these jobs were not physically burdensome, but they may have taken up as much time as the jobs they had replaced. New ideologies were also created, ideologies that reinforced new behavioral patterns, patterns that we might not have been led to expect if we had followed the sociologists' model to the letter. Middle-class housewives, the women who must have first felt the impact of the new household technology, were not flocking into the divorce courts or the labor market or the forums of political protest in the years immediately after the revolution in their work. What they were doing was sterilizing baby bottles, shepherding their children to dancing classes and music lessons, planning nutritious meals, shopping for new clothes, studying child psychology, and hand stitching color-coordinated curtains—all of which are chores (and others like them) that the standard sociological model has apparently not provided for.

The significant change in the structure of the household labor force was the disappearance of paid and unpaid servants (unmarried daughters, maiden aunts, and grandparents fall in the latter category) as household workers—and the imposition of the entire job on the housewife herself. Leaving aside for a moment the question of which was cause and which effect (did the disappearance of the servant create a demand for the new technology, or did the new technology make the servant obsolete?), the phenomenon itself is relatively easy to document. Before World War I, when illustrators in the women's magazines depicted women doing housework, the women were very often servants. When the lady of the house was drawn, she was often the person being served, or she was supervising the serving, or she was adding an elegant finishing touch to the work. Nursemaids diapered babies, seamstresses pinned up hems, waitresses served meals, laundresses did the wash, and cooks did the cooking. By the end of the 1920s the servants had disappeared from those illustrations; all those jobs were being done by housewives—elegantly manicured and coiffed, to be sure, but housewives nonetheless (compare Figures 4.1 and 4.2).

Figure 4.1 The Housewife as Manager
Source: *Ladies' Home Journal,* April 1918.

Figure 4.2 The Housewife as Laundress
Source: *Ladies' Home Journal*, August 1928.

If we are tempted to suppose that illustrations in advertisements are not a reliable indicator of structural changes of this sort, we can corroborate the changes in other ways. Apparently, the illustrators really did know whereof they drew. Statistically the number of persons throughout the country employed in household service dropped from 1,851,000 in 1910 to 1,411,000 in 1920, while the number of households enumerated in the census rose from 20.3 million to 24.4 million.[23] In Indiana, the ratio of households to servants increased from 13.5 to 1 in 1890 to 30.5 to 1 in 1920, and in the country as a whole the number of paid domestic servants per 1,000 population dropped from 98.9 in 1900 to 58.0 in 1920.[24] The business-class housewives of Muncie reported that they employed approximately one-half as many woman-hours of domestic service as their mothers had done.[25]

In case we are tempted to doubt these statistics (and indeed statistics about household labor are particularly unreliable, as the labor is often transient, part time, or simply unreported), we can turn to articles on the servant problem, the disappearance of unpaid family workers, the design of kitchens, or to architectural drawings for houses. All of this evidence reiterates the same point: qualified servants were difficult to find; their wages had risen and their numbers fallen; houses were being designed without maid's rooms; daughters and unmarried aunts were finding jobs downtown; kitchens were being designed for housewives, not for servants.[26] The first home with a kitchen that was not an entirely separate room was designed by Frank Lloyd Wright in 1934.[27] In 1937 Emily Post invented a new character for her etiquette books: Mrs. Three-in-One, the woman who is her own cook, waitress, and hostess.[28] There must have been many new Mrs. Three-in-Ones abroad in the land during the 1920s.

As the number of household assistants declined, the number of household tasks increased. The middle-class housewife was expected to demonstrate competence at several tasks that previously had not been in her purview or had not existed at all. Childcare is the most obvious example. The average housewife had fewer children than her mother had had, but she was expected to do things for her children that her mother would never have dreamed of doing: to prepare their special infant formulas, sterilize their bottles, weigh them every day, see to it that they ate nutritionally balanced meals, keep them isolated and confined when they had even the slightest illness, consult with their teachers frequently, and chauffeur them to dancing lessons, music lessons, and evening parties.[29] There was very little Freudianism in this new attitude toward childcare: mothers were not spending more time and effort on their children because they feared the psychological trauma of separation, but because competent nursemaids could not be found, and the new theories of childcare required constant attention from well-informed persons—persons who were willing and able to read about the latest discoveries in nutrition, in the control of contagious diseases, or in the techniques of behavioral psychology. These persons simply had to be their mothers.

Consumption of economic goods provides another example of the housewife's expanded job description; like childcare, the new tasks associated with consumption were not necessarily physically burdensome, but they were time-consuming, and they required the acquisition of new skills.[30] Home economists and the editors of women's magazines tried to teach housewives to spend their money wisely. The present generation of housewives, it was argued, had been reared by mothers who did not ordinarily shop for things like clothing, bed linens, or towels; consequently modern housewives did not know how to shop and would have to be taught. Furthermore, their mothers had not been accustomed to the wide variety of goods that were now available in the modern marketplace; the new housewives had to be taught not just to be consumers, but to be informed consumers.[31] Several contemporary observers believed that shopping and shopping wisely were occupying increasing amounts of housewives' time.[32]

Several of these contemporary observers also believed that standards of household care changed during the decade of the 1920s.[33] The discovery of the "household germ" led to almost fetishistic concern about the cleanliness of the home. The amount and frequency of laundering probably increased, as bed linen and underwear were changed more often, children's clothes were made increasingly out

The "Industrial Revolution" in the Home

of washable fabrics, and men's shirts no longer had replaceable collars and cuffs.[34] Unfortunately all these changes in standards are difficult to document, being changes in the things that people regard as so insignificant as to be unworthy of comment; the improvement in standards seems a likely possibility, but not something that can be proved.

In any event we do have various time studies that demonstrate somewhat surprisingly that housewives with conveniences were spending just as much time on household duties as were housewives without them—or, to put it another way, housework, like so many other types of work, expands to fill the time available.[35] A study comparing the time spent per week in housework by 288 farm families and 154 town families in Oregon in 1928 revealed 61 hours spent by farm wives and 63.4 hours by town wives; in 1929 a US Department of Agriculture study of families in various states produced almost identical results.[36] Surely if the standard sociological model were valid, housewives in towns, where presumably the benefits of specialization and electrification were most likely to be available, should have been spending far less time at their work than their rural sisters. However, just after World War II economists at Bryn Mawr College reported the same phenomenon: 60.55 hours spent by farm housewives, 78.35 hours by women in small cities, 80.57 hours by women in large ones—precisely the reverse of the results that were expected.[37] A recent survey of time studies conducted between 1920 and 1970 concludes that the time spent on housework by non-employed housewives has remained remarkably constant throughout the period.[38] All these results point in the same direction: mechanization of the household meant that time expended on some jobs decreased, but also that new jobs were substituted, and in some cases—notably laundering—time expenditures for old jobs increased because of higher standards. The advantages of mechanization may be somewhat more dubious than they seem at first glance.

As the job of the housewife changed, the connected ideologies also changed; there was a clearly perceptible difference in the attitudes that women brought to housework before and after World War I.[39] Before the war, the trials of doing housework in a servantless home were discussed, and they were regarded as just that—trials, necessary chores that had to be got through until a qualified servant could be found. After the war, housework changed: it was no longer a trial and a chore, but something quite different—an emotional "trip." Laundering was not just laundering, but an expression of love; the housewife who truly loved her family would protect them from the embarrassment of tattletale gray. Feeding the family was not just feeding the family, but a way to express the housewife's artistic inclinations and a way to encourage feelings of family loyalty and affection. Diapering the baby was not just diapering, but a time to build the baby's sense of security and love for the mother. Cleaning the bathroom sink was not just cleaning, but an exercise of protective maternal instincts, providing a way for the housewife to keep her family safe from disease. Tasks of this emotional magnitude could not possibly be delegated to servants, even assuming that qualified servants could be found.

Women who failed at these new household tasks were bound to feel guilty about their failure. If I had to choose one word to characterize the temper of the women's magazines during the 1920s, it would be "guilt." Readers of the better-quality women's magazines are portrayed as feeling guilty a good lot of the time, and when they are not guilty they are embarrassed: guilty if their infants have not gained enough weight, embarrassed if their drains are clogged, guilty if their children go to school in soiled clothes, guilty if all the germs behind the bathroom sink are not eradicated, guilty if they fail to notice the first signs of an oncoming cold, embarrassed if accused of having body odor, guilty if their sons go to school without good breakfasts, guilty if their daughters are unpopular because of old-fashioned, or unironed, or—heaven forbid—dirty dresses (see Figures 4.3 and 4.4). In earlier times women were made to feel guilty if they abandoned their children or were too free with their affections. In the years after World War I, American women were made to feel guilty about sending their children to school in scuffed shoes. Between the two kinds of guilt there is a world of difference.

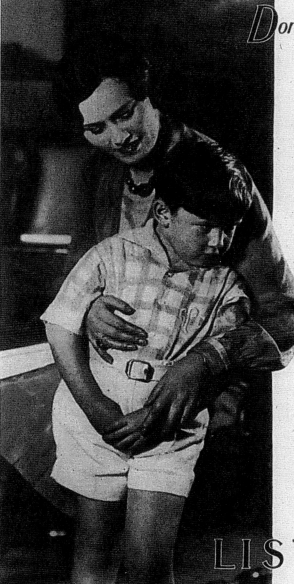

Figure 4.3 Sources of Housewifely Guilt: The Good Mother Smells Sweet
Source: *Ladies' Home Journal*, August 1928.

Figure 4.4 Sources of Housewifely Guilt: The Good Mother Must Be Beautiful

Source: Ladies' Home Journal, July 1928.

Let us return for a moment to the sociological model with which this chapter began. The model predicts that changing patterns of household work will be correlated with at least two striking indicators of social change: the divorce rate and the rate of married women's labor force participation. That correlation may indeed exist, but it certainly is not reflected in the women's magazines of the 1920s and 1930s: divorce and full-time paid employment were not part of the lifestyle or the life pattern of the middle-class housewife as she was idealized in her magazines.

There were social changes attendant upon the introduction of modern technology into the home, but they were not the changes that the traditional functionalist model predicts; on this point a close analysis of the statistical data corroborates the impression conveyed in the magazines. The divorce rate was indeed rising during the years between the wars, but it was not rising nearly so fast for the middle and upper classes (who had, presumably, easier access to the new technology) as it was for the lower classes. By almost every gauge of socioeconomic status—income, prestige of husband's work, education—the divorce rate is higher for persons lower on the socioeconomic scale—and this is a phenomenon that has been constant over time.[40]

The supposed connection between improved household technology and married women's labor force participation seems just as dubious, and on the same grounds. The single socioeconomic factor that correlates most strongly (in cross-sectional studies) with married women's employment is husband's income, and the correlation is strongly negative; the higher his income, the less likely it will be that she is working.[41] Women's labor force participation increased during the 1920s, but this increase was due to the influx of single women into the force. Married women's participation increased slightly during those years, but that increase was largely in factory labor—precisely the kind of work that middle-class women (who were, again, much more likely to have labor-saving devices at home) were least likely to do.[42] If there were a necessary connection between the improvement of household technology and either of these two social indicators, we would expect the data to be precisely the reverse of what in fact has occurred: women in the higher social classes should have fewer functions at home and should therefore be more (rather than less) likely to seek paid employment or divorce.

Thus for middle-class American housewives between the wars, the social changes that we can document are not the social changes that the functionalist model predicts; rather than changes in divorce or patterns of paid employment, we find changes in the structure of the workforce, in its skills, and in its ideology. These social changes were concomitant with a series of technological changes in the equipment that was used to do the work. What is the relationship between these two series of phenomena? Is it possible to demonstrate causality or the direction of that causality? Was the decline in the number of households employing servants a cause or an effect of the mechanization of those households? Both are, after all, equally possible. The declining supply of household servants, as well as their rising wages, may have stimulated a demand for new appliances at the same time that the acquisition of new appliances may have made householders less inclined to employ the laborers who were on the market. Are there any techniques available to the historian to help us answer these questions?

In order to establish causality, we need to find a connecting link between the two sets of phenomena, a mechanism that in real life could have made the causality work. In this case a connecting link, an intervening agent between the social and the technological changes, comes immediately to mind: the advertiser—by which term I mean a combination of the manufacturer of the new goods, the advertising agent who promoted the goods, and the periodical that published the promotion. All the new devices and new foodstuffs that were being offered to American households were being manufactured and marketed by large companies that had considerable amounts of capital invested in their production: General Electric, Procter & Gamble, General Foods, Lever Brothers, Frigidaire, Campbell's, Del Monte, American Can, Atlantic & Pacific Tea. These were all well-established firms by the time the household revolution began, and they were all in a position to pay for national advertising campaigns to promote their new products and services. And pay they did; one reason for

The "Industrial Revolution" in the Home

the expanding size and number of women's magazines in the 1920s was, no doubt, the expansion in revenues from available advertisers.[43]

Those national advertising campaigns were likely to have been powerful stimulators of the social changes that occurred in the household labor force; the advertisers probably did not initiate the changes, but they certainly encouraged them. Most of the advertising campaigns manifestly worked, so they must have touched upon areas of real concern for American housewives. Appliance ads specifically suggested that the acquisition of one gadget or another would make it possible to fire the maid, spend more time with the children, or have the afternoon free for shopping.[44] Similarly, many advertisements played upon the embarrassment and guilt that were now associated with household work. Ralston, Cream of Wheat, and Ovaltine were not themselves responsible for the compulsive practice of weighing infants and children repeatedly (after every meal for newborns, every day in infancy, every week later on), but the manufacturers certainly did not stint on capitalizing upon the guilt that women apparently felt if their offspring did not gain the required amounts of weight.[45] And yet again, many of the earliest attempts to spread "wise" consumer practices were undertaken by large corporations and the magazines that desired their advertising: mail-order shopping guides, "product-testing" services, pseudoinformative pamphlets, and other such promotional devices were all techniques for urging the housewife to buy new things under the guise of training her in her role as skilled consumer.[46]

Thus the advertisers could well be called the "ideologues" of the 1920s, encouraging certain very specific social changes—as ideologues are wont to do. Not surprisingly, the changes that occurred were precisely the ones that would gladden the hearts and fatten the purses of the advertisers; fewer household servants meant a greater demand for labor and time-saving devices; more household tasks for women meant more and more specialized products that they would need to buy; more guilt and embarrassment about their failure to succeed at their work meant a greater likelihood that they would buy the products that were intended to minimize that failure. Happy, full-time housewives in intact families spend a lot of money to maintain their households; divorced women and working women do not. The advertisers may not have created the image of the ideal American housewife that dominated the 1920s—the woman who cheerfully and skillfully set about making everyone in her family perfectly happy and perfectly healthy—but they certainly helped to perpetuate it.

The role of the advertiser as connecting link between social change and technological change is at this juncture simply a hypothesis, with nothing much more to recommend it than an argument from plausibility. Further research may serve to test the hypothesis, but testing it may not settle the question of which was cause and which effect—if that question can ever be settled definitively in historical work. What seems most likely in this case, as in so many others, is that cause and effect are not separable, that there is a dynamic interaction between the social changes that married women were experiencing and the technological changes that were occurring in their homes. Viewed this way, the disappearance of competent servants becomes one of the factors that stimulated the mechanization of homes, and this mechanization of homes becomes a factor (although by no means the only one) in the disappearance of servants. Similarly, the emotionalization of housework becomes both cause and effect of the mechanization of that work; and the expansion of time spent on new tasks becomes both cause and effect of the introduction of time-saving devices. For example the social pressure to spend more time in childcare may have led to a decision to purchase the devices; once purchased, the devices could indeed have been used to save time—although often they were not.

If one holds the question of causality in abeyance, the example of household work still has some useful lessons to teach about the general problem of technology and social change. The standard sociological model for the impact of modern technology on family life clearly needs some revision: at least for middle-class nonrural American families in the twentieth century, the social changes were not the ones that the standard model predicts. In these families the functions of at least one member, the housewife, have increased rather than decreased—and the dissolution of family life has not in fact occurred.

Our standard notions about what happens to a workforce under the pressure of technological change may also need revision. When industries become mechanized and rationalized, we expect certain general changes in the workforce to occur: its structure becomes more highly differentiated, individual workers become more specialized, managerial functions increase, and the emotional context of the work disappears. On all four counts our expectations are reversed with regard to household work. The workforce became less rather than more differentiated as domestic servants, unmarried daughters, maiden aunts, and grandparents left the household, and chores that had once been performed by commercial agencies (laundries, delivery services, milkmen) were delegated to the housewife. The individual workers also became less specialized; the new housewife was now responsible for every aspect of life in her household, from scrubbing the bathroom floor to keeping abreast of the latest literature in child psychology.

The housewife is just about the only unspecialized worker left in America—a veritable jane-of-all-trades at a time when the jacks-of-all-trades have disappeared. As her work became generalized the housewife was also proletarianized: formerly she was ideally the manager of several other subordinate workers; now she was idealized as the manager and the worker combined. Her managerial functions have not entirely disappeared, but they have certainly diminished and have been replaced by simple manual labor: the middle-class, fairly well-educated housewife ceased to be a personnel manager and became, instead, a chauffeur, charwoman, and short-order cook. The implications of this phenomenon, the proletarianization of a workforce that had previously seen itself as predominantly managerial, deserve to be explored at greater length than is possible here, because I suspect that they will explain certain aspects of the women's liberation movement of the 1960s and 1970s that have previously eluded explanation: why, for example, the movement's greatest strength lies in social and economic groups who seem, on the surface at least, to need it least—women who are white, well-educated, and middle-class.

Finally, instead of desensitizing the emotions that were connected with household work, the industrial revolution in the home seems to have heightened the emotional context of the work, until a woman's sense of self-worth became a function of her success at arranging bits of fruit to form a clown's face in a gelatin salad. That pervasive social illness, which Betty Friedan characterized as "the problem that has no name," arose not among workers who found that their labor brought no emotional satisfaction, but among workers who found that their work was invested with emotional weight far out of proportion to its own inherent value: "How long," a friend of mine is fond of asking, "can we continue to believe that we will have orgasms while waxing the kitchen floor?"

Acknowledgment

This chapter was reprinted from: Ruth Schwarz Cowan. 1976. "The 'Industrial Revolution' in the Home: Household Technology and Social Change in the 20th Century." *Technology and Culture* 17 (1): 1–23. © 1976 Society for the History of Technology. Reprinted with permission of Johns Hopkins University Press.

Notes

1. For some classic statements of the standard view, see Ogburn and Nimkoff 1955; Winch 1952; Goode 1964.
2. This point is made by Peter Laslett 1973, 28–9.
3. Ariès 1960.
4. See Laslett 1973, 20–4; Greven 1966.
5. Laslett 1973, passim.
6. For purposes of historical inquiry, this definition of middle-class status corresponds to a sociological reality, although it is not, admittedly, very rigorous. Our contemporary experience confirms that there are class differences reflected in magazines, and this situation seems to have existed in the past as well. On this issue see

The "Industrial Revolution" in the Home

Lynd and Lynd 1929, 240–4, where the marked difference in magazines subscribed to by the business-class wives as opposed to the working-class wives is discussed; Steinberg 1973, where the conscious attempt of the publisher to attract a middle-class audience is discussed; and Rainwater, Coleman and Handel, 1959, which was commissioned by the publisher of working-class women's magazines in an attempt to understand the attitudinal differences between working-class and middle-class women.

7. United States Bureau of the Census 1960, 510.

8. The gas iron, which was available to women whose homes were supplied with natural gas, was an earlier improvement on the old-fashioned flatiron, but this kind of iron is so rarely mentioned in the sources that I used for this survey that I am unable to determine the extent of its diffusion.

9. Kyrk 1933, 368, reporting a study in *Monthly Labor Review* 30 (1930): 1209–1252.

10. Although this point seems intuitively obvious, there is some evidence that it may not be true. Studies of energy expenditure during housework have indicated that by far the greatest effort is expended in hauling and lifting the wet wash, tasks that were not eliminated by the introduction of washing machines. In addition, if the introduction of the machines served to increase the total amount of wash that was done by the housewife, this would tend to cancel the energy-saving effects of the machines themselves.

11. Rinso was the first granulated soap; it came on the market in 1918. Lux Flakes had been available since 1906; however it was not intended to be a general laundry product but rather one for laundering delicate fabrics. "*Lever Brothers,*" *Fortune* November 1940, 95.

12. I take this account, and the term, from Lynd and Lynd 1929, 97. Obviously, there were many American homes that had bathrooms before the 1920s, particularly urban row houses, and I have found no way of determining whether the increases of the 1920s were more marked than in previous decades. The rural situation was quite different from the urban; the President's Conference on Home Building and Home Ownership reported that in the late 1920s, 71% of the urban families surveyed had bathrooms, but only 33% of the rural families did; see Gries and Ford 1932, 13.

13. The data above come from Giedion 1948, 685–703.

14. For a description of the standard bathroom see Sprackling 1933, 25.

15. Eastman 1927, 65. Also see Lynd and Lynd 1936, 537. Middletown is Muncie, Indiana.

16. Lynd and Lynd 1929, 96; Lynd and Lynd 1936, 539.

17. Lynd and Lynd 1929, 98; Lynd and Lynd 1936, 562.

18. On the advantages of the new stoves, see Farmer 1916, 15–20; and Lynes 1957, 119–20.

19. "How to Save Coal While Cooking." *Ladies' Home Journal* 25 (January 1908): 44.

20. Lynd and Lynd 1929, 156.

21. Lynd and Lynd 1929, 156; see also "Safeway Stores." *Fortune* 26 (October 1940): 60.

22. Lynd and Lynd 1929, 134–5 and 153–4.

23. Bureau of the Census 1960, 16 and 77.

24. For Indiana data, see Lynd and Lynd 1929, 169. For national data, see Kaplan and Casey 1958, table 6. The extreme drop in numbers of servants between 1910 and 1920 also lends credence to the notion that this demographic factor stimulated the industrial revolution in housework.

25. Lynd and Lynd 1929, 169.

26. On the disappearance of maiden aunts, unmarried daughters, and grandparents, see Lynd and Lynd 1929, 25, 99, and 110; Bok 1928, 15; "How to Buy Life Insurance." *Ladies' Home Journal* 45 (March 1928): 35. The house plans appeared every month in *American Home*, which began publication in 1928. On kitchen design, see Giedion 1948, 603–21, "Editorial." *Ladies' Home Journal* 45 (April 1928): 36; advertisement for Hoosier kitchen cabinets, *Ladies' Home Journal* 45 (April 1928): 117. Articles on servant problems include "The Vanishing Servant Girl." *Ladies Home Journal* 35 (May 1918): 48; "Housework, Then and Now." *American Home* 8 (June 1932): 128; "The Servant Problem." *Fortune* 24 (March 1938): 80–84; and *Report of the YWCA Commission on Domestic Service* 1915.

27. Giedion 1948, 619. Wright's new kitchen was installed in the Malcolm Willey House, Minneapolis.

28. Post 1937, 823.

29. This analysis is based upon various child-care articles that appeared during the period in *Ladies' Home Journal, American Home*, and *Parents' Magazine*. See also Lynd and Lynd 1929, chapter 11.

30. John Kenneth Galbraith has remarked upon the advent of woman as consumer, see Galbraith 1973, 29–37.

31. There was a sharp reduction in the number of patterns for home sewing offered by the women's magazines during the 1920s; the patterns were replaced by articles on "what is available in the shops this season." On consumer education see, for example, "How to Buy Towels." *Ladies' Home Journal* 45 (February 1928): 134; "Buying Table Linen." *Ladies' Home Journal* 45 (March 1928): 43; and "When the Bride Goes Shopping." *American Home* 1 (January 1928): 370.

32. See, for example, Lynd and Lynd 1929, 176 and 196; and Reid 1934, Chapter 13.

33. See Reid 1934, 64–8; and Kyrk 1933, 98.

34. See advertisement for Cleanliness Institute—"Self-Respect Thrives on Soap and Water," *Ladies' Home Journal* 45 (February 1928): 107. On changing bed linen, see "When the Bride Goes Shopping." *American Home* 1 (January 1928): 370. On laundering children's clothes, see, "Making a Layette." *Ladies' Home Journal* 45 (January 1928): 20; and Josephine Baker, "The Youngest Generation." *Ladies' Home Journal* 45 (March 1928): 185.
35. This point is also discussed at length in my paper "What Did Labor-Saving Devices Really Save?" (unpublished).
36. As reported in Kyrk 1933, 51.
37. Bryn Mawr College Department of Social Economy 1945; Goldwater 1947, 578–85.
38. Vanek 1973. Vanek reports an average of 53 hours per week over the whole period. This figure is significantly lower than the figures reported above, because each time study of housework has been done on a different basis, including different activities under the aegis of housework, and using different methods of reporting time expenditures; the Bryn Mawr and Oregon studies are useful for the comparative figures that they report internally, but they cannot easily be compared with each other.
39. This analysis is based upon my reading of the middle-class women's magazines between 1918 and 1930. For detailed documentation see my paper "Two Washes in the Morning and a Bridge Party at Night: The American Housewife between the Wars," *Women's Studies* (in press). It is quite possible that the appearance of guilt as a strong element in advertising is more the result of new techniques developed by the advertising industry than the result of attitudinal changes in the audience—a possibility that I had not considered when doing the initial research for this paper. See McMahon 1972, 5–18.
40. For a summary of the literature on differential divorce rates, see Winch 1952, 706; Goode 1956, 44. The earliest papers demonstrating this differential rate appeared in 1927, 1935, and 1939.
41. For a summary of the literature on married women's labor force participation, see Kreps 1971, 19–24.
42. Oppenheimer 1970, 1–15; Lynd and Lynd 1929, 124–7.
43. On the expanding size, number, and influence of women's magazines during the 1920s, see Lynd and Lynd 1929, 150 and 240–4.
44. See, for example, the advertising campaigns of General Electric and Hotpoint from 1918 through the rest of the decade of the 1920s; both campaigns stressed the likelihood that electric appliances would become a thrifty replacement for domestic servants.
45. The practice of carefully observing children's weight was initiated by medical authorities, national and local governments, and social welfare agencies, as part of the campaign to improve child health, which began about the time of World War I.
46. These practices were ubiquitous. *American Home*, for example, which was published by Doubleday, assisted its advertisers by publishing a list of informative pamphlets that readers could obtain; devoting half a page to an index of its advertisers; specifically naming manufacturer's and list prices in articles about products and services; allotting almost one-quarter of the magazine to a mail-order shopping guide that was not (at least ostensibly) paid advertisement; and as part of its editorial policy, urging its readers to buy new goods.

References

Ariès, Phillippe. 1960. *Centuries of Childhood: A Social History of Family Life.* New York: Vintage Books.
Baker, Josephine. 1928. "The Youngest Generation." *Ladies' Home Journal* 45(March): 185.
Bok, Edward. 1928. "Editorial." *American Home* 1(October): 15.
Bryn Mawr College Department of Social Economy. 1945. *Women During the War and After.* Philadelphia, PA: Curtis.
Eastman, R. O. Inc. 1927. *Zanesville, Ohio and Thirty-Six Other American Cities.* New York: Literary Digest.
Farmer, Fannie Merritt. 1916. *Boston Cooking School Cookbook.* Boston: Little, Brown.
Fortune. 1940. "Lever Brothers." *Fortune* 26(November): 95.
Galbraith, John Kenneth. 1973. *Economics and the Public Purpose.* Boston: Houghton Mifflin.
Giedion, Siegfried. 1948. *Mechanization Takes Command.* New York: Oxford University Press.
Goldwater, Ethel. 1947. "Woman's Place." *Commentary* 4(December): 578–585.
Goode, William J. 1956. *After Divorce.* Glencoe, IL: Free Press [The original article noted the publisher's location as New York—Ed.].
Goode, William J. 1964. *The Family.* Englewood Cliffs, NJ: Prentice Hall.
Greven, Philip J. 1966. "Family Structure in Seventeenth Century Andover, Massachusetts." *William and Mary Quarterly* 23: 234–256.
Gries, John M., and James Ford, eds. 1932. *Homemaking, Home Furnishing and Information Services,* Vol. 10. Washington, DC: President's Conference on Home Building and Home Ownership.
Kaplan, D. L., and M. Claire Casey. 1958. *Occupational Trends in the United States, 1900–1950.* U.S. Bureau of the Census Working Paper, no. 5. [no publisher noted], Washington, DC.

Kreps, Juanita. 1971. *Sex in the Marketplace: American Women at Work.* Baltimore: Johns Hopkins University Press.

Kyrk, Hazel. 1933. *Economic Problems of the Family.* New York: Harper and Brothers.

Laslett Peter. 1973. "The Comparative History of Household and Family." In *The American Family in Social Historical Perspective*, edited by Michael Gordon, 19–33. New York: St. Martin's Press.

Lynd, Robert S., and Helen M. Lynd. 1929. *Middletown: A Study in Contemporary American Culture.* New York: Harcourt Brace.

Lynd, Robert S., and Helen M. Lynd. 1936. *Middletown in Transition.* New York: Harcourt Brace.

Lynes, Russell. 1957. *The Domesticated Americans.* New York: Harper and Row.

McMahon, A. Michael. 1972. "An American Courtship: Psychologists and Advertising Theory in the Progressive Era." *American Studies* 13: 5–18.

Ogburn, W. F., and M. F. Nimkoff. 1955. *Technology and the Changing Family.* Boston: Houghton Mifflin.

Oppenheimer, Valerie Kincaid. 1970. *The Female Labor Force in the United States.* Population Monograph Series, no. 5. Institute of International Studies, University of California, Berkeley.

Post, Emily. 1937. *Etiquette: The Blue Book of Social Usage*, 5th ed. rev. New York: Funk and Wagnalls.

Rainwater, Lee, Richard Coleman and Gerald Handel. 1959. *Workingman's Wife.* New York: Oceana.

Reid, Margaret G. 1934. *Economics of Household Production.* New York: J. Wiley and Sons.

Report of the YWCA Commission on Domestic Service. 1915. [no publisher noted], Los Angeles.

Sprackling, Helen. 1933. "The Modern Bathroom." *Parents' Magazine* 8(February): 25.

Steinberg, Salme. 1973. *Reformer in the Marketplace: E. W. Bok and the Ladies Home Journal.* Ph.D. Dissertation, Johns Hopkins University.

United States Bureau of the Census. 1960. *Historical Statistics of the United States, Colonial Times to 1957.* Washington, DC: n.pub.

Vanek, JoAnn. 1973. *Keeping Busy: Time Spent in Housework, United States, 1920–1970.* Ph.D. Dissertation, University of Michigan.

Winch, Robert F. 1952. *The Modern Family.* New York: Holt, Rinehart and Winston.

5

Women in the Office
Clerical Work, Modernity, and Workplaces

Kim England[1]

The office and the clerical workers employed in it offer a fascinating lens through which to explore the gendered implications of economic and technological modernization alongside the emergence of cultural and urban modernity in American cities. My chapter centers on modernity in the context of the changing cultural histories and geographies of clerical workers[2] and the spatiality of the office from the late nineteenth to the mid-twentieth centuries (when more and different job opportunities opened up to women). Initially dominated by men, under modernity several clerical occupations became numerically dominated by women and discursively marked as "women's work." Clerical work captures many of the major cultural, social, and economic changes of modernity: the rise of large cities and the shift from a predominantly rural to urban population, rapid technological change, the emergence of a service-based economy powered by huge corporations, and of course the massive influx of women into paid work.

The chapter has three major sections. First, I explore the broad contours of modernity, especially in the context of gender and cities, taking note of the arrival of skyscrapers and their link to office work. The second section examines the role of technology, not only in modernity generally, but also in terms of what that meant for the tasks associated with clerical work and the expansion of offices. The third section focuses on the clerical worker herself, why employers hired her, why she was drawn to clerical work, and how she became a marker of modernity. The chapter then concludes with a brief discussion of the gendering of clerical work in the context of the cultural work associated with socioeconomic change and technological modernity.

Modernity and Cities

Modernity is notoriously difficult to define: a historical periodization or perhaps a condition associated with a variety of transformations ("modernizations") of society and everyday life; the expansion of scientific knowledge and technology premised on the human embrace of reason, rationality, and order; new ways understanding the self and identity formation; and a set of discourses about the multitude of options for reorganizing economic, political, and social life.[3] Following others, I use modernity to cover the period from the mid-nineteenth to mid-twentieth centuries in the US, a time of rapid industrialization, urbanization, and social change. I place women at the center of my analysis. Rita Felski, in the mid-1990s, pointed out that "most contemporary theories of the modern are male-centered . . . the equation of modernity with particular public and institutional structures governed by men has led to an almost total elision of the lives, concerns and perspective of women."[4] Ignoring women's experience of modern cities and their agency in shaping spaces in those cities produces an incomplete and inadequate analysis of modernity.

The initial identification of modernity with the public sphere (including the apparently ubiquitous strolling flaneur) promoted a masculinist norm, simultaneously implying that the "respectable" woman should primarily remain in the private, domestic sphere—especially if she was a white, middle-class woman—and ignores the ways women also entered into and changed public space.[5] Elizabeth Wilson was among the first to encourage feminist scholars (and others) to embrace the positive aspects of modern cities for women, to not only interpret them as dangerous places to be feared, but to reclaim them as offering women opportunities for fun, the potential freedom of anonymity, and the chance for spontaneity in otherwise closely regulated lives. As Daphne Spain points out,

> Cities provided opportunities to blur boundaries between the private and the public spheres. . . . More women used public transportation to visit, shop, or go to work in offices and stores. . . . As women in public became more common, standards of proper conduct changed as well.[6]

Scholars identify the arrival of department stores in the downtown shopping district of later nineteenth-century cities, with their plush powder rooms, elaborate lounges, and well-appointed lunch- and tea-rooms as new spaces where "respectable" women could frequent alone and linger (initially this would have been wealthy women as customers, but increasing numbers of working-class women worked as sales assistants). Women had a "respectable" reason to walk, alone even, in the public space of the streets between the stores along "Ladies' Mile" in New York or Woodward Avenue in Detroit.[7] Women, at least those who could afford it, visited department stores, theaters, and ate alone in lunch-rooms (as opposed to restaurants, where women were expected to be accompanied by a man). Such places and "the streets and sidewalks that connected them, became central to organizing exuberant woman's suffrage campaigns (from the 1890s to 1910s). Women's greater presence in public gave them the power to achieve political equality with men."[8]

In making the case for a gendered historical geography, Mona Domosh insists that "all landscapes and all places are gendered, that is shaped by gendered relationships, discourses, practices (and other topologies of power, including race, class and sexuality)," and these historical landscapes and places "can only [be] adequately understood by paying attention to relations and representations of power through which [they were] created and continue to be recreated."[9] Emphasizing the spaces of modernity, geographer David Harvey writes: "Since modernity is about the experience of progress through modernization, writings on the theme have tended to emphasize temporarily, the process of *becoming* rather than *being* in space and place."[10] Here we are urged to emphasize space in analyses of modernity. Similarly, historical geographer Richard Dennis also argues for "the active role of space" in analyzing the shaping of cities and new identities in modernity. Moreover, he argues: "Within modern cities, rationalism—the search for spatial and economic order and efficiency, as embodied in planning, zoning and regulation—made space for pluralism—an increasing diversity of social, ethnic and gendered identities."[11]

Certainly, American modernity involved the shifting and restructuring of spatial arrangements. The growth of industrial and then corporate capitalism fueled the connection of modernity with innovation and change, the rise of global capitalism, and, of course, cities. Between 1850 and 1900, US Census data indicate that the percentage of the US population in urban areas (places with populations of 2,500 or more) grew markedly, urban dwellers increasing from 15% to 40% of the population. Particularly strong urban growth occurred in the 1890s (a 56% increase in that decade alone) and 1910s (which saw a 39% increase). By 1920, 51% of Americans lived in urban places.[12] Cities were increasingly important in the spatial reorganization of both regional and the national economies. This was particularly the case for clerical work, which not only increased rapidly at the national scale; analysis of census data from 1870 to 1930 indicates that clerical work was more heavily concentrated in cities than other occupations, especially for women. Indeed, the decades of rapid urban growth match those of rapid increases in employment in clerical work, and both women's rates of labor force participation in clerical work and their share of clerical employment were greater in urban areas than for the nation as a whole.[13]

Clerical work expanded both absolutely and disproportionately, as the demand for clerical workers grew. Table 5.1 shows that prior to 1910, clerical workers (women and men) accounted for only a small proportion of all workers in the US. Between 1910 and 1930 this occupation grew by an astonishing 127%.[14] Clerical work changed from being a predominately man's occupation in 1870 (98%) to one numerically dominated by women by 1930 (the growth of women clerical workers between 1910 and 1930 was huge: 228%). And by 1930, 21% of employed women were in clerical work.

Simultaneously there was a growth of offices in size and complexity. The expansion of offices following World War I and in later decades was linked to the rapid increase in the functions and activities of the state and to the US economy becoming increasingly dominated by large, bank-financed firms and corporations with national and later international markets. The unprecedented and sustained levels of economic expansion were turning the US into the first service economy in the world, and women in clerical jobs were at the center of that transformation. This affected clerical work in a profound manner. First, functions such as record keeping, which had previously been incidental to clerical work, became its very essence. Second, as offices became more complex, the demand for clerical workers increased both absolutely and disproportionally relative to growth in overall production. Initially the largest employers of clerical workers were the government sector and insurance industries, then after World War I, banks also became major employers. By the time Harry Braverman wrote *Labor and Monopoly Capital* in 1974, he included an entire chapter on clerical workers as an example of growing working-class occupations, and his example of a "pure clerical industry" was "[b]anks and credit agencies [that] conduct only one mode of labor, the clerical, and below the managerial level the labor employed consists almost entirely of clerks who work in the offices and service workers who clean the offices."[15]

In the late nineteenth century, especially in the larger cities of the Northeast and Midwest, the built form of the modern city was taking shape. One key feature was the emergence of a distinct modern commercial downtown core: "In every big city downtown was the business district," writes Fogelson.[16] The advent of the central business district (CBD), as the Chicago School urbanists later labeled it, is tightly woven with urban modernity and the associated restructuring of urban spatial forms, functions, and practices.[17] As a material expression of the growth of the industrial city, the CBD became densely developed both in terms of land use and verticality. Such spatial changes were wrapped up in notions of progress, order, and efficiency, but also provided new opportunities for women to cautiously yet confidently venture into urban public spaces, as shoppers and increasingly as workers (see Table 5.1 for the growth in women's labor force participation). Indeed, "discourses about a new femininity emerged around the notion that respectable women could be employed in respectable jobs in offices."[18]

Many of these women office workers traveled to the CBD to their jobs, and many would be working in the larger office buildings and even skyscrapers that increasingly dominated the cityscape. Before the late nineteenth century, the tallest buildings in towns and cities had been about five stories high, the top floors only accessible by stairs. The invention of the elevator (1857) and the steel-frame

Table 5.1 Clerical Workers and Women's Employment, US, 1870–1930

	Clerical workers as percent of all employed	Women clerical as percent of all clerical jobs	Percent of women, employed	Percent of all women employed, clerical work
1870	0.7	2.2	14.8	0.1
1880	1.1	4.3	15.2	0.3
1890	2.1	16.9	17.2	2.1
1900	2.7	26.5	18.1	4.0
1910	5.1	35.9	20.9	8.7
1920	8.0	48.4	20.4	19.0
1930	8.8	52.0	22.0	20.8

Source: Hooks, 1947 (using decennial Census data).

skeleton (1885) paved the way for taller buildings, many in a beaux arts style with commanding city skylines. Office towers of 10 to 15 stories had sprouted up in major cities by the last decade of the nineteenth century.[19] For example, Chicago's Home Insurance Building (completed in 1885, demolished in 1931) was the first metal-framed "skyscraper," 10 stories tall and record-breaking for its architecture and engineering. Eight years later, Chicago had 12 skyscrapers of 16 to 20 stories. New York was slower to create its skyscraper skyline, but soon had several tall buildings. The skyscrapers and skylines of fin de siècle American cities, especially Chicago and New York, helped establish the vertical symbolism and iconography of corporate capitalism clustered in the CBD.[20]

Many of the first skyscrapers were built as "signature landmarks" for insurance companies, as a distinct material expression of their economic prowess and corporate pride. For instance, in 1909, the 41-story Metropolitan Life Insurance tower in Manhattan was completed to serve as the company's headquarters and remained so until 2005 (see Figure 5.1). For many years, the company featured the building in its advertising. As was the case in many such new tall buildings, Metropolitan Life occupied some of the

Figure 5.1 Metropolitan Life Insurance Company Home Office Building (also known as the Met Life Tower), New York City, 1912. Located on Madison Avenue, near East 23rd Street. The landmark skyscraper was completed in 1909, and until 1913 was the world's tallest building.
Source: Metropolitan Life Insurance Company (1912).

Kim England

floors and rented out the rest. The sheer amount of space in buildings like this one meant specific areas or even entire floors could be devoted to particular corporate divisions and job specializations: divisions of labor could be spatially expressed.[21] In some instances managers were on completely different floors from clerical workers: "The men who ran these corporations often occupied the offices at the top, with views looking down and over the city. . . . Occupying many of the cubicles in the stories below, however, were clerical workers."[22] The gender division of labor was thus literally built into the skyscrapers.[23]

Offices and the Technology in Them

Workplaces are sites where power and knowledge are discursively (re)produced, and they are recursively implicated in the creation of workers' subjectivities. Feminist geographers have explored several dimensions of the cultural dynamics of workplaces: the role of gender in the spatial and administrative organization of firms, the ways in which masculinities and femininities are constructed in the workplace, and how the embodied nature of work influences spatial divisions of labor within offices.[24] On the eve of the twentieth century, women were still a relative rarity in offices, and so their arrival was noteworthy, and even alarming. Although businesses employed women as stenographers, secretaries, and switchboard operators, these jobs were hidden away from the general public. When Aetna Life hired its first permanent women workers in 1911, they were told to use the back elevators so the company president would not encounter them, as he disapproved of working women.[25]

Then, as now, the embodied nature of work influenced the gendered construction of spatial (and social) divisions of labor, and vice versa. The challenge of having women in the office led to a "physical arrangement of the office [that] reinforced gender as a work category and displayed difference for all to see and experience by creating different work spaces for men and women."[26] Within office buildings it was not unusual for women clerical workers to be secluded not only from the public, but to work in completely different offices from men holding the same jobs, or if there was only one large room for clerks, women were at one end of the room and men at the other.[27] Analyses of the furnishings, fixtures, and design of fin de siècle office spaces show that executives' offices were typically furnished with fireplaces, leather chairs and rugs (even animal skins) suggestive of masculinized bourgeois domestic spaces like dens and libraries. On the other hand, the workspaces for lower status office workers were spare and more functional, often open plan allowing for little privacy and easy surveillance. It was not uncommon for a large clock on the wall to be the only ornamentation.[28]

The expansion of office work occurred alongside the invention and diffusion of new office technologies (such as the typewriter and the comptometer) in the later nineteenth century, which in turn enabled changes in both office work and corporate culture more broadly. And as Rosemary Pringle in her study of secretaries points out:[29]

> It would be difficult to imagine the office without typewriters, telephones and filing cabinets. These technologies were adopted in the later nineteenth century coinciding with the movement of women into secretarial work. They have been central to the definition of what a secretary *is*, and to the construction of the boss-secretary relationship.

Examining the expansion of office work and the machines associated with it demonstrates how technology shapes social life, as well as how understandings of technology are established through social and spatial processes and practices. Feminist science and technology studies scholars point out that a careful analysis of design and technology "reveal[s] the cultural uses and meanings of the manufactured world."[30] And Judith Wajcman employs what she calls the technofeminist framework to capture "a mutually shaping relationship between gender and technology, in which technology is both a source and a consequence of gender relations."[31] Technologies emerge and evolve within a complex web of social, economic, and political as well as technical components. Some technologies, and the tasks they help

90

accomplish, become correlated with certain feminine (or masculine) coding such that the technologies and the workers associated with them become defined through each other in gendered terms.[32]

The typewriter is a familiar example of this gendered association. For at least the first two-thirds of the nineteenth century, numerous people in Europe and North America invented and patented various sorts of "writing machines" (variously named typographers and kaligraphs, among others). In the 1860s, Christopher Latham Sholes and Carlos Glidden registered patents for a typewriter. E. Remington and Sons (the gun manufacturers and then later sewing machine manufacturers) produced a later version of the Sholes and Glidden (mounted on a sewing machine table), patenting it in 1873. Remington continued to improve the typewriter and was the only US commercial mass producer until about 1880, when competition came with the arrival of a few other brands. Establishing typewriters as office equipment was not immediate; they were expensive, each costing around $125 in the later 1870s (about $2,600 today). They were financially out of reach for many businesses, and it was only in the later 1880s that they became more common in offices.[33]

Steering clear of a technological deterministic account of the feminization of office work, Wajcman suggests that "two concurrent and interrelated processes [were] taking place as the typewriter was introduced: the gendering of the typewriter as an object and the construction of the practice of typing as feminine."[34] As a new occupation, typing was initially gender neutral, and thus had the advantage that women were not accused of stealing male breadwinners' jobs. Soon after patenting the typewriter, Remington decided to train women to demonstrate their new machines, linking typing to the supposedly feminine characteristic of manual dexterity, as embodied in the "nimble fingers" required of textile work.[35] The Remington typewriters were aggressively advertised, and in some print advertisements typewriting was linked to middle-class gentility, which displayed typewriters in the home, and likened typing to piano playing.[36] Associating typewriters with the home (at least in advertising) was a strategy that connected the machine and the typist with middle-class gendered sensibilities about the domestic sphere and appropriate activities for women. Typing and stenography jobs grew rapidly and then became labeled as "women's work": in 1870 only 4% of typists and stenographers were women; by 1910, 77% were. By 1935, *Fortune* magazine declared that "woman's place was at the typewriter."[37]

The story of the typewriter is such well-trodden ground that the other office machines invented, patented and manufactured in the same time period are all too often overlooked in historical accounts of the office. Pringle makes note of telephones and filing cabinets as indispensable office technologies, and there was also the Dictaphone, the comptometer (and other adding machines), the Hollerith, and others. Once the phonograph was invented in the late 1870s, some inventors focused on developing devices for recording and reproducing speech, specifically to be marketed to offices. Like typewriters, Dictaphones were expensive and did not sell well until the first years of the twentieth century. In 1887 the first commercially successful mechanical calculator, the comptometer (comptograph) was patented; the machines became popular as they were lightweight, reasonably inexpensive, and could be used for a variety of tasks. They had eight or nine rows of nine keys each, and a skilled comptometer operator could enter multiple digits simultaneously. At about the same time the Hollerith machine, the first commercial data processing machine, which was card-punch data processing, had been designed to speed up the tabulations of the 1890 US Census. Initially there was resistance to introducing counting machines from counting clerks and bookkeepers (both types of clerical work were dominated by men), but sales picked up by the 1910s and soon after banks in particular were the target of much of the marketing.[38]

Taken together, these new technologies mechanized and automated some aspects of office work and became important symbols of progress and modernity. However, it is important to remember that the uptake was uneven and emerged over the course of several years, sometimes decades. Certainly, with these technological innovations, correspondence and record keeping that had previously been less significant aspects of clerical work became central tasks. Mechanization meant that many clerical tasks could be routinized: subdivided into a series of steps, each completed by different people, producing maximum efficiency with minimal training.[39] By the 1920s, the case was being made for the "rationalization" of office functions by adapting the "scientific management" techniques of F. W. Taylor's extensive time and motion studies. William H. Leffingwell, who published *Scientific Office Management* in 1917, was a devotee of Taylor and his ideas, and a strong proponent of standardizing and routinizing office work practices by adapting the work practices resulting from Taylor's time and motion studies and Henry Ford's assembly line principles to office work.[40] Leffingwell's claims were, at least initially, aspirational rather than empirically widespread. Many tasks still needed to be completed by hand, and only the largest companies had the labor or the capital to afford these scientific office management systems. In many instances, workers resisted mechanization and rationalization, especially male clerical workers like bookkeepers, at least for a while, but there were savings to be made, especially when women, who could be paid less than men, could be installed as machine operators.[41]

By 1951, when Charles Wright Mills published his classic, *White Collar*, there was a proliferation of paper in the office: written records, invoices, memos, and so on (often in duplicate and triplicate). Mills used "The Enormous File" as a metaphor for the office that "produces the billions of slips of paper that gear modern society into its daily shape"[42] and was increasingly filled with what Mills called "white-collar girls." By mid-century then, the "enormous files" were large companies often with purpose-built open-plan offices with machines, desks and tasks organized around Leffingwell's office adaptation of efficient, rational, time and cost-saving "scientific management" techniques. Office technology sales skyrocketed after World War II—especially machines for bookkeeping, tabulating, billing—and as office work increased, more machines were invented or improved.[43] Employers introduced more office technology and increasingly installed women as operators to substitute (yet again with lower pay) for male clerks (Figure 5.2). Bookkeeping machines, like the comptometer,

Figure 5.2 The Stenographic Bureau, Metropolitan Life Insurance Company, New York City, 1912. The company's 1912 book explains, "Experience has shown that more efficient service is secured at less expense by grouping the stenographers" (1912: 93).
Source: Metropolitan Life Insurance Company (1912).

were especially popular, and new forms of clerical work emerged—the more routine aspects of book-keeping were split from more "skilled" aspects, with distinct gendered and social status implications. Mechanization required "office machine operators," whom Mills described as "high-school girl[s] trained in three or four months to use a machine."[44] By 1950, 83% of these operators were women. At the same time, the *profession* of accountancy, which barely existed before World War II, expanded rapidly in the post-war period; in 1950, 85% of accountants were men.[45]

Clerical Workers: Intersections of Modernity, Gender, and Space

In mid-nineteenth century offices, clerical workers worked in small, paternalistic, family-run busi-nesses. Clerks, who almost without exception were men, handled all phases of an assignment, often doing tasks that today would be considered managerial. Indeed, for a few men, clerical work was a stepping-stone to managerial positions (although these were usually the sons, nephews, or grandsons of the owner; working-class men usually worked as general clerks for their entire working lives). The paternalistic benevolence of the employer was the basis of worker control. Mutual loyalty and obliga-tion provided the incentive for clerks to work harder, and some remained with the same firm for the duration of their work lives.[46]

By the late nineteenth century the office was changing; women were increasingly employed as clerical workers, notably as stenographers, typists, secretaries, and telephone operators. As Lisa Fine writes of that time period:

> Women's entrance into clerical positions posed a direct challenge to the commonly held belief that not only was the office a male space, but also all sorts of urban settings—elevators, street cars, restaurants, boarding houses—were inappropriate for women. Women's entrance into these places set in motion a redefinition of women's sphere within the world of work and the city that continued throughout the twentieth century.[47]

At first employers were reluctant to hire women, apprehensive about their possible "distracting influ-ence" and the negative reactions to the economic competition they might pose to male breadwinners. Women's bodies in the office disrupted accepted notions of both "appropriate" embodied employ-ment and women's "proper roles"—they were constructed as "out of place" in their workplaces. The discursive constructions of bodies and the fleshy materiality of actually existing bodies are defined in and through social relations, and created in and through discursive and material spaces.[48] There were moral panics about women, especially young women in the office: would they be led astray (and reject marriage or possibility end up in prostitution), and might they attract too much attention from the public or male employees? Thus, as Kate Boyer found, "women employees were called upon to carefully moderate their behavior in order to avoid arousing male colleagues."[49] They also needed to carefully guard their respectability: "Far more than a shorthand for class, respectability was a way of speaking about and organizing gendered, racialized and sexed bodies."[50]

Despite their initial apprehensions, employers also knew that women, or more specifically edu-cated, middle-class white women, constituted a unique labor force. For instance, the potential supply of such women was substantial, not only because women were more likely than men to hold high school diplomas, but also because their range of employment opportunities was very limited, curtailed by prevailing gender stereotypes and expectations. The earliest generations of clerical workers were better educated than other women workers. Clerical workers needed to be literate and numerate. Employers preferred high school graduates, and it was not unusual for clerical workers to have also sought special training from private business or commercial schools. From the 1880s on, such col-leges taught typing, stenography, and bookkeeping. They grew rapidly and were immensely popular.[51]

However, the education requirement also served to exclude from clerical work many white women from working-class and immigrant families, as well as women of color, becoming another way to keep desirable clerical work from their reach. On the one hand, substantial numbers of working-class women were entering clerical work in the 1920s. On the other hand, African American women and other women of color were largely excluded (not so much by education, but bald-faced racism) until the 1960s and the advent of the Civil Rights Movement.[52]

Given the social meaning and cultural context of the late nineteenth and early twentieth centuries, the "breeding" and "respectability" of middle-class women made them preferable to educated working-class men. Thus, clerical work was promoted as a desirable job for young, educated white women to do for a few years prior to marriage. Emphasizing clerical work as transitory work for women was aimed at calming concerns about the potential downward pressure on wages, as well as fears that women might find paid work preferable and abandon marriage altogether. In addition, employers were keenly aware of the class background of the women they hired, and this was an important business strategy. Once employed, clerical workers were also expected to comport themselves with dignity and propriety outside the workplace. Such efforts were a form of worker control, ensuring employees stayed well within the bounds of middle-class expectations about behavior and comportment, both in- and outside of work.[53]

From the women's perspective, clerical work was desirable work. It offered greater job security, decent working conditions, and the opportunity to work in a "modern" workplace. Clerical work was mental rather than manual employment and took place in a safe, clean work environment. It was less physically demanding than other major forms of work open to women at the time, like factory work and domestic work. It had shorter working hours and offered a fixed weekly salary rather than an hourly wage, and better opportunities for promotion than most other sorts of jobs. While it is difficult to get reliable and accurate data, Rotella's detailed study of US Census data for 1890 to 1930 found that on average, women clerical worker's full-time wages in a sample of US cities were 1.8 times greater than the wages of women in manufacturing jobs in 1890, and were still 1.3 times greater in 1930.[54] Rotella also found that women clerical workers tended to be much younger (50%–60% were aged 16–25) than women workers generally (36%–43% were aged 16–25), and they were also far more likely to be unmarried, white, native-born, and better educated than other women workers.[55]

The office allowed for direct personal contact among workers (sometimes even including those of the opposite sex), and between workers and managers. Clerical work was distinctive from other jobs open to women; unlike domestic and factory work, clerical work could be considered dignified and genteel work. Certainly "industrial-era clerical workers were aware that they occupied a terrain above the labor aristocracy. The office and the selling floor were distinct from the shop floor."[56] If young women from "respectable" (white) families chose or needed to work, then clerical work was deemed appropriate, even desirable work. It was also attractive work for young women from aspiring working-class families.[57] As Sharon Hartman Strom makes clear:

> Office jobs were the best jobs available to women between 1900 and 1930. Women understood this and made rational choices for the future by investing in commercial education and taking office jobs. . . . [O]ffice work despite its gendered limits, could open the door to a wider world. Even though many women languished in boring jobs from which they longed to be freed, they also experimented with downtown amusements, pursued friendships and flirtations, and sought more education. Many others did what they considered to be worthwhile and inventive work, experimented with careers, and moved on to more expansive horizons.[58]

Not only were the working conditions attractive to young, white, middle-class women, but working in an office had a degree of panache. After working in the office during the day, the clerical worker could leave in the evening and venture into the street. In addition to the department stores, there was an increasing variety of places of "public" amusement and entertainment: dance halls, theaters, cabarets, cinemas, and nickelodeons that invited women into public spaces. Kathy Peiss notes that like "the department store, the quintessential space for women in the late nineteenth century, these vaudeville houses were palaces of consumption, amusement, and service."[59] Such venues allowed for the freedom of a non-family-centered social life and chances for unsupervised heterosocial relations. And another marker of urban modernity had emerged: "nightlife."[60] The increasing numbers of urban white-collar workers, both women and men, "were the critical element in the construction of the new commercialized 'night life.' . . . white collar workers were the most avid consumers of the commercial pleasures."[61] Their working hours were shorter and their wages higher than factory workers, and they started work later in the morning. Manual, mill, and factory workers had to get up for 6 a.m. shifts, but "clerical and sales workers could, on the other hand, stay out late, get a good night's sleep and still get to work on time."[62]

Being a typist or stenographer or more generally a "business girl" was emblematic of an exciting new urban womanhood. By the 1920s adverts for the Corry Jamestown filing cabinet and the Oliver typewriter not only showed women using this new office equipment, but included a skyscraper-filled cityscape through the window: such adverts suggest that the modern woman using modern technology in the modern city was a commonplace trope. Even before then, novels were written about her, and there were also films with the office worker as the plucky heroine. The typewriter girl literature first emerged in the 1890s, corresponding with the diffusion of the machine and its female operator in offices across the US. Lawrence Rainey explores the varied representations of typists, secretaries, and stenographers in the film and fiction of modernity, and remarks:

> The female secretary was shorthand for a recognizably modern phenomenon; she indexed a distinctly new occupational category that sprang into existence only after 1880 (in America) or 1885 (in Britain) and was indelibly linked with metropolitan experience. She was the most visible, everyday representative of the modern woman.[63]

In many typewriter novels, the typewriter girl interacts with all kinds of men, is possibly eschewing marriage, rides a bike, goes on mildly reckless adventures, and frequents the nighttime entertainment spaces of the city. As a figure of new urban womanhood, the fictional typewriter girls' spatial mobility and flamboyant autonomy were linked to the self-supporting wages, limited family supervision, and independence that, seemingly, all flowed from being a typist.[64]

These were, of course, not flesh-and-blood women, whose wages were rarely sufficient to live alone, and on closer inspection, most of the novels are steeped in moral panics about young, unmarried women "adrift in the city."[65] Nevertheless, that the imaginary geographies of everyday life in modern cities involved clerical workers and business girls as the "new urban woman" is significant. The rise and growth of the "business girl" and the "modern urban woman" was tied up with numerous broader social technological and economic trends and was suffused in raced and classed gender expectations. The point is that actual embodied women were drawn to clerical work, not merely relegated to it. All too often, accounts position the young woman clerical worker as a passive participant or a victim, duped into accepting lower wages and boring work. Yet this robs her of her agency and self-determination, of her place within this important moment in American history and cities, and indeed of being a key figure of urban modernity.

Conclusion

The clerical worker as the "new modern woman" is important in the history of women's work, while the office plays a similar role in modernity whether as an icon of a cultural moment or as an architectural style. As Elizabeth Wilson argues, modernity meant, at least for some women, a broader range of social roles and opportunities than before: "Urban life created a space where some women could experiment with new roles,"[66] including those of waged work. The expansion of the clerical sector opened up more options for certain groups of women to engage in employment, and transformed the cities they worked in: "Emblematic of modernity, typists were presented as ushering in an era full of progress and promise."[67] Initially associated with men, clerical occupations came to be statistically dominated by women and discursively marked as "women's work." In the later nineteenth century, women who did waged work were usually employed in domestic service or in the manufacturing sector. By 1930, clerical work had become one of the most significant sources of employment for women, accounting for one in five women workers.

While some office technology came to be interpreted in feminized, classed terms and was used as a means of casting clerical work and the clerical workplace as an appropriate space for white, middle-class women, it is important to keep in view that this process was not self-evident, and this particular outcome was not inevitable. That said, in the early decades of the twentieth century, clerical work provided a means by which women could claim relative freedom and autonomy, and by using a feminist lens the agency of clerical workers is emphasized, countering portrayals of them as passive participants often typical of some more standard treatments of modernity. Indeed, placing women clerical workers at the center of an analysis of modernity offers empirical evidence of Felski's argument that under modernity, "the divisions between public and private, masculine and feminine, modern and antimodern were not as fixed as they may have appeared. Or rather they were unmade and remade in new ways."[68] In short, the people, practices and places associated with the feminization of clerical work encompass some of the major markers commonly associated with modernity: technological innovation, restructured spatial relations, and the changing cultural circumstances that together created new possibilities.

Notes

1. Many of my arguments in this chapter are the result of my collaboration with Kate Boyer (University of Cardiff), who has kindly agreed to let me revisit them in this chapter. I draw from our coauthored work (Boyer and England 2008; England and Boyer 2009).

   This chapter is dedicated to my aunt, Irene Freshwater (1924–2017). She left school at 12 because of illness; however, she had a gift for mathematics and later went to comptometer college. Aunty Irene worked as a comptometer (the machine and the operator having the same name) for many years, including after she married, and she became a first-time mother in her late thirties. She was a "pioneer" and, in the context of my chapter, she is a reminder that the actual lived lives of "clerical workers" are more complex and nuanced than they can ever be represented on paper.
2. Clerical worker is a census category includes bank tellers, bookkeepers, cashiers, dispatchers, messengers, shipping clerks, stenographers and typists, and telegraph/telephone operators, among others.
3. Felski 1995, 10.
4. Felski 1995, 16; see also the introduction to this volume.
5. Felski 1995; Boyer 1998; Domosh 2014.
6. Spain 2014, 583.
7. Weisman 1992; Felski 1995; Domosh 2014.
8. Spain 2014, 583.
9. Domosh 2014, 291.
10. Harvey 1989, 205.
11. Dennis 2008, 2.
12. "Table 4: Population: 1790 to 1990." US Census. www.census.gov/population/censusdata/table-4.pdf (last downloaded November 2016).
13. Rotella 1981; Lyson 1991.
14. Growth in clerical work remained very strong from the 1940s until the 1980s, at which point growth rates began to slow, due in part to new technologies like the ATM (Boyer and England 2008; England and Boyer 2009; England 2013).
15. Braverman 1974, 208.
16. Fogelson 2001, 14.

17. Fogelson 2001; Park and Burgess 1925.
18. Wajcman 2004, 52.
19. Fogelson 2001; Willis 1995.
20. Zunz 1990; Domosh 2014.
21. Kwolek-Folland 1998.
22. Domosh 2014, 298–9.
23. As African Americans and other people of color were explicitly excluded from office work (except in businesses owned by people of color), skyscrapers also expressed the racial division of labor and other hierarchical structures of difference that shaped the modern city.
24. McDowell 1997; Boyer 2003; Rose, Dillon, and Caron 2016.
25. Strom 1992.
26. Kwolek-Folland 1998, 115. Also see Zunz 1990.
27. Boyer 2003; England and Boyer 2009.
28. Boyer 2003; Kwolek-Folland 1998.
29. Pringle 1989, 174, emphasis in original.
30. Lupton 1993, 57.
31. Wajcman 2004, 7.
32. Boyer and England 2008.
33. Robert and Weil 2016.
34. Wajcman 2004, 51.
35. Zunz 1990; Boyer and England 2008.
36. Boyer 2003; England and Boyer 2009.
37. Davies 1982.
38. Strom 1992; Wootton and Kemmerer 2007; Boyer and England 2008.
39. See Braverman 1974; Davies 1982; Fine 1990; Zunz 1990.
40. Braverman 1974; Strom 1992.
41. Kessler-Harris 2003; Wootton and Kemmerer 2007; Jeacle and Parker 2013.
42. Mills 1951, 189. See also p. 200 for the "white-collar girls" comment.
43. Jeacle and Parker 2013.
44. Mills 1951, 206.
45. Strom 1992.
46. Lockwood 1958; Braverman 1974; Davies 1982; Zunz 1990.
47. Fine 1990, 26.
48. England and Boyer 2009; England 2013.
49. Boyer 2003, 220. Also see Rose, Dillon, and Caron 2016.
50. Boyer 1998, 268. Also see Peiss 1986; Meyerowitz 1988; Rose, Dillon, and Caron 2016.
51. Davies 1982; Fine 1990; England and Boyer 2009.
52. Kwolek-Folland 1998; Kessler-Harris 2003; Bjelopera 2005. According to Elyce Rotella (1981) between 1890 and 1930, African American women made up 13 to 17% of the non-agricultural labor force, but represented less than 1% of women clerical workers until the 1940s.
53. Pringle 1989; Boyer 1998; England and Boyer 2009.
54. Rotella 1981, Appendix B. Combining the data for all the cities in the sample indicated that in 1890 men clerical workers earned $943, compared with $459 for women (the ratio of women to men's earnings being 0.46). By 1930, when women clerical workers were more of a fixture, the earnings were $1,566 for men and $1,106 for women (the ratio closing to 0.56). There was great variation across cities (and different regions of the US).
55. Rotella 1981.
56. Bjelopera 2005, 17.
57. England and Boyer 2009.
58. Strom 1992, 10. Also see Fine 1990.
59. Peiss 1986, 112.
60. Sharpe 2008.
61. Nasaw 1999, 4–5.
62. Nasaw 1999, 5.
63. Rainey 2009, 273.
64. Fine 1990.
65. Peiss 1986; Meyerowitz 1988.
66. Wilson 1991, 65.
67. Wajcman 2004, 52.
68. Felski 1995, 19.

References

Bjelopera, Jerome P. 2005. *City of Clerks: Office and Sales Workers in Philadelphia, 1870–1920.* Urbana and Chicago: University of Illinois Press.

Boyer, Kate. 1998. "Place and the Politics of Virtue: Clerical Work, Corporate Anxiety, and Changing Meanings of Public Womanhood in Early Twentieth-Century Montreal." *Gender, Place and Culture: A Journal of Feminist Geography* 5(3): 261–276.

Boyer, Kate. 2003. "'Neither Forget nor Remember Your Sex': Sexual Politics in the Early Twentieth-Century Canadian Office." *Journal of Historical Geography* 29(3): 212–229.

Boyer, Kate, and Kim England. 2008 "Gender, Work and Technology in the Information Workplace: From Typewriters to ATMs." *Social and Cultural Geography* 9(3): 241–256.

Braverman, Harry. 1974. *Labor and Monopoly Capital: The Degradation of Work in the Twentieth Century.* New York and London: Monthly Review Press.

Davies, Margery. 1982. *Woman's Place Is at the Typewriter: Office Work and Office Workers, 1870–1930.* Philadelphia, PA: Temple University Press.

Dennis, Richard. 2008. *Cities in Modernity: Representations and Productions of Metropolitan Space.* Cambridge and New York: Cambridge University Press.

Domosh, Mona. 2014. "Toward a Gendered Historical Geography of North America." In *North American Odyssey: Historical Geographies for the Twenty-First Century,* edited by Craig E. Colten and Geoffrey L. Buckley, 291–306. Lanham, MD: Rowman and Littlefield.

England, Kim. 2013. "Clerical Work." In *Sociology of Work: An Encyclopedia,* edited by Vicki Smith, 93–97. Thousand Oaks, CA: Sage.

England, Kim, and Kate Boyer. 2009. "Women's Work: The Feminization and Shifting Meanings of Clerical Work." *Journal of Social History* 43(2): 307–340.

Felski, Rita. 1995. *The Gender of Modernity.* Cambridge, MA: Harvard University Press.

Fine, Lisa M. 1990. *Souls of The Skyscraper: Female Clerical Workers in Chicago, 1870–1930.* Philadelphia, PA: Temple University Press.

Fogelson, Robert M. 2001. *Downtown: Its Rise and Fall, 1880–1950.* New Haven, CT: Yale University Press.

Harvey, David. 1989. *The Condition of Postmodernity: An Enquiry Into the Origins of Cultural Change.* Oxford: Wiley-Blackwell.

Hooks, Janet M. 1947. *Women's Occupations Through Seven Decades.* Women's Bureau, Bulletin, no. 218. Government Printing Office, Washington, DC.

Jeacle, Ingrid, and Lee Parker. 2013. "The 'Problem' of the Office: Scientific Management, Governmentality and the Strategy of Efficiency." *Business History* 55(7): 1074–1099.

Kessler-Harris, Alice. 2003. *Out to Work: A History of Wage-Earning Women in the United States.* Oxford and New York: Oxford University Press.

Kwolek-Folland, Angel, 1998. *Engendering Business: Men and Women in the Corporate Office, 1870–1930.* Baltimore: Johns Hopkins University Press.

Lockwood, David. 1958. *The Black Coated Worker.* Fairlawn, NJ: Essential Books.

Lupton, Ellen. 1993. *Mechanical Brides: Women and Machines from Home to Office.* New York: Cooper-Hewitt and Princeton Architectural Press.

Lyson, Thomas A. 1991. "Industrial Shifts, Occupational Recomposition, and the Changing Sexual Division of Labor in the Five Largest U.S. Cities: 1910–1930." *Sociological Forum* 6(1): 157–177.

McDowell, Linda. 1997. *Capital Culture: Gender at Work in the City.* Malden, MA: Blackwell.

Metropolitan Life Insurance Company. 1912. *The Metropolitan Life Insurance Company; Its History, Its Present Position in the Insurance World, Its Home Office Building and Its Work Carried on Therein.* New York: Metropolitan Life Insurance Company.

Meyerowitz, Joanne J. 1988. *Women Adrift: Independent Wage Earners in Chicago, 1880–1930.* Chicago: University of Chicago Press.

Mills, Charles Wright. 1951. *White Collar: The American Middle Classes.* New York: Oxford University Press.

Nasaw, David. 1999. *Going Out: The Rise and Fall of Public Amusements.* Cambridge, MA and London: Harvard University Press.

Park, Robert, and Ernest W. Burgess. 1925 (1967). *The City.* Chicago: University of Chicago Press.

Peiss, Kathy. 1986. *Cheap Amusements: Working Women and Leisure in Turn-of-the-Century New York.* Philadelphia, PA: Temple University Press.

Pringle, Rosemary. 1989. *Secretaries Talk: Sexuality, Power and Work.* London: Verso.

Rainey, Lawrence. 2009. "From the Fallen Woman to the Fallen Typist, 1908–1922." *English Literature in Transition, 1880–1920* 52(3): 273–297.

Robert, Paul, and Peter Weil. 2016. *Typewriter: A Celebration of the Ultimate Writing Machine.* New York: Sterling.

Rose, Damaris, Lisa Dillon, and Marianne Caron. 2016. "Lives of Their Own, A Place of Their Own? The Living Arrangements Of 'Business Girls' in Early Twentieth-Century Canadian Cities." *British Journal of Canadian Studies* 29(2): 225–248.

Rotella, Elyce J. 1981. *From Home to Office: U. S. Women at Work, 1870–1930*. Ann Arbor: University of Michigan Research Press.

Sharpe, William Chapman. 2008. *New York Nocturne: The City After Dark in Literature, Painting, and Photography, 1850–1950*. Princeton, NJ and Oxford: Princeton University Press.

Spain, Daphne. 2014. "Gender and Urban Space." *Annual Review of Sociology* 40: 581–598.

Strom, Sharon Hartman. 1992. *Beyond the Typewriter: Gender, Class, and the Origins of Modern American Office Work, 1900–1930*. Urbana and Chicago: University of Illinois Press.

Wajcman, Judy. 2004. *TechnoFeminism*. Cambridge: Polity Press.

Weisman, Leslie Kanes. 1992. *Discrimination by Design: A Feminist Critique of the Man-Made Environment*. Urbana and Chicago: University of Illinois Press.

Willis, Carol. 1995. *Form Follows Finance: Skyscrapers and Skylines in New York and Chicago*. New York: Princeton Architectural Press.

Wilson, Elizabeth. 1991. *The Sphinx in the City: Urban Life, the Control of Disorder, and Women*. London: Virgo Press.

Wootton, Charles W., and Kemmerer, Barbara E. 2007. "The Emergence of Mechanical Accounting in the U.S., 1880–1930." *The Accounting Historians* 34(1): 91–124.

Zunz, Oliver. 1990. *Making America Corporate, 1870–1920*. Chicago: University of Chicago Press.

6

Selling Desire

Gender Constructs, Social Stratification, and the Commercialization of Modern Living

Alexandra Staub

> Buying a new home allows you to start with a clean slate. The garage is empty, the kitchen is new, and the backyard offers a chance for you to design around your way-of-life.[1]

Since at least the early twentieth century, US ideas of modernity have been strongly linked to the concepts of both innovation and planned obsolescence. As a nation, the US has retained an identity as a powerhouse, not only of new technologies, but also of the processes of their production. In almost every year since 1890, the US has led the world in patent grants awarded, often producing more than twice the number of patents than the country in second place.[2] Yet innovation has been only half the story. Since the late nineteenth century, the US has embraced both a capitalist and in many respects libertarian business model. This model seeks to maximize profits through mass production rather than higher prices and, in comparison to many European countries, little regulation aside from that which guarantees "free trade."

This chapter explores how the unfettered market economy of the US has encouraged a quest for modernity in the form of up-to-dateness, and how this has affected housing production and the role of women as housing consumers in the US. I start by examining ideas of modernity in architecture and how housing producers in the US have largely rejected a focus on technology in favor of defining modernity as a constant renewal of products, leading to the marketing of modernity as an aspirational up-to-dateness. I use two product categories from the early twentieth century to serve as analogies for how current-day housing is marketed to consumers: the automobile industry and domestic products and appliances. While the automobile industry shifted its definition of modernity from mechanical advancement to aspirational representations that went hand in hand with consumers' lifestyle ambitions and desires of upward mobility, manufacturers of appliances and household products sold their consumer products by touting them as essential and convenient aids for a newly defined group of largely white, middle-class housewives. Such supposed aids were appealing to women whose worth was measured through their success in homemaking and achieving family happiness.[3]

Today, the scale of consumption has shifted. It is no longer household appliances but rather the house itself that is marketed[4] as a convenient time-saver and key to family happiness, a message that disregards the economic stratification that has become necessary to allow such aspirational lifestyles to flourish. This chapter examines how housing production companies in the US today have branded the house as a lifestyle product full of features that are marketed to women, whose role continues to be largely defined as homemaker, wife, and mother.[5] Hidden behind these consumer innovations is a harsh reality:

as the scale of consumption increases, so does the time and effort required for maintaining the upwardly mobile lifestyle. Middle-class women are thus burdened with an increase in reproductive tasks, or must outsource reproductive work to a resurgent "servant" class in an increasingly stratified society.

The expanding expectations of consumption in recent decades have had another effect on definitions of modern life: as (upscale) homes get ever larger, activities that once took place in public spaces,[6] such as parks, community swimming pools, urban cafés, or movie theaters, have been increasingly drawn into the home through the inclusion of large yards, private pools, spacious entertainment areas, and even home theaters. As a result, public spaces that in the nineteenth century were largely off-limits to upper-class women traveling alone have been made accessible to twenty-first-century women who can afford their privatization.[7]

The privatization of public life has gone hand in hand with a reversal of common readings of modernity. In much of the theoretical literature, public urban life is equated with modernity, while the home is equated with domesticity and traditionalism.[8] Drawing once-public functions into the home calls into question the continuing validity of this dichotomization. To supplement the common binary of modernity and traditionalism, I explore how the current-day process of economic stratification cloaked as social aspiration allows us to imagine the house as a body under shifting layers of agency. It is this shift of both agency and meaning that allows current-day women of leisure the pleasures of what was once only accessible within the public realm, now redefined as purchasable admittance to a freer life.

Modernity as Aspiration

The house's modernity has not always been defined through consumerism. While writers have often framed modernity in terms of urban space,[9] the Modern movement in architecture that originated in Europe after 1918 tackled the widespread lack of adequate housing for the working class through proposing technical efficiencies that would lower production costs. Attempting to solve a pressing social problem—the lack of housing—while at the same time stripping housing of what was regarded as its aspirational pompousness, the Modern movement is perhaps most provocatively summed up in Le Corbusier's seminal work *Vers une architecture* (*Towards a New Architecture*), which celebrated technical progress in the form of rationalized production combined with a materially reduced lifestyle.

Le Corbusier's book presented airplanes and automobiles as the new models for the building industry. Both, he explained, succinctly represented engineering goals, being products that went through a process of constant betterment through "*imagination and cold reason.*"[10] By contrast, he, lamented, "[t]he problem of the house has not yet been stated."[11] The house, according to Le Corbusier, needed to be reframed as a "machine for living in."[12]

It is interesting that Le Corbusier pointed to the automobile as a central model for modern housing. Whereas the car and the house were seen as bearers of technology in the 1920s, both have since become items of both mass production and aspirational desire, at least in the US. The road to mass production and consumption in the automobile industry has been clearly documented. The analogy to housing is arguably near.

Initially, automobiles were handcrafted for wealthy clients. This changed around the turn of the nineteenth to the twentieth century as Taylorism, the scientific management of workflows used to achieve efficiencies of production, created inroads in the automobile industry. It was Henry Ford who first envisioned the automobile as a mass-produced item made affordable through a systematized assembly line production that would drastically lower production costs. Coupled with new distribution networks as part of his company's focus on efficient management, the automobile became affordable for increasing segments of the population.[13] As an engineer, Ford understood "the problem of the automobile" as one of technical perfection, focusing on cars that would last and be inexpensive to repair. Historian Daniel Boorstin has argued that it was this belief in the perfectible product and Ford's failure to acknowledge consumers' love of novelty that allowed other automakers, most notably General Motors, to soon overtake Ford in sales volume.

General Motors' management success began with Alfred P. Sloan Jr., who joined the firm in 1923. He shifted the firm's focus from perfecting technology to understanding a buyer who desired a personal symbol of upward mobility.[14] In an early example of consumer profiling, Sloan introduced what would come to be known as niche marketing, introducing different makes of cars for different socioeconomic groups.[15] The car was presented as an aspirational product, with consumers encouraged to desire the next class of car as their circumstances improved (Figure 6.1). Carmakers also introduced the annual model, automobiles that were just different enough in styling from the previous year's model to make the older version seem dated. This definition of modernity as something with the latest up-to-date features became an early example of marketers' creative destruction, in which existing products are continually declared obsolete, their value destroyed, to make place for new products that are promoted as a product of creativity and innovation.[16]

Sloan was a strong proponent of free-market capitalism, believing that corporate gain would lead to national prosperity.[17] It was a view that held special credence during the first part of the twentieth century, as the US was positioning itself as the dominant world power economically, politically and, one might argue, culturally. Sloan's political focus was based on aggregate economics, not on democratic decision-making or on rectifying income disparity.[18] As such, his beliefs and actions favored a perceived meritocracy that extended to both male employees and, by extension, female homemakers whose economic identity relied on their husbands, while ignoring systemic inequalities that hindered implementation of such a system.

Defining the US as a meritocracy helps explain the role that aspirational consumption came to play in consumer choice. Advertisers created a message that upward mobility was something that everyone could somehow earn. Sloan's production of annual automobile models turned a product for the masses into a visible signal of class distinction, as marketers skillfully shaped an everyday item into one of varying degrees of status. As a tactic, the idea of aspirational consumption also translated well into the production of housing, as it developed into a manufactured consumer good of significant economic proportions.

The Car and the House

Houses and cars have in many ways developed hand in hand in the US. Not only does the housing industry employ marketing tactics that resemble those of the auto industry—the aspirational marketing that has worked to advance one works to advance the other—but the growth of the automobile industry and the growth of the single-family housing industry, which is now dominated by suburban subdivisions that rely on private transportation, are both seen as factors of social modernization. In the capital-driven system of the US, mobility has been expressed through the automobile, but also through ideas of upward mobility, as residents move frequently and planned obsolescence in the quest for up-to-dateness means houses are continually renovated or even replaced.[19] With construction systematized, housing firms have approached house production as a process similar to automobile assembly—the Levitt brothers, who built city-sized suburbs of tract houses in the 1950s, even compared their firm to General Motors[20]—and current builders continue to encourage homeowners to purchase new homes for their customizability and for features such as "safety," "energy efficiency," and "warranties,"[21] all attributes commonly associated with new cars. How has this definition of modernity affected women in the context of US housing?

To answer this question, it is useful to turn to the history of technology in the household and the marketing of appliances and other household products.[22] As Ruth Schwartz Cowan discusses in this volume, advances in household technology in the 1920s, especially in the form of appliances and products that make running the house more efficient or convenient, correlated with social changes that helped define white, middle-class women as household workers in their own homes, responsible not for *managing* a household full of servants but for taking on the tasks those servants had once

Figure 6.1 A Cadillac advertisement from 1957. The Cadillac was General Motors' most aspirational model, and its placement before an upscale home with traditional bearing was designed to underscore its exclusivity.

Source: Image used with kind permission of General Motors.

performed. The ensuing decades saw a continuation of this trend that altered class perceptions while cementing heteronormative expectations, as advertising from the post–World War II era through the 1970s focused on how the right appliances, cleaners and other household products would make the onerous parts of women's job as homemaker easier while allowing her to focus on the social aspects of this task, namely overseeing the welfare of her husband and children (Figure 6.2).

Marketing messages for household appliances and products blended in class more subtly than those seen in advertisements for automobiles (or more recently, other status-laden technical products marketed to be regularly replaced, such as mobile phones). Manufacturers' focus in the 1950s and 1960s was still on saturating the market with appliances[23] rather than suggesting their continual upgrades or replacement. Yet advertisers of the 1950s and 1960s equated middle-class comfort, tied to Hotpoint kitchens and Hoover vacuums, with white, middle-class families, ignoring the racial and socioeconomic diversity that was American reality. Advertisements were placed in magazines or in, "'wholesome' [1950s] television serials that [. . .] were early attempts to harness mass entertainment to sales of goods."[24] In time, "niche marketing" targeted a more diverse consumer base.[25] By the 1970s, protagonists portrayed in entertainment media were split into subsets based on factors such as age or race, and were directly linked to the type of advertiser that producers hoped to gain.[26] Nevertheless, being able to afford a shiny new kitchen, being able to exist on one (the husband's) income in order to pursue an unpaid job as homemaker, and the idea of using "extra time" to pamper one's family (and perhaps later, oneself) were and are prerogatives of suburban middle or upper-middle-class women, not those of the working class.

In the past few decades, housing production firms have combined class-based aspirational marketing, similar to that used in the twentieth-century marketing of cars, with the gender-based messages used by the manufacturers of appliances and other household items to present the house as an expression of status that is full of features that will make a women's reproductive labor pleasurable and trouble-free. In part, making households trouble-free for women has, since at least the early 1990s, involved outsourcing time-consuming or onerous tasks.[27] Yet manufacturers continue to portray luxurious extras and constant updates as quasi-necessities for a woman to achieve success and happiness. The result has been a vast expansion of sales opportunities, shaped by a comprehensive marketing message that includes the house, its material contents, and an aspirational lifestyle marketed as a new social standard.

Throughout the marketing process, the house's value is suggested to be a factor of features chosen by the owner, with a "custom built" house presented as expressing the owners' unique and creative personality, as the marketing message at the head of this chapter states clearly. The "pre-owned" house, by contrast, is cast as less desirable; in fact, the term "pre-owned" has for years been used as a euphemism for a used car. New homes are presented as more than simply expressions of personality; they stand proxy for achieving, or re-creating, traditional values of family and community cohesion. Gender has continued to play a central role in this process, as marketing messages emphasize women's perceived responsibility for reproductive labor, goals that are largely not defined by but rather absorbed by women.

In examining concepts of modernity, the analogy between the car and the house breaks down into one of technology versus up-to-dateness; or rather, the machine itself versus the social icon of what it represents. Just as Henry Ford's plan to engineer his vehicles as durable and affordable for the masses lost favor as General Motors' marketing of aspirational consumption spread to allow dreams of status and upward mobility through specific car ownership, European modernists' idea of establishing the house as an engineered "machine for living in" would never gain traction in a country like the US, whose strong capitalist economy favored housing based on representation and broad-scale consumption. Like General Motors in the 1920s, post–World War II housing firms came to realize that the key to selling more of their product is to keep updating it to reflect new tastes and fashions that are measured in status and social worth, even if that worth is superficial or simulated. As Dolores

Figure 6.2 A Hotpoint kitchen advertisement from 1951. Advertisers targeted an upwardly mobile middle class, suggesting that with the right appliances, women would have more time for their "extra duties," such as nurturing their families.

Hayden notes, "[M]achine-made products [of interior home décor] are all advertised as luxury goods but designed for rapid obsolescence."[28] The frivolousness of some of these updates is hidden behind claims of essential need and merit. Marketing new features as necessities for women's reproductive labor allows manufacturers to convince purchasers that their investment is based on true need, as well as social conformity masked as individual choice.

Housing, Consumerism, and Gender

The post-war US suburban housing pattern and its connection to gender-based consumerism has been criticized at least since Betty Friedan published her groundbreaking study, *The Feminine Mystique*, in 1963.[29] With chapter titles such as "The Mistaken Choice," "Housewifery Expands to Fill the Time Available," and "Progressive Dehumanization: The Comfortable Concentration Camp," Friedan made clear that she regarded the American model of women's relegation to the role of housewife as extremely problematic. In her introductory chapters, she traced the thinking that had fostered women's "choice" to become housewives to, among other things, a newly aggressive advertising industry that explained in intricate detail that women should measure their own success through the happiness and success of their husbands and children.

In 1980, Dolores Hayden followed with a further critique of US housing, linking suburban communities in the US to a hyper-capitalist economy that put an undue burden on women, especially if they worked outside the home.[30] By the 1980s, most women in the US *did* work outside the home,[31] and Hayden, pointing out that most suburbs were planned under the assumption that each house would be run by a woman serving as full-time homemaker, argued that the individualization of all aspects of such work, and an increase in products required to maintain a certain household standard, allowed manufacturers to sell ever more products while exacerbating women's double burden in performing both productive and reproductive labor. Hayden made suggestions for urban designs based on communal resources that would support employed women.

In the years since Hayden's 1980 essay, commercial service industries have sprung up to allow families to outsource reproductive labor.[32] While women working in middle-class households purportedly received some assistance through industries such as fast-food restaurants, as Hayden points out in a 2002 expansion of her earlier essay, "One woman's precarious haven was sustained by the products of another woman's small wages in this fast-growing sector of the market economy."[33] The service sector became a further industry based on principles of aspiration and social stratification: while lower-middle-class families made use of inexpensive fast-food restaurants, affluent families increasingly made use of personalized commercial services such as catering services, nannies, or even errand-running services.[34]

Hayden critiqued the effort required to maintain a system of individually managed homes to little avail: such homes have, in the past decades, became larger, requiring even more effort for their upkeep. While the average home built in the 1960s or before was less than 1,100 sq. ft. (102 m^2) in size,[35] by 2016 the median size of a new single-family home sold in the US was, at 2,497 sq. ft. (232 m^2), more than twice as large.[36] Single-family homes built in the 1980s had a median of five rooms; by 2000 the median number of rooms was seven.[37] A government analysis of housing trends found that homes built in the 2000s were more likely than earlier models to have more of all types of spaces: bedrooms, bathrooms, living rooms, family rooms, dining rooms, dens, recreation rooms, utility rooms, and of course, garages.[38] As homes became larger and included more amenities, including air conditioning, washers and dryers, garbage disposals, and fireplaces, residents reported fewer neighborhood amenities such as public transportation or day care.[39] Domestic space grew more opulent; public facilities shrank away in what would present itself as a privatization of once-public life.[40] Women were presented with choices in consumption within a cultural paradigm that seemed at odds with objective reality.

The Privatization of Public Life

The privatization of public life in the US, while seemingly gender neutral, has appeared concurrently to women's continued relegation to a role of consumer—a receiver of ideas and products developed by others (usually male). Women's role as consumers gives them a certain agency in the choice of items to consume, an agency that certainly extends to their choices in the consumption of spaces made available to them. Yet here, women's agency largely ends: throughout the centuries, women have largely been expunged from the process of defining their *role* within space and often the spaces themselves, as a few examples will show.

The erasure of women in theoretical contemplations, and the traditional banishment of "good" women from access to urban public space is the systemic malaise behind the more obvious one of women's double burden, and it helps explain some of women's struggles to control both how their identities and successes are defined. Daphne Spain argues that men control public space because they have the capital to invest in real estate and wage political campaigns. Men's control of space has also allowed them to define boundaries between public and private,[41] in a process that began in the nineteenth century and arguably continues on to the present day through limiting women's agency in the definitions of space. If women do not exist as subjects of experience and expression in theorizing space, then they have no power to determine questions or establish answers to the problem of the house. It is the continued negation of women in the theoretical discourse that has allowed their restriction in the material realm.

Diana Agrest has examined the origins of women's erasure in western architectural theory. Starting with Vitruvius's *Ten Books on Architecture* (written during the Roman Empire) and continuing on to Renaissance theoreticians including Leon Battista Alberti, Filarete, and Francesco Di Giorgio Martini, she presents how key Western theorists have ignored the very existence of women in their study of how human bodies relate to the body of a building. Filarete is especially flagrant, equating the (male) architect with the mother of the building and the architect's patron with the father, in an odd metaphor of sexualized conception and "birth." He regarded the building itself as a son; that is, both the creators and the products of the architectural process are imbued with male ideals.[42]

Agrest goes on to demonstrate how Di Giorgio's analysis of the city has further sexualized spatial order. Here the city center is compared to a navel, from where nourishment ensues to the rest of the city organism. It is, of course, a reversal of the biological process by which the unborn child receives nourishment from its mother. In Di Giorgio's version, the (male) child has claimed the role of provider, an odd twist on the logical hierarchy of the mother's body providing nourishment to her unborn child.[43] While Agrest points to the idea of immaculate conception as allowing for assertions of males giving birth, the point I wish to take from her work is that core Western architectural treatises have erased women from any role at all in spatial conception.

The reversal of creation narratives, in which women's role in creating and feeding new beings is usurped by a male architect or city planner, is telling for how it established a new mythos in which men conceive and nourish all manner of plans that women (who still exist, despite their suppression) are encouraged to adopt as reflecting the natural order of their lives. This deeper message of the male planner as executing a natural order helps explain why middle-class women of the 1920s did not revolt when asked to assume the chores of their former servants; why women did not rebel when confronted with the "comfortable concentration camp" of the suburbs analyzed by Betty Friedan in the 1960s; and why by the 1980s, when so many women were employed outside the home, they did not prioritize the communal services that would have assisted them in their daily lives. Daphne Spain has pointed out that "[a]n initial period of separatism helps marginalized groups develop independent identities and mobilize for political action."[44] Where women are kept from the collectivity of public space, they have little opportunity to engage politically. Anger at the system that has usurped her power is deflected onto the circumstances of her powerlessness, while she is granted agency to mitigate those circumstances through material changes rather than structural ones.

The erasure of women from architectural theory carries over into their erasure from the urban realm. Urban space, with its skyscrapers, automobiles, and focus on innovation, has, since at least the nineteenth century, come to represent the modern and with it the male. By contrast, the idealized domestic realm has remained a symbol of a regenerative traditionalism, popularly associated with the female.[45] Although the assertion "Wife in the kitchen. Whore in the street"[46] is an oversimplification of women's perceived role in the public realm, there is enough historical evidence to warrant a finer-grained examination of how such concepts have influenced contemporary housing design in its framing of public and private functions and their correlating spaces. While the dissolution of readily accessible public space in the US has largely been analyzed from a class-based and economic standpoint, shifting such space into a more tightly controllable private realm arguably has gender implications as well.

Setha Low has traced how in the US since the 1960s, once-public urban space has been increasingly privatized, as shopping malls, parks, and civic centers appeared within private commercial developments (i.e., developments not substantially controlled by a government entity). Low traces how the privatization of public land has intensified since the 1980s, as gated residential communities have increasingly used public tax monies to create facilities that are restricted to their members, thus effectively allowing once public and accessible land and facilities to be controlled by private entities.[47] While spaces "feel" public to those with access, they are clearly not public to those who are kept out, creating multiple perceptions of the same space, usually depending on one's social and economic status. Housing designs have also relaxed the definitions of public and private, albeit in a different way. In housing designs, privately owned spaces have taken on formerly public functions, further altering domestic landscapes and women's access to space.[48]

The shift of how public and private spaces are perceived arguably began in the early twentieth century, when electronic means of general communication such as radio and later television entered the home, setting in motion a process that blurred the lines between public happenings and the private space from which people could follow them. This process has continued as public spaces become restricted, or disappear,[49] leading to activities that once took place in public venues or urban settings increasingly taking place in private domestic spaces. In this manner, the "urban experience" of recreation and social encounters has become safely accessible for upper-class women, who retain control over domestic space. As the next section shows, the efforts of the housing industry have contributed to this process by highlighting the home as a receptacle for once-public functions, granting women who are able to purchase the requisite amenities control over spaces of entertainment and socialization.

The Housing Industry

Housing in the US is more than shelter; it is a major economic driver with a deep-rooted and well-funded political lobby.[50] Over the past 40 years, the number of housing units—located in single and multifamily dwellings—has almost doubled, from just over 70 million units in 1970[51] to over 132.4 million units in 2011.[52] Almost 83 million of these units, or 62.7%, were in detached structures.[53] The trend towards houses in suburbs[54] has equally expanded. In 1970, 51.2% of all housing was suburban.[55] Suburb types and definitions have changed since the 1970s, but in 2016, various suburb types accounted for 78% of all households in the 50 largest metropolitan areas of the US, and 84% of the household growth from 2000 to 2015.[56]

Suburban communities are often built by developers who buy a tract of land to build speculative housing. The concept is not new; such enclaves have existed in the US since the nineteenth century.[57] Suburbs gained impetus through the post–World War II housing boom, when suburban housing, such as that provided by the Levitt brothers in the form of "Levittowns," became increasingly available to the middle class.[58] Today's developments are often self-contained, and include amenities such as recreation facilities, clubhouses, and swimming pools. Access to the community is through one or more entry points that are marked, either through a gate or a low wall. Serving to isolate the community from its surroundings, such markers designate members as insiders; this is an important differentiation when it comes to use of restricted amenities such as clubhouses or pools. In 2015, the 50 largest builders in the US sold a total of 216,790 houses, with the ten largest firms constructing over 60% of the total. The following analysis explores their products and marketing practices.[59]

Large builders operate across several regions or states. Most have regional sales offices but offer the same or similar models of houses in several areas. Although large-scale builders are not the only industry that provides housing in the US, their reach is considerable. Products are developed and marketed with an eye toward customer desires and tastes,[60] with at least one developer researching "leading lifestyle brands" to determine "what's missing."[61] Many manufacturers offer several product lines at varying price points, similar to car manufacturers that offer several brands in different price ranges. Company websites present products online through images, floor plans, interactive tools, and videos; in addition, most communities display model homes that customers can visit. Customers who have chosen to purchase a home in a particular subdivision submit a down payment before picking a lot and having a house built for them based on the company's offerings, or they choose a "quick move in" home that is already constructed.[62]

Although choosing the features of a new house is more complex than choosing those of a new car, the concept is similar. In both cases, clients can choose standard features and finishes or purchase "upgrades." For a car, such upgrades might be a sunroof or leather upholstery; in a house, a sunroom or more expensive flooring. One builder that makes a point of offering common upgrades as standard even compares their houses to cars, pointing out that just as you would expect a car to include tires or headlights in the purchase price, in their houses "everything's included."[63]

Firms strive to offer a comprehensive product that includes not only the house, but also financial services such as mortgage lending or insurance. They typically offer "design centers" or personal assistance through interior decorators to assist clients in choosing appliances, finishes, and lighting from a predetermined selection.[64] Customers, and especially women, are actively encouraged to "design" or "personalize" the house. In advertising videos where consumers speak about the building process, it is not uncommon for a woman or her husband to state that it is she who has "designed" their home.[65]

In so closely determining possible aesthetic and design options, housing producers are faced with a seemingly intractable contradiction: on the one hand consumers, and especially women, are told their "creativity" and "inspiration" will lead to a "unique" home that is perfect for them, while on the other hand builders offer a fairly narrow range of options and colors to choose from based on current market trends. The key to bridging this contradiction is the producer's ability to choose emerging trends and then, through advertisements, to funnel the consumer's desire. Clients are coached on what aspirational products to purchase to enhance their own status, which is measured through the scope and contemporaneousness as well as the material value of their choices.

Once they have picked a lot, customers choose from several floor plans on offer, and then pick one of several exterior styles, which are often loosely based on historic models (Figure 6.3). Old English styles, with names such as "Tudor" or "Georgian" portray a sense of Anglo-Saxon rooted-ness; Italianate styles (often generically called "Mediterranean") suggest warmth and flair; and names such as "Versailles" and "Manor" suggest that the client has bought into royalty.[66] Floor plans have no historical bearing on the exterior and neither has historical accuracy (Figure 6.4). Richard Harris and Nadine Dostrovsky have argued that current trends towards historicist facades, which began as early as the 1960s, express developers' reactions to popular taste.[67] While this view focuses on the supposedly reactive nature of the housing industry, it also points to manufacturers' role in homogenizing popular taste, as alternatives to products deemed safely marketable are rarely developed for consumers' consid-eration. As popular styles become so widespread to be almost ubiquitous, history indicates that house style preferences shift every few generations—from the ranch houses of the 1950s and 1960s to the historicist ones common throughout the 1980s and beyond—often leading to sweeping architectural and aesthetic changes in mainstream housing.[68] Nevertheless, offerings remain based on their appeal to consumer aspirations, with current trends to historicism offering the illusion of cultural tradition and savvy that is both prearranged and purchasable.

Figure 6.3 Exterior of a Toll Brothers House. Both upscale and more modest homes have traditional facades loosely based on historical precedents.
Source: © Alexandra Staub, 2017.

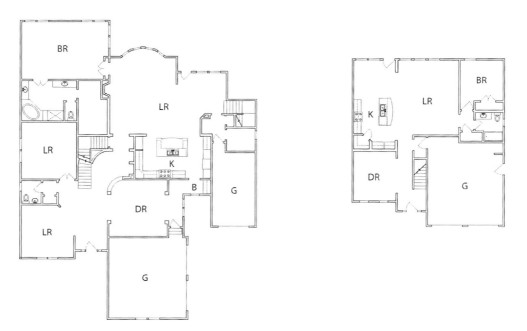

Figure 6.4 Floor plans of a Toll Brothers house (left) and a more modest D. R. Horton house (right). The homes are similarly organized, with a kitchen open to the main living area, although the larger home has a greater number of living areas (LR) and garages (G). The upscale home has an elaborate master bedroom suite (BR). Both homes have additional bedrooms and bathrooms on a second floor. Note the "butler's pantry" (B) between the kitchen (K) and dining room (DR) in the larger house.
Note: Plans are adapted from manufacturers' images.

Modernity and Interior Splendor

Interiors of new homes currently offered for sale follow several patterns. All center around a series of areas accessible to visitors, combined with more secluded areas that are reserved for the family. Public entry to the actual living spaces takes place through one or more vestibules, creating a formal entry sequence that emphasizes the homeowner's control over the visitor's spatial progression. High-end homes often have an elaborate double-height entryway, offering visitors a first impression of the home's scale. Chandeliers and curved staircases with balcony landings overlooking the entryway are not uncommon and are reminiscent of the entry to English country manors. Despite such features suggestive of nineteenth-century mansions, interiors tend to be aesthetically modern, with an emphasis on flowing spaces and abundant light (Figure 6.5).

Figure 6.5 In contrast to the traditional exteriors, interiors of developer housing, such as this Toll Brothers home, often have light-filled, open floor plans typical of modernist architecture. Living spaces and kitchens are joined to create one large room.
Source: © Alexandra Staub, 2017.

In both upscale and more modest homes, the central focus of the house's living area is the kitchen, or rather a kitchen island. Essentially a freestanding countertop, advertisements show this space as the center of home life and entertaining.[69] The kitchen is no longer a space of labor; instead, meal preparation in what is usually touted as a "gourmet" kitchen is portrayed as being simple and fast. From the kitchen, other living spaces expand so that the spaces flow seamlessly together. In more upscale homes, a separate room in the front facade is advertised as a "library" or "formal dining room," sometimes connected to the kitchen via a "butler's pantry" (see Figure 6.4). Homes may contain a finished basement, with spaces such as a play area or a home theater (Figure 6.6). Additional living spaces, often undefined, are called a "bonus room" and are often located near the children's bedrooms. Larger homes have more and larger living rooms as well as larger transition spaces between living and bedroom areas, but the general configuration of the spaces remains the same as in smaller houses.

Spaces such as a "library" or "butler's pantry" indicate the role supposedly traditional features can have in selling exclusivity. The butler's pantry, allowing discrete arrangement of dishes before they appear at the table, harks from an era in which servants in upscale homes performed the cooking and other housework out of sight, while the open kitchen marks a modern era without servants, in which the housewife's workspace has become more integrated with the rest of the house. Having lost its original function in the modern house, the butler's pantry has become a symbol of the old-fashioned grandeur associated with being served.

Figure 6.6 Upscale homes include amenities that once abounded in urban spaces, such as swimming pools or movie theaters.

Source: "Home Theater II" (original in color). From the series "Suburban Dreams" by Beth Yarnelle Edwards. © Beth Yarnelle Edwards, 2005.

The rear of the house opens to the outside and provides a third layer of living spaces including, at the very least, patios or terraces, often with outdoor furniture such as sectional sofas and chaise longues, or even outdoor kitchens with grills, a sink, and built-in counter space. Landscaped gardens or a play area for the children are common, even in modest homes. Swimming pools, often with waterfalls or other decorative features, are frequently shown in upscale houses. The backyard is often fenced in to close off this space from outside view, including from the immediate neighbors and certainly from the street.[70]

Homes have two further zones: a space producers call an "owner's suite" or "owner's retreat" (or more classically the "master" bedroom) and a further set of bedrooms that are usually grouped together and typically meant for children. In upscale homes, the owner's suite is an elaborate set of spaces entered from a hallway, with an area for the bed itself, a sitting area, and a walk-in closet making this area into a separate retreat within the home.[71] The idea of retreat, relaxation, and physical renewal extends to the attached bathroom, which is usually large and portrayed with spa-like amenities such as a freestanding bathtub, glass-enclosed shower, double sink, large mirrors, views to exterior landscapes, and costly surface treatments such as granite and decorative tile work. While such spaces are not modern in a technical or aesthetic sense, they are presented as a new standard for the twenty-first century. The combined spaces resemble an upscale hotel suite and serve as a private "getaway" for the homeowners. Hotel suites, of course, come with an array of maids and other service people to maintain them, a point that is disregarded in the advertisements.

When presented in photos, children's rooms are shown as adult-style bedrooms, with bold graphics and a more playful color scheme suggesting the youthful status of their tenants. Children are presented as younger versions of their parents; in fact advertisement videos often stress that the home will become the space where parents can bond with their children by handing down their interests and passions, in the process offering opportunities for "lasting memories."[72] These memories become part of the traditionalism that marketers claim the home will support, a traditionalism that is touted as personalized and "unique."

In the US, the role of spatial arrangement and aesthetics in housing production is clearly multilayered. While the home's exterior aesthetically alludes to deep-rooted traditions to offer emotional reassurance,[73] the interior plays a different role. Large and visibly open interiors are light and airy in a nod to architectural modernism, yet are nevertheless meant to show off social status and lifestyle acumen in the tradition of a gilded age. Former service areas, such as kitchens, have become spaces of entertaining and socialization, yet are combined with features that allude to the nineteenth-century hierarchies of upper-class society, such as a library or butler's pantry.

Housing manufacturers further bring the role of tradition into play through the functions of the spaces themselves. Advertisements tend to focus on particular aspects of reproductive labor, such as cooking, baking, or socializing, but never on more unpleasant activities, such as cleaning the large kitchen or scrubbing toilets. In focusing on the social aspects of reproductive labor, housing companies suggest that the house will serve as a representative backdrop for socializing and help establish unique family traditions, while fostering the bond between parents and children. Throughout this process, parents, and especially women, are shown as creating a nurturing environment that promises them agency in the formation of their children's experiences. Communities are presented as spaces where "memories are made"[74] and homes are presented as spaces where the neighborhood children all gather,[75] allowing parents to reminisce in the pleasures of their own childhood. Mothers are shown guiding their children, especially daughters, through domestic rituals such as schoolwork, housework, and maintaining the family's social bonds.[76] Advertisements focus on how the home will take on a central role in allowing women to successfully accomplish this aspect of reproductive labor. Entryways are designed to reduce clutter, laundry areas are designed to make washing clothing easy, spaces where women can cook and simultaneously supervise the children's homework allow mothers to effortlessly multitask, and master bedrooms are shown as a space for the woman to retreat or enjoy intimate moments with her husband.[77] The home, and the lives within it, are thus presented as being easier to maintain, the more features the home has and the more up-to-date those features are.

The lifestyle quality of many housing advertisements, and their emphasis of modern life as carefree through being up-to-date, cannot be overlooked. Social life apparently no longer takes place in public spaces (where spaces are "public" they are increasingly under private ownership); instead, photos and videos show how gourmet kitchens have superseded restaurants, private pools have replaced the community swimming pool, home theaters have made the public cinema obsolete, and generous entertainment facilities offer large-scale amusement spaces within the family home.

Reinforcing this message, the combination of modernist interiors, representing what is usually seen as private space, and traditional exteriors, in what is the house's most public display, present a reversal of the common reading of public space as expressing modernity, while the domesticity of home represents comfort and tradition. In framing the house's generous new interiors as a product of modernity, manufacturers reinforce the house's absorption of public life and public space. In emphasizing such spaces as hubs of social activity, they underscore that through purchasing, and thus privatizing, such spaces, women have gained safe, that is, controllable, access to the pleasures of public life that have so long been denied them.

Modernity in the US struggles with its dual and conflicted nature. On the one hand, modernity is defined as creative innovation; on the other hand, the homogenizing nature of capitalist consumption stifles that very innovative energy. The aspirational quality of the house's amenities have come to stand proxy for the lifestyle such amenities promise: in advertising videos, owners are shown discussing their house designs and showing off rooms in a ritual that is designed to elicit admiration and awe.[78] Women continue to be portrayed as responsible for the household's reproductive labor—a form of traditionalism that has in one way or another stayed consistent since at least the nineteenth century— while the house's features are touted as time-saving necessities.

An increase in house and room sizes has gone hand in hand with a redefinition of how such spaces are used. Larger domestic spaces are marketed as areas for a sanitized version of activities that once took place in the realm of public life, while traditional features plucked from upscale environments of the nineteenth century are set as decorative extras. The generous new spaces and functions incorporated into the domestic environment require a great deal of labor to maintain, a factor that has encouraged a resurrected service class based on unpaid or underpaid labor. As an ideology of consumption seeks to allow women access to spaces of sociability and amusement, the conflation of lifestyle freedoms, property, and the fruits of social stratification has become complete.

Acknowledgment

I am indebted to Kim England and Igea Troiani for their critical reading of early drafts of this chapter. Any errors are clearly my own.

Notes

1. D. R. Horton 2017.
2. WIPO statistical database May 2015. Up to the 1970s, European countries such as Great Britain, Germany, and France reported the second highest number of patents awarded worldwide. After 1980, countries reporting the second highest number of patents worldwide were the Soviet Union and Japan.
3. See also Ruth Schwartz Cowan's chapter in this volume.
4. Dolores Hayden makes a similar point that manufacturers have moved beyond appliances and now regard the house as a prime marketing object; see Hayden 2006, 43.
5. See also Staub 2015, 62–6.
6. The literature included many definitions of "public" vs. "private" space. In this chapter, public space is defined as space that is accessible by the general public, including spaces such as cafés or movie theaters, which require a small payment for their use. See Smith and Low 2006 for an excellent discussion.
7. For a discussion of how gender and urban space have developed in the US since the early twentieth century, see Spain 2014.
8. See the introduction to this volume.

9. Shiach 2005, and Leslie and Reimer 2003, 293, criticize the focus on urban space when exploring issues of space and modernity. Scholars from outside architecture have often limited their exploration of spatial modernity to urban space, while architects and designers have tended to take a far broader view.
10. Le Corbusier 1986 [1931], 109; italics in original.
11. Le Corbusier 1986 [1931], 107.
12. Le Corbusier 1986 [1931], 107. Le Corbusier's work has been criticized for both its class and gender aspects, points that I do not address here; see Colomina 1992.
13. Boorstin 1974, 548ff. Expanding access to car ownership was not the only social change Ford helped usher in: through management decisions such as the introduction of a "family wage" that provided a higher-than-average pay rate for males, Ford's policies introduced upper-middle-class gender divisions of labor to the working class and helped to establish an ideal of women as solely responsible for reproductive labor (see Arnesen 2006, 434).
14. Boorstin 1974, 552.
15. Boorstin 1974, 553.
16. The term "creative destruction" is largely associated with the work of economist Joseph Schumpeter 1994 [1942], and was based on Karl Marx and Friedrich Engels's analysis of crisis tendencies in capitalism.
17. Farber 2002, xii.
18. Farber 2002, xii.
19. Staub 2015, 67–71.
20. Cited in Hayden 2006, 39.
21. Terms are taken from marketing literature of several major homebuilders, such as D. R. Horton.
22. Feminist theories of technology have seen rapid development over the past few decades (see Wajcman 2010), although domestic technology was for years overlooked in the history of mechanization.
23. Coontz 2016, 231.
24. Coontz 2016, 230.
25. See Cohen 2004.
26. Coontz 2016, 231; see also Cohen 2004.
27. See Hayden 2002.
28. Hayden 2002, 151.
29. Friedan's text was based on interviews with white middle-class women; a criticism of her work is that it ignored class and racial diversity.
30. Hayden 2000 [1980].
31. See Spain 2016, 3.
32. Spain 2016, 4.
33. Hayden 2002, 98.
34. Hayden 2002, 99.
35. Sarkar 2011, 2. Square footage numbers for the older houses are inflated due to possible additions added over time.
36. Interactive table: www.census.gov/construction/chars/interactive/.
37. Sarkar 2011, 3.
38. Sarkar 2011, 3.
39. Sarkar 2011, 5.
40. For an economic analysis of this process, see also Hayden 2006.
41. Spain 2016, 16–7.
42. Agrest 2000 [1993], 362–4.
43. Agrest 2000 [1993], 364–5.
44. Spain 2016, 18.
45. See also the introduction to this volume.
46. Agrest 2000 [1993], 367.
47. Low 2006; 2008.
48. Interestingly, inverse movements have also occurred, in which public space became more "domesticized." In the late nineteenth century, feminist reformers like Melusina Fay Pierce, Frances Willard, and Jane Addams promoted a reform of urban spaces and their administration through measures taken from successful household management; see Hayden 2002, 44–8. Daphne Spain notes that feminist places such as bookstores often straddle the line between public and private, for example by creating markedly domestic interiors complete with furniture that encourages lingering; see Spain 2016, 17.
49. Smith and Low 2006, 1–2.
50. Hayden 2006.
51. U.S. Department of Commerce 1973, xv, Table A.
52. U.S. Department of Housing and Urban Development 2013, 3, Table C-01-AH.
53. U.S. Department of Housing and Urban Development 2013, 3, Table C-01-AH.

54. Suburban areas are defined here as located outside central cities but within the federal government's standard metropolitan statistical areas (SMSAs). This definition is taken from U.S. Dept. of Commerce 1973, xiv. Other definitions exist, especially as suburbs and their relationship to metropolitan areas have become spatially more complex; see Urban Land Institute 2016.
55. U.S. Dept. of Commerce 1973, xiv.
56. Urban Land Institute 2016, 2.
57. See Hayden 2003.
58. See for example Hayden 2003.
59. The top ten "housing giants" in 2016 as listed by Pro Builder were D. R. Horton Inc., Lennar Corp., Pulte-Group Inc., CalAtlantic Homes, NVR Inc., Toll Brothers, Taylor Morrison, KB Home, Meritage Homes Corp., and TRI Pointe Homes Inc. See Professional Builder 2017.
60. Many companies are reluctant to discuss how they develop their products. PulteGroup uses advanced marketing research, including focus-group interviews with potential customers as well as housing feedback via surveys. See PulteGroup 2013a.
61. TRI Pointe Homes 2016a.
62. General marketing is done predominantly through company websites and advertising videos (many companies maintain a YouTube channel). Once a customer contacts a company via the website, sales associates email the potential customer with offers to answer questions via email or a phone call, or to tour a model home in the area the customer is considering.
63. Lennar 2014.
64. PulteGroup 2012; D.R. Horton 2013; Toll Brothers 2014c.
65. For example Toll Brothers 2015b; 2015e.
66. "Versailles" and "Manor" are two exterior house styles offered by Toll Brothers. Many producers offer styles with similar names.
67. Harris and Dostrovsky 2008, 169.
68. Harris and Dostrovsky 2008, 181.
69. For example Toll Brothers 2015d.
70. For example TRI Pointe 2016b.
71. For example PulteGroup 2013b.
72. Toll Brothers 2015a; PulteGroup 2017a.
73. Harris and Dostrovsky 2008.
74. Toll Brothers 2015a.
75. Toll Brothers 2015c.
76. PulteGroup 2017a; 2017b.
77. PulteGroup 2017b.
78. Toll Brothers 2014a; Toll Brothers 2014b.

References

Agrest, Diana. 2000 [1993]. "Architecture From Without: Body, Logic and Sex." In *Gender Space Architecture*, edited by Jane Rendell, Barbara Penner, and Iain Borden, 358–370. London and New York: Routledge.

Arnesen, Eric, ed. 2006. *Encyclopedia of U.S. Labor and Working-Class History*, Vol. 1. New York: Routledge.

Boorstin, Daniel. 1974. *The Americans: The Democratic Experience*. New York: Random House.

Cohen, Lizabeth. 2004. *A Consumer's Republic: The Politics of Mass Consumption in Postwar America*. New York: Vintage.

Colomina, Beatriz. 1992. "The Split Wall: Domestic Voyeurism." In *Sexuality & Space*, edited by Beatriz Colomina, 73–130. New York: Princeton Architectural Press, 1992.

Coontz, Stephanie. 2016. *The Way We Never Were: American Families and the Nostalgia Trap*, 2nd ed. New York: Basic Books.

Farber, David. 2002. *Sloan Rules: Alfred P. Sloan and the Triumph of General Motors*. Chicago: University of Chicago Press.

Friedan, Betty. 2001 [1963]. *The Feminine Mystique*. New York: W. W. Norton.

Harris, Richard, and Nadine Dostrovsky. 2008. "The Suburban Culture of Building and the Reassuring Revival of Historicist Architecture Since 1970." *Home Cultures* 52(2): 167–196.

Hayden, Dolores. 2000 [1980]. "What Would a Non-Sexist City Look Like? Speculations on Housing, Urban Design and Human Work." In *Gender Space Architecture*, edited by Jane Rendell, Barbara Penner, and Iain Borden, 266–281. London and New York: Routledge.

Hayden, Dolores. 2002. *Redesigning the American Dream: Gender, Housing and Family Life*, 2nd ed. New York and London: W. W. Norton.

Hayden, Dolores. 2003. *Building Suburbia: Green Fields and Urban Growth, 1820–2000*. New York: Vintage.

Hayden, Dolores. 2006. "Building the American Way: Public Subsidy, Private Space." In *The Politics of Public Space*, edited by Neil Smith and Setha Low, 35–48. London and New York: Routledge.

Le Corbusier [Charles Edouard Jeanneret]. 1986 [1931]. *Towards a New Architecture*. Translated by Frederick Etchells. New York: Dover. Originally published as *Vers une architecture* in 1923. The 1986 edition I consulted is based on the 1931 English translation.

Leslie, Deborah, and Suzanne Reimer. 2003. "Gender, Modern Design, and Home Consumption." *Environment and Panning D: Society and Space* 21: 293–316.

Low, Setha. 2006. "How Private Interests Take Over Public Space: Zoning, Taxes, and Incorporation of Gated Communities." In *The Politics of Public Space*, edited by Neil Smith and Setha Low, 81–104. London and New York: Routledge.

Low, Setha. 2008. "Incorporation and Gated Communities in the Greater Metro-Los Angeles Region as a Model of Privatization of Residential Communities." *Home Cultures* 5(1): 85–108.

Schumpeter, Joseph. 1994 [1942]. *Capitalism, Socialism and Democracy*. London and New York: Routledge.

Shiach, Morag. 2005. "Modernism, the City and the 'Domestic Interior.'" *Home Cultures* 2(3): 251–268.

Smith, Neil, and Setha Low. 2006. "Introduction: The Imperative of Public Space." In *The Politics of Public Space*, edited by Neil Smith and Setha Low, 1–17. London and New York: Routledge.

Spain, Daphne. 2014. "Gender and Urban Space." *Annual Review of Sociology* 40(1): 581–598.

Spain, Daphne. 2016. *Constructive Feminism: Women's Spaces and Women's Rights in the American City*. Ithaca, NY: Cornell University Press.

Staub, Alexandra. 2015. *Conflicted Identities: Housing and the Politics of Cultural Representation*. London and New York: Routledge.

Wajcman, Judy. 2010. "Feminist Theories of Technology." *Cambridge Journal of Economics* 34: 143–152.

Online Databases, Websites and Videos Consulted

D. R. Horton. 2013. "D. R. Horton Design Center." www.youtube.com/watch?v=8B_4tQZMLRA.

D. R. Horton. 2017. "Benefits of Buying a New Home." www.drhorton.com/Home-Buyer/New-Home-Benefits.

Lennar. 2014. "Everything's Included in Your Lennar Home." www.youtube.com/watch?v=N32UX8EHqFw.

Professional Builder. 2017. "2016 Housing Giants Rankings." www.probuilder.com/2016-housing-giants-rankings.

PulteGroup. 2012. "Pulte Homes—Design to Move You." www.youtube.com/watch?v=GyGWhWWUs70&spfreload=10.

PulteGroup. 2013a. "Homeowners Inspire Pulte Life Tested® Homes." www.youtube.com/watch?v=yXVk-KDyV7c&t=3s&spfreload=10.

PulteGroup. 2013b. "The Pulte Homes Owner's Retreat: Inspired by Homeowners." www.youtube.com/watch?v=yx8MTENhLTc&spfreload=10.

PulteGroup. 2017a. "All in a Name." www.youtube.com/watch?v=xgWC6NQHXnU.

PulteGroup. 2017b. "The Tour." www.youtube.com/watch?v=j2TkZ82aEt0&t=2s&spfreload=10.

Sarkar, Mousumi. 2011. "How American Homes Vary by the Year They Were Built." U.S. Census Bureau Working Paper, no. 2011–18. www.census.gov/hhes/www/housing/housing_patterns/pdf/Housing%20by%20Year%20Built.pdf.

Toll Brothers. 2014a. "A Toll Brothers Housewarming Party." www.youtube.com/watch?v=RMZKrtt8i1M&t=6s&spfreload=10.

Toll Brothers. 2014b. "Ladies Night in the Community." www.youtube.com/watch?v=sI1j7Ir_-Tw&t=7s&spfreload=10.

Toll Brothers. 2014c. "Design Studio." www.youtube.com/watch?v=ROdyVnE9jkY&t=3s&spfreload=10.

Toll Brothers. 2015a. "Family Community." www.youtube.com/watch?v=USmpldfJiuA.

Toll Brothers. 2015b. "Three Wishes." www.youtube.com/watch?v=DQzJw3dx5L8&spfreload=10.

Toll Brothers. 2015c. "Gathering Spot." www.youtube.com/watch?v=tEs143u94_g&spfreload=10.

Toll Brothers. 2015d. "Sand Castle." www.youtube.com/watch?v=eTenEKOXDus&spfreload=10.

Toll Brothers. 2015e. "Courtyard." www.youtube.com/watch?v=9vZyi00c4WM&spfreload=10.

TRI Pointe Homes. 2016a. "TRI Pointe Group Builder of the Year 2015." www.youtube.com/watch?v=kCYAH8zVgdU.

TRI Pointe Homes. 2016b. "Aubergine at Esencia—New Homes in Rancho Mission Viejo." www.youtube.com/watch?v=dQUHBpBd10g&spfreload=10.

Urban Land Institute. 2016. *Housing in the Evolving American Suburb.* Urban Land Institute, Washington, DC. http://uli.org/wp-content/uploads/ULI-Documents/Housing-in-the-Evolving-American-Suburb.pdf.

U.S. Department of Commerce. 1973. Current Housing Reports Series H150–73A: XIV. Annual Housing Survey: 1973. United States and Regions. Part A: General Housing Characteristics. ftp://ftp.census.gov/prod2/ahsscan/h150-73A.pdf.

U.S. Department of Housing and Urban Development. 2013. *American Housing Survey for the United States: 2011.* Current Housing Reports, Series H150/11. U.S. Government Printing Office, Washington, DC. www.census.gov/content/dam/Census/programs-surveys/ahs/data/2011/h150-11.pdf.

WIPO Statistical Database. May 2015. "Patent Grants by Office and Country of Origin." *Table Generated.* www.wipo.int/ipstats/en.

7

Engendering Urban Design
An Unfinished Story

Marion Roberts

The imagery of modernist urbanism, with its high towers, gleaming glass facades, superhighways and express transit has come to dominate most of the business districts of cities on the planet. Megacities have expanded across their hinterlands, swallowing up previously rural villages, facilitating transnational and transcontinental flows of wealth, goods and information. The tropes and forms of modernist urbanism deface the suburbs too, represented by either seemingly endless rows of high-rise housing or low-rise suburban villas, arranged in so-called organic layouts, a far cry from the origins of the garden city and suburb.[1] In the face of such voracious growth, geared towards the accumulation of capital, the proposition of a gender-sensitive approach to urban design seems an impossible dream.

A gendered approach challenges traditional versions of masculinity and femininity, seeing such differences as social constructions inflected by other markers of difference and identity, for example social class, age, disability, sexual orientation and ethnicity. In contrast to viewing space as a commodity to be exploited, a gendered approach seeks to understand how spaces and places are produced and co-constructed through everyday use combined with their presence in the imagination. Feminist scholarship has interrogated key concepts in modernist urbanism and found them wanting, thereby contributing to a critique of contemporary urbanism. Gender equality is now embedded in European legislation and forms a key part of UN-Habitat's New Urban Agenda.[2] Yet there is still a large disconnect, in theory and in practice, between a gendered approach and the mainstream of contemporary city building.[3]

This chapter examines that disconnect through drawing on secondary sources and contemporary feminist scholarship. Given the breadth of the topic, the discussion is limited in geographical scope, drawing on the UK's experience to improve urban quality, the "urban renaissance." The argument will be made that while a gendered approach to urbanism is frequently at odds with the concepts of modernist urbanism, it has much in common with the preoccupations of the progressive modernist architect/planners who embraced a social welfare approach to democracy. In this specific sense, a gendered approach is a continuation of the "modernist project," but with a broader set of ideals and a greater sense of humility about the role of the designer.

Modernism and "Second Wave" Feminist Scholarship

The Charter of Athens provided a guiding document for planners and architects in the period immediately following World War II. The essential ideas promoted in the Charter were drawn from Le Corbusier's vision for a contemporary city, first published in 1929.[4] Such was the power and influence of the Charter, its proponents, and the rationale provided by the work of the early Modernists, that its shadow is still cast today, to be observed in land use zoning plans, high-rise towers, and the priority given to high-speed traffic circulation. As Tummers and Zibell point out, the functional city of the Charter "gets in the way"[5] of a gendered approach to spatial planning.

The following features of functionalist town planning have attracted criticism. The separation of distinct land uses into zoned areas of work, housing, leisure and transport disrupted the European tradition of the shop house. This form had been used from medieval times and is characterized by a narrow plot width with its commercial and work spaces on the ground floor and residential quarters above, fronting onto a street. An idealized view of suburban domesticity was inscribed into the shaping of the city, with housing firmly separated from commerce, production and manufacture. While the Charter of Athens[6] and Le Corbusier's vision have been identified here as prime documents representing modernity, it should also be acknowledged that the power of this nineteenth-century version of the domestic ideal infused other another, equally influential, vision of contemporary urban life, that is Ebenezer Howard's Garden City. Howard, who was not an architect or a planner and only provided diagrams, nevertheless strongly indicated that housing should be separated from civic functions to be located at the center of the city and industrial enterprises to be planned at the periphery.[7] He was receptive to social experimentation and while not proposing a mixture of functions, did allow some experimentation in single-sex communal living within the first Garden Cities and Suburbs.[8]

The separation of functions, sometimes cast as creating an opposition between the public and the private, central city and suburb, has been criticized at both symbolic and practical levels. Practically, a separation of functions inhibits the combination of productive and reproductive work, as multiple journeys must be made between places of employment, shops, schools and other urban amenities before even considering leisure and entertainment. This issue was recognized by the authors of the Athens Charter, who noted, "The plan should ensure that the daily cycle of activities between the dwelling, workplace and recreation (recuperation) can occur with the utmost economy of time."[9] An idealized model of family life with a male breadwinner, a housewife, and dependent children, positioned the male head of household's journey to work as the prime journey to be planned for; this journey was to be regarded as a key spatial relationship in urban layout and transport planning.[10] Bondi argued that the symbolism of suburban life as embodying a peaceful and private domesticity was still inscribed in the urban landscape at the millennium, despite substantial societal and spatial changes such as the feminizing of waged work and the blurring of the differences between inner cities, suburbs and peri-urban areas.[11]

The contrast between an idealized model of modernist urbanism and the realities of quotidian life has been crystallized in the promotion of car use. Patterns of car ownership and use were overwhelmingly dominated by men in Western Europe, such that feminist geographers could chart urban areas where women formed a passive labor force, with reduced opportunities due to their lack of mobility. While differences between male and female car uses have converged at the lower and upper end of the age groups in the global North, women continue to make shorter and more frequent trips than men (trip chaining).[12] Blumenberg's research has found that in North America, low-income women are disadvantaged by their lack of access to motorized vehicles and argues that public policy should make greater efforts to recognize this.[13]

As noted, the Charter of Athens defined four areas of life for planning, employment, housing, transport, and recreation. Tummers and Zibell point to the omission of social infrastructure, such as educational facilities and health care.[14] These were included in the neighborhood planning of the 1950s and 1960s, where typically a housing area was laid out around a school and some shops. This style of planning has been criticized by feminist scholars for its heteronormative assumptions and its implied lack of choice, redolent of a paternalism where the architect/planner foresaw all the needs of a population of workers and provided for each in a series of designated spaces.[15] Soviet planning immediately after the Russian Revolution epitomized this attention to quotidian needs, although resource constraints meant that it was rarely fulfilled and was abandoned in the Stalinist era. For example in Kharkov, Ukraine, experimental neighborhoods were built around industrial plants, and

> it was public authorities who decided how many flats and of what type were needed, as well as how many canteens, kindergartens, schools, technical school, and enterprises that address leisure and everyday needs are necessary to maintain the production work.[16]

In the UK, attention to quotidian needs also had some positive effects in setting planning standards, such as for precise quantities of open space, play space and private space to be associated with each dwelling, as well as measures for such practical issues as the collection and storage of waste.[17]

In terms of urban design, the modernism of the International Style reversed the relationship between the building as object and public space, thereby undermining the organizing principle of streets and squares intrinsic to Western European urbanism.[18] The undefined urban spaces that typically have been incorporated into modernist housing estates in the UK and US have been condemned for their association with crime and antisocial behavior. While crime has an impact on all groups in the population, there is much evidence that fear of crime impacts on women's "right to the city."[19] Nevertheless, there are some attributes of a modernist approach to the relationship between the public and private spheres that continue to have a positive impact on urban design. One of these is the provision of balconies and roof terraces, spaces that are truly private but that offer a protected view outwards from the domestic sphere and a chance of sunlight and fresh air.

Critiques of modernist urbanism were developed from the "second wave" of feminism in the 1980s and 1990s. As such, they followed the major developments in urban design theory, written by authors such as Kevin Lynch, Gordon Cullen, Christopher Alexander and Jane Jacobs, who had published their most influential works in the 1960s and 1970s.[20] It is noteworthy that Jane Jacobs cast herself as offering a "woman's-eye" view of the city, rather than a feminist one, because she made what is essentially a gendered analysis, drawing on her own everyday experiences as a mother and a community activist. While urban design theory, if it may be termed such, has since flourished, few scholars in the field have made explicit connections to gendered approaches. Cuthbert incorporates gender as one of the elements in his theorizing urban design as a spatial political economy, while Oc and Tiesdell regard gender as intrinsic to their work on cities and safety.[21] Bannerjee and Loukaitou-Sideris acknowledge the significance of gender by including a chapter on feminist approaches in their major textbook on urban design, categorized under the heading "influences" rather than as a theoretical contribution in its own right.[22]

A gendered approach to urban design has therefore been pursued outside of the most visible debates in the Anglophone world. De Madariaga points out that feminist scholarship in the built environment has suffered from a lack of recognition in what have been until very recently male-dominated professions and faculties. She comments that feminist scholars in urban design and planning have had to research and write in the mainstream of their subject areas to pursue their careers, thereby holding back theoretical exploration and empirical investigation.[23] In the next section, further waves of scholarship and professional practice are discussed in explanation of the theory and practicalities of gender-sensitive design.

Gender Mainstreaming and Gender-Sensitive Urban Design

Feminist scholarship in the 1990s was supported by the European Union's policies of gender mainstreaming. The Treaty of Amsterdam of 1997 placed a requirement on all member states, in each level of government, central and local, to guarantee equality throughout all aspects of their policy operations, including policy making and policy implementation. The Treaty of Amsterdam, in effect, required mainstreaming gender equality throughout policies and processes. While the 28 member states either were or became signatories to the Treaty, the enactment varied from country to country.[24]

The UK was particularly slow, perhaps surprisingly so given that the New Labour government that held power from 1997 to 2010 was committed to equality and social liberalism. The UK's Equality Act only passed into law in 2010. Nevertheless, many aspects of equalities legislation regarding employment, maternity rights, and the internal operations of local government had been previously either on the statute book or had been adopted as good practice.

By contrast to the UK, initiatives to provide a theoretical basis and practical experimentation in gender-sensitive urban design have come from the Nordic countries, Austria, and Germany. The most consistent and coherent set of propositions relate to the neighborhood scale of development. Here the concept of the organization of the "New Everyday Life," developed in Sweden in the 1980s, is used. This concept

> is more than a theory or a critique. It is also a vision of a more harmonious society in which people are at the centre of all concerns rather than the pursuit of a quick economic fix. Finally, it is a model for organising the basic tasks of daily life in neighbourhoods in a more integrated way.[25]

In terms of physical layout, this concept is mobilized to support a mixed-use, walkable neighborhood with a high level of commercial services and social infrastructure. Mixed-use, walkable neighborhoods on the one hand provide a break with early Modernist urbanism through integrating industry, transport, and housing, yet at the same time continue the themes of early and mid-twentieth-century neighborhood planning. The difference that gender-sensitive planning and urban design offers to the mainstream is its intention to reconcile the differential needs and requirements of different genders, ages, ethnicities, levels of capability, and differential household arrangements, regarding waged work and caring and domestic responsibilities. This reconciliation is pursued through the process of development and is made an explicit subject of debate, discussion, and the adoption of design criteria and standards. Furthermore, in doing so, the power relations between females and males are acknowledged, made visible and challenged. Caring work is made visible and treated as of equal significance to waged employment. De Madariaga and Neuman argue such an agenda offers a transformative as well as an ameliorative perspective.[26]

The prospect of transformation is taken through detailed attention to the entire development process. Damyanovic[27] puts forward a model of urban development that goes through the conventional processes of survey, analysis, proposition, development and evaluation, but crucially includes a stage of visioning. User participation and involvement is an essential part of this model. Hence, at the neighborhood level, survey data includes, for example, quantitative and qualitative data on demographics, employment, caring responsibilities, educational achievement, access and mobility and so on, with the data disaggregated by gender. The process of setting design objectives and goals, through consultation and participation, includes a questioning of values and a visioning of what could be different.[28] Damyanovic invokes Lefebvre's tripartite conceptualization of the production of space to describe this level. While the subsequent process of development would run along conventional lines, this model for a gender-sensitive approach demands a final stage of evaluation to then feed back into the process.

This approach to gender-sensitive urban design differs from a woman-centered approach. Taking gender as a guiding concept avoids the essentialism implicit in seeing women and men as homogenous categories, where women are always oppressed and victimized. The intersections of social class, ethnicity, age, sexual orientation and disability can be recognized more clearly, leading to a more inclusive process.[29] This is not to suggest that a woman-centered approach has not been of value. For example, the provision of women's centers in areas of deprivation has given particular groups of women access to safe public spaces, where they can meet, socialize, organize politically and be provided with some services such as training. However, a gender-sensitive approach recognizes that certain categories of men also suffer profound disadvantages. For example, the Irish Men's Sheds Association (IMSA) provides spaces where older men, who may be experiencing ill-health, redundancy and retirement can restore their self-esteem, improve their health and enjoy some mutual support through enjoying different sorts of practical activities together.[30]

The focus on process and visioning, establishing values and exposing power relations allows for design propositions that break with precedent. In theory, one of the most extreme modernist urban forms, the skyscraper, could be an exemplar of gender-sensitive urbanism. In countries with extremely hot climates, such as Singapore and Hong Kong, where land is at a premium, building upwards provides the only opportunity to accommodate the needs of an urban population. The early twentieth-century dream of a "city in the sky" could also be gender-sensitive, if the needs of everyday life, of production and reproduction, were reconciled. "Green" high-rise towers with outdoor spaces incorporating skygardens and skycourts are being constructed. They accommodate mixed uses, residential, office, commercial and entertainment. There is no reason why they could not incorporate social infrastructure such as clinics, dentists' offices, hairdressers, nurseries, cafés and other social facilities. Architectural ingenuity could be applied to offer a variety of accommodation for different sizes and life stages of households, with a nuanced set of relationships to public and semipublic spaces. While this example is speculative, it is based on contemporary research into new types of public and semipublic spaces in high-density environments.[31]

The "everyday routines" approach to urbanism is not without its critics. Jupp reviews a discussion among political theorists and urban geographers. They make the point that encouraging women to participate in the waged labor force meshes well with neoliberal urbanism and the priority it gives to economic growth.[32] From this perspective, the promotion of gender equality by European governments provides an uneasy alliance with feminism. Jupp goes on to argue that this apparent convergence between two ideological systems, one towards equality and the other towards laissez-faire, is most evident at a theoretical level. The next section, which reviews exemplary mainstream practice in the UK, suggests that the incorporation of an "everyday routines" approach into a development process framed by neoliberal economics demonstrates incompatibility rather than convergence.

Neoliberalism and Modernism in the UK

Gender mainstreaming had an explicit impact on spatial planning in the UK through the procedural aspects of the planning system. Here planning applications were checked for their impacts on gender equality. Sadly, studies have demonstrated that this mechanism failed to encourage vigorous questioning on what form a gender-equal development might take. At its worst, gender mainstreaming in planning degenerated into a "tick box" exercise, with untrained development control officers scrutinizing planning proposals for individual schemes and developments to assess their speculative "impact."[33] While some authors have criticized gender mainstreaming for producing a new cadre of "femocrats," it seems that a lack of specialist expertise devalued the effectiveness of infusing a gender "lens" or means of analysis into the planning process.[34]

While the formal planning system recognized gender mainstreaming procedurally, many of the attributes of gender-sensitive planning were incorporated in urban design practice during the period of New Labour's "urban renaissance."[35] Britain in the 1980s had seen the advent of neoliberalism in the economic and political sphere. Its translation into urbanism led to a deregulation of planning and a withdrawal of the state from direct provision of professional services.[36] The election of a Labour government in 1997 suggested a different track, with its "Third Way" politics, which aspired to blend the dynamism of free-market, laissez-faire economics with social protection and a social program.[37] The banking and financial systems were opened and regulation reduced, a move that subsequently proved near fatal to the global economic system. Urban design, as a practice and as a new field for education and post-professional training, was given a boost by the New Labour government. Urban design as a practice meshed well with Third Way politics, because it set down broad frameworks for the development of large sites, neighborhoods and small towns while allowing a consortia of private developers and built environment professionals to bid for smaller parcels of development. The consensus that had been building up among urban design professionals—which repudiated the "object in space" approach of modernist urbanism and sought to rework and reinterpret a traditional urbanism of blocks

123

and streets, mixed-use development, high-quality public space, and the support of public transport—found favor with the government. The publication of the report "Towards an Urban Renaissance"[38] endorsed these ideas, which were then put into practice through a program of regeneration.

Although not explicitly gender sensitive in its aims and scope, the adoption of neighborhood planning in exemplar sustainable urban extensions such as Newhall, Harlow or Upton, Northamptonshire, incorporated attention to the requirements of everyday life and sought to create "mixed communities" with different sized households and tenures, which in the UK stands as a proxy for income and social class.[39] These layouts looked back to 1950s modernism from which the concept of mixed communities came but also looked forward, providing a range of housing types beyond the nuclear family. At Upton, explicit planning for and inclusion of employment uses, shops and social facilities sought to balance the needs of everyday life between home and work. The masterplan for Upton was produced through a process of Enquiry by Design, a consultative technique pioneered by the Prince's Trust. The process resulted in a more innovative master plan and the inclusion of a more generous social infrastructure. The extension, some three miles from the market town of Northampton, was planned to be a substantial development with over a thousand dwelling units, a primary school, a health center, a nursery, live-work units, commercial offices, local shops, a community center and other facilities.[40]

Upton was promoted as an exemplar development by government agencies on a number of counts.[41] These were the consultative process itself, the degree of collaboration between different government agencies and the local authority, the use of design codes, a sustainable urban drainage system, high levels of energy saving in the housing units, the provision of housing for rent for low-income groups dispersed throughout the neighborhoods, priority given to walking over driving (see Figure 7.1), the creation of local character and identity, and the quality of architectural variety in a

Figure 7.1 A Walkable Neighborhood in Upton in 2008
Source: © Marion Roberts.

Engendering Urban Design

Figure 7.2 Contemporary Housing Design in Upton by HTA LLP
Source: © HTA LLP.

low-rise, medium-density development (see Figure 7.2). The process of building it was slow, starting with the consultative process in 2001; the scheme finally achieved completion in 2017 with the creation of the high street. The infrastructure of the shops, pub and community center was included in the last phase. The development suffered first from a lack of interest from developers in the early phases, during the boom years of the early 2000s, and then from the recession following the 2008 financial crisis. While Upton was not promoted as an explicitly gender-sensitive scheme, and a full evaluation with a gender lens would be welcome, it nevertheless demonstrates the effort that government agencies in the UK have put forth to achieve and sustain mixed-use, mixed-tenure developments with a modest level of social infrastructure.

Third Way politics inhibited a widespread adoption of this model, because the involvement of the private sector in development was aimed at partially financing rental housing for lower income groups and paying for elements of social infrastructure. Professional and scholarly attention became focused on the deals and trade-offs that had to be negotiated between developers and local authorities, and the extent to which lower income groups were either included or excluded.[42] The production of mixed-income communities proceeded at a slow pace in comparison to the fast pace of urbanism associated with rapidly urbanizing countries. Furthermore, Third Way politics only provided a regulatory mechanism and framework for public transport provision, with the impact that inhabitants of these new urban extensions still had to rely on car use even though their immediate neighborhood might be walkable.

The implication is that gender-sensitive urban design and planning is reliant on a strong social welfare program and an effective and well-resourced planning system. The attention to detail required by gender audits at the start of the process, the level of consultation needed and the generous levels of social infrastructure needed to support urban layouts geared to everyday life cannot be provided without a strong public sector. These comments apply mainly to the neighborhood level. At a regional and metropolitan scale, the challenges are greater. A "city of short distances" is only possible if either the size of the city is controlled and relatively stable and if there is a well provided-for public transport system. Regional economic planning is also required to attract and distribute investment fairly throughout the country. In the period 1997–2010 in the UK, regional councils and public bodies were set up outside London, only to be abolished and dismantled when a coalition Liberal Democrat/Conservative government took over in 2010.

Greater London remains the only region in England and Wales that has a regional planning authority and a spatial plan. It is also the richest region in the UK, such that among the "chattering classes" of the media it is commonplace to refer to London as almost a different country to the rest of the UK. In the period following the 2008 financial crisis, the remainder of the UK economy has stagnated. Planning controls have been simplified and loosened. National design guidance has been withdrawn. The brief period of a rise in quality in some housing schemes is regrettably over as volume house builders focus on quantity. Even in London, the richest region, achieving design quality is a struggle because high land prices and the crisis in housing supply drive up densities and the height of buildings. The regional authority does not monitor social infrastructure, and it is left to municipalities to agree to schemes where the profits made by developers are used to fund the construction of public buildings.

Cutbacks in public expenditure had a savage impact on equalities within UK society and between the sexes.[43] It is shocking that in the UK, the sixth richest economy in the world, nearly half a million people had to ask for emergency supplies of food in the period April 2016 to April 2017.[44] While gender-disaggregated figures are not available, it seems highly likely that the most frequent users of this "service" that is a charity and not government funded are female-headed single-parent families and single men. Meanwhile the conditions of work have become harder. "Zero-hours" contracts, whereby workers are not given fixed hours of work but are reliant on an employer calling them on a day-by-day basis (so they cannot predict their income), have entered the UK labor market. At the time of writing, nearly one million people were employed on these contracts. Women under the age of 33 make up the majority of these workers.[45] It is these conditions that have led urban scholars such as Linda Peake[46] to observe that neoliberalism has stripped away the sharp distinctions between the Global North and the Global South and to refer to an urban "precariat," that is people who are marginalized and vulnerable to destitution and illness. As such, the nineteenth-century conditions that spawned modernity have returned. Yet even though there is a severe housing crisis in the UK and many are suffering from poor living conditions with overcrowding, extortionate rents, and unfit landlords, societal changes have rendered recovering the congruence between "modernity" and gender-sensitive urban design more relevant.

Day suggests that the transfer from a gendered approach to urban policy to specific urban design measures is difficult to achieve.[47] This observation is echoed by Eva Kail, whose pioneering leadership of a women's design and construction unit in the city of Vienna for over two decades provided many examples of gender-sensitive design.[48] As Damyanovic argues, there are different levels to the social constitution of gender in spatial development, from the symbolic and utopian to the day-to-day issues such as safety, mobility and access to housing and services. From a UK perspective, the crushing of even a modest experimentation in providing social infrastructure within a neoliberal framing demonstrates the value of utopian thinking, and as Jupp also argues,[49] its assertion as a legitimate mode of theorizing.

Concluding Comments

This chapter has argued that despite its critique of the Charter of Athens, gender-sensitive planning continues many of the strands of thought and practice that made up twentieth-century modernism. The idealism of seeing the built environment as constituting an integral part of the transformation of society to respond to contemporary conditions accords with the polemic stance of early and mid-century Modernists. The detailed attention paid to quotidian realities and the aspiration to raise the quality of life for all sections of the population finds resonance with the ideals of progressive Modernist architects and planners. In striving to do so, there is an acceptance of the need for guidance to ensure qualities are embedded and inscribed in the urban landscape.

Accepting guidance carries the implication of state intervention into the development process. This chapter has noted how, in the UK—the European state that pioneered neoliberal economics in the 1980s—a commitment to guidance and a drive for quality survived for less than a decade. A gendered approach is more than the proposition of what conservative commentators would pejoratively describe as a "nanny state." Gender-sensitive urban design and planning aspires to make visible the power relations between genders through processes of participation and through detailed surveys and scrutiny of evidence. Such processes are time-consuming and demand the input of professional, trained resources.

The challenges to a market-driven approach are many and interlinked. The aspiration for a "just city," which distributes spatial resources fairly among all its citizens, runs counter to laissez-faire economics and the politics of a weak state. Not only would there be public intervention in the market for land, but there would need to be a well-resourced public sector to research and manage development. Citizens would also need to be sufficiently resourced to have the time and means to take part in a meaningful set of dialogues within the development process.

In the brief review of one exemplar development in England, the chapter has noted how traditional urban forms configured in well-defined walkable streets, carefully designed public spaces, allied with a well-resourced public infrastructure, provide many of the elements needed to balance the productive and reproductive elements of everyday life and "daily routines." There has also been a tentative suggestion that this form of neo-traditional urbanism need not be the only physical and symbolic manifestation of gender-sensitive planning. More detailed research and evaluation is needed to establish how a gendered approach can be adopted and integrated into different cultures, climates and planning regimes. As the title of the chapter suggests, engendering urban design is an unfinished story. Given the obstacles to achieving it, which this chapter has summarized rather than examined in depth, the scale of the struggle should not be dismissed.

Notes

1. Howard 1985.
2. See Item 5, www.un.org/sustainabledevelopment/blog/2016/10/newurbanagenda, accessed on August 23, 2017.
3. Perrone 2016, 548.
4. Le Corbusier 1971.

5. Tummers and Zibell 2012, 525.
6. CIAM 1933.
7. Howard 1985
8. Pearson 1988.
9. CIAM 1933, para. 78.
10. Roberts 1991.
11. Bondi 1998, 164.
12. Loukaitou-Sideris 2016, 560.
13. Blumenberg 2016, 540.
14. Tummers and Zibell 2012, 527.
15. See also Part 1 of this volume.
16. Didenko, Bouryak, and Antonenko 2016 (electronic resource).
17. See for example Mayor of London 2010, 11.
18. Rowe and Koetter 1978.
19. Whitzman et al. 2013.
20. Cullen 1961; Jacobs 1961; Lynch 1960 together with Alexander 1977 and Rowe and Koetter 1978 each contributed to the foundations of contemporary urban design.
21. See Cuthbert 2006 as well as Oc and Tiesdell 1997.
22. Day 2011.
23. De Madariaga 2016.
24. As identified by EC funded COST network genderSTE. www.cost.eu/about_cost/strategy/targeted_networks/genderste, accessed on August 23, 2017.
25. Horrelli, Booth, and Gilroy 2000, 11–12.
26. De Madariaga and Neuman 2016, 502.
27. Damyanovic 2016.
28. Damyanovic and Zibell 2013, 34.
29. Reeves, Parfitt, and Archer 2012, 20.
30. IMSA, n.d.
31. Pomeroy 2014.
32. Jupp 2014.
33. Greed 2005; Reeves 2005.
34. Burgess 2008.
35. See Punter 2010.
36. Punter 2010.
37. Giddens 2010.
38. Urban Task Force 1999.
39. Bailey, Haworth, Manzi, Paranamanage, and Roberts 2006.
40. EST 2006, 3.
41. For example, the Prince's Trust, the Commission for Architecture and the Built Environment, Architecture and Design Scotland, and the Energy Saving Trust each had case studies of Upton as an example of good practice on their websites.
42. Davidson and Lees 2010.
43. The Fawcett Society tracks gender inequalities. See https://www.fawcettsociety.org.uk/ensure-women-not-hardest-hit-economic-downturn, accessed on 10 December 2017.
44. See www.trusselltrust.org/news-and-blog/latest-stats/end-year-stats, accessed on July 18, 2017.
45. Statistics from www.ons.gov.uk/employmentandlabourmarket/peopleinwork/earningsandworkinghours/datasets/zerohourssummarydatatables, accessed on July 18, 2017.
46. Peake 2013.
47. Day 2011.
48. See Irschik and Kail 2011 and Damyanovic, Reinwald, and Weikmann 2013 for more details of the progress made in the city of Vienna
49. Jupp 2014.

References

Alexander, Christopher. 1977. *A Pattern Language: Towns, Building, Construction*. New York: Oxford University Press.
Bailey, Nick, Anna Haworth, Tony Manzi, Primali Paranamanage, and Marion Roberts. 2006. *Creating and Sustaining Mixed Income New Communities: A Good Practice Guide*. York: Joseph Rowntree Foundation.

Blumenberg, E. 2016. "Why Low-income Women in the US Still Need Automobiles." *Town Planning Review* 87(5): 525–545.

Bondi, Liz. 1998. "Gender, Class and Urban Space: Public and Private Space in Contemporary Urban Landscapes." *Urban Geography* 19(2): 160–185.

Burgess, Gemma. 2008. "Planning and the Gender Equality Duty—Why Does Gender Matter?" *People, Place and Policy* 2(3).

Congress Internationaux d'Architecture moderne (CIAM), La Charte d'Athenes or the Athens Charter, 1933. Trans. J. Tyrwhitt. Paris: The Library of the Graduate School of Design, Harvard University, 1946.

Cullen, Gordon. 1961. *Townscape*. London: Architectural Press.

Cuthbert, Alexander. 2006. *The Form of Cities: Political Economy and Urban Design*. Oxford and Malden, MA: Blackwell.

Damyanovic, Doris. 2016. Chapter 11: "Gender Mainstreaming as a Strategy for Sustainable Urban Planning." In *Fair Shared Cities: The Impact of Gender Planning in Europe*, edited by Ines Sanchez de Madariaga and Marion Roberts, e-book ed. London and New York: Routledge.

Damyanovic, Doris, Florian Reinwald, and Angela Weikmann. 2013. *Manual: Gender Mainstreaming in Urban Planning and Urban Development*. Vienna: Urban Development, Vienna.

Damyanovic, Doris, and Barbara Zibell. 2013. "Is There Gender Still on the Agenda for Spatial Planning Theories? Attempt to an Integrative Approach to Generate Gender-Sensitive Planning Theories." *DisP-the Planning Review* 49(4): 25–36.

Day, K. 2011. Chapter 11: "Feminist Approaches to Urban Design." In *Companion to Urban Design*, edited by T. Banerjee and A. Loukaitou-Sideris, e-book ed. Abingdon: Routledge.

Davidson, Mark and Loretta Lees. 2010. "New build gentrification: its histories, geographies and critical trajectories." *Population, Space and Place* 16(5): 395–411.

de Madariaga, Ies Sanchez. 2016. "Looking Forward, Moving Beyond Trade-Offs." In *Fair Shared Cities: The Impact of Gender Planning in Europe*, edited by Ines Sanchez de Madariaga and Marion Roberts, e-Book ed. London and New York: Routledge.

de Madariaga, Ines Sanchez, and Neuman, Michael. 2016. "Mainstreaming Gender in the City." *Town Planning Review* 87(5): 493–504.

Didenko, Catherine, Alexander Bouryak, and Nadiia Antonenko. 2016. "Residential Housing in Kharkov (Ukraine) 1920–1935." *ZARCH Journal of Interdisciplinary Studies in Architecture and Urbanism* (5). http://zarch.unizar.es/index.php/en/issues/published-issues/number-5/residential-housing-in-kharkov-ukraine-1920-1935, accessed on August 23, 2017.

EST. 2006. *CE 195. Creating a Sustainable Urban Extension—A Case Study of Upton, Northampton*. London: Energy Saving Trust.

Giddens, Anthony. 2010. *The Third Way Revisited*. Policy Network: Globalisation and Governance. Policy Network, London.

Greed, Clara. 2005. "Overcoming the Factors Inhibiting the Mainstreaming of Gender Into Spatial Planning Policy in the United Kingdom." *Urban Studies* 42(4): 719–749.

Horrelli, Liisa, Chris Booth, and Rose Gilroy. 2000. *The EuroFem Toolkit: For Mobilising Women into Urban and Regional Development*. Helsinki: Helsinki University of Technology.

Howard, Ebenezer. 1985. *Garden Cities of To-Morrow*. Eastbourne: Attic Books.

Irish Men's Sheds Association (IMSA). "So What Is So Special About This New Type of Shed?" Irish Men's Sheds Association. http://menssheds.ie/about-us, accessed on May 21, 2017.

Irschik, Elisabeth, and Kail, Eva. 2016. Chapter 12: "Vienna: Progress Towards a Fair Shared City." In *Fair Shared Cities: The Impact of Gender Planning in Europe*, edited by de Madariaga, Ines Sanchez, and Roberts, Marion, e-book ed. Abingdon: Routledge.

Jacobs, Jane. 1961. *The Death and Life of Great American Cities*. New York: Random House.

Jupp, Eleanor. 2014. "Women, Communities, Neighbourhoods: Approaching Gender and Feminism Within UK Urban Policy." *Antipode* 46(5): 1304–1322.

Le Corbusier. 1971. *The City of Tomorrow and Its Planning* [La Ville Radieuse], 3rd ed. London: Architectural Press.

Loukaitou-Sideris, Anastasia. 2016. "A Gendered View of Mobility and Transport: Next Steps and Future Directions." *Town Planning Review* 87(5): 546–565.

Lynch, Kevin. 1960. *The Image of the City*. Cambridge, MA and London: MIT Press.

Mayor of London. 2010. *London Housing Design Guide: Interim Edition*. London: London Development Agency.

Oc, Taner, and Steve Tiesdell. 1997. *Safer City Centres: Reviving the Public Realm*. London: Paul Chapman.

Peake, Linda, ed. 2013. *Rethinking Feminist Interventions Into the Urban*. Abingdon: Routledge.

Pearson, Lynn F. 1988. *The Architectural and Social History of Cooperative Living*. London: Macmillan.

Perrone, Camilla. 2016. "Grounds for Future Gendered Urban Agendas: Policy Patterns and Practice Implications." *Town Planning Review* 87(5): 547–564.

Pomeroy, Jason. 2014. *The Skycourt and Skygarden: Greening the Urban Habitat*. Abingdon: Routledge.

Punter, John. 2010a. "The Recession, Housing Quality and Urban Design." *International Planning Studies* 15(3): 245–263.

Punter, John. 2010b. *Urban Design and the British Urban Renaissance*. Abingdon: Routledge.

Reeves, Dory. 2005. *Planning for Diversity: Policy and Planning in a World of Difference*. Abingdon: Routledge.

Reeves, Dory, B. Parfitt, and C. Archer. 2012. *Gender and Urban Planning: Issues and Trends*. Nairobi: UN-Habitat.

Roberts, Marion. 1991. *Living in a Man-Made World: Gender Divisions and Housing Design*. London: Routledge.

Rowe, Colin, and Fred Koetter. 1978. *Collage City*. Cambridge, MA: MIT Press.

Treaty of Amsterdam amending the Treaty on European Union, the Treaties Establishing the European Communities and Certain Related Acts. 1997. Office for Official Publications of the European Communities, Luxembourg.

Tummers, Lidewij, and Barbara Zibell. 2012. "What Can Spatial Planners Do to Create the 'Connected City'? A Gendered Reading of the Charters of Athens." *Built Environment* 38(4): 524–539.

Ullmann, Franziska. 2016. Chapter 17: "Choreography of Life: Two Pilot Projects of Social Housing in Vienna." In *Fair Shared Cities: The Impact of Gender Planning in Europe*, edited by I. S. de Madariaga and M. Roberts, e-book ed. London and New York: Routledge.

Urban Task Force. 1999. *Towards an Urban Renaissance*. London: E&FN Spon.

Whitzman, Carolyn, Crystal Legacy, Caroline Andrew, Fran Klodawsky, Margaret Shaw, and Kalpana Viswanath, eds. 2013. *Building Inclusive Cities: Women's Safety and the Right to the City*. Abingdon and New York: Routledge.

8

Zaha Hadid's Penthouse

Gender, Creativity, and "Biopolitics" in the Neoliberal Workplace

Igea Santina Troiani

Zaha in Thatcher's 1970s Britain

In 1972, Iraqi-born Zaha (Mohammad) Hadid (1950–2016) (Figure 8.1) moved to London to undertake her studies at the Architectural Association (AA).[1] The daughter of the artist Wajiha al-Sabunji and the wealthy industrialist and co-founder of the left-liberal al-Ahari group and National Democratic Party in Iraq, Zaha Mohammed Hadid, came from a socialist-oriented, influential upper-class family. She studied at an Iraqi convent school for Muslims, Jews and Christians in the 1960s, "[when] women were empowered and anything seemed possible,"[2] and later attended English and Swiss boarding schools before moving to London. After graduation, Hadid worked for her former AA tutors and founders of the early OMA (Office of Metropolitan Architecture), Rem Koolhaas and Elia Zenghelis, until she opened her own architectural firm (Zaha Hadid Architects, or ZHA) in 1980, after becoming a naturalized British citizen.

One year earlier, in May 1979, Margaret Hilda Thatcher (1925–2013) was elected the first female prime minister of the UK. One of two daughters of Beatrice Ethel Stephenson and the English grocer, Methodist preacher, and politician Alfred Roberts, she grew up in provincial Grantham. According to Thatcher, her father, inspired by John Stuart Mill's *On Liberty*,[3] was an "old-fashioned liberal"[4] who believed strongly in individual responsibility and financial soundness. Having lived through the Great Depression of the 1930s and coming from a frugal but reasonably well-off middle-class family, Thatcher worked her way up the socioeconomic ladder, studying chemistry on a scholarship at the University of Oxford from 1943–1947, then becoming a barrister and a politician. As prime minister, Thatcher and the movement she spawned encouraged women and men in Britain to work hard for personal gain in order to move from depending on state welfare to becoming self-sufficient and prosperous within free, neoliberal markets. Along with US President Ronald Reagan, who was elected in 1980, Thatcher embarked on a campaign to encourage privatization of property and the deregulation of industry to facilitate global free trade and free markets that promoted global competition to restore economic power and superiority to Britain.[5] It was in the context of Thatcher's newly competitive Britain, a period coinciding with the rise of feminism, that Hadid initially struggled to build her architectural practice. But through her hard work, persistence, tenacity, and fighting spirit, she finally established an architectural empire and body of work for which she became recognized as the most famous woman architect of her time.[6]

In this chapter, I undertake a reading of Hadid's professional success through the lens of neoliberalism[7] and of Hadid herself as both a product and a producer of high-end architecture in neoliberal

Igea Santina Troiani

Figure 8.1 "Zaha Hadid at her Clerkenwell loft," September 2013
Source: © Mark O'Flaherty.

global markets. My interest is in reading Hadid through the neoliberal, gender-neutral actor *homo oeconomicus*, or economic man, and as part of a "creative class." The chapter will position Hadid in relation to the lifestyle and philosophies of her former employer, Rem Koolhaas, including his laissez-faire attitude to globalization, continuous growth, and "bigness" in architectural practice. Hadid is studied here as a successful, independent, and hardworking entrepreneur marketed through extensive publicity as a woman architect and for the unique brand of one-off pieces of high-end designer architecture and products she produced. Hadid's penthouse apartment in Clerkenwell,

London (which she did not design but refurbished internally and where she resided for two and a half years from 2006 on), is used to discuss the dominance of professional life on her private sphere. How Hadid mobilizes or enacts her gender within a neoliberal lifeworld leads to a discussion of the physical impact on her own body of her prolific global jet-setting, which I read through Michel Foucault's concept of "biopolitics" and Jonathan Crary's *24/7: Late Capitalism and the Ends of Sleep*.[8] The aim of this chapter is to consider the life of this highly acclaimed female architectural practitioner, for whom work is everything, and through doing so to highlight first, how home and work spaces for "the independent woman" can change domestically; second, how corporeal consequences of neoliberalism affect the gendered body of the architectural practitioner; and third, what a successful and fulfilling life in architecture means today.

Neoliberalism, *homo oeconomicus*, and Feminism

From 1978 to 1979—the eve of the elections of both Thatcher and Reagan—Foucault examined neoliberalism through a series of lectures he delivered in Paris that considered the relationship between governmentality (or "the art of government") and the exertion of power on the body politic. In the book of the collated lectures titled *The Birth of Biopolitics*, Foucault notes the changing association between biology and politics ("biopolitics") and the powerful role that *homo oeconomicus* plays in neoliberalism.[9] According to Foucault, economic man (who can be male or female, i.e., they can be economic man or economic woman) is competitive, driven, and singularly focused on his or her work life. Most importantly, she or he is entrepreneurial, using creativity to gain a market edge in the global economy. In her reflection on Foucault's lectures and theories, political scientist Wendy Brown argues that under neoliberalism's free market advocacy, economic man "takes its shape as human capital seeking to strengthen its competitive positioning and appreciate its value."[10] Economic man today ensures that everything is for sale. Economic rationalism demands that education, healthcare, becoming pregnant, the city, architecture, design labor, and the designer are not only commoditized but also co-opted to maximize return on investment through innovation.[11]

Homo oeconomicus, regardless of her or his gender, is highly employable and productive in their labor because they are "family-free."[12] Being family-free does not mean economic man or economic woman is without a family. *Homo oeconomicus* can be married or not, partnered, or have children. If they do have children, their freedom comes from not having primary care responsibilities, thereby giving them more time to work. Economic women and economic men with children can be family-free because their partner, a nanny, an au pair, or a boarding school takes primary care responsibilities from them.

According to Brown, women occupy two roles within the neoliberal world.

> Either women align their own conduct with this truth, becoming *homo oeconomicus*, in which case the world becomes uninhabitable, or women's activities and bearing as *femina domestica* remain the unavowed glue for the world whose governing principle cannot hold it together, in which case women occupy their old place as unacknowledged props and supplements to masculinist liberal subjects.[13]

Describing Brown's economic woman in architecture, Rochelle Martin writes,

> Women who have devoted themselves solely to their careers, attaining positions of prestige in their firms, feel that they can afford total commitment only if they are not married. This echoes a belief in the traditional career path that is structured to fit the male pattern—a young man works long hours at the beginning of his career to establish his reputation and gain necessary skills and knowledge.[14]

The difference between women choosing to become *homo oeconomicus* (in its most potentially productive form) rather than *femina domestica* occurs because of their decision not to be tied down by a partner or to have children.

It is well known that Hadid chose not to marry or have children. When queried at age 58 about her private life sacrifices, she maintained it was through her free will that she devoted her life to work, not family. "I don't think one has to get married. Nor are you obliged to have children if you don't want them."[15] "You should only have children if you can give them time. If I'd stayed in the Middle East, I could have done it. The family relationships there make it easier to look after children."[16] Being family-free has allowed Hadid to become economic woman, giving all her time to focus on her career. Conversely, Hadid's personification of economic man has come at the cost of the loss of certain aspects of her gender/femininity, questioning her typicality as a woman because of independence.

Even today, the "independent woman" is atypical for architects. When Simone de Beauvoir wrote *The Second Sex* in 1949, she set out the conundrums for "the independent woman."

> There are . . . a fairly large number of privileged women who find in their professions a means of economic and social autonomy. [. . .] [As] a minority, they continue to be a subject of debate between feminists and anti-feminists.[17]

While Hadid never claimed to be a feminist and never opposed the institutionalization of architecture through any form of activism, the relationship between capitalism and feminism established in the latter half of the twentieth century is important to understand here because the freedom for women to choose work *over* family or work *and* family has implications in the world of economic commerce and power relations.

In *Working the Spaces of Power: Activism, Neoliberalism and Gendered Labour*, Janet Newman discusses the "coincidence between feminism and global capitalism."[18] She draws out two discourses on the topic in feminist scholarship, first, "how processes of 'mainstreaming' served both to acknowledge and depoliticize feminist claims; and second, how neoliberalism appropriated identity politics."[19] Newman contends that through its ability to commoditize everything and everyone for reasons of increased marketization, "feminist-inflected activism"[20] has been erased. Under neoliberalism, working women become equal players in the marketplace. As additional "human capital," they become a productive economic market opportunity that can be exploited within the enterprise culture.[21] According to Nancy Fraser,[22] feminist critiques of patriarchy opened up women to new forms of exploitation in which women's emancipation was tied to the engine of capital accumulation.

The performativity of femininity for market advantage, defined by Goodman as "professional femininity,"[23] uses women, and in this instance the creative practice and designs by a woman architect, for increased marketization. The construction of femininity as an identity is transformed by neoliberalism into "marketable commodities."[24] Feminine skills used by professional women, such as "listening, supporting and facilitating, caring and encouraging, emotional intelligence and intuition,"[25] can be used to propose "new" modes of business management, enterprise, and products. Hadid was presented to the public as a "nice" "earth mother" who could transform, because of her commitment to the highest quality of production in her office, into a "Queen of Hearts screaming, 'Off with their heads!'"[26] In "Zaha: An Image of 'the Woman Architect,'"[27] I argue that Hadid performed femininity and masculinity as required to survive and thrive in the working world. Because women architects need to behave in traditional masculinist ways at certain times, some aspects of feminine behavior can be sacrificed, lost, or devalued in the workplace, while other aspects are used in publicity as a unique selling point (USP). Going beyond that previous research, here I contend that the professional image presented by Hadid, her creative practice, and multidisciplinary design outputs are shaped by neoliberal market forces through her participation in the "creative class."

Hadid as the "Creative Class"

The persona of the architect as a creative professional is complex, being conditioned by historic constructions of the architect in the conflicting roles of "artist" and "professional." As Nancy Levinson has written,

> Central to the mystique of architecture—in life and in the movies—is the idea of the architect as a person of marked creativity, creativity so strong it can seem a primal or religious force, allowing the architect to envision what does not yet exist, and so fundamental to [her or] his identity that others cannot help but acknowledge it, with various degrees of admiration, awe, envy, and fear.[28]

For Manuel Shvartberg,

> the popular notion of "creativity" is particularly interesting because it has become a generalized imperative of neoliberal societies: creativity (and its proxies, "innovation" and "disruption") [is] seen today as an essential component of any "competitive" worker.[29]

It is because of the ability of "creativity [to] ma[k]e new worlds out of nothing" and to "measure [. . .] that productivity as a kind of surplus value relative to other inputs"[30] that economists such as Richard Florida[31] have defined the value of the "creative class," in which avant-garde architectural designers or "starchitects" such as Hadid sit comfortably.

Nowadays the architectural "creative class" commodifies design labor through product innovation and marketing. Design as "immaterial labour gets categorized, spatialized, and monetized,"[32]—the extent of which depends on the degree of "innovation" performed by the designer within the market. Market forces allow "the creative class" to operate as gender-neutral entrepreneurs to increase their market share because the USP of their product creates global demand able to increase revenue generation. According to Richard Biernacki, "Economics instrumentalizes creativity as a factor of production."[33]

In *The Image of the Architect*,[34] Andrew Saint studies architectural practices ranging from those based on artisanship to those driven by revenue generation.[35] Starting with the creative genius with a singular artisan-driven practice (Frank Lloyd Wright), Saint moves to the large corporate practice with a business model of creative genius (Louis Sullivan) collaborating with his "salesman" business partner (Dankmar Adler)[36] to the entrepreneur architect (John Poulsen) and the developer architect (John Portman).[37] Creative or designer architects are presumed to spend substantial amounts of time designing, while good commercial practices fine-tune the timelines of productivity through delegation of labor, using partners or employees' skills as efficiently as possible to facilitate fast and efficient production of architecture (ideally large-scale architecture) in a spirit of enterprise. The business-savvy architect is seen to be hardheaded and ruthless in their attitude to staff productivity, setting tight deadlines while friendly to clients to win jobs. Saint writes, "Though the managerial and artistic approaches to architecture continue generally to appear mutually opposed, in many of the biggest and most profitable practices they have happily co-existed."[38]

Even before Thatcher came to power, the Royal Institute of British Architects (RIBA) commissioned a report in 1962, *The Architect and his Office*,[39] to survey small to large private practices in search of "a good starting point for the growth of the managerial and entrepreneurial ideal in British architecture."[40] The report's conclusions were centered on economization and rationalization of production, marketization, and an observation that larger firms had the potential to design and build more and be more economically generative so as to be more sustainable in the long term.

Between 1980 and 2013, Hadid went from "being the Architect Who Never Got Anything Built to someone who can't stop building."[41] During this period, she employed ZHA Director Patrik Schumacher, who is a strong advocate of neoliberalism.[42] The shift in productivity, however, occurred

Igea Santina Troiani

mainly because of her using digital technologies to create a marketable, curvaceous architectural brand. "According to [Frank] Gehry, Hadid's greatest strength was that she created a language that's unique to her."[43] She admitted that she was "not so focused on making money," preferring to "spend time inventing architecture instead of going and getting work."[44] Architecture critic Herbert Muschamp saw, however, that failing to build the Cardiff Bay Opera House prompted Hadid to change her behavior from being difficult[45] and self-defeating, and that this brought her more supporters and clients. Because of this, she began to build, expand her business, and win prizes and commissions of increasingly large size, thereby taking a share of what was otherwise "a white, male, [starchitect] business."[46]

Recognized as the "Queen of the Curve," Hadid's rounded products and architecture were marketed as feminine-inspired curvaceousness.[47] Through inventive business entrepreneurship, Hadid created a market share in architecture, product, fashion, and jewelry design that employed futurist smoothness. In addition to her ZHA business, Zaha Hadid Design (http://zaha-hadid-design.com/) sold and still sells Hadid-designed merchandise including chess sets, candleholders, platters, vases, dinnerware, cup and saucer sets, ties, scarves, placemats, coasters, glasses, mugs, books on her work and her lithographs, a shelving system, chandeliers, and stools. Costing up to £9,999, the designer objects are produced in limited and numbered editions, directed at the collector market. Hadid designed sets for the Pet Shop Boys; collaborated with Karl Lagerfeld to design fashion installations, namely the Mobile Art Chanel Contemporary Art Container; and furniture such as the Iceberg bench (Figure 8.2) for

Figure 8.2 "Zaha Hadid's Clerkenwell loft," September 2013
Source: © Mark O'Flaherty.

the *Z-Scape Collection* for Sawaya & Moroni. She designed handbags for Louis Vuitton and collaborated with Brazilian shoe designers to produce the Melissa shoe range, and with Pharrell Williams for Adidas. Between 2005 and 2008, she designed the *Z.Car* with Kenny Schachter/ROVE, a two-person, hydrogen-powered city car with zero emissions. As she grew in notoriety, she supported and commissioned original clothing designs by elite fashion designers. She recognized that her wanting to "wear unconventional clothes" paralleled her "not at all conventional behavior."[48]

Constructions of creative genius and authorship mean that Hadid needed to establish and perform her difference, her (literal) exceptionalness, as a kind of personal brand. Since 2006, Hadid wore for special events the "one-of-a-kind" designs by Elke Walter. Mostly black, Walter's garments created a designerly, sculptural form around Hadid's body, paralleling Hadid's curvaceous sculptural architecture. Prada and Yohji Yamamoto also designed one-off pieces worn by Hadid, "and her closet was packed with Miyake, Gigli and Miu Miu."[49] Hadid's dress image as a "creative professional" was bold, playful, entirely original, and exclusive, just like Hadid's one-off designs. It is in the very nature of starchitects that they grow from a mythological narrative and are obliged to (or rewarded for) reinforcing that myth. In the spirit of true neoliberal marketing genius, Hadid's bodily image and the image of her private penthouse become ideal subjects for publicity.

Hadid's Clerkenwell Penthouse

The penthouse, as an apartment type, has mostly been analyzed in architectural literature from the standpoint of masculinity and bachelorhood as a space of play for the unmarried, family-free man. "Playboy's Penthouse Apartment," an article first published in *Playboy* magazine, for instance, was republished in *Stud: Architectures of Masculinity*.[50] It sets out how the penthouse, with its extraordinary views and its planning focused on a large seating area, bedroom, and bathroom, allowed the playboy to accentuate his independence, masculinity, and sexual performativity. *Playboy's* penthouse was marketed as a lair to court and bed women. Domestic labors such as cooking were devalued through the inclusion of a bare-minimum kitchen with only a microwave oven. The penthouse has evolved since but remains a space for singles or family-free couples that are metropolitan wealthy (to afford the views).

In 2006, one year after having completed the BMW Central Building in Leipzig, a project Douglas Spencer describes as advertising "the world view of neoliberalism in phantasmagorial form,"[51] Hadid purchased the top-floor open warehouse of a five-story loft building and converted it into her penthouse through an uncompromising vision of whiteness. Journalist Simon Hattenstone described the space as "The whitest whiteness everywhere—white floors, white walls, white ceilings, white fibreglass sculptures that double up as white sofas"[52]—even "the AstroTurf that carpeted her roof terrace" was white.[53]

In *White Walls, Designer Dresses*, Mark Wigley writes that "The identity of modern architecture seems inseparable from the whiteness of its surfaces."[54] Analyzed at length by Wigley is the French modernist architect Le Corbusier's argument, set out in *The Decorative Art of Today*,[55] for uncluttered, white-walled, well-lit, open interior spaces that allow free movement for the demands of modern life. In "A coat of whitewash, the Law of Ripolin," Le Corbusier explains that whitewashing allows people to live healthily because whiteness demands continual cleaning to remove dirt. These two explanations for "whiteness" set off an aesthetic trajectory in contemporary architecture that continues today in the work of ZHA and remains exemplified in her penthouse.

The main living room or "studio" space in Hadid's penthouse (Figure 8.3) is an unconventional, blindingly white room, often used as a gallery stage to showcase Hadid's designs and her personal collections of designer objects. Acting more as a clutter free showroom for photo shoots of her, her paintings, furniture designs, or clothing collection, "light plays an important role, courtesy of an enormous skylight that permeates the central seating area, and a wall of windows leading to the back terrace."[56] Decorated by Kazimir Malevich–inspired ZHA digital drawings, and with her Aqua table taking

Igea Santina Troiani

Figure 8.3 "Zaha Hadid's Clerkenwell Penthouse"; note Hadid's painting (on back wall) titled "Malevich's Tektonik"
Source: © Alberto Heras. Produced by Bettina Dubovsky for *Architectural Digest*, Spain, May 2008.

center stage (sometimes photographed with or without the Rifatta Bella chairs designed by William Sawaya around it), the "studio" is undomesticated and operates more as an office foyer. "There were no books, no CDs and perilously little sign of human occupation."[57]

Another small room in the penthouse was devoted to showing her "collection of Murano glass, vases, plates [. . .] consisting of different forms and colours."[58] Designer furniture, the Marshmallow sofa by George Nelson, and Tongue chair by Pierre Paulin, were positioned around the Murano glass as a perfectly controlled complement.

On another floor was Hadid's bedroom (Figure 8.4), also starkly white, with white blinds and an adjoining bathroom. Unlike the other hard-surfaced rooms that show "perilously little sign of human occupation," Hadid's bedroom contained a large double bed with cushions and cover (which she designed for the Hotel Puerta de America, 2003–2005), a flat-screen television, and a "dressing

Figure 8.4 "Zaha Hadid's Bedroom in Her Clerkenwell Penthouse"
Source: © Alberto Heras. Produced by Bettina Dubovsky for *Architectural Digest*, Spain, May 2008.

table with dozens of perfume bottles shaped into their own skyline" (Figure 8.5).[59] It also included a small black and red work desk.

Following the typical penthouse for a bachelor with reduced kitchen, Hadid's Clerkenwell apartment was kitchenless. Hadid chose to have the existing kitchen removed because "it was 'ugly.'"[60] When she did have a kitchen, she had "someone to cook" for her, but because she went "out all the time" with clients or work colleagues, she felt no need for a kitchen in her flat.[61]

Dagmar Holub notes that

> Hadid never had her own office; she would sit right in the middle of her studio for many years. Arriving late in the morning, she would sketch for an hour or so, and then begin asking to see projects, and her employees would feed her plans and renderings.[62]

Figure 8.5 "Zaha Hadid's Dressing Table in Her Clerkenwell Penthouse"
Source: © Alberto Heras. Produced by Bettina Dubovsky for *Architectural Digest*, Spain, May 2008.

As Hadid's practice grew, she gave Schumacher more autonomy to manage the Clerkenwell office. Then she would work or have meetings at her home, which was within walking distance. Her penthouse was both inside and outside the space of the office. As ZHA grew, Hadid's penthouse became a place for working, publicity, exhibition, sleeping, and bathing, when she was not traveling overseas for work.

Globalization, "Bigness," and Big Business

Architects have always been globe-trotters, "designing structures for distant lands, getting the designs approved, and overseeing construction."[63] Michael Davis notes, however, that there are key differences between architectural globe-trotting in times past and architects engaging with globalization today. Previously, architects operated mostly within a few empires, not worldwide, and this meant that while they might have been importing one empire's architecture to another country, they "did not worry about 'globalization.'"[64] In order to generate income and create new international markets, many modern architectural firms seek out architectural and city design opportunities in the global economy.

The problem of the city was integral to teaching at the AA during the 1960s and 1970s, the period when Koolhaas studied and taught Hadid. While Koolhaas was a professor at the AA, Thatcher abolished student grants, which meant that "many English students could no longer go there" and the school opened up to internationalization "with an involuntary invasion . . . by foreign students."[65]

The debate about reverence to the historical, European city (Leon Krier) versus the modern, international city (Koolhaas/Zenghelis) that began during that time has been drawn out in the work of OMA through Koolhaas's fetishism with the modern American city. In the 1990s, this grew into an uncritical fascination with the "irrational exuberance,"[66] or heightened speculative fervor, for quickly generated new cities such as those OMA worked on in Asia.

As Ellen Dunham-Jones notes, "Equating capitalism with modernization and change, Koolhaas identified early on how global capitalism created dynamic, highly speculative urban conditions that were transforming the contemporary city."[67] For Koolhaas, new global markets provided architects with both destabilization and liberation.[68] In his book *Architecture, Ethics and Globalization*, Graham Owen quotes Koolhaas, who at the time explained, "It seems clear that somehow we [architects] should be able, when given the impossibly difficult problem of designing in two weeks a city for three million people, to respond with vigor and skill."[69] Being non-judgmental of neoliberalism has allowed Koolhaas to only see the good in its doctrine, which asserts that "free markets [. . .] result in the most efficient and socially optimal allocation of resources," and that "economic globalization [. . .] spurs competition, increases economic efficiency and growth, and is generally beneficial to everyone."[70]

Some corporate and commercial architectural practices—whether starchitect or not—aspire to continuous growth in numbers of employees and offices throughout the world through building bigger projects for, ideally, bigger profits.[71] Koolhaas argues for this desire to take on as many commissions as possible through his explanation of the "interesting topic, the economics of architecture." As Koolhaas notes, "you can never say no, because there is someone behind you who will say yes."[72] Koolhaas's writings on architects engaging with big business and its virtues are a logical next step because "bigness" is the requirement of global architectural practice. "In globalized practice," starchitects have the market advantage of using "the phenomena of celebrity—capitalized upon by architectural media and the profession alike—[to] assign identity to the work as commodity of cultural capital, as branded talent."[73] So while the revenue and cost of the labor of starchitects and their designs becomes more expensive[74] and valuable in the marketplace, exploitation of low-income labor becomes accentuated. As Brown points out, the freedom of neoliberalism accentuates social inequality rather than equality, contrary to what it falsely claims.[75]

Participating in the global economy involves architects, and the construction industry in which they operate, sometimes taking commissions from authoritarian clients, or employing workers at low rates of pay. Like many other large practices that billowed in size (OMA, Norman Foster, Steven Holl, Kisho Kurokawa, etc.), conquering more and more countries with more and more projects, ZHA came under ethical criticism because of Hadid's "apparent indifference to the suffering of workers and low-income residents [affected by her projects]."[76] Hadid's "indifference" brought into question the profession's obligation towards social justice under unfettered entrepreneurism, and with it the architect's agency. Some critics, including Guy Mannes-Abbott of the group Gulf Labor have stated that "Starchitects have acted with breathtaking contempt for the lives and wellbeing of the migrant workers building their spectacular culture shops, from which they profit so handsomely."[77] But neoliberalism takes its toll on both the poorly paid and the well paid through the Foucauldian concept of "biopolitics" because neoliberalism depletes (human) resources in order to capitalize upon them.

24/7 Architectural Work Life: Wellbeing and the Self

While Margaret Thatcher was married with twin children (born in 1953, 26 years before she became prime minister), she was devoted entirely to her political working life and practiced the neoliberal long work hours, minimal sleep culture that capitalism thrives upon in order to increase productivity.

Those who worked with her claim she only slept four hours per night during weekdays.[78] Very little sleep allowed her to put into practice her belief that disciplined long hours of hard work with little rest was the avenue to personal and economic independence and freedom.

Jonathan Crary notes that "in relation to labor, [a 24/7 work life] renders plausible, even normal, the idea of working without pause, without limits. It is aligned with what is inanimate, inert, or unageing."[79] Crary claims the "features that distinguish living beings from machines"[80] are the need for pause or rest. But "24/7 markets and a global infrastructure for continuous work and consumption"[81] undermine this. Globalized architectural practice (where a firm creates architecture 24/7 across multiple time zones in multiple countries, so that a job never stops being worked on) is not questioned in architecture. On the contrary, for many practitioners it is seen as a sign of a successful, "healthy" business. But just as the bodies of construction workers are exploited under neoliberalism, I argue here that a neoliberal, 24/7 architectural work-life is corporeally detrimental to the body and wellbeing of its star-designers, including Koolhaas and Hadid.

Koolhaas's jet-setting lifestyle of flying around the world for architectural commissions was compounded by the fact he lived between two families—one based in London with his partner and original OMA founder, the painter Madelon Vriesendorp with whom he has two children, the other in Amsterdam where he lived with his (now sole) current partner, the interior and garden designer Petra Blaisse. When he was not moving between England and the Netherlands, Koolhaas lived in hotels. But his need to travel to market and expand his practice had a profound personal and physical effect on Koolhaas's life, because he almost died from injections he was required to have to undertake work in Lagos, Africa.[82] After recovering from this near-death experience, Koolhaas changed his lifestyle, swimming daily to balance his body and mind.

In Hadid's case, not having a partner, children, or care commitments allowed her to devote herself entirely to her working life, leading to her being labeled by Stuart Jeffries as a "workaholic and single . . . destined to have only one longtime companion—galloping influenza" as the price of her global travels and success.[83] Jeffries claims that at the time of his interview with a flu-ridden Hadid in 2004, after she had won the Pritzker Prize, she hadn't stopped traveling, a pattern of continuous work she sustained from the age of 53 until her sudden death at 65.

> She's just back from Vienna, where she teaches, and will be jetting off again soon to oversee her many projects. To Rome, perhaps, where her extraordinary National Centre of Contemporary Arts [. . .] is under construction. Or to Leipzig, where her offices and technical spaces for BMW's HQ will mingle white and blue collars in a hearteningly egalitarian manner. Or to Wolfsburg, also in Germany, where she's building a science centre. Or to Italy, where her Salerno ferry terminal is being thrown up.[84]

Hadid claimed her ill-health was due to all the flying she did. She explained to Jeffries, "I don't know what they put in the air on those planes, but it is really affecting my health."[85]

Continuous work becomes a recurring theme in interviews with Hadid. In his 2010 interview with Hadid, Hattenstone states that when he asked what she did to relax, Hadid seemed to have "not quite understood the question. [Hadid replying,] 'Relax? Nothing.' But with buildings on site in France and Britain and Milan and Azerbaijan and Spain and China, there's not much time for relaxing."[86] Hadid explained the problem with women nowadays was that

> now they're liberated; they look after the home, they look after the children, they look after the work and with architecture I think it's important to have continuity. It's not like nine to five, you can't just switch on and off.[87]

While Hadid designed architecture that aimed at improving wellbeing,[88] she modeled many of her staff, female and male (and as most large starchitect and commercial firms do), into a continuous pattern of long work hours. This is a work life pattern that students from "good" architecture schools are encouraged to pursue. The life pattern develops in corporate practices into working in the office well beyond the hours of nine to five, sometimes (or often) seven days a week, and with years of work without vacation, so staff are rarely at home and able to have only limited sleep.

Rather than a site of sanctuary and rest, Hadid's bedroom doubled as a place for work. Hadid would sometimes lie awake in her white-painted apartment. However, what was going through her head wasn't the usual insomniac's litany of anxiety and regrets. "No, no, I lie awake thinking about buildings. I dream about buildings quite often and I've even trained myself to work out plans in my head, not just on paper, on a computer screen."[89] Limited or no sleep allowed Hadid to achieve maximum architectural productivity.[90]

While the reasons why women leave architecture are multifarious, as Despina Stratigakos contends, women (and men) architects made in the extreme image of *homo oeconomicus* can be so driven by neoliberal and corporate values of careerism that the physical body (not only the economic body) suffers. After suffering from and being treated for bronchitis at a Miami hospital, Hadid died of a heart attack in 2016.[91] (Three years earlier, aged 87, Thatcher died at the Ritz Hotel in London of a stroke.) Survived by her brother Haytham[92] (whom she left £500,000), Hadid's total fortune worth £67,249,458 was also bequeathed to Schumacher (£500,000), her four nieces and nephews (£1.7 million), "'past, current and future employees and office holders of the companies," and the Zaha Hadid Foundation, which was set up to promote architectural education and exhibitions of Hadid's work, and other charities.[93] Her architecture practice, ZHA, of which she was sole owner, was left in trust. "In the [fiscal year ending] April 2015, Zaha Hadid Ltd turned over £48m and employed 372 people."[94] ZHA continues its global enterprise today.

Beyond Hadid's Penthouse: Modernity, Gender, and Space After Neoliberalism

While they could not be more different in their political beliefs, Hadid and Thatcher both forged extraordinary career success for modern women in their respective fields of work. The purpose of my occasional interlacing of the two women's biographies is for comparison and to position Hadid in a context not created by her but by the governance beyond, in this instance Thatcherism. Thatcher set the scene for change in Britain for women and men to become economically "independent" workers under neoliberalism. While we imagine we are in control and free to create our own identity in the modern world through the "the ideal of individualism,"[95] it is clear that "the art of governmentality" (to return to Foucault) creates a limited set of lifeworld possibilities and trajectories, most of which perpetuate class differences inculcated in us through our merging of "cultural and parental influences, normative social orders and other ingredients."[96]

The structuralization of neoliberal corporatism creates rules and limits to the spaces (private and public) and lifestyles architectural practitioners are able to occupy and enact respectively. Hadid was a product of neoliberalism and a participant producer of neoliberal production in architecture. Her "professional femininity" was co-opted by neoliberalism for purposes of marketization, creating new markets in architecture.

Hadid's model of architectural labor reaffirms women and men architects transforming into *homo oeconomicus*, family-free, 24/7 workers. Through their "not at all conventional behavior,"[97] Hadid and Koolhaas were able to redefine definitions of gender performativity through their decisions to have no partner, or more than one partner, and to juggle their unconventional, highly demanding personal lives between their offices and homes.

Hadid's penthouse is a spatial construct of her reaffirmation of the spaces to support *homo oeco-nomicus* with a large, hard-surfaced, totally white "studio" space, bedroom, and bathroom but no kitchen. The "studio" and bedroom are no longer domestic spaces for socialization and relaxation but become a site of creative architectural labor and the socialization that supports it, including meetings, the exhibition of Hadid's design artifacts, and designer branding of her and her work as product and image. Her atypical behavior translates into a kitchenless apartment. The only signs of stereotypical femininity in Hadid's penthouse are her bedside table of perfumes and her large wardrobe. Much of her apartment appears gender neutral.

The implications of Hadid's pursuit of futuristic, hygienic, sterile "whiteness" in her penthouse conceals the labor of the unseen cleaners who maintain the penthouse's whiteness and the obsessive-ness that requires its maintenance as a showroom. Hadid's penthouse doubles as the white space of the gallery that is a constant exhibition of the art and architectural designs Hadid made and collected. Like Le Corbusier's white studio spaces, Hadid's choice of white walls shows the primary and close relationship between artists and architects. It highlights the deep overlap between neoliberal work and home through the occupant/designer's aesthetic control.

Neoliberalism makes some people "see their individual lives as the project to which they largely devote themselves. A project emblematic of modern freedom."[98] But a study of interior domestic spaces "affirm[s] the centrality of relationships to modern life, and the centrality of material culture to relationships."[99] A focus on "household material culture" shows an intertwining of historic and cur-rent social, parental, and outside influences. The household objects we select and furnish our domestic interiors with, and from which we gain comfort beyond the workplace, visually allude to our aspira-tions and engagement with the outside world.

According to Aristotle, the ultimate purpose of human existence or life is the pursuit of "eudai-monia," loosely translated as happiness. In *The Nicomachean Ethics*, Aristotle argues that eudaimonia is not about short-term pleasurable sensations but is the possible outcome of the totality of one's life, how we participate in our life and play it out.[100] There is no doubt that Hadid's total devotion to a work-centered life was her choice and that she gained great satisfaction and motivation from her work, which I would contend is not driven merely by materialist ambition. But in this chapter I have shown that while Hadid's lifestyle, a lifestyle typical of most starchitects, is seen to define a successful modern woman architect's lifestyle, it can be unsustainable. A life revolving around never-ending 24/7 work, perpetual travel, living like a "gypsy, of no fixed abode,"[101] staying in the "twilight architecture of airport terminals and distant hotel rooms" (which Koolhaas describes as "junkspace")[102] more often than your home exhausts and exploits the body of the architect. Such a singularly focused lifestyle relies on a narrow view of success, depleting us of having a fulfilling total life. So while architects might like to think that architectural production is exceptional in the area of work-life balance (that our work is our life), this chapter shows that many of the neoliberal mechanisms that exploit workers in general also apply to architectural firms and their lead architects (and the subsequent construction process), perpetuating a pattern of economic inequality, oppres-sion, and abuse of human capital.

This chapter has shown the need to facilitate improved work-life balance in architectural practice, focused on the "enterprise of [an architect's] self" rather than the "self for [architectural] enter-prise."[103] It is important to be suspicious of the motives driving neoliberal practice in architecture because it can lead to the commodification and consumption of its practitioners. Neoliberalism not only co-opts its designers into making maximum profit, but can also consume them in its 24/7 work mentality. Through this study of Hadid's penthouse I have provided a reading of the modern economic woman architect (although it can also apply to an economic man architect) and her spaces through a focus on gender, creativity, and neoliberal entrepreneurship. Hadid's extraordinary successes and failures allow reflection on the cost to the architectural "body politic" for future generations of practitioners. As David Morris explains in "Free Trade: The Great Destroyer,"

> There is no question that we have converted more and more human relationships into commercial transactions, but there is a great deal to question as to whether this was a necessary or beneficial development. [. . .] We must decide which values we hold most dear and then design an economic system that reinforces those values.[104]

Notes

1. Hadid completed her studies at the AA in 1977.
2. Hattenstone 2010.
3. Mill 2015 [1859].
4. Thatcher 1995, 21.
5. While Thatcher's personality contributed a long-term commitment to "the triumph of 'free-market' economics and . . . an aggressive emphasis on the individual as opposed to community . . . the ideology which prevailed was essentially the product of . . . other actors and factors." See Gould 2013.
6. This came through her receipt of the Pritzker Architecture Prize (2014), the Stirling Prize (2010 and 2011), and her being the first woman to be awarded the Royal Gold Medal from the Royal Institute of British Architects (2015).
7. I refer to neoliberalism here as a class-based political project aimed at new capital accumulation, as defined by Harvey 2007.
8. Crary 2014.
9. Foucault 2008.
10. Brown 2015, 33.
11. Brown 2015, 31.
12. Hochschild and Machung 1989.
13. Hochschild and Machung 1989, 104–5.
14. Martin 1989, 232.
15. Hegde 2016.
16. Hadid, quoted in Holub 2016.
17. De Beauvoir 1997 [1949], 691.
18. Newman 2012, 151.
19. Newman 2012, 151.
20. Newman 2012, 150.
21. Newman 2012, 153. "Second-wave feminism's critique of welfare state paternalism slid easily into Thatcher's critique of the nanny state and welfare protection."
22. Fraser 2009, 97–117.
23. Goodman 2013, 3.
24. Goodman 2013, 3.
25. Goodman 2013, 3.
26. Hattenstone 2010.
27. Troiani 2012, 346–64.
28. Levison 2000, 27.
29. Shvartzberg 2015.
30. Biernacki 2015, 40.
31. Florida 2002.
32. Deamer 2015, xxxiii.
33. Biernacki 2015, 40.
34. Saint 1983.
35. While *homo oeconomicus* is a phrase that is not gender specific, the word *entreprendre* meaning "to do something" comes from the thirteenth-century French masculine *entrepreneur*. Because of its use in John Stuart Mill's *Principles of Political Economy*, the term became popular and was used to describe an entrepreneur as both a risk-taker and business manager. See Mill 2009 [1884].

36. Adler was a key player in moving the American Institute of Architects towards stronger business models. See Saint 1983, 172, footnote 55.
37. "In the early days Burnham was content to leave much of the designing to the talented Root, himself acting as 'the salesman.'" Saint 1983, 87.
38. Saint 1983, 95.
39. Royal Institute of British Architects 1962.
40. Saint 1983, 142.
41. Moore 2013.
42. Hadid employed Patrik Schumacher as a student in 1988. He returned to work for Hadid in 1990 and became her long-term business partner. Today he is the principal of ZHA. See Wainwright 2016.
43. Holub 2016.
44. Hadid quoted in Hadid and Duncan 2016.
45. Muschamp 2004.
46. Moore 2013.
47. Some of Hadid's buildings have been openly compared to the shape of a vagina. See Wainwright 2013.
48. Holub 2016.
49. Holub 2016.
50. Sanders 1996.
51. See Spencer 2016, 84–94.
52. Hattenstone 2010.
53. Holub 2016.
54. Wigley 2001.
55. Le Corbusier 1987 [1925].
56. Woodward 2013.
57. Woodward 2013.
58. Woodward 2013.
59. Hattenstone 2010.
60. Hadid quoted in Hattenstone 2010.
61. Hattenstone 2010.
62. Holub 2016.
63. Davis 2009, 122.
64. Davis 2009.
65. Koolhaas 1996a, 235.
66. Dunham-Jones 2014, 150–71.
67. Dunham-Jones 2014,150.
68. Koolhaas 1996a, 232–9; Koolhaas 1996b.
69. Koolhaas, quoted in Owen 2009, 1.
70. Korten 1996, 184.
71. Mander 1996, 315–21 defines the "Eleven rules of corporate behavior" as (1) The Profit Imperative; (2) The Growth Imperative; (3) Competition and Aggression; (4) Amorality; (5) Hierarchy; (6) Qualifications, Linearity, and Segmentation; (7) Dehumanization; (8) Exploitation; (9) Ephemerality and Mobility; (10) Opposition to Nature; and (11) Homogenization.
72. Koolhaas quoted in Lubow 2000.
73. Owen 2016, 62.
74. Hadid's buildings were recognized for being costly designer objects/products, targeting the high end of the architectural market.
75. Brown 2015, 107.
76. Owen 2016, 50.
77. Mannes-Abbott 2015, quoted in Owen 2016, 50.
78. Sir Bernard Ingham, Thatcher's Downing Street press secretary, quoted in de Castella 2013: "She slept four hours a night on weekdays. I wasn't with her at weekends. I guess she got a bit more then."
79. Crary 2014, 9–10.
80. Crary 2014, 14.
81. Crary 2014, 3.
82. See Lubow 2000, "Last year, he [Koolhaas] was forced to 'go completely nothing' after he underwent 15 vaccinations in preparation for a visit to Lagos. 'The 14th injection went wrong and I developed meningitis and almost died,' he says."

83. Jeffries 2004.
84. Jeffries 2004.
85. Jeffries 2004. Hadid also traveled to teach in the Graduate School of Design at Harvard University, the University of Illinois, Columbia University, and Yale University.
86. Zaha Hadid in Hattenstone 2010.
87. Zaha Hadid in Hattenstone 2010.
88. Hadid designed the Maggie Centre in Fife, opened 2006, around ideals of calmness for wellbeing.
89. Hadid quoted in Holub 2016.
90. This model is seen to be the way towards acquiring reputational capital.
91. Hegde 2016.
92. Hadid's brother, Foulath Hadid, died in London in 2012.
93. Booth 2017.
94. Booth 2017.
95. Miller 2011, 286. Miller's research was done in collaboration with his Ph.D. student in anthropology, Fiona Parrott.
96. Miller 2011, 295.
97. Holub 2016.
98. Holub 2016, 285.
99. Holub 2016, 287.
100. Aristotle 2004.
101. Holub 2016, "Zaha described herself as a gypsy, of no fixed abode with memories in her childhood home."
102. Rem Koolhaas quoted in Adams 2006.
103. Kelly 2016.
104. Morris, "Free Trade: The Great Destroyer," in Mander and Goldsmith 1996, 224.

References

Adams, Tim. 2006. "Metropolis Now." *Observer*, June 25. www.theguardian.com/artanddesign/2006/jun/25/architecture1, accessed on May 12, 2017.

Aristotle, ed. 2004. *The Nicomachean Ethics*. Edited by Hugh Trednnick, translated by J. A. K. Thomson. London: Penguin Classics.

Biernacki, Richard. 2015. "The Capitalist Origin of the Concept of Creative Work." In *The Architect as Worker: Immaterial Labor, the Creative Class, and the Politics of Design*, edited by Peggy Deamer, 30–43. London: Bloomsbury Academic.

Booth, Robert. 2017. "Zaha Hadid Leaves £67m Fortune, Architect's Will Reveals." *Guardian*, January 16, 12.49 GMT. www.theguardian.com/artanddesign/2017/jan/16/zaha-hadid-leaves-67m-fortune-architects-will-reveals, accessed on April 7, 2017.

Brown, Wendy. 2015. *Undoing the Demos: Neoliberalism's Stealth Revolution*. New York: Zone Books.

Crary, Jonathan. 2014. *24/7: Late Capitalism and the Ends of Sleep*. London and New York: Verso.

Davis, Michael. 2009. "Has Globalism Made Architecture's Professional Ethics Obsolete?" In *Architecture, Ethics and Globalization*, edited by Graham Owen, 121–132. London and New York: Routledge.

Deamer, Peggy. 2015. "Introduction." In *The Architect as Worker: Immaterial Labor, the Creative Class, and the Politics of Design*, edited by Peggy Deamer, xxvii–xxxvi. London: Bloomsbury Academic.

De Beauvoir, Simone. 1997 [1949]. *The Second Sex*. London: Vintage.

De Castella, Tom. 2013. "Thatcher: Can People Get by on Four Hours' Sleep?" *BBC News Magazine*, April 10. www.bbc.co.uk/news/magazine-22084671, accessed on April 15, 2017.

Dunham-Jones, Ellen. 2014. "Irrational Exuberance: Rem Koolhaas in the Nineties." In *Architecture and Capitalism: 1845 to the Present*, edited by Peggy Deamer, 150–171. London and New York: Routledge.

Florida, Richard. 2002. *The Rise of the Creative Class: And How It's Transforming Work, Leisure, Community and Everyday Life*. New York: Basic Books.

Foucault, Michel. 2008. *The Birth of Biopolitics: Lectures at the College de France, 1978–79*. Basingstoke: Palgrave Macmillan.

Fraser, Nancy. 2009. "Feminism, Capitalism and the Cunning of History." *New Left Review* 56: 97–117.

Goodman, Robin Truth. 2013. *Gender Work: Feminism After Neoliberalism*. New York: Palgrave Macmillan.

Gould, Bryan. 2013. "Margaret Thatcher's Contribution to Neoliberalism." *London Progressive Journal*, April 12. http://londonprogressivejournal.com/article/view/1463/margaret-thatchers-contribution-to-neoliberalism, accessed on April 29, 2017.

Hadid, Zaha, and Jane Duncan. 2016. "Knowing Zaha a Little Bit Better: Zaha Hadid's Blend of Hands-on Design and Business Skills Makes Her a True Role Model." *RIBA Journal* 123(February): 3. www.ribaj.com/culture/knowing-zaha-a-little-bit-better.

Harvey, David. 2007. *A Brief History of Neoliberalism*. Oxford: Oxford University Press.

Hattenstone, Simon. 2010. "Zaha Hadid: 'I'm Happy to Be on the Outside.'" *Guardian*, October 9. www.theguardian.com/artanddesign/2010/oct/09/zaha-hadid, accessed on April 25, 2017.

Hegde, Sushma. 2016. "Zaha Hadid, 'Queen of the Curve' Dies of Heart Attack." April 1, 05:39 PM. https://twitter.com/sush7482, accessed on April 7, 2017.

Hochschild, Arlie with Anne Machung. 1989. *The Second Shift: Working Parents and the Revolution of Home*. London: Piatkus.

Holub, Dagmar. 2016. "Zaha Hadid's World of Fluid Freedom." May 31. www.designersatelier.co.uk/dagmars-articles/zaha-hadid-s-world-of-fluid-freedom/, accessed on April 15, 2017.

Jeffries, Stuart. 2004. "Maybe they're scared of me." April 26. www.theguardian.com/artanddesign/2004/apr/26/architecture/, accessed on December 10, 2017.

Kelly, Peter. 2016. *The Self as Enterprise: Foucault and the Spirit of 21st Century Capitalism*. London: Routledge.

Koolhaas, Rem. 1996a. "Architecture and Globalization." In *Reflections on Architectural Practices in the Nineties*, edited by William Saunders, 232–239. New York: Princeton Architectural Press.

Koolhaas, Rem. 1996b. "Understanding the New Urban Condition: The Project of the City." *GSD News*, Winter/Spring.

Korten, David C. 1996. "The Mythic Victory of Market Capitalism." In *The Case Against the Global Economy*, edited by Jerry Mander and Edward Goldsmith, 183–191. San Francisco: Sierra Club Books.

Le Corbusier. 1987 [1925]. *The Decorative Art of Today*. New York: John Wiley & Sons. First published as co-authored with Amédée Ozenfant in 1925.

Levison, Nancy. 2000. "Tall Buildings, Tall Tales: On Architects in the Movies." In *Architecture and Film*, edited by Mark Lamster, 11–48. New York: Princeton Architecture Press.

Lubow, Arthur. 2000. "Rem Koolhaas Builds." *The New York Times Magazine*, July 9. www.nytimes.com/2000/07/09/magazine/rem-koolhaas-builds.html, accessed on May 12, 2017.

Mander, Jerry. 1996. "The Rules of Corporate Behavior." In *The Case Against the Global Economy*, edited by Jerry Mander and Edward Goldsmith, 307–322. San Francisco: Sierra Club Books.

Mannes-Abbott in [N.a.]. 2015. "What can architects do about workers' rights in the Gulf?" *Icon*. www.iconeye.com/architecture.features/item/11715-what, accessed May 21. In Owen, Graham. 2016. "'I Have No Power': Zaha Hadid and the Ethics of Globalized Practice." *Candide: Journal for Architectural Knowledge* 10 (December): 41–64.

Martin, Rochelle. 1989. "Out of Marginality: Toward a New Kind of Professional." In *Architecture: A Place for Women*, edited by Ellen Perry Berkeley and assoc. ed. Matilda McQuaid, 229–236. Washington, DC: Smithsonian Institution Press.

Mill, John Stuart. 2009 [1884]. *Principles of Political Economy*. Abridged and edited by J. Laurence Laughlin. New York: Project Gutenberg e-book.

Mill, John Stuart. 2015 [1859]. *On Liberty, Utilitarianism and Other Essays*, 2nd ed. Edited by Mark Philp and Frederick Rosen. Oxford: Oxford University Press.

Miller, Daniel. 2011. *The Comfort of Things*. Cambridge: Polity.

Moore, Rowan. 2013. "Zaha Hadid: Queen of the Curve." *Guardian*, September 8.

Morris, David. 1996. "Free Trade: The Great Destroyer." In *The Case Against the Global Economy*, edited by Jerry Mander and Edward Goldsmith, 218–228. San Francisco: Sierra Club Books.

Muschamp, Herbert. 2004. "Woman of Steel: Getting Her Architecture Build Was Zaha Hadid's Most Formidable Challenge." *New York Times*, March 28.

Newman, Janet. 2012. *Working the Spaces of Power: Activism, Neoliberalism and Gendered Labour*. London: Bloomsbury Academic.

Owen, Graham, ed. 2009. *Architecture, Ethics and Globalization*. London: Routledge.

Owen, Graham. 2016. "'I Have No Power': Zaha Hadid and the Ethics of Globalized Practice." *Candide: Journal for Architectural Knowledge* 10(December): 41–64.

Royal Institute of British Architects. 1962. *The Architect and His Office: A Survey of Organisation, Staffing, Quality of Service and Productivity Presented to the Council of the Royal Institute on 6th February 1962*. London: Royal Institute of British Architects.

Saint, Andrew. 1983. *The Image of the Architect*. New Haven, CT and London: Yale University Press.

Sanders, Joel. 1996. *Stud: Architectures of Masculinity*. Princeton, NJ: Princeton Architecture Press.

Shvartzberg, Manuel. 2015. "Foucault's 'Environmental' Power: Architecture and Neoliberal Subjectivization." In *The Architect as Worker: Immaterial Labor, the Creative Class, and the Politics of Design*, edited by Peggy Deamer, 181–205. London: Bloomsbury Academic.

Spencer, Douglas. 2016. *The Architecture of Neoliberalism: How Contemporary Architecture Became an Instrument of Control and Compliance*. Bloomsbury Academic: London.

Thatcher, Margaret. 1995. *The Path to Power*. London: Harper Press.

Troiani, Igea. 2012. "Zaha: An Image of 'The Woman Architect.'" *Architectural Theory Review* 17(2–3): 346–364.

Wainwright, Oliver. 2013. "Zaha Hadid's Sport Stadiums: 'Too Big, Too Expensive, Too Much Like a Vagina.'" *Guardian*, November 28. www.theguardian.com/artanddesign/2013/nov/28/zaha-hadid-stadiums-vagina, accessed on April 25, 2017.

Wainwright, Oliver. 2016. "Zaha Hadid's Successor: Scrap Art Schools, Privatise Cities and Bin Social Housing." *Guardian*, November 24. www.theguardian.com/artanddesign/2016/nov/24/zaha-hadid-successor-patrik-schumacher-art-schools-social-housing, accessed on May 14, 2017.

Wigley, Mark. 2001. *White Walls, Designer Dresses: The Fashioning of Modern Architecture*. Cambridge, MA: MIT Press.

Woodward, Daisy. 2013. "Top 10 Architects' Homes." *AnOther*, June 22. www.anothermag.com/art-photography/2809/top-10-architects-homes, accessed on April 25, 2017.

Part 3
Socialism and Beyond

Introduction

Socialism thrust itself onto an agrarian Russian peasant society via revolution and the overthrow of the ruling monarchy in 1917. In the resulting Soviet Union, a small cadre of political elites determined economic and social policies designed to forcibly modernize the country both physically and socially through, among other things, rapid industrialization, wide-ranging housing policies, and a stated gender egalitarianism that was designed to provide the maximum number of workers for the new state. It was only after World War II, with the carving up of Central Europe into an eastern and a western sphere, that the Soviet Union expanded its influence, determining policies across a band of countries that stretched from Estonia in the north to Bulgaria in the south, scooping up countries as varied as East Germany (the former German Democratic Republic, or GDR) and Hungary along the way. Part 3 focuses on the post-war experience of socialism in the Soviet Union and the GDR before turning to post-socialist experiences in eastern Germany, present-day Russia, and Hungary.

In her chapter on "communist comfort," Susan E. Reid explores how Soviet citizens in the Khrushchev era of the 1950s and 1960s were encouraged to appropriate their new, state-provided prefabricated apartments through making them "cozy" in state-sanctioned ways. Women especially were targeted in state-sponsored lessons on homemaking practices designed to reflect a "modern" post-war Soviet citizen. Christine Hannemann, by contrast, explores the standardization of the Soviet-inspired housing estates of the GDR as a form of genderized, spatialized modernity, in which the dwelling became a manifestation of a classically patriarchal concept based on nuclear families, with women taking on full responsibility for housework in tiny, uniform apartments.

Turning to the post-GDR era, Katja M. Guenther explores how women in one eastern German city appropriated two very different built environments—one in the historic center, and one in a modernist, socialist housing estate—contrasting former state-sponsored gender ideals by creating feminist spaces in a grassroots effort with little mainstream or state support. Olga Tkach, in a further chapter on post-socialist life, examines elder care in Russia today. Analyzing the changes and challenges in domestic life that such care requires, especially for women, who bear the brunt of care work, she concludes that both a lack of adequate state-provided options and cultural bias against institutionalized care continue a genderized perception of care work as a "family issue." Finally, Nóra Séllei explores a contemporary Hungarian Film, Ágnes Kocsis's *Fresh Air*, to trace how two very different women—one middle-aged and one just savoring adulthood—inhabit and interact with spaces originally created as part of Hungary's socialist modernization.

While the first two chapters highlight some of the discrepancies between socialist theory and practice, especially with regard to modernization and women's roles in society, the latter three chapters point to the challenges and tribulations that women have faced as they adapt their socialist experiences and spaces designed for ideals of egalitarianism to the realities of their new post-socialist lives.

9

Communist Comfort
Socialist Modernism and the Making of Cozy Homes in the Khrushchev Era

Susan E. Reid

The theme of this chapter—"communist comfort" and the propagation, in Soviet mass housing of the 1950s–1960s, of a socialist modernist aesthetics of domesticity—is rich with oxymoron.[1]

First, modernism was assigned, in the Cold War's binary model of the world, exclusively to the capitalist "camp." "Socialist" and "modernist" [in the sense of the modern movement in architecture—Ed.] were positioned as incompatible. Although the conjunction of political and artistic radicalism in Soviet Russia of the 1920s is well known, the renaissance there in mid-century of socialist modernism was unthinkable in Cold War terms and has only recently begun to be taken seriously.[2]

The second contradiction is that between modernity—along with its cultural manifestation, modernism—and domesticity. Modernity and dwelling have been assumed to be at odds. Pathologized by Walter Benjamin and others as a nineteenth-century petit bourgeois addiction, domesticity and the need for comfort were to be shrugged off in favor of the freedom to roam. Homelessness, and not "homeyness," was the valorized figure of modernity.[3] In revolutionary Russia of the 1920s, the modernist avant-garde designed portable, foldaway furniture more suited to the military camp; to supplant the soft, permanent bed of home was part of their effort to make the material culture of everyday life a launch pad to the radiant future.[4] Adopting unchallenged the established cultural identification between women and the bourgeois home, modernism's (and socialism's) antipathy for domesticity was also gendered, indeed misogynistic. Its wandering, exploring hero was imagined as male, while the despised aesthetics of dwelling from which he walked away—entailing ornament, concealment, confinement and the use of soft, yielding materials, particularly textiles—was construed not only as bourgeois but as feminine.[5] That the condition of modernity was to be restless, transient and constantly on the move became, however, a source of regret and nostalgic yearning for some after the destruction and dislocations of World War II. The philosopher Martin Heidegger, writing in 1954, lamented that in modern industrial society people had lost the capacity to dwell. It was particularly hard, he found, to be at home and at peace in modern housing, which is produced as a commodity or allocated by state bureaucracies, because we no longer reside in what we or our kin have built through generations but instead pass through the constructions of others.[6]

Third, the terms "communist comfort" or "socialist domesticity" are also, at first sight, as self-contradictory as "fried snowballs." "Cozy" is unlikely to be the word that leaps to mind in association with Soviet state socialism, and least of all with the standard, prefabricated housing blocks that were erected at speed and in huge numbers in the late 1950s, which form the material context for this study. Indeed, home life has hardly been the dominant angle from which to study the Soviet

153

Union.[7] Socialism as a movement was traditionally associated with asceticism, sobriety and action; with production rather than consumption and rest; and with the collective, public sphere rather than the domestic and personal. Meanwhile, nineteenth-century socialist and feminist critiques, including those of Marx and Engels, identified the segregated bourgeois home as the origin of division of labor and alienation and a primary site of class and gender oppression. The bourgeois institutions of home and family, based on private property bonds, were supposed to be cleared away by the Bolshevik Revolution of 1917. John Maynard Keynes, speaking of left-leaning students in the 1930s, noted that "Cambridge undergraduates were never disillusioned when they took their inevitable trip to 'Bolshiedom' and found it 'dreadfully uncomfortable.' That is what they are looking for."[8]

If disdain for bourgeois domesticity was a stance sympathizers expected of the Soviet Union, neglect of human comfort was also one of the charges its detractors leveled against it. In the Cold War, Western accounts of the Soviet Union tended to focus on political repression and military hardware paraded in the public square. When Soviet Russian everyday life was addressed at all, it was in negative terms of lack and shortage, embodied in queues for basic necessities. Stereotypes of drab, austere comfort*lessness* reinforced the West's indictment and "othering" of state socialism as the polar opposite of the Western, capitalist model of ever-increasing comfort, convenience and individual, home-based consumption.[9] The Soviet home, if it came within the sights of Western attention at all, stood—by contrast with Western prosperity—for the privation of Soviet people, their *lack* of privacy, convenience, choice, consumer goods and comforts. Alternatively, it figured as a flaw in the Soviet system's "totalitarian" grasp, its Achilles' heel, a site of resistance to public values, of demobilization in face of the mobilization regime's campaigns, and even a potential counterrevolutionary threat to the interventionist state's modernizing project of building communism. Thus one Western observer surmised in 1955:

> If Russians got decent homes, TV sets and excellent food wouldn't they, being human, begin to develop a petit-bourgeois philosophy? Wouldn't they want to stay home before the fire instead of attending the political rally at the local palace of culture?[10]

Others asked,

> Can the Soviet system afford to allow a larger-scale retreat from the world of work and of collectivity to the world of cozy domesticity on the part of its women? . . . A type of socialism might appear that proved to be so pleasant that the distant vision of communism over the far horizon might cease to beckon.[11]

You could have *either* communism *or* comfort, according to this model, *not* "comfortable communism" or "communist comfort." Home and utopia—no-place—were incompatible. If comfortable homes were deemed by Cold War observers to exist at all in the Soviet Union, then it was as spaces where the official utopia of the party-state was contradicted, as sites of potential resistance and as the germ of state socialism's potential undoing.

Associated with women's traditional roles as preservers of continuity with the past, with conventional female qualities, and handed-down practices and know-how, the home's status as the recalcitrant last frontier of state modernization was gendered. Thus Francine du Plessix Gray, a Russian émigré resident in the US, represents the Soviet Russian home as an antidote to official Soviet values:

> Moscow's other havens, of course, were and remain the homes of friends: Those padded, intimate interiors whose snug warmth is all the more comforting after the raw bleakness of the nation's public spaces; those tiny flats, steeped in the odor of dust and refried *kasha* in which every gram of precious space is filled, every scrap of matter—icons, crucifixes, ancient wooden

dolls, unmatched teacups preserved since before the Revolution—is stored and gathered against the loss of memory.[12]

There, in Gray's view, authentic Russian qualities were preserved in spite of over 60 years of Soviet rule. Paramount among these is an apparently timeless and indomitable "national tradition of *uyutnost'* [*sic*]: that dearest of Russian words, approximated by our 'coziness' and better by the German *Gemütlichkeit*, denotes the Slavic talent for creating a tender environment even in dire poverty and with the most modest means." *Uiutnost'* is "associated with intimate scale, with small dark spaces, with women's domestic generosity, and with a nurturing love."[13] It represents, in Gray's elegiac account, continuity between generations of women. The womb-like embrace of the Russian home is defined by explicit antithesis to an inhospitable, inhuman public sphere and to the chiliasm and collectivism of official ideology and culture. The opposition between the home and the Soviet state's official modernizing project, which entailed rupture with the past, is represented in a series of negative/positive dyads that map onto the dichotomy public/private: bleak/snug, raw/cooked (or even re-cooked!), loss/gathering and storing, and amnesia/memory. The striving, future-oriented public project of Soviet modernity, based on Enlightenment values of rationality, science and progress, is opposed by home as a warm, hospitable, unchanging and *essentially feminine* domain of authentic human relations materialized in "scraps of matter" and unmatched teacups. The home appears as a hermetic cell, apparently untouched by historical contingency and the ruptures of the twentieth century. Padded by the accumulation of memories and memorabilia, dust and clutter, it is insulated from ideological intrusion, scientific and industrial progress—in short, from modernity and its specific Soviet mode (Figure 9.1).

Figure 9.1 Reconstruction of a Stalin-Era Domestic Interior in the Sillamae Ethnographic Museum
Photo: Dmitrii Sidorov.

One can almost hear Benjamin scream in his sleep, for the private realm Gray celebrates here is the stuff of any Marxist modernist's worst nightmares (dreams a Freudian might analyze in terms of fear of being absorbed back into the womb).[14] In such a space, even Faust might succumb to the temptation to abide and give up the quest for enlightenment. For many Soviet commentators, too, in the late 1950s and early 1960s, the period on which we focus here, the resilience of what they considered a regressive aesthetics of hyper-domesticity and bad taste among the Soviet people aroused fear of loss of political consciousness. But was the contradiction between domesticity and socialist modernity irreconcilable? Or could home be accommodated in the modernist, socialist utopia? If so, what should it look like? In what follows we will examine ways in which specialist agents in the Khrushchev era (1953–64) sought to overcome the contradiction between domesticity and socialist modernity and to delineate a modern socialist aesthetics of the domestic interior. As Gray indicated, the key Russian term in the image of homeliness is *uiut*, a word that encompasses both comfort and coziness or snugness.[15] Intelligentsia experts redefined *uiut* in modernist terms. Did popular practice follow their prescription? Or did the material practices of *uiut* remain closer to a retrospective ideal of "homeyness," as defined by anthropologist Grant McCracken, as the expression of a search for continuity, stability and a sense of rootedness?[16] In the concluding section we will turn briefly to whether the aesthetics of modern housing and modernist advice were embraced, resisted, subverted or accommodated by primarily female homemakers in their homes.

An Obsession With Domesticity

In Boris Pasternak's 1957 novel, *Doctor Zhivago*, Lara (whose name references the Lares), watching a young girl construct a home for her doll in spite of the dislocations of the Revolution, comments on her instinct for domesticity: "Nothing can destroy the longing for home and for order."[17] Unlike Pasternak's heroine, we should not take for granted, as some ahistorical, biological given, that the longing for home and order, for comfort and coziness, are mandatory for dwelling, that these are essentially feminine instincts, or that domestic spaces need necessarily be projections of the occupant's self. Along with other apparently natural categories, such as childhood, the identification of home with comfort has to be historicized as the cultural product of particular historical and material circumstances. The emergence of the concept of comfort, like that of the "private" to which it is closely aligned, was associated with industrialization, the rise of the bourgeoisie, and the segregation of the home as a private sphere and women's domain, to which the exhausted male could return from the world of work and public life.[18] In the Soviet Union, the conditions for this historical phenomenon were supposed to be swept away: bourgeois capitalism, women's confinement in the segregated home, and the idea of home as a fortress of private property values.

Yet Soviet culture of the Khrushchev era, it is no exaggeration to say, became *obsessed* with homemaking and domesticity. This was a matter both of authoritative, specialist practice and intelligentsia discourse on one hand, and of popular culture and experience on the other. Soviet public discourse, whether intentionally or as an unintended effect, naturalized coziness and comfort as essential attributes of home life and as a legitimate concern of the modern Soviet person, especially women. The domestic interior was presented not only as a place to carry out everyday reproductive functions, but also as a site for self-projection and aesthetic production, where the *khoziaika* (housekeeper or, more literally, mistress of the house) displayed her taste and creativity. It involved making things for the home and exercising judgment in selecting, purchasing, adapting and arranging the products of mass serial production. What were the historical conditions for the preoccupation with home decorating?

The material premises for the production of domesticity began, at last, to be provided on a mass scale in the Khrushchev era. The shift of priorities towards addressing problems of mass living standards, housing and consumption had already begun before Stalin's death, at the Nineteenth Party Congress in October 1952, but the pace intensified from 1957 as the provision of housing and consumer goods became a pitch on which the post-Stalin regime staked its legitimacy at home and abroad. A party decree of 31 July 1957 launched a mass industrialized housing construction campaign: "Beginning in 1958, in apartment houses under construction both in towns and in rural places, economical, well-appointed apartments are planned for occupancy by a single family."[19] The results would transform the lives of millions over the next decade. Some 84.4 million people—over one-third of the entire population of the USSR—moved into new accommodation between 1956 and 1965, while others improved their living conditions by moving into modernized or less cramped housing.[20] The construction of new regions of low-rise, standard, prefabricated apartment blocks fundamentally altered the urban—and even rural—environment, extending the margins of cities and accelerating the already rapid process of urbanization. Above all, the new flats were designed for occupancy by single families, in place of the prevailing norm of collective living in either barracks or communal apartments (Figure 9.2).

A range of bureaucracies and specialist agents of the party-state were necessarily involved in shaping the interior, given the mass scale and industrial methods of construction and the accompanying shift towards serial production of consumer goods to furnish them. At the same time, the increased provision of single-family apartments could, it was feared, foster regressive, particularist mentalities and loss of political consciousness. It was necessary therefore to work actively to forestall this. Thus architects and designers, trade specialists, and health, hygiene and taste experts were concerned not only with shaping the material structure of apartments, but with defining how people should furnish and dwell in them.

Figure 9.2 Standard Apartment Block From the Early 1960s in St. Petersburg
Photo: Ekaterina Gerasimova, 2004 for the project "Everyday Aesthetics in the Modern Soviet Flat." © Susan E. Reid.

But, the obsession with homemaking and the terms of domesticity was also shared by the millions of ordinary citizens who moved into new or modernized living quarters, or who could realistically expect to do so in the near future. Moving in, they had to furnish and decorate their homes and accommodate their standard structures to their own lives, while at the same time accommodating themselves to the new, unfamiliar spaces. As public discourse acknowledged—and some specialists regretted—the making of the domestic interior was a work with multiple authors. Architects and planners—accredited experts interpreting the priorities and briefs of the party-state—might set the parameters and determine the material structures of the house, but their power was not total. In making housing into home, it was the occupant who had the last word, however limited her room for maneuver.[21]

The negotiations between these agencies, differently positioned in relation to the authority of the state and to the material fabric of the individual home, were conventionally gendered as between a masculine public sphere and its experts on one hand, and female private interests and their amateur practices on the other.[22] Women were construed as the primary consumers and homemakers, and as such, their dominion and expertise within the domestic domain were acknowledged as a force to be reckoned with; women had to be brought on board the socialist modernizing project if the new flats were not to become nests of regressive, petit bourgeois mentalities.[23] A note of caution should be sounded, however: the gendering of the public/private, professional/amateur relationship did not necessarily correspond straightforwardly to an architect's biology. In the USSR, architecture was not so exclusively a male preserve as in the West at this time, although a gender hierarchy of specialisms did operate within it: female architects appear to have been more likely to get ahead in regard to the traditionally feminine sphere of the domestic interior than in large urban planning projects and prestigious public buildings, and the authorities who wrote on home decorating often had female names. But however they may have behaved in their personal lives, in their professional practice these female architects generally espoused the same dominant norms as their male colleagues (however patriarchal) rather than adopting eccentric or dissenting positions based on their gendered experience. A systematic examination of the gender relations within the architectural and newly emerging industrial design professions lies beyond our scope. Here, we will explore attempts both in authoritative discourse (historically and conventionally masculine), and to a lesser extent in everyday practice and experience (conventionally and in practice the domain of women) to transcend the antithesis of home comfort and communism.

Already in the 1920s, Russian avant-garde artists aspired to bring the Revolution "home" by purging from people's everyday environments things that they regarded as the trappings of petit bourgeois private life and materialization of alien class values—ornate furniture, embroidered tablecloths and antimacassars, silk lampshades and useless ornaments—and to replace them with rational, functionalist, industrial, modern and "socialist" material culture.[24] However, beginning in the discourse of the 1930s and increasing in the post-war period of demobilization and reconstruction, tablecloths, napkins and silk lampshades were reinstated as attributes of female virtue and markers of Soviet progress, signifying a modern, urban, cultured way of life (*kul'turnost'*). Vera Dunham has argued, on the basis of fictional representations, that the relegitimation of bourgeois cultural values and aspirations, as materialized in a retrospective aesthetics of homemaking and accumulation of possessions, constituted part of a "big deal" with the new Stalinist "middle class."[25] There is little historio-ethnographic research on the popular material culture of the Stalinist period by which to judge the relation between representations and reality here. But Western visitors to the Soviet Union in the 1950s also frequently commented on the overstuffed "Victorian" interiors they encountered.[26] This may be put down, in part, to a tendency to seek out confirmation of the Cold War stereotypes they brought with them (notably the contradiction between official claims for progress, based on heavy industry, and the backwardness of living conditions and consumer goods). However, the resilience or resurgence of this aesthetic through the 1930s and 1940s at least as an ideal (if not as a reality)[27] is also suggested by the fact that after Stalin's death in 1953, a laundry list of bad taste almost identical to that which the Constructivists had sought to purge in the 1920s became once again the object of a widespread campaign of anathema.

The Khrushchev era is best known for de-Stalinization—that is, for efforts to reform the most coercive aspects of Stalinism and dismantle its institutionalization of privilege. But it also saw a revitalization of utopian elements of Marx's thought concerning such matters as the relation between people and things, and the self-actualization of the individual; a restoration, in the fields of philosophy and the spatial arts, of Constructivist ideas of the 1920s about the nature of a socialist material environment, and about the relation between art, industry and everyday life; and a rapprochement with international modernism in architecture and design.[28] For cultural de-Stalinizers or modernizers, those prerevolutionary teacups and ancient wooden dolls, to which the émigré Gray clung, were the monsters brought forth by the Sleep of Reason; this home life a millstone around the neck of progress. What was needed was to fight for the liberation of man—and more particularly, given the conventional gendering of this discourse, *woman*—from the bondage of things, and to foster social forms of everyday life. Aesthetic reformers and utopian ideologues called to battle against what they disparaged as the "cult of acquisitions" and "the striving at any cost to build a nest."[29] They cast the aesthetic they repudiated as "petit bourgeois" or "philistine," a throwback to tastes and private property mentalities that were engendered by pre-revolutionary social and property relations. At the same time, this aesthetic was implicitly identified with Stalinism and, as such, an object of de-Stalinization along with the other excesses and perversions of the Revolution.[30] Taste War was a form of "class struggle" for hegemony by a sector of the intelligentsia against the bureaucratic middle-class privileged in the Stalin era, whom the aesthetic reformers cast as uncultured parvenus.[31]

The Great Transmigration

The surge of attention to housing and homemaking in the late 1950s took place against the background of a chronic housing shortage exacerbated by wartime destruction. The majority of Soviet people in the post-war period lived in barrack-type accommodation or in communal apartments, where an entire family or more would be cramped into a single room, sharing a kitchen and bathroom—if they existed—with many other families. One was lucky to have so much as a "cot-place" in a hostel—one's "private" space limited to the bed one slept in. Overcrowded, insanitary conditions and homelessness were recognized as the cause of major social and health problems.[32] Tuberculosis was rife. Recent research on post-war Soviet society presents a picture of peoples on the move, in flux, characterized by social dislocation.[33] Nomadic mobility might be embraced by modernism as a defining aspect of modernity, and it was romanticized in Soviet literature and film in the Khrushchev era (especially in regard to the Virgin Lands campaign).[34] But in life rather than fiction, after half a century of dislocation, rupture, flux and instability, to be homeless was associated with disorder, instability and marginality, and with elements of the population that eluded organization. Lack of a legitimate, registered place of residence made one a misfit in Soviet society, a marginal type (*limitchik*) or person of no fixed abode; it disenfranchised and deprived one of civic personality.[35] The dialectics of home and homelessness, dislocation and dwelling, disenfranchisement and becoming a fully self-realized Soviet person were at the center of public discourse and mass individual experience in the Khrushchev era.

In the late 1950s and early 1960s, Soviet society was on the move once again, on such a scale that the satirical magazine *Krokodil* likened this mass relocation to the "Great Transmigration of Peoples."[36] The modern-day "transmigration" was distinguished from earlier waves in Soviet history, however (resulting from collectivization, from the enforced deportation of whole ethnic groups under Stalin, and from war), in that it was caused not by the *loss* of a home, but precisely the opposite; it was a mass homecoming. People were on the move because they had been allocated new homes thanks to the intensive mass housing campaign. The fundamental changes in people's everyday environment and way of living were arguably more momentous for more people than better-known political events such as Khrushchev's

Susan E. Reid

"secret speech" to the Twentieth Party Congress in 1956, in which he denounced Stalin's excesses.[37] A new revolution took place in Soviet daily life in the late 1950s, as Svetlana Boym notes, "consisting of resettlement out of communal apartments to outlying 'micro-districts' where people were able to live in separate, albeit state-owned apartments—many for the first time in their lives."[38] As a result, the newly founded industrial design journal *Tekhnicheskaia estetika* (Technical Aesthetics) declared, "The creation of the interior of the contemporary urban apartment has become one of the most important state problems".[39] If, in the comfort of one's new home, one opened a newspaper or turned on the television (a rapidly expanding leisure pursuit and medium in terms of airtime and number of sets in the early 1960s), one would get the impression that the entire Soviet population was on the move, running around worrying about color schemes and the choice of wallpaper, furniture and lampshades (Figure 9.3).[40]

Figure 9.3 "New Furniture for New Flats"
Source: *Ogonek*, 1959.

Communist Comfort: Socialist Modernism

The new housing regions of the Khrushchev era were notorious for having sacrificed aesthetics to engineering, function and economy. One of Khrushchev's first decisive interventions, less than two years after Stalin's death in 1953, had been to denounce the extravagant, monumental style of Stalinist architecture and, seemingly prompted by modernizers in the architectural profession, to declare ornament a crime (or at least, a Stalinist "excess").[41] This implied a rapprochement with modernist principles of design dictated by function, materials and mode of production. Architects and engineers looked back to indigenous Constructivism and across the Iron Curtain to recent international developments, in particular efforts to solve the housing shortage throughout post-war Europe through system building and factory prefabrication.

The imperatives of thoroughgoing industrialization, speed and economy of construction, combined with still primitive technologies of prefabrication, required rethinking the requirements of dwelling: eliminating architectural ornament, reducing the dimensions to a functional minimum and minimizing or eliminating auxiliary spaces such as corridors.[42] Standardization was paramount: the use of a limited number of type-plans, standard modules and unembellished elevations. As Russian design historian Iurii Gerchuk describes the new flats:

> "Comfort" was also conceived in very frugal terms. . . . In the standardized housing designs accepted and applied at the turn of the 1950s–60s, ceiling heights were reduced to 2.5 m [about 8 ft.]. In the tiny, cramped flats the space for auxiliary rooms was cut to the bare minimum. The size of the kitchen was reduced from 7 to 4.5 sq. m [75 sq. ft. to 48 sq. ft.] and it opened directly off the living room. The toilet was combined with the bathroom. Convenience was sacrificed not only to save space but to simplify the construction process.[43]

Functional and featureless, the new housing estates may not count today among the monuments of world architecture, worthy of preservation orders or heritage status. On the contrary, the new flats—known as *khrushchevki* (or worse, *khrushcheby*, a contraction of "Khrushchev" and "slum")— are widely regarded as a shameful aspect of the Soviet legacy, to be purged as quickly as growing prosperity allows.[44] Yet, notwithstanding the monotonous standardization and minimum specifications of the new flats, as well as numerous shortcomings in their design, materials, construction and finish, the improvement in millions of people's quality of life cannot be overestimated. As one elderly woman told me, they are "monuments in our hearts."[45] Most significantly, the flats were planned and designed for occupancy by single nuclear families, and were equipped with mains plumbing, inside toilets and kitchens. Many people in interviews conducted in 2004–7 still recall the joy of having their own bathroom or kitchen, however diminutive, for the first time, rather than sharing with up to 50 others.[46] After a lifetime under the gaze of nosy neighbors, it was bliss to have one's own four walls to shelter one from their view, even if poor soundproofing meant you could still hear everything going on next door.[47] Along with the spread of television and car ownership, the single-family apartments have been seen, with reason, as setting in train a process of "privatization" of Soviet life. It was the state that provided the premises for this process, which was one of a number of paradoxical unintended side effects of its policies.[48] While tenants had no legal rights of ownership or disposal, and one person's apartment shared the same standard plan as another's, it was nevertheless a place to settle at last and call one's own.

Mediating the Move: Giving Public Meaning to the Separate Apartments

Housing construction gave visual dramatization to the party–state's commitment to raising living standards of the many, not just the few. The intensive housing campaign was kept in the public eye and mind through two linked themes that corresponded to the dichotomy of mobilization and settling/

dwelling: first, Happy Housewarming; and second, the process of making and maintaining a home in these government-issue spaces. Thereby the new housing was invested with public meaning as a gift that demonstrated the party-state's solicitousness for its people, and as a symptom of progress towards communism and of its superiority over capitalism.[49]

The theme of Happy Housewarming, *novosel'e* (lit. "new settling"), celebrated the dynamic, ritualized, transformative moment of moving in: turning the key in the new door for the first time, crossing the threshold, inviting friends and family inside to share one's happiness. "Housewarming is becoming the most common festival genre," declared the state newspaper *Izvestiia*.[50] "'New home—new happiness,' as the folk saying goes," began an article in the labor newspaper *Trud* in late 1959, titled "Happy Housewarming." It focused on a newly built five-story apartment block into which 56 families of workers and employees of a Moscow machine-building factory had just moved. "Bright, cozy [*uiutnye*] rooms. A joyful, festive bustle. Human happiness takes up stable and permanent residence here."[51] Housewarming was represented as a joyful rite of passage, associated with brightness, coziness, stability and happiness, through which the new Soviet person would emerge, remade, in readiness for the new life under communism. It was a mass, common celebration, but unlike the major public festivals and parades in city streets and squares, this one was celebrated by individual families with their friends and kin in their own homes.[52]

The longer dureé and mundane, everyday *process* of settling in, making home and dwelling in the new flats was harder to dramatize and keep in the public eye than the ritual moment of changing places. How to maintain public consciousness about the relation between this blessing in the present day and the future perfection to come? How to keep people mobilized for the construction of communism once they had settled in?

The duration and daily round, or *byt*, commonly designated "private life," was articulated and reproduced again and again as the subject of public discourse through pervasive advice. Allegedly in response to readers' demand, the popular press, advice manuals and television offered instruction on how to arrange one's furniture in the unfamiliar spaces, how to select elements of décor and find an appropriate color scheme, or how to maintain the new types of surface such as linoleum floor covering.[53] Housewarming and settling into one's new flat became the theme of much early television programing. Broadcasts with titles such as "For Family and Home" or "Help for the Housewarmer" represented this as the "typical" experience of the present day, presuming their viewers were either already watching in a new flat or dreaming of receiving one soon. New norms of "contemporary" (that is, modernist) "good taste" and "rational," function-based use of space were propagated through representations of model interiors in the form of ideal home exhibits and show homes, photographs and artists' impressions.[54] Advice also sought to introduce industrial, Taylorist standards of time-and-motion efficiency and mechanization into the domestic workspace of the kitchen, thereby integrating the home (via the space most implicated, in the past, in its regressive role of enslaving and stultifying women) into the public modernizing project.[55] *Izvestiia*'s "home and family" page, a significant innovation introduced in July 1959, printed articles such as that cited above, titled "New Home—New Way of Life." It argued that as millions of Soviet citizens moved to new, well-appointed apartments, it was necessary to develop the new discipline of *domovodstvo*, domestic science, "to teach how best to furnish [the new apartment] to make it more *uiutno* [cozy] to live in": "Rational nutrition, knowledge of how to dress comfortably and beautifully, and how to furnish one's apartment: all this has to be taught."[56]

Advice, addressed primarily to the female homemaker, was often a matter of informing her about consumer goods that were supposed to be available, if not now, then in the near future, and how to choose, teaching her to make wise and tasteful purchases: that is, to be a skilled consumer. New consumer goods, including furniture and appliances for the home, which were promised in the 1959 economic plan, created new civic tasks and responsibilities for the housewife; they imposed the duty of rational consumption and correct choice. Advice also functioned as socialist realism, often

Communist Comfort: Socialist Modernism

implying a greater degree of choice than was available. According to a television program on home furnishing:

> Many of us, when we receive a new apartment, want to change the color of the walls or put up wallpaper, all the more since now in Moscow you can get any kind of wallpaper you want. But, comrades!—in buying wallpaper it is necessary to make the correct choice of color, pattern and texture.[57]

Many community activities in new neighborhoods were also directed towards homemaking and making things for the home, in addition to communal campaigns to improve and maintain the external appearance of blocks of flats, monitor use of balconies, plant the yards and create children's playgrounds. The local housing administration might organize carpentry clubs for adults, exhibitions of houseplants and flower arranging, and cookery competitions, in addition to amateur art and photographic circles, musical ensembles and radio clubs.[58] Community activities included not only homecraft classes for women and girls, but also home-oriented activities for men such as woodwork. In one neighborhood carpentry club, each member began with repairing furniture, making small things such as shelves, bedside cabinets and kitchen tables, and then moved on to making more complex items such as bookshelves, TV tables or sideboards. The members got so keen that they began to spend all their free time there.[59] Such clubs aimed to attract men to keep them off the street, away from the bottle and from antisocial behavior or "hooliganism," while engaging them in activities associated with the home and fostering pride in making or mending things for their domestic space.[60] Thus, if homelessness deprived one of civic personality, becoming a homemaker (*novosel*) conversely made one a Soviet person and respectable member of the community, participating in the "typical" experience of the present day.

Although activities associated with the home were a recognized way to integrate potentially antisocial men, advice on creating the domestic interior and keeping a rational, modern, tasteful home was still addressed predominantly, if not exclusively, to women, constructing them as the primary homemakers. Men might participate, but theirs was an auxiliary role. In 1955, a *Novyi mir* reader lamented that while she and her husband might discuss how to furnish their new marital home, in practice it fell to her alone.[61] There was also a conventional gender division of skills and materials. As the community activities confirmed, work that involved structures and hard materials such as wood or metal was appropriate to men, while the aesthetic decisions, attention to surfaces, decorative touches and soft furnishings belonged to women. Making *uiut* was women's responsibility, both in authoritative discourse and, recent interviews suggest, in everyday understandings. Men are absent altogether in many of the retrospective narratives of homemaking told by women.[62] As possibilities for private car ownership grew in the course of the 1960s, cars and the spaces associated with them and their time-consuming maintenance—yard, street and garage—increasingly became an alternative male homosocial space to which men retreated to escape the home and its obligations.[63] There were some exceptions, however, where homemaking became a shared family bonding experience. One woman who had moved into a newly completed house in 1960 with her parents when she was 12 years old recalled how the whole family was involved in the process of turning the new apartment into "home." "We tried to make it nice and cozy in the apartment." Although still young, she, too, had wanted their new home to be beautiful, and actively participated in making the interior. So did her father. Forty years on, this woman still took great pride in the furniture her father had made for the family home. "Dad did everything himself!" He had made a sideboard, beds and kitchen cabinets with his own hands. He also laid linoleum. She, meanwhile, brought home fabrics for curtains and soft furnishings to decorate the interior as soon as she was old enough to work in a shop.[64]

At the same time as publicists ascribed the key role in making and maintaining the home to women, they also regularly emphasized that this was only part of their identity. If, in the past, a good

163

housekeeper was one who devoted all her time and energy to domestic affairs, the Soviet woman was not confined to her domestic role, but was also active in production and social life, which were vital to her self-realization. The conclusion the experts drew from this was not, or rarely, that the gendered division of labor in the home should be restructured but, rather, that the housewife's domestic responsibilities now included the introduction of an industrial model of efficiency or scientific management into domestic space and domestic routines. She must learn to rationalize housework—to see to it, for example, that the kitchen was arranged rationally—so that it did not absorb all her energy and time.[65]

The sheer volume of press articles on taste, advice manuals offering "help for the housewarmer," and television programs about how to make home in the new standard apartment, as well as exhibitions of new furniture designs, together focused attention on interior decorating and home improvements and rendered these a normal and even normative concern and leisure pursuit for the modern Soviet person. Even zealous Marxists who were committed to reviving the spirit of the Revolution began to endorse coziness as a legitimate aspiration along with the principle of one-family flats. For example, philosopher of material culture Karl Kantor—one of those active in reviving the suppressed legacy of the Constructivists, including the industrial modernist aesthetic they proposed as part of a reconfiguration of the relationship between people and things under socialism—distanced himself from the extreme asceticism of the 1920s. At that time, wrote Kantor,

> the struggle for the new way of life against the old bourgeois-philistine domesticity sometimes took on the form of a struggle against material comforts in everyday life, against the striving to have a separate apartment and make it comfortable. Attention to the external side of life was disparaged as little short of a betrayal of the Revolution.

However, Kantor corrected, "the liberation from enslavement to things which the Revolution brought with it, could not mean liberation from things themselves; the striving to collective forms of life does not presuppose a rejection of individual forms of dwelling."[66] "The individual should not be lost sight of behind society, nor the family for the collective." One-family flats were not per se counter-revolutionary, and concern with furnishing them was not to be confused with bourgeois fetishism or the consumerism identified with the capitalist West, he concluded. "No-one today would dream of accusing a person of betraying revolutionary ideals by taking an interest in how to furnish an apartment in a new building comfortably and beautifully."[67]

Accommodating Industrial, Standardized Construction

The main task facing Soviet citizens moving into the new flats, public discourse acknowledged, was to overcome standardization: how to create *uiut* in a mass-produced, concrete, prefabricated box. It was assumed that the new occupants would need and want to customize and interiorize their look-alike, industrially mass-produced living space to fit it to themselves. The official media encouraged the idea that the raw interiors of the prefabricated concrete blocks had somehow to be processed and worked over, to make them into cozy homes. While standardization was acknowledged as a necessary condition of industrial production, it was represented more as a problem that needed to be mitigated, rather than as a virtue on account of its homogenizing potential (with the exception that the elision of differences in living conditions between city and country was represented as a major benefit of extending such housing construction to rural areas). Responses to a 1968 survey of residents who had moved into new Moscow apartments in 1966 indicated that they saw standardization as antithetical to *uiut*. Twenty-one out of 85 respondents named this as a defining characteristic of the interior, and 20 percent said they did not want their apartment to look like their neighbors' apartment.[68] Many thought lack of choice of consumer goods exacerbated the problem of standardization of interiors. One wrote: "Standard, lack of *uiut*: if one were to judge from the contemporary home it might seem that everyone has identical characters." Conversely, *uiut* must presumably require a degree of individualization.[69] It was *uiut* that made the difference between mere living space and a lived-in place, home.[70]

The problems and paradoxes of making "private life" in both public and commodified housing—as a common problem of industrial modernity identified by Heidegger, for example, in his 1954 essay— have received much attention from anthropologists, design historians and others in different national contexts since at least the 1980s. They emphasize that residents do not passively submit to the given structures and the norms they materialize. As Marianne Gullestad, Daniel Miller and Nicky Gregson demonstrate, even if most people no longer reside in homesteads built with their own hands but in commodified or state-allocated housing, "most do engage in sets of activities that are about seeking to constitute these dwelling structures as appropriate sites of habitation for them"; that is, they accommodate those spaces to their own lives, a process that includes both appropriation and compromise.[71] Studies of social housing in Britain, including Daniel Miller's important analysis of how residents of council housing overcame alienation, and Judy Attfield's work on how residents of rented public housing in Harlow New Town made themselves "at home" in its modernist, open-plan structures, focus on the material practices of appropriation of space.[72] McCracken, in his 1989 study of North American owner-occupied homes, similarly found that individuals sought to mediate their relationship with the larger world, "refusing some of its influences, and transforming still others" by creating "homeyness."[73] At issue is the possibility of exercising agency, control over boundaries and what Wolfgang Braunfels calls "the freedom to participate in the design of one's own urban living environment."[74]

The possibility of such agency and mutuality has often been denied by Western commentators in regard to the Soviet context. Writing of Soviet mass housing, historian Blair Ruble cites Braunfels with the gloss: "The Western alienation from residence . . . was magnified in the Soviet Union, where all planning is done for strangers."[75] Yet Soviet residents were expected to make a large input into transforming the concrete shell of their apartment into a livable space. Experts writing in the popular and specialist design press in the Khrushchev era emphasized the labor of making the standard apartment into home, that is, the agency and responsibilities of the homemaker. People did not passively move in, or "consume" the apartment as a ready-made, fully finished commodity, either in representations or in practice. If only because of shortcomings in the construction and finishing (rather than as a matter of state policy and design), this required personal investment of effort, resourcefulness and skill on the part of the homemaker: people actively made the standard space into home through their purchases, taste decisions, and by making or adapting things. Many manufactured goods also presupposed the need for work on them by the user.[76] Advice literature assumed the necessary input of the tenant and included very practical directions on how to adapt or fit cupboards, equipment and labor-saving devices.[77] Some authors even acknowledged that choosing and arranging things for the new home was a semiotic process: an exercise in self-expression and differentiation. That one could and even *should* inscribe one's individuality upon the plan and walls of the new apartment and make the givens of the standard architecture personally meaningful and communicative of self-image and social position was an unexamined premise of much advice literature.[78]

Nevertheless, the degree of individualism envisaged was not only narrowly circumscribed by the physical structure of the building and by shortcomings of centrally planned production and distribution (shortages and lack of choice of consumer goods); it was also subject to widely promulgated norms and regimes of taste. Residents were not supposed to exercise their agency just anyhow, but in ways that accorded with the ideal identity of the Soviet person and with modernist norms of good taste, rationality and hygiene—as these were defined by intelligentsia experts. Communism presupposed voluntary self-regulation, the internalization of and submission to social norms, and accommodation of personal desires to the best interests of the collective. And this consciousness extended beyond "communist morality" to matters of aesthetics.

Susan E. Reid

Rationalization and Modernization of *Uiut*

Uiut remained the central term in discussions of domesticity in the context of Khrushchev-era remodernization. There was much ambivalence, however, about the will to coziness, and this was often expressed in misogynistic terms. Anxieties included, as Christine Varga-Harris summarizes, "trepidation over the rise of bourgeois desires, tastes and mores (gendered female); the emasculation of men within the household (metonymic of the emasculation of the working class as a whole, gendered male); and the disruption of social relations."[79] Even as the search for *uiut* was legitimated and encouraged, the dream of a private realm such as Gray presented, seemingly insulated from the public sphere and from the forces of modernization and sovietization, was denigrated as "philistine" and regressive by authorities on the interior. Thus Boris Brodskii, writing in the new design journal *Dekorativnoe iskusstvo SSSR* (*Decorative Art of the USSR*), condemned the idea of home "as an island where one could build one's personal [*lichnuiu*] life 'as I like.'" Repudiating this conception of privacy as a throwback to "petit bourgeois" values of the past, he, like other taste reformers, firmly identified it with a particular treatment of domestic space and residue of clutter: ornate furniture, embroidered tablecloths and antimacassars, and silk lampshades. These trappings of "private life" not only failed to cement relations between people, Brodskii argued, but were fetishes that alienated them. "The struggle with philistinism is the struggle for man's liberation from the bondage to things, which . . . appear to him more significant (and thence more beautiful) than they in fact are."[80] A direct, seemingly causal link was assumed between things of a particular quantity, kind and style and a home-centered mentality, segregated from the public sphere. Such possessions chained people—especially women—to the home and inhibited their engagement with public life. The assumption that padded and cluttered interiors stultified the individual was rationalized by reference to hygiene and women's enslavement to the unproductive labor of dusting, which (along with the "kitchen slavery" Lenin had denounced as the source of women's stereotypical lack of political consciousness) prevented them from realizing themselves as unalienated, all-round individuals.[81]

Brodskii and other publicists sought to distinguish the proper, socialist attitude towards the new apartments from the bourgeois "home-is-my-castle" mentality in aesthetic terms. To prevent the new one-family apartments from becoming nests of particularist and regressive mentalities, their solution was to promote a modernist style known as the "contemporary style." The contemporary interior must be fitted to assist the process of opening up everyday life into the public sphere, to make the boundary between public and private transparent and shift the center of gravity of everyday life out of the room or flat and into the public sphere. Thus, while *uiut* remained vital to homemaking in the "new type of small-scale apartment for one family," and continued to be identified with "the idea of an attentive female hand," the challenge was to produce it in ways that did not reproduce petit-bourgeois relations. *Uiut* must be redefined in austere, modern, hygienic terms explicitly opposed to those of the bourgeois and Stalinist past and appropriate to the present period of scientific technological revolution and imminent transition to communism.

What this modernized socialist *uiut* repudiated was clear already to the reader of the highbrow literary journal *Novyi mir*, cited above: it was *not* "rubber plants with dusty leaves, nor a herd of marble elephants put out to pasture on one's dressing table 'for good luck.'"[82] If in the past, *uiut* was identified with confinement and encumberment, entailing the use of all means "to *reduce* living space, associated with cushions and drapes, dust and warmth," the (ideal) contemporary Soviet person, by contrast, strove for her home to be hygienic and spacious, to have more light and fresh air, to be furnished simply and conveniently with simple and beautiful objects of everyday life.[83] Modern beauty and comfort under socialism were the product of reason, dictated by function, convenience, hygiene, openness, stylistic homogeneity and good taste. Prime targets for the modernist broom were the accumulation of dust, clutter, useless ornaments and mementos—that is, precisely those things which, in Gray's and other accounts of the (traditional) Russian home, were most closely

Communist Comfort: Socialist Modernism

identified with its female occupant and the status of the interior as an expression of femininity, identity and memory.

Among the most unforgivable taste gaffes were ersatz rugs hung on walls on which swans, kittens, tigers, women's heads or portraits of important people were painted in oils.[84] These painted rugs, sold at stations and provincial markets, were a form of popular culture that had emerged in spite of the state, filling a vacuum left by the command economy. Producing them was a way in which collective farm peasants supplemented their income (Alexander Solzhenitsyn referred to them in his *One Day in the Life of Ivan Denisovich*, 1962).[85] Not only did such artisanal production occupy a shady area outside the state's economic planning and regulation, but it also undermined the intelligentsia's cultural hegemony. That it eluded quality control and aesthetic regulation by the professional artistic organizations was a matter of concern to taste experts in the late 1950s, as well as to the Komsomol (Party Youth League).[86] Moreover, to use rugs as wall hangings was a traditional practice of Russia's hinterland (while all negative practices tended to be branded indiscriminately as "petit bourgeois," their origins were often also rural and regional or ethnic), and attacks on this practice were part of a condescending *mission civilisatrice* by modernizing urban professionals to reform and indeed westernize popular practice. An architect instructed *Rabotnitsa*'s women readers in 1959:

> rugs hung on walls—that's bad! They are spread on the floor to muffle footsteps and keep feet warmer, or are hung behind a divan without a back so that one does not lean against the cold wall and also above the bed so as not to scratch the wall. Don't get carried away with rugs because they collect dust.[87]

Other traditional uses of textiles were also inappropriate. A manual for teenage girls, *Podruga* (Girlfriend), showed "before" and "after" images of the same interior done in retrograde and good contemporary taste, where the key difference was the disappearance, along with little ornamental marble elephants, of the scalloped and embroidered cloths that covered every surface in the "before" image (Figure 9.4). "Many imagine that the more napkins, lampstands and sideboards, the cozier [the interior]," lamented a Novosibirsk taste manual, also for young people—but they were wrong! Along with beds covered in satin bedspreads and mountains of white, lace-covered cushions, intended proudly to proclaim the family's prosperity, they merely betrayed the householders' lack of discernment and failure to understand what beautifies and what spoils the appearance of the home (Figure 9.5).[88] Because all spaces and furniture in the modern Soviet flat had to serve multiple functions and the bedroom became the living room during the day, the bed had to double as a settee, not be set apart as a site of display of wealth.[89] Dust-catching and unhygienic, embroidered cloths were a throwback to petit bourgeois models of domesticity and homebound femininity. They were associated with the trousseau and the private property functions of the bourgeois and feudal family; with ostentatious display; with irrational, time-wasting practices of housekeeping; and with an anachronistic conception of women's role, tied exclusively to the home. Embroidery testified to the confinement and oppression of women in the past, who were treated as chattels to be exchanged accompanied by a trousseau, rather than as free, equal and entitled to develop their individuality, as they were supposed to be under socialism.[90]

Textiles had been used traditionally in Russian culture, including in the communal apartment from which many occupants of new flats had moved, to screen and conceal: nets hid intimate life from neighbors, valances around bedsteads concealed the things stored beneath them, and curtains were widely used to hide messy shelves.[91] Victor Buchli insightfully analyzes the ways in which, in the Stalin period, embroidered cloths were deployed to "individualize" space and for the purpose of "interiorization" or "privatization" and "withdrawal."[92] The approved modernist aesthetics of transparency

Figure 9.4 "Good" and "Bad" Taste in Home Furnishings. From M. Chereiskaia, "Zametki o khoroshem vkuse"
Source: *Podruga* [Girlfriend], Moscow 1959, 220–21.

was conceived, by contrast, as opening up the "private" interior onto the public space beyond, and maximizing space and light.

> Don't clutter up the apartment with things. Let there be more space and light. Every item of furnishing you acquire must be essential for you. . . . Choosing furniture don't buy cumbersome things, [. . . they] make it crowded and look very old-fashioned. The most important thing is stylistic unity.

Communist Comfort: Socialist Modernism

Figure 9.5 Kazan' Interior
Photo: Sofia Chuikina, 2005, for the project "Everyday Aesthetics in the Modern Soviet Flat." © Susan E. Reid.

If you have only just started to equip your apartment then get contemporary, light, elegant and, at the same time, very simple furniture [Figure 9.6].[93]

Writing in *Rabotnitsa*, the magazine for women workers, architect Irina Voeikova, a frequent commentator in the popular press on how to furnish homes, instructed new homemakers to purchase furniture that left as much free space as possible. Thus "huge bedsteads on high legs disappear from our lives along with patterned valances," for "everyone knows that one doesn't hang valances nowadays." They

169

Figure 9.6 "Contemporary" Furniture (imported from Finland), Mid-1960s, St. Petersburg
Photo: Ekaterina Gerasimova, 2004, for the project "Everyday Aesthetics in the Modern Soviet Flat." © Susan E. Reid.

were to be replaced by "convenient divans and chairs that easily transform into beds without taking up a lot of space."[94]

Others exhorted: "Contemporary furniture must be convenient to use, compact, light and without carving or moldings (scrolls, cornices), which are hard to wash and clean" (Figure 9.7). "Contemporary lamps must be simple, light, hygienic, modest and elegant."[95] Functional zoning was recommended, applying the modernist principle of spatial separation of functions in conditions where a single room had to serve multiple purposes. But this could be achieved without blocking off areas and daylight with solid partitions, by using differentiated color schemes or light, open shelving units. Voeikova recommended a light frame with vertical cords above a narrow trough for plants. Trained to climb up the cords, the vegetation would form a light trellis, which corresponded with the fashionable aesthetics of transparency, lightness and irregular vertical lines.

Communist Comfort: Socialist Modernism

Figure 9.7 Model Interior in the "Contemporary Style"
Source: O. Baiar and R. Blashkevich, *Kvartira i ee ubranstvo*, Moscow, 1962.

Home as a Site for Display of Cultural Level and Aesthetic Discernment

One of the sins associated with embroidered cloths and lace pillows was that they served purely for display and were non-functional or even inhibited the proper use of an object or space. Was there any place at all for displays, mementos, ornaments and other decorative elements in the socialist modern interior? In his 1954 call for industrialized construction, Khrushchev had condemned non-functional decoration in architecture as an expensive waste of resources, a luxury associated with Stalinist "excess," which was unwarranted in modern socialist society. Signaling Soviet architecture's reorientation towards international modernism, with its minimalist aphorisms such as "less is more" (widely attributed to modernist architect Ludwig Mies van der Rohe) and its identification of ornament with criminality, degeneracy and regression to a primitive evolutionary stage (Adolf Loos), the First Secretary's intervention (reinforced by subsequent decrees against "excess") rendered all forms

171

of decorative art aesthetically and morally suspect.[96] Specialists extended the prohibition on "superfluous" decorative elements to the domestic interior; these must be reduced to the minimum or eliminated, along with anything else that served purely the purpose of display or concealment. "Some think that decorations create *uiut*. That's not quite right. . . . To create genuine *uiut* in the apartment the main thing is convenience for people."[97]

As in earlier modernist discourse in the West (and in the rants of nineteenth-century male taste reformers, for example in Great Britain), the decorative was identified, negatively, with the feminine, along with anything that was a matter of surface rather than substance. Women were represented as the chief perpetrators of clutter, hoarders of superfluous things and accumulators of knick-knacks.[98] But they were also their chief victims, taste experts cautioned, for useless decorative paraphernalia were among the chains that bound women into domestic slavery, because it fell to them to dust and polish them. As women saw the light of communist consciousness, they were expected to recognize the tyranny of trash as an aspect of their oppression in the past, clinging to which was false consciousness. Ridding their lives of this dust-collecting ballast was in their own best interest. Combined with simplifications of the forms of furniture—stripping off the ornate moldings from older items of furniture, for example—it would not only make their apartment look more contemporary, but would reduce the time they spent on cleaning, freeing them up for social and cultural activities.[99] As the 1955 *Novyi mir* reader had already grasped, ornaments popular in the recent past, such as miniature elephants, were out, as was the dysfunctional display of family status and wealth that characterized the bourgeois home.

Memory objects were particularly problematic, along with women's traditional role as custodians of memory. Public discourse represented moving into the new flat as a clean break with the past and its material and ideological residue, while taste experts' insistence on the unified contemporary style for all elements of the interior delegitimized alternative principles of unity based on biography, affect and personal ties. After repeated relocations and losses, in addition to the fear-induced excision of evidence associated with purged friends or family members, the material repositories of memory had often been reduced to the portable and concealable form of a small treasure box. But if any remaining material links with family history and repositories of personal memories had survived after decades of upheavals, destruction and loss, they were now to be cast away on the tide of progress, left behind in the move to the radiant future. This was often a physical necessity in practice: old pieces of furniture were too big to bring into the small flats. Their abandonment was also an imperative of modernity, according to advice that exhorted those moving to new apartments to do so unencumbered by the material trace of the past.[100]

There were mixed messages, however, concerning decorative touches in the apartment. These related to the centrality of aesthetics in the vision of the communist future. How to make the industrially prefabricated interior into a work of beauty and self-actualization? The importance of aesthetic education in the formation of the fully rounded future citizen of communism was emphasized by philosophers and ideologues in the Khrushchev era, informed by a return to Marx (especially his earlier writings), and was written into the new Party Program ("the Communist Manifesto of the present era") ratified in 1961. All Soviet people should have the opportunity to develop their aesthetic sensibilities and taste through access to art and aesthetic education. Moreover, they should themselves become producers of aesthetic value.[101]

The domestic interior was potentially a key site for daily encounter with art and for cultural activity. The household's cultural level (rather than its wealth, as in the past) was manifest, for example, through the presence of a piano or books.[102] Unique paintings might not be accessible for all, or even desirable in the modernist interior, according to some aesthetic specialists, because of their dust-collecting frames and spatial illusionism, which disrupted the flat plane of the wall. Judiciously chosen art prints were advocated, however, especially those in which decorative, formal qualities took precedence over naturalistic representation.[103] Voeikova recommended calm tints for walls on the grounds that these were easy on the eye, allowed one to use decorative fabrics for curtains and soft furnishings, and made a good background for prints, paintings, photographs and decorative elements. "In such a room a brightly patterned rug or colorful decorative cushions on a divan will not look excessive, nor a vase in a saturated color or picture on the wall."[104] The choice, restrained deployment of such objects in the interior created contemporary beauty and revealed aesthetic discernment, and was quite distinct from mindless, eclectic, tasteless accumulation or vulgar display of luxury.

Moreover, creating the beautiful, tasteful interior was in itself a form of aesthetic production and not only of consumption.[105] For, as two television viewers (a married couple, both engineers) put it, writing in to the program on homemaking mentioned earlier: "Everyone must become an artist in their home!"[106] A specialist in the new discipline of Technical Aesthetics indicated that, notwithstanding the value of rationalization and standardization, there was a place for purely expressive, aesthetic gestures. While advocating thoroughgoing standardization of utilitarian routines and domestic fittings, because this would combat the regressive influence of the nuclear household and of any fetishistic tendencies that the increased availability of consumer goods might foster, she forestalled possible objections that fitted furniture would prevent the manifestation of individuality. For, the specialist asserted, the occupant's individuality would find full expression in the *aesthetics* of interior decoration.[107]

Handicraft

It will be clear by now that this did not mean open season: only certain kinds of decorative objects, discerningly deployed in moderation, were acceptable. In regard to curtains or wallpaper, for example, bold, abstracted patterns were deemed "contemporary," but naturalistic designs that dissembled the flatness of the fabric or wall by creating a spatial illusion were in bad taste. Not only was discrimination to be exercised according to the specific formal treatment, but there were also hierarchies of virtue pertaining to the materials and mode of production, where artifacts were made, and by whom. The painted rugs discussed earlier were anathema not only for the romantic and nostalgic images depicted on them and because they were "dishonest"—a cheap ersatz for woven rugs—but also because they were a form of unregulated artisanal production for provincial bazaars, neither "authentic" folk craft nor industrial manufactures.

Certain kinds of handmade objects, in limited numbers, were, however, acceptable within the modern, industrially produced interior, notably traditional "genuine" folkcraft and unique works of decorative art. Even in journals such as *Dekorativnoe iskusstvo SSSR*, which staunchly promoted the stripped-down modernist "contemporary style," authors widely acknowledged that an increasingly standardized, industrially mass-produced environment engendered an aesthetic need for the *faktura* (texture, surface qualities that bear the trace of the process of making) of handmade things. They also discussed approvingly the discerning use of folk ornaments, craft and handmade *objets d'art* in the mass-produced modern interior. Illustrations of ideal modern interiors regularly included carefully selected items of handcraft—a well-placed, hand-thrown vase or a rough, handwoven tapestry—amid the stripped-down lines of the new furniture.[108] The Estonian home decorating magazine *Kunst ja kodu* (*Art and the Home*, also published in Russian as *Iskusstvo i domashnii byt*) celebrated handcraft as part of the ideal modern interior (as it was in contemporary Scandinavian modernism, an important model for Estonian design in this period).[109] Taste experts advocated the restrained, discerning use, in the contemporary apartment, of traditional folkcraft identified with the specific traditions of various ethnic groups, regions and national republics of the Soviet Union. "The inexhaustible imagination and varied forms and colors of folk craft provide unlimited choice of works of decorative-applied art to beautify any room." Voeikova recommended ceramics such as statuettes or dishes hung on the wall, vases, painted figures from Viatka, Georgian black-fired pottery, carved wooden figurines from Transcarpathia or Karelia, along with folk rugs, weavings, Vologda lace and other traditional textile arts from various national republics.[110] A limited number of well-chosen and subtly deployed items of folkcraft was desirable in the industrial, standard urban apartment, then, for the splash of color or contrasting texture they added.

But what of amateur handicraft produced by women in the home? "What is the amateur of handicraft to do?" Voeikova put this question: "Do embroidery and lace, executed by the mistress of the house (*khoziaika*) herself have a place in the new décor?" Could the definition of everyday aesthetic production embrace even embroidery, needlepoint and crochet? As we have seen, the legitimacy of deploying in the interior cloths and embroidered napkins, which had played a significant role among the repudiated forms of homemaking, had been under question in recent years. Needlework, along with other uses of textiles, was suspected of harboring regressive relations, as well as dust.[111] Yet Voeikova answered her own rhetorical question: "Not only do they go [in the interior], but these artifacts beautify the room."[112] Her affirmation of amateur needlework's legitimacy in the modern interior should not automatically be explained by her gender. In part, this was a matter of finer distinctions to do with authenticity, allowing original or traditional designs appropriate to the medium and handmade (but not machine) lace. Needlepoint reproductions of popular, sentimental, naturalistic paintings based on crude patterns, sold in bazaars and in the hobby shop *Rukodelie* (handicraft), were still considered vulgar perversions.[113] It may also have been a compromise with the assumed tastes of Voeikova's readership, this being an article published in the magazine for women workers (a highbrow modernist aesthetic that excluded embroidery and crochet was still consistently pursued in the more specialist design magazine *Dekorativnoe iskusstvo SSSR*). Written in 1964, her willingness to admit amateur embroidery may also be an early indication of a growing critique, even among design professionals, of socialist modernism's asceticism and deracination. By the end of the 1960s, the tide had turned decisively. Intelligentsia discourse increasingly acknowledged the material and psychological losses entailed by industrial progress, by purging material links with the past and by the insistence on stylistic unity. It called instead for an "ecology of culture" and sought to reconnect with suppressed personal and collective memories, as well as to embrace the heterogeneity of "national" styles. In this changing climate of ideas, textiles, thread and tapestry began to be used as positive metaphors to reimagine the relationship between present identities and the past, revaluing the kind of connection between generations of women that needlework artifacts, patterns and skills materialized (Figure 9.8).[114]

Figure 9.8 "All of this is my mother's [work]. She did the housekeeping and crocheted." Evgeniia's mother's needlework with a tapestry received as a gift, c. 1965.
Photo: Ekaterina Gerasimova, 2004, for the project "Everyday Aesthetics in the Modern Soviet Flat." © Susan E. Reid.

Practice

Whatever misgivings the arbiters of taste held in the Khrushchev era, needlework and handicraft of various sorts remained popular leisure practices in Soviet urban homes throughout the 1950s to the 1980s. Not only were large quantities of needlework produced and deployed in the interior, but they were also carefully preserved through the years, even though storage space was at a premium in these small apartments.[115] Textiles in various forms, deeply enmeshed in traditional notions of comfort, homecraft and female worth, remained essential material for creating home, a means to appropriate and individualize space and personalize standard goods. Rugs provided sound and heat insulation while curtains were used to keep out drafts or to screen off areas of the shared main room (a niche where a child slept, for example) and demarcate functions. They also remained essential for creating privacy in the sense of concealment from external, uninvited eyes; although the separate apartments gave much greater privacy in this sense, a feature of their design was relatively large windows. In interviews and even in published accounts of moving in, the first thing a housewife has in mind when she says to her daughter "we should start making it cozy" is to hang curtains or nets in order to enclose the interior.[116] The woman cited earlier who was proud of her father's cabinetmaking recalled that making the apartment cozy had entailed the use of napkins, for example, to cover the television, and spreading a tablecloth when guests came.[117]

In this respect, the voluminous advice literature appears to have had little direct effect on many people's material practices of *uiut*, which were still determined by their habitus and remained closer to McCracken's "homeyness" as the expression of a search for continuity, stability and a sense of rootedness than to the modernist contemporary style.[118] When prototypes of furniture for mass production were presented to the population at an exhibition of model interiors in 1961, many who wrote in the visitors' comment books found the new style "primitive," ugly, poorly finished and anonymous, lacking in "national" characteristics. Many also found it priced well beyond their means, and moreover, it was still unavailable in the shops.[119] One respondent in the 1968 survey of new Moscow homes may have spoken for many when she denied that the minimal, "contemporary" aesthetic that was so widely propagated could be either cozy or convenient to live in. On the contrary, for all that the modernizers condemned the way the old "petit-bourgeois" (or Stalinist) interior subordinated function to non-functional display, the same criticism could, she pointed out, be leveled against the contemporary style they advocated. Its modernist minimalism and cool perfection rendered the interior like one in an exhibition or an illustration in a design magazine. *Uiut*, for this resident, depended on signs of being lived in.[120] Others identified it with the warmth of human relations or the presence of a nice cat.[121]

We can recognize this response to the socialist modernist "contemporary style" as a version of the stock complaint about the unlivableness of the modernist interior familiar in the West. However, it would be wrong to represent this as a thoroughgoing or universal rejection of the new modernist style—and indeed of socialist modernity—regardless of social class, ethnicity or personal dispositions. Alongside the negative responses to the model interiors exhibited in 1961, there were many who welcomed the new, light and simple furniture, and who would simply be glad to have an opportunity to buy any furniture whatever. The look of many of the apartments in the 1968 survey, according to its author Elena Torshilova, conformed to the official aesthetic of the contemporary style. And, when asked "How is *uiut* achieved?," 81% of the informants rehearsed its widely promoted principles: "through cleanliness" and "a small number of things," "convenience," "unity of style" and "harmony of the whole ensemble of the interior."[122] That small survey made no claims to be representative, however. The informants, residents of an apartment block belonging to a Moscow research institute, included an unrepresentatively large number of people with higher education and doctorates. It is probable that take-up was highest among this, the same social stratum as the specialists who promoted the cosmopolitan modernist contemporary style, who were also more able to afford the new furniture. A much larger sample than Torshilova's or than the interview and visual data I have been able to gather

Susan E. Reid

from some 70 households would be necessary to draw meaningful generalizations concerning class, ethnic and urban-rural (first- or second-generation urban dwellers, etc.) distinctions. The available evidence would suggest, however, that the effort to propagate the contemporary style met with neither universal acceptance nor with total rejection, but had a varied and mixed response. While take-up was limited by factors ranging from taste and habitus to price and shortage, and adoption of the approved style in popular practices of homemaking and ideals of beauty and *uiut* was patchy and selective, many interiors were hybrids of new and old: not an outright rejection of the modern, but its accommodation and absorption/integration into an established conception of *uiut*.

Conclusion

This chapter has explored attempts in authoritative discourse to transcend the antithesis of home comfort and communism, coziness and socialist modernity, and to redefine coziness in ways that could be reconciled with the Enlightenment values of progress, science and reason through a modernist aesthetics. To a large extent this discourse was addressed to women, aiming to reform their notions of taste and delegitimate traditional practices of homemaking. The hegemony of the state, as materialized in the invasive effects of modern housing, is often seen as an assault on women's domain and dominance within the domestic sphere. Yet, while architects and planners set the parameters of the new housing, and specialists sought to shape the ways in which women made home in the new flats, they were dependent on individual householders to materialize the norms of the contemporary aesthetic. Home, and women's practices in it, tested the jurisdiction of the state. The continued production of decorated cloths and the use of textiles by women and girls in many homes are just two of the ways in which advice on good taste and rational living was ignored in everyday practice.

How are we to interpret this? Is this a case of what anthropologists in other contexts have described as resistance by female occupants who persist in traditional practices and uses of space even when these have been designated "irrational," or otherwise denigrated or countered by "creative and sometimes subversive alternatives"?[123] For Henri Lefebvre, home is inherently an oppositional, "private" space that "asserts itself . . . always in a conflictual way, against the public one."[124] Moreover, as we saw, the "private" space of home in the Soviet scheme of things was regarded by outside observers as communism's "other," a flaw in the Soviet system's supposedly "totalitarian" grasp or consummate grid of surveillance, where the state project of socialist modernity was contradicted. We should not resort to this model uncritically, however, it being one of the binaries that sustained and legitimated the Cold War and blinkered Western understanding of Soviet experience. The Soviet discourse we have analyzed was aimed precisely at overcoming this antithesis and accommodating home comfort within socialist modernity. Did that spell the beginning of the end of communism, as Cold War observers predicted? Was the preoccupation with nest-making a symptom of degeneration of the Soviet project, marking a retreat from building communism into private values, personal consumption and "home-is-my-castle" mindsets? Or was it, rather, a way to sustain the Soviet regime and lend new legitimacy to the project of building communism?

So large a question cannot be resolved here. To construe the practices of homemaking as resistance to the hegemony of the state or the cultural elitism of intelligentsia specialists, however, invests them with too much conscious, programmatic intention. They are more accurately described by the model of ad hoc coping tactics and making do, as vernacular, everyday ways of negotiating and coming to terms with the material constraints and possibilities of their lives, as suggested by Michel de Certeau.[125] As Attfield found in British social housing in the same period of the mid-twentieth century, residents made themselves "at home" in a variety of ways that mitigated the homogeneous unity of modern design:

> Yet it cannot be said that tenants rejected modernity as such, even when they clung to family heirlooms and traditional furnishing conventions. On the contrary, it was the adaptability with

which tenants took over their domestic space, stubbornly arranging it in contravention to the designers' intentions, that shows how they appropriated modernity to their own designs.[126]

Soviet homemakers took what they could afford or get hold of and incorporated it as best they could into their conception of beauty and *uiut*. In the course of the 1960s, as prosperity and consumer goods production grew, many people gradually acquired the new modular furniture to replace the older bulky items that wouldn't fit or looked out of place in the new flats—and learned to live with and even to love it. Incorporating the new into eclectic, hybrid combinations along with older pieces in more ornate styles, with handmade things and with memory objects, they assimilated them into their domestic space and routines, accommodating modernity and socialism in ways that allowed them and their families to live comfortably within these givens. Thus home was where the contradiction between the forward thrust of modernity and chiliasm of communism on one hand, and dwelling on the other, was accommodated: a heterotopia rather than a counter-utopia.

Acknowledgment

This chapter was reprinted from *Gender & History* ISSN 0953–5233. Reid, Susan E. 2009 November. "Communist Comfort: Socialist Modernism and the Making of Cosy Homes in the Khrushchev Era." *Gender & History* 21 (3): 465–498. © The author 2009. Journal compilation © Blackwell Publishing Ltd. 2009, 9600 Garsington Road, Oxford OX4 2DQ, UK and 350 Main Street, Malden, MA 02148, USA.

Notes

1. This chapter is drawn from a larger project, "Everyday Aesthetics in the Modern Soviet Flat," generously supported by the Leverhulme Trust RF/5/RFG/2004/0095. Over 70 interviews were conducted between 2004 and 2007 in St. Petersburg, Kazan, Samara, Kaluga and Tartu, with people who had moved into new apartments in the early 1960s. On paradox as inherent in modernity see Kotsonis 2000.
2. Conference, "Different Modernisms, Different Avant-Gardes" (Reid and Crowley 2000; Betts and Pence 2007; Reid 2006a; Reid 2006b).
3. Reed 1996; Heynen 2005; van Herck 2005. For "homeyness," see McCracken 1989.
4. Matich 1996; Boym 1994, 73–88; Benjamin 1986, 48; Benjamin 1978; Heynen 2005, 17; Kettering 1997; Kiaer 2005.
5. Gronberg 1993; Parker and Pollock 1987; Elliott and Helland 2002; Sparke 1995; Attfield 2007; Wolff 1990, 51–66 and 34–50; Rendell, Penner, and Borden 2000.
6. Heidegger 1978 [1954], 348; Gregson 2007, 21–3.
7. Exceptions include Buchli 1999; Gerasimova 2000; Harris 2003; Varga-Harris 2005.
8. Cited in Skidelsky 1992, 519; de Grazia 2005, 113.
9. Compare Richard Nixon's position in dispute with Nikita Khrushchev: BBC News: On This Day, 24 July 1959. http://news.bbc.co.uk/onthisday/hi/dates/stories/july/24/newsid_2779000/2779551.stm, accessed on September 7, 2009.
10. Higgins cited in Mace 1963, 187.
11. Mace 1963, 187–8; Gould and Gould 1957, 176.
12. Gray 1989, 2.
13. Gray 1989, 2–3.
14. Benjamin 1999, 220; Heynen 2005, 17.
15. Gray 1989, 2; van Herck 2005, 141 *n*. 3; Buchli 1999, 56–62; Gullestad 1992, 79–80.
16. McCracken 1989; Matt 2007, 283–4.
17. Pasternak 1957, 443–4; Pasternak 1958, 360; Mace 1963, 186–7.
18. Crowley 2000; Ariès 1973; Ariès and Duby 1991. Literature on the public/private dichotomy and on the gendered segregation of spheres is extensive: see e.g., Helly and Reverby 1992; Weintraub and Kumar 1996; Siegelbaum 2006b.
19. Central Committee CPSU 1957 (1960), 332–48; Khrushchev 1959.
20. Andrusz 1984, 157, table 7.5; Harris 2003; Zhukov 1964, 1.
21. Merzhanov and Sorokin 1966, 4; RGALI, f. 2329, op. 4, ed. khr. 1388, ll. 51–2, 1961; Brodskii 1965, 65–9; Brodskii 1963, 25; Baiar 1957, 17–20; Voeikova 1962, 30; Attwood 2004, 189, 200–1, *nn.* 72–3. Cf. Miller 2001, 9–11.

Susan E. Reid

22. These negotiations are examined more fully in the wider project from which this article is drawn "Everyday Aesthetics in the Modern Soviet Flat" (see endnote 1).
23. For detail, see Reid 2004; Reid 2002.
24. Kiaer and Naiman 2006.
25. Dunham 1976; Fitzpatrick 1992, 216–37; Kettering 1997.
26. See e.g., Mace and Mace 1963, 187–8; Gould 1957, 176; Rau 1959, 5.
27. Paucity of consumer goods, overcrowding and the loss of homes and possessions in the course of serial dislocations structure life stories of this period as narrated in interviews conducted under my project "Everyday Aesthetics in the Modern Soviet Flat" (see endnote 1).
28. Renkama 2006; Gilison 1975.
29. Brodskii 1963, 24.
30. For further discussion, see Reid 1997, esp. 190–2.
31. Boym 1994, 39–40.
32. Andreeva 1956, 23–4; Sosnovy 1959, 1–21; Sosnovy 1954, 114–15.
33. Filtzer 2006; Manley 2006; Zubkova 1998; LaPierre 2006. Tuberculosis was frequently cited in cases considered for rehousing in new apartment blocks. TsAGM, f. 62, op. 15, d. 267; TsAGM, f. 62, op. 15, d. 266.
34. Boym 1994, 73–88; Clark 1985, 227–33; Pohl 2004.
35. For the identification between housing registration and civic identity or enfranchisement, see Mandel'sham, cited in Boym 1994, 93; TsGALI SPb, f. 341, op. 1, d. 357, l. 32; Manley 2006, 233; Papernyi 1993; Kotkin 1993. Corten 1992, 31. This spatial organization of the population was not new. See Kotkin 1995.
36. Semenov 1964.
37. See also Harris 2006, 171.
38. Boym 1994, 125. The role of such public agencies in the ownership of housing increased in the 1950s, giving the "state" a virtual monopoly over urban housing construction, although cooperatives represented an alternative. Sosnovy 1959, 9.
39. Zhukov 1964, 1; Buchli 1997.
40. See e.g., the TV script Rybitskii 1963; Roth-Ey 2007.
41. Khrushchev 1955; Ruble 1993.
42. A decree of 23 April 1959 extended the moratorium on superfluous embellishment to public interiors: Central Committee CPSU 1959, 166–71; see also Harris 2003 chap. 8, 467–546.
43. Gerchuk 2000, 88.
44. Movchaniuk 1998; Shvarts 1998.
45. Concierge, Union of Architects, St. Petersburg, April 2005.
46. Interviews for "Everyday Aesthetics"; Adzhubei 1989, 118.
47. Harris 2006.
48. Shlapentokh 1989; Siegelbaum 2006a; Reid 2006c; Field 2007.
49. See special issue on the gift, *Journal of the Royal Anthropological Institute* (*N.S.*) 12 (2006); Brooks 1999.
50. Nikol'skaia 1959.
51. "Schastlivoe novosel'e" 1959.
52. For fuller discussion of representations of *novosel'e*, see Reid 2009.
53. See e.g., *Izvestiia*'s "For Home and Family" page and the illustrated magazine *Ogonek*'s rubric, "Women—This Is For You"; Merzhanov and Sorokin 1966; Field 1996, 41; Kelly 2001.
54. See e.g., the 1958 novel by Daniil Granin 1964 [1959]; Baiar and Blashkevich 1962; regular features in magazines such as *Ogonek* (e.g., 11 (8 March 1959) back cover), *Dekorativnoe iskusstvo SSSR, Kunst ja kodu, Sem'ia i shkola*. Among exhibitions of model interiors, the most significant was "Iskusstvo—v byt" (Art Into Life), held in Moscow 1961.
55. For argumentation, see Reid 2005.
56. Nikol'skii 1959. See also Lapin 1959.
57. Rybitskii 1963.
58. TsAGM, f. 4, op. 139, d. 35: ll. 12–16.
59. TsAGM, f. 4, op. 139, d. 35, ll. 8–12.
60. TsAGM, f. 4, op. 139, d. 35. On efforts to engage men with domesticity, see Edel' 1958, 12.
61. "Tribuna chitatelia" 1955, 247.
62. Interviews for "Everyday Aesthetics."
63. Siegelbaum 2006, 97.
64. Interview with L. G., St. Petersburg 2004, "Everyday Aesthetics."
65. Abramenko and Tormozova 1959, 4. See also Reid 2005.

Communist Comfort: Socialist Modernism

66. Kantor 1963, 26–48; Cf. Strumilin 1960, 213; Baranov 1967, 17.
67. Kantor 1963, 29–30.
68. Torshilova 1971, 141–3.
69. Torshilova 1971, 141–3.
70. Chereiskaia 1959, 220.
71. Gregson 2007, 23; Gullestad 1992; Miller 2002.
72. Miller 1988; Attfield 1999.
73. Hill 1991, 300, with reference to McCracken 1989, 179.
74. Braunfels 1988, 38; cf. Hill 1991.
75. Braunfels 1988, 38; Glazer 1990, 507–18; Ruble 1993, 243–4.
76. On the input of labor by the consumer, which Soviet consumer goods presupposed in the "post-commodity" phase before the item could be used or assimilated, see Gerasimova and Chuikina 2004; See also Orlova 2004.
77. See e.g., Baiar and Blashkevich 1962, 15; "Svoimi rukami," 1961, 48–9; and regular features in *Kunst ja kodu*. Cf. Vysokovskii 1993, 284; RGALI, f. 2329, op. 4, ed. khr. 1391, l. 29, l. 47 (visitors' book for exhibition "Iskusstvo—v byt," Moscow 1961).
78. Sharov and Poliachek 1960, 66–79. See also Chereiskaia 1959, "Zametki o khoroshem vkuse," 220; Buchli 1999.
79. Christine Varga-Harris, "Homemaking: Keeping Appearances and Petticoat Rule." Paper presented at conference "The Thaw," Berkeley, May 2005.
80. Brodskii 1963, 24.
81. Sidorov 1960; Lenin 1970, 24.
82. "Tribuna chitatelia" 1955, 247.
83. Chereiskaia 1959, 220; Torshilova 1971, 140; *Kunst ja kodu* 1962, 1–2; Voeikova 1964, 30–1; Gol'dshtein 1959, 30; Krasnova 1960, 44–5.
84. Sharov and Poliachek 1960, 73.
85. Solzhenitsyn 1963, 192.
86. RGASPI, f. M—1, op. 32, d. 972, ll. 58–63; Jenks 2006.
87. Gol'dshtein 1959, 30.
88. Sharov and Poliachek 1960, 73.
89. On beds as outdated "prejudice," see Briuno 1960, 46; Voeikova 1962, 30; Buchli 1997.
90. On the gendered meanings of textiles and on modernism's delegitimation of women's aesthetic practices, see Sparke 1995; Attfield 2007; Attfield 2000, 129–36; Heynen 2005.
91. Interview with L. G., St. Petersburg, female.
92. Buchli, *Archaeology*, p. 128.
93. Voeikova 1964, 30; Baiar 1956, 47–8; Baiar and Blashkevich 1962.
94. Voeikova 1964, 30; Voeikova 1962, 30.
95. Gol'dshtein 1959, 30.
96. The Austrian architect-journalist Adolf Loos's influential essay "Ornament and Crime" written in 1908, tied the elimination of ornament to progress in a Darwinian argument. See Loos 1966, 226–31. In the 1920s, Le Corbusier denounced ornament in *The Decorative Art of Today* and *Towards a New Architecture*.
97. Gol'dshtein 1959, 30.
98. One speaker in a discussion considered entresol storage "a superfluous seedbed of rubbish, which housewives always have and which must simply be liquidated." TsGALI SPb, f. 341, op. 1, d. 386, l. 16 (1954).
99. Abramenko and Tormozova 1959, 4; Nikol'skaia 1959; Chereiskaia 1959, 220–34; Nikol'skaia 1958b, 46–7; Nikol'skaia 1958a, 42–4. See also Buchli 1997; Reid 1997; Gerchuk 2000.
100. The contemporary interior as a site of memory, and women's use of objects and embroidery to materialize memories, are central issues of interviews for "Everyday Aesthetics" and, as represented in painting, of Reid 1993.
101. "Programme of the CPSU," in Hodnett 1974, 255–6.
102. Books were an essential attribute of the cultured home, for the absence of which no amount of luxury could compensate. GARF f. 6903, op. 26, d. 449, item no. 459, script of program for Moscow Television: "Dlia doma, dlia sem'i: vasha lichnaia biblioteka," 2 February 1963. However, a piano in a home where nobody played was a useless ornament. Sharov and Poliachek 1960, 70–2.
103. Voeikova 1962, 30; Krasnova 45; Interview with I. A., St. Petersburg, b. 1927, engineer, female; Filatov, (1961), 177.
104. Voeikova 1964, 30–1.
105. Briuno 1960, 4; "Khudozhnik prishel na kvartiru," 1963, 26; Liubimova 1964, 15–18.
106. "Dlia doma, dlia sem'i. V pomoshch' novoselam," 5 January 1963, GARF, f. 6903, op. 2, d. 449.
107. Liubimova 1964, 16.
108. *Kunst ja kodu* 1962. Goncharov 1960, 24; Krasnova 1960, 45.
109. Kalm 2002, 52–65.

Susan E. Reid

110. Voeikova 1964, 31; Goncharov 1960, 24.
111. See Buchli 1999, 128.
112. Voeikova 1964, 31.
113. Suvorova 1962, 46.
114. For detail, see Reid 1993, 161–87.
115. "Everyday Aesthetics" interviews, 2004–07, St. Petersburg, Tartu, Samara, Kaluga, Kazan.
116. Interview with I. A., St. Petersburg, b. 1927, engineer, female; Edel' 1959, 12.
117. For the affective meanings of textiles, and their close identification with the human body, see Attfield 2000, 129–36; Heynen 2005, 1–29.
118. McCracken 1989, 168–83.
119. RGALI, f. 2329, op. 4, ed. khr. 1391; TsAGM f. 21, op 1, d. 125, d. 126, d. 127 (visitors' book for exhibition "Iskusstvo- v byt!," 1961); Torshilova 1971.
120. Torshilova 1971, 140.
121. Ekaterina Gerasimova, interview for project "Intelligentsia and Philistinism in Russian History and Culture," funded by Finnish Academy of Sciences, 2000–2, accessed with kind permission of Timo Vihavainen. See also Vihavainen 2004.
122. Torshilova 1971, 138–9.
123. Birdwell-Pheasant and Lawrence-Zuñiga 1999, 23–8.
124. Lefebvre 1991, 361–2.
125. De Certeau 1984.
126. Attfield 1999, 81.

References

Abramenko, I., and L. Tormozova, eds. 1959. *Besedy o domashnem khoziaistva*. Moscow: Molodaia gvardiia.
Adzhubei, Aleksei. 1989. *Te desiat' let*. Moscow: Sovetskaia Rossiia.
Andreeva, N. I. 1956. "Gigienicheskaia otsenka novogo zhilishchnogo stroitel'stva v Moskve (period 1947–1951 gg.)." *Gigiena i sanitaria* 1956(6): 23–24.
Andrusz, Gregory D. 1984. *Housing and Urban Development in the USSR*. London: Macmillan.
Ariès, Philippe. 1973. *Centuries of Childhood*. Harmondsworth: Penguin.
Ariès, Philippe, and G. Duby, eds. 1991. *History of Private Life, Volume 5: Riddles of Identity in Modern Times*, 5 Vols., edited by Antoine Prost and Gerard Vincent, translated by Arthur Goldhammer. Cambridge, MA: Belknap Press of Harvard University Press.
Attfield, Judy. 1999. "Bringing Modernity Home: Open Plan in the British Domestic Interior." In *At Home: An Anthropology of Domestic Space*, edited by Irene Cieraad, 73–82. Syracuse, NY: Syracuse University Press.
Attfield. Judy. 2000. *Wild Things: The Material Culture of Everyday Life*. Oxford: Berg.
Attfield, Judy. 2007. *Bringing Modernity Home: Writings on Popular Design and Material Culture*. Manchester: Manchester University Press.
Attwood, Lynne. 2004. "Housing in the Khrushchev Era." In *Women in the Khrushchev Era*, edited by Melanie Ilič, Susan Reid, and Lynne Attwood, 177–202. Basingstoke: Palgrave Macmillan.
Baiar, Ol'ga. 1956. "Sdelaiem kvartiru udobnoi i uiutnoi." *Sovetskaia zhenshchina* 1956(7): 47–48.
Baiar, Ol'ga. 1957. "Dekorativnoe ubranstvo kvartiry." *Dekorativnoe iskusstvo SSSR*, Jubilee edition (Moscow): 17–20.
Baiar, Ol'ga, and Rimma Blashkevich. 1962. *Kvartira i ee ubranstvo*. Moscow: Stroiizdat.
Baranov, A. 1967. "Sotsiologicheskie problemy zhilishcha." In *Sotsial'nye problemy zhilishcha*, edited by A. G. Kharchev, S. M. Verizhnikov, and V. L. Ruzhzhe. Leningrad: LenZNIIEP.
Barkov, V. 1982. *Kniga novosela (domovodstvo dlia muzhchin)*. Alma-Ata: Kainar.
Benjamin, Walter. 1978. "Moscow." In *Reflections: Essays, Aphorisms, Autobiographical Writings*, edited by Walter Benjamin, 97–130. New York: Schocken.
Benjamin, Walter. 1986. *Moscow Diary*. Cambridge, MA: Harvard University Press.
Benjamin, Walter. 1999. *The Arcades Project*. Cambridge, MA: Harvard University Press.
Betts, Paul, and Katherine Pence, eds. 2007. *Socialist Modern: East German Everyday Culture and Politics*. Ann Arbor: University of Michigan Press.
Birdwell-Pheasant, D., and D. Lawrence-Zuñiga. 1999. "Introduction." In *HouseLife: Space, Place and Family in Europe*, edited by D. Birdwell-Pheasant and D. Lawrence-Zuñiga, 23–28. Oxford: Berg.
Boym, Svetlana. 1994. *Common Places: Mythologies of Everyday Life in Russia*. Cambridge, MA: Harvard University Press.

Braunfels, Wolfgang. 1988. *Urban Design in Western Europe: Regime and Architecture, 900–1900.* Translated by Kenneth J. Northcott. Chicago: University of Chicago Press.

Briuno, A. 1960. "Vasha kvartira." *Sem'ia i shkola* 1960(10): 46.

Brodskii, Boris. 1963. "Novyi byt i kamufliazh meshchanstva." *Dekorativnoe iskusstvo SSSR* 1963(8): 23–28.

Brodskii, Boris. 1965. *Khudozhnik i gorod.* Moscow: Iskusstvo.

Brooks, Jeffrey. 1999. *Thank You Comrade Stalin! Soviet Public Culture From Revolution to Cold War.* Princeton, NJ: Princeton University Press.

Buchli, Victor. 1997. "Khrushchev, Modernism, and the Fight Against Petit-Bourgeois Consciousness in the Soviet Home." *Journal of Design History* 10(2): 161–176.

Buchli, Victor. 1999. *An Archaeology of Socialism.* Oxford: Berg.

Central Committee of CPSU and USSR Council of Ministers. 1957 (1960). Decree "O razvitii zhilishchnogo stroitel'stva v SSSR," 31 July 1957, *Pravda,* 2 August 1957.

Central Committee of CPSU and USSR Council of Ministers. 1959. Decree "Ob ustranenii izlishestv v otdelke, oborudovanii i vo vnutrennem ubranstve obshchestvennykh zdanii." *Sobranie postanovlenii pravitel'stva SSSR* (23 April 1959). Moscow: Gosiurizdat (1959), 166–171.

Chereiskaia, M. 1959. "Zametki o khoroshem vkuse." In *Podruga,* edited by R. Saltanova and N. Kolchinskaia, 220–34. Moscow: Molodaia gvardiia.

Clark, Katerina. 1985. *The Soviet Novel: History as Ritual,* 2nd ed. Chicago and London: University of Chicago Press.

Corten, Irena H. 1992. *Vocabulary of Soviet Society and Culture: A Selected Guide to Russian Words, Idioms and Expressions of the Post-Stalin Era, 1953–1991.* Durham, NC: Duke University Press.

Crowley, John. 2000. *The Invention of Comfort: Sensibilities and Design in Early Modern Britain and Early America.* Baltimore and London: Johns Hopkins University Press.

De Certeau, Michel. 1984. *The Practice of Everyday Life.* Berkeley: University of California Press.

De Grazia, Victoria. 2005. *Irresistible Empire: America's Advance Through 20th-Century Europe.* Cambridge, MA: Belknap Press of Harvard University Press.

Dunham, Vera S. 1976. *In Stalin's Time: Middleclass Values in Soviet Fiction.* Cambridge: Cambridge University Press.

Edel', M. 1958, 30 April. "Divan." *Krokodil* 12: 12.

Elliott, Bridget, and Janice Helland, eds. 2002. *Women Artists and the Decorative Arts 1880–1935: The Gender of Ornament.* Aldershot: Ashgate.

Field, Deborah A. 1996. *Communist Morality and Meanings of Private Life in Post-Stalinist Russia, 1953–1964.* Ph.D. Dissertation, University of Michigan.

Field, Deborah A. 2007. *Private Life and Communist Morality in Khrushchev's Russia.* New York: Peter Lang.

Filatov, Iu. 1961. "Veshchi, sovremennost, 'zhivopis.'" *Zvezda* 1961(2): 176–179.

Filtzer, Donald. 2006. "Standard of Living Versus Quality of Life: Struggling with the Urban Environment in Russia During the Early Years of Post-war Reconstruction." In *Late Stalinist Russia: Society Between Reconstruction and Reinvention*, edited by Juliane Fürst, 81–102. London and New York: Routledge.

Fitzpatrick, Sheila. 1992. "Becoming Cultured: Socialist Realism and the Representation of Privilege and Taste." In *The Cultural Front: Power and Culture in Revolutionary Russia*, edited by Sheila Fitzpatrick, 216–237. Ithaca, NY: Cornell University Press.

Gerasimova, Ekaterina. 2000. *Sovetskaia kommunal'naia kvartira kak sotsial'nyi institut: istoriko-sotsiologicheskii analiz.* Ph.D. Dissertation, European University, St. Petersburg.

Gerasimova, Ekaterina, and Sof'ia Chuikina. 2004. "Obshchestvo remonta." *Neprikosnovennyi zapas* 2004(34).

Gerchuk, Iurii. 2000. "The Aesthetics of Everyday Life in the Khrushchev Thaw in the USSR (1954–64)." In *Style and Socialism: Modernity and Material Culture in Post-War Eastern Europe*, edited by Susan E. Reid and David Crowley, 81–100. Oxford: Berg.

Gilison, Jerome M. 1975. *The Soviet Image of Utopia.* Baltimore: Johns Hopkins University Press.

Glazer, Nathan. 1990. "The Prince, the People, and the Architects." *The American Scholar* 59: 507–518.

Gol'dshtein, A. 1959. "Chto takoe uiut?" *Rabotnitsa* 1959(1): 30.

Goncharov, A. 1960, 16 October. "Vkhodi v nash dom, narodnoe iskusstvo." *Ogonek* 42: 24.

Gould, Bruce, and Beatrice Gould. 1957. "We Saw How Russians Live." *Ladies Home Journal* (February): 58–61, 176, 179.

Granin, Daniil. 1964 [1959]. *Posle svad'by.* Leningrad: Sovetskii pisatel.

Gray, Francine du Plessix. 1989. *Soviet Women Walking the Tightrope.* New York: Doubleday.

Gregson, Nicky. 2007. *Living With Things: Ridding, Accommodation, Dwelling.* Wantage, UK: Sean Kingston.

Gronberg, Tag. 1993. "Decoration: Modernism's 'Other.'" *Art History* 15(4): 547–552.

Gullestad, Marianne. 1992. *The Art of Social Relations*. Oslo and Oxford: Scandinavian University Press.

Harris, Steven. 2003. *Moving to the Separate Apartment: Building, Distributing, Furnishing, and Living in Urban Housing in Soviet Russia, 1950s–1960s*. Ph.D. Dissertation, University of Chicago.

Harris, Steven. 2006. "'I Know All the Secrets of My Neighbors": The Quest for Privacy in the Era of the Separate Apartment.'" In *Borders of Socialism: Private Spheres of Soviet Russia*, edited by Lewis Siegelbaum, 171–190. New York and Basingstoke: Palgrave.

Heidegger, Martin. 1978 [1954]. "Building, Dwelling, Thinking." In *Basic Writings: Martin Heidegger*, edited by D. Farrell Krell, 347–363. London: Routledge.

Helly, Dorothy, and Susan Reverby, eds. 1992. *Gendered Domains: Rethinking Public and Private in Women's History*. Ithaca, NY: Cornell University Press.

Heynen, Hilde. 2005. "Modernity and Domesticity: Tensions and Contradictions." In *Negotiating Domesticity: Spatial Productions of Gender in Modern Architecture*, edited by Hilde Heynen and Gülsüm Baydar, 1–29. London and New York: Routledge.

Higgins, Marguerite. 1955. *Red Plush and Black Bread*. Garden City, NY: Doubleday.

Hill, Ronald. 1991. "Homeless Women, Special Possessions, and the Meaning of 'Home': An Ethnographic Case Study." *Journal of Consumer Research* 18: 298–310.

Hodnett, Grey, ed. 1974. *Resolutions and Decisions of the Communist Party of the Soviet Union, Volume 4: The Khrushchev Years 1953–1964*. Toronto: University of Toronto Press.

Jenks, Andrew. 2006. "The Art Market and the Construction of Soviet Russian Culture." In *Borders of Socialism: Private Spheres of Soviet Russia*, edited by Lewis Siegelbaum, 47–64. New York and Basingstoke: Palgrave.

Kalm, Mart. 2002. "Sauna Party at the Summer Cottage: Soviet Estonians Play at Being Western." In *1960s: Universal/Individual*, edited by Pekka Korvenmaa and Esa Laaksonen, 52–65. Helsinki: Alvar Aalto Academy.

Kantor, Karl M. 1963. "Chelovek i zhilishche." *Iskusstvo i byt* 1963(1): 26–48.

Kelly, Catriona. 2001. *Refining Russia: Advice Literature, Polite Culture, and Gender From Catherine to Yeltsin*. Oxford: Oxford University Press.

Kettering, Karen. 1997. "'Ever More Cosy and Comfortable': Stalinism and the Soviet Domestic Interior, 1928–1938." *Journal of Design History* 10(2): 119–135.

Kiaer, Christina. 2005. *Imagine No Possessions: The Socialist Objects of Russian Constructivism*. New Haven, CT: Yale University Press.

Kiaer, Christina, and Eric Naiman, eds. 2006. *Everyday Life in Early Soviet Russia: Taking the Revolution Inside*. Bloomington: Indiana University Press.

Khrushchev, N. S. 1955. *O shirokom vnedrenii industrial'nykh metodov, uluchshenii kachestva i snizhenii stoimosti stroitel'stva*. Moscow: Gospolitizdat.

Khrushchev, N. S. 1959. *O kontrol'nykh tsifrakh razvitiia narodnogo khoziaistva SSSR na 1959–1965 gody*. Moscow: Gospolitizdat.

"Khudozhnik prishel na kvartiru." 1963. *Sluzhba byta* 1963(6): 26.

Kotkin, Stephen. 1993. "Shelter and Subjectivity in the Stalin Period." In *Russian Housing in the Modern Age*, edited by William Brumfield and Blair Ruble, 171–210. Cambridge: Cambridge University Press.

Kotkin, Stephen. 1995. *Magnetic Mountain: Stalinism as a Civilization*. Berkeley: University of California Press.

Kotsonis, Yanni. 2000. "Introduction: A Modern Paradox." In *Russian Modernity*, edited by David Hoffmann and Yanni Kotsonis, 1–16. Houndmills: Palgrave.

Krasnova, E. 1960. "Khoroshii vkus v ubranstve zhil'ia." *Sem'ia i shkola* 1960(1): 44–45.

Kunst ja kodu (Iskusstvo i domashnii byt). 1962. "Editorial." 1962(2): 1–2.

LaPierre, Brian. 2006. "Private Matters or Public Crimes: The Emergence of Domestic Hooliganism in the Soviet Union, 1939–1966." In *Borders of Socialism: Private Spheres of Soviet Russia*, edited by Lewis Siegelbaum, 191–210. New York and Basingstoke: Palgrave.

Lapin, A. 1959. "Malen'kie zaboty bol'shogo novosel'ia." *Izvestiia*, November 14.

Le Corbusier. 1960. *Towards a New Architecture*. Translated by Frederick Etchells. New York: Praeger.

Le Corbusier. 1987. *The Decorative Art of Today*. Translated by James Dunnett. Cambridge, MA: MIT Press.

Lefebvre, Henri. 1991. *The Production of Space*. Oxford: Blackwell.

Lenin, V. I. 1970. "Velikii pochin. (O geroizme rabochikh v tylu)." In *Polnoe sobranie sochinenii*, 5th ed., Vol. 39. Moscow: Izdatel'stvo politicheskoi literatury. 1–29.

Liubimova, G. 1964. "Ratsional'noe oborudovanie kvartir." *Dekorativnoe iskusstvo SSSR* 1964(6): 15–18.

Loos, Adolf. 1966. "*Ornament und Verbrechen* ["Ornament and Crime"]." Translated and reprinted in *Adolf Loos: Pioneer of Modern Architecture*, edited by Ludwig Münz and Gustav Künstler, 226–231. New York: Praeger.

Mace, David and Vera Mace. 1963. *The Soviet Family*. London: Hutchinson.

Mandel'sham, Nadezhda. 1990. *Kniga vtoraia*. Moscow: Moskovskii rabochii.

Manley, Rebecca. 2006. "'Where Should We Resettle the Comrades Next?' The Adjudication of Housing Claims and the Construction of the Post-War Order." In *Late Stalinist Russia: Society Between Reconstruction and Reinvention*, edited by Juliane Fürst, 233–246. London and New York: Routledge.

Matich, Olga. 1996. "Remaking the Bed: Utopia in Daily Life." In *Laboratories of Dreams: The Russian Avant-Garde and Cultural Experience*, edited by J. Bowlt and O. Matich, 59–78. Stanford, CA: Stanford University Press.

Matt, Susan J. 2007. "Why the Old-Fashioned Is in Fashion in American Homes." In *Producing Fashion: Commerce, Culture, and Consumers*, edited by Regina Lee Blaszczyk, 273–292. Philadelphia: University of Pennsylvania Press.

McCracken, Grant. 1989. "'Homeyness': A Cultural Account of One Constellation on Consumer Goods and Meaning." In *Interpretive Consumer Research*, edited by Elizabeth C. Hirschman, 168–183. Provo, UT: Association for Consumer Research.

Merzhanov, B., and K. Sorokin. 1966. *Eto nuzhno novoselam*. Moscow: Ekonomika.

Miller, Daniel. 1988. "Appropriating the State on the Council Estate." *Man* 23(2): 353–372.

Miller, Daniel, ed. 2001. *Home Possessions: Material Culture Behind Closed Doors*. Oxford: Berg.

Miller, Daniel. 2002. "Accommodating." In *Contemporary Art and the Home*, edited by Colin Painter, 115–130. Oxford: Berg.

Movchaniuk, Vadim. 1998. "Reshaetsia sud'ba 'khrushchevok': v interesakh grazhdan." *Etazhi* 2, March 1.

Nikol'skaia, E. 1958a. "Blagoustroistvo zhilishcha." *Sem'ia i shkola* 1958(1): 42–44.

Nikol'skaia, E. 1958b. "Uiut i obstanovka v dome." *Sem'ia i shkola* 1958(11): 46–47.

Nikol'skaia, E. 1959. "Ob uiute v obstanovke kvartiry." In *Besedy o domashnem khoziaistva*, edited by I. Abramenko and L. Tormozova, 7–56. Moscow: Molodaia gvardiia.

Nikol'skii, M. 1959. "Novyi dom—novyi byt." *Izvestiia*, December 19.

Orlova, Galina. 2004. "Apologiia strannoi veshchi: 'malen'kie khitrosti' sovetskogo cheloveka." *Neprikosnovennyi zapas* 2004(34).

Papernyi, Vladimir. 1993. "Men, Women and Living Space." In *Russian Housing in the Modern Age*, edited by William Brumfield and Blair Ruble, 149–170. Cambridge: Cambridge University Press.

Parker, Roszika, and Griselda Pollock. 1987. *Old Mistresses: Women, Art and Ideology*, 2nd ed. London: Pandora.

Pasternak, Boris. 1957. *Doktor Zhivago*. Milan: Feltrinelli Editore.

Pasternak, Boris. 1958. *Doctor Zhivago*. Translated by Max Hayward and Manya Harari. London: Collins Harvill.

Pohl, Michaela. 2004. "Women and Girls in the Virgin Lands." In *Women in the Khrushchev Era*, edited by Melanie Ilič, Susan E. Reid, and Lynne Attwood, 52–74. Basingstoke: Palgrave Macmillan.

Rau, Santha Rama. 1959. *My Russian Journey*. New York: Harper & Brothers, 5.

Reed, Christopher, ed. 1996. *Not at Home: The Suppression of Domesticity in Modern Art and Architecture*. London: Thames & Hudson.

Reid, Susan E. 1993. "The Art of Memory: Retrospectivism in Soviet Painting of the Brezhnev Era." In *Art of the Soviets*, edited by M. Cullerne Bown and B. Taylor, 161–187. Manchester: Manchester University Press.

Reid, Susan E. 1997. "Destalinization and Taste, 1953–1963." *Journal of Design History* 10(2): 177–202.

Reid, Susan E. 2002. "Cold War in the Kitchen: Gender and Consumption in the Khrushchev Thaw." *Slavic Review* 61(2): 211–252.

Reid, Susan E. 2004. "Women in the Home." In *Women in the Khrushchev Era*, edited by Melanie Ilič, Susan E. Reid, and Lynne Attwood, 149–176. Basingstoke: Palgrave Macmillan.

Reid, Susan E. 2005. "The Khrushchev Kitchen: Domesticating the Scientific-Technological Revolution." *Journal of Contemporary History* 40(2): 289–316.

Reid, Susan E. 2006a. "Toward a New (Socialist) Realism: The Re-Engagement with Western Modernism in the Khrushchev Thaw." In *Russian Art and the West: A Century of Dialogue in Painting, Architecture, and the Decorative Arts*, edited by Rosalind P. Blakesley and Susan E. Reid, 217–239. DeKalb: Northern Illinois University Press.

Reid, Susan E. 2006b. "Khrushchev Modern: Agency and Modernization in the Soviet Home." *Cahiers du Monde russe* 47(1–2): 227–268.

Reid, Susan E. 2006c. "The Meaning of Home: 'The Only Bit of the World You Can Have to Yourself.'" In *Borders of Socialism: Private Spheres of Soviet Russia*, edited by Lewis Siegelbaum, 145–170. New York: Palgrave.

Reid, Susan E. 2009. "Happy Housewarming." In *Petrified Utopia: Happiness Soviet Style*, edited by M. Balina and E. Dobrenko, 133–160. London: Anthem Press.

Reid, Susan E., and David Crowley, eds. 2000. *Style and Socialism: Modernity and Material Culture in Post-War Eastern Europe*. Oxford: Berg.

Rendell, Jane, Barbara Penner, and Ian Borden, eds. 2000. *Gender, Space, Architecture: An Interdisciplinary Introduction*. London: Routledge.

Renkama, Jukka. 2006. *Ideology and Challenges of Political Liberalisation in the USSR, 1957–1961: Otto Kuusinen's "Reform Platform," the State Concept, and the Path to the 3rd CPSU Programme*. Helsinki: Suomalaisen Kirjallisuuden Seura [Bibliotheca Historica 99].

Roth-Ey, Kristin. 2007. "Finding a Home for Television in the USSR, 1950–1970." *Slavic Review* 66(2): 278–306.

Ruble, Blair. 1993. "From *Khrushcheby* to *Korobki*." In *Russian Housing in the Modern Age*, edited by William Brumfield and Blair Ruble, 232–270. Cambridge: Cambridge University Press.

Rybitskii, V. 1963. *Dlia doma, dlia sem'i. V pomoshch' novoselam.* 5 January 1963. Script for television program. State Archive of the Russian Federation (GARF), f. 6903, op. 2, d. 449.

"Schastlivoe novosel'e." 1959. *Trud*, November 7.

Semenov, I. 1964, 10 August. "Velikoe pereselenie narodov" (cartoon). *Krokodil* 22: 8–9.

Sharov, Iu. and G. Poliachek. 1960. *Vkus nado vospityvat' (besedy dlia molodezhi).* Novosibirsk: Novosibirskoe knizhnoe izdatel'stvo.

Shlapentokh, Vladimir. 1989. *Public and Private Life of the Soviet People: Changing Values in Post-Stalin Russia.* Oxford: Oxford University Press.

Shvarts, Mikhail. 1998. "'Krushchevki' eshche postoiat." *Etazhi* 2, March 1.

Sidorov, I. 1960. "Tsvety v komnate." *Ogonek* 24(June), inside back cover.

Siegelbaum, Lewis. 2006a. "Cars, Cars, and More Cars: The Faustian Bargain of the Brezhnev Era." In *Borders of Socialism: Private Spheres of Soviet Russia*, edited by Lewis Siegelbaum, 83–103. New York: Palgrave.

Siegelbaum, Lewis, ed. 2006b. *Borders of Socialism: Private Spheres of Soviet Russia.* New York: Palgrave.

Skidelsky, Robert. 1992. *John Maynard Keynes.* London: Papermac.

Solzhenitsyn, Alexander. 1963. *One Day in the Life of Ivan Denisovich.* Translated by Ralph Parker. Harmondsworth: Penguin Books.

Sosnovy, Timothy. 1954. *The Housing Problem in the Soviet Union.* New York: Research Program on the USSR.

Sosnovy, Timothy. 1959. "The Soviet Housing Situation Today." *Soviet Studies* 11(1): 1–21.

Sparke, Penny. 1995. *As Long as It's Pink: The Sexual Politics of Taste.* London: Pandora.

Strumilin, Stanislav. 1960. "Rabochii byt i kommunizm." *Novyi mir* 1960(7): 203–220.

Suvorova, I. 1962. "Na urovne plokhogo rynka." *Dekorativnoe iskusstvo* 1962(6): 46.

"Svoimi rukami." 1961. *Dekorativnoe iskusstvo SSSR* 1961(3): 48–49.

Torshilova, Elena. 1971. "Byt i nekotorye sotsial'no-psikhologhicheskie kharakteristiki sovremennogo zhilogo inter'era." In *Sotsial'nye issledovaniia. Vypusk 7: Metodologicheskie problemy issledovaniia byta*, edited by A. G. Kharchev and Z. A. Iankova, 137–144. Moscow: Nauka.

"Tribuna chitatelia: O vospitanii vkusa." 1955. *Novyi mir* 1955(2): 247–254.

van Herck, Karina. 2005. "'Only Where Comfort Ends Does Humanity Begin': On the 'Coldness' of Avant-Garde Architecture in the Weimar Period." In *Negotiating Domesticity: Spatial Productions of Gender in Modern Architecture*, edited by Hilde Heynen and Gülsüm Baydar, 123–144. London: Routledge.

Varga-Harris, Christine. 2005. *Constructing the Soviet Hearth: Home, Citizenship and Socialism in Russia, 1956–1964.* PhD diss., University of Illinois at Urbana-Champaign.

Varga-Harris, Christine. 2005 "Homemaking: Keeping Appearances and Petticiat Rule." Paper presented at conference "The Thaw," Berkeley, May.

Vihavainen, Timo. 2004. *Vnutrennii vrag: bor'ba s meshchanstvom kak moral'naia missiia russkoi intelligentsii.* St. Petersburg: Kolo.

Voeikova, Irina. 1962. "Vasha kvartira." *Rabotnitsa* 1962(9): 30.

Voeikova, Irina. 1964. "Uiut-v prostote." *Rabotnitsa* 1964(10): 30–31.

Vysokovskii, Aleksandr. 1993. "Will Domesticity Return?" In *Russian Housing in the Modern Age*, edited by William Brumfield and Blair Ruble, 271–308. Cambridge: Cambridge University Press.

Weintraub, Jeff, and Krishan Kumar, eds. 1996. *Public and Private in Thought and Practice.* Chicago: University of Chicago Press.

Wolff, Janet. 1990. *Feminine Sentences: Essays On Women and Culture.* Cambridge: Polity Press.

Zhukov, K. 1964. "Tekhnicheskaia estetika i oborudovanie kvartir." *Tekhnicheskaia estetika* 1964(2): 1.

Zubkova, Elena. 1998. *Russia After the War: Hopes, Illusions, and Disappointments, 1945–1957.* Translated by Hugh Ragsdale. Armonk, NY: ME Sharpe.

Archives

Central Moscow City Archive/ Tsentral'nyi arkhiv goroda Moskvy (*TsAGM*).

TsAGM, f. 62 (Moskovskii gorodskoi sovnarkhoz), op. 15, d. 267 (Perepiska o zhiloi ploshchadi i zaselenii doma v Nov. Cheremushkakh kvartal 23 korpus 8, 1964).

TsAGM, f. 62, op. 15, d. 266 (Perepiska s Upravleniem, 1964).

TsAGM, f. 21, op 1 d. 125, d. 126, d. 127, and others (visitors' book for exhibition "Iskusstvo- v byt!" 1961).

TsAGM, f. 4, op. 139, d. 35 (Stenog. otchet soveshchaniia ob opyte agitatsionno-massovoi raboty sredi naseleniia po mestu zhitel'stva 4/01/1961).

Russian State Archive of Literature and Art (RGALI).
RGALI, f. 2329, op. 4, ed. khr. 1388, ll. 51–2 (transcript of discussion of exhibition "Iskusstvo—v byt!" June 6, 1961).
RGALI, f. 2329, op. 4, ed. khr. 1391 (visitors' book, exhibition "Iskusstvo—v byt!" Moscow 1961).

Central Archive of Literature and Art, St. Petersburg (TsGALI SPb).
TsGALI SPb, f. 341, op. 1, d. 357 (meeting in Leningrad in December 1953 between architects and workers).
TsGALI SPb, f. 341, op. 1, d.386, l. 16 (discussion of new housing blocks, Leningrad 21 May 1954).

State Archive of the Russian Federation (GARF).
GARF, f. 6903, op. 2, d. 449 ("Dlia doma, dlia sem'i. V pomoshch' novoselam," Script of program for Moscow Television. January 5, 1963; February 2,1963).

Russian State Archive for Social and Political History (RGASPI).
RGASPI f. M-1, op. 32, d. 972, ll. 58–63 ("O merakh bor'by s antikhudozhestvennymi, khalturnymi izdeliiami," March 1959).

10

Women as "Socialist" Dwellers

Everyday Lives in the German Democratic Republic[1]

Christine Hannemann

Dwelling in the Former German Democratic Republic (GDR): Social Determinants and Premises

In "socialist" cities women, as city residents, resided in many spaces simultaneously: in their living areas within the dwelling, in their apartment house, in their neighborhood, and in the city. Although planners assumed gender equality, what did it really mean to be female in a "socialist" city, in a newly designed "socialist" city quarter, or in a "socialist" apartment? What characterized the housing and the various social spaces in the new "socialist" estates, and how did these spaces affect women? How did cities reflect a governmentally decreed gender equality?

In East Germany's (the GDR's) state ideology,[2] housing was considered part of the societal conditions and structures that were defined through socialism. The GDR was one of several countries that had an extensive "top-down modernization program" as one of the satellite states under the control of the former Soviet Union:

> The largest attempt to modernize a society through social upheaval started with the Russian revolution in the early 20th century, a revolution that set off a series of economic and social experiments by communist regimes that represents a broad attempt at comprehensive social, as well as technical reform.[3]

Ideological concepts for housing were translated into traditionally conceived patriarchal housing structures catering to the nuclear family, in what would nevertheless be defined as socialist micro-housing.[4]

In the case of the GDR, the ideological concept of the *Platte* (the common term for buildings made of prefabricated panel housing) must be examined with some caution, as the relationship between ideology and the resulting architectural and urban configuration of mass-produced housing is anything but simple or straightforward. Housing complexes in urban residential areas in the GDR cannot simply be analyzed as spatial translations of abstract ideological ideas. Any socio-historical understanding of the industrialized building processes in the GDR, as well as the buildings this process produced, must take into account three political and historical parameters: first, the political and institutional context, not only in the GDR as a specific society, but in all societies in the Eastern Bloc that were based on a bureaucratic "state-socialism"; second, the difference between industrialized housing for the lower and the middle classes as developed in the 1920s and 1930s by modernist architects (e.g., modernist architects working in the Weimar Republic) and the realization of those technocratic ideas through

GDR housing policy; and third, the origins and content of socialist housing and living concepts within the historical context of the GDR, especially with regard to positions on dwelling and family espoused by the SED (Socialist Unity Party, the ruling party of the GDR).

In comparison to Western countries, where industrialized housing construction was largely seen as a question of technology, socialist countries and especially the GDR imposed the *Platte* as a political doctrine. Beginning in the 1950s, socialist countries linked the planning and realization of newly constructed housing estates with debates about the "socialist city" that had originated in the late 1920s and early 1930s. During this earlier period the Soviet Union had developed numerous urban projects for "new socialist cities" in Siberia, such as Magnitogorsk, Orsk, and Nowokusnezk. These cities were developed in cooperation with modern architects such as Ernst May and Hans Schmidt. The new urban projects were based on the concept of Fordism and were designed to organize the city by function. Housing areas were designed to foster a "socialist lifestyle." A city block was thus developed to be seen as a spatial unit that included not only housing, but also community facilities, everyday infrastructure, and green areas. During these years the essential theoretical and practical foundation for the "socialist housing complex"[5] was developed—a complex that became the heart of the "socialist city."

In the GDR, as in all other socialist countries, the "socialist housing complex" became the dominant urban model during the mid-1950s. The transition to industrial housing construction went hand in hand with standardization and the development of building typologies that influenced both building production and housing schemes. The size of these housing schemes was planned as a catchment area for about 4,000 to 5,000 residents and containing a school. The walking distance between an individual housing block and common facilities, such as day care centers, schools, stores, and public transportation, was used as a metric to determine dimensions and spatial constructions. Housing estates were planned to be strictly residential areas and offered few employment possibilities. The spatial division between public and private that one finds in bourgeois social models did not exist, because private space was renounced. On the basis of the distances between the buildings and the open spaces, areas were planned and realized in the form of undifferentiated green areas, playgrounds and open spaces where laundry could be dried.

Newly constructed housing developments were based on the guidelines of "socialist housing complexes" and on the increased use of prefabricated concrete panels (the *Platte*). The repetitiveness of uniform housing complexes, constructed without regard to their existing surroundings, finally led to spatial and architectural monotony. This monotony became a defining feature of the GDR's large housing estates, the basic feature of which was the "de-differentiation" of dwelling types. A logical consequence of the socialist concept for society was thus the monofunctional and uniform layout of that society's built environments, which was seen as expressing a *sozialistische Lebensweise*, or a socialist lifestyle. Following official SED ideology, people were expected to realize and fulfill their identity as socialist human beings in all dimensions of collective life: as part of a nuclear family, a *Hausgemeinschaft* (households in the same building), the political activities of the *Nationale Front*,[6] as well as the many other clubs and societies for sport, leisure, culture and consumption.[7] In terms of urban planning, architects and engineers were not to work on the endless differentiation of individual dwelling typologies but rather to materialize the collective essence of socialist life into living spaces. Put another way, planners were to design a clear and legible relationship between the individual household (family), the housing block, the housing estate (neighborhood), and the heart or center of the city itself. This mandate became a strong programmatic concept that was put forward as the very ideological argument for a fully rationalized and industrialized system of building construction.

Three ideological aspects became the driving force behind industrialized building itself: (1) a belief in technology and in social progress through industrialization as based on Marxism-Leninism; (2) a fixation on the socialist nuclear family; and (3) the ideology of social equality. In the following paragraphs I discuss these three elements.[8]

Christine Hannemann

A Belief in Technology and Social Progress

In the Moscow "All Union Congress" of 1954, the GDR's political direction was clearly laid out: The only possible way to realize socialist housing would be to adopt mass production techniques in the building sector. The early years of the GDR had seen the KPD (Communist Party of Germany) and later the SED lay out the fundamental principles of unlimited industrialization of the building process. Over the next several years, these two organizations were able to initiate sweeping political and socioeconomic changes. Their actions removed the independent bureaucratic institutions that had been based on a central democratic system, and replaced them with models dictated by the Soviet Union. As a result, the GDR began mirroring all of the Soviet Union's sociopolitical reforms, a factor that remained unaltered until Mikhail Gorbachev's perestroika policies took hold in the late 1980s.

Certainly, one could consider industrial production methods as necessary for tackling the problem of housing shortages. The GDR, however, implemented a centralized building system that was expanded in the 1970s by the introduction of *Wohnungsbaukombinate* (building cooperatives), an implementation that was driven primarily by ideology and politics. The goal of industrializing the building sector was based on a tenet of Marxism-Leninism as developed by Lenin and his followers. Socialism was to set free the productive forces that would allow a transition to communism. Industrialization of the building process was therefore not a purely technical problem but rather the incarnation of social progress. This process reflected the Marxist-Leninist theory whereby "'a fixation on craft' in production [would be overcome]. This refers to a process of moving from primitive manual production to industrialized mass production."[9] The stated goal behind the theory was to encourage technological progress.

The ideas espoused in the GDR did not differ greatly from those promoted in West Germany (the Federal Republic of Germany, or FRG) with respect to improving the post-war building sector. In the FRG, public housing as an ideal was never fully realized for various reasons, even though the government and building industry went to great lengths to try to implement subsidized housing as a strategy for providing cost-efficient housing in the 1960s and 1970s. Internationally, the industrialization of housing production was viewed as a means to modernize and rationalize construction technology, with industrialized nations such as France, Germany, the US, and the Scandinavian countries forerunners in this process.[10]

The *Platte* had symbolic power: it designated a belief in progress. If one considers industrialization of the building process as a part of modernism, then within architectural theory the *Platte* follows the ideas of the Modern movement as developed in the 1920s. Within social and political theory, however, the *Platte* follows the tradition of Leninism. Lenin hoped to use socialism to establish a political avant-garde that would in turn enforce modernism. Large-scale industrialization was designed to cater to the economic principles of socialism. Instead of allowing disproportionate and anarchical developments, which were seen as a hallmark of capitalist industry, the GDR government made a conscious decision to base the national economy on what was perceived as the peoples' needs. In formulating this abstract theory, government officials neglected to include a strategy for industrialized building, and from the beginning of the GDR, officials found that they were unable to overcome systemic management and planning problems as well as a shortage of building materials.[11] In order to justify the industrialization of housing, socialist theorizers cited passages from Marx's *Kapital*[12] about "machinery and large industry," even though Marx never theorized industrialization.

The most important result of all these theoretical considerations was the establishment of "socialist building" as an economic and social process. All state and political ideologies were forthwith used as a means to enforce building typologies in the field of housing. The development of such typologies culminated in the 1970s with the nationwide introduction of housing that would be known as the WBS 70, a standardized apartment unit made of modular concrete panels.

188

Fixation on the Nuclear Family

The concept of the socialist family further determined the development of housing in the GDR. The socialist family was regarded as the smallest "cell" of society. The sociology of the family in the GDR demonstrated that this main social unit corresponded to the regime's political-ideological goal. The composition of the nuclear family was defined as one or two parents with one or more children. As noted by Jutta Gysi, "91.5% of all households [with more than one person] in the GDR fit this definition."[13] In the GDR, non-standard lifestyles were rare, and it was the two-generation nuclear family that determined the development and layout of industrialized housing, starting with a 1950s model known as the Q3A, up to the WBS 70 model that became ubiquitous in the 1970s. The floor plan of each apartment type was limited by the ceiling span and by the location of installation walls for kitchens and bathrooms. Although design choices were theoretically numerous, economic constraints and the technical organization of the building process allowed only seven floor plan possibilities for the WBS 70 model.

Not only the floor plan concept but also the community infrastructure planned for housing estates was fraught with consequences. Because the party line held that the nuclear family model was to be combined with women's full-time employment, it was necessary to include social facilities within the housing complexes so that families could be relieved of some of their domestic burdens. In addition to housing, the goal was thus to build a day care facility and a kindergarten, a school, a supermarket and a service center in each complex, although these goals were not always realized. Nevertheless, facilities such as schools and a supermarket were considered the minimum acceptable level of social infrastructure, and were regarded as essential for the workforce, particularly for women. This not only showed the situation women found themselves in, but also reflected contemporary communist social constructs, which assumed that "labor [would be] the primary purpose of life."

The Ideology of Social Equality

Generally, social change in the GDR was characterized by the regime's and political party's claim that the development of social structures was to be centrally planned and had to correspond to economic goals. The main structural components of this system were ownership, education, professional qualification, labor and income. The central ideological leitmotif was the rapprochement of classes and an end to class stratification as it pertained to essential conditions for life, such as income, education and housing. Siegfried Grundmann, a leading urban sociologist who practiced at the GDR's Academy of Social Sciences (a scientific research institute of the SED) described this concept as follows: "The existence of class struggle and the deepening of social differences shall no longer rule the social structure of cities. Instead, cities shall be regulated through a step by step reduction in social differences."[14] Implementing this ideal meant that equal and decent housing had to be created for all.

The call for equal and decent housing appeared in urban concepts, especially those of the late 1960s and 1970s, of which the urban and housing plans of Halle-Neustadt can be regarded as exemplary.

> The city housing complex under socialism is not marked by the differentiation of job levels, income or any other factors. [. . .] [T]here are no socially caused differences in residential quarters. Everybody lives under the same circumstances in the same apartments. A director and a delivery person from the chemical plant live side by side in the same building, and the town mayor lives in the same housing block as a janitor from the energy plant and the urban planner who planned the town.[15]

In general, social change in the GDR was characterized by the fact that it was

> shaped by the demands of the state and party leadership from the beginning. The development of social structures in all its essential components—ownership structure, education structure,

qualification structure, employment structure and income structure—required central planning and governing according to economic aims.[16]

Until the end of the 1970s and with regard to essential conditions of life such as income, education, and housing, the concept of an increasing rapprochement between all classes and levels of society thus remained the regime's central ideological leitmotif.

The principle of equality called for a "women's policy," which was formally defined through the principle of equal rights for women. In fact, women were already seen as mostly equal in the sense of having equal legal rights. Nevertheless, in some aspects of daily life, equality still needed to be established. This is documented by social policy, in particular the mothers' policy of the 1980s, during the last years of the GDR's existence as a state. While such policies sounded progressive on the surface, their ambivalent nature emerged through linguistic formulations such as the "compatibility of work and motherhood."

The idea of "equal rights" was reflected in the ideological premises for the GDR's housing development program, implemented in 1971, which had the aim of solving the "housing problem" by defining it as a social problem. In its technical and spatial implementation, this meant constructing large new city quarters, thus reducing urban development to the construction of residential buildings augmented by minimal infrastructure facilities. Such facilities included day cares, kindergartens, schools, and facilities for medical and service-related care, positioned so that residents could easily reach them on foot. Residential-area infrastructure was seen as necessary, because a high percentage of working-age women were employed outside the home.[17] On the one hand, high female employment levels expressed the success of social policies that encouraged women's equality. On the other hand, this female employment was objectively an economic and personal necessity resulting from the GDR's political organization of economic and thus also income systems.

The social conditions of the workday defined the objectives and, above all, the time schedule for residential activities, including working times, daily or weekly rhythms, the stressful working experience, and the opening hours of shops, medical institutions, and governmental authorities. Women researchers in the GDR's Academy of Sciences researched the "GDR woman" and characterized her in a text called "The Woman Question as Part of the Social Question" as follows:

> The woman [of the GDR] is employed full time; she is active in all fields of activity and all social classes and strata; her income is in the middle range [for the GDR], she does not, in the majority of cases, work as a shift worker, and she has few leadership roles within the GDR economy. Normally, she has a 10th-grade education [which meant she completed a polytechnic secondary school—Ed.], one or two children, and is married.[18]

In the GDR, living in a nuclear family was typical, with the nuclear family defined as a heterosexual family comprised of two genders (male and female) and encompassing two parents or one parent with child(ren). Women had to work at the reproduction of the labor force, namely mothering, and all family nurturing and household work. In spite of the fundamentally desired equality of women in all essential areas of life in the GDR, domestic work was still seen as predominantly women's work. Time budget analyses demonstrated that women (usually mothers) performed three quarters of housework and family-related work in addition to being employed outside the home 40 to $43 - \frac{3}{4}$ hours per week, plus breaks and time spent commuting.[19]

Housing in large estates was a consequence of the building policy pursued by the SED's single-party system and became a way of life for millions of people in the GDR, as illustrated by the following figures: of the total housing stock of approximately seven million apartments in the GDR, 2.1 million were housing units built after World War II.[20] At an average household size of 2.5 persons, those 2.1 million new units housed at least 5.25 million people, or about a third of the GDR's population.

Women and their families tended to live in units built as part of the WBS 70 system. This apartment type was erected in large housing estates located for the most part at the periphery of industrial and administrative centers (the so-called main housing estates). This standardized housing type constituted the basis of the housing construction program of the GDR, with typical floor plans shown in Figure 10.1.

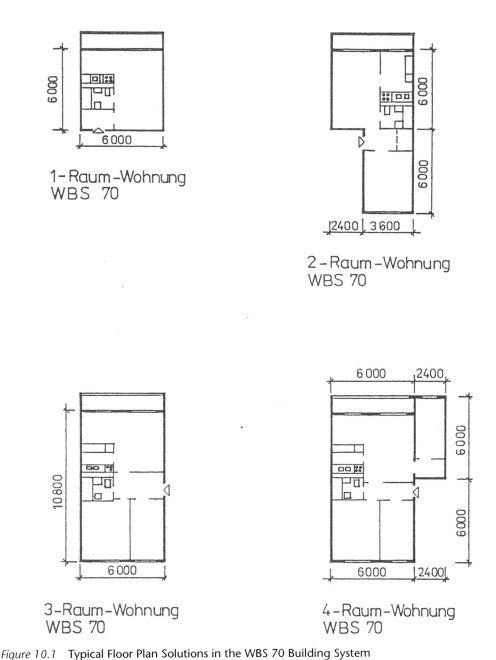

Figure 10.1 **Typical Floor Plan Solutions in the WBS 70 Building System**
Source: C. Hannemann, based on drawings of the former Bauakademie der DDR, Institut für Wohn- und Gesellschaftsbauten, Abteilung Prognose.

Christine Hannemann

In the next section, I would like to provide examples that combine certain aspects of women's lives in large estates with the results of sociological research conducted in three GDR cities with major post-war housing developments. The studies are the result of urban and residential sociological investigations carried out in post-war housing estates located in two industrial cities with a high degree of new construction: Hohenstücken, built in 1987 in the city of Brandenburg; and Lobeda, constructed in Jena in 1988. Furthermore, I was able to use the results of a longitudinal study carried out in newly built residential areas of Berlin-Marzahn in 1981, 1983, and 1986. A secondary analysis done by Kirsten Gurske examined women's lifestyles in more detail.[21]

Brandenburg, a steelmaking and manufacturing center in the administrative district of Potsdam with a population of about 95,000 in 1988, was a city of industrial workers. Industries included the district's factories for housing components, a transmission plant, services based on the presence of the military,[22] a wool yarn spinning mill (the largest "female" employer in the city), and other light industry. Because of the economic importance of Brandenburg's industrial base, a number of housing estates were built in the city. One of the largest was Hohenstücken, located on the eastern edge of the city. A typical residential area of the 1980s, it was constructed to house 21,000 people.

Jena-Lobeda, the second case study, is located on the southern edge of Jena. A former industrial, university, and administrative town with a population that was once about 100,000 residents, Jena was one of the largest cities in the GDR. Because of its importance as an industrial center—the *Volkseigenes Kombinat Carl Zeiss Jena*, which produced optical lenses, was located here—Jena became a point of focus in the construction of new housing estates. Nine years after the GDR was founded in 1949, Jena became the first city in which "complex housing" was constructed, defined as housing created with industrial methods and planned with a certain level of infrastructure located within the housing estates. Jena, founded in 1230 and almost completely destroyed during World War II, was literally rebuilt from 1949 to 1989. The newly developed area of Jena-Lobeda (the largest new complex in the city) had about 40,000 inhabitants in 1988. The social infrastructure in the different parts of this large housing estate (Lobeda-West, Jena-Winzerla, and Jena-Lobeda-Ost) included 11 schools, six supermarkets, two youth clubs, the Lobeda cultural center, and a sports complex with an indoor swimming pool and sauna.

The third case study, the newly built district of Berlin-Marzahn on Berlin's eastern edge, had approximately 150,000 inhabitants in 1988—the size of many medium-sized towns—making it the largest peripheral housing estate of the GDR. The initial impetus for the construction of Berlin-Marzahn came as the result of a 1976 decision made by the Politburo of the Central Committee of the SED and the Council of Ministers of the GDR to "further socialist development of the capital of the GDR." According to this declaration, 300,000–330,000 apartments were to be created between 1976 and 1990 in (East) Berlin—Figure 10.2 shows a view across the area—through both new construction and the modernization of existing dwellings. The entire project involved the construction of 33,000 apartments with all necessary housing-related infrastructure, such as supermarkets, schools, bus stops, and kindergartens (see Figure 10.3): "In total, eight residential complexes were to be built, including compact centers with overlapping functions."[23] Because of an increased need for housing, however, planned infrastructure remained unbuilt and the areas reserved for infrastructure were used for additional housing blocks. The cuts in infrastructure mainly affected cultural institutions, services, and health care.

Due to the strong similarity of the structural-spatial parameters of post-war GDR housing and the general uniformity of the ways of life in the GDR, the findings discussed below can stand in for many new development areas of the GDR.

Figure 10.2 View Across Berlin-Marzahn, 1984
Source: Bundesarchiv.

Figure 10.3 The GDR's large estates were meant to be family friendly. Here, day care workers go for a walk with their charges in a large housing estate in 1970.
Source: Bundesarchiv.

Social and Demographic Characteristics of New Construction Areas in the Former GDR

A characteristic feature of the new housing estates in the former GDR is that the population structure followed state housing policies. Because older, inner-city buildings were seen as inadequate for families, young families tended to move from the inner city to the new residential areas once they were finished.

This led to a relatively homogeneous age structure in the new complexes, with a low median age and a higher number of children than in the inner cities. Thus, in 1988, 57% of the adult female population of the Jena-Lobeda sample ($n = 126$) was under 40 years of age and a further 25% was under 55. New construction areas were only of relevance for retirees if they lived in a retirement home located in the complex. In the context of "complex housing construction" (see earlier definition), retirement homes were only placed at the periphery of the new housing estates.

The population of the new residential areas differed from that of the inner-city areas in terms of their professional makeup as well. There were fewer unskilled and semiskilled workers than in the inner cities. Women with higher education levels and technical qualifications were overrepresented. A gender-specific analysis of the planned economy by industrial sectors reflected the employment structure of women in the new housing estates. For the most part, the residents of newly built areas worked as white-collar employees or as members of the "intellectual class,"[24] whereby women were typically qualified as skilled workers or had a technical education. In Marzahn, for example, 40% of the adult female residents were white-collar employees or members of the intellectual class, and more than 50% had a technical education certificate.[25] The main areas of employment for women were trade, the service and health sectors, and education.

How can we characterize the typical woman living in a large housing estate in the GDR? She was 25–45 years old, married or living with a significant other (whereby a quarter lived without a partner), and had one or two children. As far as her social status went, she was a skilled worker or a member of the intellectual class.

The new housing areas were predominantly residential. Due to the mono-functional nature of the estates, few women were able to find work near their place of residence. In Marzahn, 13% of women worked in an adjoining industrial district, while about one-fourth—predominantly university graduates—worked in the inner city of East Berlin. Because of the burdens associated with employment and caring for the family, a high proportion of women (29%) switched their workplace after moving to the new housing estates, while 13% wanted a new job, but had not yet found anything suitable. Men, on the other hand, changed their jobs far less frequently.

A small number of residents of the new housing estates were single parents. That this number was not larger can be explained by the sociopolitical aims of the housing allocation system, which favored "young marriages." Children of unmarried mothers were thus born in older buildings.[26] Single-parent families in the newly built areas were mainly headed by divorced women. About 12% of the women in Jena-Lobeda and 15% in Berlin-Marzahn were divorced. Three-quarters of these women had children. In their age structure and qualifications, they were otherwise not different from the "typical" inhabitant of a large housing estate. In Berlin-Marzahn, for example, more than 50% of single women had a degree or a higher education qualification, while 40% had a skilled worker qualification. Living without a second adult in the household, the commute to work (in Marzahn, residents often needed 45–60 minutes to reach their inner-city jobs), childcare, and the location and infrastructure of the residential areas often lead to problems in coordinating everyday life, problems that were particular to women.

The Gender-Specific Use of New Apartments

The "classic" new apartment described earlier provided a framework for gender-specific behavior. This can be demonstrated through case studies of housing use, which were carried out in Jena-Lobeda in 1988.[27] They showed that there were interrelationships between gender-specific use of space, housing images, and how people lived. The spatial organization of the new apartments was restricted by the average unit size of 57 m^2 and by the hierarchical, function-specific floor plan design described below.

A special focus of the case studies was the analysis of special features, which resulted from the continuation of professional activities and/or work-intensive hobbies at home. Typically this consisted of activities such as repairing one's car, tending a vegetable garden, or sewing one's own clothes. Such activities were important as they circumvented deficiencies in the GDR such as the lack of professional auto-repair facilities, lack of fresh produce, or lack of consumer goods such as fashionable clothing. Over two-thirds of the men engaged in such "work after work," while women's after-hours work consisted of maintaining the household.

The newly built apartments offered few possibilities for arranging an undisturbed workplace. Altering the set use of the rooms contradicted traditional living arrangements, which were defined as consisting of a living room, bedroom, and children's rooms. Figure 10.4 (right side) shows a floor plan based on a GDR code called the "technical standards, goods regulations, and delivery conditions," while the left drawing shows the husband's permanent or temporary workplaces in the living room, marked with an "A." Having the husband's work area in the living room blocked this space for family use, and it explains why the wife usually did the housework in the kitchen or in the bathroom (where she did the laundry), while the husband was "working."[28]

Christine Hannemann

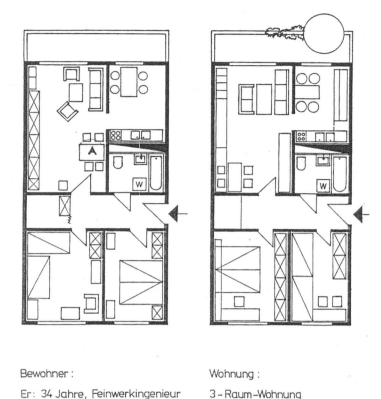

```
Bewohner:                                Wohnung:
Er:  34 Jahre, Feinwerkingenieur         3 - Raum-Wohnung
Sie: 32 Jahre, Finanzökonom              WBS  70
Es:  9 Jahre, 2 Krippenkinder            11 - Geschosser,  TGL 9552
```

Figure 10.4 Case Study Jena-Lobeda
Source: C. Hannemann, based on drawings of the former Bauakademie der DDR, Institut für Wohn- und Gesellschaftsbauten, Abteilung Prognose.

How Did Women in the Large Housing Estates Rate Their Living Conditions?

Large estates have generally been regarded negatively in Germany. Even in the former GDR, they were seen as gray, boring, and anonymous, and as bedroom cities. Yet the new housing estates were also the highest attainable residential standard for many people, especially if such housing was located in East Berlin, which as the capital offered better supplies of everyday goods than any other city in the GDR.

Residents and non-residents reported significant differences in their assessment of the new estates. Residents positively remarked on factors such as comfort, pleasant play facilities for toddlers, traffic calming, and noise and pollution control. For example, 75% of married women reported feeling comfortable in their homes. This meant that women resigned themselves to the deficiencies of their housing's architectural design. When residents offered negative comments, these generally pertained more to the residential areas than to the apartments themselves.

Residents regarded both room sizes and apartment floor plans as problematic. The apartments were designed with occupancy loads based on GDR housing policy norms, in which a two-room apartment was to house two to three people, a three-room apartment three to four people, and a four-room apartment four to five people. A typical allocation was a three-room apartment for a family with two children, which residents regarded as too small for a family of this size. Residents consistently criticized the children's room and the bathroom as too small, the kitchen as too narrow, and storage space as inadequate. Women also criticized the lack of variability in the use of rooms. In apartments where the living room and the kitchen were directly connected, for example, the largest room (designed to be the living room) could not be used as a children's room.

In interviews, women rarely addressed the fact that Marzahn had ample greenery in the form of interior courtyards and playgrounds, but deficits in cultural and sports infrastructure. Women expressed dissatisfaction with the lack of recreational facilities. Particularly criticized, especially compared to older neighborhoods, were courtyard designs and playgrounds. Women saw courtyards as offering too little privacy, few sheltered places, too few trees, and no evergreen trees or shrubs to offset the gray of the concrete buildings. Playgrounds were seen as unimaginative, with a lack of padding, and not enough fixtures or vegetation that would provide shade. In all, women criticized that there were too few playgrounds and public spaces with benches and trees.

Interviews with women showed that in the residential areas, women and families lacked possibilities for communication. Restaurants, cafés, and shopping were also criticized, as were available options for sporting activities. Women preferred swimming pools and saunas, which were usually overcrowded or had problematic opening times. Woman rejected state-sponsored clubs (usually located in stand-alone community centers—Ed.). Women supported equal opportunities for access to sports facilities. Woman living in Marzahn found possibilities for sports and cultural activities lacking, especially those that allowed joint activities for women and their children.

Ultimately, it was obvious that women, who had to manage the time they had available, would first save time by reducing time spent on the "culture" of everyday work and family. The discrepancy between leisure interests and being able to realize such interests was much greater for women than for men. Women in Marzahn were more interested in the offerings of the so-called high culture than were men. For one-fifth of the women, (East) Berlin's cultural opportunities were the most important factor in their attachment to the city, followed by their place of work. Nineteen percent mentioned social contacts at work as the most important factor (not the work itself), and another 19% stated that their partner was the most important aspect of their attachment to Berlin. By contrast, men ranked their workplace first when asked for their reasons for living in Berlin.

In general, the gender-specific analysis of urban and residential sociological studies shows that women and men have clear similarities in their values concerning housing. On the one hand, this resulted from real "equality" in housing conditions. On the other hand, the "myth that existed in the minds of many women of having already achieved equal rights meant they were blinded to the real disadvantages [that they faced in everyday life]."[29] Gender-typical differences can be found in the job structures of housing complexes and in the use of social-spatial facilities. In particular, there were gender differences in how residents drew from the surrounding urban area and how they used their more immediate living area.

Gender-specific differences in housing use in the former GDR can be summarized as follows:

- Women were more invested in their communities. They performed more community service activities in the neighborhood, for example by taking care of their neighbors' children.
- For women, the immediate residential environment's leisure quality was less important than outdoor activities (such as gardening and crafts).
- Women more frequently spent their leisure time at home with their family than did men. Men were more frequently in the city center.
- Men used cars significantly more often than did women. Women drove less, and biked, walked, or used public transportation more, even when making big purchases or traveling to recreational areas.
- To save time, women often chose to work close to home, accepting lower earnings or employment for which they were overqualified.

Christine Hannemann

Also in the GDR: "Female as Usual"

At first glance, urban and residential research results from the GDR and the FRG show striking similarities, as women's assessments of their problems as city dwellers were not very distinguishable in the two systems. The "socialist" manner of developing urban and living space in the context of societal structures also resulted in social differences that can be judged as critical for women. In both systems, new housing areas proved to be inadequate as places for women's work, while everyday life remained differentiated into male and female spheres. Empirical studies showed that most women remained within the patriarchally dominated arena of "hierarchical differences."

The result of social changes in the cities of the GDR can be summarized as follows: on the one hand, infrastructure in the new housing estates provided a basic socio-spatial condition for the emancipation of women; that is, such spaces were designed to make it possible for women to participate in social life, and especially in professional life. On the other hand, the socio-spatial structures that were developed, from the concept of the dwelling to the monostructure of housing areas, formed a specific example of a patriarchal urban development and residential building practice. Such spaces represented the sociocultural transformation of a gender-specific division of labor into systematically planned spatial patterns.

The difference between the planners' intent and the sociologically measured result is extremely interesting, especially when seen in the context of a broader socialist movement that was meant to solve the "woman question." Planners followed modernist tenets on a spatial level, including a separation of functions in both urban plans and floor plans. This modern planning proved to be a good proxy for a "modern" society.

The one- to four-room prefabricated apartment that became the new standard for the GDR was designed to enable socialist dwelling. At the same time, it was also the outcome of "modernity." The GDR used its own standardization codes, which provided the basis for the apartment's functional structure, dimensioning and furnishing. The codes governing housing, known as the "TGL 9552-dwelling house," had similarities to codes that were developed as part of Western modernity.[30]

Modern dwelling typologies are determined by ideological and policy-driven configurations, as well as technical norms, such as the West German "DIN" code (*deutsche Industrienorm*, or German Industrial Norm). Within the FRG there were 600 to 750 DIN codes in the 1970s and 1980s that referred to the construction industry. State-subsidized housing in the FRG and public housing of the GDR were both characterized by standards that determined dwelling sizes as well as details such as storage and service spaces, circulation spaces, and circulation areas for the residents' physical movement. The corresponding codes used in the GDR, called TGL ("*Technischen Normen, Gütevorschriften und Lieferbedingungen*," or "technical norms, quality specifications and delivery terms") and the DIN codes used in the FRG were similar, differing only in their title and wording, as well as slight differences in technical parameters such as minimum height requirements for living rooms.

The summary presented in Table 10.1 illustrates the similarities and differences between the two norm systems.[31]

The drawings in Figure 10.1 show a generic floor plan including the parameters presented. These types of floor plans, which were additively stacked into apartment buildings, were arranged in two ways: first, as five- to six-story slab buildings with double-loaded stairwells, or as 11-story towers with two apartments per floor. The standardization of the newly built apartments guaranteed that particular dwelling functions would be assigned to particular rooms. This was true for the kitchen and the bathroom because of their installation walls, but also held true for the apartment's other spaces.

In the GDR, planners developed WBS 70 housing with the aim of creating equal and comfortable housing conditions for a majority of the population. The regime attempted to use technical and organizational means to further the basic processes of a socialist society as well as to accelerate the convergence between classes and social strata. But in the final result, all of the ideas and efforts presented were simply a variation on the ideas of modernity. In order to more fully understand this, the historic roots of the GDR's industrially built apartments, and especially their floor plans, need to be explained.

Women as "Socialist" Dwellers

At the beginning of the 1920s, floor plan typologies for publicly subsidized housing in Germany were developed so that a typical small apartment had, on average, an area of 65 m². The result was that in public housing, requirements were formulated so that a high percentage of dwellings were built for households with similar social structures. Against this historic background we can begin to understand how ages-old social differentiations in housing conditions were spatially recorded, and how in the GDR such differentiations were altered in favor of a statewide use of uniform typecast buildings and floor plans. The impact of public housing of the 1920s and 1930s, which was influenced by structural and spatial concepts of upper-class nineteenth-century housing, has been widely documented. Schema 10.1 shows this coherence conclusively.

Table 10.1 Technical Norms in the Federal Republic of Germany (FRG) and in the German Democratic Republic (GDR)

FRG	GDR
DIN 18011:	TGL 9952/01:
Dwelling; metrics and mapping of the rooms	Dwelling house; generic claims concerning the homes and apartments
DIN 18022	TGL 9952/02:
Kitchen, bathroom and water closet inside the residential construction; planning guide	Dwelling house; kitchen, kitchenette TGL 9952/04:
DIN 18025	Dwelling house; constructional fire protection
Apartments for disabled people	TGL 9952/03:
	Dwelling house; sanitary rooms

Schema 10.1 The Formal Principles of Apartments Throughout the Centuries

Scheme A: formal principle of the upper-middle-class dwelling of the nineteenth century

1)   Representation and household area
living room, dining room and kitchen
day area

2)   Family area
children's room, bedroom and bathroom
night area

3)   Servants area

Scheme B: formal principle of public housing in 1920s and 30s

1)   Representation and household area
living room, dining room, kitchen
day area

2)   Family area (private space)
children's room, bedroom and bathroom
night area

Scheme C: formal principle of the prefabricated apartment in the GDR

1)   Family and household area
living room, children's room, dining place and
kitchen (especially kitchen inside)
day area

2)   Individual area
bedroom and bathroom, partly children's room
night area

See also Hannemann (1989, 63f); Wahrhaftig (1985, 69).

Christine Hannemann

Notes

1. An early version of this chapter was published as: Christine Hannemann. 1991. "Wenn Frauen 'sozialistisch' wohnen—zur Lebensweise in 'Hauptwohnbaustandorten' in der DDR." In: *FrauenPläne (Frauen Pläne)—Stadtumbau, sozialer Wandel und Fraueninteressen*, edited by B. Martwich, 123–136. Darmstadt: Wohnbund Verlag für Wissenschaftliche Publikationen. Furthermore, I would like to express my thanks to Antonia J. Krahl for her assistance.
2. The GDR ceased to exist as a state after German unification in 1990.
3. The quote is taken from Alexandra Staub's introduction to this volume.
4. A *microraion* was a primary administrative unit and residential area in the Soviet Union and in some former communist states as well as the former GDR. Residential districts in most of the cities and towns in Russia, the republics of the former Soviet Union and in the early GDR were built in accordance with this concept. See Goldzamt 1974; and also Hannemann 1996.
5. See Sozialistische Wohnkomplex (Der) 1959.
6. This was the SED's politically motivated merging of all parties and societal organizations.
7. See Engelberger 1958/59.
8. See Hannemann 1996.
9. Vogée 1967, 30.
10. See Hannemann 1996.
11. See Reidemeister 1972.
12. See Marx 1977 [1867], 391ff.
13. Gysi 1988, 510.
14. Grundmann 1984, 205.
15. Autorenkollektiv 1972, 85.
16. Wielgohs and Schulz 1990, 23.
17. In 1970 the percentage of employed women among the employed population of the GDR was 77%, and in 1980 it was 80.5%. See Winkler 1990, 78.
18. Erhardt and Weichert 1988, 531.
19. Hannemann 1991, 125.
20. Winkler 1990, 157.
21. For this section, I was able to use unpublished research by Kirsten Gurske (cf. Niederländer, Gurske, Schumann, and Richter 1987). Niederländer, Gurske, Schumann, and Richter (1987) is based on unpublished studies from 1981, 1983, and 1986. Gurske evaluated Niederländer et al.'s three studies with regard to women's issues. The result can be considered a precursor to the article she published in 1987 titled "*Zur Entwicklung eines Neubaugebiets der Hauptstadt der DDR.*"
22. These included an army base, Brandenburg penitentiary, and offices of the State Security Service (*Staatssicherheitsdienst*).
23. Kuhirt 1983, 227.
24. "The special role of the intelligentsia [. . .] finds its expression in certain occupations and activities requiring high qualifications which as a rule presuppose a university, technical college, or other specialized education" (Baylis 1974, 64). This group of employees included all persons who carried out specific activities in various areas of the social reproduction process that were not directed towards the production of a material product. The intelligentsia included all persons with a university degree or technical qualification. (For a discussion of employees and intelligence in Marxist-Leninist sociology, see Grundmann 1978, 307, and Baylis 1974, 64). The ambiguity of the concepts is evident when one regards their definitions. The information given here is based on the subjects' self-classifications.
25. Niederländer, Gurske, Schumann, and Richter 1987, 81.
26. Schmidt 1990, 26.
27. These results are derived from nine case studies that focused on residential behavior with regard to the relationship between work and housing. This qualitative investigation was used as a supplement to a representative survey on urban development and housing in Jena in 1988. The case studies were drawn up in the form of daily protocols.
28. Hannemann 1989, 61ff.
29. Nickel 1990, 39.
30. Hannemann 1999, 406ff.
31. Hannemann 1999, 407f.

References

Autorenkollektiv. 1972. *Halle-Neustadt. Plan und Bau der Chemiearbeiterstadt.* Berlin: VEB Verlag für Bauwesen.

Baylis, Thomas A. 1974. *The Technical Intelligentsia and the East German Elite: Legitimacy and Social Change in Mature Communism.* Berkeley, Los Angeles, and London: University of California Press.

Engelberger, Otto. 1958/59. "Zum Stand unserer städtebaulichen Entwicklung unter den Bedingungen der Industrialisierung des Bauwesens." *Wissenschaftliche Zeitschrift der Hochschule für Architektur und Bauwesen Weimar* 6(3): 161–168.

Erhardt, Gisela, and Brigitte Weichert. 1988. "Einige soziologische und sozialpolitische Aspekte zur Entwicklung der Frau im gesellschaftlichen Arbeitsprozeß." In *Jahrbuch für Soziologie und Sozialpolitik,* edited by Akademie der Wissenschaften der DDR, Institut für Soziologie und Sozialpolitik, 525–533. Berlin: Akademie Verlag.

Goldzamt, Edmund. 1974. *Städtebau sozialistischer Länder: soziale Probleme.* Berlin: VEB Verlag für Bauwesen.

Grundmann, Siegfried. 1978. "Intelligenz." In Wörterbuch der marxistisch-leninistischen Soziologie, edited by G. Assmann, W. Eichhorn I, E. Hahn, G. Heyden, H. Jetzschmann, A. Kretzschmar, M. Puschmann, H. Taubert, and, R. Weidig, 307–310. Opladen: Westdeutscher Verlag.

Grundmann, Siegfried. 1984. *Die Stadt.* Berlin: Dietz Verlag.

Gysi, Jutta. 1988. "Familienformen in der DDR." In *Jahrbuch für Soziologie und Sozialpolitik,* edited by Akademie der Wissenschaften der DDR, Institut für Soziologie und Sozialpolitik, 508–524. Berlin: Akademie Verlag.

Hannemann, Christine. 1989. "Zur Geschlechtsspezifik des Wohnens von Frauen in der DDR." In *Frauen erneuern ihre Stadt. Kritische Frauenblicke auf Stadterneuerung in Hamburg und Berlin,* edited by M. Allers, B. Brakenhoff, U. Martiny, B. Martwich, M. Pedersen, H. Rake, and S. Stern, 61–70. Hamburg: Self-published.

Hannemann, Christine. 1991. "Wenn Frauen 'sozialistisch' wohnen—zur Lebensweise in 'Hauptwohnbaustandorten' in der DDR." In *FrauenPläne (Frauen Pläne)—Stadtumbau, sozialer Wandel und Fraueninteressen,* edited by B. Martwich, 123–136. Darmstadt: Wohnbund Verlag für Wissenschaftliche Publikationen.

Hannemann, Christine. 1996. *Die Platte.* Wiesbaden: Vieweg Verlag.

Hannemann, Christine. 1999. "Normiertes Glück Ost und West. Über Standard, Norm und Sozialstaatlichkeit." In *Ernst Neufert. Normierte Baukultur im 20. Jahrhundert,* edited by W. Prigge, 405–429. Frankfurt and New York: Campus Verlag.

Kuhirt, Ullrich. 1983. *Kunst der DDR 1960–1980.* Leipzig: Seemann.

Marx, Karl. 1977 [1867]. *Das Kapital,* Vol. 1. Berlin: Dietz Verlag.

Nickel, Hildegard Maria. 1990. "Frauen in der DDR." *Aus Politik und Zeitgeschichte. Beilage zur Wochenzeitung Das Parlament,* B 16–17/90: 39–45.

Niederländer, Loni, Kirsten Gurske, Wolgang Schumann, and Karin Richter. 1987. *Zur Entwicklung eines Neubaugebiets der Hauptstadt der DDR, Berlin.* Berlin: Self-published.

Reidemeister, Andreas. 1972. "Zur Entwicklung der Produktivkräfte und der Produktionsverhältnisse im Bauwesen der DDR." *Kursbuch 27 Planen, Bauen, Wohnen*: 139–167.

Schmidt, Gudrun. 1990. "Sozialdemographische Wirkungen bisheriger Stadtplanung." In *Frauengerechte Stadt??!,* edited by C. Hannemann, G. Schmidt, and H. Vetter, 23–27. Berlin: Self-published.

Sozialistische Wohnkomplex (Der). 1959. *Deutsche Bau-Enzyklopädie.* Offprint. Berlin: Deutsche Bauakademie.

Vogée, Hans Dieter. 1967. *Das Bauwesen in der Deutschen Demokratischen Republik.* 4th ed. Berlin: VEB Verlag für Bauwesen.

Wahrhaftig, Myra. 1985. *Emanzipationshindernis Wohnung. Die Behinderung der Emanzipation der Frau durch die Wohnung und die Möglichkeit zur Überwindung.* 2nd ed. Cologne: Pahl-Rugenstein.

Wielgohs, Jan and Marianne Schulz. 1990. "Reformbewegung und Volksbewegung. Politische und soziale Aspekte im Umbruch der DDR-Gesellschaft." *Aus Politik und Zeitgeschichte, Beilage zur Wochenzeitung "Das Parlament"* B 16–17/90: 15–24.

Winkler, Gunnar, ed. 1990. *Sozialreport '90. Daten und Fakten zur sozialen Lage in der DDR.* Berlin: Verlag die Wirtschaft.

11

Reclaiming Space for Women

Negotiating Modernity in Feminist Restorations in Post-socialist Eastern Germany

Katja M. Guenther

Kröpeliner-Tor-Vorstadt is a trendy neighborhood adjacent to the city center of Rostock, a northeastern German port city curled around the mouth of the Warnow River as it meets the Baltic Sea. Kröpeliner-Tor-Vorstadt comprises residential and industrial buildings mostly built between 1875 and 1940. With sections damaged during World War II, the neighborhood was largely left to decay during the socialist period. After the collapse of state socialism in 1989, the neighborhood experienced a wave of restoration and soon became known for its nightlife and hipster vibe, thanks to the large representation of students and recent graduates from the University of Rostock, whose campus partially lies within the neighborhood. The neighborhood offers coffee shops, health food stores, and bars, as well as quieter residential side streets lined with early twentieth-century apartment buildings, many of which were built to house workers at the nearby wharf (see Figure 11.1). Although some of the housing is distinctively student-quality, rents per square meter in this neighborhood are easily double those of properties in the city's many peripheral neighborhoods in which the high-rise, socialist-era *Plattenbau*, the prefabricated concrete panel apartment buildings that became the signature of East German housing policy, are dominant.[1]

A bright pink apartment building stands out among the more muted buildings on one side street in Kröpeliner-Tor-Vorstadt. The vivid color suggests something unusual about the house and, indeed, this is not a typical apartment building. Rather, this is Amandahaus (Amanda House), a residential collective for single mothers. Restored by a group of women between 1994 and 1996, Amandahaus is an effort to maintain affordable housing for single women in one of the city's more desirable central neighborhoods. Beyond providing below-market rents, Amandahaus is also organized to ensure that the women help each other with childcare, emotional support, and friendship.

The Beginenhof, a building that has been central to feminist organizing in Rostock since the collapse of state socialism in 1989, is located in Rostock's Südstadt neighborhood. Although just over 3 kilometers (2 miles) away, the Südstadt feels like a world apart from Kröpeliner-Tor-Vorstadt. In place of four- and five-story historic row houses stand massive complexes of *Plattenbau* that the East German government erected en masse in cities and towns across the country in an effort to quell a housing crisis and provide low-cost, modern housing to East German workers. The Südstadt was developed between 1961 and 1965 with the construction of nearly 8,000 apartments intended to house about 20,000

Figure 11.1 Margaretenplatz in Kröpeliner-Tor-Vorstadt, Rostock. The residential buildings in this area date from the late nineteenth century.
Source: © Helge Busch-Paulick, 2010.

Figure 11.2 Prefabricated GDR housing blocks in Rostock's Südstadt neighborhood in an image from 1967
Source: Bundesarchiv.

residents. Figure 11.2 shows an image of the neighborhood from the late 1960s. Built in parallel rows of buildings with green lawns between them, a scheme designed to maximize natural light and airflow, the *Plattenbau* neighborhood is divided by several large promenades and a series of smaller side streets. The original development included a shopping center that was expanded in 1993; the neighborhood is also home to many of the scientific and technical departments of the University of Rostock, including the medical school and medical center.

The Beginenhof is a two-story building nestled in an expanse of greenery between the taller *Plattenbau* and is built around a courtyard in the same flat-roofed panel style as the neighboring high-rises. Originally built as the city's first day care, or *Kita*, the building became a home for feminist organizations in 1994. In contrast to the cozy and historic feeling of Amandahaus, the Beginenhof—which comprises a mixture of office and social spaces—evokes an institutional setting.

In this chapter, I examine how feminist activists in Rostock have negotiated the spaces of Amandahaus and the Beginenhof. How do feminists claiming and restoring existing buildings to use as feminist centers draw on historical and contemporary ideas about feminism, space (including design and architecture), and place? How do they negotiate GDR-era built environments? How are these spaces and feminists' relationships to them tied to socialist and post-socialist understandings of modernity? I identify layered meanings in how feminist organizations relate to competing eastern and western German discourses of modernity, which are expressed through the architecture and planning decisions of the East German and unified German states. A flashpoint in these conflicting visions of modernity is the *Plattenbau* buildings and the neighborhoods they constitute. *Plattenbau* were intended to be pinnacles of modernity and of the worker's state, but after unification they quickly fell into disfavor as symbols of state-planned housing gone awry. Shifting ideas about modernity as a consequence of unification contributed both to changes in ideas about desirable built environments and in gender norms and systems. Here, I link those changes, drawing on analyses of interview and ethnographic data collected between 2000 and 2015 to reveal how feminists conceptualize their spaces vis-à-vis feminism, modernity, and the East German past.

The first section of the chapter provides a brief historic context of both the gender politics and housing politics of the German Democratic Republic (GDR). Although an ideal more than a reality, the GDR prided itself on supporting modern women, or women who were engaged in paid labor and enjoyed equal rights with men. The West German gender structure, which was pushed eastward through unification, instead has a more ambivalent relationship with gender and modernity, promoting contradictory ideas of modern womanhood as entailing the same rights and entitlements as men, but also unabashedly tied to reproduction and the domestic sphere. The end of the GDR catalyzed a crisis of gender in eastern Germany as well as an economic crisis that involved, among other elements, a major shift in housing markets. A rapid emphasis on *Sanierung*, or restoration and "modernization" of older buildings, followed the collapse of state socialism and had a distinct emphasis on Western housing norms as being modern—comfortable, convenient, and safe—and socialist housing as outdated and inadequate. The second and subsequent sections turn to examine how feminist organizations and activists made sense of shifting ideas about built environments and community as they carved out spaces for their organizations.

Renovating Rostock: Gender and the Building Boom of the 1990s

German unification in 1990 ushered in multiple layers of change in the social, political, and economic life of eastern Germans, involving gender, space, and competing ideas about modernity. Western conceptualizations of modernity focus on individual liberties and the right of self-actualization, rendering modernity an inherently non-socialist concept. In contrast, the East German state asserted its advances towards being modern by linking social progress (or what would be called modernization in the West) to social equalization.

East German modernity also involved a stated (if not always realized) commitment to gender equality. In the GDR, women and men were both expected to engage in paid labor, and East German women held the world record for labor force participation rates. Women remained primarily responsible for the domestic sphere, but the East German state could claim that its incorporation of women into the workforce facilitated social equality.

With the collapse of state socialism in 1989 and the unification of East and West Germany in 1990, newly introduced gender norms and policies from western Germany that construct women as mothers and wives and minimize women's economic activity, coupled with a substantial economic recession in eastern Germany, resulted in conditions that made it increasingly difficult for women to remain in the labor market in eastern Germany.[2] Western German state policies did away with woman-friendly policies from the GDR, such as accessible state-funded day care for working mothers, stigma-free access to birth control, abortion on demand, and relatively easy, no-fault divorce.[3] As unemployment soared in eastern Germany in the early and mid-1990s, women were seen as the least deserving of workers, and they found limited political or social support from the unified German state for their continued access to employment. Some women—especially young women and those with higher levels of education—left the region in search of opportunities elsewhere. Others found themselves laid off and either underemployed or temporarily employed in government-funded positions. Many women lost their connection to workplaces that had been important to them and found themselves relegated to domestic spaces. This involved both a shift in where women spent their time and in their identities. Women whose social value once rested on their roles as workers and mothers now found their social value tied primarily to their roles as wives and mothers.[4]

Even as eastern Germans enjoyed new political freedoms and the freedom to consume in a capitalist economy, economic contraction and policy change attempted to shift gender norms, largely to the detriment of women.[5] Eastern Germans as a whole were second-class citizens in the unified Germany, constructed as backwards and infantile relative to western Germans. Dominant images of eastern German women in the unified Germany were particularly unforgiving, representing them as cold-hearted mothers (*Rabenmütter*) and indifferent wives who left their children in state-run day care centers to pursue employment in pursuit of socialism's false promise of equality.

In the immediate unification period of 1989–90, eastern German women organized extensively to resist threats to women's rights and status, albeit with little visible impact on national policy discourse.[6] Most feminist activism focused on the local, where women worked together to develop services that had long been needed, but which were unavailable in the GDR, such as domestic violence intervention and rape crisis centers, or on services that were now needed because of the end of the GDR, such as job training and reeducation programs. Although the GDR's stated goal—which the state routinely implied was already achieved—was social equality, including gender equality, women in the GDR nonetheless experienced workplace discrimination, the double burden of employment and motherhood responsibilities, and gender-based violence.[7] Unification created new possibilities for women to organize around these issues, which they also rightly feared would become more severe and pronounced through unification.[8]

Feminists not only organized in the rapidly changing political and economic environment of German unification; they also did so against a backdrop of powerful physical transformation in eastern Germany. Economic challenges facing the GDR resulted in delays in maintaining and expanding infrastructure and housing. Some historically significant sites had remained untouched since the end of World War II. The best known of these is the Dresden Frauenkirche, which GDR leaders left in ruins as a war memorial, but cities like Rostock also typically had historic centers that had been ruined or left to decay. The built environment in the GDR in 1989 is thus often described as cold, drab, and dilapidated: although the GDR initiated and completed many new building projects, including an ambitious albeit not fully realized program to provide new housing for all of its residents by 1990, the lack of access to materials and the need for cost-effectiveness meant the mass-produced buildings appeared monotonous, and once built, were often poorly maintained.

Following unification, eastern Germany became a country of construction. For western German developers and preservationists, eastern Germany represented a treasure trove. While urban planning in western Germany in the 1960s and 1970s often laid waste to historic areas, eastern Germany's historic buildings were in a state of decay, but usually nonetheless intact. As anthropologist Jason James notes,

> Given the stigmatization in the unified Germany of the GDR and most East Germans' pre-1990 biographies, architectural heritage offers an important and rare occasion for Easterners to claim a positive contribution to the unified nation. To an extent, it even redeems their relative deprivation under socialism, since the survival of so much "historic substance" now appears as a fortunate (if unintended) effect of the GDR's economic failings.[9]

Although Rostock is a peripheral city in eastern Germany, its city center remained a target for investment and was quickly renovated following unification, restoring color and architectural detail to previously neglected Gothic, neo-Gothic, and baroque buildings. In the economic spasms that dominated eastern Germany in the early 1990s, city planners were eager for investment, and the federal government created numerous subsidies and tax incentives to redevelop real estate in the former GDR.[10] In eastern Germany, many apartments in pre-war buildings shared bathrooms located on stairway landings; virtually none had appliances like dishwashers or washing machines. Dilapidation was common and was especially acute in the pre-war neighborhoods and the *Plattenbau* communities built before the 1970s. Both the government and private investors poured hundreds of millions of euros into renovating socialist-era housing to achieve West German standards, which generally involved major renovation to meet building codes for safety and energy efficiency. Overall, western Germany spent an estimated two trillion euros on redevelopment efforts between 1990 and 2008, including public infrastructure and employment programs, as well as private sector investment.[11]

During this transformation, *Plattenbau* buildings largely fell out of favor, even as many eastern Germans continued to rely on them for affordable housing. From a western German perspective, *Plattenbau* buildings were the ugly and cheap evidence of a disastrous social experiment and became synonymous with East German backwardness. *Plattenbau* buildings projected "an image of eastern Germany as visually undernourished and less eventful, suggesting that East time had lagged behind West time."[12] As city centers, which had been grossly neglected during the GDR era, were restored and became viable and desirable places to live in the early 1990s, the social value of the *Plattenbau* areas decreased.[13]

At the time of unification in 1990, much of the housing in Rostock was *Plattenbau* erected in outlying neighborhoods to house workers and their children. In the GDR, Rostock experienced substantial development, including the construction of new neighborhoods designed to house tens of thousands of people.[14] The neighborhoods of Dierkow, Evershagen, Groß Klein, Lichtenhagen, Lütten Klein, Reutershagen, Schmarl, and Toitenwinkel saw the construction of over 70,000 apartments, and in 1989, over 70% of Rostock's population lived in *Plattenbau* buildings, compared to a national average in the GDR of about 25%.

The GDR's version of modernity, as physically expressed through the *Plattenbau* building program, was different from that of the West: rather than emphasizing the connection between technology and individual freedom like the West, the GDR emphasized the connection between technology and social equality. The *Plattenbau* buildings were developed as a great equalizer that would offer all workers similar standards of accommodation and a shared community experience. The construction of the *Plattenbau* neighborhoods helped maintain the GDR's political legitimacy as it fulfilled a core promise to provide modern housing for the proletariat. Heavily celebrated as important innovations and a key contribution to the socialist project, *Plattenbau* buildings enabled East Germans to experience the pleasure of shiny new apartments with central heat, private indoor plumbing, and appliances. Relocating citizens from dilapidated housing in urban cores to the *Plattenbau* areas outside of city centers also removed people from their daily reminders of life before socialism.[15] The residents of the city center—where bathrooms were shared and buildings heated with coal—included dissidents and others who failed to comply with state policies and ideologies, and who thus were given lowest priority for housing assignments.

At the time of unification in 1989, much of the GDR's housing was substandard compared to that in Western Europe. At the same time, in the years following unification, depopulation reduced housing demand, even as government incentives to renovate substantially increased supply, resulting in a market slump in the mid-to late 1990s. In Rostock, the population declined from 250,000 to barely 200,000 in the first five years after unification. Renovated pre-war buildings close to the city center became desirable housing, while high-rise neighborhoods became less popular and were viewed as options primarily for the lowest classes and recent immigrants. Neo-Nazi riots against asylum-seekers

Katja M. Guenther

in 1992 in the *Plattenbau* neighborhood of Lichtenhagen solidified the reputation of *Plattenbau* areas as home to low-class reactionaries.

Creating a Feminist Home: Amandahaus

Feminist organizations participated in the restoration of buildings against this backdrop of massive social change, repurposing buildings for new feminist groups in ways that reflected complex and often contradictory responses to East and unified German discourses of modernity. Amandahaus emerged as a semi-collective apartment building specifically for single mothers to enable such women to live close to the city center with other women who could help share in childcare and offer other forms of support. Amandahaus emerged from a working group of the local chapter of the *Unabhänginger Frauenverband* (UFV, or Autonomous Women's Association), an East German feminist organization that developed shortly before the fall of the Berlin Wall in 1989. The UFV first sought to incorporate feminist perspectives into the calls for reform of the GDR and later, when the GDR collapsed, promoted the interests of eastern German women during and after the process of German unification.[16] Particularly active between 1989 and 1991, the UFV existed as a loose federation of local chapters that sought to respond to local, regional, and national feminist concerns.[17] Reflecting its roots in the GDR, the UFV emphasized women's right to economic participation, while also integrating issues more visible in Western feminism, especially violence against women, which was a largely unacknowledged issue in the GDR.

The social upheavals accompanying unification created numerous pressures for women. Although many of the changes they were confronted with originated in policy and economic transformations at the national and even global levels, women often experienced major changes in their everyday lifeworlds. Women lost their jobs, which had been key sources of identity and daily anchors in the realms of economic and social activity. They saw their neighborhoods transformed. The schools their children attended introduced new curriculums and systems of organization. Suddenly, no one learned Russian and everyone took English courses. A rush of unfamiliar consumer goods and technologies became must-have items, even as familiar goods disappeared.

The early 1990s were a period of possibility, excitement, and anxiety for eastern German women. The UFV was one site where women could meet with other women concerned about women's rights and the maintenance of policies and practices from the GDR that helped women and supported their economic integration.

The women who conceptualized Amandahaus were strangers to each other prior to unification, but met during the wave of activism that contributed to the collapse of the GDR and the following feminist mobilization. All were active in the UFV and other organizations that were part of the Beginenhof, which I discuss shortly. After unification, these women saw life in *Plattenbau* housing as undesirable and isolating because of the depopulation of *Plattenbau* neighborhoods and the focused redevelopment of the city center. Of particular concern for the women of Amandahaus was that *Plattenbau* were located mostly in peripheral neighborhoods that quickly became known for their various indicators of social decay, such as high vacancy rates, business closures, graffiti, and neo-Nazi or other countercultural activity.

The influence of population shifts and housing policy on these perceptions cannot be underestimated. Rostock's total population shrank by 20% between 1990 and 2000, with a marked decrease in the mid-1990s. The departing migrants were primarily younger residents seeking economic opportunities elsewhere. At the same time, more and more housing was being renovated with the support of the federal government, and with particular interest in historic city centers. The population thus shifted within the city: many people moved toward the city center and out of the *Plattenbau* neighborhoods, leaving some feeling like ghost towns. For single women, these communities even felt scary; the eruptions of neo-Nazi activity in some of these areas made feminists feel especially unwelcome and disconnected from the populations there. *Plattenbau* buildings also presented a logistical problem for collective housing: there was not enough interest or funding for the founders of Amandahaus to buy a five-story (or taller) apartment building. The only smaller multifamily buildings were those in the city's older neighborhoods. Because the success of the Amandahaus model also depended on full occupancy, the founders were concerned about investing in communities with unstable housing markets, where it might be difficult to find tenants in the future. Taken together, these factors made the *Plattenbau* neighborhoods undesirable for Amandahaus' founders, even if not all of the founders were averse to the type of housing or the neighborhoods.

Living close to the city center posed its own challenges. Housing stock was limited, and the building the Amandahaus collective purchased was basically a ruin. They undertook renovations almost entirely by themselves, working evenings and weekends for two years until they could move in. Because of structural constraints, they ended up with one studio apartment, and decided to rent this apartment to a woman who had raised children as a single mother in the GDR but now lived alone. The remaining flats, as planned, were for women with children. All of the initial residents were involved in the planning, design, and construction of the house.

The narratives of the founding members of Amandahaus reveal the complexities of making sense of the post-unification transformations, including rapid shifts in the housing market, the introduction of consumer opportunities (especially those focused on domesticity), and the rising cost of living. Most clearly, the founders saw having a modern apartment not as a status symbol, as it so often was in the West, but as evidence of freedom. In my conversations with the women of Amandahaus, the ability to *choose* and to individuate were central to their housing choices, reflecting capitalist beliefs around self-fulfillment but not of accumulation. "We wanted to live nicely!" one of them recalls. Further conversation revealed that "nicely" meant apartments with modern amenities, natural light, high ceilings, and proximity to public transportation and the central commercial areas of the city. Living "nicely" meant living freely in physical spaces that felt open and connected.

While their narratives reflect an interest in self-fulfillment, Amandahaus was born out of a desire to make sure single mothers could afford to live in the city center. This reflected a GDR-era emphasis on social equality, and an insistence that income and occupation should not unduly limit residential choices. Combining the socialist emphasis on class equality, a feminist recognition that single mothers are uniquely economically disadvantaged, and a capitalist interest in self-fulfillment, the founders of Amandahaus integrated diverse ideologies.

For the Amandahaus residents, living in the city center after unification meant having greater access to resources valued under capitalism, particularly consumer opportunities such as shops and restaurants. It also offered access to pedestrian culture, which can provide a further sense of community and belonging. Amandahaus residents came to see *Plattenbau* neighborhoods as unstable, as it was unclear to them who would live there, what it would cost, or what the overall future of these neighborhoods would be. Moving to the city center afforded a greater sense of security on these fronts. Although the founders of Amandahaus recognized many positive attributes of life in the GDR, they ultimately found living in a rebuilt historic building more freeing *and* more stable than remaining in neighborhoods that in the GDR had once promised equality and stability.

Still, residents at Amandahaus with whom I spoke consistently acknowledged the importance of *Plattenbau* for life in the GDR and as a continuing symbol of the GDR's efforts at social equality. In reflecting on her move from an apartment in a high-rise to Amandahaus, Carolina acknowledges the major loss of space she experienced: she gave up a spacious multiroom apartment to move into a studio in Amandahaus as the sole resident with no children living at home (she raised two children as a divorcee in the GDR). As she recounts:

> Amandahaus was the best thing—excepting my kids of course—that I have experienced in my life. I [previously] had a nice, big apartment, but I was lonely in the *Plattenbau* neighborhood, and

> I gave it all up to live in this studio, but the quality of my life, and how the architect worked with me so I have lots of light and some space—I feel totally comfortable here. I have a small closet, but I have taken on a leftist philosophy that I don't need so much. And I will be able to afford this place when I am old. You never know how rental markets will change, but I will be able to afford this place.

For Carolina, being part of a community of women was most important in her decision to move, but she also very much wanted to live in the city center, an area that had previously felt off-limits to her. Having come of age in a rural area before living in a *Plattenbau* neighborhood for most of her adult life, moving to Kröpeliner-Tor-Vorstadt felt to her like she was moving to the heart of the city. She found the stores, restaurants, bars, and street life invigorating. She also found important financial reasons for her move: in addition to the stability of mutual support from other residents, the rent is tied to the original property loan, not to the apartment's market value, so rent rates barely increase. Although she moved in during her forties, she has since retired, and having a stabilized rent is significantly advantageous when living on a fixed retirement income. Paradoxically, living in the historic city center is important to her because of access to consumer opportunities, but she does not have the space (or the financial resources) to buy things.

For many eastern Germans who grew up in the GDR, the consumer opportunities of capitalism are overwhelming. For the founders of Amandahaus, the most important part of being in the city center was not to be able to consume more, but to be able to observe consumption. Seeing consumer opportunities is a fascination and trying new things is like a sport. The women routinely discuss what they have seen for sale, often mocking consumer culture even as they seem entertained by it. Although these women have dedicated substantial energy and time to building their own home, they largely reject consumer-based notions of domesticity, preferring simple and sometimes homemade items to decorative items sold in stores.

The founders of Amandahaus share a narrative of desirability and modernity that focuses on a combination of location, function, and affordability. Following the GDR's position that housing can serve as a social equalizer, they developed Amandahaus as a way to resist rising inequality. They especially feared that single mothers would be pushed out of the newly desirable central core of the city because of their lower income. Insistence on living in the central city was also an effort to resist capitalist pressures: they refused to be priced out because they were single women with children, arguing that everyone has a right to live in the city center, not only the wealthy. They also wanted to build a community, not just a space. As one founder states:

> The point here is not the money, but the advantages of living here together in the house with a sort of a surrogate family. We all help watch the kids, and we have an environment here to support single mothers who work and are socially engaged, and we want to make things easier for such women through small favors or help.

The model of living at Amandahaus still respects modern, Western notions of privacy, for example that each family should have a separate apartment with its own kitchen and bath. The only communal spaces in the building are a spare room in the basement and the backyard. In terms of living habits, this was not a collective in the sense of countercultural movements of the 1960s. But when people are home, their doors to the stairwell are open or unlocked, and residents (who have all become close friends) move between apartments with little concern about intruding or being an inconvenience. Children scamper freely across apartments, looking for attention, treats, and/or mischief.

Amandahaus supports a family type that is viewed by some as modern and by others as a social ill associated with modernity: the single-parent family. Residents reject such criticisms, instead asserting that society needs to do more to support *all* family types, and pointing to women's lower earnings as the primary reason why single-mother households often struggle. Choosing to be a long-term or even permanent single mother is a key part of Amandahaus residents' identities. The house is not intended to serve as a way station for single women as they seek a partner, but rather to offer women who foresee longer-term single parenting an affordable and supportive home.

Moving in and letting go of the idea of partnering is a big step for women. In a society obsessed with romance and partnering, Amandahaus residents expect no imminent change in partnership status. For many women, this can be difficult to acknowledge. As one of the founders and original residents of Amandhaus observes:

> I think it is a big step to make this decision [to live here]. There is an acknowledgement that you are taking control of your own life and no longer waiting for some prince to come and take you away. You stop waiting for rescue, and instead say, "I am living here now, and this is my choice." There are not that many women who will take that step. It is a big step in life.

The women who live in Amandahaus also acknowledge that their home is often misunderstood. They report that people always ask if men are allowed in the apartments at all—"as if we would tie them up in the cellar and pour lead over them!" one of them jokes. When they first began work on the building, some neighbors feared they were really opening a brothel, or that the house was a home for lesbians. Men are welcome in the space, and many of the residents date or even have serious (albeit non-cohabiting) relationships with non-residents. However, if and when a resident partners and wants to cohabit, she must move out of Amandahaus.

Amandahaus presents an opportunity for women and their children to live apart from men in a built environment that is an unapologetic modernization of a historic building in a central neighborhood. Pushed out of the *Plattenbau* neighborhoods over the uncertainty about their future character, cost, and the scale of the buildings, and pushed into the city center by a desire for something new and different from the common living experiences of the GDR, the founders of Amandahaus have integrated elements of socialist and capitalist visions of modernity into their space. The community orientation reflects GDR-era values, as does their insistence on the right of all people, not just wealthier people, to live in neighborhoods seen as desirable. At the same time, they accept much of what the new capitalist real estate market deems desirable.

Building a Feminist Community: The Beginenhof

The Beginenhof is the women's center in Rostock. The building houses numerous organizations, the composition of which has changed since the Beginenhof opened in 1994. During and immediately following unification, the Beginenhof's founding women's groups, including the UFV, the local crisis center for survivors of gender-based violence, and a women's educational and job training organization, shared space in a former military barrack in the city center. The original location was inadequate for the growing number of women's groups and the services they sought to offer. The women's groups thus banded together to incorporate an umbrella organization, Rostock Women's Initiatives, that could negotiate for a new property. After considering other possibilities, Rostock Women's Initiatives signed a 25-year lease on a building in the Südstadt they named the Beginenhof after the Beguines, women who formed semi-monastic communities between the thirteenth and eighteenth centuries, and who were known residents of Rostock, where they cared for the ill and infirm.

The Beginenhof represents a space physically very different from Amandahaus. The structure was originally built as a childcare center. Two stories of prefabricated concrete panels with a washed concrete exterior, the building is nestled among high-rises with a similar aesthetic and simply looks like a lower, smaller version of the neighboring residential buildings. A driveway approaches the building on one side and the opposite side abuts a large grassy area. The interiors of the building feel modern and bright, if institutional. The floorplan is something of a maze because the building is in the shape of a ladder, with two main wings and a set of rung-like hallways connecting them horizontally. These connecting halls create courtyards that pour light into the building. Interior spaces feel simple and modern with only the occasional visual cue—such as a feminist mural in a stairwell—that the building is a women's center.

Feminist activists involved in member groups in the early 1990s selected this building in part because of limited options in the city; a common theme I heard from women who were involved in the Beginenhof's early days was their frustration looking for a space to house a women's center. The feminist groups negotiated with the city of Rostock for a subsidized location, yet in spite of an apparent glut of available real estate, the city was slow to find suitable matches. The building ultimately chosen was the only option of a size feminists thought was adequate. Although some members argued in favor of a location in the city center (and some groups later broke away and moved to a building directly in the center), many feminist participants saw the siting of the building within a neighborhood of *Plattenbau* buildings as enhancing the building's connection to the community and promoting its accessibility to women from different classes and age cohorts. Several women involved with the founding of the Beginenhof recalled their hopes that a location in a *Plattenbau* area would help demystify feminism by encouraging local residents to come to the center and engage informally with other visitors and with staff. They recognized the city center as taking on new meaning as a social hub and residential area for educated and affluent people, and wanted the Beginenhof to feel accessible to women who didn't fit into the trendy, slick urban core.

Women involved in establishing the Beginenhof at its inception also rejected negative depictions of the *Plattenbau* neighborhoods. In a conversation with one founder of a member organization, she resisted views she characterized as "*wessie*" (a hostile term for western Germans) that the *Plattenbau* houses were "shabby" and "ugly," instead pointing to positive characteristics including large windows and brightness, financial accessibility, and convenience. Another feminist activist from the Beginenhof lived in a *Plattenbau* house, and when I met her in her apartment, she proudly detailed how important the *Plattenbau* community was to her: she enjoyed the amenities of her apartment and its surroundings, including her neighbors, and described moving into the *Plattenbau* apartment as a positive turning point in her life, because it was her first time living independently. Living in the "*Platte*" made her feel like a "true GDR woman."[18]

The space of the Beginenhof is defined by safety, accessibility, and technology. The most important aspects of the building are what it contains: safe spaces for women to congregate and build community, and technologies—particularly computers—that women can use to enhance their job market prospects. At the Beginenhof, the use of space is focused on achieving professional norms of modernity while bringing in elements that would help make it feel woman-friendly. Due to financial limitations, the renovations to the building did not fundamentally alter the interior spaces or the exterior appearance of the building, but the existing interior spaces—a cafeteria, classrooms, and offices—lend themselves well to the building's new use. Developing an open communal space was particularly important in the Beginenhof. A café that provides lunch, snacks, and drinks for workers and visitors was intended as a central social hub for the building and facilitates conversations between staff members at different organizations. Beyond serving as a dining option for those working or participating in activities at the Beginenhof, the café is open to anyone who wants an afternoon snack, and it has become a well-liked spot for birthday celebrations.

Other spaces within the building focused on creative outlets for women, which organizers believed would help women negotiate the stresses of unification and build a sense of community with other women. A dance studio offers a range of movement classes. In the 1990s and into the early 2000s, a ceramics studio original to the GDR-era day care center afforded a space in which visitors could work on creative projects and informally interact with other women. Seminar rooms are available for established and fledgling groups to hold meetings. Women come from throughout the city to make use of services.

Not all of these spaces have proven sustainable. Unlike Amandahaus, where the primary financial outlay was at the outset and subsequent funding was made possible through a steady stream of income from rents, funding needs at the Beginenhof are ongoing. To remain a vibrant site for women in the community, the Beginenhof's member groups needed continued funding for employees as well as for supplies and other resources. During the mid-1990s, numerous government-funded temporary employment programs made it possible for member organizations to maintain at least one paid staff person, and towards the late 1990s, some organizations were eligible for funding through the European Union. However, the general funding climate became more and more challenging as time went on. The Independent Women's Association ceased to operate in Rostock in the early 2000s. A feminist organization focused on women's art and culture relocated to a space in the city core, which the director felt would be more accessible to a greater number of women than the former location in the Beginenhof building. A day care center occupying about half of one floor took over the ceramics studio, so this is no longer a space for women. How the space is organized has thus shifted over time, with some organizations (like a crisis center for sexual and domestic violence) expanding and utilizing more rooms, while some smaller organizations moved elsewhere or ceased to exist.

With the exception of some feminist art on some walls, the Beginenhof's spaces appear very much like those of any other office building. During my multiple visits to the building between 2000 and 2009, the guiding design principle appeared to be professionalism: contemporary furniture, standard office technology, and bright lighting. As the tenants in the building shifted over time, the interior spaces increasingly took on the familiar shape of corporate offices. The director of the Rostock Women's Initiatives changed many times because the position was funded through short-term government job programs, but each director I met stressed her efforts at achieving a "welcoming" and "professional" environment in the building, using limited resources to keep the building looking "fresh."

The Beginenhof's member organizations have been overwhelmingly dependent on local, federal, and European Union government funds to support their work and continued existence. Although state surveillance of the building seems to be minimal—one local official is a regular visitor, and some EU staffers made periodic site visits to member organizations receiving funds in the early 2000s—the Beginenhof aligns itself with the professionalized expectations of the state. In response to the demands of funding organizations for staff members with relevant educational backgrounds (such as degrees in counseling, psychology, social work, or pedagogy), the women who worked at the Beginenhof also shifted from feminist activists to professionals who worked there because it was a job.[19] An upper-level staff member whose professional training is in childcare has a typical narrative: after unification, she moved to western Germany, but when her son was born, she returned to Rostock to be near her family. When she sought work, she wanted to:

> work on community issues, but I never imagined I would work in the area of women and girls. [. . .] But I couldn't find a position in my exact field with at-risk kids. When I got this job, I got used to it pretty quickly, and of course now I think violence against women is an important issue.

As the Beginenhof's small workforce increasingly professionalized, and most women who had been involved in the activism in 1989–90 moved on to other activities, the physical space also came to be more like an office building. This aligns with pre- and post-unification notions of modernity as involving the work of specially trained professionals in appropriate occupations, and rejects feminist precepts particularly common in Western feminisms that the shared experience of womanhood is a sufficient basis for supporting survivors of violence and guiding feminist organizations.

One important difference from other types of office buildings is that access at the Beginenhof varies across genders. Since its inception, the Beginenhof has housed crisis-focused organizations for girls and women who have experienced gender-based violence like rape and domestic violence. For girls and women who have survived traumatic violence, having men in the space could be problematic.

Other organizations, like the educational training center, had offerings for women and men, and sought to support technological education for both women and men, with a focus on the former. In alignment with East German gender politics, wherein women and men were seen as allies in the socialist project, feminist activists in Rostock generally welcomed men to participate. However, a small group of women felt men should be excluded from the building to encourage women's solidarity, and to ensure women felt safe in the building. Ultimately, it was decided that men would be excluded from the Beginenhof's café (except for private events), as well as from areas where survivors of gender-based violence were likely to be present. This is a marked difference from women's centers in western Germany, where radical feminist ideologies generally preclude men from entering women's spaces. Among most feminists in Rostock, fostering women's interests—including providing economic opportunities, reducing violence, and providing childcare—are understood as relevant for women and men.

The Beginenhof ultimately reflects notions of modernity from East Germany and unified Germany, as well as elements common to the two. Embracing its location in a *Plattenbau* building demonstrates acceptance of the social and aesthetic value of this type of structure. Like many eastern Germans, the founders and current employees at the Beginenhof do not see the *Plattenbau* in the same negative light as western Germans, but they also recognize that *this* version of a *Plattenbau* building—which they believe is safely constructed, energy efficient, and has fully functioning systems that support current technologies—would not have been possible in the GDR. Breathing new life into the building, and helping to ensure its occupancy throughout its 25-year lease, has been a point of pride for many of the women I spoke with who worked there.

Conclusion

German unification created a complex set of social transformations in which socialist and capitalist ideas about modernity came into direct contact and sometimes conflicted. Eastern Germans abruptly had to negotiate contradictory ideas about what is modern and how a modern society incorporates women. Feminists in Rostock negotiated this complex terrain by asserting a model of women's emancipation that sought to bring the GDR's stated goals into reality, a model that rejected western German ideas about women's primary contributions as belonging to the domestic sphere. Given western German hegemony in the unification process, this was impossible, and GDR women's rights and status eroded as a consequence of unification. Still, eastern German women held fast to their beliefs that a modern society is one in which all people have equal opportunities and live free from violence.

Amandahaus and the Beginenhof provide two windows into how feminist organizers have claimed space in Rostock since the end of state socialism, and developed relationships to those spaces through the lenses of modernity and feminism. Both Amandahaus and the Beginenhof emerged from the feminist activism sparked by the end of the GDR and German unification, and both have persisted for almost 30 years. Feminist organizers pushed to secure space for themselves during a period of massive redevelopment when feminist concerns were largely sidelined. For Amandahaus, this meant buying private property that would become a women's space. For the Beginenhof, this involved negotiating with the city of Rostock to lease a government-owned property to house feminist groups and organizations. In both cases, feminists insisted on a right to belong, and to have a physical presence in the city's social fabric and built landscape.

The financing of these spaces reflects inverse trajectories that in turn also reveal the shifting strength of feminist presence in Rostock. That Amandahaus had to seek funding from a western German bank points to the lack of recognition of women's housing concerns among city and local officials in Rostock. The space of Amandahaus was not seen as having social value, and was perhaps even shunned by funders because of its echoes of socialism. In spite of the struggle of securing funding for construction, upon completion of the building project, Amandahaus had a sustainable funding model, and remains solvent and successful.

The Beginenhof, in contrast, was far more successful in advocating for a physical space in the city, receiving city and local state support. In part by participating in what was basically an occupation of a military barrack during the tumultuous unification period, the Beginenhof established a precedent for a feminist presence in the city. City and state officials accepted the need for services for women during the unification period, and supported the transformation of the day care center into a women's center. As time went on, however, and funding sources dried up, the financial situation of some organizations that were part of the Beginenhof grew more precarious, and while some organizations grew, others ceased to exist. Once the perception of an initial crisis for women as the result of unification ended and eastern Germany was deemed "modernized," it became difficult for feminists to make claims for support and space. In unified Germany, then, feminist visions for gender equality have been largely sidelined, and the most mainstream organizations that are also most similar to feminist organizational types in western Germany (such as domestic violence shelters and rape crisis centers) are also the most successful and persistent. These are also the organization types that now dominate at the Beginenhof.

The experiences of finding and developing spaces for women reflect the complexity of German unification and the negotiation of East German and unified German identities and politics. As Rethmann (2009) notes, German unification resulted in "the opening up of a large arena of contradictory responses and experiences, an arena in which multiple meanings rubbed against each other with considerable friction."[20] The founders of Amandahaus developed a housing arrangement with strong socialist underpinnings, even as they rejected the *Plattenbau* neighborhoods and seemingly bought into the idea that the city center is highly desirable. The organizers of the Beginenhof, who generally followed a state-centered model of organizing and became more and more professionalized over time, moved into a *Plattenbau* area, holding on to an idea that these structures were designed to be open and accessible to all, unlike the increasingly exclusive and costly city center. Thus, we see fascinating contradictions between spatial choice and ideology that reveal how individuals and organizations living through major social upheaval may pick and choose from available ideologies.

Notes

1. See Hannemann, this volume.
2. Guenther 2010.
3. Dölling 1991; Rosenberg 1991; Maleck-Lewy and Ferree 2000.
4. Kolinsky 1999; Duggan 2003.
5. Miethe 1999; Guenther 2010; Dodds and Allen-Thompson 1994.
6. Kahlau 1990; Hampele-Ulrich 1993, 2000; Miethe 2008.
7. Ferree 1993.
8. Ferree 1994.
9. James 2009, 20.
10. Michelsen and Weiß 2010.
11. Risen 2009.
12. Oye 2007, 113.
13. Bräunert 2010.
14. Hannemann 1996.
15. Rubin 2016.
16. Hampele-Ulrich 1993; Ferree 1994.
17. Hampele-Ulrich 2000.
18. See again Hanneman's contribution to this volume for an analysis of residents' views of the *Plattenbau*.
19. Guenther 2010.
20. Rethmann 2009, 23.

References

Bräunert, Svea. 2010. "Transformationsraum Fotografie: Berlin-Hellersdorf am Übergang von DDR zu BRD." *German Life and Letters* 63(4): 1468–1483.

Dodds, Dinah, and Pam Allen-Thompson. 1994. *The Wall in My Backyard: East German Women in Transition*. Amherst: University of Massachusetts Press.

Dölling, Irene. 1991. "Between Hope and Helplessness: Women in the GDR After the 'Turning Point.'" *Feminist Review* 39(Autumn): 3–15.

Duggan, Lynn. 2003. "East and West German Family Policy Compared: The Distribution of Childrearing Costs." *Comparative Economic Studies* 45: 63–86.

Ferree, Myra Marx. 1993. "The Rise of 'Mommy Politics': Feminism and Unification in (East) Germany." *Feminist Studies* 19(1): 89–115.

Ferree, Myra Marx. 1994. "'The Time of Chaos Was Best': Feminist Mobilization and Demobilization in East Germany." *Gender and Society* 8(4): 597–623.

Guenther, Katja M. 2010. *Making Their Place: Feminism After Socialism in Eastern Germany*. Stanford: Stanford University Press.

Hampele-Ulrich, Anne. 1993. "The Organized Women's Movement in the Collapse of the GDR: The Independent Women's Organization (UFV)." In *Gender, Politics, and Post-Communism: Reflections From Eastern Europe and the Former Soviet Union*, edited by Nanette Funk and M. Mueller, 180–193. London: Routledge.

Hampele-Ulrich, Anne. 2000. *Der Unabhängige Frauenverband: Ein Frauenpolitischen Experiments im Deutschen Vereinigungsprozess*. Berlin: Berlin Debatte Wissenschaftsverlag.

Hannemann, Christine. 1996. *Die Platte: Industrialisierter Wohnungsbau in der DDR*. Berlin: Vieweg+Teubner Verlag.

James, Jason. 2009. "Retrieving a Redemptive Past: Protecting Heritage and Heimat in East German Cities." *German Politics & Society* 27(3): 1–27.

Kahlau, Cordula. 1990. *Aufbruch! Frauenbewung in Der DDR*. Munich: Verlag Frauenoffensiv.

Kolinsky, Eva. 1999. "Women, Work, and Family in the New Länder: Conflicts and Experiences." In *Recasting East Germany: Social Transformation after the GDR*, edited by Chris Flockton and Eva Kolinsky, 101–125. London: Frank Cass.

Maleck-Lewy, Eva, and Myra Marx Ferree. 2000. "Talking About Women and Wombs: The Discourse of Abortion and Reproductive Rights in the GDR During and after the Wende." In *Reproducing Gender: Politics, Publics, and Everyday Life after Socialism*, edited by Susan Gal and Gail Kligman, 92–117. Princeton, NJ: Princeton University Press.

Michelsen, Claus, and Dominik Weiß. 2010. "What Happened to the East German Housing Market? A Historical Perspective on the Role of Public Funding." *Post-Communist Economies* 22(3): 387–409.

Miethe, Ingrid. 1999. "From 'Mother of the Revolution' to the 'Fathers of Unification': Concepts of Politics Among Women Activists Following German Unification." *Social Politics* 2(Spring): 1–22.

Miethe, Ingrid. 2008. "From 'Strange Sisters' to 'Europe's Daughters'? European Enlargement as a Chance for Women's Movements in East and West Germany." In *Gender Politics in the Expanding European Union: Mobilization, Inclusion, Exclusion*, edited by Silke Roth, 118–136. New York: Berghahn Books.

Øye, Inger-Elin. 2007. "The Feeling for Gray: Aesthetics, Politics, and Shifting German Regimes." *Social Analysis* 51(1): 112–134.

Rethmann, Petra. 2009. "Post-Communist Ironies in an East German Hotel." *Anthropology Today* 25(1): 21–23.

Risen, Clay. 2009. "Underestimating East Germany." *The Atlantic*. www.theatlantic.com/magazine/archive/2009/

Rosenberg, Dorothy. 1991. "Shock Therapy: GDR Women in Transition from a Socialist Welfare State to a Social Market Economy." *Signs* 17(1): 129–151.

Rubin, Eli. 2016. *Amnesiopolis: Modernity, Space and Memory in East Germany*. Oxford: Oxford University Press.

12

Kin-Related Elder Care in Russian Families

Challenges for Homemaking

Olga Tkach

Introduction

Scholars working in the social sciences have criticized visions of home as a static space of uniqueness, stability and security.[1] Their standpoint reflects the social history of the twentieth century, when the ideal of domesticity as being exceptionally comfortable and consistent across generations was called into question. Urbanization, with its mass migrations and dramatic social transformations, caused some of this change, as did revolutions and wars that uprooted millions of people from their homes. Old concepts of home were also swept away by state policies and ideologies of mass housing and domesticity. For instance, in the Bolshevik era and Soviet Russia, home ceased to be a private matter, a fortress of private property and comfort, of bourgeois capitalism, or of women segregated into their own domain.[2]

Studies of intergenerational and geographic mobility as well as feminist scholarship and research on marginalized social groups have significantly contributed to our understanding of the multisited house, unstable home and unpredictable domestic life. The first showed that houses, homes and related place identities change with family dynamics and the stage of one's life cycle.[3] The latter broke out of a cycle that romanticized the intimate private domain, exposing how it can provoke feelings of frustration, unfairness, alienation, humiliation and fear. These feelings, studies showed, come about because of an unequal division of domestic labor or a traumatizing experience of domestic violence and segregation.[4] Both constructions of home are relevant and heuristic for the research of home–based kin-related elder care.

In the literature on care, aging and family, few studies have considered the accommodations made to private dwelling spaces as a result of such care.[5] This chapter examines the junction of home and care through an analysis of interview data collected in three Russian cities: Kazan and Samara in the Volga region, and Arkhangelsk, located near the White Sea.[6] In our interviews with people who had decided to live with their elderly relatives and provide them with care on a daily basis, we collected stories that are representative for Russia, where long-term care, sometimes spanning many years, remains a family responsibility and an issue almost completely hidden within the private sphere. Neither in the Soviet Union nor in current-day Russia have public institutions managed to solve the problem of elder care adequately. In recent years, the connection between elder care and

Olga Tkach

home settings has become even tighter, due to both a neoliberal weakening of the welfare state and the advancement of a conservative family discourse. Private citizens, especially women, perform unpaid caregiver work, which in hours can amount to a full-time job. Women must often combine these tasks with regular paid employment. Additionally, care work is improvised in homes that are not spatially and materially designed for infirm and dying people. Families must change the layout and materiality of the home and provide access to other sites of care, such as clinics and health care services. New boundaries, or rather frontiers, of privacy must appear within the home and between the home and the outside world; additionally, there are internal domestic boundaries related to an aging body.[7]

Our chapter explores how home-based kin-related elder care affects homemaking practices and the micro-geography of homes. After describing the empirical data, I turn to a conceptualization of contemporary care patterns and then map out the Russian example. I then analyze how homes change in terms of material culture, homemaking strategies and residents' feelings as they are confronted with elder care. After that, I examine internal and external boundaries as well as conflicts that exist in several improvised "nursing homes," where caregivers and care-receivers co-reside. Finally, I discuss the sociopolitical significance of home as a primary locus of kin-related elder care in contemporary Russia.

Research Data and Method

The overall sample used for this study comprises 23 in-depth focused interviews with the primary caregivers co-residing with their elderly, dependent parents, grandparents or in-laws.[8] Our interviewees were both men and women ranging in age from 26 to 61. Highly educated, they worked in both the public and private sector in Kazan, Samara and Arkhangelsk. All of them remained employed in order to keep their income and outside activities as an escape from the totality of care work. The majority of our interviewees were married, although several were single or divorced. Most had children and some had grandchildren. The age of care receivers varied from 60 to 96 years old. Various somatic and mental disorders, as well as disabilities due to age, prevented them from living on their own.

In tracing the chronology and the daily routines of their care work, our interviewees carefully recounted their challenges and the transformations that their homes underwent because of co-residing with a dependent elderly relative. The views and activities of those who were cared for have been reconstructed from the narratives of their younger relatives. Our interview partners all lived in the same city or region as their parents, even before care became necessary. Out of 23 care stories, ten care receivers moved to their caregiver's apartment; seven caregivers moved to live with care receivers; and in six cases, the different generations lived together prior to care becoming necessary. Elderly relatives relocated either from their own urban flats or from private houses in the nearby countryside, or sometimes from other relatives who refused to continue care work for different reasons. The majority of caregivers moved from flats that they owned; only in one case did a caregiving couple move from a rental apartment. After relocation, households included three to four generations and up to seven people. Our sample contained housing from one- to four-room flats (see Figures 12.1 and 12.2). The housing varied considerably in quality and scale, from centrally located two- or three-storied wooden apartment blocks lacking hot water, central heating, sewage systems, or individual bathrooms and kitchens (Figure 12.3) to more modern multistory blocks of flats, either built during the Soviet era or afterwards (Figure 12.4).

Figure 12.1 A 64-year-old caregiver and her 90-year-old father sit in the kitchen of a three-room apartment in Samara that he moved into several years ago.
Source: © Natalia Zolotova, 2017.

Figure 12.2 One of three rooms in a Samara apartment. It is used as a caregiver's bedroom and is also occupied by her children when they visit.
Source: © Natalia Zolotova, 2017.

Figure 12.3 A three-story wooden barrack in downtown Arkangelsk, built in the 1930s. The house has no central heating, hot water, sewage lines, private bathrooms or kitchens. The residents occupy one or two rooms rather than flats.
Source: © Olga Tkach, 2017; commentary by Natalia Kukarenko.

Figure 12.4 A nine-story block of flats built in 1979 in the outskirts of Samara. The block consists of some 300 private two- or three-room apartments. The building has eight entrances.
Source: © Natalia Zolotova, 2017.

Localization of Elder Care: Variety of Modern Patterns

Ideas and practices related to elder care are largely driven by local cultural practices and attitudes towards aging. Culturally and structurally grounded patterns of elder care shape welfare policies and the development of social institutions, as well as public opinion regarding intergenerational bonds, the elderly, and primary loci of care. In the late 1980s to mid-1990s, Arlie Russell Hochschild developed the concept of four gendered cultural models of care that reflect the "care deficit" in both private and public life and the public discourse.[9] Although these models were drawn decades ago from the research of American families, they still remain internationally appropriate for (post)modern societies. The first is the traditional model represented by the image of the homemaker mother providing unpaid care. The second is the postmodern model, represented by the working mother who "does it all," with no additional help from any quarter (or at best, a man doing little at home) and no adaptation in her work schedule. The third is the cold-modern model represented by impersonal institutional care in year-round ten-hour day care and old-age homes. The fourth is the warm-modern model, in which institutions provide some care of the young and elderly, while women and men join equally in providing the remaining care needed. It is modern because public institutions become part of the solution, and warm because we do not relinquish all care to them.[10] The models differ by the degree of modernization, and among them the fourth model seems the most institutionally advanced and gender balanced. Hochschild also points out that various developed nations respond differently to similar care deficits they face, and adopt either pure or synthetic models, or are in transit from one model to another.[11]

Following the idea of national cultural politics of care or care cultures, and focusing particularly on elder care, current European research distinguishes two cultures and types of care localization. The Southern European model, also called the Mediterranean familist or residential care model, relies mainly upon unpaid female labor in a private domestic setting. It presumes the co-residence of several generations and is based on the solidarity and resources of an extended family.[12] This model also prevails in post-socialist contexts, where familist care compensates for underdeveloped social security, public health and pension systems. In post-socialist contexts, intergenerational care provides for the wellbeing, health and leisure of the elderly.[13] Researchers comparing Western capitalist and post-socialist patterns of elder care have found that in countries with harsher living conditions, multigenerational co-residence remains prevalent.[14] In Hochschild's terms, this model reflects both traditional and postmodern and in part warm-modern models. In contrast to the familist model, the Northern European model of elder care, similar to Hochschild's cold-modern model, is provided primarily by professionals working in institutional settings, such as nursing homes.[15] In addition to Scandinavia, where this model has been studied and described, this form of care exists in many Western countries, where family solidarity remains strong but is much less likely to involve co-residency.[16] In these alternative models, the main responsibility for care or its delegation to institutions belongs to (extended) families, rather than just women.

The dichotomy of familial and institutional care has become less pronounced, as a rollback of the European welfare state has led to professionals or volunteers as well as migrant nurses providing care to elderly people residing in their own homes. Various policy options exist, such as providing a diverse stock of housing and "staying put" programs, which help older people keep their homes, maintain their social networks, live in safe housing, and obtain needed care.[17] Depending on the particular case, various programs that allow the elderly to age in place can be seen as either a cold- or warm-modern form of elder care, as they do not rely solely on traditional support structures, such as extended families. A further global trend is the commercialization of care, including elder care.[18] Researchers still distinguish between states that institutionalize social welfare, where formal and informal markets predominate as social service providers, and those where communities of volunteers, such as families, friends and neighbors provide care, usually in the spaces of the home. The different approaches have led to intense debates over whether states, markets or families provide the best care in terms of affordability, efficiency and care ethics.[19] Regardless of what type of care is considered mainstream in a particular society, home care retains its sociopolitical significance either by replacing an underdeveloped public sector, or by humanizing or "warming up" cold care provided by modern institutions.

The Culture of Familial Co-residence and (Elder) Care in Russia

Like many post-socialist countries, Russia tends towards traditional or postmodern models of care, similar to the familist care culture of southern Europe. Like many nations worldwide, Russia is aging: the percentage of retired citizens in the overall population is growing (see Table 12.1), and life expectancy rates, while still lower than those of most wealthy countries, have also been increasing. Not surprisingly, the incidence rate (number of new cases per population at risk in a given time period) among elderly citizens is higher than that of other age groups.[20] Some 80% of citizens older than retirement age (55 years for women and 60 years for men) have multiple chronic pathologies, with patients over 60 having an average of four to five different chronic diseases, including a wide range of somatic and mental disorders, such as dementia.[21]

The Russian state admits that systemic approaches are necessary to solve these issues. In 2016, the government approved the "Strategy of Actions in the Interests of the Citizens of the Older Generation in the Russian Federation until 2025" (hereafter "Strategy") to further an elder policy that had been

Table 12.1 Population of the Russian Federation by Year (January Figures)

	2008	2009	2010	2011	2012	2013	2014	2015[1]	2016	2017[2]
General population, in thousands	142,747.5	142,737.2	142,833.5	142,865.4	143,056.4	143,347.1	143,666.9	146,267.3	146,544.7	146,804.4
Population over retirement age[3]	30,160.8	30,540.9	31,186.1	31,808.9	32,433.5	33,099.6	33,788.6	35,163.4	35,986.3	36,685.1
Percentage of the population over retirement age in the general population	21.1	21.4	21.8	22.3	22.7	23.1	23.5	24.0	24.6	25.0

1 As of 2015, figures include the Crimean Republic and the city of Sevastopol.

2 Preliminary data.

3 Defined as males over 60 years old and females over 55 years old. In order to make this range more precise, elder policy distinguishes three age cohorts of elder citizens: (1) 60–64 years old—socially and economically active, often employed'; (2) 65–80 years old—less active, many of them needing health care and social services; (3) above 80 years old—citizens having serious health issues and requiring help and care. See Strategiia 2016, 2.

Source: *Rosstat*, May 17, 2017.

Olga Tkach

Table 12.2 Explanations Given by Elderly Citizens in 2011 and 2014 of Why They Avoid Public Health Care (in Percentages)

Explanation	2011	2014
Elderly preferred self-directed treatment	73.1	49.6
Elderly are not satisfied with the level of services offered by the clinic	21.3	30.7
Elderly do not expect effective treatment	14.6	24.7
Elderly required services that can only be obtained for pay	5.9	12.5
Elderly are not able to get to the clinic without help	5.3	10.3
It was complicated to get to the clinic	7.9	9.7
Elderly were not aware of where to get required health care	0.4	1.4
Elderly did not have time	4.4	7.8
Other reasons	2.6	7.0
Total	100	100

Source: Rosstat, cited by Trubin et al. (2016, 11).

under development since the mid-1990s. The Strategy combines elements of both welfare and neoliberal policies. It acknowledges elderly citizens as facing health issues, loneliness and a lack of mobility, making them subjects of social care. The Strategy also assumes state responsibility for "increasing elderly citizens' quality of life."[22] According to official statistics, 87.6% of citizens over 65 need care offered by public institutions. Although municipal social workers provide care both in institutions and in clients' homes, they are able to provide services for only a fraction of eligible patients.[23] Not only are services rare, but their quality remains unsatisfactory, as Table 12.2 makes clear.

As a newly neoliberal state, the Russian government has signaled that it considers the elderly to be an economic burden, stressing that a patient over 70 years old costs seven times more to treat than one who is 16–64 years old.[24] So-called optimization measures have reduced the number of specialized institutions, available spots in them and social workers. In a trend towards reducing or commercializing social welfare, the Russian state has attempted to encourage non-governmental organizations (NGOs), socially responsible businesses or families and private citizens to fill the ensuing gap. The latter are seen as having the primary responsibility for elders' care, which has resulted in a conservative discourse about the traditional family model and the need to strengthen family values.[25] As the Strategy states:

> In Russia, the family has traditionally been the main institution of intergenerational care. The support of an elderly person by family members, and the contribution of elderly people in caring for younger generations, are of great social importance.[26]

Russian policies exalt that "large multigenerational families have always been the main type of family in traditional Russian culture, where close relationships between several generations of relatives exist."[27] Propagating relatives' support of the elderly,[28] the state uses an ideology of intergenerational bonding to revive family members' natural interest in and perceived responsibility for care work.

In their narratives, most of our interviewees echoed such state propaganda clichés. When asked to imagine alternatives to home-based care, they defined the private realm as the only possible care domain, and family as a main source of elder care. They rated people who take elderly parents to a nursing home as uncaring and ungrateful sons and daughters. Our interview partners described institutionalized care as a violent withdrawal of elderly people from the family, using terms such as "to send out," "to give away," "to forsake" and "to abandon." Similarly, in a 2013 national survey, 53%

of respondents who had visited public nursing homes for the elderly claimed that the living conditions in such homes were bad, while 57% considered the relocation of aging people to such homes as abnormal and unacceptable for people with children or close relatives. Half of the respondents who considered relocation as unacceptable were convinced that children must take care of their parents. In the national sample, 94% of the respondents claimed that they have never had relatives living in nursing homes[29] (although social stigmatization may have prevented respondents from admitting the contrary). In a national survey conducted in July 2016, 17% of the respondents aged 40–54 and 22% of the respondents over 55 were reluctant to move out of their parents' home because their elderly relatives "need constant custody and care."[30]

On the one hand, such representations reveal people's agency in solving family issues. On the other hand, I would interpret such perceptions as a defense mechanism for families who find themselves standing face to face with the necessity of home-based care with almost no public support. Although the Soviet Union had an extensive welfare system on paper, social services were either scarce or did not meet citizens' needs, so that families had to rely on intergeneration bonds in order to compensate for the lack of services.[31] Our interviewees recounted that they would not have survived or been able to maintain a work-life balance without the solidarity of their family circle:

> When I grew up and got married, we lived with [my mother] for three years. We got along very well. We ran the household together, and she helped us with our child. [. . .] It was a very hard time. I was writing my thesis and we were short on money. And she helped us, she took our child to school, helped her with homework. Overall, she helped us a lot.
>
> *(Firuza, 50, takes care of her mother, 73 in Kazan)*

Another interviewee recounted:

> [My parents] took care of their granddaughter a lot. Dad picked her up from school; mom cooked for us. It was a tremendous help.
>
> *(Irina, 55, takes care of her mother, 81, and father, 83, in Samara)*

During the economic crisis of the 1990s, older relatives supported many young Russian families.[32] It is still an option for many. Our research has found that one reason people continue work after formally retiring is to support their children and grandchildren by paying for their education, mortgages, or other expensive purchases.[33] Often, grandparents lived with their children to care for their grandchildren. Although the Soviet Union had policies in place to provide each family with an apartment,[34] flats were often occupied by several generations due to a de facto lack of housing. Co-residence continues to be the norm for many families today. A national survey conducted in July 2016 found that younger generations prefer the advantages of living with their parents. Respondents aged 18–25 in particular mentioned motives such as, "I would not be able to manage domestic chores" (43%), "I need constant support and advice from my parents" (29%) and, "Living alone means extra costs that can be avoided" (37%).[35] Intergenerational residential attachment does not necessarily mean strong family bonds and affection towards other family members, but rather a flexible and reliable solidarity that can be mobilized on demand. Still, within such cultures, kin-related, home-based elder care is regarded as a fair and anticipated payback for the older generation's childcare.

In contemporary Russia, a number of cultural, economic and political factors come together in the discourse and practice surrounding the perceived family responsibility for elderly care. A large number of people who are now in their fifties and sixties have assumed care for their aging and infirm parents, considering it as a "normal thing," something that becomes inscribed into their biographical scripts uncontested. They face a certain dilemma. On the one hand, even if it causes them hardships, they opt

Olga Tkach

for residential, kin-related elder care because this decision is structurally and culturally determined. On the other hand, they take on the responsibility for their parents' care deliberately and on goodwill.

Preparations for Generational Co-residence

The turning point where middle-aged family members decide to provide home-based care is the elderly relative's inevitable dependency,[36] that is, the irreversible decline of their energy and health, and loss of their mental and/or physical activity and autonomy. In some cases, decline can be slow, accompanied by constant and visible changes of somatic or mental health, worsening of eyesight and/or hearing, and of the ability to move around. In other cases, a drastic and unexpected event such as a sudden fall, stroke or massive heart attack, or loss of a spouse leading to heavy depression and other diseases, can result in a need for care. In both cases, elderly people may lose the ability to maintain their household, use appliances, pursue well-loved hobbies or maintain proper hygiene. Constant supervision in the form of co-residence is then clearly needed.

An elderly person with set habits, a difficult nature and constant demands is not welcome for many relatives. The elderly person thus moves in with those relatives who are able to live with him or her. Care, understood as commitment, sacrifice or compromise, becomes a final argument for those who have great confidence in their nuclear family members, such as spouses and adult children. In this respect, a nuclear family, or rather married couple, is one of the most solid bases for kin-related, home-based elder care. Lena from Kazan tells how she, together with her husband and sons, came to the decision to take her peevish mother in to live with them:

> [My mother] has a very difficult nature. She is an irreconcilable person, especially with regard to my brother's family. [. . .] My mother is a person who does not need anyone. Moving in with that kind of person is contentious, of course. She was always plotting against my husband, turning my husband against me and the children against us, etc. It's an unpleasant situation. We talked to her, and she agreed to live with us. I also spoke with my husband, since this is my mother. He agreed [to the move]. And I also told our children that we would take grandma in. So, she's been living with us for over four years.
> *(Lena, 51, takes care of her mother, 71, in Kazan)*

Sometimes, housing conditions do not allow an extended family to live together, so members of a nuclear family must temporarily split up in order to provide elder care. Alexander (57 years old) from Samara had to leave his wife and move in with his 89-year old mother, who had suffered a stroke. He decided that it was better not to take his wife to live in a small flat in a wooden house with no hot water and no private bathroom, especially as his wife needed time and energy to look after her own elderly mother, who lived on her own.

When possible, moving in with an elderly relative begins with a family project of redistributing, joining, exchanging or enlarging real estate and living space. Our sample consists of representatives of the lower-middle classes, for whom the purchase of a new flat was seen as problematic. An extended family, however, often owned several smaller apartments, which belonged to or were shared by various relatives. This modest family accruement of real estate could be traded up or down when an emergency or significant life changes necessitated it.[37] In the following case, real estate was distributed in favor of the youngest generation of a family:

> When our older daughter told us she wanted to start her own family, [all the relatives] decided that we would pool our flats and [trade them in for] a three-room flat and a studio apartment. We would give [our daughter] a studio apartment, while moving in with [my husband's] parents to take care of them.
> *(Tatiana, 49, takes care of her mother-in-law, 85, and father-in-law, 88, in Samara)*

Another option was to trade in several smaller flats for a larger one:

> When [my mother] moved in, we felt our flat was too small for all of us [. . . .] We sold her flat, bought a new one, and moved out from the one the institute had provided [in the Soviet era]. We live together now; we have a three-room flat. She lives in one room. Our daughter lives in another. The room where my husband and I live is also used as a living and dining room. It's OK with us.
>
> *(Firuza, 50, takes care of her mother, 73, in Kazan)*

If selling flats and buying new ones is not possible, family members arrange for caregivers to co-reside with an elderly person in whatever flat is available. This means that elder care is sometimes provided in an apartment that is owned by a family member who does not live there. Andrei (28 years old) from Arkhangelsk and his partner moved to Andrei's 60-year-old father, who is partially paralyzed on the right side of the body. He lives on the outskirts of the city in a three-room flat owned by Andrei's mother and younger brother. Because both Andrei's mother and brother were not able to perform the care work, Andrei and his partner had to move from their rental flat in the central city to his father's flat.

The question of housing in the context of elder care can obviously be solved in many ways. The most widespread solution is that the middle generation co-resides with dependent parents, while their children, who themselves are often married with children, live separately. When an extended family makes a temporary or final decision about who moves in with whom, the home must be adjusted to the new care tasks. The following sections consider the materiality and domesticity, as well as the feelings of the inhabitants towards this new home, by examining the ensuing boundaries and conflicts.

Elder Care and Homemaking: Materiality, Practicality, Sensuality

In most cases, an elderly person experiences relocation as something painful, as it requires shifting from an independent owner or dweller to a dependent family member or guest. A loss of things left in the former apartment as well as social networks that cannot be moved might lead to frustration and loneliness. Raisa recalls that her mother was able to accept the fact of relocation only after getting back a shawl that she had forgotten in her former flat:

> [My mother] calls herself a migrant, because she had to move out of her flat and leave her "nest" behind. [. . .] She left things that she had acquired over the course of years. She moved into a new place, and felt like a stranger. And she identifies us with this disaster that happened to her. [. . .] I acted with the best of intentions, but she didn't feel well. We did not take the goods that [she had] acquired over the course of years. It was bad for her. We did not take her fluffy shawl. She reminded me about it for two years, until I went [to her old place] and got it for her. [. . .] So, you know, it's physiologically difficult for her. Everything [in the new place] is not hers.
>
> *(Raisa, 61, takes care of her mother, 96, in Samara)*

Although Raisa was a good caregiver, her mother still felt like an newcomer for whom relocation led to an identity crisis. To her, the old shawl was a familiar item that signified her own home, a feeling of comfort and an ability to manage life.[38]

Even if some old items cannot be kept or taken from the former apartment, in most cases the dependent elderly person might require new things or special equipment such as wheelchairs, crutches, portable toilets or other paraphernalia. Able-bodied relatives not only purchase new goods but also make special devices they cannot buy, or adapt things that are at hand. Zinaida recalls how she made use of an air mattress:

> I was sitting and thinking, "Oh, my God, how am I supposed to bathe mom?" [. . .] Then I had an idea. Now I recommend it to all my friends who have the same problem. I have an air mattress. We used to take it on vacations. I inflated it, and put it in the bathtub as a seat. And then I carefully placed [my mother] onto it. It meant she was able to sit comfortably.
>
> *(Zinaida, 53, took care of her mother for seven years in Kazan)*

Our research shows that multigenerational co-residence has a positive influence on the daily life of the elderly, in particular as the home becomes more predictable, safer and better adjusted to their needs. Yet elderly relatives who have memory lapses or who are inattentive or physically weak make the everyday life of the whole family unpredictable and even dangerous, as the elderly relative's actions can result in fires, floods or burglaries. Caregivers must increase precautionary measures such as hiding sharp kitchenware, or locking up access to gas appliances, water faucets, the kitchen or even the front door when they go to work. Younger relatives adapt the apartment, widening doorways or removing thresholds, to facilitate movement around the apartment and make their elderly relatives more comfortable.[39]

The domestic life of a caregiving family is dominated by the constant care work that the middle generation (most commonly a married couple) performs. The division of labor for the caregiving couple is quite traditional and corresponds to overall trends in Russian families: women perform routine housekeeping tasks, such as cleaning and cooking, as well a range of physical care work, such as spoon-feeding, bathing, shaving or required medical care. Men warm up prepared meals, take out the garbage, do the shopping and drive when needed.[40] To a certain extent, all members of the household are involved in elder care and share all responsibilities. Elderly people with deteriorating health often spill or drop things, forget to close doors or turn off appliances, and generally make a mess that has to be cleaned up. Relatives have to help the elderly with everyday tasks and bodily functions. If a building is not equipped with an elevator, and an apartment does not have hot water or heat, both housekeeping and care work become tremendously difficult. The family operates as a team, and for many, care work becomes a family bonding experience. Nonetheless, women—the daughters or daughters-in-law—manage the care process. The woman constantly monitors the situation, gives calls to other family members to check if everything is being done properly and on time, and coordinates schedules:[41]

> Everyone does everything, depending on the situation. For example, when I work, my daughter calls me and asks, "Did grandma eat anything?" My husband also calls and asks, "Is grandma fed?" My son-in-law comes home at lunchtime, and also asks, "Did anyone give a food to grandma?" or "Did she use the toilet?" Thus, everyone knows what to do next. This is how it usually goes.
>
> *(Lena, 51, takes care of her mother, 71, in Kazan)*

Caregivers must constantly be on the alert, monitor the elderly person's health and maintain his or her diet and treatment schedule. In fact, the elderly person's feeding and medication regimen determines the schedule for the rest of the household, as relatives spend most of their time at home devoted to elder care. Zaituna from Kazan describes her normal day as follows:

> We get up at 6 am, check [mother's] blood pressure, then we give her blood pressure medication, and then have breakfast. After breakfast she goes to bed again and watches TV . . . she can switch it on herself . . . I go to work. I have lunch at noon. I run home and give her lunch, check her blood pressure again, she takes her medication again if needed, and then I go to work. I get back at 7.30 p.m., we have dinner . . . Sometimes, when her blood pressure changes rapidly, I ask

neighbors to help. I leave the key with a neighbor who lives on the second floor. This is how my normal day goes.

(Zaituna, 50, takes care of her mother, 80, in Kazan)

The main caregivers must balance the totality and unpredictability of home-based care with their professional lives. Usually, they must scale back their career aspirations and, if possible, arrange for a more flexible work schedule.

When a dependent elderly relative moves in, it also adds new sensual experiences to the domestic environment. The tempo gets slower or faster, and noise levels increase or decrease. At night, elderly residents might wander about, watch TV with the volume on high or ask for help. Not everyone is able to adjust their biorhythms to provide night care:

My son is scared to stay overnight with his grandma. She's been known to get up, turn on the gas, and forget about it. I used to wake up immediately. He is young; he does not wake up. Once, she turned on the gas but he did not hear it. That's why he's scared. He says, "I will not sleep at all, then." This is very annoying. But I wake up right away. She gets up—I wake up.

(Alexander, 57, takes care of his mother, 89, in Samara)

Another common problem is illustrated by Tatiana's father-in-law, who suffers from senile dementia accompanied with hyperexcitability. Tatiana and her husband consciously rejected an extensive medication regimen in order to allow her father-in-law a more normal life. She explains what the entire family experiences every night:

[My father-in-law] walks 24 hours a day. He passes by our room shuffling, he turns on the light everywhere, he flips switches. He goes to the toilet and back, flips again, and then turns the water on for 10 minutes straight. This is just Nazi torture, when you toss and turn the whole night listening to running water. Then he leaves [the bathroom], and in two minutes he forgets he was there. His operational memory doesn't work at all. He doesn't even make it back to his room before starting to follow same procedure again. This endless walking happens day and night.

(Tatiana, 49, takes care of her father-in-law, 88, and mother-in-law, 85, in Samara)

New bodily experiences divide those who are able to tolerate unpleasant sights and smells, as well as family members' annoying habits, from those (mainly grandchildren) who cannot overcome the feeling of irritation and disgust. Caregivers try their best to conceal unpleasant smells with cleaning products. Yet boundaries related to the aging body do not seem to be the primary source of conflict. The next section considers other internal and external boundaries and conflicts that make up the micro-geography of home.

External Boundaries and Internal Conflicts of the "Caring Home"

Even if an apartment is fully equipped for care and the elderly person surrounded by loving and responsible relatives, the middle-aged relatives cannot perform their tasks without the assistance of qualified healthcare. Almost all interviewees and their (grand)parents reported negative experiences with public healthcare and related services, resulting in a tendency to perceive these external spaces as a type of "counter-home." Underdeveloped urban infrastructure and public transportation and a lack

Olga Tkach

of medical staff, as well as outdated or poor equipment in public clinics and hospitals, create many issues for a terminally ill person and his or her relatives:

> The hospital is very uncomfortable, because it has high thresholds and steep stairs. When we climbed up with [my mother], everybody looked at us with sympathy and even supported us verbally, because they saw that it was very difficult for her. So this is why I can't take her anywhere.
>
> *(Lena, 51, takes care of her mother, 71, in Kazan)*

When elderly parents have to stay in the hospital for any length of time, caring relatives accompany them, sometimes for weeks, to act as informal nurses. Relatives must endure unfavorable conditions, as well as the staff's hostile attitudes. They persist, believing that their presence might mean better service and security for their parents. Nevertheless, the most urgent issue that our interviewees identified was that doctors and nurses demonstrate a careless and irresponsible attitude towards older patients. Elderly people are often diagnosed as suffering from "old age," for which treatment is pointless. Caregivers vie for doctors' attention with bribes, or attempt to find a private clinic. Another way to compensate medical doctors' disregard is to transform the home into an amateur clinic or hospice, which unlike public and private hospitals feels engaged, safe and secure.[42] Gradually, caregivers learn to be experts in particular illnesses and provide necessary medical procedures. They feel proud and empowered when, against the prognoses of medical doctors, they are able to get their relatives back on track and prove that the family's warm and loving attention is much more effective than any hospital.

Most of our interviewees rejected outside help. Unfamiliar paid helpers were often rejected by the elderly relatives themselves:

> A friend of mine has a mother with diabetes. She has already lost both legs and eyes. She abuses all the nurses my friend hires. Nobody wants to work with her. They pay 10000–11000 rubles [per month],[43] but nobody wants to stay, even for that money.
>
> *(Zaituna, 50, takes care of her mother, 80, in Kazan)*

The cared-for desperately try to keep their lives private and home boundaries closed, for they feel embarrassed about their dependent status, weaknesses and disabilities. Caregivers themselves also distrust both public social workers and private nurses. For this reason, and because they consider services to be of low quality, they do not hire nurses. Other relatives rarely provide a significant amount of service, as they live in other housing, other cities or even abroad. They can only contribute financially, or take over for the primary caregivers occasionally if the elderly relative agrees.

The "soft" variant of involving outsiders is to rely on neighbors and friends who live nearby. These are usually female pensioners who, over decades, have become part of a territorial urban microcommunity. Such communities are common in apartment buildings that were built in the 1960s to 1980s and that have housed the same families for generations (Figure 12.4). Able-bodied relatives can easily leave their keys with trusted neighbors, who provide free or inexpensive help either regularly or on occasion. Because our interviewees were all employed and thus absent from home during the day, cooperation with the neighbors meant someone could call an ambulance, bring medicine or food, pop in once in a while to check on things, or take the elderly person for a walk or to sit on the bench by the front door (Figure 12.5).

After their morning routine, elderly people stay at home alone, unless relatives or neighbors stop by during the day. Elderly people generally stay in bed, watch television (news and series are popular), read newspapers and books, sit by the window or on the balcony, make phone calls, knit, take care of pets and houseplants, play solitaire, write poems, play musical instruments and sing songs. Despite this range of activities, the elderly suffer from loneliness. Their social isolation can be quite dramatic, as Russian cities lack infrastructure for people with special needs. Doorways, corridors and stairs are

Figure 12.5 A bench by one of the entrances to a nine-story block of flats in Samara. The bench is a favorite resting spot for elderly people living in the house or the surrounding neighborhood.
Source: © Natalia Zolotova, 2017.

narrow, and ramps and elevators rare. Under such conditions, even taking an elderly family member for a walk every day becomes challenging:

> When the weather is beautiful and warm, especially in the summer, I take [grandmother] for a walk in a wheelchair. We live on the ground floor, and the building has no accommodations for the disabled. First, I take out the wheelchair, and then my mother and I walk grandma out together. One person would not able to do it, for the front stoop is very high. That is why we have to walk her out together.
>
> *(Stepan, 29, takes care of his grandmother, 86, in Arkhangelsk)*

Although Russians prefer not living on the ground floor, in buildings without an elevator the caregivers said they were happy to live there, to make it easier to exit the house and go for a walk.

When family members arrive back from work, they do not always have enough time or energy to make up for the lack of communication during the day. The care stories show that the instrumental aspects of caregiving, such as washing, cleaning and feeding, prevail over the communicative or emotional aspects of care work.[44] Still, families try their best to improve their elderly relatives' environment and try to find extra time to keep them company. Primary caregivers might organize a family reunion, encourage other family members to visit elderly relatives or ask grandchildren to call their grandparents. An elderly relative has to attract attention through numerous demands, inquiries and whims that cannot be ignored. By compelling their family members to constantly be on the move, the elderly compensate for their dependent position and social isolation, become more involved in family life and demonstrate their authority.

Caregivers reported that their social life also decreased. Because caring for an elderly person involved maintaining silence and calmness at home, having guests over was rare:

> Guests don't come over any more. We had a bunch of friends we've known since school. Since [mother] moved in, we've lost our freedom. If someone comes over, she appears in the corridor and stands there. She has poor eyesight, and tries to recognize who it is. It's not comfortable for a person to be scanned like that. So people come to have fun, and she tries to join us—an elderly woman, grey hair, with a teacup. You know, it's disturbing.
>
> *(Raisa, 61, takes care of her mother, 96, in Samara)*

Home becomes confining, limiting or excluding mobility and any chance to relax. The caregivers have to reduce the frequency of business trips, doctors' appointments, vacations, leisure time and dating. They see their lives, bodies and time as belonging to the relatives they care for:

> Certainly, I'm not free. I can't go anywhere at night. I have a schedule: work, home. [. . .] I can't do what I like to do, because I spend all my time at home, cooking, helping [my mother], and performing everyday medical procedures for her. This is what I do, day after day, with no weekends.
>
> *(Liubov, 56, takes care of her mother, 80, in Arkhangelsk)*

The emotional and physical pressures on able-bodied family members cause them to experience psychological burnout and physical exhaustion to the point of declining health. Observing a parent's process of aging and dying on an everyday basis can be psychologically difficult. Our interviewees admitted that they were often not able to interact with their parents on equal terms. As parents' personalities and communication skills underwent dramatic changes, they lost their ability to clearly articulate their thoughts:

> Only recently, [my mother] was able to hear, but now she is practically deaf. So, you know, I can't speak with her tenderly, because I have to repeat everything five times, and by the fifth time I have to yell, of course. Yelling is by default not kind. If I ask her, "Did you take your pill?" I repeat it five times. So care has become a source of irritation.
>
> *(Raisa, 61, takes care of her mother, 96, in Samara)*

Under such circumstances, many caregivers are not able to negotiate control over their own spaces and everyday lives. The narratives reveal that the uncontested ideology of kin-related, home-based elder care runs counter to a reality in which amateur "nursing homes" are beset by frustrations and conflicts. Suppressing one's irritation becomes a crucial aspect of emotional work. In this context, the outside world is imagined as a space of desire, relaxation and emancipation, in contrast to the home environment that is characterized by self-discipline, self-control, exhaustion and unwanted attachment. Only caregivers who have enough resources, either material (e.g., a *dacha* [summer house])[45] or social (relatives' support), can afford to leave home and let out their negative emotions:

> Honestly, mom pisses me off. I can hardly hold back. Sometimes, I feel so irritated. I try to leave home, because if I answer rudely, then I won't forgive myself. [. . .] I lose my temper, and my nerves are shot. When I come home after a 24-hour shift, and she asks me to do something with her, then I . . . feel guilty. [. . .] I think if you're tired, it's better to go out, to walk, go somewhere

if you have someone to replace you. I have a person like that. Regardless, I control my temper, and go for a walk.

(Olga, 47, takes care of her mother, 81, and father, 83, in Kazan)

Internal conflicts give some caregivers cause to reflect on the ideology of intergenerational reciprocity and openly criticize it as a hypocritical pitfall. One has to take care of one's parents, even if one harbors no warm feelings towards them. This ideology is seen as a relict of a premodern, extended rural family. To critics, it has seemingly lost its significance in today's urbanized societies. Our interviewees believe that the chafing and interdependent relationships between relatives still exist in Russia today because of the lack of adequate housing, coupled with the lack of privacy that generations of Soviet citizens came to see as normal. Raisa from Samara likened her situation to a *kommunalka* (apartment shared by several families) to describe the dwelling genealogies that have evolved in Russian cities:

> We have lived in *kommunalkas* our whole lives. First, our parents lived with their parents, then we lived with ours, and then our [grown] children lived with us. That is why phrases like, "I brought you up, and you owe me," are still widespread. I think this is wrong. We want to live in dignity and independently of each other. I cannot live my own life now. I want to go in a certain direction, but someone says, "Come here." This attitude needs to change; it is our future. So far this issue could not be resolved in our country because of our mentality and our politics. [. . .] Overall, I think we need nursing homes where people can *live*, not nursing homes like we have here in Russia. [We need] decent, adequate ones where an elderly person can have his or her own room and communicate with others. [. . .] They have to have good meals, a nurse who can measure blood pressure and give necessary medication.
>
> *(Raisa, 61, takes care of her mother, 96, in Samara)*

Interestingly, Raisa equates sharing an apartment with one's parents as similar to living in a *kommunalka*, where unrelated strangers compete for an apartment's shared spaces such as hallways, kitchens and bathrooms.[46] Raisa uses the term to refer to the lack of privacy due to overcrowded flats, stifling intergenerational bonds and a tendency toward mutual control. Her reference also points to a certain hopelessness, as people feel trapped in their living situation due to cultural inertia, leading to feelings that one is doomed to live like this forever. Raisa calls for modernization, defining it as residential separation and the emancipation of generations from each other, as well as the development of public services. Still, she does not assume that such modernization could ever take place in Russian society, due to existing socioeconomic, cultural and political paradigms.

Based on Italian data, Barbara Da Roit has shown that ideas of intergenerational solidarity are stronger in economically deprived social milieus, while wealthier social groups move to transform conservative care patterns.[47] Russian scholars have also observed the separation and spatial emancipation of upper-class and upper-middle-class families who can afford to purchase their own flats and hire domestic workers without having to rely on elder relatives' help.[48] With less wealthy families, however, generational emancipation would require better social infrastructure. Our interviewee Raisa points to this very issue in contemporary Russian society. There is a high demand for decent social support networks and a separation between domestic spheres and nursing homes. Such separation would allow apartments to be limited to nuclear families while permitting alternatives to home-based care and the ideology of intergenerational reciprocity, yet such alternatives have not been realized. In Hochschild's terms, Raisa's statement reflects a desire to make Russian care culture a bit colder than the traditional or postmodern one, as private citizens do not have energy or institutional resources to warm it up.

Olga Tkach

Conclusion

This chapter analyzed family narratives in which a small urban apartment becomes a site of elder care. Russian families have kept a kin-related pattern of care similar to the Southern European familist version, a postmodern care culture where private citizens have to balance work and family life with almost no public support. In the Russian context, this pattern is due to the lack of social welfare and professional nursing assistance, the marginalized status of elderly patients in the health care system, and a continued ideology of intergenerational reciprocity among people born in the 1950s and 1960s. Even during Soviet times, elder care was almost entirely family-based by choice. Both the authorities and society were unwilling to invest in the development of professional nursing services; consequentially people relied on traditional structures by default.[49] Current-day Russia has become a neoliberal state under the cloak of a social welfare system, and remains wed to conservative family policies that promote strong intergenerational bonds. This leaves families no choice but to take responsibility for their terminally ill or infirm relatives. Yet, as Hochschild notes, "the private realm to which conservatives turn for a solution to the care deficit has many problems itself."[50] Able-bodied relatives must adapt their private dwelling space to be used as an improvised nursing home. Families, predominantly working women, manage the private sphere as caregivers, domestic workers, amateur medical doctors and psychologists in order to compensate for deficiencies in or the lack of public care. To a certain extent they are successful, although they pay a high price in terms of privacy, comfort, and health.

The processes of aging, dying, and death interrupt daily routines and call into question the home as a space of safety, relaxation, and freedom. Residential elder care can lead to the physical and social isolation of family members from the external world. It also results in the home being split into two spheres that remain firmly interrelated: that of the caregivers and that of the care receivers. The boundary and conflicts between them can be described in terms of dirt/cleanliness, demolishing/renewing, complexity/simplicity, someone's belongings/one's own belongings, and so forth.[51] Despite the caregivers' best efforts, such discrepancies cannot be resolved. Instead, they evoke the feeling that their efforts are futile, due to a lack of resources and skills for providing effective elder care.

Clearly, private homes where unpaid residential elder care is provided have enormous public and political significance. They replace public institutions of care almost completely, therefore compensating for deficits in the availability of elder care. The lack of options, along with cultural biases, means that the demand for modern elder care cannot be satisfied. What would the modernization of elder care in Russia look like, considering that such care has been a family matter for centuries? Feeling exhausted by residential care work, our research participants understand the modernization of elder care as drifting to a cold-modern rather than a warm-modern model. For many, taking an elderly parent to a nursing home, even one of excellent quality, continues to raise the ethical dilemma of taking a loved relative away from the family. I would argue that they do not consider the warm-modern model an option because for various reasons their worldview does not allow a partnership between private citizens/families and (in the broadest sense) public institutions in caring for the elderly. Under current structural conditions, public and private elder care seem mutually exclusive to them. Thus, caregivers prefer to keep care culture warm in private, while still lamenting about less modernized institutional care. A lack of substantial government and business initiatives in the realm of elder care, as well as an unequal division of elder care work within families, will most likely impede changes in the current situation as well as Russia's transition to a warm-modern society.

Notes

1. Since about the 1980s, the most prominent contribution to this criticism has been made in the areas of migration research and studies of transnationalism. For the most recent overview see Boccagni 2017.
2. Reid 2009, 469. In the 1920s, the struggle for *novyi byt* (a new daily routine) presumed not only women's emancipation through active participation in mass production, but also the opening up of domesticity to the gaze of the Soviet collective.

Kin-Related Elder Care in Russia

3. See Bertaux-Wiame and Thompson 1997; Cuba and Hummon 1993.
4. Blunt and Dowling 2006, 10, 15–21, 25.
5. Martin-Matthews 2007, 246.
6. In January 2017, Kazan had 1,231,878 inhabitants, making it Russia's sixth largest city. Samara had 1,169,719 inhabitants and Arkhangelsk 352,128, making them Russia's ninth and 54th largest cities respectively. This chapter is based on a sample that was a part of an interregional research project called "Gender Arrangement of Private Life in Three Russian Regions," carried out by the Gender Program of the European University at St. Petersburg, Russia in 2008–10, and funded by the Ford Foundation, Grant No. 080–1405, and Novartis International AG. The first version of this text was published in Russian as Tkach, Olga. 2015. "'Zabotlivyi dom': uhod za pozhilymi rodstvennikami i problemy sovmestnogo prozhivaniia." *Sotsiologicheskie Issledovaniia* 10: 94–102.
7. Martin-Matthews 2007, 239; Wiles 2005, 85.
8. All names have been changed.
9. In private life, the care deficit is most palpable in families where working mothers, married and single, lack sufficient help from partners or kin. In public life, the care deficit can be seen in government funding cuts for services to poor mothers, the disabled, mentally ill, and the elderly (Hochschild 1995, 332).
10. Hochschild 1995, 332, 338–42.
11. Hochschild 1995, 342.
12. Da Roit 2007; Zechner 2004.
13. See Tchernina and Tchernin 2002, 561.
14. For example, in Lithuania and Russia, more than 60% of women aged over 85 live in an extended family; see Gaymu 2003, 216.
15. Hockey 1999, 111–16; Kröger 2009, 400.
16. Gaymu 2003, 216.
17. Howden-Chapman, Signal, and Crane 1999, 24–5.
18. Kremer 2011, 134; see also Folbre and Nelson 2000, 134; and Dyck, Kontos, Angus, and McKeever 2005. This is also true for southern European countries, where despite slow development of social infrastructure, relatives refuse to take full responsibility for elder care work, citing their right to privacy and a career. See Da Roit 2007, 253, 256–7.
19. Harmonious co-existence of various sources of care, including family, and private and public institutions, is the closest to the warm-modern model described in Hochschild 1995. For a fuller discussion about hybrid and multi-sited elder care, see Smith 2005, 1–2; Fine 2005, 249; Da Roit 2007, 254; Martin-Matthews 2007, 230; Lawson 2007, 6; and Thomas 1993, 652.
20. See Trubin, Natalia, Marina, and Gavdifattova 2016, 10–11.
21. *Strategiia* 2016, 8.
22. *Strategiia* 2016, 4, 23.
23. See Trubin, Natalia, Marina, and Gavdifattova 2016, 25–6.
24. Strategiia 2016, 8.
25. Chernova 2012, 91.
26. Strategiia 2016, 20.
27. *Rossiiskaia Gazeta* 2014.
28. Strategiia 2016, 20.
29. FOMnibus 2013.
30. Levada Centre 2016.
31. See Rotkirch, Tkach, and Zdravomyslova 2012.
32. Tchernina and Tchernin 2002, 552–3.
33. Centre for Independent Social Research "Working Pensioners in the Russian City: Forming of Occupation Niches and Possibilities of Labour Market (Case of St. Petersburg)" funded by the Institute for Public Planning, Moscow, Russia, Grant No.179/K (02/2012–09/2012), which analyzed 30 in-depth biographical interviews with working pensioners in various market segments (unpublished report).
34. See Reid 2009, 469. In 1986, Mikhail Gorbachev made the last Soviet housing pledge, launching the national program "Housing 2000," which promised that by 2000 every Soviet family would be living in a separate apartment or house.
35. Levada Centre 2016.
36. Fine and Glendenning 2005, 612; Folbre 2007, 186.
37. For instance, in the case of someone's marriage, childbirth, divorce, graduation or illness. See Bertaux-Wiame and Thompson 1997; Shpakovskaya 2009. In the Soviet era, the majority of citizens lived in state-owned apartments (Reid 2009, 475). In 1991, Boris Yeltsin signed into law "On the Privatization of Housing in RSFSR," which granted residents ownership rights to their flats. By 2010, 75% of all housing falling under the

new law had become privatized, although this percentage varies across regions (see Information Agency of Russia. 2016. http://tass.ru/info/3426534). The majority of our interview partners and their relatives owned their flats.

38. In other cases, if children or grandchildren moved in with an elderly relative, he or she desperately resisted any renovations or decluttering. Soviet citizens' lifelong attachment to goods has been extensively studied (cf. Gerasimova and Tchouikina 2004; Gurova 2004; Orlova 2004).

39. See Gaymu 2003, 214, 225 for how multigenerational co-residence can considerably alter the elderly person's living conditions, especially when faced with economic crises and poverty. Moving to live with their children, parents benefit from the improved socioeconomic position of the younger generation.

40. An exception is sons helping their fathers to bathe.

41. Women also manage the domestic sphere when it comes to childcare and domestic work; see Tkach 2009; Zdravomyslova 2009; Rotkirch, Tkach, and Zdravomyslova 2012.

42. See Smith 2005, 13.

43. About $300–350 in 2011.

44. See Folbre and Nelson 2000, 129.

45. For research of Russian dacha see Lovell 2003; Caldwell 2011.

46. For a discussion see Boym 1995; Gerasimova 2002; Reid 2009; Utekhin 2015.

47. Da Roit 2007, 261–2.

48. See Gladarev and Tsinman 2009; Shpakovskaya 2009; Rotkirch, Tkach, and Zdravomyslova 2012.

49. See Lawson 2007, 3.

50. Hochschild 1995, 336.

51. Hockey 1999, 108–10, 118.

References

Bertaux-Wiame, Isabelle, and Paul Thompson. 1997. "The Family Meaning of Housing in Social Rootedness and Mobility: Britain and France." In *Pathways to Social Class: A Qualitative Approach to Social Mobility*, edited by Daniel Bertaux and Paul Thompson, 124–182. Oxford: Clarendon Press.

Blunt, Alison, and Robyn Dowling. 2006. *Home*. London and New York: Routledge.

Boccagni, Paolo. 2017. *Migration and the Search for Home: Mapping Domestic Space in Migrants' Everyday Lives*. New York: Palgrave Macmillan.

Boym, Svetlana. 1995. *Common Places: Mythologies of Everyday Life in Russia*. Cambridge, MA: Harvard University Press.

Caldwell, Melissa. 2011. *Dacha Idylls. Living Organically in Russia's Countryside*. Berkeley and Los Angeles: University of California Press.

Chernova, Zhanna. 2012. "New Pronatalism? Family Policy in Post-Soviet Russia." *Region* 1(1): 75–92.

Cuba, Lee, and David Hummon. 1993. "Constructing a Sense of Home: Place Affiliation and Migration Across the Life Cycle." *Sociological Forum* 8(4): 547–572.

Da Roit, Barbara. 2007. "Changing Intergenerational Solidarities within Families in a Mediterranean Welfare State: Elderly Care in Italy." *Current Sociology* 55(2): 251–269.

Dyck, Isabel, Pia Kontos, Jan Angus, and Patricia McKeever. 2005. "The Home as a Site for Long Term Care: Meanings and Management of Bodies and Spaces." *Health and Place* 11(1): 173–185.

Fine, Michael. 2005. "Individualization, Risk and the Body: Sociology and Care." *Journal of Sociology* 41(3): 247–266.

Fine, Michael, and Caroline Glendenning. 2005. "Dependence, Independence or Inter-dependence? Revisiting the Concepts of 'Care' and 'Dependency.'" *Ageing and Society* 25(4): 601–621.

Folbre, Nancy. 2007. "Measuring Care: Gender, Empowerment, and the Care Economy." *Journal of Human Development* 7(2): 183–199.

Folbre, Nancy, and Julie A. Nelson. 2000. "For Love or Money—Or Both?" *Journal of Economic Perspectives* 14(4): 123–140.

FOMnibus. 2013. "O domah prestarelyh." http://fom.ru/TSennosti/11148, accessed on July 6, 2017.

Gaymu, Joëlle. 2003. "The Housing Conditions of Elderly People." *Genus* 59(1): 201–226.

Gerasimova, Katerina. 2002. "Public Privacy in the Soviet Communal Apartment." In *Socialist Spaces: Sites of Everyday Life in the Eastern Bloc*, edited by David Crowley and Susan E. Reid, 207–230. New York: Berg.

Gerasimova, Katerina, and Sofia Tchouikina. 2004. "Obshchestvo Remonta." *Neprikosnovennyi zapas* 2(34): 70–77.

Gladarev, Boris, and Zhanna Tsinman. 2009. "Dom, shkola, vrachi i muzei: potrebitel'skie praktiki srednego klassa." In *Novyi byt v sovremennoi Rossii: gendernye issledovaniia povsednevnosti*, edited by Elena Zdravomyslova, Anna Rotkirch, and Anna Temkina, 189–221. St. Petersburg: European University at St. Petersburg Press.

Gurova, Olga. 2004. "Prodolzhitel'nost' zhizni veshchei v sovetskom obshchestve: zametki po sotsiologii nizhnego bel'ia." *Neprikosnovennyi zapas* 2(34): 78–83.

Hochschild, Arlie Russell. 1995. "The Politics of Culture: Traditional, Cold Modern, Post Modern and Warm Modern Ideals of Care." *Social Politics: International Studies in Gender, State, and Society* 2: 331–346.

Hockey, Jenny. 1999. "The Ideal Home: Domesticating the Institutional Space of Old Age and Death." In *Ideal Homes? Social Change and Domestic Life*, edited by Tony Chapman and Jenny Hockey, 108–118. London and New York: Routledge.

Howden-Chapman, Philippa, Louise Signal, and Julian Crane. 1999. "Housing and Health in Older People: Aging in Place." *Social Policy Journal of New Zealand* 13: 14–30.

Kremer, Margareta. 2011. "Caring for the Elderly at Home: Developments in the Long-term Care Sector in Austria." In *Politics of Care*, edited by Majda Hrženjak, 121–140. Ljubljana: Peace Institute.

Kröger, Teppo. 2009. "Care Research and Disability Studies: Nothing in Common?" *Critical Social Policy* 29(3): 398–420.

Lawson, Victoria. 2007. "Geographies of Care and Responsibility." *Annals of the Association of American Geographers* 97(1): 1–11.

Levada Centre. 2016. "Prozhivanie vmeste s roditeliami." August 12. www.levada.ru/2016/08/12/zhit-vmeste-s-roditelyami/, accessed on July 6, 2017.

Lovell, Steven. 2003. *Summerfolk: A History of the Dacha, 1710–2000*. Ithaca, NY: Cornell University Press.

Martin-Matthews, Anne. 2007. "Situating 'Home' at the Nexus of the Public and Private Spheres: Ageing, Gender and Home Support Work in Canada." *Current Sociology* 55(2): 229–249.

Orlova, Galina. 2004. "Apologiia strannoi veshchi: 'malen'kie hitrosti' sovetskogo cheloveka." *Neprikosnovennyi zapas* 2(34): 84–90.

Reid, Susan E. 2009. "Communist Comfort: Socialist Modernism and the Making of Cosy Homes in the Khrushchev Era." *Gender & History* 21(3): 465–498 (reprinted in this volume).

Rossiiskaia Gazeta. 2014. "Kontseptsiia gosudarstvennoi semeinoi politiki v Rossiiskoi Federatsii na period do 2025 goda." August 29. https://rg.ru/2014/08/29/semya-site-dok.html, accessed on July 6, 2017.

Rosstat (The Federal State Statistics Service of the Russian Federation) http://www.gks.ru/wps/wcm/connect/rosstat_main/rosstat/en/figures/population/

Rotkirch, Anna, Olga Tkach, and Elena Zdravomyslova. 2012. "Making and Managing Class: Employment of Paid Domestic Workers in Russia." In *Rethinking Class in Russia*, edited by Suvi Salmenniemi, 129–148. London: Ashgate.

Shpakovskaya, Larissa. 2009. "'Moi dom—moia krepost.' Obustroistvo zhil'ia novogo srednego klassa." In *Novyi byt v sovremennoi Rossii: gendernye issledovaniia povsednevnosti*, edited by Elena Zdravomyslova, Anna Rotkirch, and Anna Temkina, 222–261. St. Petersburg: European University at St. Petersburg Press.

Smith, Susan J. 2005. "States, Markets and an Ethic of Care." *Political Geography* 24: 1–20.

Strategiia deistvii v interesah grazhdan starshego pokoleniia v Rossiiskoi Federatsii do 2025 goda. 2016. February 5. http://government.ru/media/files/7PvwlIE5X5KwzFPuYtNAZf3aBz61bY5i.pdf, accessed on July 6, 2017.

Tchernina, Natalia V., and Efim A. Tchernin. 2002. "Older People in Russia's Transitional Society: Multiple Deprivation and Coping Responses." *Ageing and Society* 22(5): 543–562.

Tkach, Olga. 2009. "Uborshchitsa ili pomoshchnitsa? Variatsii gendernogo kontrakta v usloviiakh kommertsializatsii byta." In *Novyi byt v sovremennoi Rossii: Gendernye issledovaniia povsednevnosti*, edited by Elena Zdravomyslova, Anna Rotkirch, and Anna Temkina, 137–188. St. Petersburg: European University at St. Petersburg Press.

Thomas, Carol. 1993. "De-Constructing Concepts of Care." *Sociology* 27(4): 649–669.

Trubin, Vladimir, Nikolaeva Natalia, Paleeva Marina, and Sofia Gavdifattova. 2016. *Pozhiloe naselenie Rossii: problemy i perspektivy.* Sotsial'nyi Biulleten,' no. 5. Analytical Centre under the Government of the Russian Federation, Moscow.

Utekhin, Ilya. 2015. "The Post-Soviet Kommunalka: Continuity and Difference?" In *Everyday Life in Russia, Past and Present*, edited by Choi Chatterjee, David L. Ransel, Mary Cavender, and Karen Petrone, 234–251. Bloomington: Indiana University Press.

Wiles, Janine. 2005. "Home as a New Site of Care Provision and Consumption." In *Aging and Place: Perspectives, Policy, Practice*, edited by Gavin J. Andrews and David R. Phillips, 79–97. London and New York: Routledge.

Zdravomyslova, Elena. 2009. "Niani: Kommertsializatsiia zaboty." In *Novyi byt v sovremennoi Rossii: Gendernye issledovaniia povsednevnosti*, edited by Elena Zdravomyslova, Anna Rotkirch, and Anna Temkina, 94–136. St. Petersburg: European University at St. Petersburg Press.

Zdravomyslova, Elena, and Olga Tkach. 2016. "Kul'turnye modeli klassovogo neravenstva v sfere naemnogo domashnego truda v Rossii." *Laboratorium: Russian Review of Social Research* 3: 68–99.

Zechner, Minna. 2004. "Family Commitments Under Negotiation: Dual Careers in Finland and Italy." *Social Policy and Administration* 38(6): 640–653.

13

Space, Body and Subjectivity in Ágnes Kocsis's Film, *Fresh Air* (2006)

Nóra Séllei

Fresh Air is about the relationship between a single mother and her daughter living in a derelict housing estate in post-communist Hungary. Their space features not only as part of the visually powerful narrative of the film, but also as a constitutive element in the subjectivity of the protagonists. Working as a public toilet attendant at a metro station, the mother desperately tries to appropriate her space, which is both abject and brutal, whereas the daughter, studying to be a dressmaker, pushes her spatial boundaries by designing dreamlike dresses. In their claustrophobic physical, psychological and social space, their femininity and female sexuality play a key role: although different, they are exposed to gazes, bullying and brutality, while also struggling with each other in a space that is both the simulacrum of a dream world and their everyday post-communist reality.

As a result of the powerful and definitive presence and mutual construction of urban spaces and female bodies, Ágnes Kocsis's *Fresh Air* can be interpreted from the perspective of how Elizabeth Grosz sees the interconnection between urban spaces, bodies and subjectivities, inasmuch as

> [T]he body [. . .] is not distinct, does not have an existence separate from the city, for they are mutually defining. [. . .] [T]here may be an isomorphism between the body and the city. But it is not a mirroring of nature in artifice. Rather, there is a two-way linkage which could be defined as an *interface*, perhaps even a cobuilding. What I am suggesting is a model of the relations between the bodies and the cities which sees them, not as megalithic total entities, distinct identities, but as assemblages or collections of parts, capable of crossing the thresholds between substances to build linkages, machines and often temporary sub- and microgroupings.[1]

Fresh Air seems to comprise such an isomorphism. It invites the viewer-interpreter to enter a cinematic world with a powerful visuality and spatiality, in which there is a strong connection and impact between spaces and bodies: an impact that mutually constructs spaces and bodies, while at the same time does not fully fix or pin down the subjects. Although most of the time in the film narrative the modern urban space looks deterministic from the perspective of subjectivity, including the body as an element of subjectivity, the space at the same time is also shaped by the presence of the desiring and embodied subjects. Furthermore, there is an inevitable mutuality between the bodies and the spaces of the two protagonists; thus, the film creates an isomorphism between the spaces and the bodies, or rather, the spaces of the bodies and the bodies of the spaces alike.

This cinematic world—or the urban space of this cinematic world—is rather uncanny in the Freudian sense of the word, too: known and unknown, familiar and strange at the same time,[2] particularly for those having experienced the period of state socialism and its aftermaths. The urban framework is

Space, Body and Subjectivity: *Fresh Air*

provided by the run-down, rigid and claustrophobic spaces that define the place of the two female protagonists, who have drifted on the periphery, which contributes to the construction of their subjectivity. In turn, the two women are active participants in constructing the spaces, and their process of space construction indicates—and symbolically reproduces—the changes in their rather loaded intersubjective relationship. In this story about the public toilet attendant mother and her 17-year-old daughter studying in a vocational school specializing for the textile and clothing industry, both protagonists are searching for themselves, for their sense of self, for their space and for their body, while also for each other. This process is full of ambivalence rooted in the body, in the female body, sexuality and desires, and the ambivalence is caused by the attraction and repulsion implicated in the process.

The relationship between bodies and spaces appears in a complex way in this cinematic text, partly due to the consistent color symbolism applied to both protagonists. The mother's colors are the sexually charged red and purple, evoking in one's cultural imagination the lush brocade wallpapers in brothels. The daughter's color, on the other hand, is grayish green, which can be seen as a camouflage color, particularly in contrast to the mother's red and purple. Yet, as she also applies this color to the dresses she designs, it also evokes the cultural image of the mermaid, which—by definition—has an irresistible seductive power, as suggested by the mother's color symbolism. In this way, what looks at first sight to be an irreconcilable but actually only apparent contrast between mother and daughter turns into a communication pattern that is visually expressed by the color symbolism of the cinematic text. This pattern is also based on the gradually reconstructed external and internal spaces related to the protagonists, while the lyrical visuality of the film, showing multiple layers of the body and the subject, keeps up the ambivalence of the central symbols, too.

The subjects, as they emerge in and as a result of the filmic representation, are clearly defined by the spaces. Almost in a cliché-like or catalog-like way, while also reflecting on them as clichés, the film enumerates a great number of derelict, dreary and often desolate post-socialist spaces of modernity that enframe, decolor, impair and limit the protagonists' subjectivities, including their bodies, sometimes creating ironic or even grotesque contrasts. The opening scene takes place in the derelict local cultural center that must have had its heyday, but is now the congenial and appropriate space for socially and culturally peripheral subjects looking for emotional and social stability. Viola, the mother, goes to the event organized by a matchmaking agency called "Hearts Found." The musician, playing a Roland synthesizer and wearing a lilac jacket and a shirt with huge patterns, plays "romantic hits" while the master of ceremonies tries to keep control over the uncontrollable: the attraction and repulsion of bodies. While he is trying to arrange the people into a paired-off order of mutually found hearts, or rather bodies (which by definition cannot be brought about and arranged from the outside), *his* body is the clear indicator of the incongruity of his intention and the result of his attempt. Obviously thinking himself elegant in his white suit that is far too tight on his fat belly, back, shoulders and arms, and wearing non-matching shoes and a tie with incongruently big patterns, his greasy hair smoothed down and reaching his nape, his unhygienic and unkempt appearance is in sharp contrast to his own self-image, and predicts the failure of his undertaking to create sexually attracted, matching pairs out of those desperate human bodies and desiring subjects (Figure 13.1).

The opening scene, thus, has a key role in this film, in which one of the central questions is the controlling or repressing of desires, or quite the contrary, the possibility of living up to one's desires and accepting the body as part of one's subjectivity within a very clearly defined sociocultural and semiotized space. This is what both mother and daughter are struggling with. They approach this question from two opposite ends of the scale, as indicated by their respective color symbolism: the inverse color of red is green and vice versa. They mutually include each other, even if inverted, but are inevitably related to one another, and their relationship is best described as a form of implication. The mother Viola's experienced—and obviously wounded and at the same time repressed—sexuality implicates Angéla, the daughter, who can be seen as the result of her own mother's troublesome relationship to her body. Angéla, seeing her mother's experiences of bringing her up on her own (as suggested, most probably

Nóra Séllei

Figure 13.1 A lonely-hearts-dance event marks the incongruencies of self-images.
Source: © Ferenc Pusztai and Ágnes Kocsis, producer and co-producer/director of *Fresh Air*.

abandoned by the father of her child), and not having any meaningful relationships, opts for repressing her own desires, while at the same time longing to experience her own sexuality. This is evidenced by her fairy-tale inspired dress designs evoking mermaids and princesses, even though she cannot or does not want to admit to herself the reason why she reacts with enmity and hatred to her own mother and her mother's body. For Angéla, it is her own mother who embodies both literally and in a more abstract sense whatever she wants to exclude from her own subjectivity and keep at a distance from her own identity in a process that can be best described using Kristeva's notion of the abject.[3] Angéla's mother's body represents what looks for the daughter, based on the body's functioning, as something repulsive, disgusting or heterogeneous. She wants to define herself as against the heterogeneity of the mother's body, as a subject with a homogeneous identity, which is a vain attempt because the abject, which she intends to distance from herself, keeps returning as her repressed uncanny, breaking into the space of her subjectivity, and haunting her until she accepts it and makes it an integral part of her own identity. At that moment, even the material, abject body undergoes a transubstantiation.

The various stages of this subject construction process take place partly in—and as a result of— urban spaces, creating an interface (in the sense of Elizabeth Grosz's term) between spaces and bodies. The film presents three kinds of urban spaces: first, the run-down housing estate; second, geometrically represented road junctures, railway stations, derelict viewing towers and a hospital; and third, a public restroom. The housing estate can be seen as an iconic post-socialist space:

> Originally intended as affordable accommodation for a society in the quest for a perfect future, panel buildings, as symbolic promises of a new life, soon came to signify the failure of these promises and became permanent homes for dwellers who were no longer idealistic travellers but hopeless prisoners.[4]

Viola, the single mother who works as a restroom attendant and lives in the closed space of a flat in a housing estate, can certainly be seen as a prisoner who, on the other hand, does not seem to give up her desire of finding a partner and creating a functional relationship.

Space, Body and Subjectivity: *Fresh Air*

Figure 13.2 Mother and Daughter in Their Socialist-Era Apartment
Source: © Ferenc Pusztai and Ágnes Kocsis, producer and co-producer/director of *Fresh Air*.

Her desire to create another space for herself is indicated by the large-scale poster on the wall of her room in their flat. It shows the image of an autumn forest and is both a contrast to her totally alienated urban environment characterized by cold gray colors, rectangular and geometrical shapes and lifeless materials, and also a simulacrum in the sense that the simulacrum raises

> a question of substituting the signs of the real for the real, that is to say, of an operation of deterring every real process via its operational double. [. . .] Never again will the real have the chance to produce itself.[5]

In this case, the poster covers a whole wall behind the sofa, the central piece of furniture in the sitting room from where mother and daughter watch television and apparently share the space in their total alienation (Figure 13.2). Nevertheless, the poster is obviously an enlarged photograph, so in this way it does have a reality. Its function, however, is still that of a simulacrum because it represents a nostalgic evocation of a never-existing reality from the perspective of the inhabitants of this flat, and in this way its function perfectly complies with how Baudrillard explains the logic of the simulacrum: "Simulation is the master, and we only have a right to the retro, to the phantom, to the parodic rehabilitation of all lost referentials."[6] These wall-size megaposters were typical of the socialist period, but also those of the 1990s, and in many cases the exotic landscapes with tropical beaches signified—at least from the cultural and social spaces where they were on display—the unreachable, the never-existing dreamland, the desire to create a dream and the desire to create another space by integrating this wall-size simulacrum into the everyday (Figure 13.3).[7]

In analyzing the use of colors in an exhibition space about concrete panel buildings, Zsolt Györi asks the question:

> After all, what could be a more evident sign of the desire to transcend the monotony, achromatism, uniformity, and coldness of building materials and patterns than to introduce into it spatial variety, coziness, and individuality through color, arrangement, and ornamentation? Such a desire also carries a compensatory function as it hopes to counterbalance the de-individualizing effects of centralized and economic planning of space.[8]

Nóra Séllei

Figure 13.3 The Everyday, Represented by the Mundane
Source: © Ferenc Pusztai and Ágnes Kocsis, producer and co-producer/director of *Fresh Air*.

The wall-size megaposter undeniably serves the very same purpose: it is meant to go against what Eszter Zsófia Tóth describes as the prefabricated housing estate's unsuitability for living, an environment from which nature seems an unreachable dream.[9] The poster is also meant to bring individuality into the home, to break the gray monotony of the concrete panel, and to create variety. Yet paradoxically, even this wall-size megaposter is part of the very same logic of how the concrete panel buildings are made—the posters are not free from prefabrication, from technologized production, from replicated multiplication. Whereas they were meant to bring individuality and contrast to industrial mass production, their widespread use made them panels in the manner of the elements of the flats whose monotony they were supposed to break.

The prefabricated panel apartment in a deteriorated area has further characteristics in this cinematic text, creating a deterministic and at the same time isomorphic architecture around the characters' bodies as their third skin. The flat is presented as an emphatically closed and claustrophobic space, with a rather narrow corridor, with dark and small spaces, with a kitchen where one can hardly take a step, let alone cook and dine properly. Fish swim about in a miniature aquarium that both the mother and the daughter gaze at, sitting on the same chair in the same position, as if observing and pondering upon their own entrapment and lack of freedom. The only window the viewer can see opens onto the internal, cantilevered corridor of the building itself, offering no view, no perspective, no vistas. Yet, even without a view, the window is still used as a liminal space by Angéla, the daughter, who every now and then sits on the windowsill, some drawings of her own in the mildly lit room in the background. Even the external space consists of a reinforced concrete structure, offering no freedom of choice but leading into one direction, into what looks a narrowing dead end (Figure 13.4).

The second kind of spaces—the external, public or institutional spaces—function similarly in the film. They are iconic spaces of urban alienation and technology: bridges, a railway station, a multilevel motorway junction, Angéla's school and the hospital where the mother is taken. All of them are characterized by grayness and sharp geometrical patterns, offering no sign of either homeliness

Space, Body and Subjectivity: *Fresh Air*

Figure 13.4 Angéla sits in the dreary concrete structure that is home.
Source: © Ferenc Pusztai and Ágnes Kocsis, producer and co-producer/director of *Fresh Air*.

or teleology, even if for a while the urban space of the road deceptively seems to be leading somewhere. Angéla, as a talented student of the textile vocational school, gains the chance to participate in a competition in Italy, but she cannot finance her trip, so she leaves home to hitchhike to Rome. On the Italian border she falls asleep, and on waking up, she notices a car with Roman license plates, so she asks the occupants to take her along. Not speaking any foreign language she cannot make herself understood, and when they arrive at their destination she realizes that she has returned to the very multilevel road junction where she started off a day before. The only direction that is available here is the roundabout, the dead end, the U-turn, the non-perspectival circularity, even when roads seem to be available (Figure 13.5). In some scenes, Angéla literally imitates flying, but even in these instances, she is either locked up by the apartment buildings that serve as a backdrop to her "flight" on the steel bar used to clean rugs, or she goes around in circles, her arms stretched wide, on the edge of round concrete shapes that used to be the boundaries of sandboxes on a playground. All the meanings of the external urban spaces direct her into one-way or dead-end directions, and define her body and subjectivity in disciplinary, confining and deterministic ways, with sharp geometrical angles and in many cases "fearful symmetries."[10] The most fearfully symmetrical space in the film is a hospital, where the staircase is photographed as a system of bars and at the same time a labyrinth. Here, not only the patient but also their relatives are lost and exposed to the institutionalized disciplining of the bodies.

The third kind of marked space in the film is the public restroom,[11] where Viola, the mother works. This space bears multiple significations. First of all, it is located in one of the stations of the metro system, which in itself is a heavily semiotized external urban space. The public restroom is thus included and in terms of power and ideology deeply implicated in a structure provided by the metro station. Discussing this space in both Eastern European and Western films, György Kalmás argues that "[t]he empty yet threateningly alive spaces of the metro" are both "ghost-like" and "psychotic spaces" that are also used in "cinematic allusions. [. . .] [A]ll these films take the spectator to the margins of human existence, to a no man's land, where human beings face some kind of a crisis, where there are monsters lurking around the corner."[12] The surrounding metro system

243

Nóra Séllei

Figure 13.5 Roads that are roundabouts, dead ends, and U-turns, leading nowhere.
Source: © Ferenc Pusztai and Ágnes Kocsis, producer and co-producer/director of *Fresh Air*.

exemplifies the complexity of the ideological investments into urban spaces by offering an insight into the existence of various cultural and social layers and aspects. Like missionaries with a religious zeal offering spiritual and physical healing, ideology enters the very space that cannot be healed yet obviously cries for healing. No less meaningful is the empty yet consciously structured pre-metro foyer with its series of columns and corridors that define the human subjects entering this space. Exposed to the coldness and hardness of the fake marble surface, the human bodies follow the logic of isomorphism as they stiffen, feel threatened and are menaced with being violated. This experience emphatically pertains to women, whose bodies by definition do not belong to public spaces and are therefore more vulnerable when exposed to empty spaces, particularly at night and particularly in the metro. The fact that the public restroom is located in the underground space of the metro system creates an external environment to Viola's workplace that defines its functions and potentials and is inscribed with multiple significations.

Apart from being embedded in this par excellence space of power inscribed in—and by—the cityscape, the public restroom (or toilet) is loaded with psychoanalytical meanings that contribute to the construction of the subject. The toilet is directly related to the body, especially to the abject parts of the body, and as such the phrase "public toilet" is a contradiction in terms inasmuch as a public space is staked off for the functions of the body that culture defines as most private, the functions that culture does not even want to know of or acknowledge, but paradoxically cannot *not* acknowledge, having to create a space for them within the space of the public. The public toilet thus includes what is denied by culture, what is to be rejected by culture, but what, as follows by the logic of the supplement, cannot be ultimately removed from within the boundaries of culture. The public toilet itself is a cultural phenomenon and institution, in the same way as the abject cannot be removed from within the boundaries of the body. In our culture, everything that takes place in the restroom is a most private function of the body, made invisible, literally flushed under the surface or, as derived from the original meaning of the phrase "water closet," washed off with water, cleansed off from the body. It is not by chance that the toilet (or in another expressive phrase, the privy, referring back to its private function) is usually located in the most hidden or innermost part of the house. Looking at it also from this

Space, Body and Subjectivity: *Fresh Air*

Figure 13.6 Viola in her place of work, a public toilet
Source: © Ferenc Pusztai and Ágnes Kocsis, producer and co-producer/director of *Fresh Air*.

perspective, the public toilet is an oxymoron because at least in modernity it shifts the most private into the space of the public, making the public toilet arguably an iconic urban space of modernity.

The public restroom (or toilet) is therefore a trope for the paradoxical feature of the abject: its function is to control, in a space cut off from the public, the ultimately uncontrollable primary bodily functions unacknowledged by culture. It is not by chance that this is where Viola works, in a space primarily (but not exclusively, as it will be pointed out) containing human waste, and the abject that needs incessant wiping off. In the first cinematic sequence at the toilet, the mother is mopping the floor (Figure 13.6), carrying on her incessant struggle with the constantly reproduced, self-reproduced filth that permeates even her own body. On the bus on the way home, she keeps sniffing at her hands, checking out if traces of the toilet's smell can still be discerned on the surface of her body. On her getting home, however, her daughter hysterically starts opening all the windows of the flat and locks herself up into her own space, her room, where the mother is prohibited even to enter. In most of the film, the spaces of the mother and the daughter exclude each other; they are each other's opposites. For that very reason, they are also inevitably related to each other, and the film can be interpreted as a process of the daughter slowly accepting, accommodating, inhabiting and appropriating the mother's spaces.

Although the daughter, Angéla, does everything to exclude from her body and subjectivity anything that the mother's body means and signifies, their home and the space of the public toilet also correlate. Returning home, the mother obsessively tries to clean her body in the same way she wants to keep the public toilet clean: by cleansing off all the deposited layers of what she considers disgusting filth. The gestures of purification are the same: even the whiteness of her back brush evokes the toilet brush. By projecting these images upon each other, there comes about an equation or at least in Grosz's term an isomorphism between the body and the space. The public restroom is not only a space but also the mother's body, something she has an incessant struggle with and which, however, she keeps decorating, in the process making more emphatic what she represses in herself: her sexuality. Within the public restroom, between the women's and the men's part, she has an inner space, a room of her own, where she sits all day and where she keeps perfect order. Here, she stitches the smallest rip in the wall hanging and sweeps the smallest morsel off her table in a space that she decorates with the same colors and objects that define the space of her sitting room at home. Purple and red are the two colors that signify her desires and subjectivity that, in turn, are repulsive and filthy from the perspective of her daughter. At the beginning of the film, the daughter can relate to her mother's active female sexuality—of which she herself is the result—with disgust because she is a child who does not know her father, having been raised exclusively by her mother.

From the perspective of both the mother's and the daughter's subjectivity—and for the interpretation of the film—William A. Cohen's theoretical insight into the formation of subjectivity is relevant. Cohen claims that people are declared filthy when they are "unassimilably others," either because their noticeable features repel the observer or because the physical aspects of their body (their smell, appearance, or shabbiness) do the same. Actions, behavior and ideas are filthy where they are part of the immoral, inappropriate, obscene or unacceptable. These all are value judgments that are usually unconsciously experienced and bear cultural codes. In all the varieties of filth there is a shared feature: from the perspective of the judge they serve the purpose of distinguishing, "*That* is not me." For this reason, filth is so disturbing that it jeopardizes the integrity of the subject who faces it. When confronting filth and rejecting it, we are already late, as the subject is already contaminated."[13]

As we deduce from a haphazard sentence between her daughter and her daughter's friend, Viola is not even willing to tell her daughter who her father is, which obviously contributes to the fact that Angéla makes a connection between the smell of her mother's body on her return home from the public restroom and what she finds not only physically disgusting but also morally improper. Angéla looks at and smells her mother's body with such undisguised disgust that it becomes clear that the unpleasant smell extends beyond itself. Angéla's disgust derives from the position of the mother's female sexuality in the public space, and also from the abject elements of the male and female bodies that can be linked to the public restroom. The daughter thus projects both physical and cultural filth upon her mother's body, while wanting to define the differences between her mother's and her own body by the forced construction of the boundaries between their spaces, as if wanting to claim, using all the symbolic elements of the film, "*That* is not me." The consciously built boundaries are almost trenches, yet they gradually crumble in the film. Together with the boundaries, binaries that looked distinct and serve as the foundation for the mother's and the daughter's exclusive subjectivities implode as well, at least from the daughter's perspective. By the end of the film, Angéla accepts her mother's space, but paradoxically, instead of being contaminated by it the daughter assumes her mother's subject position, suddenly realizing the beauty it implies that before she could only perceive as rejectable filth that must be kept at a distance.

In the closing scene, Angéla is sitting in for her mother as the attendant in the public toilet because her mother was attacked here, after the toilet had been closed for the night. Viola was beaten up, and the day's income was taken away from her. The scene signifies both symbolic and physical violence simultaneously because Viola is taken in and then seriously violated by two men. As a result of the beating, Viola assumes her daughter's typical colors, consisting of various shades of green and blue. The attack can be understood as the various ways in which women are exploited and abused. It recalls the economic and symbolic vulnerability of single mothers, a woman who society perceives as having no one—no man—by her side to protect her in the middle of the night. (In its own way, this also presumes that in this culture a woman needs someone to protect her, as if "protectors" could not also function as abusers either within or outside the domestic space). The attack also evokes the position of prostitutes—the archetype of sexualized women—who work on their own at night, exposed to violence of all kinds. This violence is all the more called to mind as Viola's room in the public restroom, wedged between the male and female spaces, inserts her body between two panes of glass, and thus turns her into the object of observation. This paradoxically means that what is inhabited by her as her own space is actually a space that creates a unique isomorphism with her body inasmuch as she is turned into a sexualized object exposed to and on display for the public. When she is beaten up and assumes her daughter's colors, which are also camouflage colors (or rather when she is stigmatized by those colors), her sexuality is denied and broken by her attackers. Damaged as a desiring subject,

Space, Body and Subjectivity: Fresh Air

Viola's sexuality—her active female sexuality—is stigmatized by the green and blue "stains" that have been stamped onto her body.

As her employer threatens to fire Viola while she is being treated in the hospital, her daughter takes over her job as a substitute restroom attendant. Although she enters her mother's (work)place holding a tissue in front of her nose and trying to fend off the smell she has always found unbearable, she can now see more than the abject and the rejectable in this space. The space opens up for her in its complexity, including its beauty and order. While the mother is in the hospital (where not only her own body wears the blue and green marks of being beaten up, but the whole space creates the impression of grayish green), her daughter, at this moment already wearing *red* dotted trousers, enters the innermost, almost sanctuary-like space of her mother. Showing the daughter's gradual transformation, the mother's space opens up for her via a relatively obvious, yet paradoxically both lyrical and ironic symbolism. She turns on the table light, a red electronic flower that opens its petals when turned on. (Even the toilet paper is shaped into a flower in bloom.) She then opens her mother's most secret cabinet—or closet—where she keeps all her air fresheners. Like a maniac, her mother has been searching for the perfect air freshener for years, one capable of camouflaging what culture and its subjects want to reject—and eject—from their body. This is what the public toilet symbolizes in its complexity, and she has been looking for an air freshener that is capable of turning that which it is supposed to cover up into not only acceptability but also beauty.

This is how this ambivalent space comes about: Angéla settles in her mother's innermost space and takes over her subject position in its ambiguity, which includes both the abject and the filth. They are no longer rejected (ejected) from the subject; quite the contrary, the abject is integrated into the subject, while this process of integration also creates beauty, no matter how artificial. Angéla takes her place at her mother's table, she assumes her red work smock (or habit, in both senses of the word), while she takes up her drawing pad (Figure 13.7). In this way, she not only assumes her mother's subjectivity, including her maternal-material legacy, but also integrates her own creative and desiring identity into her newly emerging subjectivity. In the closing shot, however, the gradually receding camera—in contrast to the opening petals of the electronic flower—turns the space into a narrow

Figure 13.7 Angéla takes over for her mother in the public toilet.
Source: © Ferenc Pusztai and Ágnes Kocsis, producer and co-producer/director of *Fresh Air*.

corridor that evokes all the other claustrophobic, corridor-like spaces of the film: the small entrance hall to Viola and Angéla's flat in the concrete block, and the closed space of the school workshop where the teacher responds to Angéla's creativity with derisive comments, as this is hardly a space where the freedom of creation is possible. While the camera withdraws from the internal space of the restroom attendant, it inevitably merges with what surrounds the internal, partly self-made and protected, partly exposed and vulnerable closet: the external urban space that keeps looming large as a threat, as a space that—along with its more "legitimate" users and inhabitants—can at any time violently break into the socially, culturally and gender-wise vulnerable space of the mother—and by this time, that of the daughter.

By evoking these other spaces, the closing shot creates a short-circuit closure and locks Angéla into both the claustrophobic spaces and their semiotic meaning. In this sense, the closing scene evokes all the other spaces of the film. As a result of the isomorphism between the spaces and the gendered bodies, the finale also implicates the subjects in the semiotically and multiply loaded spatiality of the cinematic weave. Undoubtedly, by settling in the mother's space, the daughter assumes her mother's subject position. The maternal body, and its mature-female, sexually desiring subjectivity no longer appear as the abject Other one can reject, causing the clear binary opposition between the mother and daughter to implode. The camera withdrawing from the inner space to create a claustrophobic corridor evokes the broader cultural-social space construction (Figure 13.8) that—beyond *this* emblematic space of the public restroom—is their shared space. Even if in the hospital scenes there is no communication between the mother and daughter, the symbols and colors create the connections. While the internal space of the (water) closet is reconstructed and resemiotized through the isomorphism between the bodies, the newly reconstructed subjectivity of Angéla, and the inner space of the public restroom, the same cannot be said of the other, external spaces. The ambivalent beauty (a beauty that includes the abject) as revealed in the inner space cannot be extrapolated into other social spaces. This ambiguous complexity remains inevitably closed into the space of the public toilet. It is a space that,

Figure 13.8 The claustrophobic corridor leading to the public toilet symbolizes the lives of Viola and Angéla in post-socialist Hungary.
Source: © Ferenc Pusztai and Ágnes Kocsis, producer and co-producer/director of *Fresh Air*.

Space, Body and Subjectivity: *Fresh Air*

along with its functions, culture does not want to be aware or take account of but paradoxically cannot afford to ignore. While Angéla's subjectivity changes as a result of her changed attitude towards her mother's body and *micro*space, the surrounding sociocultural construction remains unreconstructed, as Angéla cannot change the structure of the *macro*spaces. In contrast to culture's legitimate spaces, whatever is constructed in the symbolic structures of the public restroom will remain an invisible and improbable inclusion.

Notes

1. Grosz 1992, 248.
2. See Freud 1955 [1919].
3. See Kristeva 1982, 56–89 and 207–10.
4. Győri 2016, 29.
5. Baudrillard 2000, 2.
6. Baudrillard 2000, 38–9.
7. At one point in the film, a wall-size image of a beach also appears: when the daughter Angéla is on a date in a café, a beach is painted on the background wall. This is an updated form of the "prefab" wall-size poster, but its function is the same: escape into what from the perspective of reality is an unreal or even surreal non-space (Figure 13.3).
8. Győri 2016, 29.
9. Tóth 2010, 149–50.
10. See William Blake, "The Tyger."
11. For Ágnes Kocsis as auteur-director, the restroom is a semiotized space in another film as well. Eszter Ureczky argues that in Kocsis's second feature film, *Pál Adrienn* (2010), she also uses the restroom as an ambiguous space: it is both the most private, and at the same time an alienated and claustrophobic space. See Ureczky 2016, 171.
12. Kalmár 2016, 114.
13. Cohen 2005, ix–x.

References

Baudrillard, Jean. 2000. "The Precession of Simulacra." In *Simulacra and Simulation*, translated by Sheila Faria Glaser, 1–42. Ann Arbor: University of Michigan Press.

Blake, William. "The Tyger." Available at: https://www.poetryfoundation.org/poems/43687/the-tyger"

Cohen, William A. 2005. "Introduction: Locating Filth." In *Filth: Dirt Disgust, and Modern Life*, edited by William A. Cohen and Ryan Johnson, vii–xxxvii. Minneapolis: University of Minnesota Press.

Freud, Sigmund. 1955 [1919]. "The 'Uncanny.'" In *The Complete Psychological Works*, Vol. XVII, edited by James Strachey, translated by Alix Strachey, 217–256. London: Hogarth Press.

Grosz, Elizabeth. 1992. "Bodies—Cities." In *Sexuality and Space*, edited by Beatriz Colomina, 241–253. Princeton, NJ: Princeton University Press.

Győri, Zsolt. 2016. "Concrete Utopias: Discourses of Domestic Space in Hungarian Cinema." In *Cultural Studies Approaches in the Study of Eastern European Cinema: Spaces, Bodies, Memories*, edited by Andrea Virginás, 28–49. Newcastle upon Tyne: Cambridge Scholars.

Kalmár, György. 2016. "Apostate Bodies: Nimród Antal's *Kontroll* and Eastern European Identity Politics." In *Cultural Studies Approaches in the Study of Eastern European Cinema: Spaces, Bodies, Memories*, edited by Andrea Virginás, 112–130. Newcastle upon Tyne: Cambridge Scholars.

Kocsis Ágnes, dir. 2006. *Fresh Air*. Distributed by MOKÉP. Budapest: KMH Film.

Kristeva, Julia. 1982. *Powers of Horror: An Essay on Abjection*. Translated by Leon S. Roudiez. New York: Columbia.

Tóth, Eszter Zsófia. 2010. *Kádár leányai: Nők a szocialista időszakban*. Budapest: Nyitott Könyvműhely.

Ureczky, Eszter. 2016. "Post-Bodies in Hungarian Cinema: Forgotten Bodies and Spaces in Ágnes Kocsis' *Pál Adrienn*." In *Cultural Studies Approaches in the Study of Eastern European Cinema: Spaces, Bodies, Memories*, edited by Andrea Virginás, 168–191. Newcastle upon Tyne: Cambridge Scholars.

Part 4
Modernism vs. Traditional Values

Introduction

Modernity, often couched in the form of westernization, was a foreign import in many countries, including Iran and Turkey, the examples covered in Part 4. Trade and a cultural secularism were the hallmarks of such modernity, which included a rewriting of spatial practices and the role of women within them.

Rana Habibi examines Iran's capital city Tehran during the era of Mohammad Reza Pahlavi in the middle of the twentieth century, a time when women were required to go in public without the Islamic veil as a sign of their westernization. Parallel to women's unveiling, Habibi finds that buildings also "unveiled," with balconies and other openings allowing new exchanges between the public street and the private home. Bülent Batuman then turns to present-day Turkey, examining mosque spaces during a time when a conservative ruling party is attempting to use religious icons to foster tradition-alism and eradicate state secularism. He discusses how the new state leaders have given women greater roles in both the design and use of mosque spaces in an attempt to further integrate them into the new order. Finally, Eda Acara discusses how rural women in the Thrace region of Turkey have learned to become activists in order to counter the pollution of the river that helps provide their livelihood. This new activism has helped rewrite these women's sense of modernity while transforming everyday geographies of their village.

Collectively, these chapters point to the tensions inherent between modernity and traditionalism in areas with strong cultural identity politics and the differing roles that women play in this process.

14

Unveiled Middle-Class Housing in Tehran, 1945–1979

Rana Habibi

Mass housing development was a key part of urban modernization for most Middle Eastern cities. It gradually began in the mid-1940s and lasted until the late 1970s. The discourse around mass housing construction, beginning with the form of modern neighborhoods, was introduced in Iran in 1946 with the establishment of the Association of Iranian Architect-Diplom (*Anjoman-e-Architect-ha-ye-Diplom-e-ye-Iran*), or AIAD. It was further advanced in 1952 with the executive cooperation of the Construction Bank (*Bank-e-Sakhtemani*). Over the next 18 years, mass housing projects were systematically constructed in Tehran and other Iranian cities under the supervision of *Bank-e-Sakhtemani* and AIAD. After 1964, with the establishment of the Housing and Development Ministry and a law requiring foreign partnerships for housing construction, most of the mass housing projects were assigned to the private sector, a situation that continued until the Iranian Revolution of 1978–9.

The discourse and discussions of mass housing construction furthered the spread and publication of ideas on a new, modern way of living and dwelling among greater segments of the population. The use of housing as an instrument of extensive national modernization was an approach that only came about in Iran following World War II. The process of modernization in Iran had already begun in the nineteenth century (specifically by Nasir-al-Din Shah Qajar in 1846), and the country was vastly transformed by Reza Shah Pahlavi during his reign from 1925 until 1941. In this period, however, the country's modernization concerned only specific social classes, which were largely elites. Architecturally, modernization was limited to governmental buildings, monuments, and villas. It was only after the formation of new neighborhoods for the middle classes, in suburbs located mostly in the eastern part of the city, that the structure and image of Tehran dramatically changed, leading to the unfolding of a new, modern lifestyle among its citizens. With Mohammed Reza Pahlavi's ascent to the throne in 1941, his attempt to disseminate the notion of modern living became a noticeable force behind Iran's modern political will. The Iranian government, like its Middle Eastern peers, "used public-housing projects as an instrument of nation-building in an attempt to gain the allegiance of the new citizenry."[1] Hence, mass housing projects were not only matters of urban development, economic responses to a housing crisis, and pressures from rural–urban migration, but they were also part of a larger framework that provided ideological justification for Iran's place in the network of modern nations and made the country a part of the "civilized world." The mass housing constructed was not only part of new, modern neighborhoods; it represented a new, modern nation and a new middle class.

The emergence of middle-class neighborhoods following World War II was prefaced by the Anglo–Soviet coup d'état, the deposal of Reza Shah, and the instatement of his son, Mohammad Reza Shah, to the throne. Mohsen Habibi, an Iranian scholar of architectural modernism, divides this Cold war period in Iran into four specific periods: 1941–1953, the parliamentary period, when technocrats had the most power of execution; 1953–1962, the reconsolidation of the state and redefinition of the socioeconomical

253

Rana Habibi

position of Iran; 1962–1971, the peak period of modernism in Iran, when the speed of modernization increased and the manifestation of internationalism became more visible both in the city and in political actions; and 1971–1979, the oil boom era, when international companies moved into Iran and, at the same time, the bottom-up modernization that led to the revolution of 1979 began to form.

This chapter focuses on roughly the same time period (1945–1979) and is divided into four themes positioned within non-Western modernism studies: (1) the institutionalization of modernism through mass (public) housing projects; (2) citizen adaptation of ideal modernism and popular modernism; (3) the spread of modern taste through mass housing; and (4) the adaptation of a transnational model. The analysis is based on four case studies and the architectural discourses and practices evident in each: four mass public housing projects in Tehran (Chahrsad Dastgah, Narmak, Kuy-e Farah, and Ekbatan) that were designed and constructed under the supervision of Bank-e-Sakhtemani and AIAD members in the period between 1946 and 1969; and one mass housing project (a second stage of Ekbatan), designed and constructed by the private sector in 1975.

Iran and Modernity

Starting with Nasir al-Din's Qajar reign in 1846, Iran was repeatedly frustrated by the superior military power of its neighbors: Russia to the north and the British Empire to the east and south.[2] Apart from the strong internal will for modernization during the Kings of Qajar era, the presence of the Russian army in the nineteenth century and the discovery of oil by the British in the early twentieth century impacted the process of modernization.[3] With the start of Reza Shah's reign in 1941 and the newly created central government, the modernization process was applied more internally. Other Western powers, predominately France and Germany, while showing no explicit territorial ambitions for control over Iran exercised political pressure by influencing culture and pedagogy.[4] Even though the 1941 Anglo-Soviet invasion had destroyed Reza Shah's rule, it left the Pahlavi state intact.[5] The central government at this time was managed by Parliament, which was divided into the Liberal, Nationalist and Left parties. According to the constitution, the new Shah, Mohammad Reza Pahlavi, would not have any executive power. Instead, a new generation of technocrats maintained power from 1941 until the Anglo-American coup of 1953. These technocrats had recently graduated from universities in France, Germany, Belgium, Italy, and England, and continued the modernization process in Iran over this 12-year period.[6] After a coup d'état in 1953, during which the US removed Prime Minister Mohammad Mosaddegh in favor of a strengthened monarchy, the US began to exert more influence on the process of modernization in Iran. Unlike other Middle Eastern countries, which were directly under control of one of the empire powers, Iran thus experienced very mixed and diverse models of modernity.

Revolution in the Meaning of Public and Private

The initiation of a modern way of living and the evolution of Iranian domestic culture is a consequence of internal socioeconomic, cultural, and political transformations. This internal transformation, however, is influenced—and sometimes driven—by a complex transnational web of connections. Iran received a steady flow of imported educational reforms, new laws, urban planning principles, and household commodities over several decades.

The transitions of domestic culture and family life are long processes. These changes had already started during the nineteenth century through transforming the system of production.[7] The establishment of Anglophonic and Francophonic missionary schools for girls by British and American missionaries entering Iran in the early twentieth century also contributed to this process.[8] Missionaries believed they had a responsibility to replace traditional ways of life with more rational Western norms. Their schools were established to educate women in matters of housekeeping and family care, and to familiarize them with a new understanding of everyday life with topics such as "problems and principles of

254

social living" and "practical hygiene," introduced in order to rationalize their pupils' habits and routines. Missionaries' homes served as models for deconstructing traditional dwellings, while rationalizing the home's activities was the main mission of these schools.[9] Domesticity is often considered to be part of a civilizing mission and, as such, the importance of domesticity was a crucial factor in the colonial encounter.[10] Another influence was, of course, the elites and the furnishings that they imported.[11]

The transformation of domestic culture was neither a central part of social reformation nor an instrumental tool of modern nation building until after the formation of a central government by Reza Shah in 1921. Subsequently, the spontaneous internal and international flows of exchange and change concerning social policies were intertwined with strong governmental ambitions, plans, and actions. Among those actions, some were of fundamental importance: unveiling women, a new dress form for men, the establishment of modern family laws by Reza Shah in the 1930s, and the Truman Point IV program for women, titled "home economics," and introduced in the 1950s. Last but not least, the Kennedy Doctrine and its "modernism ideology"[12] had an enormous impact, as it advocated for "a good way of living for all nations."[13] Exporting American expertise in urban planning and architecture was an important element in the physical implementation of the American Doctrine. It is evident that there was a direct connection between the emergence of the domestic ideal on the one hand and the rise of industrial capitalism and imperialism on the other.[14]

These internal and international actions and influences that contributed directly or indirectly to the transformation of domestic culture embodied themselves explicitly in the architecture of the modern house and consequently, the city and urban form. Modernism, as a coherent architectural doctrine and practice, delivered the practical knowledge required for the introduction of new housing forms and systems. In other words, the "modern house" at the architectural scale and the "modern neighborhood" at the urban scale became the cultural embodiments of modernist socioeconomic actions, programs, and influences.

Revolutionizing the domestic culture was a well-known tool of modern nation building (including societal modernization) in the region at that time.[15] Reza Shah, like his Turkish peer and neighbor Mustafa Kemal Atatürk,[16] imposed social reforms through legislative initiatives, such as "family laws" (including the divorce law of 1934 and the "women unveil law" of 1935). These were the first and major steps in the creation of new family structures and a new, modern society.[17]

In addition to the laws that allowed this change in traditional family structures, the radical transformation of the production system produced further societal changes. During the intertwined processes of urban modernization, spontaneous rural to urban migration, and production system transformation, the traditional production of handcrafts decreased, as did the proportion of the agricultural population. Urban women no longer took part in income-generating activities.[18] These changes in Tehran have been referred to as "housewife-ization," a phenomenon also evident during the same period in Turkey and Egypt and usually coinciding with the process of capitalist modernization and rural–urban migration.[19]

Along with the transformation of domestic culture and the formation of new family structures (from the collective family to the nuclear family), the Truman Point IV program[20] began to modernize home education and rationalize the lives of Iranian housewives as "home economic" courses were instituted, supervised by the US Department of Education.[21] The main goal of this program was to modernize Iranian lifestyles by upgrading housewives' use of modern household commodities and improving domestic "decorative taste." Like other homemaker's institutes in the Middle East, the task of the institutes was not to question women's primary vocation as homemakers, but simply to make this vocation more scientific (rational) and contemporary (modern).[22]

The transformation of social and daily life was reflected in the housing and the urban lives of Iranians as well. In the 1940s, Iran experienced dramatic changes in its urban forms, as worldwide modernization movements were embodied in new "modern" neighborhood units in Tehran. Proposals for these neighborhoods, like those in other countries, not only included new housing typologies, but also aimed to alter existing social structures and facilitate nation building. The government of Iran advanced the modernization of the state by "unveiling" and promoting a new social "spirit" that took the form of new urban districts. Discussions and proposals regarding new neighborhoods centered on creating healthy, suitable, low-cost housing for new government employees, a group emblematic of Iran's newly established, modern middle class.

The appearance of the middle class led to changes in Iranian urban development through the formation of "modern neighborhoods." The social reproduction of the modern middle class was the literal unveiling reformation of 1933. In approving this law, Reza Shah set out to standardize and Europeanize the appearance of the nation.[23] By the mid-1930s, there were at least 4,000 women—almost all in Tehran—who ventured into public places without veils, or at least without wearing the full-length covering known as the *chadour*.[24] Unveiling in urban and social terms was the most pronounced sign of modernization in Iran. Urban public spaces would not only displace men's activities but also women's.

Iran's social reformation affected the forms of housing and the dialogue between private and public space, inside-outside and hidden-manifest. Traditional, introverted Iranian houses that had no opening towards public spaces suddenly opened up to the street and public squares through windows and balconies (Figure 14.1). This new urban landscape emerged out of the country's socio-urban

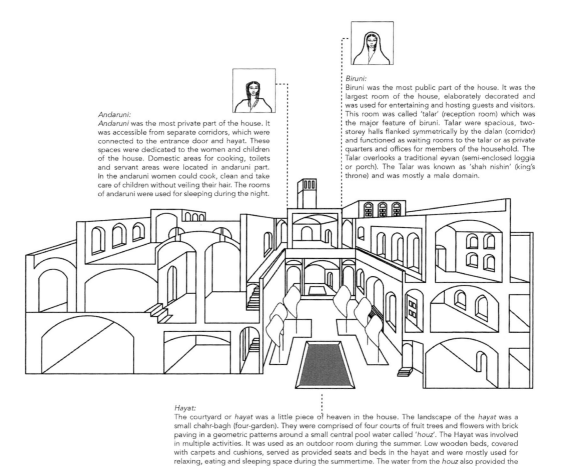

Figure 14.1 **Diagram of Traditional Iranian House**
Source: © Rana Habibi, 2017.

transformation and attempts by the reformers to define a modern Iranian culture. However, these changes were not always acceptable to extremely traditional and conservative citizens.

Architect and AIAD member Vartan Hovanesian described the influence of the unveiling law upon housing models:

> Unveiling the old-fashioned Iranian society by Reza Shah, which was the most progressive social reformation in the last fifty years in Iran, led to the unveiling of Tehran as well. The houses of this city, like women in traditional society who were covered with dark veils, were surrounded by monotonously high muddy walls and had no aperture to the outside world except a wooden door. In that age, who could break this sad and dark hedge? Who could open the window from his living room towards the street or build a balcony for looking outside? Only after the unveiling law and return of our Iranian architects from Europe could a new model for housing find its way to Iranian society.[25]

The urban transformation was initially not that radical. As we can see in Chaharsad Dastgah—the first modern, middle-class neighborhood in Tehran—while houses redefined the spatial characteristics of the traditional courtyard house, the balconies still looked towards private backyards, and only balconies of the housing blocks around the main public square opened to the public domain (Figure 14.2). The main spatial structure of houses included two stories linked by a staircase, which functioned as an independent volume and modern object, offering a new representation of spatial division (*hashti*) in a traditional house. In a traditional house, spatial divisions separated the internal (*andaruni*), private spaces, like the kitchen and other "female" spaces, from external (*biruni*) or public spaces, like the living room, guest room, and other "male" spaces. The staircase had exactly the same function of spatial division (*hashti*) in the modern houses of *Chaharsad Dastgah*. The kitchen was designed on the ground floor, while the balcony (*ayvan*), linked to the guest living room (*otagh pazirayi*), was located on the first floor. The balcony (*ayvan*) in traditional houses looked out onto the private yard (*hayat*) instead of looking into public space.

Abbas Adjdari, one of the designers of Chaharsad Datsgah, explains this choice of housing typology:

> The climate situation of Tehran and the cultural lifestyle of Iranians necessitate individual houses with a courtyard and surrounding walls. It means each single house needs a small pool (hauz), water storage, and walls for hiding the yard from the public. So, an Iranian house costs more in comparison with European houses. The Europeans don't need a small pool (hauz) in their houses because they spend their lives more indoors than outdoors, while Iranians use a yard (hayat) as an outdoor room of the house. Also, Europeans, based on their culture, don't need to hide their family (wife and children) from public eyes. Therefore, they can live in apartments with several floors and share some equipment, such as laundry, kitchen, and bathrooms, with each other. Hence, their solution for mass housing production is more affordable. Unfortunately, at this moment, the apartment typology cannot be successfully applied to [an] Iranian lifestyle. We, as architects, should find a solution for our housing crisis, and rather than imitate European apartments, we should find a compromise that suits the Iranian way of life.[26]

From Ideal Modernism to Popular Modernism

Although the modernization process in Iran, as in many other countries, first started with revolutionary ideals, in practice it had to go through a process of moderate steps. Through moderation and appropriation, an idealistic modernist vision was made more practical, based on pre-existing sociocultural characteristics and typological elements in architecture and urban settings. Ultimately, this local version of modernism became accepted, provoked urban reactions, and produced some unexpected social consequences. Narmak, a modern, middle-class neighborhood constructed from 1952–1958, exemplifies this journey from an ideal modernity to an ordinary one.

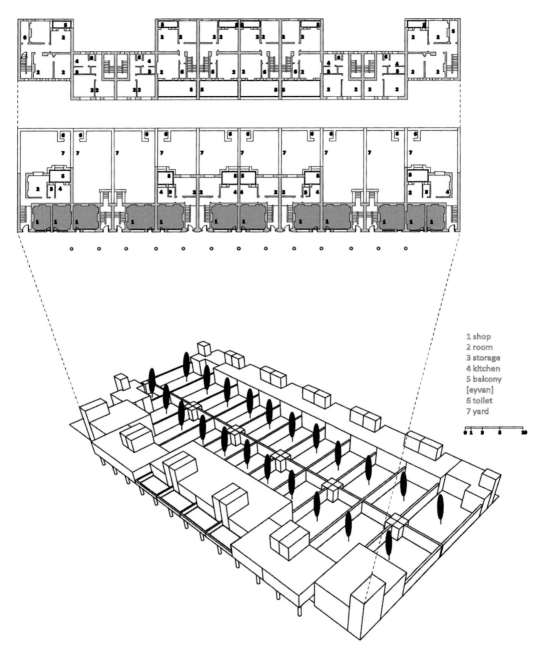

Figure 14.2 Chaharsad Dastgah Housing Units with Balconies towards the Square and Private Backyards
Source: © Rana Habibi, 2017.

The Narmak project was intended to be absolutely modern, but vernacular elements found their way into this new, modern world. In this case, the vernacular discriminately co-operated with and infiltrated the modernization process, and a new form of modernity emerged from the dialectical interaction.

The design of the housing units was based on an imported French prefabrication system, KALAD. This concrete system, which permitted the construction of two- to three-bedroom houses with

Unveiled Middle-Class Housing in Tehran

concrete panels of 1.10 m × 4.40 m (approx. 3′6″ ×14′5″) in one day, was positioned as a "housing factory."[27] The architects proposed one-story, semidetached homes with a private yard and two, three, or four bedrooms (Figure 14.3).[28] According to the architects, KALAD was not only a system for housing standardization, but was also "representative of the beautiful and affordable modern house."[29]

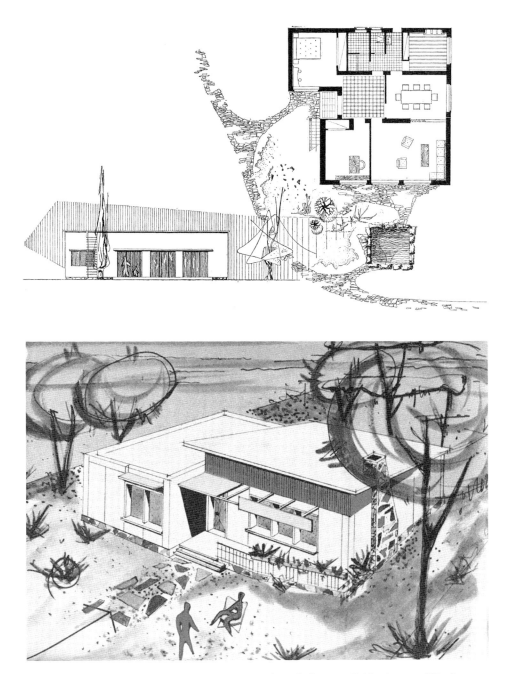

Figure 14.3 Kalad Houses and the Iranian Version of a Kalad House With *Houz* and Yard
Source: *Journal of Bank-e-Sakhtemani* 1956, 2–4.

The two-bedroom type had a living and dining room separated by a service area. The service area included a kitchen and bathroom with a hallway linking the spaces together. This functional division (between daytime activities in the living and dining rooms, and nighttime activities in the bedrooms) also applied to the volume of the respective rooms. Narmak architects used this same general layout for all of the typological variations. In this way, modernist architecture—as a way of building, a knowledge product, a style-of-life consumer item, and above all, a symbol of modernity—had traversed national boundaries in the form of prefabricated housing designed for the middle class.[30]

While architects in Iran were preaching the universal applicability of modern architecture, Iranian dwellers had other things on their minds. Narmak's middle-class women homeowners made requests that were eventually published in the *Journal of Bank-e-Sakhtemani*: a source of water in the yard for washing clothes and rugs, and a stairway from the yard to the roof as an alternative sleeping space for the summer topped the wish list.[31] The owners desired an extension of the house from the inside to the outside, for the modern neighborhoods were missing the outside spaces that traditionally structured daily practices of domesticity. Mina Marefat emphasizes the crucial role of the yard (*hayat*) in traditional Iranian houses:

> The *hayat* was landscaped as a small *chaharbāgh* (literally four-gardens) with trees and flowers and brick paving in geometric patterns around a small, central pool of water. Sleeping outdoors in the *hayat* or on the roof was customary in the warmer seasons when the courtyard was sprinkled with water in the evening for use as an outdoor room.[32]

Architects thus had to provide an Iranian yard for the modern prefabricated houses. The yard and house juxtaposed both domains of the project: the house, as a representation of the international modernist paradigm; and the garden, as a customized, localized space to meet the traditional needs of homeowners. In the end, the master plan of Narmak was never realized. The house owners and builders divided the lands and built their own houses based on the definition of home that they knew.

Modern Taste and Mass Housing

During the Cold War, the Iranian modernization process, as in so many other countries, faced a choice between the influence of communism or US-led capitalism. At the advent of the 1960s, however, the American Century was celebrated in much of the world. "Some scholars point out that between 1945 and 1970, most international construction and exportation came from the US."[33] The US systematically exported its own ideology of modernism to other countries during the early 1960s through the Kennedy Doctrine, whereby the US attempted to contain communist influence, especially in Latin American countries, resulting in "a series of integrally related changes in economic organization, political structures, and system of social values."[34] The Kennedy Doctrine targeted traditional societies and aimed for integration with the modern world. Considering the interdependency between political and socioeconomic changes, the Kennedy government concluded that "the progress of developing societies can be dramatically accelerated through contact with developed ones."[35]

The export of American commodities, comprehensive planning, and architecture were the forms of "contact" used to build "consumer societies" for American products. Imported commodities not only fueled a culture of consumption in various societies but also transformed the spatial structure of that country's houses. In this vein, furnishings based on Western or imported commodities had a significant impact on the interior spatial structure of the "modern" Iranian house. The gradual introduction of Western household commodities that started in the nineteenth century with the dinner table and chair grew rapidly during the 1960s. Gradually, furnishings based on imported household commodities introduced new tastes and modern domestic culture to Iranian families. Importing a washing machine, vacuum cleaner, and other time-saving appliances eliminated the need for a maid; thus the vacated maid's room became another bedroom.[36] As early as 1950, many Iranians (including those in smaller cities) had already begun to remodel their homes based on newly available commodities and technologies.

Unveiled Middle-Class Housing in Tehran

If we consider commodities—and their economic value in general—as a particular type of social potential and even more as a form of material culture transferred from one nation to another, it becomes clear how imported household commodities create a pluralistic global imagination of an "equipped kitchen," "standard house," and the notion of a "good life" that is at the core of modernism based on a capitalist system. As commodities "in motion" illuminate their human and social context,[37] they also become indicators of lifestyle and modes of modernity.

The *Kuy-e Farah* housing development shows the transformation of the interior of Iranian houses based on new imported commodities (Figure 14.4). A significant aspect of the Kuy-e Farah housing

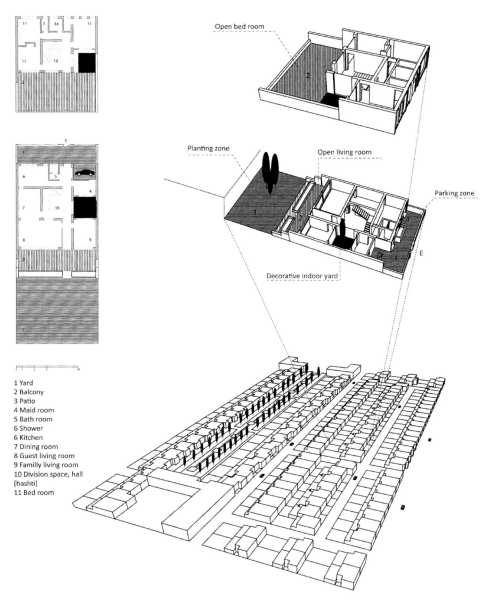

Figure 14.4 Kuy-e-Farah Housing Development
Source: © Rana Habibi, 2017.

units was an L-shaped configuration of the kitchen, dining room, and living room. The kitchen and dining room formed the long part of the "L" shape, while two connected living rooms made up the short part. The "L" form for the distribution of kitchen, dining, and living rooms was developed from international precedents that rationalized living space.[38] The conceptual transformation of the kitchen in the new houses was not only because of international exchanges, but also because of the modernization of technology. As Chehabi points out:

> Traditionally, the kitchen was placed far away from the living area in the houses. This was due to the smoke and soot produced by the ovens, and made possible by the availability of a permanent staff to do the cooking. When Western style houses replaced the traditional Iranian house centered on a courtyard, the kitchen became a separate room not far from the dining room and living room, an arrangement that became even more common after butane gas was introduced to Iran in the 1960s, an innovation that rendered kitchens cleaner.[39]

Kuy-e Farah, like other contemporaneous houses in the world, offered a "rationalized kitchen" that was well connected to the dining and living rooms. The kitchen was based on the housewife's movement between three main elements: the washing basin, oven, and refrigerator. The kitchen was connected to the porch directly with a door, and it had two other connections to the corridor and dining room. The reception room (*utaq-e pazirayi*) and living room (*neshiman*) were perpendicular to the kitchen and dining room. Bedrooms were located upstairs and connected to the other rooms by a staircase. Three bedrooms and two bathrooms on the upper floor were indicative of the nuclear family model of the modern house. The maid's room on the ground floor with a separate door to the yard illustrates the economic level of the middle class in the beginning of the 1960s in Iran. The design of modern houses at the time was based on specific "movements" towards the modern resident, and it proposed very defined functional or rationalized spaces for specific activities. In this way, the last generation of single-family row houses became the nuclear family model and embodiment of all domestic cultural transformation that occurred since the modernization process had first begun in Tehran.

Kuy-e Farah is representative of the late 1950s and early 1960s modern middle-class houses, as well as a last generation of single-family row houses. One of the significant characteristics of the 1960s Tehran districts, and of Kuy-e Farah specifically, is the priority given to cars rather than pedestrians. With the establishment of several car production factories (such as *Sherkat-e-Sahami-e Am-e Sanati va Tolidi-e Moratab*) in the late 1950s, the number of private cars increased exponentially. In 1966, with the production of an Iranian car under the name of *Sherkat-e-Khodrosazi-e Saipa*, the private car became an integral member of the modern Iranian house. Since that time, accommodating the car has been a key challenge and priority. The place for the car in relation to the house and the neighborhood became a central planning issue of structural importance:

> Without any doubt, nowadays, one of the main desires of citizens in large cities is having an automobile. Therefore, one of the main problems that cities face is the lack of parking places. With increasing wealth and quality of life, people demand more cars and so the city and houses will need more parking space.[40]

The presence of cars had a major impact on the function of the yard. Traditionally, the *hayat* (yard) in the Persian house (an open space on the ground floor) was defined through orchards and a *hauz* (small pool of water) in the middle of the yard; however, this changed dramatically in Kuy-e Farah houses. The yards in Kuy-e Farah had traditional domestic uses, but included a new element for urban life: a parking space for an automobile. The vernacular "yard" was, in a way, decomposed into four to five separate elements: the backyard as a place for plants and flowers; a platform on the ground floor as an extension of the living room; a vast balcony on the first floor extending the bedrooms; a small patio inside the house used as a small orchard-garden and light catcher; and the front yard that was now defined as a parking space. For typologies with only a front yard, plant space and parking space merged together, and for the ones with only backyards, the street was used as for parking. Extension spaces, namely the courtyard, balcony, and patio, remained the same for all variations. In sum, the spatial organization of the Kuy-e Farah neighborhood yards was fundamentally transformed. The car, as a new status symbol, was integrated into the courtyard and it became, in many ways, a new piece of furniture. Technological innovation and oversizing of the housing units also contributed to the transformation of the yard concept. Ali Saremi explains the role of plumbing in the transformation of the yard in general:

> Plumbing left no use for the pool in the middle of the courtyard. The pool was therefore filled and covered with mosaic, allowing a more clear space within the yard for parking an automobile. Bringing the car into the yard also required the removal of little flower boxes, the widening of the traditional vestibule, and the replacement of the small wooden double-entry doorway by a large metal gate.[41]

The Modern House as a Transnational Model

The role of the car in shaping living spaces was accelerated by the first master plan of Tehran, designed by Victor Gruen, an Austrian-American planner, and Aziz Farmanfarmaian, an Iranian architect who graduated from the École des Beaux-Arts in Paris. Gruen had extensive experience in the design of shopping malls and was known as "the designer who gave architectural shape to American consumerism."[42] The Comprehensive Plan for Tehran that Gruen and Farmanfarmaian developed addressed the city's most pressing problems, such as housing shortages, overcrowding, inadequate services, unemployment, and incessant migration.[43] Gruen and Farmanfarmaian responded to these challenges by proposing the creational of ten central urban units:

> The urban centers were to be connected by public transit lines, and large green areas separated the districts. The design of the urban centers resembles Gruen's designs for shopping malls and renovation plans for city centers in the United States.[44]

Programmed to accommodate commercial markets and to facilitate the movement of automobiles, the Comprehensive Plan not only proposed new spaces and urban structure, it also aimed to stabilize a new domestic culture:

> The habit of the people of the United States of America is that women usually take their husbands to work, then drop off their children at schools, and go shopping on their way home. The same trend is gradually becoming evident in Tehran, and the degree of its success at the end of the plan depends on the efficiency of the public transportation network. Yet, in terms of planning, the use of private vehicles should be the basis of future developments.[45]

The Comprehensive Plan offered new residential complexes that were developed around shopping malls. Residential areas, administrative buildings, and new recreational centers were linked together by highways and metro lines. The ideas of the Comprehensive Plan were furthered in housing projects of the 1970s.

Tehran of the 1970s was regarded as the oil capital of Iran and the Middle East. As such, it captured the interest of international investors, many from the US. As a result, Iran, particularly Tehran, faced a wave of internationalism during this decade. To cope with Tehran's housing crisis, massive building projects were undertaken in cooperation with international companies. These housing projects were indicative of the "open to internationalization" mindset, while at the same time emblematic of the search for Iran's own "local" culture. The projects accommodated elements of the local along with an international way of life, providing a transnational model in Iran. In Tehran, however, this combination of lifestyle was, in comparison to previous decades, more in line with international standards than with vernacular rules. The construction of various types of towers and high-rises in the city during the 1970s demonstrates this new application of international architectural standards. These international standards became a common destination of discourse and practice for Iranian modernists, who had often spent years of their professional lives abroad, as well as for international architects who came to Iran to complete internships or pursue projects as well-established figures in the field. The housing projects such architects completed were the outcome of imported ideas adapted to local Tehran realities, or rather "transferred models" based on global contemporary models that were re-interpreted in their new environment.

The Ekbatan housing project is representative of this so-called transferred model in Tehran, in which an accelerated diffusion of Western ideas around the world presented several ideological models that were transferred and shaped urban environments and spaces worldwide. Newer urban–architecture practices served as models that were imported and adapted, more or less, to local needs and conditions.[46] These transformed models were not a one-way road, as both importers and exporters as well as the interpreters of models had a role to play in creating this new urban environment. The models were transformed, conveying networks of local and foreign actors, flows of ideas, exchanges and adaptations, while illustrating the understanding of "planning culture and of a milieu of professionals who shape the urban environment."[47] The flows of ideological models and interactions of many local and international intermediaries led to a transnational model. This transnational model, with its introduction and rapid diffusion to other urban landscapes, encapsulates several "domesticated modernities," defined as forms of modernism that were modified by the cultures and societies they encountered. The transnational model is a process of intertwined histories in which the role of locals and the scale of influences is important. The case of Ekbatan illustrates that despite internal cultural challenges and a search for a modern identity, the housing complex remains a translated version of an international model.

The head of management and the executive director of the Ekbatan project was the architect Rahman Golzar, who also personally owned the 220-hectare site in West Tehran on which Ekbatan would be built. The design team was comprised of Iranian, US, and South Korean architects. The Gruzen Partnership[48] was one of the US firms that operated as a design partner. Another major design partner was the Korean avant-garde architect Kim Swoo Geun, already well-known for adapting modernism to Korean culture. The combination of local and foreign designers and builders made Ekbatan into a transnational experiment that began as a foreign model, but that evolved into a domestic production with both international and local characteristics.

The architecture of Ekbatan, with its exposed rough concrete and very large modernist block forms, is undoubtedly largely derived from Brutalism.[49] Situated in a park, the design combined rough concrete, continuous ribbon windows, and *pilotis* to suggest one of the icons of modernism: Le Corbusier's Unité d'Habitation (first built in 1952 in Marseille, France). At second glance, however, it is striking how much Ekbatan resembles models of residential buildings in New York of the 1940s that experimented with Y, U, and X-shaped building plans, as well as the well-known prototypes developed by Marcel Breuer for the notorious Stuyvesant competition (Figure 14.5).

The "towers in the park" idea (a concept developed by Le Corbusier) and Y-shaped buildings designed for New York in the 1940s ultimately served as prototypes for solving the middle-class housing shortage in 1970s Tehran. Moreover, significant differences existed between Phases 1 and 2 of the project. Phase 1 was designed by a team of Iranian and American architects, while Phase 2 was designed largely by South Korean architect Kim Swoo Geun. Each block of Phase 1 has three major steps in height, from five to nine to 12 floors, and each block rests on *pilotis*. The blocks in

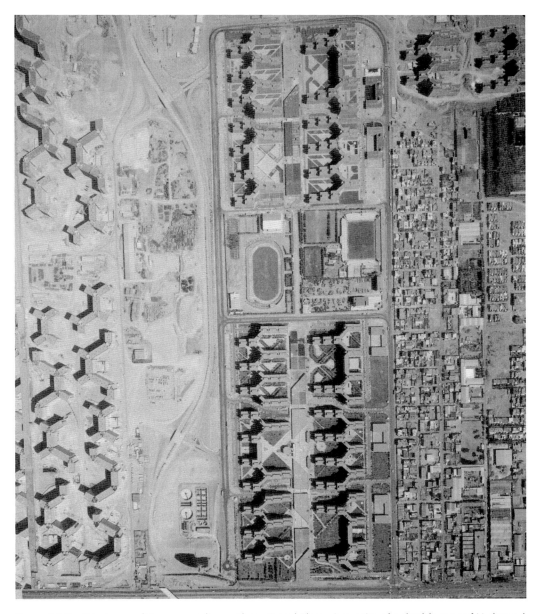

Figure 14.5 Ekbatan and its surroundings. Phase 1 and Phase 3 consist of a double row of U-shaped apartment buildings, while Phase 2 buildings have an incomplete Y-shape.
Source: National Cartography Center [Iran], image from April 2014.

Phase 2, by contrast, were built as massive 12-story buildings without any steps in levels. Further differences are found in the design approaches to the shopping centers that form the center of the generously sized, continuous, and predominantly open public areas. Even the manner that housing is integrated into the park and the realization of housing typologies within the variously shaped blocks differs between phases, a result of the evolving interaction between diverse local and international actors.

Rana Habibi

Epilogue: Neglecting Internationalism and Continuations of Modernism in Practice

The population of Iran increased dramatically during the country's 30-year modernization process. Urbanization was largely due to uneven capitalist development and the corresponding unequal distribution of the society's wealth and resources among the growing population. Despite increases in the country's wealth, the 1970s oil boom merely increased the gap between rich and poor.[50] State-sponsored modernization attempts were more focused on big cities and upper- and middle-class society rather the urban poor, so the modernization programs did very little to improve the situation of widespread poverty.[51] Housing was still a very big issue; 70% of urban migrants did not have a proper house. This disparity fostered a hostile attitude among the urban poor and other urban social groups towards modernization; it engendered their negative reaction to the imposition of Western-oriented culture, which they correspondingly viewed as the root cause of their predicament.[52]

The failure to balance economic and social modernization among all classes led to alternative movements against modernization and its resulting consumer culture. These alternative movements advocated for the "local" and "traditional" over Western-oriented culture (cited in Mirsepassi 2000, 77).[53] The anti-Western sentiment that developed, popularly known as *Gharbzadegi* (West-intoxication), was present even among Iranian intellectuals.[54] They portrayed Iranian modernization (westernization) as a disease that had infected Iranian society from the outside and debased Iranian life and cultural integrity.[55] In response to this perceived "disease," traditionalist Iranian intellectuals became proponents of a "return to the roots" movement, trying to undo the reconciliation of the universal culture of modernity with Iranian culture, as was seen in the example of housing at Ekbatan.

While the poor were frustrated with the uneven distribution process of urbanization and one-sided economic changes, Iranian intellectuals were undergoing an identity crisis. Religious institutions, which were deeply embedded in Iranian family life, especially among the poor, had remained quiet during the modernization process; however, religion found its way to the forefront through the leadership of Ayatollah Khomeini after the Iranian Revolution of 1979. Devout religious adherents initiated social movements, countering the top-down White Revolution (1962) of Mohammad Reza Shah; they became increasingly more visible and public in the 1970s. The intellectuals leading this countermovement worked hand-in-hand with the Leftist Party. Those suffering from the imbalanced economy took to the modern boulevards in protest and demanded change. In the wake of the protests in February 1979, the Shah left Iran, and most foreign parties and international offices were forced to follow suit. The long road to modernization that began in 1921 was forced to take a new path following the Revolution in 1979.

Even so, the housing project of Ekbatan continued more or less along its initial trajectory even after the Revolution, and it remained popular among residents. Like every other modern apartment building in Iran, most of the balconies have been covered and their functions revised to become room extensions or storage rooms. Residents admire the complex's independence from the city, as it has its own school, shopping center, and mosque, and is considered a safe place for children.[56] After the revolution, Ekbatan was the subject of films, novels, and an art exhibition created by a younger generation of residents,[57] with the main theme being the paradox of modernity. Ekbatan residents have strong feelings for their neighborhood and are proud to live in one of the most modern neighborhoods in Tehran. In online social networks, for example, there is a page specifically for *Ekbatan* residents, where they remain closely informed about each other and changes to the complex, and where they discuss any neighborhood issues.[58] Although built by an international consortium, Ekbatan has become a local neighborhood and maintains a strong collective identity among its residents.

266

Notes

1. Habibi 2006.
2. Grigor 2009, 9.
3. Following Nasir al-Din Shah's assassination in 1896, Iran saw a vital new period due to the expansion of modern schools and the growth of publications with themes ranging from geographical discoveries and political conflicts to scientific developments and adventure novels. These educational venues afforded the Iranian public insight into the world beyond their own country. For more information, see Karimi 2012; Amanat 1999.
4. Grigor 2009, 9.
5. The two allies, joined by the US in December 1941, realized that Iran could be useful in achieving control over the Persian Gulf's oil resources. They took the main transport routes from the Gulf to the Soviet Union and split Iran into two zones, much like in World War I, with the Russians taking the North and the British the oil-rich South. However, they left the actual administration of the country to the central government.
6. See: Abrahamian 1982; Abrahamian 2008; Jahanbegloo 2004; Mirsepassi 2000.
7. Mansour Moaddel (1994, 9) in his book chapter "Tobacco Rebellion of the 1890s" has pointed out that in the late nineteenth century, many Iranian handicrafts were replaced by Western manufactured goods, causing a dramatic change in the traditional production system:

   > In the past, high quality textiles were manufactured in Isfahan since everyone—from the highest to the lowest—wore local products. But in the last few years, the people of Iran have given up their body and soul to buy the colorful and cheap products of Europe. In doing so, they incurred greater losses than they imagined: local weavers, in trying to imitate imported fabrics, have lowered their quality; Russians have stopped buying Iranian textiles; and many occupations have suffered great losses. At least one-tenth of the guilds in this city were weavers; not even one-fifth has survived.

8. For more information, see Rostam J. Kolayi 2008.
9. Karimi 2012.
10. Tranberg Hansen 1992.
11. Chehabi 2003.
12. The term "modernism ideology" is taken from Latham 2000.
13. Latham 2000.
14. Heynen 2005.
15. Heynen 2005.
16. For more information about Turkish domestic culture transition, see Bozdogan 2003.
17. Chehabi 1993.
18. Moghadam 2000.
19. Moghadam 2000.
20. The Point IV program in Iran addressed mainly the modernization of health and education, embodied in building dams and roads, improving rural life and eradicating numerous contagious diseases by building several hospitals, and establishing a "home economics" department in the government.
21. See Karimi 2012.
22. Bozdogan 2003.
23. Chehabi 1993, 9.
24. These women were mostly Western-educated upper-class daughters, foreign wives of recent returnees from Europe, and middle-class women of religious minority groups.
25. Hovanesian 1960, 5.
26. Adjdari 1946, 15.
27. Khodayar 1957.
28. Khodayar 1957.
29. Khodayar 1957.
30. Lu 2012.
31. Sarafian 1960, 17.
32. Marefat 1988.
33. Cody 2012.
34. Latham 2000.
35. Latham 2000, 2.
36. Saremi 2005, 34.
37. Appadurai 1986.
38. See for example Henderson 2007, 252.

39. Chehabi 2003, 51.
40. Badie 1962, 18.
41. Karimi 2012, 133.
42. Hardwick 2004, 55.
43. Gruen and Farmanfarmaian 1966.
44. Madanipour 1998, 43.
45. Gruen and Farmanfarmaian 1966.
46. Nasr and Volait 2003, xv.
47. Nasr and Volait 2003, xi–xxxi.
48. The Gruzen Partnership was originally founded as Kelly & Gruzen in 1936. They were a staunchly modernist American firm with a legacy of federal housing projects. After graduating from MIT and spending his internship in Italy, Jordan Gruzen started work at his father's firm. Peter Samtond joined him, and the name of the company changed to Gruzen and Partners and then to Gruzen Partnership. Peter Samton explained in an interview with MIT *Graduated Journal* how they became involved in the design of Ekbatan:

> We had a small but very international class at MIT. One student was Kyu Lee, an architect from Korea by way of Japan's royal family. He was pretender to the throne of Korea. He was my roommate and a very good designer. Another classmate was from Tehran. When we did work for the Shah in 1976, the four of us had a reunion in Tehran. The internationality of our class opened our eyes to the larger world.

> *MIT School of Architecture and Planning n.d.*

49. Brutalism, a movement characterized by large forms and exposed concrete construction, was developed after World War II in Great Britain and the US.
50. Abrahamian 2008, 124; Mirsepassi 2000.
51. Mirsepassi 2000, 74.
52. Mirsepassi 2000, 75.
53. Ernest Gellner characterizes the same predicament in an eloquent way:

> The romanticization of the local tradition, real or imagined, is a consequence of the desire to maintain self-respect, to possess an identity not borrowed from abroad, to avoid being a mere imitation, second-rate, a reproduction of an alien model.

54. Two intellectual figures, Jalal Al-e-Ahmad and Ali Shari'ati, are representative of *Gharb-zadegi* theories. Al-e-Ahmad (1923–69) as a short-story writer and novelist, essayist, social critic, and translator of French literature, represents a generation of Iranian intellectuals, who in the earlier part of their lives, were impressed with modernization ideology but then abandoned international modernity to embrace a local and authentic solution. Ali Shari'ati was led by a French-educated Shi'i ideologue. He attempted to construct and popularize a "modern" Shi'i ideology in response to the existing secular ideologies. Therefore the poor and the intellectuals came to the same conclusion: the simultaneous rejection of modernization and the romanticism of local cultures. For more information, see Abrahamian 2008; Mirsepassi 2000.
55. For example, Al-e-Ahmad populist Islam did not reject modernization as such, but would seek to reimagine modernity in accordance with Iranian-Islamic tradition, symbolism and ideology. Mirsepassi 2000.
56. Refer to the fan page of Ekbatan residents on Facebook, www.facebook.com/groups/the.ekbatan/?fref=n.
57. For example, see the photography exhibition of Behnam Sadighi, *Ekbatan West of Tehran*, www.behnamsadighi.com/site/articles.aspx?id=2014&galleryItem=1946. Refer also to the 2014 film *Ekbatan* created by Mehrshad Karkhani and the book *Street Number 38 of Yousef-Abad* written by Sina Dadkhah, where youth life in Ekbatan is described, along with Yousef-Abad other modernist neighborhoods in Tehran built in the 1940s.
58. See the fan page of Ekbatan residents on Facebook, www.facebook.com/groups/the.ekbatan/?fref=nf.

References

Abrahamian, Ervand. 1982. *Iran Between Two Revolutions*. Princeton, NJ: Princeton University Press.
Abrahamian, Ervand. 2008. *A History of Modern Iran*. Cambridge: Cambridge University Press.
Adjdari, Abbas. 1946. "Housing Problems in Tehran and Other Iranian Cities." *Architecte* 1(1): 15–16.
Amanat, Abbas. 1999. "Qajar Iran: A Historical Overview." In *Royal Persian Paintings: The Qajar Epoch 1785–1925*, edited by L. Diba and M. Ekhtiar, 22–30. London: I. B. Tauris.
Appadurai, Arjun. 1986. *The Social Life of Things: Commodities in Cultural Perspective*. Cambridge and New York: Cambridge University Press.

Badie, Naser. 1962. "The New Neighborhoods of Tehran [Title in Persian: Mahalleh-ha-ye Jadid-e Tehran]." In *Investigation in Social Problems of Tehran* [Title in Persian: Barresi-Masael-e-Ejtemaee-ye-Shahr-e-Tehran], edited by M. Motmaeni and M. Hakemi, 10–13. Tehran: Tehran University Press.

Bozdogan, Sibel. 2003. "Living Modern: Cubic Houses and Apartments." In *Modernism and Nation Building: Turkish Architectural Culture in the Early Republic*, edited by S. Bozdogan, 193–240. Seattle and London: University of Washington Press.

Chehabi, Houchang E. 1993. "Staging the Emperor's New Clothes: Dress Codes and Nation-Building Under Reza Shah." *Iranian Studies* 26(3/4): 209–229.

Chehabi, Houchang E. 2003. "The Westernization of Iranian Culinary Culture." *Iranian Studies* 36(1): 43–61.

Cody, Jeffery W. 2002. *Exporting American Architecture, 1870–2000.* New York: Routledge.

Grigor, Talinn. 2009. *Building Iran: Modernism, Architecture and National Heritage Under the Pahlavi Monarchs.* New York: Periscope.

Gruen, Victor, and Aziz Farmanfarmaian. 1966. *Comprehensive Plan of Tehran.* Tehran: Municipality of Tehran Press.

Habibi, Mohsen. 2006. *Intellectual Trends in the Contemporary Iranians Architecture and Urbanism.* Tehran: Cultural Research Bureau.

Hardwick, Jeffery M. 2004. *Mall Maker: Victor Gruen, Architect of an American Dream.* Philadelphia: University of Pennsylvania Press.

Henderson, Susan R. 2007. "A Revolution in the Women's Sphere: Grete Lihotzky and the Frankfurt Kitchen." In *Housing and Dwelling: Perspectives on Modern Domestic Architecture*, edited by B. Miller Lane, 221–247. London and New York: Routledge.

Heynen, Hilde. 2005. "Modernity and Domesticity: Tensions and Contradictions." In *Negotiating Domesticity: Spatial Productions of Gender in Modern Architecture*, edited by H. Heynen and G. Baydar, 1–29. London: Routledge.

Hovanesian, Vartan. 1960. "The Introduction." *Modern Architecture Journal* 1(1): 4–9.

Jahanbegloo, Ramin. 2004. *Iran Between Tradition and Modernity.* Lanham, MD: Lexington Books.

Karimi, Pamela Z. 2012. "Dwelling, Dispute, and the Space of Modern Iran." In *Governing By Design: Architecture, Economy, and Politics in the Twentieth Century*, edited by Aggregate, 95–119. Pittsburgh, PA: University of Pittsburgh Press.

Khodayar, Ahmad. 1957. "The First KALAD House in Narmak Neighborhood." (Title in Persian: Avalin Khaneh-ye-KALAD—dar-Kuy-e-Narmak). *Journal of Bank-e-Sakhtemani* 6: 10–15.

Kolayi, Rostam J. 2008. "Origins of Iran's Modern Girls' Schools: From Private/National to Public/State." *Journal of Middle East Women's Studies* 4(3): 55–88, Special Issue: Innovative Women: Unsung Pioneers of Social Change.

Latham, Michael E. 2000. *Modernization as Ideology, American Social Science and 'Nation Building' in the Kennedy Era.* Chapel Hill: University of North Carolina Press.

Lu, Duanfang. 2012. "Entangled Modernities in Architecture." In *Handbook of Architectural Theory*, edited by G. Crysler and H. Heynen, 231–246. London: Sage.

Madanipour, Ali. 1998. *Tehran: The Making of a Metropolis.* Chichester: John Wiley.

Marefat, Mina. 1988. *Building to Power: Architecture of Tehran 1921–1941.* Ph.D. Dissertation. MIT University, Boston.

Mirsepassi, Ali. 2000. *Intellectual Discourses and the Politics of Modernization: Negotiating Modernity in Iran.* Cambridge: Cambridge University Press.

MIT School of Architecture and Planning. n.d. "Plan 78: Peter Samton (BArch '57 and Jordan Gruzen (BArch '57)." https://sap.mit.edu/article/alumni-profile/peter-samton-barch57-and-jordan-gruzen-barch57, accessed on September 16, 2017.

Moaadel, Mansour. 1994. "Tobacco Rebellion of the 1890s." In *A Century of Revolution, Social Movements in Iran*, edited by J. Foran. 5–20. Minneapolis: University of Minnesota Press.

Moghadam, Valentine M. 2000. "Hidden From History? Women Workers in Modern Iran." *Iranian Studies* 33(3/4): 377–401.

Nasr, Joe, and Mercedes Volait. 2003. "Transporting Planning." In *Urbanism Imported or Exported? Native Aspirations and Foreign Plans*, edited by J. Nasr and I. Volait, xi–xxxi. West Sussex: Wiley-Academy.

Sarafian, Iman. 1960. "A Brief History of Housing." (Title in Persian: Seir-e-Ejmali-ye-Maskan). *Journal of Bank-e-Sakhtemani* 2: 16–19.

Saremi, Ali. 2005. "Iran: An Unaccomplished Modernization in Architecture." *Mimar Journal* 7(2): 31–36.

Tranberg Hansen, Karen. 1992. "Introduction: Domesticity in Africa." In *African Encounters with Domesticity*, edited by K. Tranberg Hansen, 9–16. New Brunswick, NJ: Rutgers University Press.

15

Appropriating the Masculine Sacred
Islamism, Gender, and Mosque Architecture in Contemporary Turkey

Bülent Batuman

The mosque has been a major architectural element in Islamic societies. Representing the materialization of religion in the public sphere, mosques have also emerged as landmarks in cities of the Islamic world. As a space of prayer as well as socialization, they have served as a means of maintaining the sense of community and the spatio-practical production of identities built on shared religion. In this respect, their significance has lasted into the modern era. Yet, this does not mean that the social and iconographic functions of the mosque have remained unchanged. On the contrary, mosques have gone through significant transformations under the influence of historical dynamics. This chapter aims to discuss the mosque as a field of contestation regarding two intertwined themes of gender and modernism through the case of Turkey.

Mosque architecture in Turkey has always been controversial due to the country's republican history marked by radical secularism, which has significantly influenced the cultural dynamics of both gender and modernism. One outcome of Turkish secularism was the limiting of religion to the private sphere, denying the mosque a place in the public realm. In contrast to other Muslim societies where mosques have been used as public spaces of gathering and socialization, Turkish mosques have been treated as strictly religious spaces. As I will show, a significant—if unintentional—outcome of this policy was the discouraging of women from attending the mosque and the designation of home as the feminine space of worship and socialization.

While the Turkish state succeeded in creating a modern society that has adopted a secular lifestyle, this top-down modernization process has also triggered conservative discontent. The ensuing tension politicized mosque design in the second half of the twentieth century and led to the identification of modernism with state-led secularization. The mimicry of classical Ottoman mosque architecture, in response, emerged as an expression of conservatism. The last decades of the century witnessed the rise of Islamism as a political force in Turkey, similar to other parts of the Islamic world. As a result, all of the cultural signs, symbols, and performances of Islam and Islamism gained visibility in the public sphere. This was simultaneously a process of liberalization and one of scrutiny: in particular, the gendered aspects of piety were subject to criticism raised by female Islamic intellectuals. Mosque architecture has not been free from this process of increased scrutiny. Especially after the rise to power of an Islamist party, the Justice and Development Party (AKP), in 2002, the field of mosque design witnessed an unforeseen level of plurality along with criticisms of the mosque space's patriarchic character.

In this chapter, I will discuss modernism and gender in relation to mosque architecture through the example of two recent mosques built in Ankara and Istanbul. These examples embody significance

270

in terms of the long-lasting tension between modernity and tradition in mosque architecture. Interestingly, both of these mosques were originally designed by male architects but were "appropriated" by female interior designers throughout their construction processes. I will argue that the political tension that has defined modernism in mosque architecture, together with the rising (feminist) criticisms of the intrinsic patriarchy of the social use of mosque space, have opened room for women's intervention not only as users but also as designers of mosque space.

The Mosque in Republican Turkey

In Turkey, the radical secularism of the single-party regime that lasted until the end of World War II resulted in the strict control of the religious domain by the state. One of the first measures taken by the young nation-state was the establishment of the Directorate of Religious Affairs (hereinafter Diyanet) in 1924 to control all religious activity in the country, including the administration of the existing 12,500 mosques.[1] Within this context, mosque building was merely a response to communal needs. The mosques built in this period were relatively small in size, and no major examples were executed. They were built by builders who followed local traditions in the provinces and followed the example of the existing Ottoman mosques in the larger cities. Mosque architecture was not part of the cultural manifestations of nation building throughout the early republican years, which made Turkey an exceptional case among the nation-states established in countries with Islamic populations. This in turn resulted in the lack of a debate on the iconography of the mosque until the 1950s. Ottoman mosque architecture was continued due to the persistence of building traditions.

While the radical modernism of a single-party regime enforced in the early republican years was hostile to the mosque as a national symbol, the Democrat Party that came to power in the wake of World War II sought reconciliation with the country's Islamic identity. Although the Democrat Party also supported secular modernization, it did not hesitate to use the mosque as a symbol of national identity. Thus, the party initiated the construction of a mosque in Ankara, the new capital and the modern showcase of the republic. The winning project of a national competition in 1957, the Kocatepe Mosque project by Vedat Dalokay and Nejat Tekelioğlu, displayed a modernist design. The scheme followed the traditional mosque layout in its central dome, minarets, and physical organization. Yet, its innovative thin concrete shell structure defined the main prayer hall as a unified space flooded with light from all sides. The corners where the shell touched the ground were marked with four slender minarets, which, with their abstracted forms resembling rockets, were perceived as quite alien (Figure 15.1).[2]

While the government proudly embraced the modernist mosque design, conservative circles raised subdued criticisms. Interestingly, in the wake of a military coup toppling the Democrats in 1960, the modernist design of Kocatepe Mosque (which was still under construction) was identified with the military intervention and understood as yet another symbol of radical modernism. Under increasing conservative pressure, the project was abandoned and its foundations destroyed in 1966. A new project, a colossal Ottoman replica mostly imitating the sixteenth-century Şehzade Mosque, was approved in 1967 after a speedy competition and its construction was begun. Not only the style but also the size of the mosque was dramatically changed to house ten times as many people.[3]

The termination of the modernist project for Kocatepe Mosque was a breakpoint. After that, mosque design in Turkey reverted to the conscious mimicry of classical Ottoman examples, which for the conservatives was both a victory of tradition over modernism and a nostalgic representation of imperial power. Aside from a few exceptions, the neo-Ottoman mosque form became a paradigm for the following decades. This would only change with the rise of the AKP to power in 2002 and the emergence of a pious bourgeoisie as patrons of new mosques. The establishment of an Islamist government for the first time would also trigger new debates in gender politics, as a parallel to Islam's visibility in the public sphere.

Figure 15.1 Unbuilt Project for Kocatepe Mosque, Designed by Vedat Dalokay and Nejat Tekelioğlu
Source: Vedat Dalokay Archive.

Turkish Islamism and Gender Politics

Islam as a political force began its global rise in the 1960s. The decline of secular nationalist governments in the post-colonial Islamic world, the disappointment of the Arab-Israeli War in 1967, and the suppression of left-wing movements against the backdrop of the Cold War led to the rise of Islamism as a political force.[4] This trend gained pace with the end of the Cold War, as Islam began to assume a global identity as a populist response to neoliberalism across the Third World. With the dismantling of welfare mechanisms, Islamic networks of solidarity, successfully deployed by the Ikhwanul Muslimin ("Muslim Brotherhood") in the Middle East, became more influential than ever. Especially where authoritarian regimes were marked by corruption and the failure to maintain popular consent, political Islam rose as the major oppositional power.

A similar process took place in Turkey. Parallel to various cases in the Middle East, Islamism had a largely middle-class character, yet also spoke to the poor with its emphases on morality and religion.[5] Islamism was spearheaded by provincial entrepreneurs who had felt marginalized by the dominant establishment since the 1970s. Beginning in the late 1980s, Islamists succeeded in developing grassroots ties in larger cities as well as in the provinces, and expanded their electoral base under conditions of deprivation caused by neoliberal restructuring.[6] Their first success was winning the municipalities of various cities including Istanbul and Ankara in 1994. After that, they consolidated and expanded these grassroots networks, which led to the rise of the AKP to power in 2002.[7] Female activists played an important role in this process.[8] House visits were an important activity and they were vital to the early grassroots organization of the Turkish Islamists as well as the making of female activist identities.[9] It is crucial to note the spatial character of this activist political activity: the home emerged as an important space for not only Islamist mobilization but also for the making of an Islamic habitus. Coded as a feminine space, home became a key locus. On the one hand it was the space of activist work, allowing direct contact with the household. On the other hand, as an essential metaphor in the Islamic imagination, it derived its sacred significance from its feminine character.[10]

While face-to-face networking contributed to Islamist mobilization, it empowered the women seeking self-help and individual achievement. Saba Mahmood, in her study on Cairo, discusses the empowerment of women through Islamist organizations.[11] She argues that what is at stake is not emancipation in a progressive sense, but empowerment through the organizational performances of the Islamist networks. Obedience to the patriarchy embedded within religious teaching also creates possibilities of active female agency, which the activist women make use of. Otherwise put, despite the dominance of patriarchy, it would be an error to dismiss the role of female agency within Islamist mobilization. As I will show, the expansion of their activity allowed women to appropriate physical and institutional spaces promoted by Islamist politics.

The rise of the AKP to power marked a new episode in relation to women's position within the Islamist movement. Although a detailed discussion is beyond the scope of this chapter, what is significant for my discussion is the transformation of the mosque as social space through the gradual increase of women's involvement. This involvement did not only concern an increase in the number of women attending the mosque. More importantly, they demanded to have a say in the spatial organization of women's sections in the mosques, because men had always controlled the segregated spatial organization of the mosques. While women were not excluded from the mosque, women's sections had generally been organized poorly, in basements or behind curtains. In particular, the neglect to women's ablution spaces had discouraged them from attending the mosque.

The body politics of women's presence in mosque space is too complex to elucidate in detail here. For instance, the anxiety about bodily cleanliness, a characteristic of Islamic teaching, becomes a challenge when it comes to the imprecise nature of menstruation.[12] Hence, women voluntarily prefer to stay out of the mosque in the face of such anxiety.[13] Moreover, the patriarchal character of mosque space undermines individuality and reduces the women to merely their sex, which allows for the disdainful treatment of women by men.[14]

Beginning in the 1990s, feminist critiques from within the Islamic world began to emerge. A significant aspect of these critiques concerned the spatial forms of gender segregation inside the mosque. In different places within the Islamic world, Muslim women raised the demand for men and women to perform the prayer together and asked for the possibility of woman-led prayers in Islam.[15] Although there were parallel endeavors in Turkey in the 1990s,[16] female-led prayer, unlike in other parts of the Islamic world, has never even been discussed. Nevertheless, women's demand for equal space inside the mosque gradually gained ground, due on the one hand to the increased social mobility of pious women, and on the other hand to the perception for the first time of women's exclusion from the mosque space as discrimination.[17] Therefore, beginning in the 1990s, Muslim women challenged the de facto assignment of home as the space of worship for women.

Women's demands to participate in the mosque as public space received positive response from the AKP government seeking to promote religious performance within public spaces. In response to criticisms from female Islamic intellectuals on the inadequacy of proper spaces for women and the miserable conditions of the existing women's sections, the Mufti Office (a branch of Diyanet) in Istanbul launched a project to assess the state of Istanbul's mosques with regard to their women-friendliness. The study revealed that half of the approximately 3,000 mosques in Istanbul were not suitable for women to perform their prayers.[18] While presenting the findings of the study to the two stakeholders (the Diyanet officials and the architectural community) at a symposium on mosque architecture, the female Diyanet officer Kadriye Erdemli did not confine herself to the statistical data. She allocated more than half of her presentation to theologically argue for women's right to an equal place within the main prayer hall, with visual access to the *mihrab* and the *minbar*.[19] This presentation was a critical illustration of how mosque space was becoming a topic of gender politics.

Representing the Pious Bourgeoisie

Throughout the 1990s, a pious bourgeoisie had already emerged and declared its support for the Islamist parties. This new faction of businessmen played an important role in the AKP's rise to power in 2002. The freedom enjoyed by religious groups during the rule of the AKP also contributed to the emergence of the mosque as a signifier of distinction. For the first time, mosque architecture outside architectural mimicry began to receive popular approval. Although there were minor examples before, the 2000s witnessed the emergence of devout patrons and the rise of heterogeneity in the architectural vocabulary of mosque design.

The stylistic choices of new mosques ranged from historicist interpretations of traditional mosques to innovative experiments. An example of the former category is Başyazıcıoğlu Mosque in Ankara, built in 2007. This mosque was a small-scale imitation of Al-Masjid an-Nabawi in Medina, one of the holiest sites of Islamic faith. A significant example of the latter category is Emre Arolat's Sancaklar Mosque, built in 2013 to great architectural acclaim. In order to create a worship space free of cultural and temporal links, Arolat proposed "dissolving" the mosque into the landscape. In his scheme, the prayer hall is a cave-like space located underground and signaled with a vertical prism representing the minaret.[20] Here, it is interesting to note that such heterogeneity also legitimized the hitherto marginal lineage of modernist mosque design, and a new generation of prominent Turkish architects identified the opportunity to put forward innovative proposals.

Perhaps the most controversial example of such new mosques was Şakirin Mosque, which was built by the philanthropist Şakir family in memory of İbrahim and Semiha Şakir. The mosque is situated inside Karacaahmet Cemetery, the largest cemetery in Turkey, and was built from 2005 to 2009. The family employed Hüsrev Tayla, the designer of the neo-Ottoman Kocatepe Mosque, although Tayla had been experimenting with domical shell structures in his later career. Tayla proposed the same scheme for the new mosque, which strikingly resembled Dalokay's abandoned project for Kocatepe (Figure 15.2).

The small mosque has a floor area of 500 m² (5,400 sq. ft.) and sits on a 3,000 m² (32,300 sq. ft.) platform. The main prayer hall is covered by a freestanding dome that touches the ground on only four corners, allowing for an unprecedented level of transparency. The domical volume is supplemented with a 650 m² (7,000 sq. ft.) courtyard, following Ottoman tradition, and two detached 35 m (115 ft.)

Appropriating the Masculine Sacred

Figure 15.2 Şakirin Mosque in Istanbul
Source: © Bülent Batuman.

minarets. Tayla proposed to control transparency in two levels by dividing the facades horizontally. He designed the lower levels following traditional examples, with thick walls containing window niches, and he covered the upper levels with geometrical patterns of stained glass. His proposal for the interior also adhered to traditional design methods.

Meanwhile, the family demanded that Zeynep Fadıllıoğlu, the granddaughter of Semiha Şakir, be in charge of the interior design. The architect insisted that he should be solely responsible for the comprehensive design of the structure and its interior. The dispute could not be resolved, and the architect left the project, waiving his rights to the design. At this point, Fadıllıoğlu took control of the project and made revisions to the architectural blueprints.

According to Fadıllıoğlu, the structural simplicity of the dome was tasteful and required matching features that would "bring the project closer to the modern architecture of the present-day."[21] Accordingly, the concrete dome was covered with fish-scale aluminum panels. To continue the contemporary image of the mosque, the facade organization was also drastically changed. A double-layer facade formation was proposed to reduce transparency and control daylight. The outer layer was an oblique curtain of aluminum mesh, which fit into the curved openings of the shell structure. By contrast, the inner layer enveloping the interior space comprised frameless glass curtain walls. The glass panes at the worshippers' eye level imitated the pages of the holy Quran, in which the spaces between the lines of the page were gilded to create a similar effect (Figure 15.3). The traditional ablution fountain at the center of the courtyard was interpreted in the form of a water sculpture, where water flowed through the reflective surface of a stainless steel sphere.

Figure 15.3 Şakirin Mosque, interior. Note the gilded glass panes imitating pages of the Quran and the unusual designs of the *mihrab*, the *minbar* and the chandelier.
Source: © Bülent Batuman.

Typical elements of a traditional mosque interior were also interpreted in unusual forms. The *mihrab*, the niche marking the direction of Qibla, was designed as a freestanding element in the form of a turquoise-colored crescent. The *minbar*, the pulpit where the imam delivers the sermon, was also designed as a sculptural object inspired by the pendentives of the dome's inner surface. Finally, the chandelier was designed to bring a modern interpretation to traditional precedents that held candles on large circular iron frames. Here, three circular frames were fixed at different angles to create a three-dimensional composition. They carried Quranic verses as well as glass drops hanging from the frames that diffracted light from the spotlights of the chandelier.

The unified space of the domical shell allowed for an interesting opportunity for the women's section. In this rare situation, the women's section, organized as a balcony on the entrance facade, was under the central dome, thus sharing the atmosphere of the prayer hall (Figure 15.4). While there are numerous examples where women's sections have been created with balconies, here the section was also treated with an unusual level of transparency through making the parapets of the same metal mesh as was used on the facades. In a way, the partition visually separating the genders was as transparent as the aluminum curtain separating the interior of the mosque from the exterior. Moreover, Fadıllıoğlu underlined her particular interest in the women's section:

> I positioned them on the upper balcony, because during prayer the women must be behind the men. But I also decided to make the balcony level one of the most beautiful areas, with the chandelier crystal droplets just in front, and where you can see the *mihrab* from the best angle.[22]

After its inauguration, the mosque immediately attracted attention. Fadıllıoğlu's office undertook an extensive public relations campaign to publicize the mosque as "combining the modern and the traditional."[23] She appeared on television programs and gave interviews to international media, promoting the mosque as the first one designed by a woman.[24] While this self-proclaimed title did not reflect reality, it greatly contributed to the promotion of the mosque.[25] In this way, the design of the mosque was attributed to Fadıllıoğlu, to the dismay of the architect. For instance, CNN's coverage was

Figure 15.4 Şakirin Mosque, the Women's Section
Source: © Bülent Batuman.

later amended—possibly after a notification from the original architect—to acknowledge Tayla as the designer of the mosque itself.[26] Moreover, Fadıllıoğlu's identity as a non-practicing Muslim who did not even wear a headscarf (the most visible sign of piety for Muslim women) was already a reflection of the fusion of tradition and modernity. Fadıllıoğlu did not even hesitate to pose inside the prayer hall without a headscarf, which would not normally be tolerated inside a mosque. Breaking traditions, the designer called attention to her project in the national and international media by successfully utilizing her association with the client as well as her international connections.

Not all comments about the mosque's design were positive. The architectural community in Turkey, composed largely of professionals with modernist training who favor modern designs over imitations of traditional mosques, responded harshly. Although the effort to break away from neo-Ottoman imitations was affirmed, critics frequently pointed out that Tayla's freestanding dome was a repetition of Dalokay's project for Kocatepe.[27] The harshest criticisms were reserved for the interior design. Prominent architectural historian Doğan Kuban criticized the transparency of the prayer hall, claiming that it had been reduced to a "garden pavilion."[28] The chandelier, the fountain of the courtyard, and the *mihrab* and *minbar* were all criticized as overdesigned and lavish. According to Behruz Çinici, the designer of the Aga Khan Award–winning mosque inside the Turkish Parliamentary complex, the interior design comprised "fetishistic elements" and "it would be sin to call this building a mosque."[29] Tayla himself was also very vocal in expressing his discontent at being excluded from the design process and at the designer's disregard for his possible suggestions for the interior space. According to him, the interior design "damaged his architecture."[30]

Criticism of the mosque concentrated on a few themes. Architecturally, the dome and its shell structure presented a simple and powerful form, yet they also created problems of enclosure and functional organization such as transparency and the organization of ablution facilities at the lower level. Tayla's proposals for the facades were seen as inconsistently traditional in relation to the structural system he proposed. On the level of interior design, the criticisms were extraordinarily harsh, especially considering the few examples of mosques that diverged from the traditional Ottoman mosque form.

The disapproval of the interior design as lavish and kitsch arguably conceals multiple tensions regarding professional ideology, including intertwined issues of modernism vs. tradition, professional competence, class, and gender.[31] The identities of the client and the interior designer troubled the conventions of the architectural profession. The pious bourgeoisie sought an original architectural expression that dared to unsettle not only the conventions of tradition but also those of modernist paradigms. Yet, as middle-class professionals with a modernist and secularist ethos, Turkish architects were equally far removed from pompousness and the ahistorical reproduction of tradition. They equated the former with the nouveau riche, and the latter with religiosity and conservatism. In their eyes, the pious bourgeoisie represented the combination of these two traits. Moreover, the multidimensional identity of the designer, a bourgeois woman who was not formally educated as an architect, was also troublesome. She was simultaneously utilizing power networks of the pious bourgeoisie, the international media, and state institutions. Yet, she was also bold enough to shatter professional conventions in which the architect is detached from "his" creation. On the contrary, she appeared within the space she had designed as a woman, while her bodily performance without a headscarf defied the masculine codes of the profession as well as of religion.

At this point, it would be interesting to note how Islamist women perceive the Şakirin Mosque. In a comment on the mosque, Islamic intellectual Yıldız Ramazanoğlu reflected an awareness of the criticisms cited above, yet strove to propose alternative interpretations.[32] For instance, although she agreed with the perception that ornamentation and glitter are excessive, she argued that this could be attributed to the importance given to the congregation using the space. Similarly, she argued that the unusual level of transparency creates a sense of praying within nature. Perhaps the most striking divergence of interpretations concerned the women's section. While prominent architect Cengiz

Appropriating the Masculine Sacred

Bektaş dismissed the mezzanine floor allocated to women as an obstacle preventing the perception of the overall space at the entrance, Ramazanoğlu interpreted this space as an architectural expression of democracy, presenting women's equal space under the main dome as having visual access to the *mihrab* and the imam leading the prayer.[33]

A State Mosque for an Islamist Government

While construction on the privately commissioned Şakirin Mosque was underway, the government also commissioned a mosque, this one designed to reflect the government's Islamist ideology. While the new Diyanet campus outside the city center of Ankara provided the initial impetus for construction of the new mosque, the AKP was further motivated through its struggle with the armed forces, which in 2007 used a memorandum to block the election of an Islamist president. Although the AKP responded to the military memorandum with early elections that would net them a landslide victory, they saw the iconography of the mosque as an opportunity to articulate their worldview. The mosque's architecture and even its name continued to reflect the conflict between the Islamist government and the secularist establishment. Cynically named "VIP mosque" in the secular media, the government later chose to name it after Ahmet Hamdi Akseki, the first director of Diyanet.

Although the pious bourgeoisie's experiments with mosque architecture constituted a small portion of mosques built, their importance was magnified by the architectural debates they triggered outside the architectural community. Interestingly, even Diyanet searched for alternatives to the innumerable poor imitations of classical mosques. Through a number of symposia, Diyanet sought collaboration with the architectural community in order to develop a new architectural idiom for contemporary mosques. Meanwhile, the AKP government endorsed the neo-Ottoman typology as representing contemporary Turkish Islamism, with references to the sixteenth-century imperial image of Turkish Islam.[34] It would require a consolidation of power for the Islamists to build monumental neo-Ottoman mosques, a feat that they had not yet achieved in 2007. During the time that the Ahmet Hamdi Akseki Mosque was being planned, the delicate balance of power between the Islamist government and the secularist state bureaucracy thus forced the former to seek negotiations regarding the architecture of the first state mosque they would build.

These negotiations help explain why the Ahmet Hamdi Akseki Mosque, which is among the largest in Turkey with its dome of 33 m (108 ft.) diameter, is characterized by a modernist appearance (Figure 15.5). Similar to the unbuilt proposal for Kocatepe and the Şakirin Mosque, it presented an austere interpretation of the traditional Ottoman mosque characterized by a central dome. In the Ahmet Hamdi Akseki Mosque, the dome's structure rests on four arches standing on four pillars. The massing of the volumes creates an image where the dome is sitting on top of another, rather flat, domical surface that defines galleries on all four sides of the dome. The plan's symmetrical organization is further emphasized by the four corner minarets as well as the elimination of the traditional Ottoman courtyard.

Although the Diyanet officials accepted a modernist aesthetic, they demanded that the mosque embody Ottoman and/or Seljuk elements that would link it to traditional Turkish Islamic architecture. A significant element that would become the subject of ideological negotiations was the facade design (Figure 15.6). Earlier versions of the design reveal that Salim Alp, the architect, faced a problem similar to that faced by Tayla, the architect of the Şakirin Mosque, namely the facade's transparency resulting in excessive daylight within the mosque. To address this problem, Alp proposed horizontal sunshades behind glass surfaces. In his scheme, the main entrance to the north was defined by a prismatic projection conforming to the lines of the sunshades. In a second version, he put forth a different solution, proposing vertical blank strips on the eastern and western facades to limit daylight (as well

279

Bülent Batuman

Figure 15.5 Ahmet Hamdi Akseki Mosque in Ankara
Source: © Bülent Batuman.

as transparency), and reworking the main entrance to include a large curvilinear canopy that matched the arched eaves of the roof. The final version departed significantly from the earlier proposals and included a massive block on the north facade, with a tall gate that imitated historical Seljuk portals. Seljuk patterns decorated both the surface of this block and larger vertical strips added to the east and west facades. With these additions, which were made during construction over the objections of the architect, the modernist aesthetic of the mosque was hybridized.[35] During its inauguration in 2013, it was presented as a "neoclassical mosque."[36]

Although construction was completed by the end of 2010, the building's interior design and finishing took another three years. The delay was significant given that another monumental mosque—the neo-Ottoman Ataşehir Mimar Sinan Mosque in Istanbul—was built in less than two years, between

Figure 15.6 Ahmet Hamdi Akseki Mosque, Early Proposal for the Entrance Portal (above) and Built Version of the Entrance Portal (below)
Source: © Salim Alp Architecture.

2010 and 2012. The delay on the Ahmet Hamdi Akseki Mosque had nothing to do with external obstacles. It should rather be understood in relation to the ideological conflict between modernism and tradition represented in the mosque's architecture. Ahmet Hamdi Akseki Mosque was the first attempt in the search for a new form for Islamism, a search that was not free of tensions and contradictions. The traditional Ottoman form was an ideological reference that the AKP did not wish to abandon. However, the secular establishment also associated the mosque with Islamism, and in 2007 was still powerful enough to force the AKP to negotiate. Meanwhile, Diyanet officials were less rigid about the ideological connotations of architecture and welcomed contemporary experiments. However, they had their own conservatism regarding the conventions of prayer, which I will discuss. Finally, the overall image of the mosque hinted at divergence from traditional forms, which would be expected to continue in the detailing of the project in the hands of the architect. Hence, the interior design was delayed, during which time the architect was eliminated from the project and the AKP consolidated its power through successive elections in 2007 and 2009.

While the mosque's fate was being debated, Diyanet organized a limited competition for the interior design, inviting some 20 firms.[37] This list was twice shortened, first to five firms and then to three. After a lengthy waiting period, a female architect, Sonay İlbay, was awarded the project. Although the choice could not be reduced to her gender, it is plausible to say that the Diyanet officials were pleased to be working with a female designer, despite her lack of expertise in mosque design.[38] A female designer was in tune with their ongoing attempts to promote women's participation in the mosques. The job was supervised by a construction company that appointed art historians and acoustics experts as well as artisans as consultants for the traditional techniques of murals, calligraphy, inlay, stained glass, and woodwork. Thus, the designer's lack of expertise was compensated by the efforts of the company overseeing the further construction process. This was also a means to guarantee both the quality and the dominance of traditional decorations.

The use of traditional methods in the decorative arts was also politically complicated. On the one hand, these elements were seen as the sole reference to tradition, given the modernity of the mosque's overall form. On the other hand, work on the Ahmet Hamdi Akseki Mosque was also informed by the controversies surrounding Şakirin Mosque. Fadıllıoğlu's bold, postmodern interpretation of traditional decorative elements inspired designers but alarmed Diyanet. İlbay's various details, such as a chandelier reminiscent of the one in Şakirin Mosque, were thus rejected. This did not mean that all details of the interior followed tradition and were dictated to the designer (Figure 15.7). İlbay designed the Qibla wall to be orthogonally geometric, incorporating Seljuk patterns and religious calligraphy. Moreover, the interior of the dome contained a novel design. Traditionally, the inner surfaces of the central domes contain either concentric decorative patterns or radial lines creating a static representation of the heavens. In the Ahmet Hamdi Akseki Mosque, radial lines were interpreted in the form of eight curvilinear strips creating a rotation effect. The designer was also successful in persuading critical officials to accept transparent parapets at the edge of the women's section, a design problem that was solved through placing balconies within the side galleries rather than beneath the central dome.

Upon its inauguration in 2013, the mosque was widely praised as a synthesis of tradition and contemporary technology. Curiously, publications of the building almost always focused on the decorations and interior design, to the extent that the name of the architect was almost never mentioned in the press coverage. Even the lengthy description of the building on the website of the construction company mentioned the names of nine designers (and artisans) and eight consultants, but not the architect.[39] When President Abdullah Gül visited the mosque, it was the staff of the construction company and not the architect who accompanied and briefed him on the architecture of the mosque.[40] The interior designer, on the other hand, was named and praised for her work. In the mainstream media, it was İlbay who was interviewed about the mosque, with emphasis on her gender.[41] In 2007, the AKP and established secularists had come to a tacit agreement that the Ahmet Hamdi Akseki

Appropriating the Masculine Sacred

Figure 15.7 Ahmet Hamdi Akseki Mosque, Interior
Source: © Bülent Batuman.

Mosque would be built as a modernist structure. By 2010, this had changed, and traditional decorative arts had come to dominate the interior. When the mosque was inaugurated in 2013, it was the traditional elements that were highlighted in media coverage, turning the mosque's interior into a subtle political statement against the mosque's initial modernism.

Gender Politics of the Mosque

The rise of the AKP to power triggered various changes in both politics and social life in Turkey. The mosque as a social space as well as its architecture have been influenced by these changes. The government reorganized Diyanet in order to simultaneously extend its religious services outside the mosques and bring new social functions into them. This was crucial because the mosque in Turkey has traditionally been used exclusively for prayer, in contrast to other countries in the Middle East where the mosque is frequently used for socialization.[42] Expanding religious life into social life while allowing social life into the mosque space has taken on many forms. For instance, the directorate issued a circular in 2009 to encourage expanding the functions planned for new mosques to include tea rooms, playgrounds, sports facilities, health clinics, libraries or reading rooms, exhibition and conference rooms, bookstores, and soup kitchens, among others.[43] It even encouraged imams to improvise in creating social spaces within the mosque, which resulted in extreme examples such as offering karate lessons inside the prayer hall.[44]

Women's increasing attendance rates had already begun to change not only the quality of the mosque as a social space but also its architecture. The demand for gender equality in terms of spatial use went hand in hand with the empowerment of women in relation to the definition of these spaces. Initially defined as a problem of "beautification of the women's section in mosques," pious women and especially Islamist intellectuals demanding spatial equality resulted in the introduction of specific architectural elements such as functionally organized ablution spaces and a better location of women's sections in relation to the *mihrab* and the central dome.

Both the pious bourgeoisie and the Islamist government were seeking new forms for mosque architecture in a quest for new Islamic architectural expressions. Their efforts met with obstacles as the secularist state bureaucracy remained hostile to all symbols of Islamism from the start. Architectural professionals, too, objected to the new direction. The professional community was not against mosques in general, but was quite unsympathetic to Ottoman imitations. Experiments in modernist mosque design were generally praised; however, such praise was limited to austere interpretations of modernism. This narrow view of the modernist aesthetic helps explain the architectural community's harsh criticisms toward the Şakirin Mosque. Diyanet, which appeared as an intermediary, had a flexible approach that tolerated divergence from neo-Ottomanism, but remained rigid with regard to the spatial organization as it related to the performance of prayer.

Within this complicated power network defining mosque architecture, gender emerged as a suitable instrument to overcome opposing positions through acts of political correctness. In cases of disputes between architects and their clients, female designers were invited to override professional conventions. For the government, such instrumentalization was further useful to suppress ideological opposition in mosque architecture. For instance, when the government came up with a plan to build a colossal mosque on a hilltop in Istanbul, the architectural community opposed the project. After a controversial competition that was boycotted by the Chamber of Architects, the government awarded the project to two young and inexperienced female architects who had proposed an Ottoman imitation, emphasizing both their gender and their piousness to rationalize their selection. Having assured the conservative architectural direction of the mosque in this way, the government soon cast aside the winning architects, continuing the Ottoman design under new direction.[45]

Increasing attention to gender, even for the sake of power struggles among men and their institutions, represented the agency and empowerment of women. The instrumentalization of women's agency for Islamist politics also opened up possibilities for appropriation and empowerment. Whether Islamist or secular, women appropriated spaces opened under these new circumstances and increased their visibility in mosque architecture as users, critics, and designers. While the facilities used by women within the mosques had been ignored before, their spaces became distinctive ones of the new mosques. Even neo-Ottoman imitations were legitimized through referring to the attention paid to women's sections. For instance, Ramazanoğlu Mosque (2006–2014), built in Adana, was advertised as "women-friendly," claiming to respond to the needs of women in its design.[46] Transforming mosque spaces to attract women, moreover, extended beyond the mere improvement of women's sections. Millet Mosque (opened in 2015), located within the new Presidential Compound in Ankara, included a plastic playground inside the prayer hall by the staircase to the women's section. The striking contrast between the bright colors of the playground and the dark interior and overall gravitas of the state mosque is a fine example of the transformation of the physical space of the mosque under interacting forces of religion, politics, and everyday life.

It is not simply the transformation of spaces used by women that is at stake. While the design of mosques by women has been extremely rare in Turkey, over the course of a few years women's agency with regard to mosque architecture went through a remarkable transformation. After the Şakirin Mosque was built, women produced further new mosque projects, including the aforementioned Ramazanoğlu Mosque, which was designed by four female architects. If the ongoing political struggles among patriarchal agents was one factor that led to women's greater involvement in mosque architecture, another was the implicit collaboration between women, such as Islamist intellectuals and secular professionals, with different viewpoints.

Notes

1. Karaman 2008, 286.
2. For discussions on Kocatepe Mosque, see Meeker 1997; As 2006; Batuman 2016.
3. I have developed a detailed discussion on the significance of the Kocatepe Mosque elsewhere. See Batuman 2016.
4. Mandaville 2007, 49–95.
5. Bayat 2013, 172–3; Mandaville 2007, 98–101.
6. White 2002; Tuğal 2006.
7. For a detailed discussion on the Islamists' success in urban politics, see Batuman 2013 and Batuman 2018.
8. Göle 1996; Saktanber 2002; Arat 2005.
9. White 2002, 199.
10. Saktanber 2002, 39–41; Yılmaz 2015, 220–4.
11. Mahmood 2005.
12. Mernissi 1991, 74.
13. Yılmaz 2015, 220.
14. For a personal narrative of an Islamic intellectual on her experience with men in her attempt to perform prayer in the main prayer hall, see Ramazanoğlu 2011.
15. Elewa and Silvers 2011. A key figure juxtaposing activism and scholarship towards gender equality in Islam was Amina Wadud. For her groundbreaking work, see Wadud 1992 and Wadud 2006. For a recent collection honoring Wadud's work and providing a view to the global state of scholarship, see Ali, Hammer, and Silvers 2012.
16. For an analysis via the case of prominent Islamist-feminist intellectual Konca Kuriş, see Keskin-Kozat 2003.
17. Yılmaz 2015, 207–20.
18. Erdemli 2013, 127.
19. Erdemli 2013, 126.
20. For a scholarly review of the mosque, see Gür 2017.
21. Fadıllıoğlu 2011, 135–6.
22. McKenzie 2014.
23. McKenzie 2014.
24. Anon. 2010.
25. See for instance Cihan Aktaş's research on architect Makbule Yalkılday, who was born in 1914 and worked extensively on restoration of mosques and also designed one: Aktaş 2015.
26. McKenzie 2014.
27. Güzer 2009.
28. Kuban, Tekeli, Çinici, and Bektaş 2009.
29. Kuban, Tekeli, Çinici, and Bektaş 2009, 41.
30. Tayla 2009.

Bülent Batuman

31. Here it is worth mentioning that the general public regarded the mosque more positively than did the professional community. The mosque triggered curiosity and became a topic of discussion in various internet forums even before its inauguration. Once it was opened for worship, many users took photographs, shared them online, and commented positively on its architecture and decoration. For such a forum topic on Şakirin Mosque, see http://wowturkey.com/forum/viewtopic.php?t=52770&start=0, accessed on May 16, 2017.
32. Ramazanoğlu 2015. It is worth noting that the text discusses the overall work of Tayla, although the author does not refrain from commenting positively on the interior design of Şakirin Mosque.
33. Kuban, Tekeli, Çinici, and Bektaş 2009, 43; Ramazanoğlu 2015, 201.
34. The promotion of the neo-Ottoman mosque as a political signifier by the Turkish government also had a transnational character. See Rizvi 2015.
35. Interview with Salim Alp, July 25, 2017.
36. Directorate of Religious Affairs 2013.
37. Interview with Sonay İlbay, March 21, 2017.
38. İlbay had 20 years of experience in the construction unit of a public bank before starting her own office. Her work in Ahmet Hamdi Akseki Mosque led to new commissions on mosque interiors in Turkey and abroad.
39. "Ahmet Hamdi Akseki Camii." http://enderinsaat.com/Icerik.ASP?ID=1316, accessed on February 8, 2016.
40. Anon. 2013a.
41. Anon. 2013b.
42. Bayat 2013, 68–80.
43. Özaloğlu and Gürel 2011, 346.
44. Anon. 2012.
45. For details, see Batuman 2016, 336–9.
46. Anon. 2011.

References

Aktaş, Cihan. 2015. "Makbule Yalkılday." In *Türk Mimarisinde İz Bırakanlar*, Vol. 2, edited by Şahin Torun, 153–161. Ankara: Ministry of Environment and Urbanization.

Ali, Kecia, Juliane Hammer, and Laury Silvers, eds. 2012. *A Jihad for Justice: Honoring the Work and Life of Amina Wadud*. Akron: 48 Hour Books.

Anon. 2010. "Profile: Zeynep Fadillioglu." *BBC*, October 8. http://news.bbc.co.uk/2/hi/programmes/real_cities/9060045.stm, accessed on March 21.

Anon. 2011. "Kadınlara Özel Cami." *AljazeeraTurk*, August 9. www.aljazeera.com.tr/haber/kadinlara-ozel-cami, accessed on August 14.

Anon. 2012. "Camide Karate Kursu." *Milliyet*, July 15. www.milliyet.com.tr/camide-karate-kursu/gundem/gundemdetay/15.07.2012/1567107/default.htm, accessed on August 17.

Anon. 2013a. "Cumhurbaşkanı Gül soruları cevapsız bıraktı." *Haberturk*, April 26. www.haberturk.com/gundem/haber/839315-cumhurbaskani-gul-sorulari-cevapsiz-birakti, accessed on August 2.

Anon. 2013b. "Sonsuzlukta kadın imzası." *Akşam*, April 24. www.aksam.com.tr/guncel/sonsuzlukta-kadin-imzasi/haber-198976, accessed on August 2.

Arat, Yeşim. 2005. *Rethinking Islam and Liberal Democracy: Islamist Women in Turkish Politics*. Albany: State University of New York Press.

As, İmdat. 2006. "The Digital Mosque: A New Paradigm in Mosque Design." *Journal of Architectural Education* 60: 54–66.

Batuman, Bülent. 2013. "City Profile: Ankara." *Cities* 31: 578–590.

Batuman, Bülent. 2016. "Architectural Mimicry and the Politics of Mosque Building: Negotiating Islam and Nation in Turkey." *Journal of Architecture* 21: 321–347.

Batuman, Bülent. 2018. *New Islamist Architecture and Urbanism: Negotiating Nation and Islam Through Built Environment in Turkey*. Abingdon and New York: Routledge.

Bayat, Asef. 2013. *Life as Politics: How Ordinary People Change the Middle East*, 2nd ed. Stanford, CA: Stanford University Press.

Directorate of Religious Affairs. 2013. *Diyanet İşleri Başkanlığı Ahmet Hamdi Akseki Camii*. Ankara: Directorate of Religious Affairs.

Elewa, Ahmed, and Laury Silvers. 2011. "'I Am One of the People': A Survey and Analysis of Legal Arguments on Woman-Led Prayer in Islam." *Journal of Law and Religion* 26: 141–171.

Erdemli, Kadriye A. 2013. "Cami Mimarisinde Kadınların Yeri ve İstanbul Müftülüğü Camilerin Kadınlar Bölümünü Güzelleştirme Projesi (3T Projesi)." In *1. Ulusal Cami Mimarisi Sempozyumu Bildiri Kitabı*, 113–128. Ankara: DİB Yayınları.

Fadıllıoğlu, Zeynep. 2011. "Şakirin Camii Tasarım ve Uygulama Süreci." In *İstanbul'da Karacaahmet Tarihi Mirası İçinde Şakirin Camii*, edited by Önder Küçükerman, 131–158. Istanbul: Semiha Şakir Vakfi.

Göle, Nilüfer. 1996. *The Forbidden Modern: Civilization and Veiling.* Ann Arbor: University of Michigan Press.

Gür, Berin F. 2017. "Sancaklar Mosque: Displacing the Familiar." *International Journal of Islamic Architecture* 6: 165–193.

Güzer, Abdi. 2009. "Modernizmin Gelenekle Uzlaşma Çabası Olarak Cami Mimarlığı." *Mimarlık* 348: 21–23.

Karaman, Fikret. 2008. "The Status and Function of the PRA in the Turkish Republic." *Muslim World* 98: 282–290.

Keskin-Kozat, Burçak. 2003. "Entangled in Secular Nationalism, Feminism and Islamism: The Life of Konca Kuriş." *Cultural Dynamics* 15: 183–211.

Kuban, Doğan, Doğan Tekeli, Behruz Çinici, and Cengiz Bektaş. 2009. "Şakirin Camisi ve Çağdaş Cami Tasarımı." *Yapı* 333: 38–43.

Mahmood, Saba. 2005. *Politics of Piety: The Islamist Revival and Feminist Subject.* Princeton, NJ: Princeton University Press.

Mandaville, Peter G. 2007. *Global Political Islam.* London and New York: Routledge.

McKenzie, Sheena. 2014. "Meet the Mosque Designer Breaking the Mold." *CNN*, November 17. http://edition.cnn.com/2014/09/23/world/meast/divine-design-the-mosque-architect/, accessed on March 21.

Meeker, Michael E. 1997. "Once There Was, Once There Wasn't: National Monuments and Interpersonal Exchange." In *Rethinking Modernity and National Identity in Turkey*, edited by Sibel Bozdoğan and Reşat Kasaba, 157–191. Seattle: University of Washington Press.

Mernissi, Fatima. 1991. *The Veil and the Male Elite: A Feminist Interpretation of Women's Rights in Islam.* New York: Perseus Books.

Özaloğlu, Serpil, and Meltem Ö. Gürel. 2011. "Designing Mosques for Secular Congregations: Transformations of the Mosque as a Social Space in Turkey." *Journal of Architectural and Planning Research* 28: 336–358.

Ramazanoğlu, Yıldız. 2011. "Camilerde Kadının Yeri Neresi." *Zaman*, May 3.

Ramazanoğlu, Yıldız. 2015. "Hüsrev Tayla." In *Türk Mimarisinde İz Bırakanlar*, Vol. 2, edited by Şahin Torun, 201–208. Ankara: Ministry of Environment and Urbanization.

Rizvi, Kishwar. 2015. *The Transnational Mosque: Architecture and Historical Memory in the Contemporary Middle East.* Chapel Hill: University of North Carolina Press.

Saktanber, Ayşe. 2002. *Living Islam: Women, Religion and the Politicization of Culture in Turkey.* London and New York: I. B. Tauris.

Tayla, Hüsrev. 2009. "Şakirin Camisi'nin Mimarı Hüsrev Tayla ile Söyleş." *Yapı* 333: 44–46.

Tuğal, Cihan. 2006. "The Appeal of Islamic Politics: Ritual and Dialogue in a Poor District of Turkey." *Sociological Quarterly* 47: 245–273.

Wadud, Amina. 1992. *Qur'an and Woman.* Kuala Lumpur: Fajar Bakti.

Wadud, Amina. 2006. *Inside the Gender Jihad: Reform in Islam.* Oxford: One World Publishers.

White, Jenny. 2002. *Islamist Mobilization in Turkey: A Study in Vernacular Politics.* Seattle: University of Washington Press.

Yılmaz, Zehra. 2015. *Dişil Dindarlık: İslamcı Kadın Hareketinin Dönüşümü.* Istanbul: İletişim.

16

The Emergent Gender of Rural Modernities in Turkey

Eda Acara

In contemporary Turkey, one in every five women lives in a rural area, and half of all farmers are women.[1] It is not a coincidence that we have recently witnessed rural women in active, leading, and visible roles in protests against hydroelectric and fossil fuel power plants and mega-projects, specifically against highways.[2] What is the common denominator in these conflicts that provokes women's motivations and actions? In this chapter, drawing on the activist, peasant women's experiences living close to one of the most polluted rivers in contemporary Turkey, the Ergene River, I explore the ways that emergent neoliberal rural modernity is manifested in gender relations, more precisely in women's political subjectivities of the new rural politics. The village that constitutes the main subject of inquiry held the first village protest against river pollution, organized under women's leadership, at a regional scale in 2009, and it has grown into an annual march ever since.[3] Here, I concentrate on how women's political engagement generates new rural landscapes that disturb rural domestic ideology and patriarchal gender relations, while also transforming everyday geographies of the village. I argue that rural women use modern capitalist contradictions to negotiate their history and place in the village's political and economic life. It is within this context that their environmentalism against the pollution of the Ergene River is also a socio-spatial struggle. It can further be argued that gender relations are useful in comprehending the full scope of the metabolic rift that pollution creates in a village's life. This article derives from fieldwork in a small village by the Ergene River during the summer of 2012.[4]

The Ergene River, a tributary of the Maritza (Meriç) River crossing the border between Bulgaria, Greece, and Turkey, is a "dead river" with level-four pollution.[5] It is found in Thrace, at the crossroads of the Middle East and Europe, an area that has witnessed rapid industrialization and its environmental consequences. As Figure 16.1 shows, Turkey is located at the intersection of the Middle East and Europe. The country has undergone enormous industrial and environmental changes in the past decade, leading to severe water pollution. The greatest water pollution in Turkey is found in large metropolitan areas such as Istanbul and in their peripheries. The Marmara region, which encompasses various industrial zones located on the Thracian periphery of Istanbul, has the most polluted water.[6] River pollution plays an extensive role in the contamination of soil and of surface and underground water, endangering animal, human, and plant life. Several studies have found traces of hard metal toxicity in agricultural lands in the vicinity of the Ergene River, which is worsened by pesticide contamination.[7] The accountability of factories and, for that matter, the state and its institutions, is still very limited when it comes to the issue of pollution.[8]

Despite the historical prioritization of urbanization and industrialization over environmental protection,[9] agricultural and dairy production have continued at a regional scale, regardless of the concerns of civil society regarding food quality and health.[10] The authoritarian, neoliberal, and extractive policies

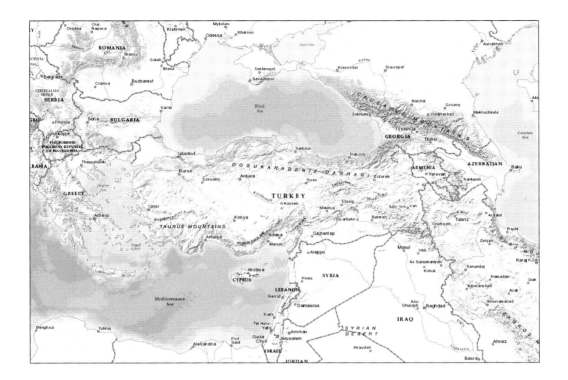

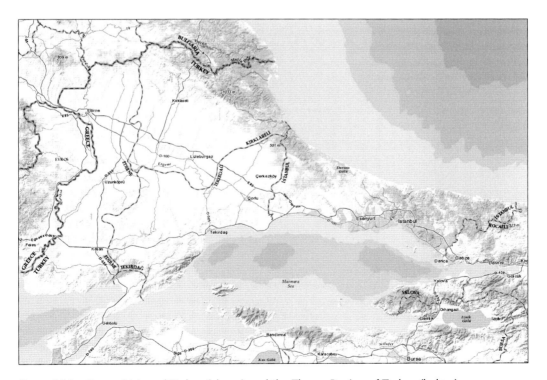

Figure 16.1 General Map of Turkey (above) and the Thrace Region of Turkey (below)

of the ruling Justice and Development Party have continued to raise further risks in environmental cycles at a regional scale: in the areas between the city and the countryside, the frontier subregion of the Thrace region and the megacity Istanbul, and agricultural lands and industrial production sites. These policies consist of the construction of fossil fuel power plants[11] and housing projects in addition to the construction of an artificial canal that came to be known as *Kanal İstanbul*.[12] These policies construct and reshape rural modernities in the peripheral regions of metropolitan areas in contemporary Turkey.

The experience of modernity is multiple and complex. The ways modernity takes "place" depends on multiple histories and spatial processes that shape a certain locale. Moving away from a romantic understanding of place and instead conceiving of a spatiotemporal location where complex and multiple particularities of socio-spatial relations are formed.[13] Place is not inherently or naturally imbued with politics, nor is it a locational site in which progressive politics are automatically an end result; rather, place posits complex structures of spatialities that shape experience. Place is "integral to the very structure and possibility of experience,"[14] in which experience is an active engagement with the world. And, it is through this understanding of place that space possesses constraining and enabling aspects for political engagement.[15] This underlying conceptual and theoretical framework feeds into the analysis I present here, of the rural experience of pollution and the place of gender within it.

I first dwell on the meanings of rural modernity and its conceptual significance in understanding gender, place, and modernism within the Turkish context. Then, in the next two sections, I explore the political geographies of a village close to the polluted Ergene River, where women emerged as political subjects of a regionally renowned protest. In the final section, I develop the concept of rural modernity and gender for future research on geographies of uneven spatial development.

Contradictions of Rural Modernity in the Thrace Region of Turkey

> While water-power is necessarily rural, steam-power is by no means necessarily urban. It is capitalist utilization which concentrates it mainly in the towns and changes factory villages into factory towns.[16]

Modernity is best associated with the urban expansion of capitalism, an act of colonization and domination over what are considered to be "not modern" geographies and the people living in those geographies, which are "seen to lack . . . capacity for reflective reasoning."[17] Urban expansion is a product of "the first great division of labor in society,"[18] where "each individual industrial capitalist is constantly striving to get away from the large towns necessarily created by this production, and to transfer his plant to the countryside."[19] Urban and rural separation, a form of the uneven production of space, has been necessary for the capitalist expansion of modernity, and has made capital accumulation possible. Thus "the factors of modernity lie not outside the logic of capital but are contained in it."[20] It is within this context that infrastructure consists of technologies that contain, regulate, and make flows possible between urban and rural areas, as best illustrated in *Anti-Dühring* by Engels and Marx, as cited in this section's epigraph.[21]

Capitalist modernity and class contradictions coexist. This coexistence is well established in the geographical and historical literature on infrastructure and the city.[22] Geographers Maria Kaika and Erik Swyngedouw, in their piece on the water networks of Europe and how and where they were constructed and used by people during early modernity, discuss the fetishization of these urban networks, which reinforces an ideology of progress. The sites where these urban water networks were built, such as dams, water towers, apartment buildings with tap water, and pipes, became places that symbolized progress, and which consequently became desired images for the working classes.[23] This idea of infrastructural progress was very influential in later modernity as well; in Turkey this led to the fetishization of the "modern" apartment and came to shape modern urban housewifery.[24] Modernity rests on the invention of urban spatiality,[25] and theories of modernity have largely been about the cities. The exploration of what happens in rural areas is crucial, however, as recent urban studies literature discusses increasing rates of uneven spatial development as a factor of the present era of neoliberal urbanization. Contemporary urban

The Emergent Gender of Rural Modernities

phenomena manifest themselves in expansions of urban territory around and within cities, horizontally and vertically, forming what we know as metropolitan areas and/or city regions.[26]

It is important to explore the question of "what happens to the rural in relation to the urban expansion of neoliberalism in the contemporary world?" Here, I take river pollution as a major peak point of urban expansion. Formerly, the overall economy of the village under study rested on a combination of wheat, sugar beets, and dairy production, at least from the 1960s through the 1980s.[27] It is very hard to find precise production figures for the village in question, as it is only possible to find figures with regard to production at the Lüleburgaz county level. Therefore, I am inferring this argument from the fact that in comparison to the surveys by the Ministry of Rural Affairs in 1965,[28] surveys by the same ministry in 1984[29] differed in terms of the variety of agricultural production. These surveys were conducted at the county, regional, and city scale, aggregating village calculations. Nevertheless, it seems that Lüleburgaz increased its sugar beet production from the mid-1960s to the mid-1980s. However, the average amount of increase in production is not necessarily reflected in the village economy, as each village has its unique land use. Based on the interviews and observations in the village, it is safe to argue that the village economy was founded on water-intensive production, because water from the river was immediately available without further costs of drilling. Access to water is the reason why losing the river's irrigation capabilities had a significant impact on the village economy. The Ergene River's pollution therefore constituted a major reason for women's protests in the village.

The Ergene River's pollution reflects the devaluation of agricultural production in the face of expanding urban and industrial activities in the overall regional economy. Restructuring Istanbul's industries and moving them to the Thrace region, specifically to the organized industrial zones in the Çerkezköy and Marmara regions, started in 1971 when the State Planning Organization designated them as underdeveloped regions to be advanced through governmental incentives. One of the main reasons for decentralizing Istanbul's industry was the improvement in transportation across the Bosporus Peninsula, binding Asia Minor to Europe.[30] Currently, there are six organized industrial zones, one European Free Trade zone, and 18 small-size industrial sites, which taken together accommodate more than 2,000 industrial facilities.[31] These figures only show the legal and registered industrial ownership; it is reported that 70% of the industrial activity in Thrace occurs outside of the legally established organized zones.[32]

Urban theorist Tarık Şengül characterizes the post-1980 era by drawing attention to the urbanization of capital where urban entrepreneurialism produced multiscalar governance models.[33] The era after 2000 witnessed the competition of these models.[34] In parallel, economic reforms introduced in 2000 signified a complete transition to a neoliberal agrarian system, which included the elimination of support prices and the withdrawal of support for the unions of agricultural cooperatives. Among other laws that primarily influenced producers in the Thrace region was the Sugar Law, enacted in 2001, through which more extensive quotas gradually decreased the amount of sugar production and limited contracts with the farmers.[35]

The neoliberal turn after the 1980s, particularly in the agrarian sector, in conjunction with the decentralization of Istanbul's industry into the Thrace region, led to the proletarianization of farmers in the region from the late 1970s onwards,[36] along with second generations migrating to more industrialized centers such as Çorlu, Tekirdağ, and Istanbul.[37] A consequence has been an aging and much decreased rural population, especially in the villages located in close proximity to the Ergene River. Men tend to work in the more urbanized centers of the region, because agricultural productivity has considerably decreased.[38] As a result, women tend to be more visible and active in village social, economic and political life, even if their labor is not valued. Here, women and the gender question within the contemporary context of capitalist modernity in Turkey often becomes more observable as urban and industrial expansion becomes symptomatic in the rural hydrological and food production regimes through severe water pollution.

Modernity is a gendered project of hegemony, "where spatial categories of private and public were mapped onto temporal distinctions between past and present," and in the discourse of modernity, women in general have come to symbolize the non-modern "by being outside the dehumanizing structures of

Eda Acara

the capitalist economy as well as the rigorous demands of public life."[39] It is through such categorization that women also become an object of modernity: recent literature on rural modernity suggests that women become part of modernist narratives by voicing modernist concerns.[40] This phenomenon has been well established in two separate studies during agrarian crises in between the two world wars, where "farm women," as an image and a political subjectivity, were politicized and instrumentalized by the elites for the needs of the modern nation, specifically in Germany and Japan. However, these farm women were also actively involved, even if silently, by their presence in conservative modernist politics. Moreover, it was farm women's discontents and their capability to voice them that made governments target them, both as objects for desired modernization and then as political subjects of their constituencies.[41]

In countries like Turkey that were established as a result of imperial dissolution and that have arisen out of competitive nationalisms,[42] the process of nation-state building has been influential in determining the gender complexities of modernity. The early republican era, which most of the literature on urbanization, architecture, and modernization focuses on, illustrates the state-led formation of a network of economic spaces to facilitate interregional integration. Urbanization and industrialization were used as a spatial strategy in this regard, where state-owned factories, model villages and towns, educational buildings (i.e., village institutes), and agricultural cooperatives served as examples for the new nation's subjects.[43] These economic spaces were fundamental to the formation of urban and rural elites. The urban elites and the Turkish state acted on rurality and the peasantry by trying to tame them through education and/or by integrating them into the active labor force.[44] As such, until the 1980s, the state-led and state-pioneered modernization of villages and towns constituted the backbone of this hegemonic relationship between the state and the peasants in Turkey.[45]

Within this context, rural space and rural women were viewed by many of the modernist nation(alist) state projects as antithetical to modern cityscapes,[46] and thereby women became a significant target for education.[47] Nevertheless, many of the developmentalist nation-states like Turkey rest on women's rural labor.[48] That is because production is bound by household production, where women, children, and the elderly, for a majority of the time, work for free or for less money than men.[49] Here, rural women and their embodiment become symbols of backwardness and tradition opposed to Western modernity. This gendered spatial association is also the reason why any kind of traditional symbol, such as the headscarf, further becomes a rural-urban demarcation.

It is my contention that this idea of rural backwardness also legitimized the phenomenon of rural modernity in Turkey and ordered the economic spaces of the village in distinct ways. In the next section, using a village tour guided by a woman village dweller, I will show how village geography has changed and how women living in the village narrate and temporalize these changes around the gendered idea of a rural modernity. Their temporalization also served as the basis of their collective action, and as both an enabling and a constraining factor for women's spatial routines in participating in village politics. It is, however, important to emphasize that this temporalization is not an absolute representative of a singular rural modernity in Turkey, because, as explained at the beginning of the article, modernity produces multiple experiences.

Gender-Walking and Remembering Past Rural Modernities

The Village Social Cooperation and Solidarity Association was established in 2008.[50] Contrary to the gender-neutral name of the association, it was set up by women and it was mainly pioneered by four of them. These four women live in what is called the downstream of the river. They grew up in the village, left it for work and/or education, but then came back for personal health and/or financial reasons. They still own land very close to the Ergene River—to the point where when the river sometimes floods they are not able to grow anything except purslane. In addition to the march they organized in 2009, which is now held annually, they further set up trainings for themselves on agriculture and husbandry.[51]

The Emergent Gender of Rural Modernities

Auyero underlines the significance of spatial routines that stand at the heart of collective action. Spatial routines are "the mundane spatial structures of everyday life."[52] In order to examine how spatial routines were formed historically, I will use a tour of the village, undertaken by Alev.[53] Alev was a 52-year-old dairy farmer residing in the village. She dropped out of university during her first year, after which she worked for several factories. The village tour she conducted, I will argue, played with a very peculiar idea of village nostalgia, and renarrated the history of the village in order to lash out at the transforming rural modernities in the region. In the middle of this transformation lies the pollution of the Ergene River.

During the first days of my fieldwork in 2012, I met Alev on the streets of the county, marching with a group of students, protesting against the pollution of the Ergene River. After a brief introduction, she invited me to a small village gathering where activists from Istanbul and other regional locations participated. At our second meeting in the village with a crowd of young activists, Alev gave a long tour of the village. This tour was especially important to grasp the spatial routines that formed the structure of collective action in the village. Not least, it also unraveled the abandoned, forgotten, and at some point erased past due to the changing economic structure of the village.

Alev started the tour at the village square, situated between the village coffeehouse and the shuttered school and its garden. The school was closed due to low population. According to an interview with the local newspaper *Görünüm*, 180 households resided in the village, which was not legally enough to keep the community clinic and the school open.[54] The village's overall population is currently 491. During Alev's childhood years, perhaps in the late 1960s, the school, overlooking the Ergene River, was a place where students used to obtain agricultural training in a vocational program for rural populations that Alev referred to as "getting an education while simultaneously laboring" (*üretim içinde eğitim*). The school was also a place where young people used to come together to play the traditional *saz*. Here, Alev seemed to recall the popular memory of Village Institutes and People's Houses, which during the 1940s provided an applied education for the peasants from the surrounding villages. These peasant students were raised to become teachers who were capable of construction, taking care of village hygiene, playing music, and teaching multiple courses. In other words, they were expected to disseminate the village ideals. The Village Institutes were closed in the 1950s, as they were accused of disseminating communist ideals. Lüleburgaz had a strong tradition of teachers from one of the Village Institutes known as Kepirtepe Village Institute. It is within this context that Alev was recalling with nostalgia a historical time frame where villages were seen as the core of economic, social, political, and cultural production and dissemination.

In a different context in Ankara, feminist historian Akşit Vural tackles what she refers to as the "politics of decay," a form of spatial and social exclusion exercised by the central state and municipalities in a multi-ethnic non-Turkish district. She suggests that the politics of decay involves daily negotiation between the acts of remembering while forgetting, as the decaying objects are marked by their decaying characteristics.[55] Similarly, the decaying school, the school library and the theater in the village were instances of an active forgetting of the past. Alev underlines the coexistence of girls and boys at school, "Something that is different in the villages now." Imagining the village in secular terms resonates with Özyürek's conceptualization of republican nostalgia, as a way to counteract Islamism, Kurdish separatism, and also the interventions by the International Monetary Fund (IMF) and European Union in the economic and political realms. Özyürek's conceptualization was empirically based on research on the middle classes and bureaucratic elites of Turkey in the 1990s.[56] In Lüleburgaz, however, Alev was in a sense counteracting Islamism in the village space, against a crowd of students who viewed the village to be backward at all times, without history. Instead, Alev's narrative was reconstructing the village past around modernity and gender. This reconstructed past was strategically an empowering narrative for women, as it opened up a renewed space to voice their gendered concerns about the declining village economy and the Ergene River's pollution.

Alev's counternarrative not surprisingly touched on the morning of the coup d'état in 1980, when the books at the school library were burned and the village cooperative (*Köy-Koop*) was shut down. Village cooperatives have a distinctively strong place in regional history compared to the rest of Turkey. They were broadly responsible for development and enhancing agricultural production. Teachers who lived in the villages established a small number of them in the Thrace region between 1973 and 1974. From 1976 to 1980 the number of cooperatives increased from 7 to 100, all within the region. Producing and selling milk was the predominant regional economic strategy, followed by food marketing. Village co-ops in the Thrace region even held village food markets where the members exchanged milk for vegetables and other agricultural production to cut the cost of mediators.[57] However, co-ops were shut down by the state during the coup d'état in 1980.[58] Between 1988 and 1989, the village co-ops returned and started to sell milk to SEK, a state owned factory for dairies. SEK was then privatized in 1995. In opposition to SEK's privatization and in order to raise its profits, the Village Cooperatives Union was, as of this writing, constructing a milk factory alongside a cultural facility in Poyralı of the Thrace region.[59] Figure 16.2 shows an example of a village coop, which played an active role in the village economy up to the 1980s.

Figure 16.2 A Village Coop
Source: © Eda Acara, 2017.

The Emergent Gender of Rural Modernities

Figure 16.3 Water Box for Animals
Source: © Eda Acara, 2017.

On the tour with Alev, the next stop was the place where the village bull had been tied in the past (Figure 16.3). The village was a hub for other villages to bring their cows to breed. Peasants would either jointly buy the village bull,[60] or state-owned farms sometimes provided the villages with a bull. Alev emphasized that because certified cows are now in demand, village bulls and local breeds are largely erased from the village landscape, leaving the village bull's space empty.

Alev showed these economic spaces from the village's history, spaces that physically stand right at the center of the village. The weakening of village cooperatives along with the decay of previous village spaces were narrated by Alev as an overall state strategy that showed the destruction of the village and its production capabilities, and the dispossession of its peasants. According to her, this process has turned peasants into factory workers, whose numbers have vastly increased in Çorlu and Çerkezköy.

In the past, the village had a dairy farm. As Alev states: "[Owning the means of production] is the thing that gives you existence."[61] The next stop on the tour was the long-abandoned, communally owned dairy farm. Alev explained that milk produced in the village is currently given to a multinational dairy company for free, as this company built the modern milking facility in exchange for milk for the next five years. Setting up so-called modern milking facilities in the villages of the Thrace region was part of a joint partnership between the company, the Agricultural Bank, and the Ministry of Agriculture and Rural Affairs.[62] In a controversial part of her conversation with the students, however, Alev warned them about the milk that was produced and bought by the company. She specifically stressed that the milking facility did not test for the contamination of the milk from the pollution of the Ergene River. Later that day, we saw groups of cows grazing along the river bank.

Eda Acara

While raising questions about the hygiene of the milk that they sell to the company, she also criticized labor conditions. She recalled a memory of when she brought the milk to the factory and a worker hit the bucket harshly before carrying it in. To her, this memory illustrated the peasants' slavery and the devaluation of their labor:

> I was once a factory worker and at the factory, you only sell your labor. You've got nothing else to earn from. However, when you produce milk in a village, you have to buy a cow, grow corn and barley, you have to build a barn and so, you need to prepare a certain infrastructure, you need to have money. So you put money, your labor, produce milk, and transport the milk and then a guy hits your milk. Then you are not a producer any more, but you become a slave.

To sum up, the village tour involved biographical aspects of Alev's migrant life, back and forth between rural and urban living arrangements. It also involved the migrant life of the village in between two different phases of capitalist modernity. These two transformational moments, perhaps best marked by the pollution of the Ergene river, also gave women a voice in the village, an unanticipated political subjectivity. This political subjectivity, however, narrates a specific nostalgia for the past, where the village economy and culture are politicized for women's activism. It is through such a political endeavor that a new rural modernity and gendered concerns arise in contemporary Turkey.

Women's Activism and the Changing Political Geographies of the Village

The village built a repertoire of protest against the Ergene River's pollution long before women's activism. In the 1990s, the village co-ops led an action against river pollution.[63] In 2001, a march organized by the members of the Freedom and Solidarity Party (*Özgürlük ve Dayanışma Partisi*, or ÖDP) passed through the village.[64] Then, a petition campaign organized mainly by TEMA, a mainstream environmental association, was held in six villages.[65] This continuous repertoire of action was a depository aspect of the village space—"the enabling and constraining aspects of spaces for engaged politics"[66]—that perhaps enabled the idea of a village march in the first place.

Apart from the history of a repertoire of action in the village, women's stronger activism and participation was possible through the integration of elder and conservative women into the circle of conversation. In this regard, Alev specifically emphasized one single elder woman named Selcan who made their association trustworthy. When Alev first came back to the village, she occasionally went to village ceremonies, such as circumcision (*sünnet*) ceremonies and weddings, not only to make herself a place within the village community, but also to explore whose social circles and influence was the best. That is how she came to meet Selcan. It is not always typical to encounter religiosity and conservatism in gendered rural modernities as an enabling aspect of social space for political engagement. This is because religiosity creates an accountable, trustworthy, and familiar safe space for diverse women, whether religious or not, to participate in collective action. This accountability was emphasized by Alev more than once, and it further indicates how when rural women's discontents became vocal, they need to be contained and made "accountable."

Women's activism further played a controversial role in the village because women were not expected to have active political voices and actions, specifically from the perspective of the men in the village. In addition, immobility often constituted the main characteristic of village life for women, and the fact that women belong inside the house has been a well-documented and historical fact in village life.[67] During my stay, it was possible to observe on many occasions how political protest definitely made women more mobile between the village and the surrounding counties and cities. However, it is not easy to consider this increasing mobility as total emancipation. Engaging with politics clearly empowered women in gendered negotiations with regard to mobility. Also, women's activism drew more visitors with either political or research interests to the village. These visitors, including myself

296

for example, served once or twice as an excuse to loosen some of the restrictions on women's mobility in the village and fields, especially at night.

The social and political geography of the village changed not only in terms of women's mobility. Women's activism created a silent polarization and tension regarding support for the mukhtar (*muhtar* in Turkish, a local mayor) versus support for the Association in village affairs. Alev dated the beginning of the tension with the mukhtar back to the time when she wrote a newspaper article about how economic and social life in the village had deteriorated over the years. The article was based on a conversation with Selcan. According to Alev, on many occasions, village men expected women to inform them of their discontent about village issues before it got out to a wider public, such as in the situation of the newspaper article. The mukhtar once attempted to beat Alev to shut her down while she was criticizing him about things that could have been done about the pollution in the Ergene River. Selcan prevented the beating; while blocking the mukhtar's hand, she warned him, "drunk talk is sober thought."[68] Women's discontent was largely seen as a matter of dishonor in the village. It is through this domestic ideology that men control women's bodies and their social and political lives in the household and the village.[69]

While pointing to a polarization on several occasions during and after the time that the village march was first organized, Alev also underlined that she had to "rub the mukhtar in the right way" so that he would get used to women's presence in village politics and remain cooperative when the march was organized. Village dwellers, both women and men that I interviewed living on the north side of the river close to the main highway to Istanbul, started referring to the women living by the river as downstreamers. In rural vocabulary, downstream/upstream is usually a traditional marker of village wealth. That is because downstreamers are close to running water, and in the case of our village, this area stands as the most vulnerable to pollution. On the other hand, upstreamer villagers are far away from the river, and their lands are less affected by river pollution. Politically, upstreamers were also supporters of the head of the village, the mukhtar.[70] With such a transformed social and political geography, it was possible to witness a silent polarization in village politics, where the river and gender played key roles in contested negotiations over women's place in rural modernity.

Conclusion: Reflections and Further Studies on the Gender of Rural Modernity in Turkey

River pollution, like many other environmental problems, is often viewed as needing a technological or planning fix. That is why its socio-spatial and political consequences are mostly unrecognized. It is my contention that the Ergene River's pollution must be seen as an end result of a metabolic rift in the wider Thracian geographies of urbanization and industrial development. And this metabolic rift, together with the reconstructed rural modernities in contemporary Turkey after the 1980s, provides rural women with newly emerging political spaces in the villages. It would be wrong, however, to conceptualize these political spaces as merely emancipatory. Rather, as I have tried to argue, these political spaces empower women in their daily negotiations of place within the overall village economy. In other words, rural women, in the case of this village, try to find their place amid the cracks of capitalist contradictions in rural geographies while renarrating their own histories and places, and imprinting them on the space of the village and its abandoned economic spaces through village tours to younger generations.

While exploring the village's gendered and political spaces, I also suggested that rural modernity as a concept is useful in understanding historical differences in the emerging urban and rural geographies in Turkey. Contemporary urbanism and urban power geometries exacerbate urban expansion into rural areas while also depopulating villages. Here, rural modernity is constituted by a gendered experience of economic spaces, built into the fabric of the village. It is gendered in the sense that the old rural modernity that is now abandoned in the contemporary village—solidified in the decaying

Eda Acara

school building, in the absence of the village bull, and in the weakened place of the village co-op in the village's economy to the point that it has been replaced by a milking facility, debited to the village by a multinational company—has been renarrated as a modern aspect of the village. Regardless of whether these aspects are modern or not, I think they point to different capitalist and urban moments and relations, producing rural spaces. Historicizing different rural modernities carries the utmost importance if we would like to be able to analyze and understand the gender and class contradictions that are located in diverse economic spaces.

Notes

1. Talu 2015.
2. There is a growing literature on women's participation in the protests against hydroelectric power plants. For example, see Akbaş, Bozok, and Bozok 2016; Şendeniz and Yavuz 2013.
3. I interviewed ten women who participated in the planning of these protests. I also had a chance to hold shorter interviews with four women and one man who did not support the protests at all.
4. This research was supported by the Social Sciences and Humanities Research Council of Canada (SSHRC), Queen's University (Ontario, Canada), and the American Association of Geographers.
5. This is the highest level of pollution.
6. Turkish Ministry of Environment and Forestry 2004.
7. Avşar, Gürbüz, and Kurşun 1999; Arıcı et al. 2000.
8. For more on Turkish formal and informal policies on pollution, see Acara 2015a.
9. For a review of historical, economic and political tensions in hindering the balancing of the needs for industrial development and environmental protection in Turkey, see Orhan and Scheumann 2011.
10. For a review of health risks in the region, see Acara 2015b.
11. A protest was held in February 2017 against the potential construction of such a fossil fuel power plant. See Tek Silivri 2017.
12. For a review report on the project, see Zeren Gülersoy, Erdemli Mutlu, and Yazıcı Gökmen 2014.
13. This sense and/or definition of place is very common with Doreen Massey's scholarship. See Massey 1994, 2005. See also Malpas 1999.
14. Malpas 1999, 32.
15. Auyero 2006.
16. Engels and Marx, *Anti-Dühring*, 281.
17. Felski 1995, 14.
18. Engels and Marx 2010, 277.
19. Engels and Marx 2010, 282.
20. Feng 2006, 256.
21. Engels and Marx 2010.
22. Dutton, Seth, and Gandhi 2002; Gandy 1999; Konvitz, Rose, and Tarr 1990; Roy 2005; Kaika 2005; Kaika and Swyngedouw 2000.
23. Kaika and Swyngedouw 2000.
24. Gürel 2009.
25. Harvey 2014; Şengül 2009.
26. Brenner 2004; Brenner, Peck, and Theodore 2010; Brenner and Theodore 2002.
27. Köyişleri ve Kooperatifler Bakanlığı 1984.
28. Köy İşleri Bakanlığı 1965.
29. Köyişleri ve Kooperatifler Bakanlığı 1984.
30. Tekeli 2013.
31. Trakya Kalkınma Ajansı 2010.
32. Inci 2010.
33. Şengül 2009.
34. Bayırbağ 2010.
35. Aydın 2010.
36. Mortan, Özgen, Özkan, and Tekin 2003.
37. İstanbul Kalkınma Ajansı 2010; TKA 2010.
38. Trakya Kalkınma Ajansı 2013.
39. Felski 1995, 18.
40. Jones 2009; Tamanoi 1998.

41. Jones 2009; Tamanoi 1998.
42. Ahmad 2008; Zürcher 2007.
43. Keskinok 2010; Karakaya 2010.
44. On the experience of People's Houses, for example, see Karaömerlioğlu 1998a and Arı 2004; also for the experience of Village Institutes in Turkey, see Karaömerlioğlu 1998b; on labour, see Arnold 2012; Nacar 2009.
45. Karaömerlioğlu 2002; 1998a, 1998b.
46. Göle 1996; Secor 2002, 2003; Aksit 2005; Saktanber & Çorbacıoğlu 2008
47. On women's education in rural areas, Aksit Vural (2005) specifically underlines, for example, ethnic inequalities in accessing educational facilities based on overall rural power geometries.
48. Karkıner 2014; Toksöz 2015.
49. Kandiyoti 1997.
50. Goncagül 2009.
51. Yıldız 2009.
52. Auyero 2006, 573.
53. This is a pseudonym.
54. Yıldız 2009.
55. Akşit Vural 2010.
56. Özyürek 2006.
57. "Köy-Koop Atakta" 1995.
58. The military intervention in 1980 lasted for three years.
59. See "Süt Birliği Olmaz, İnsan Birliği Olur" 1997. The memory and economic accountability of village cooperatives are still very much alive to the point where, for example, agricultural irrigation costs are still organized within cooperatives, rather than irrigation unions (*sulama birliği*). This is quite distinctive to the Thrace region compared to the rest of Turkey.
60. Arabacı 2016.
61. Alev's words when giving the tour.
62. Ministry of Agriculture and Rural Affairs 2009.
63. Ayan 2009.
64. Atış 2001b.
65. Atış 2001a.
66. Auyero 2006, 569.
67. Kandiyoti 1997.
68. Rephrased from Alev's narration of the incident. The original in Turkish was *"burası sarhoş masası değil."*
69. For more on a review of the ideology of domesticity, see for example Little 2006.
70. Women challenged the mukhtar's group during the 2014 municipal elections. The challenge was resolved nevertheless for the favor of the current village administration, and women decided to abandon their candidacy in the elections.

References

Acara, Eda. 2015a. *Conflict Geographies of Water Pollution in Thrace Region of Turkey*. Dissertation, Department of Geography and Planning, Queen's University.

Acara, Eda. 2015b. "Ergene Havzası'nda bir yönetim taktiği olarak Yönetimsizlik, Kirlilik ve Sağlık." *Toplum ve Bilim* 134: 86–102.

Ahmad, Feroz. 2008. "Politics and Political Parties in Republican Turkey." In *The Cambridge History of Turkey, Turkey in the Modern World*, edited by Reşat Kasaba, 226–265. Cambridge and New York: Cambridge University Press.

Akbaş, Meral, Mehmet Bozok, and Nihan Bozok. 2016. "'Bizim Dereyi Kim çaldı?': Doğu Karadeniz'de Yaşlı Kadınlar ve Yaşlı Erkeklerin Doğa Anlatıları." In *Sudan Sebepler, Türkiye'de neoliberal Su-Enerji Politikaları ve Direnişler*, edited by Cemil Aksu, Sinan Erensü and Erdem Evren, 247–269. Istanbul: İletişim Yayınları.

Aksit Vural, Elif Ekin. 2005. *Kizlarin Sessizligi* [*Silence of the Girls*]. Istanbul: İletişim Yayınları.

Akşit Vural, Elif Ekin. 2010. "Politics of Decay and Spatial Resistance." *Social and Cultural Geography* 11(4): 343–357.

Arabacı, Elçin. 2016. "Köy Boğası Nedir?" *Anneanneyle Bursa Sözlü Tarihi*, March 15. http://bursasozlutarih.blogspot.com.tr/2016/02/koy-bogasi-nedir-anneannemle-her-ogle.html.

Arı, Eyal. 2004. "The People's Houses and Theatre in Turkey." *Middle Eastern Studies* 40(4): 32–58.

Arıcı, M., T. Gümüş, F. Atansay, M. Turan, A. Kubaş, and O. Gaytancıoğlu. 2000. *A Research on Determining of Some Heavy Metals, Aflatoxins and Crop Losses in Rice Irrigated With Industrial Waste Water in Thrace Region.*

AGROENVIRON 2nd International symposium on new Technologies for Environmental Monitoring and Agro-Applications, Tekirdağ, October 18–20, 2000.

Arnold, Caroline E. 2012. "In the Service of Industrialization: Etatism, Social Services and the Construction of Industrial Labour Forces in Turkey (1930–1950)." *Middle Eastern Studies* 48(3): 363–385.

Atış, İbrahim. 2001a. "Köylülerden Ergene için imza kampanyası." *Görünüm*, April 26: 1.

Atış, İbrahim. 2001b. "ÖDP Ergene için yürüdü." *Görünüm*, July 21: 1.

Auyero, Javier. 2006. "Spaces & Places As Sites & Objects of Politics." In *Contextual Political Analysis*, edited by Charles Tilly and Robert E. Goodin, 564–594. New York: Oxford University Press.

Avşar, F., M. A. Gürbüz, and İ. Kurşun. 1999. *Ergene Nehrinden Sulanan Çeltiklerin Bazı Mikrobesin Elementi ve Bazı Ağır Metal İçerikleri*. Trakya'da Sanayileşme ve Çevre Sempozyumu III, Edirne, November 11–13, 1999.

Ayan, Bülent. 2009. "Ayan-Beyan." *Görünüm*, November 16: 2.

Aydın, Zülküf. 2010. "Neo-Liberal Transformation of Turkish Agriculture." *Journal of Agrarian Change* 10(2): 149–187.

Bayırbağ, Mustafa Kemal. 2010. "Local Entrepreneuralism and State Rescaling in Turkey." *Urban Studies* 47(2): 363–385.

Brenner, Neil. 2004. *New State Spaces, Urban Governance and Rescaling of Statehood*. Oxford: Oxford University Press.

Brenner, Neil, Jamie Peck, and Nik Theodore. 2010. "Variegated Neoliberalization: Geographies, Modalities, Pathways." *Global Networks* 10(2): 182–222.

Brenner, Neil, and Nik Theodore. 2002. "Cities and the Geographies of 'Actually Existing Neoliberalism.'" In *Spaces of Neoliberalism, Urban Restructuring in North America and Western Europe*, edited by Neil Brenner and Nik Theodore, 2–32. Oxford and Malden, MA: Blackwell.

Dutton, Michael, Sanjay Seth, and Leela Gandhi. 2002. "Plumbing the Depths: Toilets, Transparency and Modernity." *Postcolonial Studies* 5(2): 137–142.

Engels, F., and K. Marx. 2010. *Collected Works, Volume 25, Engels*. Translated by Emile Burns and Clemens Dutt. London: Lawrance & Wishart.

Felski, Rita. 1995. *The Gender of Modernity*. Cambridge, MA and London: Harvard University Press.

Feng, Ziyi. 2006. "A Contemporary Interpretation of Marx's Thoughts on Modernity." *Frontiers of Philosophy in China* 1(2): 254–268. doi:10.1007/s11466-006-0007-6.

Gandy, Matthew. 1999. "The Paris Sewers and the Rationalization of Urban Space." *Transactions of the Institute of British Geographers* 24(1): 23–44.

Göle, Nilüfer. 1996. *The Forbidden Modern: Civilization and Veiling*. Ann Arbor: University of Michigan Press.

Goncagül, Şenol. 2009. "Kadına İmkan ve Fırsat Eşitliği Verin." *Trakyagündemi*, July 13. www.trakyagundemi.com/kirklareli/11781005/-kadina-imkan-ve-firsat-esitligi-verin-.html, accessed on May 2, 2017.

Gürel, Meltem Ö. 2009. "Defining and Living Out the Interior: The 'Modern' Apartment and the 'Urban' Housewife in Turkey During the 1950s and 1960s." *Gender, Place and Gender* 16(6): 703–722.

Harvey, David. 2014. *Seventeen Contradictions and the End of Capitalism*. Oxford: Oxford University Press.

Inci, Osman, ed. 2010. *Trakya (Istanbul'un Isgaline) Direniyor*. Istanbul: Cumhuriyet Kitaplari.

İstanbul Kalkınma Ajansı. 2010. *2010–2013 İstanbul Bölge Planı* [Istanbul Regional Plan for 2010–2013]. Edited by İstanbul Kalkınma Ajansı [Istanbul Development Agency]. Istanbul: İstanbul Kalkınma Ajansı (IKA) [Agency of Development for Istanbul].

Jones, Elizabeth B. 2009. *Farm Women and the Politics of Labor in Germany, 1871–1933*. London and New York: Routledge.

Kaika, Maria. 2005. *City of Flows: Modernity, Nature, and the City*. New York: Routledge.

Kaika, Maria, and Erik Swyngedouw. 2000. "Fetishizing the Modern City: The Phantasmagoria of Urban Technological Networks." *International Journal of Urban and Regional Research* 24(1): 120–137.

Kandiyoti, Deniz. 1997. "Cinsiyet Rolleri ve Toplumsal Değişim: Türkiyeli Kadınlara İlişkin Karşılaştırmalı Bir Değerlendirme." In *Cariyeler, Bacılar, Yurttaşlar*, 21–49. Istanbul: Metis Yayınları.

Karakaya, Emel. 2010. *Construction of the Republic in City Space: From Political Ideal to Urban Planning*. Unpublished Master's Thesis, Urban Design in City and Regional Planning, Middle East Technical University.

Karaömerlioğlu, Asım. 1998a. "The People's Houses and the Cult of the Peasant in Turkey." *Middle Eastern Studies* 34(4): 47–73.

Karaömerlioğlu, Asım. 1998b. "The Village Institute Experience in Turkey." *British Journal of Middle Eastern Studies* 25(1): 47–73.

Karaömerlioğlu, Asım. 2002. "Agrarian Populism as an Ideological Discourse of InterWar Europe." *New Perspectives on Turkey* 26(Fall): 59–93.

Karkıner, Nadide. 2014. "Anadolu'da Devletten Oğula Ataerkil Tarım: Küçük Köylü Mülkiyeti ve Küçük Meta Üreticiliği." In *Köylülükten Sonra Tarım, Osmanlıdan Günümüze Çiftçinin İlgası ve Şirketleşme*, edited by Abdullah Aysu and Serdar M. Kayaoğlu, 195–236. Ankara: Epos.

Keskinok, Çağatay H. 2010. "Urban Planning Experience of Turkey in the 1930s." *METU JFA* 27(2): 173–188.

Konvitz, Josef W., Mark H. Rose, and Joel A. Tarr. 1990. "Technology and the City." *Urban History* 5(2): 32–37.

Köy İşleri Bakanlığı. 1965. *Köy Envanter Etüdlerine Göre Kırklareli*. Ankara: Köy İşleri Bakanlığı.

Köyişleri ve Kooperatifler Bakanlığı. 1984. *Köy Envanter Etüdü, Kırklareli-1981*. Ankara: Köyişleri ve Kooperatifler Bakanlığı.

"Köy-Koop Atakta." 1995. *Gündöndü*, March 15–April 1: 1 and 5.

Little, Jo. 2006. "Gender and Sexuality in Rural Communities." In *The Handbook of Rural Studies*, edited by Paul Cloke, Terry Marsden and Patrick Mooney, 365–378. London, Thousand Oaks, CA and New Delhi: Sage.

Malpas, Jeff. 1999. *Place and Experience: A Philosophical Topography*. Cambridge: Cambridge University Press.

Massey, Doreen B. 1994. *Space, Place, and Gender*. Cambridge: Polity Press.

Massey, Doreen B. 2005. *For Space*. Thousand Oaks, CA: Sage.

Mortan, Kenan, Nese H. Özgen, Müge Özkan, and Barış Tekin. 2003. *Lüleburgaz icin Kent Stratejisi* [*Urban Strategy of Lüleburgaz*]. Lüleburgaz: Lüleburgaz Belediye Baskanlığı.

Nacar, Can. 2009. "'Our Lives Were Not as Valuable as an Animal': Workers in State-Run Industries in World-War-II Turkey." *IRSH* 54(suppl.): 143–166.

Orhan, Gokhan, and Waltina Scheumann. 2011. "Turkey's Policy for Combating Water Pollution." In *Turkey's Water Policy: National Frameworks and International Cooperation*, edited by Aysegul Kibaroglu, Anika Kramer, and Waltina Scheumann, 117–139. Berlin, London, and New York: Springer.

Özyürek, Esra. 2006. *Nostalgia for the Modern, State Secularism and Everyday Politics in Turkey*. Durham, NC and London: Duke University Press.

Roy, Ananya. 2005. "Urban Informality: Toward an Epistemology of Planning." *Journal of American Planning Association* 71(2): 147–158.

Saktanber, Ayşe, and Gül Çorbacıoğlu. 2008. "Veiling and Headscarf-Scepticism in Turkey." *Social Politics: International Studies in Gender, State and Society* 15(4): 514–538.

Secor, Anna J. 2002. "The Veil and Urban Space in Istanbul: Women's Dress, Mobility and Islamic Knowledge." *Gender, Place & Culture* 9(1): 5–22.

Secor, Anna J. 2003. "Citizenship in the City: Identity, Community and Rights Among Women Migrants to Istanbul." *Urban Geography* 24(2): 147–168.

Şendeniz, Özlem, and Şahinde Yavuz. 2013. "HES Direnişlerinde Kadınların Deneyimleri: Fındıklı Örneği." *Fe Dergi* 5(1): 43–58.

Şengül, Tarık. 2009. *Kentsel Çelişki ve Siyaset, Kapitalist Kentleşme Süreçlerinin Eleştirisi*. Ankara: İmge Yayınevi.

"Süt Birliği Olmaz, İnsan Birliği Olur." 1997. *Görünüm*, August 5: 10–12.

Talu, Nuran. 2015. *Türkiye'de İklim Değişikliği Siyaseti*. Ankara: Phoenix Yayınevi.

Tamanoi, Mariko Asano. 1998. *Politics and Poetics of Rural Japanese Women*. Honolulu: University of Hawai'i Press.

Tekeli, Ilhan. 2013. *İstanbul'un Planlanmasının ve Gelişmesinin öyküsü*. Istanbul: Tarih Vakfı Yurt Yayınları.

Tek Silivri. 2017. "Trakya'da termik santral tepkisi giderek artıyor." Last Modified February 26, 2017. http://teksilivri.com/haber/termik-santral-tepkisi-giderek-artiyor-2920.html, accessed on April 5, 2017.

Toksöz, Gülay. 2015. "Kalkınmada Farklı Yörüngeler." In *Geçmişten Günümüze Türkiye'de Kadın Emeği*, edited by Ahmet Makal and Gülay Toksöz, 143–169. Ankara: İmge Kitabevi.

Trakya Kalkınma Ajansı (TKA). 2010. *T21 Trakya Bölge Planı* [*T21 Thracian Regional Plan*]. Tekirdağ: Trakya Kalkınma Ajansı [Development Agency of Thrace].

Trakya Kalkınma Ajansı. 2013. *TR21 Trakya Bölgesi 2014–2023 Bölge Planı Taslağı* [*Draft Regional Plan of Thrace for the Years From 2014 to 2023*]. Tekirdağ: Trakya Kalkınma Ajansı [Development Agency of Thrace].

Turkish Ministry of Environment and Forestry. 2004. *Çevre Atlası* [*Environmental Atlas*]. Ankara: Turkish Ministry of Environment and Forestry. http://www.cedgm.gov.tr/CED/Files/cevreatlası/atlas_metni.pdf, accessed on September 1, 2010.

Yıldız, Semih. 2009. "Karamusul'da 'Beyaz Hareket.'" *Görünüm*, November 12: 11–12.

Zeren Gülersoy, Nuran, Özgül Erdemli Mutlu, and Esra Yazıcı Gökmen, eds. 2014. *İstanbul'un Geleceğini Etkileyecek Üç proje 3. Köprü, 3. Havalimanı, Kanal İstanbul: TEMA Vakfı Uzman Görüşleri*. Istanbul: Atölye Osman Maybaa Sanayi ve Ticaret A.Ş.

Zürcher, Erik-Jan. 2007. "The Ottoman Legacy of the Kemalist Republic." In *The State and the Subaltern*, edited by Touraj Atabaki, 111–123. London: I. B. Tauris.

Part 5
A Rapidly Globalizing World

Introduction

Part 5 explores the experience of countries that have gone through rapid development through globalization; often, but not always, going hand in hand with neoliberal policies at a national or local level. The first three chapters examine cases taken from China and the last three look at developments in India.

C. Cindy Fan examines rural-urban migration in China, and how such population shifts have transformed the modern Chinese family. She finds an ambivalence towards modern city life, as migrants organize gendered resources in order to access urban work opportunities while maintaining deep connections to their rural villages of origin. Penn Tsz Ting Ip follows with an analysis of a specific experience of rural-urban migration. Her chapter examines young migrant women who learn to be "modern Chinese women" by consciously shedding their rural appearance and adopting habits of consumption and appearance learned in their new urban setting. Duanfang Lu discusses the experiences of a different urban worker, that of the young women who work for Foxconn, a major electronics manufacturer tied to a global labor regime. Examining space, gender, and everyday life in the Foxconn factory complex, she explores how rural migrant women learn to be urban while coping with the stresses of their employer's extensive social control.

In the chapters that examine modernity, space, and gender in India, Madhavi Desai makes a historic sweep, discussing the colonial typology of the bungalow as it evolved in twentieth-century Gujarat and showing the role this structure played in a rethinking of tradition and culture, especially as they relate to women's spaces and women's social roles. Aparna Parikh then turns to current-day Mumbai, exploring the lives of women who work the night shift in in India's call center industry, and tracing women's coping strategies as they grapple with gendered expectations of household chores and family caregiving. Finally, Shelly Pandey examines the lives of Sikh refugees from Afghanistan, where women find their gender-based experiences and access to public space vastly changed in their new lives in Delhi.

In the three examples from China, we see a state-sanctioned modernization expressed through a rapid expansion of commerce and industry, with women migrants shedding their rural habits—in some cases ambivalently—to adopt a more prestigious urban habitus in an uneasy alliance between modernity and traditionalism. In the Indian examples, conversely, globalization and the ensuing social changes have come in multiple stages. On the one hand, Western influence through contact with colonial powers led to the evolution of common Indian housing, resulting in hybrid spaces that challenged traditional living patterns as well as gender roles. On the other hand, current global patterns threaten to burden women disproportionately with the demands of their "modern" life through increased workplace and domestic demands. Finally, as Shelly Pandey shows, women's empowerment to break tradition and move freely across spaces once denied them can come in small increments that feel liberating nevertheless.

17

Migration, Gender and Space in China

C. Cindy Fan

The documentary *Last Train Home* opens with a husband and a wife stranded at a train station, among tens of thousands of migrant workers waiting to go home for the Chinese New Year—also referred to as Spring Festival (春节)—amid a snowstorm that has stopped trains from running. Meanwhile, back home in a village in Sichuan Province, the couple's teenage daughter and son, who live with their grandmother, wait for the parents to return for a once-a-year reunion. Over a phone call, the mother asks, "Have you received your report card? Did you do well, huh? So-so? You have to keep studying hard. We haven't gotten the train tickets yet. It will take a few more days . . . Are you there?" After showing us both heartwarming and heart-wrenching episodes of human stories in the family, the documentary closes with the daughter deciding to become a migrant worker herself, to the disappointment of her parents.

Stories like this are commonplace in China. Rural families are split between the city and countryside, in order for the husband, or both the husband and wife, to take advantage of urban job opportunities while maintaining their roots in the countryside. Left-behind wives, children and elders not only guard the farmland but also are key to the gender and intergenerational divisions of labor that enable migrants' pursuit of urban work. This chapter aims to explain the logic of such a household strategy, identify the role of gender in migrant households' spatial and social practices and highlight the impacts of those practices on women. The next section outlines the relationship between rural-urban migration, the *hukou* (户口) system, and the split-household strategy. This is followed by a section on gender norms and division of labor as well as left-behind wives. The two sections that precede the chapter's conclusion focus on the intergenerational division of labor that enables both the husband and wife to pursue migrant work, and the persistence of transactional marriages that motivate rural Chinese to use remittances to build big houses and transform rural villages.

Migration, *hukou*, and Household Strategy

Historically, population mobility in China was low, due in part to the agrarian nature of the traditional economy that bound people to the land. But mobility has increased rapidly since the 1970s and especially since the 1980s. The "floating population," a stock measure of the number of migrants who are not living at their place of registration (or *hukou* location), increased from two million (about 0.2% of China's population) in 1983 to 298 million (21.8% of the population) in 2014.[1] Even if intra-city and intra-county moves are excluded, the number in 2014 still stood at 253 million.[2] Such massive migration, primarily from rural to urban areas, has been the key driver of China's rapid urbanization, which was only 18% in 1978 and reached 56% by 2015.[3]

A unique feature of Chinese rural-urban migrants is their practice of circularity and household-splitting. Except for the few who have left the countryside for good, rural migrants tend to straddle the city and countryside, splitting their households between two or more places for an extended period of time, and traveling back and forth between home villages and the locations of migrant work. Some migrants may have lived and worked in cities for over two decades, but they still consider the village and not the city their home. They return to the home village infrequently, typically once a year—during the Chinese New Year—or even less often, due to transportation costs and the demands of urban work. Nevertheless, they tend to circulate rather than settle down permanently in cities. A popular explanation for the persistence of circularity and split households is the *hukou* system.

Numerous papers and books on the *hukou* system have been published, thus this chapter does not seek to repeat the details.[4] Suffice it to say that the *hukou* system was formally put in place in the late 1950s by the Chinese government to manage resources by segmenting the country into separate rural and urban worlds. Rural Chinese were given access to farmland as their main source of livelihood, whereas urban Chinese were entitled to state subsidies and benefits. Without urban local *hukou*, rural migrants' access to housing, education, health care and desirable jobs such as government jobs in cities is severely constrained. Accordingly, rural-urban migration was kept at a very low level until the economic reforms in the late 1970s unleashed rural labor to access rapidly increasing urban job opportunities. However, very few migrants intend to or are able to stay in the city for good or consider it their permanent home.

While *hukou*'s impacts are certainly profound, it does not adequately address two seemingly counterintuitive phenomena: most rural migrants do not intend to stay in the city permanently, and most do not want urban *hukou*. First, contrary to the myth that rural Chinese want to settle down permanently in cities, researchers have revealed that the majority of rural-urban migrants intend to eventually return to the countryside.[5] Second, while *hukou* reforms since the 1980s have made it much easier for rural migrants to obtain urban *hukou* in medium-sized and small cities and towns, study after study has shown that responses to such opportunities have been less than enthusiastic.[6]

In other words, despite the advantages of urban areas over rural areas and of urban *hukou* over rural *hukou*, rural migrants do not plan to stay in the city permanently and are not enthusiastic about obtaining urban *hukou*. In order to understand this paradox, an explanation that centers on household strategy is necessary. I argue that migrants split the household between urban and rural areas in order to access both urban and rural resources as part of a long-term household strategy. This challenges a conventional view that migrants' vision is short term and focuses only on immediate monetary return from migrant work. On the contrary, a split-household strategy shows that migrants' understanding and comparison of the long-term sustainability offered by the city and countryside underlie their migration and household decisions.

Urban areas offer jobs and wages but not a sustained economic future or a sense of social belonging. Migrant jobs typically are not stable, do not offer career mobility, and cannot support the high urban cost of living. Migrants are seen as outsiders and inferior to urbanites, and they are not integrated into urban society. Against the backdrop of *hukou* barriers, the high cost of living, social segregation, and poor career prospects in the city, migrants are not motivated to consider cities more than just a place to earn wages and augment household income, let alone a place to take root.

On the other hand, it is in migrants' interest to keep their roots in the countryside.[7] The countryside continues to be a source of social support via migrants' immediate and extended family and fellow villagers. For example, migrants leave behind family members to farm or they lease out farmland to others—usually without collecting rent—not because of economic gain from agriculture, but in order to protect and maintain their farmland, again for their anticipated return in the future. Farmland constitutes migrants' source of economic security in the event that urban work opportunities subside. Migrants' homes in the countryside, in many cases already expanded or renovated using remittances, are a permanent place to stay that they can rely on, as opposed to temporary residences in the city. This in part explains migrants' building new houses and expanding existing houses in the village despite their constant absence, and some have decided to purchase a house or apartment in nearby towns in order to engage in non-farm work upon their return.[8]

Through household-splitting, migrants can earn urban wages, support the rest of the family at a rural and lower cost of living, save for large expenses such as expanding their house and financing a wedding, and protect their rural livelihood and residence for possible eventual return. Indeed, return migrants are not an uncommon phenomenon; they may return due to advanced age, urban work hardship, family needs and other reasons, and they may return to the home village or nearby towns.[9]

Given that the city is merely a place to work and a source of wages and remittances but not where most migrants plan to stay ultimately, leaving behind some or most of the household members in the countryside is an investment for the family's future as well as a logical arrangement. The next two sections focus on how the split-household arrangement is organized, especially via gender and intergenerational divisions of labor.

Gender Division of Labor and Left-Behind Wives

The Confucian ideology that has guided social relations in China for over 5,000 years prescribes individuals' roles according to their positions relative to other members of society. For example, students are positioned with respect to teachers, and employees are positioned with respect to employers. Likewise, the roles of women and girls are relative and subordinate to those of men and boys in their lives. Specifically, a daughter is subordinate to her father before marriage (*zaijia congfu* 在家从父); a wife is subordinate to her husband (*chujia congfu* 出嫁从夫); and an elderly mother is subordinate to her sons (*laolai congzi* 老来从子). While Mao's notion of women shouldering "half the sky" has increased their labor force participation since the 1960s, patriarchy is deeply rooted in Chinese society. The traditional norms of male dominance and male preference persist. A case in point is the grossly lopsided sex ratio at birth, officially 1.18 to 1 in 2010.[10] Such excess of males over females is due to sex-selective abortions, female infanticide, and underreporting of female births, all reflecting parents' response to the one-child policy that lasted from 1979 to 2015, and which has severely limited the number of births and accordingly the chance of having sons.

Patriarchy is manifested spatially in multiple ways: patrilocal exogamy, gender inside-outside division of labor, patrilineal inheritance and transactional marriage. I shall address the first two in this section and the last two in the next two sections. First, Chinese marriages abide by the patrilocal tradition; namely, the wife leaves her natal family and moves to join the husband's family. In an agrarian economy, a daughter getting married also means that the natal family loses her labor. The eventual and inevitable loss of daughters through marriage undermines girls' value and discourages parents from investing in their education,[11] as illustrated by the age-old saying that "daughters married out are like water spilled out." Patrilocal exogamy also explains the prevalence of early marriage, because parents of sons are eager to recruit a daughter-in-law not only for her labor but also her reproduction, which sustains both lineage and labor supply through her children.

Second, Chinese families traditionally define gender roles in terms of inside and outside spheres—women's place is inside the home, including caregiving, whereas men are responsible for the outside, including making the earnings to support the family (*nan zhu wai nu zhu nei* 男主外女主内).[12] In the countryside, such spatial division translates into the gendered "men till, women weave" work division,[13] which constrains women's sphere to the physical home. In other words, traditional gender norms restrict women's physical mobility, to the extent that the extreme and inhumane practice of foot-binding not only was allowed but was celebrated, further and severely immobilizing women.

In recent decades, as migrant work has become a norm for rural Chinese, new gender inside-outside divisions have come into being. Jacka[14] argues that the husband leaving home for migrant work is an extension of the traditional inside-outside division of labor; namely, upon marriage and

C. Cindy Fan

Figure 17.1 A Mother and Her Children in a Chinese Village
Source: © Cindy Fan, 2014.

the husband's pursuit of migrant work outside the home, the wife then shoulders the responsibility of not only domestic work but other village activities, especially farming, all included as part of the woman's inside sphere. Indeed, a wife-inside and husband-outside division of labor has been one of the most common split-household arrangements for migrant households. During the 1980s and 1990s, single migrants (an adult unmarried child) and sole migrants (one of the spouses, usually the husband) leaving home for urban work were popular household arrangements, the latter resulting in the phenomenon of left-behind wives in the countryside (Figure 17.1).[15]

By 2010, the number of left-behind wives was estimated at 47 million.[16] While remittances from migrant husbands improve the household's standard of living, left-behind wives face a larger workload and even hardship, having to care for the children and elderly and do household chores as well as farm.[17] Research has found that left-behind wives are less healthy, both physically and mentally, than wives of non-migrant men because of increased workload and stress.[18] Their shouldering of rural economic activities has been referred to as agricultural feminization.[19] While women's central and heavy participation in agriculture may be empowering because in the husbands' absence they are in positions of making decisions, research shows that traditional gender hierarchy within rural households remains strong. Regardless of whether the husbands are migrants or non-migrants, the tradition of women subordinating to men and of men making "big decisions" persists,[20] as illustrated by this male return migrant who was interviewed as part of household surveys in Sichuan and Anhui:

> Men are the family's main source of income, and therefore are the decision makers. On a daily basis and internally, my wife and I are equal. But it's different externally. When I host male guests,

my wife is not allowed to sit at the table. If the guests include women, then my wife can sit and accompany me.[21]

In addition, left-behind wives are not physically and economically mobile because they rely on the husband's remittances, further reinforcing women's status as subordinates and dependents. In short, rural marriages facilitate gender division of labor, enable men's pursuit of migrant work, foster the feminization of agriculture and undermine women's independent participation in economic and earning activities. Research has also found that left-behind wives suffer feelings of loneliness, insecurity and abandonment, and that husbands' outmigration adversely affects marital relations.[22]

Intergenerational Division of Labor

Patrilineal inheritance refers to a traditional practice whereby a father at an advanced age would divide his inheritance among his sons. This practice is referred to as *fenjia* 分家, or household division.[23] In the case of rural Chinese families, inheritance primarily includes farmland, a house or portions of a house, and other properties. It is a process of transmission of economic control from one generation to the next, thus allowing adult sons to establish their own households.[24] Daughters are traditionally excluded from inheritance, an extension of the patrilocal tradition under which they are expected to join the husbands' family and as such will no longer be members of the natal family.

The prevalence of migrant work among rural Chinese has, however, motivated a rethinking of the onset and formulation of *fenjia*. Specifically, to Chinese migrants who began migrant work in the 1980s, remittances helped them to overcome poverty and made their subsistence possible.[25] Over time, migrants who have achieved subsistence are motivated to use remittances to finance household expenditures, including house construction or renovation, weddings, children's education, and agricultural and entrepreneurial activities. As such, migrant work and split households have become a way of life in rural China, so much so that couple migration—both spouses pursuing migrant work and leaving their children behind—has become increasingly common since the 1990s.[26] This is a departure from the traditional inside-outside gender division of labor and instead illustrates a new outside-outside organization, where both the husband and wife work outside the home *and* the village. While some migrants bring their children to the city, the proportion of migrant workers moving as a family is still small. Therefore, unlike the sole migrant model, where one of the parents stays behind, couple migrants must rely on other non-migrant family members to care for the farmland and left-behind children. Research has shown that the amount of remittances that migrants send back is a function of the extent of caregiving provided by the non-migrants who stay behind.[27] Postponing *fenjia*, at least in form if not in timing, allows members of the extended family, especially parents of the migrant couple, to help. Such a split-household strategy underscores the value and practicality of an extended family living under one roof. In short, intergenerational collaboration among the extended family facilitates migrant work, and as a result migrant households may skip or postpone *fenjia* and opt for leveraging extended family ties instead. Even if *fenjia* takes place as planned, the fact that migrants' parents and siblings reside in the same village facilitates an intergenerational division of labor, which also motivates migrants to renovate and expand their houses to accommodate the extended family (see also the next section).

Indeed, many rural villages in China now have a hollowed-out age structure whereby only the young and the old stay behind (Figure 17.2).[28] According to the 2010 census, left-behind children under the age of 18 amounted to 61 million, accounting for about 22% of all Chinese children and 38% of rural children.[29] Although the number of migrant children in urban areas was already 36 million by 2010 and the number is on the rise,[30] their access to education is still constrained, and many must return to their hometowns in order to prepare for the appropriate curriculum prior to taking the national university entrance examination.[31] In short, leaving children behind remains a common practice for migrants.

Figure 17.2 Elderly Residents and Children in a Chinese Village
Source: © Cindy Fan, 2014.

Research has shown that remittances sent by migrants have enabled improvement in financial support for the left-behind elders,[32] who by taking on childcare and farming responsibilities make it possible for their adult children to pursue migrant work. Such skipped-generation organization is prevalent in rural China.[33] In fact, it is not uncommon for left-behind children to see their parents only once or twice a year or even less.[34]

When family needs arise that require migrants to return, wives are more inclined to return than their husbands. This is especially the case when the couple's children are young or when school-age children need supervision and care, which once again reflects the persistent gender norms about women as nurturers.[35] Once one of the spouses returns, the intergenerational division of labor shifts back to the gender division of labor, illustrating migrants' flexibility and fluidity in household organization and arrangement but also the persistence of gender hierarchy. A woman who has a young child shares her aspiration:

> I wish that I had income that I could decide how to use, and that I sat at the dinner table with my family. I would very much like to go out for migrant work after my child gets older. Right now I can't because I need to take care of the child.[36]

Transactional Marriage and the Rural House

While women's increased mobility signals changes in the gender division of labor that enable more rural Chinese to access urban income opportunities, it is questionable if such changes have fostered fundamental shifts in gender norms and hierarchy. The persistence of transactional marriages and how they are manifested by rural houses suggest that such norms and hierarchy show no signs of weakening.

Despite Maoist policies that increased women's labor force participation, age-old traditions that undermine women's status remain strong in China. Gender inequalities in education and the labor market remain large.[37] The belief that marriage defines women's "happiness" (*xingfu* 幸福) is prevalent, especially in the countryside.[38] Most rural women have few means other than marriage to escape poverty and achieve upward mobility.[39] Traditionally, hypergamy—moving up through marriage—is expected of and has been pursued by women in China.[40]

In Chinese villages traditionally dominated by households sharing the same lineage, village exogamy is necessary for avoiding kin marriages and for natal families to diversify risks and enlarge networks.[41] For thousands of years, rural women have been encouraged to marry men in nearby villages. This form of traditional marriage migration occurs over short distances.[42] A survey in the late 1980s found that most rural marriages did not exceed a 25 km (15-mile) radius.[43]

Not unlike many other parts of the world, the mate-selection process in China has been, and still is, pragmatic and transactional. Specifically, it involves evaluation of a potential spouse's attributes (*tiaojian* 条件), such as age, education, occupation, income and economic ability, physical characteristics (e.g., height and appearance), health, class, personality, family background and resources.[44] Attributes can also be functions of specific political economic contexts. During the Maoist collective period, for example, former landlords connoted bad class origins for marriage, and Communist Party membership was considered a good attribute.[45] Attribute matching centers on the relative similarity in status between the prospective spouses, subject to the hypergamy principle, which stipulates that husbands should be somewhat "superior" to wives in terms of age, height, education and occupation.[46] It is strongly and widely believed that marriages involving households with similar socioeconomic statuses ("matching doors" or *mendang hudui* 门当户对) will be stable and successful.

Attribute trade-off refers to the ways in which a desirable attribute can compensate for or offset a less desirable attribute and vice versa. For example, a prospective husband's older age may be offset by his wealth. Trade-off can also facilitate matching if a desirable (or less desirable) attribute of a prospective spouse is offset by another desirable (or less desirable) attribute of the other spouse. For example, a prospective husband's lack of education may be offset by the prospective wife's less desirable physical appearance. The emphasis on attribute matching and trade-off explains the need for "introducers" (*jieshaoren* 介绍人) or matchmakers (*meiren* 媒人),[47] whose role is to bring together prospective spouses who are fitting (*dengdui* 登对) to one another. While the younger generations do not rely on matchmakers as much as their parents and grandparents, the formality of having a go-between remains a required step of the marriage process, as illustrated by this man who got married at 29:

> I met my wife in 1995, in Shanghai. We are from the same village, but we hadn't met each other before. After we met, and after having a *jieshaoren* who formally introduced us to each other, we got married in 1997.[48]

For a rural woman who has few options other than marriage to improve her socioeconomic status, the socioeconomic status and potential of the prospective husband's village and family are important factors in marriage decision-making.[49] Hence, spatial hypergamy has always existed in China. Given that decollectivization of the rural economy since the 1980s has removed the commune shelter and has increased household opportunities as well as risks, it is likely that calculations of costs and benefits of decisions such as marriage are more elaborate than previously.[50] The prospective husband's economic status is an even more crucial consideration for marriage than in pre-reform years. A tangible indicator of such status is the size and condition of a house, either newly built for a son of marriageable age or built to be inherited by the son in the future.

The patrilocal exogamy tradition, where the wife moves out of the natal family to join the husband's family, is rooted in marriage being practiced as a contract negotiated between two families involving the transfer of rights over women and their production and reproduction. In this connection, the prospective husband's economic capacity becomes important. A new house or an expanded house—often judged in terms of size—is one of the determining factors of men's competitiveness in the marriage market. Due in part to the draconian birth control policy in place since the late 1970s, the lopsided sex ratio in China (more men than women) has become even more skewed.[51] Accordingly, the marriage market has stiffened for men and is even more competitive in the countryside and in poorer parts of the country. A new and large house increases a son's competitiveness in the marriage market and is a strategy especially appealing to rural households who have access to significant or sustained remittances. Accordingly, Chinese villages that have sent out migrant workers typically have both new and large houses as well as smaller and older houses, the former reflecting positive outcomes from migrant work and the latter associated with non-migrant households or households with limited remittances (Figures 17.3 and 17.4). In fact, parents often feel responsible for building a new house or expanding and renovating an existing house in preparation for their sons' marriages, which

Figure 17.3 Entrance of an Old House in the Countryside
Source: © Cindy Fan, 2012.

Migration, Gender and Space in China

Figure 17.4 A New House in Rural China
Source: © Cindy Fan, 2012.

in turn motivates the pursuit of migrant work and remittances to fund house projects, as illustrated by this father in Anhui:

> The children are growing up in front of our eyes. I had only a straw house with three rooms. Under those circumstances, it would be difficult for my sons to find wives, let alone to get rich. . . . I had no choice but to leave the village for migrant work.[52]

Another father who has two sons and two daughters plans to leave his houses to the sons:

> I have three houses. One is a straw house built in the early 1960s; it's worth nothing. This year I built two new houses—all funded from migrant work—to be used by my two sons when they get married.

Notably, however, it is not uncommon to find that the insides of large houses are quite empty, both in terms of furniture and actual usage (Figure 17.5). This is probably because during much of the year migrants are not living in the village, and because the house size is motivated more by marriage competitiveness than by household need. The empty spaces in such houses contrast starkly with the high-density living condition of migrants in cities. They tolerate the tight spaces, knowing that urban living is temporary and that their houses back home are much more spacious. Such calculus signifies

313

Figure 17.5 The Living Room of a New House in Rural China
Source: © Cindy Fan, 2012.

migrants' insecurity about the city, which motivates them to maintain roots in the countryside. At the same time, the prevalence of large houses underscores the persistence of patrilocal and transactional marriage traditions and of gender norms and hierarchy.

Summary and Conclusion

The massive rural to urban migration starting in the 1980s has transformed China's social and economic landscape. While migrant workers have fueled industrialization, urbanization and export growth at skyrocketing rates, Chinese rural families have experienced unprecedented changes. Migrants straddle and circulate between the city and countryside, accessing urban work opportunities while protecting and maintaining rural land, housing and economic resources. Such a strategy, which causes the rural household to split between two or more places, reflects not only a response to the restrictive *hukou* system but also migrants' calculus about the sustainability and viability of the city versus the countryside as their future permanent home.

Gender is a key component of the rural households' spatial strategies, which in turn reinforce the persistence of gender norms and hierarchy in rural China. Marriage allows men to pursue migrant work because wives who are left behind will be responsible for caregiving, farming, household chores and other rural activities. Such gender division of labor is a manifestation of age-old inside-outside social and spatial spheres ascribed differently to men and women. Left-behind wives' loneliness and heavy workloads likely affect their mental and physical health adversely, despite the improved standard of living brought about by remittances. While left-behind wives have taken on more central roles in rural economic activities, there is little evidence that deeply rooted gender hierarchies have changed as a result. Intergenerational division of labor allows both the husband and wife to pursue migrant work, leaving behind their children to be raised by grandparents. Women continue to be identified with nurturing duties, however, and are the ones who return when caregiving needs arise.

Migrants' plans to eventually return to the countryside are vividly illustrated by their use of remittances to build, expand and renovate houses. Houses built this way tend to be large, an ironic outcome given that for much of the year migrants are away and do not stay in the houses. The explanation is once again gendered; namely, a large house increases a son's competitiveness in the marriage market. Thus, the persistence of transactional marriages and patrilocal exogamy is expressed spatially through practices of house-building, which in turn motivates migrant work for the remittances it generates.

All in all, a gender lens is crucial for understanding how migration shapes spaces in rural China and spatial practices of Chinese rural households. Household-splitting, house-building and gender and intergenerational divisions of labor all point to the persistence of traditional gender norms, ideology and hierarchy, which have proven to be far more stubborn than Mao's "half the sky" intervention.

Notes

1. NBS 2015; Zheng 2013; Zhu, Xiao, and Lin 2015.
2. NBS 2015.
3. Jiang 2016, 23; Wu 2016.
4. See e.g., Alexander and Chan 2004; Chan and Buckingham 2008; Solinger 1999; Wang 2005; Zhang and Treiman 2013.
5. See e.g., Cai and Xu 2009; Chen and Fan 2016; Fan 2011; Yue et al. 2010; Zhu and Chen 2010.
6. Chen and Fan 2016.
7. Fan and Wang 2008; Tan 2007; Xu 2010; Zhu 2007.
8. Duan and Ma 2011.
9. Chunyu, Liang, and Wu 2013; Duan and Ma 2011; Wang and Fan 2006.
10. Shi and Kennedy 2016.
11. Lu 1997.
12. Mann 2000.
13. Entwisle and Henderson 2000, 298; Hershatter 2000.
14. Jacka 2006.
15. Fan 2016.
16. Li 2015.
17. Xiang 2007.
18. Jacka 2012; Li 2015; Xu 2009.
19. Davin 1998; Jacka 2006.
20. Meng and Ye 2015.
21. Fan 2015. Quotes in the rest of the paper are all from surveys in Sichuan and Anhui provinces conducted during the Spring Festivals of 1995, 2005 and 2009, with supplementary visits in 2012. The surveys were part of a joint project with Renmin University of China and included in-depth interviews with 300 households in 12 villages (Fan 2015).
22. Xu 2009.
23. Jacka 2012.
24. Wakefield 1998.
25. ACFTU 2010; Wang, Liu, and Lou 2011; Yue et al. 2010.
26. Fan and Chen 2013; Xiang 2007; Ye and Pan 2008, 301.
27. Fan and Wang 2008; Fan, Sun, and Zheng 2011.
28. Duan 2015; He and An 2015; Ma and Zhou 2008; Xiang 2007.
29. CLB 2016; Davin 2014.
30. CLB 2016.
31. CLB 2016; Davin 2014.
32. Cong and Silverstein 2011; Du et al. 2004; Guo, Aranda, and Silverstein 2009.
33. Lu 2012; Tan 2011; Ye and Murray 2005.

C. Cindy Fan

34. CLB 2016.
35. Wu and Hu 2015; Zheng 2013.
36. See note 21.
37. Cheng 2009; Dasgupta, Matsumoto, and Xia 2016.
38. Wang and Hu 1996, 287.
39. Honig and Hershatter 1988; Wang 2000.
40. Croll 1981, 97.
41. Davin 1999, 141–2; Potter and Potter 1990, 205.
42. Wang and Hu 1996, 283; Zhuang and Zhang 1996.
43. Renmin Ribao 1989, 4.
44. Fan 2000.
45. Croll 1981, 86–93.
46. Lavely 1991; Yang 1994, 220.
47. Croll 1981.
48. See note 21.
49. Li and Lavely 1995.
50. Han and Eades 1995.
51. Cai and Lavely 2003; Shi and Kennedy 2016.
52. See note 21.

References

ACFTU. 2010. "Guanyu Xinshengdai Nongmindong De Yanjiu Baogao" ["A Research Report on the New Generation Migrant Workers"]. http://news.xinhuanet.com/politics/2010-06/21/c_12240721.htm, accessed August 29, 2016.

Alexander, Peter, and Anita Chan. 2004. "Does China Have an Apartheid Pass System?" *Journal of Ethnic and Migration Studies* 30(4): 609–629.

Cai, Ling, and Chuqiao Xu. 2009. "Nongmingong Liucheng Yiyuan Yingxiang Yinsu Fenxi: Jiyu Wuhan Shi De Shizheng Diaocha" ["A Study on Affecting Factors of Migrant Workers' Decision for Settlement: A Case Study in Wuhan City"]. *Zhongguo Nongye Daxue Xuebao (Journal of China Agricultural University)* 26(1): 40–46.

Cai, Yong, and William Lavely. 2003. "China's Missing Girls: Numerical Estimates and Effects on Population Growth." *China Review* 3(2): 13–29.

Chan, Kam Wing, and Will Buckingham. 2008. "Is China Abolishing the *Hukou* System?" *China Quarterly* 195: 582–606.

Chen, Chuanbo, and C. Cindy Fan. 2016. "China's Hukou Puzzle: Why Don't Rural Migrants Want Urban Hukou?" *China Review* 16(3): 9–39.

Cheng, Henan. 2009. "Inequality in Basic Education in China: A Comprehensive Review." *International Journal of Educational Policies* 3(2): 81–106.

Chunyu, Miao David, Zai Liang, and Yingfeng Wu. 2013. "Interprovincial Return Migration in China: Individual and Contextual Determinants in Sichuan Province in the 1990s." *Environment and Planning A* 45(12): 2939–2958.

CLB. 2016. "Migrant Workers and their Children." *China Labour Bulletin*. www.clb.org.hk/content/migrant-workers-and-their-children, accessed August 18, 2016.

Cong, Zhen, and Merril Silverstein. 2011. "Intergenerational Exchange Between Parents and Migrant and Non-migrant Sons in Rural China." *Journal of Marriage and Family* 73(1): 93–104.

Croll, Elisabeth. 1981. *The Politics of Marriage in Contemporary China*. Cambridge: Cambridge University Press.

Dasgupta, Sukti, Makiko Matsumoto, and Cuntao Xia. 2016. "Women and Men in China's Labour Market: Is Inequality on the Rise?" In *Transformation of Women at Work in Asia: An Unfinished Development Agenda*, edited by S. Dasgupta and S. S. Verick, 259–294. Geneva: ILO.

Davin, Delia. 1998. "Gender and Migration in China." In *Village Inc.: Chinese Rural Society in the 1990s*, edited by F. Christiansen and J. Zhang, 230–240. Surrey: Curzon Press.

Davin, Delia. 1999. *Internal Migration in Contemporary China*. London: Macmillan Press.

Davin, Delia. 2014. "Demographic and Social Impact of Internal Migration in China." In *Analysing China's Population: Social Change in a New Demographic Era*, edited by I. Attane and B. Gu, 139–162. Dordrecht: Springer.

Du, Peng, Z. Ding, Q. Li, and J. Gui. 2004. "Nongcun Zinv Waichu Wugong Dui Liushou Laoren De Yingxiang" ["The Impact of Children's Migration on the Elderly Who Stay Behind"]. *Renkou yuanjiu (Population Research)* 28: 44–52.

Duan, Chengrong. 2015. "Woguo Liudong Ertong He Liushou Ertong De Jige Jiben Wenti" ["Several Basic Issues About China's Left-Behind and Migrant Children"]. In *Zhongguo Nongcun Liushou Renkou – Fansi Fazhanzhuyi De Shijiao (Left-Behind Population in Rural China: A Critique of Developmentalism)*, edited by J. Ye, H. Wu and X. Meng, 3–11. Beijing, China: Shehui kexue wenxian chubanshe (Social Science Academic Press).

Duan, Chengrong, and Xueyang Ma. 2011. "Dangqian Woguo Xinshengdai Nongmingong De Xin Zhuang-kuang" ["A Study on the New Situation of the Younger Generation of Farmer-Turned Migrant"]. *Renkou yu jingji (Population & Economics)* 4: 16–22.

Entwisle, Barbara, and Gail E. Henderson. 2000. "Conclusion: Re-drawing Boundaries." In *Re-drawing Boundaries: Work, Households, and Gender in China*, edited by B. Entwisle and G. E. Henderson, 295–303. Berkeley: University of California Press.

Fan, C. Cindy. 2000. "Migration and Gender in China." In *China Review 2000*, edited by C.M. Lau and J. Shen, 423–454. Hong Kong: Chinese University Press.

Fan, C. Cindy. 2011. "Settlement Intention and Split Households: Findings From a Survey of Migrants in Beijing's Urban Villages." *China Review* 11(2): 11–42.

Fan, C. Cindy. 2015. "Migration, Remittances, and Social and Spatial Organization of Rural Households in China." In *Transnational Labour Migration, Remittances and the Changing Family in Asia*, edited by B. Yeoh and L. A. Hoang, 194–226. Basingstoke: Palgrave Macmillan.

Fan, C. Cindy. 2016. "Household Splitting of Rural Migrants in Beijing, China." *Trialog: A Journal for Planning and Building in a Global Context* 116/117: 19–24.

Fan, C. Cindy, and ChenChen. 2013. "The New-Generation Migrant Workers in China." In *Transient Urbanism: Migrants and Urbanized Villages in Chinese Cities*, edited by F. Wu, F. Zhang and C. Webster, 17–35. London: Routledge.

Fan, C. Cindy, Mingjie Sun, and Siqi Zheng. 2011. "Migration and Split Households: A Comparison of Sole, Couple, and Family Migrants in Beijing, China." *Environment and Planning A* 43: 2164–2185.

Fan, C. Cindy, and Wenfei Wang. 2008. "The Household as Security: Strategies of Rural-Urban Migrants in China." In *Migration and Social Protection in China*, edited by R. Smyth and I. Nielsen, 205–243. Singapore: World Scientific.

Guo, Man, Maria P. Aranda, and Merril Silverstein. 2009. "The Impact of Out-Migration on the Inter-Generational Support and Psychological Wellbeing of Older Adults in Rural China." *Ageing & Society* 29: 1085–1104.

Han, Min, and Jeremy Seymour Eades. 1995. "Brides, Bachelors and Brokers: The Marriage Market in Rural Anhui in an Era of Economic Reform." *Modern Asian Studies* 29(4): 841–869.

He, Congzhi, and Miao An. 2015. "Fazhan Huayuxia Zhongguo Nongcun Liushou Laoren De Fuli Zhi 'Tong'" ["The Pain of China's Rural Left-Behind Elderly's Welfare in the Development Discourse"]. In *Zhongguo Nongcun Liushou Renkou – Fansi Fazhanzhuyi De Shijiao (Left-Behind Population in Rural China: A Critique of Developmentalism)*, edited by J. Ye, H. Wu and X. Meng, 213–239. Beijing, China: Shehui kexue wenxian chubanshe (Social Science Academic Press).

Hershatter, Gail. 2000. "Local Meanings of Gender and Work in Rural Shaanxi in the 1950s." In *Re-drawing Boundaries: Work, Household, and Gender in China*, edited by B. Entwisle and G. Henderson, 79–96. Berkeley: University of California Press.

Honig, Emily, and Gail Hershatter. 1988. *Marriage*. Stanford, CA: Stanford University Press.

Jacka, Tamara. 2006. *Rural Women in Contemporary China: Gender, Migration, and Social Change*. Armonk, NY: M. E. Sharpe.

Jacka, Tamara. 2012. "Migration, Householding and the Well-Being of Left-Behind Women in Rural Ningxia." *China Journal* 67: 1–21.

Jiang, Yihua. 2016. *Renkou Qianyi Yu Xianyu Chengzhenhua Yanjiu (Research on Population Migration and County Urbanization)*. Beijing: Jingji kexue chubanshe.

Lavely, William. 1991. *Marriage and Mobility Under Rural Collectivization*. Berkeley: University of California Press.

Li, Jiang Hong, and William Lavely. 1995. "Rural Economy and Male Marriage in China: Jurong, Jiangsu 1933." *Journal of Family History* 20(3): 289–306.

Li, Qiang. 2015. "Zhangfu Waichu Dui Liushou Funv Shenti Jiankang De Yingxiang" ["The Impacts of Husbands' Labor Migration on the Health of Left-Behind Wives"]. In *Zhongguo Nongcun Liushou Renkou: Fansi Fazhan Zhuyi De Shijiao (Left-Behind Population in Rural China: A Critique of Developmentalism)*, edited by J. Ye, H. Wu and X. Meng, 161–177. Beijing: Shehui kexue wenxian chubanshe (Social Science Academic Press).

Lu, Li. 1997. "Funu Jingji Diwei Yu Funu Renli Ziben Guanxi De Shizhen Yanjiu" ["Women's Economic Status and their Human Capital in China"]. *Renkou yanjiu (Population Research)* 21(2): 50–54.

Lu, Yao. 2012. "Education of Children Left Behind in Rural China." *Journal of Marriage and Family* 74: 328–341.

Ma, Zhongdong, and Guowei Zhou. 2008. "Isolated or Compensated: Impact of Temporary Migration of Adult Children on the Wellbeing of the Elderly in Rural China." *Geographical Review of Japan* 81(1): 47–59.

Mann, Susan. 2000. "Work and Household in Chinese Culture: Historical Perspectives." In *Re-drawing Boundaries: Work, Household, and Gender in China*, edited by B. Entwisle and G. E. Henderson, 15–32. Berkeley: University of California Press.

Meng, Xiangdan, and Jingzhong Ye. 2015. "Nongye Nvxinghua Dui Jiating Xingbie Guanxi De Yingxiang" ["The Impacts of Agricultural Feminization on Gender Relations Within the Family"]. In *Zhongguo Nongcun Liushou Renkou: Fansi Fazhan Zhuyi De Shijiao (Left-Behind Population in Rural China: A Critique of Developmentalism)*, edited by J. Ye, H. Wu and X. Meng, 192–209. Beijing: Shehui kexue wenxian chubanshe (Social Science Academic Press).

NBS. 2015. *China Statistical Yearbook 2015*. Beijing: China Statistics Press.

Potter, Sulamith Heins, and Jack M. Potter. 1990. *China's Peasants: The Anthropology of a Revolution*. Cambridge: Cambridge University Press.

Renmin Ribao. 1989. "Duoshu Nongmin Tonghunchuan Bu Chaoguo 25 Gongli" ["Most Rural People's Marriage Boundaries Are Less than 25 km"]. *Renmin Ribao (People's Daily)*, August 11.

Shi, Yaojiang, and John James Kennedy. 2016. "Delayed Registration and Identifying the 'Missing Girls' in China." *China Quarterly* 228: 1018–1038.

Solinger, Dorothy J. 1999. *Contesting Citizenship in Urban China: Peasant Migrants, the State, and the Logic of the Market*. Berkeley: University of California Press.

Tan, Kejian. 2007. "Nongmingong Chengshi Dingju Yingxiang Yinsu Yanjiu" ["A Study on Factors Affecting Migrant Workers' Settlement Intention in the City"]. *Zhongguo shanxisheng dangwei dangxiao xuebao (Academic Journal of Shanxi Provincial Committee Party School of Communist Party of China)* 30(2): 46–48.

Tan, Shen. 2011. "Zhongguo Liushou Ertong Yanjiu Shuping" ["Left-Behind Children in Rural China: A Research Review"]. *Zhongguo shehui kexue (China Social Sciences)* 1: 138–150.

Wakefield, David. 1998. *Fenjia: Household Division and Inheritance in Qing and Republican China*. Honolulu: University of Hawaii Press.

Wang, Dianli, Baojun Liu, and Suping Lou. 2011. "Xinshengdai Nongmingong De Chengshi Rongru—Kuangjia Jiangou Yu Diaoyan Fenxi" ["New Generation of Migrant Workers Integrating Into Urban Society—Frame Construction and Survey Analysis"]. *Zhongguo xingzheng guanli (Chinese Public Administration)* 2: 111–115.

Wang, Fei-Ling. 2005. *Organizing Through Division and Exclusion: China's Hukou System*. Stanford, CA: Stanford University Press.

Wang, Feng. 2000. "Gendered Migration and the Migration of Genders in Contemporary China." In *Re-drawing Boundaries: Work, Household, and Gender in China*, edited by B. Entwisle and G. Henderson, 231–242. Berkeley: University of California Press.

Wang, Jianmin, and Qi Hu, eds. 1996. *Zhongguo Liudong Renkou (China's Floating Population)*. Shanghai: Shanghai Caijing Daxue Chubanshe (Shanghai Finance University Press).

Wang, Wenfei Winnie, and C. Cindy Fan. 2006. "Success or Failure: Selectivity and Reasons of Return Migration in Sichuan and Anhui, China." *Environment and Planning A* 38: 939–958.

Wu, Guoxiu. 2016. "Gov't Report: China's Urbanization Level Reached 56.1%." http://landportal.info/news/2016/04/govt-report-chinas-urbanization-level-reached-561, accessed August 28.

Wu, Huifang, and Penghui Hu. 2015. "Funv Jiating Zhaoliao Zeren Guhua Yu Nongcun Xingbie Guanxi Bianqian ["The Firming Up of Women's Family Care-Giving Responsibilities and the Changes of Rural Gender Relations"]. In *Zhongguo Nongcun Liushou Renkou: Fansi Fazhan Zhuyi De Shijiao (Left-Behind Population in Rural China: A Critique of Developmentalism)*, edited by J. Ye, H. Wu and X. Meng, 178–191. Beijing: Shehui kexue wenxian chubanshe (Social Science Academic Press).

Xiang, Biao. 2007. "How Far Are the Left-Behind Left Behind? A Preliminary Study in Rural China." *Population, Place and Space* 13(3): 179–191.

Xu, Chuanxin. 2009. "Nongcun Liushou Funu Yanjiu: Huigu Yu Qianzhan" ["Studies on Left-Behind Women in Rural Areas: Review and Prospects"]. *Renkou yu fazhan (Population and Development)* 15(6): 55–56.

Xu, Tianceng. 2010. "Nongmingong Dingjuxing Qianyi De Yiyuan Fenxi: Jiyu Beijing Diqu De Shizheng Yanjiu" ["An Analysis on Migrant Workers' Settlement Intention: A Case Study of Beijing"]. *Jingji kexue (Economic Science)* (3): 120–128.

Yang, Yunyan. 1994. *Zhongguo Renkou Qianyi Yu Fanzhan Di Changqi Zhanlue (Long Term Strategies of Population Migration and Development in China)*. Wuhan: Wuhan chubanshe.

Ye, Jingzhong, and James R. Murray. 2005. *Guanzhu Liushou Ertong (Left-Behind Children in Rural China)*. Beijing: Social Science Academic Press.

Ye, Jingzhong, and Lu Pan. 2008. *Beiyang Tongnian: Zhongguo Nongcui Liushou Ertong (Differentiated Childhoods: Children Left Behind in Rural China)*. Beijing: Shehui kexue wenxian chubanshe (Social Science Academic Press).

Yue, Zhongshan, Shuzhuo Li, Marcus Feldman, and Haifeng Du. 2010. "Floating Choices: A Generational Perspective on Intentions of Rural-Urban Migrants in China." *Environment and Planning A* 42: 545–562.

Zhang, Zhuoni, and Donald J. Treiman. 2013. "Social Origins, *Hukou* Conversion, and the Wellbeing of Urban Residents in Contemporary China." *Social Science Research* 42: 71–89.

Zheng, Zhenzhen. 2013. "Zhongguo Liudong Renkou Bianqian Ji Zhengce Qishi" ["Change of Floating Population in China and Its Policy Implications"]. *Chinese Journal of Population Science* 33(1): 36–45.

Zhu, Yu. 2007. "China's Floating Population and their Settlement Intention in the Cities: Beyond the *Hukou* Reform." *Habitat International* 31(1): 65–76.

Zhu, Yu, and Wenzhe Chen. 2010. "The Settlement Intention of China's Floating Population in the Cities: Recent Changes and Multifaceted Individual-Level Determinants." *Population, Space and Place* 16: 253–267.

Zhu, Yu, Baoyu Xiao, and Liyue Lin. 2015. "Changing Spatial and Temporal Patterns of China's Floating Population: Findings From the 2010 and 2000 Censuses." In *Handbook of Chinese Migration: Identity and Wellbeing*, edited by R. R. Iredale and F. Guo, 48–70. Cheltenham: Edward Elgar.

Zhuang, Shanyu, and Maolin Zhang. 1996. "Chabie Renkou Qianyi Yu Xingbie Goucheng Diqu Chayi De Kuodahua" ["Migration Between Different Regions and the Enlargement of Regional Sex Composition"]. *Renkou xuekan (Population Journal)* 1: 3–10.

18

Migrant Women Walking Down the Cheap Road

Modernization and Being Fashionable in Shanghai

Penn Tsz Ting Ip

If Modernity and Progress reside in the city, and if the city monopolizes modern culture, then the countryside is the city's emaciated other.[1]

Introduction

Tu (土)? It is just like how other people say: you dress like this, you must have just arrived here [Shanghai] from *xiangxia* (乡下 "countryside"). To give an impression of *tu* is that you are coming from *xiangxia*. It is because people in *xiangxia* dress more *tu*. Actually, I do not agree that they are *tu*. It is just that people dress more comfortably there. The fact is that people in the cities do dress the same.

Elaine, 28-year-old dessert shop waitress, Hubei

Under the Economic Reform and the Open Door Policy announced by Deng Xiaoping in 1978, China put great effort into modernization, resulting in drastic economic growth, which has formed the socioeconomic spatial politics between rural and urban China.[2] Through the implementation of the nationwide *hukou* (户口 "household registration") system, China is divided into rural and urban populations[3] upon which different social values are imposed: urban citizens become the center of modern culture and rural people are assigned to the lower class.[4] The discourse of modernity in the post-Mao era, as Yan Hairong comments, "produces the countryside both materially and ideologically as a wasteland stripped of state investment and inhabited by moribund tradition, with the two dimensions mutually reinforcing each other."[5] Addressing rural/urban politics, Yan argues that "the post-Mao culture of modernity is an epistemic violence against the countryside that spectralizes the rural in both material and symbolic practices"; therefore, "young migrant women's pursuit of a modern subjectivity, situated in the culture of modernity produced by post-Mao development, has to be understood in the context of a reconfigured rural–urban relationship in China's structured political economy."[6] Within this discursive context, the "countryside cannot function as the locus of a modern identity for rural young women."[7] Thus, rural women may grow to despise the countryside's backwardness, and desire a more modern, fashionable city lifestyle.

This grand narrative of a rural/urban dichotomy, brought about by the post-Mao state, is transforming under the political rule of Xi Jinping, the seventh president of the People's Republic of

China (PRC).[8] Framed as "The Chinese Dream" by Xi's government, the nation expresses its desire for continuous prosperity that must be executed by developing rural and inland China, in conjunction with the integration of individuals' aspirations, including all citizens from rural and urban regions, to achieve personal wellbeing.[9] Therefore, the National New-Type Urbanization Plan (2014–2020) has been put into effect,[10] together with the Ministry of Housing and Urban-Rural Development (MOHURD),[11] to facilitate urbanization and modernization in rural China.[12] Nonetheless, Wanning Sun reminds us:

> A different China, consisting of myriad marginalized social groups, remains largely hidden. The members of these groups, each with the modest dream of greater equality and less discrimination in their lives, cast a disquieting shadow over the vision of a rejuvenated China with common prosperity that is the stuff of President Xi Jinping's "China Dream."[13]

Focusing on one of these marginalized social groups, this chapter questions how and to what extent gendered "subalterns"[14]—rural migrant women—gain access to the Chinese Dream. To answer this, I look at the lives of rural migrant women as providing a response to the impetus for modernization and the national political goal.

As mentioned by Elaine, one of my research participants from rural China, the way in which people from the countryside dress is seemingly "the same" as the way those from the global city (Shanghai)[15] dress. In this way, the negative attachment of *tu*, literally earth, soil, or clay, which is imposed on rural bodies to signify a sense of backwardness in post-reform China, can be erased through embracing urban fashion. Fashion is a promising site to negotiate the conceptual distinctions between rural and urban, as well as the material culture of modernization. Accordingly, this chapter studies the lives of rural migrant women who, in the process of migration, are negotiating definitions of the "Chinese modern woman." I focus on the ways these women are interpellated as *potentially* modern and fashionable at a specific site, the so-called "Cheap Road" in Shanghai. The *Qipulu* Clothing Wholesale Market, known as the Cheap Road by foreigners, is a wholesale district targeting fashion buyers from Shanghai and nearby regions. Having begun as a small shopping street in 1978,[16] the Cheap Road has become a symbol of modernization reflecting the development of the market economy and witnessing the fashion trends of post-reform China. Following Miller's *A Theory of Shopping*,[17] shopping is read as not merely a form of hedonism or materialism and should not be extrapolated to the negation of consumerism and global capitalism.[18] Rather, Miller argues, "shopping is not just approached as a thing in itself. It is found to be a means to uncover, through the close observation of people's practices, something about their relationship."[19] I aim to study fashion shopping and its nuances, because fashion can allow "subjective thoughts and existences to take on greater autonomy."[20] This chapter suggests that understanding fashion consumption makes a vital contribution to migration studies because it exemplifies the dilemmas of identity and subjectivity as faced by migrant women.

(Un)fashionability of Rural Migrant Women

Under the *hukou* system, rural migrant workers are labeled as *nongmingong* (农民工 "peasant-worker"), which "refers to a group of industrial and service workers with rural *hukou*."[21] *Nongmingong* work "in urban jobs (and chiefly in towns and cities), yet legally they are not considered urban workers."[22] Moreover, the rural labor workforce is gendered;[23] for instance, the young female workers in the factories are known as *dagongmei* (打工妹—literally, "working sister" or "working girl").[24] These female workers are marginalized in the cities due to their rural *hukou* and their alleged low *suzhi* (素质 "quality").[25] The political significance of geography intricately attaches to rural migrant women's bodies and affects their lives, yet little has been done to capture the impact of fashion or to make sense of how rural migrant women transform themselves to cope with these unequal social circumstances. How does modernization manipulate and shape the bodies and looks of migrant women?

Historically, fashion has been adopted as a tool to shape female subjectivity in China. During the Republican period (1912–49), intellectuals shed light on the definition of the ideal *xin nüxing* (新女性 "new woman")[26] as part of the political agenda for modernization.[27] Being able to "speak a little English" and wear "flamboyant Western clothes" became the image of "modern woman."[28] In the Mao era (1949–76), women were advised to wear gender-neutral outfits to mobilize the female population to join the workforce.[29] This erasure of femininity came to an end in the post-Mao period because the Reform State encouraged the beauty economy.[30] As Xiaoping Li states, "Since then, both the meaning of 'fashion' and clothing styles have undergone considerable transformation in accordance with larger societal changes" because "a high fashion modeled on elite fashion in capitalist consumer culture has come to dominate."[31] Hence, urban women have to face the challenge to be fashionable. Matthew Chew's study of *qipao* (旗袍) explains, "Fashionable yet not outlandish, sexy yet subdued, *qipaos* represent one of the solutions in China's present fashion market that alleviates urban women's fashion dilemma."[32] While urban women struggle for a balance between socio-moral pressures and global fashion,[33] rural migrant women come to the city and feel the urge to transform themselves by embracing modern femininity.[34]

As Lisal Rofel proposes, "modernity persists as an imaginary and continuously shifting site of global/local claims, commitments, and knowledge, forged within uneven dialogues about the place of those who move in and out of categories of otherness."[35] Generally, modernity "assumes a noncontinuous break with what it constructs as the irrationalities of tradition."[36] In China, rural migrants' imaginaries of modernity are strongly attached to two contradictory conceptions: *tu* and *xiandai* (现代—literally, "modern"). As shared by Xiaomei, a 16-year-old salesperson from Jiangxi working in a fashion shop on the Cheap Road, the antonym of *tu* is *xiandai*. She clarified that *xiandai* is about the cities, and the Cheap Road is "modern" because it is a place that sells *shishang* (时尚 "fashion"). Her understanding of *tu* and *xiandai* reveals the intricate relationship between *tu*, *xiandai*, and *shishang*. In this chapter, I use Rofel's theorization of modernization to study rural migrant women's perceptions of *tu* and *xiandai* and to explore the ways in which modernization seeps into their lives.

Methodology

During fieldwork research conducted between September and December 2014, May and July 2015, and in October 2016, I conducted 88 in-depth interviews with rural migrant women through the "snowball" method, including one shop owner and four salespersons working on the Cheap Road. These research participants, aged 15 to 54 at the time of the interviews, are from different rural regions of China, and mainly work as service workers in Shanghai, in the food and beverage service industry, beauty parlors, and domestic service.

Drawing on my fieldwork data, this chapter first examines the self-narratives of rural migrant women, particularly with regard to their migration experiences, to investigate how they transform themselves in response to imaginaries of the "modern urban woman" in Shanghai. During the in-depth interviews, I asked semi-structured questions, including what the women brought from their hometowns to Shanghai, where they usually shop in the city, and how much they spend on fashion shopping. Additionally, I asked them how they feel when they go back to their hometown. As Miller argues, "[shopping] is found to be a means to uncover, through the close observation of people's practices, something about their relationship."[37] In light of his argument, I examine young migrant women's new "modern" consumer experiences as revealing of their social relationships with Shanghai's cityscapes and the women's hometowns.

Second, the chapter analyzes the ways in which the Cheap Road addresses, through its spatial organization and commercial strategies, rural migrant women's aspiration to become a "modern woman." In her study of advertisements in Republican Shanghai, Barbara Mittler, following Mirzoeff's work, argues that "[v]isual culture used to be seen as a 'distraction from the serious business of text and history' while images can in fact also be seen as a locus of cultural and historical change."[38] This chapter follows Mittler's study to analyze the advertisements and commercial images found on the Cheap Road in relation to emerging imaginaries of the "modern woman."

The third section of this chapter focuses on the "go-along"[39] interview technique with Elaine. Before the go-along, I interviewed her about her fashion-shopping habits. Then, during the two-hour walk with her on the Cheap Road, she led me along her usual route and I video-recorded her commenting on her shopping experiences. Allowing Elaine to follow her usual path, this method enabled me to observe the "social architecture"[40] created by her path. After the go-along, I arranged a one-hour interview with her to inquire how she felt about our walk. Last, I analyze Elaine's fashion style and trace how it has gradually "developed" through shopping, and suggest that by developing their fashion style through shopping, rural migrant women become the "Chinese modern *rural* woman" who must find a point where their identities as migrant women and Shanghai women meet.

The Materiality of the "Modern"

This section studies the narratives of rural migrant women living between rural China and the city to capture the social relationships forged between the rural female migrant identity and "Chinese modern culture" through fashion shopping.

First, it is significant to point out that among all personal belongings, clothes are "undesirable things" for rural migrant women to bring with them from their hometowns. When asked what they brought from their home to Shanghai, their answers are enlightening:

> I do not take clothes [from her rural home]. [Researcher: Why don't you bring clothes?] Basically, I purchase clothes here [Shanghai].
>
> *Miumiu, 26-year-old senior hairstylist, Anhui*

Miumiu is not the only one who does not bring clothes from home. Her junior colleague Vivi shared:

> When I first left [home], I brought only a few clothes for temporary use. Then, I bought new clothes. It is heavy to bring clothes. It is troublesome.
>
> *Vivi, 18-year-old hairstylist apprentice, Anhui*

Although Miumiu and Vivi shared that clothes in Shanghai are more expensive than in their hometowns, they still decided to buy new clothes to avoid the burden of carrying clothes from their home to Shanghai. The reason for this is not only that clothes are "heavy to bring." Miumiu confided:

> I work in the fashion industry as a hairstylist. It is better not to wear or buy clothes from my hometown because those fashion items are more *tu*. If I bring those clothes from home to Shanghai, I would not wear them. It would be a waste.
>
> *Miumiu, 26-year-old senior hairstylist, Anhui*

In Miumiu's case, shopping is done out of need, as clothes from home do not fit well in the urban workplace. It is the need for fashion shopping that gives these female migrants a chance to experience self-transformations.

Second, I explore how rural migrant women's friends and family in their hometowns commented on their new outfits:

> They think I am too fashionable. Therefore, every time I go back home, I wear the most *xiuxian* (休闲 "casual") clothes. Actually, some people are jealous. Although I am not a high-profile

Penn Tsz Ting Ip

person, I want to be more low-profile. My family was poor when I was young. [. . .] Now, people can feel that our condition is getting better. However, I do not want to *xuanfu* (炫富 "flaunting one's wealth"). It is better to be simpler.

Eileen, 31-year-old senior hairstylist, Jiangsu

Eileen joined the beauty service industry 15 years ago, starting as a hairstylist's apprentice without any income. She now earns RMB 10,000 (about $1,455) per month as a senior hairstylist in a high-class salon. The effort she has made in the service industry has helped her to live a better life; however, she decides not to be "too fashionable" in her hometown. Moreover, Pang Yuan shared:

PANG YUAN: One time when I went back home for Chinese New Year, someone said to me, "This is really ugly! Why do you dress like this?"

RESEARCHER: Is it about the clothes you brought from Shanghai?

PANG YUAN: I think they dress weirdly and very *xiangqi* (乡气 "rustic"). However, they think I am very *tu* because what I wear has a lack of colors.

RESEARCH ASSISTANT: Is that black, gray, and white?

PANG YUAN: Yes, exactly! "Can you wear more colors [colorful clothes]? You are so young but dress up so *tu*," they commented. My response was, ok, fine. "I am very fashionable here [in Shanghai], all right?" This is what I thought; however, I didn't say it out loud.

Pang Yuan, 25-year-old hairstylist, Hunan

Because red is the traditional color for New Year celebrations,[41] Pang Yuan's choice of colors is considered unusual by her rural community. Both Pang Yuan's and Eileen's experiences show the responses of their rural communities where their rural peers may not appreciate their new fashion style. Thus, these rural migrant women become dislocated in their hometowns, someone to be gazed upon because a sense of "fashion style" is not only subjective, but also closely linked to history and culture.[42] More importantly, *tu* is not a stable concept—there is a discrepancy between what *tu* is in Shanghai and what *tu* is in the rural communities. In short, both Pang Yuan and Eileen are aware of a certain level of transformation of their bodily images as they become more fashionable, putting them into a position to negotiate the unstable conception *tu*. Significantly, rural migrant women have learned to employ the sense of *tu* to measure the suitability of their rural male counterparts.[43] As Pang Yuan confided, she felt that rural men are less attractive than the men in Shanghai. It is less likely that Shanghai men will want to marry her, however, because of the embedded social hierarchy between urban and rural residents; therefore, she remains single. Thus, rural men are the "emaciated other" for rural migrant women.

Third, *tu* is an adjective that is frequently used by my research participants. Etymologically, the character *tu* denotes earth, soil, or clay. But what is *tu* to rural migrant women? When *tu* refers to nature, why is it used in such a negative way in their conversations? When asked what *tu* is, I collected the following answers:

Perhaps it is a feeling given to others that one has darker skin and dresses less clean. Then it gives an impression of *tu*. It is not wearing very nice clothes and being a bit darker. Then, you are *tu*. Just like this.

Elaine, 28-year-old dessert shop waitress, Hubei

I don't know how to define *tu*. I think it is to look down upon [a person]. How to describe *tu*? It feels that it means people from the countryside.

Dongmei, 17-year-old salesperson at Qipulu, Henan

Tu refers to the ways in which one dresses and talks.

Xiaomei, 16-year-old salesperson at Qipulu, *Jiangxi*

By their definitions, *tu* is similar to "hick" in English, signifying a backwards person from the countryside. Elaine's point about *tu* being about "darker skin" suggests agricultural work exposing one to the sun. When modernization creates imaginaries of the cities as being better than the countryside, *tu* becomes negatively associated with rural bodies. Yet it is more problematic when young rural women come to work in Shanghai, as they are not peasants but workers; some of them do not have the agricultural skills to accurately be called *nongmingong*.[44] As Phoebe, a 21-year-old migrant from Jiangxi shared, she feels more comfortable to be labeled as "Shanghai *wailai wugong*" (上海外来务工—literally, Shanghai migrant worker).

In her research, Zheng Tiantian documented how female migrant hostesses spend large amounts of time and money on hair products and hairstyling to avoid being associated with their rural backgrounds by their customers.[45] As Zheng writes, "According to the hostesses, dirty or unfashionable hair reveals your rural background. They often critically comment on each other's hair, saying, 'That is so hick (土气 *tuqi*)!'"[46, 47] While working in different sectors, my research participants share a similar desire to avoid being connected to their rural backgrounds. Hence, being "modern" is a way to learn how to navigate the city without being looked down upon by the city residents. Therefore, fashionable clothes become an immediate resource used by rural migrant women. To comprehend the commercial images selling rural migrant women the imaginaries of the "Chinese modern woman," the following section will examine the visual culture on the Cheap Road.

Visualizing the "Modern"

Drawing on Mittler's approach to Shanghai's modern advertisements, this section analyzes the spatial organization and commercial strategies found on the Cheap Road in relation to emerging imaginaries of the "modern Chinese woman."

Qipulu Clothing Wholesale Market, aka the "Cheap Road," is located in the former downtown Zhabei district, which emerged as a business district, Jing'an, in 2015. The Cheap Road is situated close to the Bund and to Nanjing East Road, areas known for attracting tourists and business activities. Although the Cheap Road focuses on wholesale business, the fashion shops also sell clothes to retail customers, attracting enormous numbers of tourists and low-income migrants. People like to shop at the Cheap Road not only because goods are sold at wholesale prices, but also because the products are the trendiest.[48] Moreover, transportation to the Cheap Road is extremely convenient, as it is located next to the Tiantong Road Metro Station. Malls have been constructed close to each other along the Cheap Road, and there are now 11 main wholesale market malls (see Figure 18.1). The first time I visited this shopping area, its high density of shops and pedestrians impressed me greatly. Drawing on my observations, I will summarize the three main commercial practices used to advertise imaginaries of the "modern": first, the displaying of goods; second, the branding of shops; and third, advertising through billboards.

Displaying fashion products is the most common practice that shops use to attract customers. Because the shops are so densely arranged in the malls, this makes the visual experience on the Cheap Road very intense. Each mall consists of a basement and four or five floors with hundreds of small shops on each floor. On the Cheap Road, malls have different opening hours: some are open from 5:30 a.m. to 4:30 p.m., and some from 7:00 a.m. to 6:00 p.m. During the periods that salespeople are working on their wholesale orders and are busy packing batches of clothes into big plastic bags, the malls become extremely chaotic and uncomfortable for retail shoppers. Fashion items, plastic bags,

Figure 18.1 "Cheap Road" Street View
Source: © Penn Ip, 2016.

dust, and dirt are scattered on the floors, which even makes it difficult to walk there (see Figure 18.2). Retail customers have to tolerate the mess, but it is not solely a bad experience because they are able to touch the goods and feel their texture, and more importantly to judge their quality and size. Due to the dense spatial arrangement, retail customers not only have intimate contact with the commodities, but also with other customers and workers. In this way, the visual experience is not only intense but also compressed into a crowded space where every step creates a new sensual experience. As Mittler writes, "images, more than texts, offer the opportunity for the communication of excitement, mood and imagination."[49] The image of the densely displayed goods in the malls is the best advertisement, affording customers direct access to the imaginaries of the fashionable world.

On the Cheap Road, the second strategy of shop-branding is not only closely connected to fashion trends and popular culture, but also to history and politics. Many businesses have adopted Korean characters in their shop's names in response to the popularity of Korean culture in China.[50] There is even a Korean-themed shopping mall called S&S Fashion Plaza on the Cheap Road, which was built in 2009. As I observed, the shops on the Cheap Road closely follow trends and sell clothes and accessories that are prominently featured in popular Korean TV dramas and movies, such as *My Love From the Star*[51] and *Descendants of the Sun*.[52] Significantly, while Korean culture is dominant in this shopping district, Japanese culture is almost absent, although Japanese design plays an important role in the global fashion industry.[53] Out of curiosity, I asked my research participant Elaine and she replied:

> After all, Chinese do not like Japanese. On the Cheap Road, I seldom see Japanese products. There are more Korean [products]. They do not say it is Japanese goods. They only say it is *waimao* (外贸 "foreign trade").

Figure 18.2 After Rush Hour on the "Cheap Road"
Source: © Penn Ip, 2016.

Elaine described how Chinese people "do not like Japanese" due to the two World Wars. Japanese goods have become an exceedingly sensitive issue in the country. To avoid the possibility of being attacked if a boycott of Japanese goods occurs again,[54] shop owners do not use Japanese characters as names for their shops. The absence of Japanese culture indicates how the Cheap Road is not only a place for wholesale or retail activities, but also a geopolitical place with a particular political consensus.

Third, the huge billboards displayed on the Cheap Road are a key medium for rural migrant women to access imaginaries of the "Chinese modern woman." The first time I visited the Cheap

Figure 18.3 Large Billboards on the "Cheap Road"
Source: © Penn Ip, 2016.

Road, the large billboards on all sides of the shopping malls caught my attention immediately. The billboards are unlike the advertisements of the luxurious high-class shopping malls in the Jing'an district. Most of the billboards on the Cheap Road have extremely simple visuals: usually only a female model wearing a fashionable outfit is represented (see Figure 18.3). These models are mainly white, with only a few Asians, marketing a global concept of fashion. They are dressed colorfully, with

Figure 18.4 A Billboard Model Poses Seductively on the "Cheap Road"
Source: © Penn Ip, 2016.

stylish attire and modest makeup. More importantly, all of them are posing confidently, and sometimes seductively, giving them a classy, international, and modern charisma (see Figure 18.4). Their poses holding bags, purses or other fashionable accessories, and doing nothing related to the home, distances them from the domestic sphere. Thus, a sense of modern, globalized femininity and confident, public individuality is constructed (see Figure 18.5).

Figure 18.5 Western Models Are Common on the "Cheap Road"
Source: © Penn Ip, 2016.

The billboards are positioned on top of all the shopping malls on the Cheap Road, arranged neatly next to each other. It is unavoidable for customers to see these images as they walk along the Cheap Road because of their size. The impression is similar to the moment of "subconscious reception," as Mittler describes people flipping the pages of a magazine and seeing the advertisements without looking closely at the texts.[55] This "subconscious reception" is a "visual event"—"the interaction of visual sign and viewer."[56] In the case of the billboards, a visual event is created when pedestrians scan the parade of the female models as they walk along the road.

This visual event resembles the worshipping of a goddess. Here, I use the analogy of worshipping the goddess as a ritualized event, extending the meaning of goddess to the "modern" female subjects who are commonly termed *nüshen* (女神 "goddess") in Chinese popular culture. Nowadays, women who meet the aesthetic standard of the popular online terminology, *baifumei* (白富美—literally, white, rich, and beautiful), are commonly named *nüshen*. Hence, the female models on these billboards can be seen as the "modern" *nüshen* that rural women look up to, and from whom they learn how to dress.

In short, imaginaries of the "modern" are being visualized through these three main advertising techniques: a touch of the "modern" is made accessible in which rural migrant female women can feel fashion items before purchasing them; fashion shops reflect the trendiest designs, including a sense of politics and history; and the billboards are a visual event for female customers to worship the "goddesses" of a "modern" heaven. As Mittler writes, "advertising is involved in the 'manipulation of social values and attitudes,' and thus may even be said to fulfill 'the function of art and religion in earlier days'!"[57] The advertisements displayed on the Cheap Road enable rural migrant women to understand modern Shanghai culture. As Rofel reminds us, "modernity persists as an imaginary."[58] The Cheap Road provides an ideal shopping environment for lower-class women to feel, touch, and consume a sense of the "modern," and helps rural migrant women to envision what a "Chinese modern woman" is. However, Mittler warns, "Advertising is a world that is prescriptive and pre-emptive at the same time: it offers impossible dreams and warns of possible realities; it shows and it judges alternatives."[59] Although the dream of being a modern goddess seems within reach for rural migrant women, the reality is perhaps different due to their marginalized status. In the following section, I will follow one of my research participants to explore the extent to which she feels she can transform herself by shopping on the Cheap Road.

The Spatiality of *Tu* and "Modern"

Elaine, a 28-year-old migrant from Hubei, was a hairstylist when I first met her in 2015. Since then she has changed her job and started working in a dessert shop in the hope of one day opening a dessert shop of her own. During our second interview in 2016, she shared with me that she is married and lives together with her husband and her brother and sister-in-law. Previously, she lived with another rural migrant woman, whom I met in 2015. After ten years as a migrant worker in Shanghai, Elaine's life has drastically changed, but she still meets with her former housemate and shops on the Cheap Road with her regularly. Elaine goes shopping on the Cheap Road at least ten times a year. My analysis incorporates both interviews and the go-along method to document Elaine's experiences on the Cheap Road, with a one-hour interview before the go-along and another afterward. Allowing Elaine to follow her usual path, this method enabled me to observe the "social architecture"[60] created by her path and to explore the ways in which the shopping experiences of a female migrant worker are affected by the structures of the malls.

During our walk, Elaine shared her view that people from the countryside are seemingly the same as Shanghai people. Her thoughts about this sameness are worth a closer reading. When asked about how she feels about the Cheap Road before our go-along, Elaine stated:

> *Qipulu* ("The Cheap Road") is one of the clothing wholesale markets in China. It is different from other shopping malls. It is a district for wholesale in Shanghai. Therefore, people from other regions will come to purchase clothes. Many people go to *Qipulu* to *tao* (淘—literally, hunt for nice goods). After *tao*, they will polish the clothes and put them in their boutiques. The clothes will then look finer, and can be sold for different prices.

Elaine's explanation clarifies the nature of the Cheap Road, which targets buyers from retail shops as a wholesale market. Fashionable clothes being sold in Shanghai can be transported to other regions in

China through the retail shops' buyers from different provinces, giving rural consumers a chance to purchase them. This allows rural people to dress the same as established Shanghai residents. As Elaine reminds us, rural people are not *tu*: they only wear simpler attire. Her claim is a rejection of the urban/rural geopolitics that people from the countryside are more backward.

When asked about the difference between the Cheap Road and other shopping malls, Elaine explained the hidden rules that retail consumers have to follow:

> If you purchase clothes in *Qipulu* ("The Cheap Road"), you cannot return them. It's unlike any other shopping mall. Sometimes he/she [shopkeeper] may exchange another item with you, but it is for sure he/she will not refund it.

Beside this rule, Elaine shared that shops offer no discounts, but consumers can bargain with the shopkeepers. There are generally no price tags on products, meaning one has to ask the salesperson or the shop owner for a price. Given these specific circumstances, Elaine has learned to hunt for good quality, low-price products:

> By touching the products, you can feel them and judge if you will feel comfortable when you wear them. You cannot feel it if you buy it in *Taobao* [an online shopping mall]. I do not buy winter clothes in *Taobao* for sure. *Qipulu* is a *shishizaizai de defang* (实实在在的地方 "real place").

While online shopping is extremely popular in present-day China, Elaine considers the Cheap Road as a "real place" for shopping. She spends more than RMB 1,000 (about $145) per shopping trip on the Cheap Road when she finds nice clothes that she likes and that are of good quality. Earning RMB 5,000 per month, Elaine spends roughly RMB 5,000 (about $730) per year on clothes. This pre-go-along interview helped to understand her shopping habits as well as the hidden rules for retail customers.

During our two-hour go-along, Elaine walked with me on the Cheap Road following the route she walks with her friends, and explained to me how she usually shops. Following Elaine's route, we first walked to the Xingwang Clothing Wholesale Market, and she explained that after entering this mall, she and her friend would stay inside, walking to Shanghai Xingwang International Clothing City through the bridge that connects these two malls on the second floor. They have developed a shopping route based on the spatial arrangement of these two malls—each floor consists of different streets, and they walk sequentially from one street to another in order not to miss or repeat any shop. She skips the ground floor because the goods there are the cheapest and are of a similar style and quality to those she can find in her rural hometown. In Elaine's words, clothes on the ground floor are more *tu*. Therefore, they start shopping on the first floor, and then move upstairs to the higher floors where the better products can be found. She explained that because she earns more now than ten years ago, she aims to buy products of better quality even though the price is higher. This practice suggests on the one hand the "sameness" she finds on the ground floor, and on the other hand the "otherness" she desires to acquire in relation to the distinction between *tu* and *xiandai*. In this sense, walking from the ground floor (the cheapest goods), to the fourth floor (the most expensive products), the spatial structure is similar to walking from her rural hometown to Shanghai. This shopping experience thus helps Elaine to understand the distance between *tu* and "modern."

After walking in these two malls, Elaine guided me to the Korean-themed shopping mall. As per her suggestion, we skipped walking through the other shopping malls because they are not part of her usual routine. Then, we went to the last shopping mall, Baima Mansion, which is one of the wholesale shopping malls specifically dedicated to middle-age fashion. There, Elaine wanted to look for clothes for her parents, and eventually we walked to the shop owned by one of my research participants, Qiu Laoban, a 40-year-old migrant woman from Wenzhou. The three of us had a pleasant conversation, which was a new experience for Elaine because she had never chatted with a salesperson or shop owner on the Cheap Road except when she wanted to bargain.

During our post-go-along interview, Elaine shared that her affective experiences as a customer have been modified after working for ten years in Shanghai. Ten years ago, when Elaine first arrived in Shanghai, she found herself *tu*:

> I was young at the time. I felt that I was a bit *tu*. I was fresh. I did not have money to buy nice clothes to dress myself up.

As a new migrant worker ten years ago, Elaine found Shanghai a stunning city where people "looked attractive." She felt the urge to transform herself, especially because she was working in the fashion industry:

> When I was promoted as hairstylist, I had to buy new clothes. It is important to be fashionable and modern to gain trust from clients.

In the service sectors, services workers are required to meet fashionable, modern standards; therefore, workers have to undergo a certain level of physical transformation.[61] Hence, Elaine confided:

> The Cheap Road is a necessity for the working class. It is because people of low income cannot afford shopping for fashion in Shanghai. But the Cheap Road, where we can find cheap fashion, becomes a necessity.

In her opinion, the Cheap Road provides an alternative for the working class to consume low-price fashion. Because the fashion clothes are "cheap," the Cheap Road earns its name and becomes a necessity as highlighted by Elaine.

Rural migrant women's fashion style can be gradually transformed through shopping in Shanghai, yet becoming a "Chinese modern woman" remains challenging. As Elaine shared:

> Clothes in Shanghai are comparatively more fashionable and look more stylish. However, the clothes I buy are not so fashionable. I mainly buy clothes that are more *xiuxian*.

Elaine explained that she likes fashionable clothes, but somehow she cannot handle the *kuazhang* (夸张 "hyperbole") style because her personality does not fit well with it. Elaine explained that when she returns to her rural hometown, she also dresses a bit more casually because it is comfortable. Therefore, she does not have to restyle herself for the rural environment. Yet dressing casually does not mean not being "modern" enough to walk the streets of Shanghai:

> At that time I found that Shanghai women looked attractive. The white-collar women were different than other women here. Now, I feel that Shanghai women are more or less the same, because they wear casual and comfortable clothes.

Her observation of how Shanghai women have changed their fashion style during the past ten years is crucial, because she has learned from these city women that wearing casual and comfortable clothes is a possible fashion style. However, the "sameness" she found has not dissolved the social hierarchy between rural and urban people. Elaine said that she is aware of the discrimination against *waidiren* (外地人 "outsiders"—literally, non-local people) in Shanghai. After working in Shanghai for ten years, Elaine dreams of returning home. She planned to earn more money in Shanghai in order to save sufficient capital to start a business in her hometown or her husband's.

Penn Tsz Ting Ip

She also said that living in her hometown is more comfortable because her home is much more spacious than the rented apartment in Shanghai. Her dream echoes the national promotion of the Chinese Dream in which the nation attempts to persuade rural migrants to return home for rural modernization.

Conclusion

Drawing on this analysis, I suggest that it is inadequate to analyze rural migrant women through the lens of the "Chinese modern woman" without taking the rural/urban divide and rural political identity into account. Rural migrant women's dilemmas in fashion are different than those faced by urban women[62] because they have to learn to be modern in the city to avoid discrimination, and simultaneously find a sense of comfort when they return home. For Pang Yuan, her relatives applied pressure on what she chose to wear during Chinese New Year, where Eileen had chosen to dress simply in order to keep a low profile in her hometown. In Elaine's situation, the "casual" fashion style is seemingly a balance she found to navigate in both Shanghai and her hometown. As Pierre Bourdieu reminds us, "Social subjects, classified by their classifications, distinguish themselves by the distinctions they make, between the beautiful and the ugly, the distinguished and the vulgar, in which their position in the objective classifications is expressed or betrayed."[63] In this sense, rural migrant women can transform themselves to be more fashionable, yet they always have to deal with the socio-moral pressures between rural and urban China, where both localities have their different moral and fashion standards.[64] Hence, rural migrant women should not be analyzed as merely "Chinese modern women" because they are "Chinese modern *rural* migrant women" who must find a point where their identities as migrant women and Shanghai women meet.

This chapter reveals that *tu* is an unwanted, undesirable element imposed on rural female's bodies. Focusing on the commercial strategies on the Cheap Road, I conclude that the imaginaries of "Chinese modern woman" are being visualized through three main advertising techniques: a sense of the "modern" is made accessible by allowing rural migrant women to intimately judge the commodities on offer; fashion shops reflect the trendiest fashion culture, but with political and historical sensitivity; and billboards provide a visual event for female customers to worship "goddesses" from the "modern" heaven.

Significantly, rural migrant women have learned to employ the sense of *tu* to measure the suitability of their rural male counterparts. Thus, rural men are the "emaciated other" for single rural migrant women. As discussed by C. Cindy Fan in this volume, single men and their parents must build large houses to attract single women in rural China. Doubtlessly, rural migrant women can enjoy a certain degree of self-transformation and autonomy, yet their identity is deeply entangled with their rural *hukou*. In other words, they remain marked as rural migrant women by local people in the cities. Respectively, "Chinese modern *rural* migrant women" can seemingly gain access to the Chinese Dream by embracing a sense of "modern" through fashion shopping, yet in achieving their personal wellbeing and livelihood they remain constrained by their rural identity, gender, and social hierarchy. Finally, this chapter suggests that future research could involve the perspectives of city dwellers and urban customers to explore the degree to which rural migrant women manage to counter stereotypes through dressing fashionably.

Notes

1. Yan 2008, 44.
2. Chan 2012; Solinger 1999; Sun 2014.
3. Fan 1999.
4. Yan 2008.

5. Yan 2008, 44.
6. Yan 2003, 579.
7. Yan 2008, 44.
8. Taylor 2015.
9. Ahlers 2015.
10. Taylor 2015.
11. See www.mohurd.gov.cn.
12. Mars and Hornsby 2008, 20.
13. Sun 2014, 27.
14. Sun 2014, 27.
15. Farrer and Field 2015.
16. Huang 2008, 133.
17. Miller 1998.
18. See Pun 2003.
19. Miller, Daniel. 1998. *A Theory of Shopping*. New York: Cornell University Press, 4.
20. Lipovetsky 1994, 10.
21. Chan 2010, 663.
22. Chan 2010, 663.
23. Fan 2003.
24. Pun 1999.
25. Anagnost 2004.
26. In the interval, inspired by modern Western culture, the concepts of gender evolved from the ingrained connection of females to the social relationship within *jia* ("home"), that is *nu* ("daughters"), *fu* ("wives"), and *mu* ("mothers"), to a more individual concept, that is *nüxing* ("woman") (Chong 2013, 244; see Barlow 1994).
27. Edwards 2000.
28. Yen 2005, 165.
29. Chen 2001; McWilliams 2013.
30. Yang 2011.
31. Li 1998, 74.
32. Chew 2007, 159–60.
33. Chew 2007, 160.
34. Otis 2012.
35. Rofel 1999, 3.
36. Rofel 1999, 11.
37. Miller 1998, 4.
38. Mittler 2007, 14–15.
39. Kusenbach 2003.
40. Kusenbach 2003, 474.
41. Kommonen 2011, 371.
42. Lipovetsky 1994.
43. Gaetano 2015, 102–3.
44. Zhang 2015.
45. Zheng 2003, 163.
46. The Chinese characters 土气 (*tuqi*) are not included in the original text in Zhang's work.
47. Zheng 2003, 163.
48. *World Market* 2003.
49. Mittler 2007, 16; Dyer 1982, 86.
50. Hong 2014.
51. Jang 2013.
52. *Descendants of the Sun* 2016.
53. Slade 2009.
54. China Daily 2005.
55. Mittler 2007, 16.
56. Mittler 2007, 16–17.
57. Mittler 2007, 15; Dyer 1982, 2.
58. Rofel 1999, 3.
59. Mittler 2007, 27.
60. Kusenbach 2003, 474.
61. Otis 2012.

Penn Tsz Ting Ip

62. Chew 2007.
63. Bourdieu 1984, 6.
64. Yan 2008, 180.

References

Ahlers, Anna L. 2015. "Weaving the Chinese Dream on the Ground? Local Government Approaches to 'New-Typed' Rural." *Journal of Chinese Political Science* 20: 121–142.

Anagnost, Ann. 2004. "The Corporeal Politics of Quality (*Suzhi*)." *Public Culture* 16(2): 189–208.

Barlow, Tani E. 1994. "Theorizing Woman: *Funü, Guojia, Jiating.*" In *Body, Subject & Power in China*, edited by Angela Zito and Tani E. Barlow, 253–298. Chicago and London: University of Chicago Press.

Bourdieu, Pierre. 1984. *Distinction: A Social Critique of the Judgment of Taste.* Translated by Richard Nice. Cambridge, MA: Harvard University Press.

Chan, Kam Wing. 2010. "The Global Financial Crisis and Migrant Workers in China: 'There Is No Future as a Labourer; Returning to the Village Has No Meaning.'" *International Journal of Urban and Regional Research* 34(3): 659–677.

Chan, Kam Wing. 2012. "Crossing the 50 Percent Population Rubicon: Can China Urbanize to Prosperity?" *Eurasian Geography and Economics* 53(1): 63–86.

Chen, Tina Mai. 2001. "Dressing for the Party: Clothing, Citizenship, and Gender-formation in Mao's China." *Fashion Theory* 5(2): 143–172.

Chew, Matthew. 2007. "Contemporary Re-emergency of the Qipao: Political Nationalism, Cultural Production and Popular Consumption of a Traditional Chinese Dress." *China Quarterly* 189(March): 144–161.

China Daily. 2005. "Boycotting Japanese Goods Makes No Good." *China Daily*, April 23. www.chinadaily.com.cn/english/doc/2005-04/23/content_436720.htm, accessed on February 25, 2017.

Chong, Gladys Pak Lei. 2013. "Chinese Bodies that Matter: The Search for Masculinity and Femininity." *International Journal of the History of Sport* 30(3): 242–266.

Descendants of the Sun. 2016. Directed by Eung-bok Lee and Sang-hoon Baek. Written by Eun-sook Kim and Won-seok Kim. KBS, Next Entertainment World, Barunson Inc., and Descendants of the Sun SPC. KBS2.

Dyer, Gillian. 1982. *Advertising as Communication.* London: Routledge.

Edwards, Louise. 2000. "Policing the Modern Woman in Republican China." *Modern China* 26(2 April): 115–147.

Fan, Cindy C. 1999. "Migration in a Socialist Transitional Economy: Heterogeneity, Socioeconomic and Spatial Characteristics of Migrants in China and Guangdong Province." *International Migration Review* 33(4 Winter): 954–987.

Fan, Cindy C. 2003. "Rural–Urban Migration and Gender Division of Labor in Transitional China." *International Journal of Urban and Regional Research* 27(1): 24–47.

Farrer, James, and Andrew D. Field. 2015. *Shanghai Nightscapes: A Nocturnal Biography of a Global City.* Chicago: University of Chicago Press.

Gaetano, Arianne M. 2015. *Out to Work: Migration, Gender, and the Changing Lives of Rural Women in Contemporary China.* Hong Kong: Hong Kong University Press.

Hong, Euny Y. 2014. *The Birth of Korean Cool: How One Nation is Conquering the World Through Pop Culture.* London: Simon & Schuster.

Huang, Shilong. 2008. "Xinpinpu: Shanghai shoujia niuzai fushicheng" ["New Pinpu: Shanghai's First Denim Clothing City"]. *Beijing Textile Journal* 6: 133.

Kommonen, Kirsi. 2011. "Narratives on Chinese Colour Culture in Business Contexts: The Yin Yang Wu Xing of Chinese Values." *Cross Cultural Management: An International Journal* 18(3): 366–383.

Kusenbach, Margarethe. 2003. "Street Phenomenology: The Go-Along as Ethnographic Research Tool." *Ethnography* 4(September 3): 455–485.

Li, Xiaoping. 1998. "Fashioning the Body in Post-Mao China." In *Consuming Fashion: Adorning the Transnational Body*, edited by Anne Brydon and Sandra Niessen, 71–89. Oxford: Berg.

Lipovetsky, Gilles. 1994. *The Empire of Fashion: Dressing Modern Democracy.* Translated by Catherine Porter. Princeton, NJ and Oxford: Princeton University Press.

Mars, Neville, and Adrian Hornsby. 2008. "Introduction." In *The Chinese Dream: A Society Under Construction*, edited by Neville Mars, Adrian Hornsby, and Haijing Wen, 20–29. Rotterdam: 010 Publishers.

McWilliams, Sally E. 2013. "'People Don't Attack You If You Dress Fancy': Consuming Femininity in Contemporary China." *Women's Studies Quarterly* 41(1–2 Spring/Summer): 162–181.

Miller, Daniel. 1998. *A Theory of Shopping.* New York: Cornell University Press.

Mittler, Barbara. 2007. "Gendered Advertising in China: What History Do Images Tell?" *EJEAS* 6(1): 13–41.

My Love From the Star. 2013. Directed by Tae-yoo Jang. Written by Ji-eun Park. HB Entertainment. SBS.

Otis, Eileen. 2012. *Markets and Bodies: Women, Service Work, and the Making of Inequality in China*. Stanford, CA: Stanford University Press.

Pun, Ngai. 1999. "Becoming *Dagongmei* (Working Girls): The Politics of Identity and Difference in Reform China." *China Journal* 42: 1–18.

Pun, Ngai. 2003. "Subsumption or Consumption? The Phantom of Consumer Revolution in 'Globalizing' China." *Cultural Anthropology* 18(4): 469–492.

Rofel, Lisa. 1999. *Other Modernities: Gendered Yearnings in China After Socialism*. Berkeley: University of California Press.

Slade, Toby. 2009. *Japanese Fashion: A Cultural History*. Oxford: Berg.

Solinger, Dorothy. 1999. *Contesting Citizenship in Urban China: Peasant Migrants, the State, and the Logic of the Market*. Berkeley: University of California Press.

Sun, Wanning. 2014. *Subaltern China: Rural Migrants, Media, and Cultural Practices*. London: Rowman & Littlefield.

Taylor, Jon R. 2015. "The China Dream Is an Urban Dream: Assessing the CPC's National New-Type Urbanization Plan." *Journal of Chinese Political Science* 20: 107–120.

World Market. 2003. "Yongyuan Renao De Qipulu" ["The Forever Lively Cheap Road"]. *World Market* (September): 58–59.

Yan, Hairong. 2003. "Specialization of the Rural: Reinterpreting the Labor Mobility of Rural Young Women in Post-Mao China." *American Ethnologist* 30(4): 578–596.

Yan, Hairong. 2008. *New Masters, New Servants: Migration, Development, and Women Workers in China*. Durham, NC: Duke University Press.

Yang, Jie. 2011. "*Nennu* and *Shunu*: Gender, Body Politics, and the Beauty Economy in China." *Signs: Journal of Women in Culture and Society* 36(2): 333–357.

Yen, Hsiao-pei. 2005. "Body Politics, Modernity and National Salvation: The Modern Girl and the New Life Movement." *Asian Studies Review* 29(June): 165–186.

Zhang, Xia. 2015. "One Life for Sale: Youth Culture, Labor Politics, and New Idealism in China." *Positions: East Asia Cultures Critique* 23(3): 515–543.

Zheng, Tiantian. 2003. "Consumption, Body Image, and Rural-Urban Apartheid in Contemporary China." *City & Society* 15(2): 143–163.

19

Space and Gender in the Chinese Workplace

Past and Present

Duanfang Lu

Gender relations have been radically restructured since the founding of the People's Republic of China in 1949. In traditional China, men were considered the threads that connected the lineage system over time, while women, whose lives were subordinated to the patriarchal order and bound to the domestic sphere, were deemed as accessories to this system.[1] After the socialist revolution, a series of changes greatly improved the legal, economic, and social status of women in Chinese society: the introduction of the marriage law in 1950, the mass mobilization of urban women to participate in production in the late 1950s, and the state's continuing commitment to gender equality in the subsequent decades.[2] The peculiar spatial features of the work unit (*danwei*)—the socialist enterprise or institute that integrated work and living spaces—further enhanced the conditions for women not only in social terms, but also in material terms. During the socialist period, most factories, schools and government offices were organized into a state administrative system; the work unit was the basic unit of this system.[3] The latter functioned not only as the workplace but also as the principal social institution in which the lives of most urban residents were organized.[4] The fundamental importance of the work unit in Chinese society lay in its unique combination of economic, political, and social functions.[5] The work unit offered its employees lifetime employment and attendant welfare such as public housing and medical care.[6] A typical work unit integrated production, residence, and social facilities within one or several walled compound(s). It ran a variety of social services such as canteens, clinics, and nurseries, which supported the lives of working women well.[7] Despite state-imposed gender equality in the public sphere, however, traditional gender relations persisted in domestic spaces, with women shouldering most of the housework at home. There were also urban-rural differences in gender relations. Instrumental to the government in collectivization, the patriarchal order remained strong in the countryside.[8]

Economic reforms since 1978 have brought enormous changes to Chinese society. While femininity was deemphasized in the Maoist era, there has been a revival of belief in traditional gender relations.[9] The urban employment rate for working-age women fell from over 90% at the end of the 1970s to 61% by 2010.[10] The work unit has gradually declined as the fundamental socio-spatial unit of the Chinese city. With the rise of the private sector, millions of new job opportunities have been created for rural migrants. While the work unit is adapting to the new opportunities brought by the reforms, some of its features are reproduced in private factories, many of which continue to provide dormitories for workers. Among others, Foxconn, the multinational electronics contract manufacturing company, has planned and constructed its various facilities across China in ways similar to the work unit. However, as a private firm whose primary objective is to drive workers to meet production demands, Foxconn also differs from the socialist *danwei* in significant aspects.

This chapter offers a comparative study of space and gender in the Chinese work unit and in the Foxconn factory. It will show how urbanism and gender systems have transformed in the radical transition of the Chinese economy's restructuring, from one based on centrally planned heavy industry with permanent employment and comprehensive social welfare for urban workers to one that relies on export-oriented industries with the massive use of rural migrant workers.[11] This chapter will first provide an examination of the work unit as an urban form, with a discussion of its gender-specific socio-spatial effects. This will be followed by an investigation into space, gender and everyday life in the Foxconn factory complex. The chapter closes with a comparative analysis.

The Work Unit as an Urban Form[12]

Typically, the site planning of a new work unit was carried out by professionals, but the subsequent development was often planned by the work unit's own Department of Basic Construction. Beginning with essential production structures and dormitories for single workers, the work unit grew naturally, expanding as the enterprise matured. There were wide variations in the spatial layout, resources and size of individual work units. Work units in suburban and rural areas were generally well equipped, while units near downtown areas and in small towns were less so. Work units also differed greatly from one another in area and population size, from those of a few hundred square meters with dozens of members, to those of thousands of square meters with hundreds to thousands of residents.

Every work unit was a walled enclosure, or, if large enough, a cluster of several walled enclosures. The wall, in most cases made of brick, set the work unit physically apart from its surroundings. There were usually several entrances through the wall from city boulevards. The main entrances were staffed by security personnel and fortified with heavy, wrought-iron gates. The level of security at entrances varied from unit to unit. Some institutions, such as major administrative offices and military-related units might subject all persons to identification procedures. Others were relatively easy to enter. The gate was closed at midnight and opened in the early morning. Once closed, coming and going for both residents and outsiders became difficult. Passage could only be obtained by waking the understandably displeased gatekeeper, who would only open the door for unit members he (rarely she) recognized. The working and living quarters were usually circled by separate walls. The gates between them might remain closed during work hours to prevent employees from slipping back home.

The work unit provided public housing for its employees and their families. Usually, the living quarters (*shenhuo qu*) were close to the workplace. The only exceptions were factories that polluted the environment and work units located in highly developed urban areas where land was scarce and housing space was limited. In these cases, employees might live in separate housing areas, or spilled over into downtown neighborhoods or residential tracts managed by the municipal government. Some work units provided bus links between residences and work. Small work units might have their workplace and residence within a compact area, while larger ones tend to separate them into distinct areas with walls or roadways. Residences included apartments for families and dormitories for single workers, both housed in modern-style buildings in orderly rows. The oldest ones were two to six stories high with stairwells; some of the newest ones were high-rise buildings equipped with elevators. The design of both dormitories and apartments presented a realistic trade-off between social, utility and housing spaces by externalizing social activities and utilities from housing units. As a number of functions were removed from the private domain and accommodated instead in unit social facilities, the size of the residence was reduced significantly. In the case of dormitories, while centralized common restrooms were provided on each floor, there were no kitchens, dining rooms or shower rooms; people were expected to eat in unit canteens and take showers in public bathhouses. Each room accommodated four to eight persons and was fitted with bunks. Some furniture was provided by the

Figure 19.1 People Biked or Walked to the Canteen in their Work Unit in Beijing, 2005.
Source: © Duanfang Lu.

work unit, including desks and chairs in addition to the bunks. Men and women were usually housed in separate dormitory buildings.

The work unit provided various community facilities. Small work units had canteens, social halls, clinics and public bathhouses (Figure 19.1). Medium-sized units might add nurseries, kindergartens, parks, libraries, sports fields, guesthouses and shops. Large work units, especially factories in remote suburban or rural areas, had such elaborate social service systems that they resembled a miniature city. In addition to the facilities listed above, they had food markets, hospitals, post offices, banks, movie theaters, workers' clubs, barbershops, and primary and high schools. While facilities in small work units were scattered in buildings throughout the unit compound, large units might have a district set aside for social services, which formed an area similar to a city's downtown. Children's playgrounds, bicycle sheds, sports fields, parks, and other recreation spaces were provided in the open areas between buildings. All these facilities were designed for the exclusive use of unit members, but enforcing such exclusivity depended on the strength of individual work units. In some cases, neighboring units cooperated to support the joint use of facilities such as schools and hospitals.

The close proximity of work, housing and social facilities resulted in a peculiar pattern of local comings and goings. Many unit residents could carry out their daily business within the unit compound, although some did travel daily beyond the unit walls. Children of small work units went to schools outside the compound. Adults living with their spouses or parents in work units other than their own had to commute by bus or bicycle. Weekends were a time when many made trips a good distance away from their work units: shopping downtown, playing in parks or visiting relatives and friends who lived in other parts of the city. However, the daily routine of many unit members was confined by the unit compound.

The design of the work unit created an institutionally non-sexist environment that supported the activities of employed women and their families. Since the late 1950s, urban women were expected to have paid employment, with homebound women being the exception. The work unit's integration of production, residence and social services on a manageable scale greatly facilitated the functioning of two-worker families. Public canteens offered alternatives to cooking at home, nurseries within the unit compound reduced the time spent in commuting, and nursing rooms near workshops helped mothers to get back to work (Figure 19.2). The support for women in the Maoist city therefore

Space and Gender in the Chinese Workplace

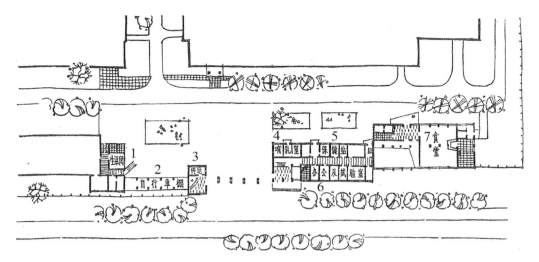

Figure 19.2 The Front Yard of a Factory, Published in 1963: (1) "Life Room"; (2) Bicycle Shed; (3) Janitor's Room; (4) Nursing Room; (5) Clinic; (6) Office and Laboratory; (7) Canteen
Source: *Jianzhu xuebao* 1963, 5.

contrasts sharply to the Western capitalist city, which was fundamentally dependent on the subordination of women, as recognized by a vigorous feminist critique since the 1970s.[13] As a result of gender-based planning, childcare is rarely available near offices; the transportation pattern assumes the woman is available as a full-time driver; and the whole idea of the suburbs is indeed based on the assumption of the self-reliant home with a full-time operator—the woman.[14]

The stress on gender equality in China resulted in a desexualized culture during the Maoist period, when women not only became part of the traditional domain of male labor but also conformed to a genderless appearance. Nevertheless, behind the official celebration of gender equality in the socialist workplace, residual patriarchal authority survived in Chinese domestic space; women were almost invariably expected to spend more time on housework and childcare than men. Without modern household appliances such as washing machines and modern ovens, homemaking at the time was arduous.[15] Women's double burden of work and domestic responsibilities sometimes resulted in household crisis.[16] In response to women's particular needs, every work unit had a women's committee, which dealt with a broad range of women's concerns and family disputes.

The Foxconn Factory: Continuity and Change[17]

The changes brought by economic reforms since 1978 have been accompanied by enormous transformations of urban China. The work unit has gradually declined as the fundamental socio-spatial unit of the Chinese city, but some of its features are reproduced in private companies. Corinna-Barbara Francis's study of Beijing's high-tech sector, for example, reveals that private firms in Haidian District have adopted paternalistic approaches to management similar to those employed by the work unit.[18] This section will focus on similarities and differences in spatial organization and management style between *danwei* and the factories of the Foxconn Technology Group. Found by Terry Guo in Taiwan in the 1970s, Foxconn is currently the largest electronics producer in the world. It produces half of the world's electronic products for a large number of companies such as Apple, Dell, Microsoft, Sony, HP and Nokia, with Apple being its largest client. About 40% of Foxconn revenues are from Apple. Foxconn employs over 1.4 million workers in China, with factories in major cities such as Shenzhen,

Figure 19.3 The Living Quarters of Foxconn Kunshan, Wusongjiang in 2015
Source: © Duanfang Lu.

Beijing, Shanghai, Tianjin, Chengdu and Chongqing, as well as in 15 provinces throughout the country. From the very beginning of its operation in mainland China, the spatial organization of Foxconn factories reproduced a range of features of the work unit. In 1988, Foxconn set up its first offshore factory with 150 workers in Shenzhen. Despite being very small in scale, the all-in-one factory building had a canteen on the ground level and workers' dormitory on the sixth floor.[19] As Foxconn expanded, its various factory complexes have come to feature an elaborate sphere of reproduction quite similar to large work units. For example, with 430,000 workers, Foxconn Longhua in Shenzhen has dormitories, a library, soccer fields, basketball courts, a track and field, swimming pools, clinics, shops, canteens, restaurants, banks, bookstores and a post office.[20] In other, smaller-scale Foxconn facilities, the living quarters also offer the most essential living services (Figure 19.3).

The common physical features of the Foxconn factory and the work unit can be summarized as (1) a walled and gated enclosure, (2) a well-integrated internal circulation system, (3) close association of work and residence, (4) a high level of provision of social facilities and (5) rationalist architectural layout and style. Like members of the work unit, Foxconn workers may conduct most daily affairs without leaving the factory complex. In both cases, the design of dormitories is based on the concept that housing requirements for single employees are less complex than for married employees, and thus space expectations are lower. While common restrooms are provided, there are no kitchens, living rooms or dining rooms. Each room accommodates six to eight persons and is fitted with bunks, desks and chairs. Female and male employees are accommodated in separate dormitory buildings. Like the work unit, the living quarter of Foxconn is also called *shenghuo qu*, and the trade union is in charge of managing workers' welfare.

Despite these parallels, however, unlike the work unit, which provides family housing and supports a variety of family needs, the Foxconn factory complexes, with most of their employees in their late teens to mid-twenties, do not provide family housing or any family-related services for workers.[21] Whether the worker is single or married, he or she is assigned a bunk space for one person. Married couples have to rent apartment flats outside the factory if they wish to live together. After they have children, they usually need to send them back to their hometown, as children without local residency status do not have access to public schools. Unlike the work unit, where permanent employment is the norm, there are quick turnovers in Foxconn, as most workers do not see opportunities for career advancement. In addition, random dormitory assignments often break up existing social networks, hindering communication and interaction between workers. As a result, workers often experience distrust and loneliness.

While both the Foxconn factory and the work unit feature clear boundaries and security gates, the level of security at entrances is much higher at the Foxconn factory complex. Most work units are relatively easy to enter; only those obviously not belonging to the work unit would be stopped for an identity check by the gatekeeper. In contrast, at Foxconn complexes, all persons are subject to identification procedures (Figure 19.4). Passage can only be obtained by showing Foxconn staff ID. Even family members cannot enter the living quarters. The strict control of coming and going often becomes a source of conflict between workers and security personnel.

Mao's mass-line doctrine of the work unit is replaced by Foxconn's strict management regime. Its 13-level management hierarchy with clear lines of command is organized in a pyramid.[22] At the bottom are ordinary workers, whose wages and welfare are minimal. They face multiple layers of management from assistant line leaders, line leaders, team leaders, and supervisors at the middle level, who are rewarded by housing and monetary benefits. At the upper level are decision-making leaders, rewarded by the company with share dividends and job tenure. At the tip of the pyramid is Foxconn CEO Terry Guo. As in the previous socialist period, when people regularly recited *Chairman Mao's Quotations* in political campaigns, Foxconn staff members are asked to write Guo's Quotations from memory in tests

Figure 19.4 The Gate of Foxconn Kunshan, Zizhulu, 2015
Source: © Duanfang Lu.

Duanfang Lu

for promotion.[23] Factory-floor managers give speeches to workers at the beginning and end of the work day. Workers get yelled at when they make mistakes during work. It is believed that only through a military style of management do young rural migrant workers become disciplined laborers.[24]

While there is generally a lack of discipline among workers in *danwei*, Foxconn has developed an intensive mode of production and management in order to meet price, quality and time-to-market specifications. The level of work intensity is much higher in Foxconn factories than in *danwei*. Foxconn managers use computerized devices to test the capacity of the workers. The target is increased gradually until workers' capacity reaches the maximum. Excessive overtime often occurs when Foxconn speeds up the production to meet Apple's short delivery deadline, which puts workers under high pressure. In 2012, for example, the shift in production from the iPhone 4S to the iPhone 5 led to intensive working conditions for workers in Foxconn Taiyuan, who could not even take one day off in a week for two consecutive months.[25] On September 23, 2012, after security officers beat three workers for failing to show staff IDs, a riot erupted. Thousands of workers smashed security offices, production facilities, shops, and canteens in the factory complex.[26]

Until a few years ago, many Foxconn workshops only hired female workers. Due to their supposed docility and attention to detail, women were considered better workers than men on some labor-intensive production lines. More male workers have been hired in recent years, but female workers still very much outnumber male workers. A direct result of this is that male workers are very popular, and it is relatively easy for them to find a girlfriend there. In fact, finding a suitable wife has been the main reason some male workers from poorer areas work in Foxconn factories.[27] Unlike in *danwei*, at Foxconn, male workers and female workers cannot enter each other's dormitories. Breaking this rule means their work ID cards are taken away by the security guards and they may even be dismissed. The strict dormitory access system therefore prevents intimate activities from taking place within the complex. This in turn forces workers to go beyond the factory complex to use what the city offers for dating and other social activities. Notably, more female workers choose to rent a flat instead of the factory dorms. My study at the Zizhulu factory of Foxconn Kunshan showed that around 40% of its female workers currently live in rental flats. As a result, a significant portion of the Foxconn dormitories are now empty. There are a number of reasons behind this phenomenon. Women value privacy and hygiene more than men. Also, renting a flat means that their boyfriends do not need to spend that much money on urban facilities such as hotels and restaurants, therefore female workers with rental residences become more attractive than those living in the factory dormitories.

Unlike existing studies of Foxconn focusing on labor issues, my study highlights the fact that the Foxconn factory complex is not just a place where rural migrant workers learn to labor. For most of them, it is their first stop in the city where young workers learn to be urban. What surprised me during my field research was how fashionable their outward appearances are. With chic clothes and hairstyles, most of them looked just like any urban youngsters. While gender differentiation was de-emphasized in the Maoist era, market forces and the rise of consumerism have reintroduced a sexually dimorphic conception of gender. Under a new discourse that serves to enhance consumers' desire for feminine beauty and sexuality, women have increasingly become active consumers of fashions, beauty care products and services. In the case of rural female workers, they have often been through a quick transformation from a rural feminine appearance to an urban one within a few months.[28] Within a year or two, some of them are ready to move on to become beauty care providers. From my conversations with them, I learned that peer learning has greatly contributed to the development of their urban appearance. Most Foxconn workers are in their late teens to mid-twenties. An agglomeration of young bodies without the usual monitoring from older people that one would usually find in the village or family setting means that young people can pursue the most updated ways of expressing their identities more freely. In the past few years, the spread of social media platforms such as QQ and WeChat has changed the speed and scope of urban learning for young migrant workers. Like urbanites, they are

344

exposed to urban news and knowledge through the networks beyond their immediate work environment. WeChat official accounts, in particular, offer free articles with images that can be easily accessed and forwarded to friends through smartphones, which have greatly facilitated urban learning beyond the spatial confines of the factory complex.

Traditionally, migrants have had a strong family and hometown orientation. Their tolerance of hardship in the city is often predicated on the expectation of eventually returning to their villages for recuperation. Their success is measured by the amount of savings they can bring to the village for housing construction. In contrast, the new generation of migrant workers live for now rather than for the future. They are more willing to spend money on urban consumption: dining with friends in restaurants, going to movie theatres, and shopping in local malls. Nonetheless, many continue to consider themselves rural, despite their enhanced urban knowledge and skills. As they still remain highly economically disadvantaged in comparison to urbanites, they feel that they lack the resources to take full advantage of the opportunities and services in the city. With the current *hukou* system, there is a discrepancy between rural and urban welfare and access to education.[29] As long as rural migrants are placed asymmetrically in urban society in economic and social terms and are denied social recognition as equals, feelings of inferiority continue. In addition, with the increased consumerism in society and communication across different social strata, the new generation of migrant workers suffers not only from poverty but also from relative deprivation.

Still, for many rural female workers, factory life can be liberating and empowering in contrast to their previous lives in the village. The traditional view that daughters are temporal members of their natal family still prevails in the countryside. Daughters are considered inferior to sons in many families. Parents are less willing to invest in the education of their daughters (rural female workers have about a year less schooling than male workers, on average). In contrast, female workers are not treated as inferior members in the factory; instead, they receive career development opportunities based on performance rather than gender. Factory life also introduces them to an enlarged arena for developing their subjectivities and skills. Many female workers I interviewed, for example, mentioned various sorts of training certificates they received, showing their strong motivation to grasp opportunities offered by the city to change their lives. They are also quite willing to discuss workplace grievances with friends, either through face-to-face conversations or through social media. The improved status and level of freedom have also enabled many woman workers to become more confident and more aware of their rights than their male counterparts. As China Labour Bulletin, a Hong Kong-based non-governmental organization (NGO), noted in a March 19, 2013 report, "about a fifth of strikes in Guangdong since the beginning of the year had been in factories and other workplaces with largely female staff."[30] It was also reported that women were "some of the most active workers posting information online about strikes and protests, and in seeking out legal assistance for problems at work."[31]

From the Work Unit to the Foxconn Factory: A Comparative Perspective

Both the work unit and the Foxconn factory feature the close association of work and residence, a gated enclosure, and a high level of provision of social facilities. This peculiar way of spatial organization has a few advantages for the enterprises:

1. With housing costs internalized, workers can be paid less.
2. Workers' physical strength is reproduced at the lowest cost possible with their daily routines organized efficiently.
3. Outside distractions are minimized through the spatial confines.
4. Reducing commuting distances saves time, commuting costs and energy consumption, and allows for longer working hours.

Both *danwei* and the Foxconn factory share some characteristics of the company town in capitalist society, defined as a settlement built and operated by a single business enterprise.[32] Dependent on resource sites, company towns were often situated in remote, isolated locations, where the companies had little alternative but to build housing and related services for workers.[33] In contrast, most work units and Foxconn factories are located in cities or on urban fringes. My book *Remaking Chinese Urban Form* reveals that the building of living facilities within work units was often accomplished through construction outside the state-approved plan, resource hoarding and exchanges via informal channels.[34] This certainly did not happen automatically. Instead, it was a result of the conflicted relationship between the state, work units and planners in the construction of essential consumption facilities. With the immense scarcity of consumption facilities causing severe political tension and strife during the 1950s, the state responded by imposing the responsibility of urban provision upon the work unit. Faced with political pressure from employees below and administrators above, unit leaders strived to meet the needs of their workers. Due to the lack of the competitive mechanisms characteristic of capitalism, work units were willing to develop the essential means of consumption for their own workers, despite a low return on investment and other liabilities. The Chinese redistribution system was designed so that it was possible for work units to switch a portion of capital from production to consumption via both formal and informal channels. The integral spatial form of the work unit was therefore the unique outcome generated by the conflicts between the needs of capital accumulation and the necessity of labor reproduction within a peculiar socialist/Third World context.

In the reform era, accelerating marketization has resulted in the increasing mobility of capital and labor across the borders of the work unit. Some work units have transformed themselves into commercial companies listed on the stock market, some have collaborated with other private companies to develop new projects, and still others have leased part of their offices or laboratories to foreign firms. Ironically, at a time when the work unit has gradually declined as the fundamental socio-spatial unit of the Chinese city, the Foxconn dormitory-factory regime has flourished rapidly in China. Its phenomenal growth needs to be situated within the structure of global modernity. In the early twenty-first century, the advancement of telecommunications technologies has made the acceleration of outsourcing possible. More and more businesses in the Global North have chosen offshore outsourcing as a way to reduce operating costs, bring in expertise from the outside, reduce labor costs and avoid excessive government regulations. The workforce of nations in the Global South such as China and India are paid only a small fraction of what would be the minimum salary in the Global North.[35] Therefore, they provide a favorable environment for offshore contractors to grow. China, in particular, offers a range of advantageous conditions for industrial development. While other developing countries may also be able to provide abundant cheap labor, in most cases their land is under private ownership. Not only is land much more expensive to acquire, infrastructural support is often poor and uneven. In contrast, as local governments compete to get Foxconn to set up new factories in their territories in order to boost gross domestic product (GDP) growth, Foxconn's development in China has been facilitated through the provision of extensive cheap land and infrastructural support by local governments.[36] Hence, it is worthwhile to build extensive living facilities despite the availability of these services in the city. With the low cost of the spatial advantages listed at the beginning of this section, Foxconn manages to deliver scale and quality at rock-bottom prices, which enables it to remain highly competitive in the global manufacturing arena. In the past decade, Foxconn has grown to be the world's largest electronics contractor manufacturer and the largest private employer in China.

The gendered experience within the work unit and the Foxconn factory needs to be read against the backdrop of these larger contexts. To highlight women's different access to resources in these two spatial forms, I would like to characterize women's experience with the work unit as one of "settling" and with the Foxconn factory as one of "battling." Developed under the centrally-planned socialist economy the work unit provided permanent employment and comprehensive social welfare for its employees. Working women and their families settled well in the work unit, supported by the close proximity between the workplace and residence as well as various facilities such as public canteens, kindergartens, shops and clinics. They enjoyed significant access to resources other than monetary ones. At times of crisis, the work unit's women's committee took responsibility for helping them deal with a range of issues, including family disputes. In contrast, the Foxconn factory has developed in the context of an economy based on export-oriented industries with a massive use of rural migrant workers. As a private firm, its primary objectives are to maximize profits and drive workers to meet production demands. The Foxconn factory used to be a highly female-gendered space. The choice of employing female workers was not, however, made because of women's rights, but due to the exploitation of females' perceived docility and dexterity. Foxconn only supports single workers' needs, and assumes workers would either leave the job or make arrangements by themselves once they start a family. For most of its workers, the Foxconn factory is a transitional stage of their career rather than the end point. As such, factory life, especially for highly motivated female workers, has been a battle in an enlarged field (in comparison to their previous village life) to acquire more skills, rights, and economic, social and cultural capital.

With worker expectations for higher wages and a better quality of life balanced by outside scrutiny and a tighter labor market, the model of the Foxconn dormitory-factory regime is currently facing multiple challenges. In 2010, a series of workplace suicides at Foxconn stirred profound concerns about Foxconn as a global labor regime.[37] In response to negative publicity surrounding labor conditions, Foxconn has conducted some progressive labor policy reforms since then, including increasing workers' wages, addressing the overtime problem and allowing workers to hold direct elections for union representatives. According to a 2012 China Labor Watch report, two Foxconn factories were the top performers in a number of aspects among the ten electronics factories under survey, including wages, working hours, rewards and penalty measures, food and dormitory, and channels for appeals.[38] While in 2010 the basic monthly wage for assembly line workers of most Foxconn factories fell in the range between 950 CNY (or about 147 USD) and 1,200 CNY (or 186 USD), Foxconn Kushan workers now receive 1,800 CNY (or 279 USD) as the base monthly wage.[39] They are allowed regular ten-minute breaks every 45 minutes, and excessively long working hours are no longer allowed. Foxconn also installed safety nets for dormitories. However, on August 4, 2010, a 23-year-old female worker jumped from the third floor of Foxconn Kunshan Wusongjiang factory.[40] Her body tore through the newly installed safety net and she died. In many ways, the Foxconn dormitory-factory regime is not unlike the weak safety nets it installed: the unbearable lightness of the nets can no longer hold its workers' urban dreams, which have become more and more substantial.

My research shows that a new generation of migrant workers of both genders, being well equipped with new means of social networking, tend to learn enterprise bargaining skills and disseminate any workplace grievances quickly. The increasingly speedy processes of their urban learning have been made possible by smartphones and associated social networking software. Notably, it is precisely through the cheap labor they offer in the first place that smartphones have become widely affordable, providing workers with new means of social engagement. Many female workers are now well aware of their rights and are willing to fight for them. While in the previous socialist era, gender equality was largely a state-imposed agenda, the rise of new digital public spaces means that women themselves are developing a feminist consciousness. It remains to be seen how this newly independent feminist consciousness unfolds amid radical changes in the Chinese workplace.

Acknowledgements

Research for this chapter has been supported by the Australian Research Council (FT110101119). Parts of this chapter appear in my book *Remaking Chinese Urban Form* (Lu 2011 [2006]) and an earlier book chapter on this topic (Lu 2015).

Notes

1. Baker 1979.
2. Stacey 1983.
3. Schurmann 1968.
4. Lü and Perry 1997, 3–20; Walder 1986; Henderson and Cohen 1984.
5. Whyte and Parish 1984, 25.
6. During the pre-reform era, the government allocated 95% first jobs in urban areas; once one was assigned to a specific work unit, job changes were difficult. See Naughton, Barry: "Danwei: The Economic Foundations of a Unique Institution." In: *Danwei*, edited by Xiaobo Lü and Elizabeth J. Perry, 169–194. New York: East Gate.
7. Lu 2011[2006], chapter 3.
8. Stacey 1983.
9. Yang 1999.
10. Fincher 2013.
11. Eng 1997, 554–68.
12. The research is based on my fieldwork in Beijing, Wuhan, Guanzhou, Shanghai, Xiamen and Gaobei in 2000, a survey of work units conducted in Beijing in 2000–2001, my own experience with several work units and related publications.
13. Sandercock and Forsyth 1992.
14. I owe this account to Manuel Castells's lecture series on "Comparative Urban Policies," 1997, University of California, Berkeley.
15. Whyte and Parish 1984.
16. Wolf 1985.
17. My research on Foxconn factories was conducted in Kunshan, Langfang, Beijing and Chengdu in 2015.
18. Francis 1996.
19. Pun and Chan 2012, 383–410.
20. Pun and Chan 2012.
21. Interview with workers at Foxconn Kunshan Zizhulu by author, March 7, 2015.
22. Pun and Chan 2012, 394.
23. Pun and Chan 2012, 396.
24. Interview with workers at Foxconn Chengdu Bi County by author, September 20, 2015.
25. Chan, Pun, and Selden 2013.
26. Lin and Huang 2012.
27. Interview with workers at Foxconn Kunshan Zizhulu by author, March 7, 2015.
28. See also Penn Tsz Ting Ip's chapter in this volume.
29. Fan 2002.
30. *The Economist* 2013.
31. *The Economist* 2013.
32. Garner 1992.
33. Allen 1966.
34. Lu 2011[2006], chapter 4.
35. Dahlman 2011.
36. China.org.cn 2009.
37. Balfour and Culpan 2010.
38. China Labor Watch 2012.
39. Interview with workers at Foxconn Kunshan Wusongjiang by author, March 8, 2015.
40. Song, Sun, and Liu 2010.

References

Allen, James B. 1966. *The Company Town in the American West*. Norman: University of Oklahoma Press.
Baker, Hugh. 1979. *Chinese Family and Kinship*. New York: Columbia University Press.
Balfour, Frederik, and Tim Culpan. 2010. "A Look Inside Foxconn, Where iPhones Are Made: A Postmodern Chinese Industrial Empire that Was Blighted by Suicides." *Bloomberg Businessweek* 9, December 2010.
Chan, Jenny, Ngai Pun, and Mark Selden. 2013. "The Politics of Global Production: Apple, Foxconn and China's New Working Class." *New Technology, Work and Employment* 28(2): 100–115.
China Labor Watch. 2012. "Tragedies of Globalization: The Truth Behind Electronics Sweatshops." www.china laborwatch.org/report/52, accessed on January 20, 2015.

China.org.cn. 2009. "Cities Vie for Terry Gou's Money." October 28, 2009. www.china.org.cn/business/2009-10/28/content_18784806.htm, accessed on December 12, 2013.

Dahlman, Carl J. 2011. *The World Under Pressure: How China and India Are Influencing the Global Economy and Environment.* Stanford, CA: Stanford University Press.

The Economist. 2013. "Factory Women, Girl Power." May 11, 2013. www.economist.com/news/china/21577396-supply-female-factory-workers-dwindles-blue-collar-women-gain-clout-girl-power, accessed on May 15, 2017.

Eng, Irene. 1997. "The Rise of Manufacturing Towns: Externally Driven Industrialization and Urban Development in the Pearl River Delta of China." *International Journal of Urban and Regional Research* 21: 554–568.

Fan, Cindy C. 2002. "The Elite, the Natives and the Outsiders: Migration and Labour Market Segmentation in Urban China." *Annals of the Association of American Geographers* 92: 103–124.

Fincher, Leta Hong. 2013. "China's Entrenched Gender Gap." *New York Times*, May 20. www.nytimes.com/2013/05/21/opinion/global/chinas-entrenched-gender-gap.html, accessed on May 12, 2017.

Francis, Corinna-Barbara. 1996. "Reproduction of *danwei* Institutional Features in the Context of China's Market Economy: The Case of Haidian District's High-tech Sector." *China Quarterly* 147: 839–859.

Garner, John S. 1992. *The Company Town: Architecture and Society in the Early Industrial Age.* New York: Oxford University Press.

Henderson, Gail E., and Myron S. Cohen. 1984. *The Chinese Hospital: A Socialist Work Unit.* New Haven, CT: Yale University Press.

Lin, Qiling, and Yuhao Huang. 2012. "Taiyuan fushikang qunou chixu 4 xiaoshi, juchen yin bao'an daren yinfa" [Taiyuan Foxconn Riot Lasted for Four Hours; It Was Said that It Was Caused by Security Guards Beating Workers]. *Xinjing bao* [*Beijing News*], September 25, 2012. http://news.qq.com/a/20120925/000118.htm, accessed on December 12, 2014.

Lu, Duanfang. 2011 [2006]. *Remaking Chinese Urban Form: Modernity, Scarcity and Space, 1949–2005.* London: Routledge.

Lu, Duanfang. 2015. "The Work Unit and the Foxconn: A Comparative Perspective." In *Beijing Danwei: Industrial Heritage in the Contemporary City,* edited by Filippo De Pieri, 36–55. Ostfildern, Germany: Hatje Cantz.

Lü, Xiaobo, and Elizabeth J. Perry, eds. 1997. *Danwei: The Changing Chinese Workplace in Historical and Comparative Perspective.* New York: East Gate.

Naughton, Barry. 1997. "Danwei: The economic foundations of a unique institution." In *Danwei: The Changing Chinese Workplace in Historical and Comparative Perspective,* edited by Xiaobo Lü and Elizabeth J. Perry, 169–194. New York: East Gate.

Pun, Ngai, and Jenny Chan. 2012. "Global Capital, the State, and Chinese Workers: The Foxconn Experience." *Modern China* 38(4): 383–410.

Sandercock, Leonie, and Ann Forsyth. 1992. "A Gender Agenda: New Directions for Planning Theory." *Journal of the American Planning Association* 58: 49–59.

Schurmann, Franz. 1968. *Ideology and Organization in Communist China.* Berkeley: University of California Press.

Song, Bin, Wenxiang Sun, and Qiong Liu. 2010. "Juzi xiujian fanghuwang, nanzu kunshan fushikang zhuilou beiju" [Huge Amount of Money Spent on the Installation of Safety Nets, Hard to Prevent Foxconn Employees From Jumping]. *Diyi caijing ribao* [*The First Finance Daily*], August 9, 2010. www.yicai.com/news/387716.html, accessed on November 3, 2014.

Stacey, Judith. 1983. *Patriarchy and the Socialist Revolution in China.* Berkeley: University of California Press.

Walder, Andrew G. 1986. *Communist Neo-Traditionalism: Work and Authority in Chinese Industry.* Berkeley: University of California Press.

Whyte, Martin, and William Parish. 1984. *Urban Life in Contemporary China.* Chicago: University of Chicago Press.

Wolf, Margery. 1985. *Revolution Postponed: Women in Contemporary China.* Stanford, CA: Stanford University Press.

Yang, Mayfare. 1999. "From Gender Erasure to Gender Difference: State Feminism, Consumer Sexuality, and Women's Public Space." In *Spaces of Their Own,* edited by Mayfare Yang, 35–67. Minneapolis: University of Minnesota Press.

20

The Bungalow in the Colonial and Post-colonial Twentieth Century

Modernity, Dwelling and Gender in the Cultural Landscape of Gujarat, India[1]

Madhavi Desai

Modernity as a dominant paradigm had a major influence on Indian society. Its physical and stylistic manifestation was the Modern Movement, which attempted to transform the concept of time and space and create a new order in architecture. The Modern Movement was also a major cultural force to be reckoned with. Its appropriation and distinction as well as the spirit of adaptation and assimilation in the Indian landscape expressed a diversification of modernity that is yet to be fully understood. After 1947, in the post-independence period, modern architectural expressions dealt with multiple and complex regional realities that were intertwined with history and tradition. Closely integrated with the visual arts, modernist ideas of universalism and rationalism had an impact on not only architecture but also on urban design and city planning.

Modernism came to India as a dominant paradigm that was intrinsically connected to colonial rule, especially the British Raj, which officially began in 1858 but had existed earlier in the form of the East India Company. Urbanism can be considered one of the most lasting legacies of the Raj. The 200-year-long imperial rule brought about fundamental changes in Indian urban development by introducing new concepts of town planning and architecture. The imperial rulers used buildings as representations of their identity, authority and superiority. The colonial urban experience left an immense impact on the entire country: "Cities became the sites of the modernist enterprise, the most visible expression of the cultural upheaval in all its destructive and creative glory."[2]

Although several housing patterns and types were developed during the British Raj, the most famous and lasting legacy has been that of the "bungalow," the detached, individual dwelling that is found everywhere in India. It is a building type that spread almost all over the colonial world. Towards the turn of the twentieth century, the bungalow emerged as a new and "modern" urban dwelling form on the domestic landscape as an alternative to the medieval system of dense housing that existed in the crowded inner cities of India (Figure 20.1). Although the affluent sections of society often lived in large houses such as the *Havelis* in Gujarat or the *Wadas* in Maharastra, the bungalow was an altogether new and modern type that came about as a result of a historical revolution in the plan, form and structure of the dwelling unit. The type gradually grew more sophisticated and opulent, coming closer to the European villa in concept. There were variations in size, style and ornamentation as the form went through a spatial evolution along with the political, technological, and cultural changes in society due to the growing influences of modernity as the twentieth century progressed. The bungalow remained a favorite option during the heyday of the Modern Movement until the 1970s, in the state of Gujarat as well as the rest of India.[3]

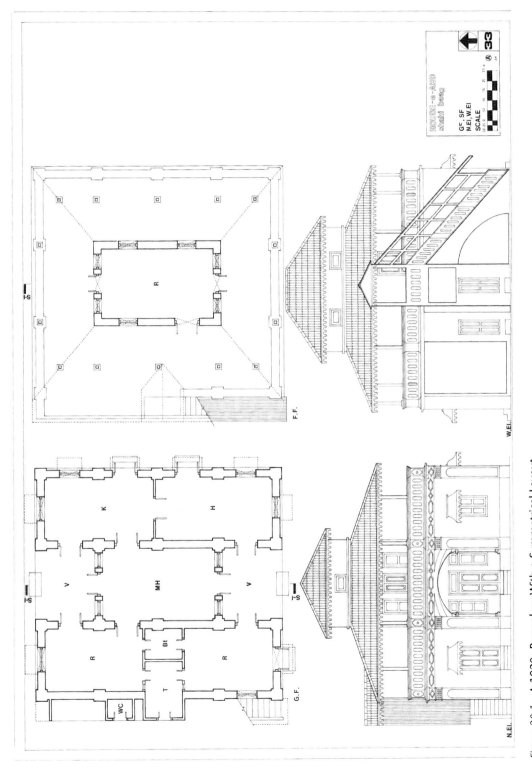

Figure 20.1 A 1920s Bungalow With a Symmetrical Layout
Source: © Miki Desai, Archicrafts Archives.

Madhavi Desai

As established by Amos Rapoport, there is a close relationship between sociocultural factors in a community and house forms.[4] The built environment is a cultural artifact, and architecture is the physical expression of culture. Space is socially constructed.[5] As a product of culture, space is not innate but is the setting of life and its various rituals and activities. Cultural rules that are often internalized govern the use of space, and codes regulate behavior between genders. Thus, the physical form mediates and structures gender relations. It has been widely argued that house forms are influenced by the gender roles embedded in family structures. As society changes, the built environment also responds through modifications and alterations.

This chapter attempts to analyze the typology of the bungalow in the State of Gujarat as it evolved during the twentieth century as a modern house form deeply embedded in the interrelationship of society, regional culture and gender. Beyond the biological differences between men and women, gender differences are shaped by several determinants such as history, culture, religion and environment. Being in a diverse, unequal and plural nation of various ethnic, religious and language groups, an Indian woman's identity is ever-shifting, informed by the country's colonial past, the modern era and the rapidly changing, "globalizing" present, where she is often in transition. Therefore, this chapter will be looking at middle-class women in general and will resort to certain generalizations in spite of the heterogeneity of women's backgrounds such as caste, community, religion, and economic strata.

Feminism and the Idea of the Modern

The concept of feminism is fluid; it changes with time and context. It has long been controversial in a postcolonial context in India, mainly because of the problematic construction of feminism along the lines of Eurocentric liberalism as understood by the Indian society at large. An examination of Indian architectural discourses in history and theory reveals that, for the most part, issues of race, gender or class do not figure in the scholarship, as opposed to a number of other disciplines where gender research has a strong presence and where feminist thinking has affected the production of knowledge and modes of representation. But within the discipline of architecture, the marginalization of feminism in oral or written mainstream discussions has affected both theory and practice. This exclusion has also submerged the role of feminist knowledge in the historical narrative of architecture—an issue this chapter attempts to address.

In addition, "the idea of the modern in India is deeply gendered."[6] In post-colonial narrative, the modern woman is expected to embody both the traditional cultural identity of "Indian" and the modern reality of changing social structures. In the colonial as well as post-colonial periods, the internal and external forces working on Indian society brought tradition and modernity together. It has been assumed that gender equality is built into the discourse on modernity because independent India's constitution has proclaimed it as a part of being a "modern" nation. However, with the predominant position being that the built environment is gender neutral, there is a huge lacuna in the study of the relationship of space and gender, especially the influence of technological and spatial modernity on women's everyday lives and domestic architecture, which this chapter attempts to address through the evolution of the bungalow. Rooted in the colonial house form, the bungalow grew in response to political, social, cultural and technological changes in society. From a military dwelling in the cantonment, it became an imperial villa and finally a modernist house. At the same time, from a barely educated woman with many children, being a part of a joint family while fully engaged in cooking and household activities, the Gujarati woman gradually began living in a nuclear family, going to college and then taking up professional courses and controlling her number of children, thus becoming a product of modernity. How this change was reflected in the development of the bungalow is the key inquiry.

352

Women and Society in Gujarat

Located on the west coast of India, the State of Gujarat has the longest coastline among all states in India. Until the medieval period, it could boast of several excellent ports such as Khambhat, Bhrugukutch, Surat, Ghoga, Rander and Mandavi, through which the people of Gujarat established trade connections with Africa, Southeast Asia and West Asia. It also had a network of land routes for trade that went as far as China via northern India, as well as to the Middle East via Afghanistan and Iran. The intense commercial activities made Gujarat a cultural melting pot of civilizations and empires and also gave rise to prosperous urban centers and settlements that evolved in response to myriad forces including foreign influences in the form of commerce, travel or invasions.

At the turn of the twentieth century, Gujarat society had a rather provincial and medieval mentality with its moorings in the traditions of entrepreneurship, astuteness, and a lifestyle that nurtured family life. Unlike Tamil Nadu, Kerala and Uttar Pradesh, society was not dominated by the Brahmin caste. The people were practical, accommodating and progressive.[7] Agriculture was the major occupation in rural areas, while trading was predominant in urban centers. The social structure of the pre-colonial period in Gujarat was strictly based on community and caste. There was adherence to social roles and traditional customs as prescribed by the community. Within this social context, the individual self was rather insignificant. Typically a woman was married after puberty and spent her life bringing up numerous children and looking after the house and the family. However, there began to be a gradual change in this situation from the mid-nineteenth century onwards due to new political, economic and educational institutions and processes, including the effects of modernization during colonial rule.

Further structural changes took place in society from 1920 to 1970. The role of women underwent a slow but definite transformation, although the system of a joint family largely remained in place, at least until the 1950s. Girls' education, social awareness against child marriages and widow remarriages, the beginning of participation in economic activities like the service sector and the professions and the creation of social organizations brought about a gradual transformation of women's lives[8] (Figure 20.2). The crucial factor became the freedom struggle against the British rule led by Gandhi, in which women began to take part in a major way, because

> by the 1920s, two quite different rationales for women's rights were being expressed: the one that women's rights should be recognized because of women's socially useful role as mothers; the other that women, having the same needs, desires and capacities as men, were entitled to the same rights.[9]

Mahatma Gandhi established the Sabarmati Ashram in Ahmedabad and lived in the city from 1915 to 1930. His presence, activities and thoughts were significant at the national level in general, but also in the local context in particular by inspiring women's leadership. He gave women new self-worth and dignity by encouraging them to join public life and participate in the freedom struggle against the British.[10]

By 1940s, education for women was an accepted norm in urban areas. Women came out of their narrow domestic world struggling for political as well as social freedom. From passive spectators, they became active agents of change. As the century progressed, many women's institutions and organizations arose. There were also other changes like a reduction in the number of children born to couples, the introduction of modern amenities that reduced women's household labor and the diminishing number of servants per household.

Figure 20.2 A Woman Graduate in 1947
Source: Personal archive.

Women and the Domestic Realm

Indian society being predominantly patriarchal, a woman is closely associated with the domestic built environment because the notion of "home" is intricately intertwined with her self-image. A woman bears almost the entire burden of nurturing and housekeeping, whether she is working in the public domain or not. "A woman's competence and worth were judged by her ability to preserve order and maintain harmony in the family and house, in short, as a homemaker."[11] The home is at the center of a woman's life as well as her daily activities. Along with ritual, caste and kinship, gender plays an important role in the negotiation of space.[12] It accommodates the male/female dichotomy symbolically and spatially. It determines the way in which the relations between men and women are socially constructed and how this construct affects their roles in society.

The Traditional Pre-colonial Dwellings in Gujarat

Most premodern urban settlements in Gujarat were dense and compact towns contained by a peripheral wall. The social division of the population was reflected in the morphology of the town. The settlement was segregated into micro-neighborhoods called *pols* based on well-defined, cohesive

The Bungalow in the Twentieth Century

communities/castes such as Suthar, Brahmin and Bania. A system of mixed land use existed in response to the traditional social structure of the period when retailing, manufacturing, and living formed a close symbiosis. In a hierarchical circulation pattern, the main roads, secondary streets and the *bazaar*s became public spaces. Open spaces were restricted to small squares. The street was a social space, primarily an area of communication and reciprocal social exchange. Many activities took place outside the house, in the streets. Typologically most houses (between two parallel walls) were deep with three (or four) sequential rooms, one behind the other, and a narrow frontage with a highly ornamented facade that opened onto a street. The spatial organization of the dwelling was inward-looking with a small courtyard in the center[13] (Figure 20.3). Broadly, the front rooms belonged to the men and the back areas to the women, while the centrally located courtyard acted as a transitional space.

The spatial divisions within the private space were fluid and multifunctional. This resulted in complex negotiations by the women, responding to social notions of ritual pollution, morality and social hierarchy. These traditional dwellings are inhabited even today, albeit in a modified social and physical form, with the settlement having a more heterogeneous population in contrast to the past.

The bungalow arrived as an alien alternative house form, a counter-concept to the more or less socially geared, community-oriented, collective lifestyle that was manifest in the urban dwellings of organic settlements in medieval India. In addition, the grid system of the newly developed suburbs looked sparse and orderly. Roads, wide lanes and the frontage gave the bungalow a sought-after image of a "modern" home. As the status of women changed in society, the spatial and symbolic layout of the bungalow responded to it. This chapter will try to decode this intense cultural/spatial relationship manifest in the bungalow, while deconstructing the real and imaginary gender boundaries and understanding the creation of modern gender identities.

Figure 20.3 The Courtyard as a Transitional Space
Source: © Miki Desai, 2012.

355

The Bungalow as a New Concept[14]

The bungalow was a "generic 'building type' from which that general range of buildings and these basic principles of construction could be said to have derived."[15] It represented a spatial autonomy and a form that clearly expressed the social and political divide between the rulers and the masses:

> The location of the bungalow-in-its-compound, away from places of Indian settlement, expressed the political and social relationship between the occupants of both. Spatial distance reflected social distance. The closely clustered houses of the Indian town or village were functional not just in terms of climate or existing technology and transport; they also expressed the basic social and economic relationship of their inhabitants.[16]

It was a symbol of the imperial culture that was transformed into a sophisticated, stylistic version of the house. The British in India also viewed this bungalow type with a lot of nostalgia, as they attempted to create a home away from home. Gradually the bungalow got absorbed into Indian culture when adopted by the middle class, mainly due to the population's desire for a healthy environment and their eagerness to appear modern and progressive. Thus, it developed, through the nineteenth and even twentieth century, as an alternative and distinctive dwelling form in the subcontinent. As we will see later, the form was regionalized in Gujarat (and elsewhere) in response to the people's lifestyle, local climate, materials and building techniques.

British Bungalows in Cantonments

The cantonments developed in most Indian cities in order to house the increasing numbers of British civil and military personnel away from the chaos and squalor of the "native" part of the city, which was generally overcrowded and lacked basic amenities. The civil lines contained the administrative offices and courts as well as residential areas for the officers. They invariably had large open spaces and roads that were built according to a plan, with administrative buildings occupying a central position. While maintaining a physical and social distance from the masses, the design of cantonments also aimed to create an environment similar to a European one:

> The stations were laid out on a grid-pattern of spacious avenues lined with pretty classical bungalows. Each bungalow, designed with a veranda on three sides, was set in its own garden compound and shaded by bougainvillaea, climbing plants and shaded trelliswork. Large open areas were laid out as parade grounds for drill and training, whilst the bigger garrisons had their own clubs, racecourses and parks. The focus for most cantonments was the church.[17]

The typical early bungalow located in the military cantonments of the cities of Gujarat, such as Baroda and Ahmedabad, was a single-storied structure with the clear territorial definition of a walled compound.[18] It was simple, austere and utilitarian. It was a largely symmetrical composition with a generous hall in the center and spacious rooms (dining, study and bedrooms) with very high roofs at the corners off the hall. Bathrooms were provided separately on the outside; however, later on they were attached to the bedrooms. Invariably there was a wide, multifunctional and extensive veranda around three (or four) sides of the house for climatic protection. The veranda was an important transitional social space that was neither as public as the street nor as secluded as the house itself. The structure was built in response to the hot-dry or hot-humid climate of Gujarat. Thick walls, high ceilings, a ventilator system, flat or high-pitched roofs (or a combination of both) and semi-open spaces were used. The sociopolitical superiority of the British was expressed through classical ornamentation and European references in design, particularly in the facades.

The Bungalow in the Twentieth Century

For the British, India offered a kind of lifestyle that they could never have imagined in their own country:

> [The British] bride found her life subordinated to that of her husband, as his was to the Raj, a patriarchal hierarchy shot through with a rigid protocol. . . . In India a girl who was too plain or too poor to find a husband in Britain would be showered with proposals; and she and her husband would live life at a much higher standard than either could at home, with a retinue of servants, spacious bungalows and all the sport you could wish.[19]

On the other hand, the life of the wives of the British officers in India was also rather difficult and alien. Away from their native lands and familiar surroundings, they did not feel very comfortable in the almost hostile climatic conditions of the Indian plains. While their husbands were on duty, the wives had little to do. The tropical heat did not allow them any outside life, nor did the unhygienic and filthy towns hold any appeal for them. The ladies eventually brought with them, from England, all sorts of paraphernalia like furniture, curtains, cupboards and chinaware. They also developed the art of gardening, growing some of the native plants as well as bringing from their hometowns various flowering and non-flowering plants. They spent their time in setting up their household in as "English" a manner as possible and entertaining guests. They had the privilege of employing several servants; therefore, leisure time, combined with plentiful Indian labor, encouraged entertaining and social gatherings. Thus the role of the *memsahib* of the house was rather ceremonial. The kitchen, servants' quarters and service areas were always located to the rear of the house, often joined to the main unit by a roofed corridor.[20]

The Bungalow as a Villa

The westernization of domestic life in Gujarat, like the rest of India, began at the top of the socio-economic ladder. The first of the bungalows were built at the turn of the twentieth century by the wealthy and westernized elites of Gujarat who preferred the new housing form for reasons of health, sanitation and social prestige. They generally owned horse carriages and were able to move out of the traditional parts of the cities to live in the new type of housing located at a distance, in favorable surroundings and with greater quiet and privacy. For example, in Ahmedabad and Surat, the first bungalows came up to the edges of the walled cities, often on the banks of the river on which the original town was situated. Later on they began to be built farther away as the suburbs developed. Besides status consciousness, a desire to live a more individual lifestyle as opposed to collective community living was the motivation that made the concept of the bungalow a success. The new bungalow was a typical villa-like, spacious mansion set in large grounds that had a garden and recreational facilities. The compound was landscaped with flower beds, lawns, fernery, tall trees, perhaps a fountain in the center and amenities such as tennis and badminton courts. There were porches at the front verandas. Influenced by the neoclassical style of the public buildings of that time, these bungalows were generally brick structures having facades adorned with features of Grecian or other European classicism blended in (Figure 20.4). Thus, the bungalow truly presented an architecture of "social mobility and distinction" as the owners attempted to imitate the imperial rulers.

Since the nineteenth century, there has been a distinct progressive trend due to the westernized education of Indian men. Men wanted to transform women's private spheres of household and family, to make them more fitting mothers, efficient housewives and enlightened companions. As girls were encouraged to get an education, the roots of traditional bondage to the home were shaken and gradual change began. Therefore, the first half of the twentieth century, with increasing exposure to European lifestyles, women were sharply caught between tradition and modernity. The rich and elite women living in the villas in Gujarat basically looked up to and emulated the British. They went to college,

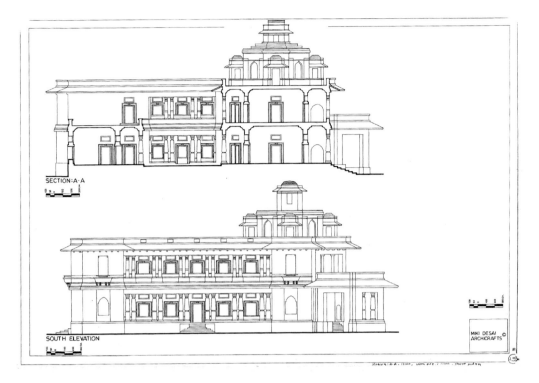

Figure 20.4 The Bungalow as a Mansion With "Indianized" Elements
Source: © Miki Desai, Archicrafts Archives.

played tennis and took piano lessons. But the extended family structure was still the prevalent norm, with three generations often living together under one roof in a largely traditional and patriarchal household.[21] These rich families had extensive outside help in the form of cooks, servants, *ayahs*, a driver, sweepers, and gardeners, most of whom were provided accommodation in the bungalow compound. The layout reflected the social hierarchy. In spite of the apparent modernity in lifestyle, gender divisions existed in social interactions in the residential space.[22]

The Bungalow as a Middle Class Home

At the turn of the twentieth century, the bungalow gradually began to become popular in Gujarat, although traditional house types also continued to be utilized. By the 1930s, there was substantial growth of an educated, westernized middle class in Gujarat. The bungalow ideology became democratized and accessible to this class of city dwellers. As it became adopted by a growing section of this society, its meaning and social value subtly changed, and it also became compact as the plot size diminished. Housing societies, plotted development layouts and city planning with motorized vehicles for the modern age began to take shape. Co-operative housing societies were a popular trend in 1920s and 1930s in Gujarat. The suburbs had begun to develop in new areas on the fringes of the cities away from the historic walled cities. For example, in the town of Bhavnagar planned plotted development was proposed for the people:

> In India, suburbanization is related to the shift of population in newly developed areas with new housing structure and new pattern of interaction. But even in modern suburban societies there are

The Bungalow in the Twentieth Century

certain ways of traditional lifestyle, e.g. caste system, which has regulated Indian rural life for several centuries and which plays an important role in the growth of the process of suburbanization.[23]

People of the same caste or community pooled their resources and collectively bought land in the new suburbs in order to move out of the inner cities. Films and magazines showed images of houses and interiors, promoting the modern lifestyle. In addition, the use of pattern books in one or another form, some even in regional languages, affected the development and aesthetics of the bungalow. For example, booklets that promoted the use of cement carried views of modern houses. The Indian Cement Company began producing cement in India in 1914, but it became popular as a modern material only in the 1940s and 1950s. Thus, a large clientele for the bungalow emerged from a traditional society that had thus far been hesitant to adopt the new mores.

The ramifications of this new type of housing on neighborhood planning and the resulting urban fabric were immense, and the residential and urban patterns of the cities changed completely. Compared to the close-knit, rather organic morphology of the inner city, the new geometrical layouts had road networks with plots for the bungalows. In contrast to the familiar *pols*, the bungalow was an object in space, a building placed in the middle of a well-defined and protected area. For women, it brought relative isolation, both personally and socially, particularly as their mobility was restricted in comparison to that of men. Their social world was more or less confined to the neighborhood. At the same time, in the new location, caste and kinship began to play a less significant role in their lives, creating a new sense of freedom. Nevertheless, there was no doubt that the new dwelling type signified a high socioeconomic status for men and women at that time.

Within the house, there was clear gender segregation in social interaction. There was a separate kitchen area behind or at the back of the bungalow where servants and the women of the house undertook cooking and supervising activities. The hall was the most elaborately decorated, formal space, with colonial furniture. The men entertained there, and the women often segregated into another space for interaction. In day-to-day living, women were closely associated with the kitchen and utility areas. The central hall and the front veranda were designated as predominantly male domains. As observed by Kumar:

> [A]ttempts were made to carve out the space of "women's work" which, for both middle class and poor women, centred on her biologically defined qualities of motherhood. Women's skills, it seems, were seen as "nurturing" ones, such as nursing, cooking, cleaning, teaching, or those which followed from their traditional household duties, such as food processing and handicrafts.[24]

The Nationalist Ideology

Along with the westernizing influence, there was another growing force that was affecting society throughout India during the first half of the twentieth century. Strong nationalistic sentiments, a result of the freedom struggle against the imperial rule, brought about revivalism in architecture. During this period the bungalow was gradually modified to respond more to the regional lifestyle, climate and culture of the people in Gujarat, as well as to nationalist sentiments. Gandhi's presence in Ahmedabad from 1915 to 1930 was crucial to Gujarati elites and the middle class in their search for an alternative expression of their "Indian" identity.

The book *Grihvidhan* by Virendraray C. Mehta, a visionary and an engineer, was published in the Gujarati language in 1937.[25] *Grihvidhan*, which can be considered a pattern book or a handbook, is a masterpiece that is copiously illustrated. It contains a wealth of information, particularly concerning the domestic architecture for Gujarat during the early twentieth century. The material of the book had the unique value of reviving what was best in the indigenous tradition as well as adopting

Western concepts to make them fit Indian traditions and environment. The first half of the book covered theoretical background, construction details and specifications; the other half consisted of numerous varieties of dwelling designs (plans and elevations), which attempted to reflect the socio-cultural and economic patterns within the society at large.[26] In plan after plan, we find that although these houses and bungalows were spacious and included a hall as well as an office specifically for the men (at times), a large room designated as being the "women's room" was always provided for the collective use of the women and children living in the joint family system, where they could change clothes, feed the babies, keep the cradles and perhaps take a nap in the afternoon between household tasks.

Towards the 1930s, the growing sense of revivalism began to introduce a transformation in the facades of the houses, bringing in references from the past. A humanized scale, sloping overhangs, arches, corbelling, decorative precast cement *jalis* and motifs from Hindu and Islamic architecture were the elements that brought about a distinct change in the image of the bungalow. The plan organization responded to the social reality of regional lifestyles. A courtyard was introduced to respond not only to the climate, but also to the social set-up; that is, the joint family with its gender divisions. Many spaces such as a storeroom, a *puja* room, and a sewing room were added to match the extensive lifestyle of a Gujarati family, specifically where women's household work was concerned. This work included the yearly making of pickles, the yearly cleaning and drying of grains, and many ancillary functions. Rituals regarding pollution[27] were practiced strictly. Often there was a special bathroom for the ritual baths of menstruating women. The daily movements of the women in the family were centered around the courtyard and the kitchen areas, where elaborate food-related activities took place.

> The concept of equality, as a correlate of the concept of individual freedom, is alien to Indian society. It was first introduced into Indian culture through western education and through the exposure of western-educated Indians to liberalism, at the beginning of the nineteenth century. But it did not become an operational principle of Indian life until the country achieved independence and adopted a democratic system of governance.[28]

The Art Deco Influence

The bungalow simultaneously began to respond to the fashionable styles Art Deco and Streamline Moderne, which were introduced to metropolitan areas in India via images from Europe and the US and first used on commercial buildings in India from the 1930s onwards. Bungalows built in this mode often had a curved veranda at the ground floor and a balcony on the first floor (Figure 20.5). Flat terraces characterized the style, in addition to an abstract ornamentation, embossed emblems, decorative grilles made of steel and built-in furniture. The buildings that used "Indian" elements of the past, as mentioned earlier, were called "Indo Deco" buildings.

Art (or Indo) Deco buildings generally had an asymmetrical spatial organization, which was also reflected in the facades. The kitchen was now a part of the main house, particularly in middle-class homes where servants were comparatively fewer and the land available was limited. The outhouses and servants' quarters continued to be built behind the main house. The bungalow had now become more utilitarian than luxurious. The courtyard often acted as a buffer zone for protecting the privacy of the women. In Saurashtra, where the Gujarati society is more conservative, an additional stair was provided in at the back part of certain houses so that women's movements could be separate from those of the men. Joint families[29] were beginning to break up. The living and dining areas were designed as adjoining but separate spaces. On ceremonial and religious occasions, men and women sat separately, being segregated along gender lines.[30] The living room and the front veranda remained male domains, while women interacted in the dining room or an ancillary room during social functions.

The Bungalow in the Twentieth Century

Figure 20.5 An Art Deco Bungalow
Source: © Miki Desai, 2017.

By the time India gained political independence in 1947, it had embarked on an ambitious project of modernization. The policies of the nation-state and its constitution revolved around making India a modern nation: "[T]here was a strong desire among the political leadership, more specifically the first Prime Minister Jawaharlal Nehru, to employ architecture as a means of expressing the vitality, progress and 'modern-ness' of the emerging nation state."[31] Modernization brought about gradual structural transformation of Indian society with changes in culture, values and social norms. The bungalow, at that moment, was on the threshold of embracing the principles of the Modern Movement, already well established in Europe and America.

Modernist Houses

In the post-independence period, the bungalow continued to be popular in Gujarat, as suburban housing increased at a fast rate between 1950 and 1970. By then, the notion of "home" as a detached building enclosed by land had become deeply rooted in the Gujarati society. With technological and economic changes and the dominance of Modern Movement principles, the bungalow underwent yet another transformation, as architects in Gujarat developed a completely different vocabulary and used new building materials and structural systems, denouncing the old-world order to embrace the new. They consciously "shed" ornamentation, separating form from decoration, and avoiding it as irrelevant to the purity and honesty of the building. Geometric patterns and abstract composition dominated the visual form. Of significance are the bungalow examples in the international and the Brutalist modes, where roofs were flattened and a new syntax of space-making was introduced, while

Madhavi Desai

features such as the porch, the veranda and the balcony were retained. By the 1960s and 1970s it was no longer called a "bungalow" but became a "modern" house. The house was a composition in space, indirectly changing as well as reflecting women's evolving relationship to home.

> Traditional gender segregation becomes difficult to maintain [in a modern house]. Space, together with changes in social and economic structure, causes a breakdown in gender barriers. The restructuring of gender roles in the direction of greater egalitarianism contributes to the process of social change in a modernizing society.[32]

Caste and kinship had begun to play a much less significant role in an individual's life by the 1960s. This was accompanied by a growing privatization of family life. Simultaneously, feminist ideas gained influence as more and more women joined the workforce as well as new professions:[33]

> Now the pattern is changing and many women, after obtaining better education, either earn their living because of a need to augment family resources, or take up professional jobs because they want to enlarge their horizons and become responsible citizens who can contribute to the national effort.[34]

By 1970s, there was a clear preference for a nuclear family structure, and the family size was consciously limited by having two or three children. The role of women had definitely undergone a change whereby her individuality was recognized. Relatively speaking, "nuclear family life leads to an equalization of the marital relationship and this is already visible in Indian professional classes."[35] In a nuclear family, women had more time for a lifestyle that was relatively leisure-oriented and consumerist, even though there were fewer servants available. There were radical transformations in the notions of privacy as well as personal space. The definition of a wife came close to that of a companion to whom one can turn, and with whom one can share joys and sorrows.

In the modernist tradition, floor plans became more open. Most of the practicing architects in Gujarat were Western educated and fairly influenced by masters such as Le Corbusier and Frank Lloyd Wright. The living and dining spaces were combined as the major public space in the house (Figure 20.6). The interior space was beginning to draw special attention as a designed space:

> One of modernist architecture's key propositions was a total redefinition of the nature and significance of the interior of architectural structure, the domestic dwelling among them. They eradicated the idea of gendered spaces in the home and instead opened up the interior to become an extension of the exterior.[36]

There was a considerable stylistic change in the making of the interiors, furniture design and surface treatments due to the modern influence. As the importance and role of the woman of the house increased, the kitchen spaces also began to be constantly upgraded with newer finishes, detailing and modern gadgets. The kitchen was integrated into the living-dining configuration, instead of being at the back. As a result, the space became more gender inclusive while modifying the dynamics of social interaction. The living room was used mainly for relaxation, and recreation or interaction within the family and with guests. The bedroom was the space that gave the woman of the house her private territory in relative terms. The modernist house, however, remained a symbol of social mobility or socioeconomic status. It was here that the consumerist lifestyle manifested itself. After 1980, skyrocketing land prices in urban areas brought in the decline of the bungalow typology as people had to resort to other, emerging, alternative forms of housing, such as walk-up apartments and row houses, as well as high-rises.

The Bungalow in the Twentieth Century

Figure 20.6 A Modernist House
Source: © Miki Desai, 1997.

Conclusions

In this chapter, I have attempted to portray the evolution of a dominant urban house type in Gujarat in the twentieth century with respect to the construct of gender, including the spatial interpretation of concepts of modernity. The chapter traces the transformation of the bungalow as it evolved from a dwelling unit with a symmetrical layout in the military cantonment to a modernist house, a transformation that parallels the social path, role and position of women in Gujarat. At the turn of the twentieth century, the architectural expression in Gujarat was the result of the coming together of two cultures: an external colonial imposition of form and aesthetic style and an internal, regional (Gujarati) force based on sociocultural patterns and people's lifestyles. One can sense an inherent conflict of tradition with modernity. The main forces of social change were increasing education for women, transition to the nuclear family system, a limited number of children and radical changes in the notions of the self.

The bungalow as a type symbolized "modernity," as it was a distinct break with building traditions of pre-colonial times. It was also a means for the people of Gujarat to define themselves and their modern identity. It is evident that as the twentieth century progressed, a less sharp division of the spatial divide between genders became evident, with a gradual shift occurring towards a more egalitarian status for women in the family. We find that from the rather ceremonial role of a British housewife living in the early bungalows, the Indian woman had come to achieve more spatial control and better social status in the 1970s, particularly within the nuclear family structure. The family's spatial organization shifted from having gender segregation and the limitation of a designated "women's room" to more egalitarian open and integrated floor plans in the modernist house, as women's personal and marital spaces became socially legitimate.

With the new clustering pattern, the modern gridiron neighborhood introduced a degree of isolation in the lives of the women, yet at the same time increased their sense of privacy and control over space. Although the facades were symmetrical and highly articulated, the plan organization reflected the lower status of women, social change being slower than aesthetic and stylistic modifications. The location of the kitchen was, moreover, crucial to the changing social position of women in Gujarat. From a separate structure behind the house to a location towards the back of the house, the kitchen moved to being next to the living and dining spaces as time passed. Changes such as the common bath, a purely utilitarian space in a joint family structure of the pre-independence period, were replaced by a bath attached to the master bedroom, a luxurious space symbolizing the acceptance of the idea of pleasure and a sense of companionship in matrimony. However, with cooking and nurturing still being the women's responsibilities, their connection to the kitchen and utility areas remained (and to this day remains) strong, whether in a joint or a nuclear family. Women still have a long journey towards a completely egalitarian social attitude and house form.

Notes

1. This chapter is further developed from Desai 2007b.
2. Hosagrahar 2005.
3. See Desai and Desai 1995.
4. Rapoport 1969.
5. Weisman 1992.
6. Chaudhury 2012.
7. As early as in 1902, two women in Gujarat completed their education from Bombay University; see Panchal, Taylor, and Shukla 2002.
8. Desai 1983.
9. Kumar 1993.
10. "The coming of British rule brought in western modern ideas like secularism, democracy, equality and rights to the individual. Alongside, there also developed indigenous ideas of nationalism. Both these developments led to an introspection of one's own society." Colonialism in India: The Gender Question-Virtual Learning Environment 2017, Nationalist Agenda for Social Reformers and Women, last modified June 29. http://vle.du.ac.in/mod/book/view.php?id=11512&chapterid=21974, accessed on March 8, 2017.
11. Hirschon 1985.
12. Niranjana 2001.
13. Desai 2007a.
14. Several explanations exist about the etymology of the word "bungalow." The most accepted one is that it came from the vernacular hut of Bengal, a thatched house with walls of mud or matting that the military engineers of the East India Company of England based their shelters early on.
15. Scriver 1994.
16. King 1984.
17. Davies 1985.
18. This entire concept was new in contrast to the dense housing of India's inner cities.
19. Telegraph 2017. www.telegraph.co.uk/history/9408142/The-women-who-flocked-to-India-to-bag-a-husband.html, Last modified March 9, 2017.
20. Bhatt 1998.
21. Observing the joint family system elsewhere in India, the Webbs noted in 1912:

> There were three separate houses joined together by covered passages—a large handsome guest house of the ordinary European style of these parts, a house for women and children . . . and a smaller, shabbier edition for the servants. The family consisted of our host and his wife, two widowed sisters and some 30 or 40 young people of two generations—sons and nephews and their wives and their children. The ladies were 'Purdah,' and lived in seclusion, and never left their establishments except on pilgrimages, or in the case of the married ladies to visit their own mothers.
>
> *(Webb and Webb 1992)*

22. Gendered divisions existed within the servants too. The men generally worked in the public areas of the house such as the living/dining/kitchen while the women took care of and had access to bedrooms of children and couples.

23. Sengupta 1988.
24. Kumar 1993.
25. Mehta 1939.
26. Desai and Desai 1993.
27. In the Hindu religion, as per tradition, menstruating women used to be considered impure and had to follow certain rules. During their menses, they were not allowed to enter the kitchen and temples or touch other males and females, among other behavioral constraints. These rules hardly exist now in urban areas.
28. Chitnis 1988.
29. A joint family, which was a norm in India, is one where members of a unilineal descent group (descent through the male line) live together with their spouses and offspring in one homestead and under the authority of one of the members.
30. This is true to a great extent even today, definitely in rural areas and most often in urban areas.
31. Desai 2017.
32. Sinha 1991.
33. "In this century Indian women have undergone a social revolution rather more far-reaching and radical than that of men. In fact this quiet revolution (it also had its spectacular moments in the nationalist struggle) is the most important element in the social changes that have occurred in modern India" (Lannoy 1971).
34. Lannoy 1971.
35. Lannoy 1971.
36. Sparke 1995.

References

Bhatt, Vikram. 1998. *Resorts of the Raj: Hill Stations of India.* Ahmedabad: Mapin.
Chaudhury, Maitreyee. 2012. "Indian 'Modernity' and 'Tradition': A Gender Perspective." *Polish Sociological Review* 2(178): 277–289.
Chitnis, Suma. 1988. "Feminism: Indian Ethos and Indian Convictions." In *Women in Indian Society: A Reader*, edited by Rehana Ghadially, 81–95. New Delhi: Sage.
Davies, Philip. 1985. *Splendours of the Raj: British Architecture in India 1660–1947.* Middlesex: Penguin Books.
Desai, Madhavi. 2007a. *Traditional Architecture: House Form of Bohras in Gujarat.* Pune: NIASA.
Desai, Madhavi. 2007b. "Women and Architecture of the Colonial Bungalow in Gujarat: 1920 to 1970." In *Gender and the Built Environment in India*, edited by Madhavi Desai, 146–168. New Delhi: Zubaan.
Desai, Madhavi. 2017. *Women Architects and Modernism in India: Narratives and Contemporary Practices.* London and New York: Routledge.
Desai, Madhavi, and Miki Desai. 1993. "Grihvidhan: A Discourse on House Form." *Architecture+Design* 10(2): 43–47.
Desai, Madhavi, and Miki Desai. 1995. "The Adaptation and Growth of the Bungalow in India." In *Environmental Design: European Houses in Islamic Countries*, edited by Attilio Petruccioli, 104–121. Rome: Journal of the Islamic Environmental Design Research Centre.
Desai, Neera. 1983. *Gujaratma Ognismisadima Samajik Parivartan.* Ahmedabad: University Granthanirman Board [in Gujarati].
Hirschon, Renee. 1985. "The Woman-environment Relationship: Greek Cultural Values in an Urban Community." *Ekistics* 310 (January/February): 15–21.
Hosagrahar, Jyoti. 2005. *Indigenous Modernities: Negotiating Architecture and Urbanism.* London and New York: Routledge.
King, Anthony D. 1984. *The Bungalow: The Production of a Global Culture.* London: Routledge & Kegan Paul.
Kumar, Radha. 1993. *The History of Doing: An Illustrated Account of Movements for Women's Rights and Feminism in India, 1800–1900.* New Delhi: Kali for Women.
Lannoy, Richard. 1971. *The Speaking Tree: A Study of Indian Culture and Society.* New Delhi: Oxford University Press.
Mehta, Virendraray, C. 1939. *Grihavidhan.* Bhavnagar: City Improvement Office [in Gujarati].
Niranjana, Seemanthini. 2001. *Gender and Space: Femininity, Sexualization and the Female Body.* New Delhi: Sage.
Panchal, Shirish, Bakul Taylor, and Jaydev Shukla. 2002. *Vismi Sadinu Gujarat*, Vol. 23. Vadodara: Samvad Prakashan [in Gujarati].
Rapoport, Amos. 1969. *House Form and Culture.* Englewood Cliffs, NJ: Prentice-Hall.
Scriver, Peter. 1994. *Rationalization, Standardization and Control in Design: A Cognitive Historical Study of Architectural Design and Planning in the Public Works Department of British India: 1855–1901.* Ph.D. Dissertation. Technische Universiteit Delft, Netherlands.

Sengupta, Smita. 1988. *Residential Pattern of Suburbs*. New Delhi: Concept.

Sinha, Amita. 1991. "Women's Local Space: Home and Neighbourhood." In *Bridging Worlds-Studies on Women in South Asia*, edited by Sally Sutherland. Berkeley: University of California Regents. (Occasional paper series/Center for South Asia Studies, University of California at Berkeley).

Sparke, Penny. 1995. *As Long As It Is Pink: The Sexual Politics of Space*. London: Pandora.

Telegraph. 2017. "The-women-who-flocked-to-India-to-bag-a-husband.html." Last modified March 9, 2017. www.telegraph.co.uk/history/9408142/.

Virtual Learning Environment. 2017. "Nationalist Agenda for Social Reformers and Women." Last modified June 29. http://vle.du.ac.in/mod/book/view.php?id=11512&chapterid=21974, accessed on March 8, 2017.

Webb, Sidney, and Beatrice Webb. 1992. *The Webbs in Asia: The 1911–1912 Travel Diary*. Edited by George Feaver. Basingstoke: Palgrave Macmillan.

Weisman, Leslie K. 1992. *Discrimination by Design: A Feminist Critique of the Man-Made Environment*. Urbana and Chicago: University of Illinois Press.

21

Gendered Household Expectations

Neoliberal Policies, Graveyard Shifts, and Women's Responsibilities in Mumbai, India

Aparna Parikh

In 1991, under the aegis of Manmohan Singh—the then finance minister of the Nationalist Congress Party (and subsequently the prime minister of India from 2004 to 2014)—the Indian state adopted neoliberal policies, resulting in reduced government spending on public institutions and infrastructure, and increased support to facilitate private development and foreign investment. As part of neoliberal restructuring, the state enacted policies to facilitate direct investment in call centers. India was a favored location for this sector, primarily because of a large English speaking and technically skilled workforce. Call centers prefer hiring women, stating that women are "naturally" docile and can nurture, making them well suited for this job.[1] Women constitute 51% of the workforce in call centers,[2] a higher gender ratio than any other jobs in the IT (information technology) sector in India.[3] The night shift required for such work also causes changes in domestic life, requiring female workers to alter strategies for social reproduction.[4]

I conducted semi-structured interviews and participant observation to investigate how women adapt household responsibilities while working the night shift in call centers. From women's narratives of their daily routines and life cycle, I gleaned implicit or explicit references to discourses of tradition and modernity that guided their choices. I identified trends that illustrate the nature of adaptations across my research participants. I find that several women justify their entry into a paid workforce—particularly jobs involving night shifts—through a household "crisis" narrative that necessitated this decision. For these women, as well as several others, entering the paid workforce does not reduce their sphere of household responsibility, often resulting in reduced hours of sleep to manage both. This continued gendering of social reproduction also transfers to an extended chain of dependence on other people, primarily female kin members, for services including childcare, cooking, and cleaning. Thus, traditional ideas of gendered household responsibility continue even as women play a significant role in the functioning of neoliberal modernization. This chapter contributes to feminist scholarship focusing on social reproduction, particularly demonstrating the centrality of "tradition" in continuing expectations for gendered responsibility even as women enter the "modern" workforce.

Outsourced Call Centers in India

Since the 1980s, advanced telecommunications systems have presented a "spatial fix"[5] in unprecedented ways,[6] reducing the cost of information flows and coordination of industries across space. These efficient technologies are considered essential for the smooth flow of capital. Buttressed by technological advancements, neoliberal policies have resulted in increased capital flows between nation-states, and a geographic dispersal of services for marketing and production. While there is increased networking through telecommunications and flows of capital, there is fixed capital invested in built forms and the relative immobility of labor required to conduct service operations in outsourced sites. These sites are located primarily in major urban centers in the Global South.

The outsourcing of call centers mushroomed in the late 1990s as corporations sought to lower the cost of telephone-based customer service support. India became the favored location, gaining advantage over other countries because of lower minimum wages and the presence of a large English-speaking workforce with technical know-how. This was facilitated by an economy that had recently adopted free-market principles and liberalized controls on foreign direct investment.[7] Call centers in India operate primarily at night to accommodate daytime hours in the US. This night shift work has increased the number of people who work the night shift in Mumbai, India.[8] Unlike other outsourced sectors, particularly manufacturing industries, call centers have proliferated within cities (Figure 21.1). As a result, urban landscapes around call centers have been transformed, with altered transportation networks and hours of business (Figure 21.2). In 2015, the Indian government allocated about $74.5 million[9] to make urban India competitive for the call center industry

Figure 21.1 Call Center in Mumbai, India, 2015
Source: © Aparna Parikh.

Figure 21.2 Informal Activity on the Street Near Call Centers in Mumbai, India, 2015
Source: © Aparna Parikh.

in response to an acceleration of call centers in the Philippines.[10] The allocation is consistent with neoliberal tenets, with state support for the private sector through provision of infrastructure and incentives.

Call centers prefer hiring women, stating that women are "naturally" docile and have the ability to nurture, which makes them well suited for this job.[11] Women constitute 51% of the workforce in call centers,[12] which is a higher gender ratio than there is with any other jobs in the IT sector in India.[13] The graveyard shift requires women to traverse urban space at night while negotiating security concerns and the stigma of women in public space at late hours.[14] In this chapter, I focus on gendered expectations for household reproduction, through which I shed light on the intertwining of discourses of tradition and modernity in the functioning of the outsourced call center industry in India. Most women working in call centers in India are in their twenties or early thirties, have a college degree, and are middle-class urban women.[15] Call center employees intend this work to be a stepping-stone in their careers. However, many remain within the industry, often quitting one call center only to join another, as they are unable to find better paid work with their academic qualifications, or find that their skill sets from call center work are inadequate for other jobs.[16]

While many women working the night shift in Indian call centers quit after marriage, fearing disapproval from their in-laws,[17] some believe such work can be managed through an understanding between partners.[18] Unmarried or married, local or migrant, studies find that working the night shift entails a multiplicity of adaptations. In social life, this involves curtailed opportunities to meet

Aparna Parikh

friends and an inability to fulfill family obligations during religious events and festivals.[19] In domestic life, it involves changing arrangements for grocery shopping, cooking, cleaning, and childcare. This is particularly pressing for women as they are primarily responsible for social reproduction[20] as well as the "reputation" of the family.[21] Thus, the hours of operation have an impact on women that is distinct from the impact of such hours on their male co-workers, requiring careful negotiation between professional and domestic responsibilities.

Theoretical Framework

The entry of women into the "modern" workplace of outsourced call centers has been accompanied by the persistence of traditional norms regarding respectable femininity,[22] which in India is marked by a confluence of nation, gender, and class. In this chapter, I examine how a focus on household responsibility allows for an examination of the interplay between discourses of tradition and modernity, purported as dichotomous, in contemporary India.

In emphasizing women's choices and experiences, I examine the centrality—and continuity—of gendered social reproduction *even when* women are directly involved in processes of production. Feminist scholars have emphasized the importance of social reproduction for processes of production, particularly examining its centrality to capitalism.[23] Social reproduction involves "activities and attitudes, behaviors and emotions, responsibilities and relationships directly involved in the maintenance of life on a daily basis, and intergenerationally."[24] Women and minorities have historically borne a greater burden for social reproduction across contexts.[25] Feminist geographers have emphasized women and their geo-historical context as pivotal for examining social reproduction,[26] as well as its link to globalization.[27] There has been an emphasis on the exacerbation of individualized social reproduction through the diminishing presence of institutions associated with social reproduction following the introduction of neoliberal policies. However, others have pointed out the danger of this critique being applied uncritically across contexts, as it can involve a romanticizing of the past where the state played a significant role in providing for citizens, which is untrue in numerous settings, particularly in the Global South. In the Nepalese context,

> the old discriminatory structures [hinged on caste and ethnicity] have combined with international competition to keep poor women from traditionally oppressed groups at the bottom of the labor hierarchy. Although human rights rhetoric has helped to raise women's political awareness as measured by the conventional indicators, in reality the traditional discriminatory social structures have been shifted to the modern jobs as well.[28]

Building on these scholarly insights, I examine women's roles in social reproduction in relation to their entry into a neoliberal workforce.

I also build upon arguments by feminist geographers who have suggested the importance of the intimate as a starting point for understanding the global.[29] I argue that women working the night shift in outsourced call centers embody the link between the local and the global, where their altered strategies for social reproduction helps illuminate the impact of the outsourced call center industry, helping us to reconstrue the boundaries and synergy between modernity and tradition. The outsourced call center industry is hailed as one of the "strongest pillars" for achieving modernity in India.[30] Scholars argue that the IT[31] and outsourced sectors[32] are often conceived in opposition to tradition, and show how processes of modernization are often accompanied by a renewed emphasis on tradition,[33] or by a selective rejection of tradition to allow for desirable modernity.[34] In fact, in certain villages in southeastern India, dowry was *first introduced* in 1996.[35] The dowry was used to sponsor visas to Australia for IT jobs, thus indirectly facilitating a transnational IT industry, and

370

elevating the social status of the family. Xiang's findings demonstrate an adoption of hitherto absent regressive social practices and challenge assumptions of modernity associated with the IT industry. This instance helps disrupt a conception of modernity that is decoupled from or in opposition to tradition and emphasizes what cultural theorist Homi Bhabha[36] contends as the problematic "binary division of past and present." Bhabha argues that tradition often involves an evocation of a past "that is not necessarily a faithful sign of historical memory but a strategy of representing authority in terms of the artifice of the archaic."[37] Thus, the reference to "tradition" becomes a tool to perpetuate societal power relations, even while welcoming certain changes in political economy.[38] I find that there is a persistence—and even exacerbation—of "traditional" gendered practices for social reproduction, even as women work night shifts in outsourced call centers and participate in the functioning of the outsourced call center industry.

These continued gendered household roles rely on what Bhabha describes as the importance of the stereotype:

> The stereotype is not a simplification because it is a false representation of a given reality. It is a simplification because it is an arrested, fixated form of representation that, in denying the play of difference (which the negation through the Other permits), constitutes a problem for the *representation* of the subject in significations of psychic and social relations.[39]

This simplified representation is key to analyzing the narratives that facilitate the continuity of gendered social reproduction at the scale of the household. While these stereotypes do not stay static over time, the changes in the characterization of the ideal of Indian women continue to rely on patriarchal understandings of gendered household responsibility.[40]

This chapter contributes to the literature on social reproduction within neoliberal regimes through a focus on entry into a paid workforce, the continued gendering of household responsibility, and a reliance on kinship and other networks in adapting to night shift work. Drawing on details of everyday life within the broader realm of social reproduction, including the buying and preparation of food, upkeep of the household, and so on, I elaborate on the relation between social reproduction and gendered household responsibility within the context of neoliberal transitions.

Emerging Themes

This chapter is based on findings from ethnographic fieldwork around outsourced call centers in Mumbai, India, including semi-structured interviews with forty women and twelve men working night shifts, seven focus groups and participatory mapping with fourteen women working night shifts in call centers. About half of my female research participants were married, providing me perspective on variations of expected responsibilities between married and unmarried women. Women's marital status also played a salient role in how they presented their entry into call center work. In each of the interviews, a point of focus was on daily and weekly routines, as well as motivation to join the call center industry. While I obtained several contacts, I faced challenges setting up interviews with call center employees. This is because in addition to hectic work and domestic schedules, their shifts often varied on a weekly basis, receiving a roster for the following week only on Friday evening. The roster includes their shift timings as well as their weekly times off. This made it challenging to set up interviews, as participants often had to cancel because of last-minute changes in household chores based on the weekly roster. Each Saturday afternoon, I would contact potential research participants and attempt to set up interviews for the following week. We would go back and forth for a few weeks before managing to set up an interview slot. I was told by common acquaintances that it would be easier to get an interview slot with men working in the call center, because they "were free" after work, whereas women usually

Aparna Parikh

"had something or the other going on at home." This explanation provided me an indication of continued household responsibility by women, which was confirmed in numerous interviews thereafter. In the following three sections, I expand on how women working night shifts in outsourced call centers in Mumbai justified their entry into night shift work, managed household responsibility, and the networks they relied on to do so. I do so through a focus on experiences of exemplary women in each instance.

Crisis as Justification

I spoke with Anahita[41] during a break in her night shift at an outsourced call center. She was married, had two children, and lived in an intergenerational household with her husband's parents. This arrangement is typical in many Indian families. Anahita had a college degree and had worked in the call center industry for three years at the time I conducted the interview. Her current workplace was the second call center she had worked in. While she described her life as being "fairly reasonable" now, Anahita was sad as she narrated her entry into night shift work in call centers. Anahita explained that she had never thought of working in a call center, as she had been dubious of the "respectability" of those working night shifts. She clarified, saying:

> [N]ot only the character of these women, but also how everyone looks at them. But now of course, I know the other side. Now I'm here. And I see that a lot of my colleagues are just like me, from respectable families, and trying to make money. Well, trying to make money for their families. And many have similar reasons as me for doing night work.

Anahita's claims indicate the widespread stigma associated with night shift work. While stigma towards night shift work in India is not new, its contemporary iteration relies on a fear of promiscuity that can presumably result from corrupt Western influences that accompany the growth of the IT sector.[42] The assumptions regarding promiscuity are gendered, and materialize most acutely in night shift work. When the outsourced call center industry entered India, it was received dubiously due to stigmatized perceptions of night shift work,[43] and the industry made efforts to advertise women working in call centers as the "good women who work at night."[44] While contemporary Indian women are situated in contrast to those of previous generations, as well as lower-class, lower-caste women,[45] they are also distinguished from presumably promiscuous Western women through a focus on respectability, invoking discourses of "balance, restraint, and 'knowing the limit.'"[46] Thus, I find that women articulate their respectability while working night shifts in a modern industry by upholding traditional Indian values involving gendered household responsibility.

Like Anahita, numerous research participants spoke about the questions regarding women's respectability they had, or which were posed to them by family members or friends. This stigma was associated with the personality of those choosing to work night shifts, or the "bad habits" women would presumably acquire once they worked in call centers. Despite her apprehension, Anahita began working night shifts following a family crisis in 2013, in which her husband had an accident, was disabled, and unable to continue working. These circumstances forced her to take up work that was well paid given her qualifications, while giving her what she hoped would be sufficient time to take care of household work. Further, her in-laws "permitted" her to take up night work because of the extenuating circumstances in which they had found themselves, in which the sole breadwinner of the family had been rendered disabled. Anahita clarified that it was only because of her family's financial difficulties that she was comfortable being employed in the paid workforce, particularly in night shifts. For Anahita as well as her in-laws, these views of her suitability for night shift work in call centers shifted dramatically in the face of a crisis that met their household. Her husband had always maintained, even before she took up call center work, that she was "permitted" to enter the "formal" workforce, as long as she could manage the household. Like Anahita, numerous research participants expanded on extenuating circumstances that propelled their choice to work night shifts in call centers. These reasons included illness in the family (as in Anahita's case), unexpected shutting down of a small family business, or moving from an intergenerational family into a single-family setting. The last of these involved a significant financial investment in buying or renting a flat that necessitated two breadwinners in a household, as well as slightly increased autonomy (with a reduced role of in-laws) to make decisions about working night shifts.

Prior to working at a call center, Anahita had a garment business that she operated from home. She obtained fabrics from a supplier, and sold these to her neighbors and friends for a small profit. However, this did not take up a lot of time and did not pay very highly. As an introvert, she was nervous about entering the "formal" paid workforce, and was apprehensive about not fitting in. The shift in doing paid work from home to entering the "formal" workforce is a significant marker. Paid work from home is typically informal, and often part time. This work is often thought of as supplemental to household income, not crucial to it. Women working from home rarely earn more than their husbands—helping maintain gendered power dynamics between spouses that hinge upon financial measures. It is crucial to note that of the women who claimed to be entering the workforce for the first time, several had taken up paid work previously but categorized such work as distinct because it entailed working from home. The notion of a crisis, as explained earlier, came up across several interviews. This was a significant point for several of my research participants to characterize their entry into the industry. While that was certainly not true of every female research participant, I found it to be true of every woman who entered the industry after she was already married.

It is crucial to note that for women entering night shift work, they continued to be primarily responsible for household work. In fact, some of them took up night shift work to be able to continue doing household chores during the day. I expand on this in the next section.

Continued Household Responsibility

Meena was enthusiastic about being interviewed, and told me that no one had ever taken any interest in her life prior to this. Jokingly, she remarked: "I don't know how long you will stay interested though, once I tell you about my life. It's just regular you know. Nothing special—just like everyone else." Like Anahita, Meena's family, too, faced a crisis that compelled her to join an outsourced call center. Unlike Anahita, however, Meena said she was extremely outgoing, and was enthusiastic about interacting with office colleagues and taking part in telephone conversations. Upon graduating from college, Meena had worked in a clerical position for eight months before getting married, following which she quit her job. As she put it:

> My in-laws didn't say no for me to work. But you know, it takes a while to get settled in a new house and with new responsibilities. I can't just come home from office and tell my mother-in-law—get me food—like I told my sister or mother, or even my younger brother sometimes. It's different you know. So I thought I'll leave work for some time to get used to, . . . then kids, then just life is busy. But then . . . I had to again work.

When she started working at a call center, Meena was re-entering the paid workforce after twelve years. She is now the prime breadwinner in her household, supplemented by her father-in-law's post-retirement part-time work. Her husband, meanwhile, wants to launch a new venture. Meena was extremely concerned about "how society will look at this type of arrangement, where the wife earns

Aparna Parikh

more," but claimed that earning money for her children was more important to her, and hence she entered the paid workforce.[47] However, Meena chose to take up the night shift so she could be at home with her children during the day.

Meena explained to me that she made an extra effort for household upkeep after entering the paid workforce. This helped her prove to neighbors and extended family members that she could still be a "good" mother, wife, and daughter-in-law even while working night shifts. While few research participants claimed to make "extra efforts," most of them continued to bear significant household responsibility. Arguably, this continuation itself entails an increase in effort, which often became distributed along gendered kinship networks, which I will expand on in the next section. For Meena, her routine involved getting home early in the morning from the night shift. Once or twice a week, she would buy groceries for the household on her way back. The water supply at her house was for two hours each morning, so Meena had to ensure she was home by that time. After placing buckets to fill water, she warmed the milk to make tea for the household, and then prepared lunch for the family and filled in her children's tiffins (packed lunch) to take to school. Meena proudly told me that her daughter, at nine, is now old enough to start packing her own lunch, and her brother (seven) also tries and helps her. Once lunch is prepared, she helps her children get dressed, following which her father-in-law drops them at their bus stop for school. Following this, she does some chores, and then sleeps until mid-afternoon, getting under five hours of sleep each day. Her children come home from school at three, after which she helps them with their homework, and then prepares dinner before leaving for her shift. Her husband sometimes tries to help, but Meena said that she doesn't try to teach him, because in her opinion, that would take longer than doing the chores herself. When I suggested that while this would probably be true once, and he would be able to help her thereafter, she shrugged and said, "*Haan, shaayad* (yeah, maybe). But still, how to do that in front of his parents. Maybe it would be odd for him. I don't know. This is just how things are."

Like Meena, many female research participants continue to be primarily responsible for household chores. This involves buying groceries, food preparation, packing lunch, getting children dressed, and helping them with school assignments. The continuation of gendered household responsibility supports findings from other research examining this sector in India:

> Meetings are typically scheduled [all day] from 8 a.m. to 9 p.m. But nobody complains as it is seen as an essential part of the industry, given its very rapid growth rate. However, this is a serious problem for women, who have to work long hours at office and then take care of the household too. They have no personal time left and exhaustion is common. Most men work long hours and then go home and relax.[48]

Entering the paid workforce is thus accompanied by the persistence of gendered household responsibility. Further, the pressure to be a "good" wife, mother, or daughter-in-law to combat stigmatized perceptions of working the night shift exacerbates gendered household responsibility. These increased responsibilities are not always borne individually, however, and women rely on extended gendered kinship and other networks to manage their household responsibilities.

Adaptation Networks

As discussed in the previous section, women working the night shift in outsourced call centers were primarily responsible for household chores. However, several research participants professed to being perpetually tired due to lack of adequate sleep, and they relied on various kinship networks to help them adapt to working night shifts. The adaptation primarily involved a redistribution of

Gendered Household Expectations

responsibility for household upkeep, which occurred overwhelmingly along gendered lines. Feminist scholars, particularly those focused on social reproduction, have observed adaptation for childcare and other household roles in response to the feminization of migration, and following the entry of women in various capacities to the workforce where they were hitherto absent.[49] This adaptation network has been articulated as a "transfer chain" of filial kin work.[50] Building off this line of thinking, I present how women draw upon kinship networks, primarily women, to adapt household responsibility while working the night shift in outsourced call centers.

Payal, an unmarried woman who worked the night shift in a call center and lived with her parents and unmarried brothers, claimed to have lesser responsibilities than most of her female colleagues who were married and/or had children. When she began this job, Payal had thought working night shifts would not entail any change in her routine, other than her sleep schedule. She said: "After all, I don't have any real responsibilities, you know. No husband, no children. And my mother and the maid do the cooking, so yeah."

However, a few weeks into the job, Payal realized that numerous household tasks formed part of her routine, which she claimed had been "almost invisible" in her mind. She said:

> I never realized only what all I do. Fold clothes after they have dried, put them in people's rooms, clear up after eating, pick up things from the *kariyana* (grocery store). *Kuch na kuch. Aise itna sochti hi nahi thi mein—bas kar diya kaam* (There's always something or the other. I never gave it much thought, but just did the tasks). Now, when I want to get every minute of sleep I can, I realize all the things I did. Because you know, now my time is more valuable. Because time to sleep is valuable to me.

Despite valuing every extra minute to sleep, Payal does continue to do these "little household tasks" that she had never given much thought to. She said one is required to compromise something—in this case her sleep—because "boys will not do anything." Like Payal, other research participants, too, recognized the various "mundane" tasks they performed daily, once they faced challenges in completing them. However, unlike Payal, not all research participants continued to do such chores, relying on other family members to take up the slack. Neema, an unmarried female call center employee, felt overwhelmed once she began to work night shifts, and relied on her mother for tasks she had earlier carried out, including preparing her younger brother's tiffin. Neema said her mother had been unhappy when she began working at a call center, as she was unable to help at home, and was hoping she would quit soon, despite higher wages than other jobs she was qualified for.

Priya, a single mother with two young children, relied extensively on her kinship networks in order to work night shifts. Every evening, her sister's teenage son would come to her house and spend the night with her children while Priya went to work. Her sister also sent food for the family with her son. Her children would take this food for lunch, while it would serve as Priya's dinner when she returned home early in the morning. The presence of her teenage nephew provided Priya mental reassurance of knowing that her children would not be alone while she was away each night. In this way, Priya's extended kinship network is integral for her to adapt to working night shifts. While the specific nature of adaptations varied, I found that most of my research participants depended on other family members, primarily women, to help them adapt to working night shifts. Men working night shifts in call centers told me that their wives and/or mothers had had to adjust their cooking routine to ensure that they could pack fresh food for their husband's/son's tiffin, while also cooking at other times for children's meals. As Aman, a male research participant told me, "I sometimes eat outside the call center in the shorter break, but I like to get dinner from home. But I have a wife, so that's fine." Further, I found that some male research participants increasingly relied on women to conduct tasks they previously carried out, such as household finances, because they were tired due to lack of adequate sleep.

Aparna Parikh

For chores including washing and drying clothes, dusting, sweeping, and mopping the house, all of which occurred daily—particularly in intergenerational households—most research participants enlisted domestic help, who came in for an hour or two each day. They clarified that even prior to working in call centers, this system of domestic help had been in play. However, their dependence on domestic help had increased after joining night shifts, as suggested by Ila, who said:

> I used to do all the shopping for my house myself. But now I'm tired in [the] afternoon sometimes, so I ask my *bai* (female domestic help) sometimes to go get something I forgot. I even give her a little extra [money] to do this. Really, it's not too much to do.

It is important to note that while Ila characterized the additional tasks her domestic help had to take on as "not too much to do," she still found these tasks excessive, and hence relied on domestic help to do them. While dependence on primarily, although not exclusively, female domestic help is common in middle-class households across Mumbai and various parts of India, there appears to be an increase in their responsibility following the entry of middle-class women into the paid workforce. While discussing the social networks that facilitated their adaptation to working the night shift, many of my research participants did not mention domestic help. On being asked who undertook certain household tasks following their entry into the paid workforce, women explained the role of domestic help. Arguably, similar to the "mundane" tasks that women only realized they did once every minute of sleep became precious, the role of domestic help in maintaining households (before or following night shift work) is significant to point out. This dependence perpetuates historically embedded caste-based inequalities, and manifested through my research as well. While such inequalities were implicitly suggested through my interviews, I do not fully flesh out caste dynamics and domestic help in this chapter. I found that research participants who came from lower-middle-class backgrounds, residing in *chawls*[51] or shared tenements, could not afford domestic help, and hence increased their reliance on gendered kinship networks for household chores. Thus, there was a transfer chain of household responsibility from women working in outsourced call centers to a network primarily constituted by other women who were domestic help or kinship members.

Conclusion

In this chapter, I examine the everyday lives of women working in outsourced call centers in Mumbai, India, to suggest a centering of traditional notions of gendered roles within households even as women enter the paid workforce and work night shifts. The narrative of a crisis appears to be commonly used by various women to justify working outside the house, particularly at night. However, even with this change in social patterns, there appears to be a continuation of gendered household responsibility. In fact, for some women, this tends to exacerbate their role in attempting to prove that they are "good" wives, mothers, or daughters-in-law. As such, a good woman is one who adheres to traditional norms. Further, I find that adapting to working night shifts has entailed reliance on an extended network that is made up primarily of female kinship members or domestic help. Thus, these themes show how the introduction of a modern workforce is not at odds with the continuation of traditionally held gendered expectations regarding household responsibility. This chapter contributes to feminist scholarship focusing on social reproduction, particularly demonstrating the centrality of "tradition" in continuing expectations for gendered responsibility even as women enter the "modern" workforce in contemporary Indian society.

Notes

1. Hegde 2011.
2. Batt et al. 2005.
3. Dube, Dube, Gawali, and Haldar 2012; Sudan 2010.

Gendered Household Expectations

4. Vora 2010.
5. In keeping with David Harvey's (2001) conceptualization, the term "spatial fix" is used to connote a resolution to a problem, as well as pinning something down in a locus.
6. Harvey 2001.
7. Hegde 2011, 178–95.
8. While outsourced call centers are present in numerous Indian cities, and there has been a push to increase their numbers in smaller cities, Mumbai and New Delhi have the highest number of outsourced call centers. This is largely attributed to the presence of infrastructure and other multinational industries, as well as large numbers of an educated, English-speaking populace. See Patel 2006.
9. Ghosh 2015.
10. Bajaj 2011.
11. Hegde 2011.
12. Batt et al. 2005.
13. Dube, Dube, Gawali, and Haldar 2012; Sudan 2010.
14. Patel 2006.
15. Gupta 2012.
16. Aneesh 2012; Gupta 2012.
17. Tara and Ilavarasan 2009.
18. Ng and Mitter 2005.
19. Mirchandani 2005.
20. Patel 2010; Poddar 2010; Kelkar, Shrestha, and Veena 2002.
21. Tara and Ilavarasan 2009.
22. Radhakrishnan 2009.
23. Laslett and Brenner 1989; Picchio 1992; Katz 2001; Federici 2004.
24. Laslett and Brenner 1989, 382.
25. Laslett and Brenner 1989; Katz 2001.
26. Mitchell, Marston, and Katz 2004.
27. Katz 2001.
28. Acharya in Bakker and Silvey 2012, 69.
29. Mountz and Hyndman 2006.
30. Ghosh 2015.
31. Xiang 2007.
32. Freeman 2000.
33. Bhabha 1994.
34. Narayan 2013.
35. Xiang 2007.
36. Bhabha 1994, 51.
37. Bhabha 1994, 51–2.
38. Narayan 2013; Radhakrishnan 2009.
39. Bhabha 1994, 107, emphasis in original.
40. Radhakrishnan 2009.
41. All names throughout this chapter are pseudonyms.
42. Radhakrishnan 2009.
43. Hegde 2011.
44. Parikh 2013.
45. Chatterjee in Sinha 2000, 624–5.
46. Radhakrishnan 2009, 211.
47. Clark and Sekher 2007 and Tara and Ilavarasan 2012 find that call centers provide women with relatively high-paying jobs that were previously unavailable, a finding echoed by some of my research participants as well.
48. Kelkar, Shrestha and Veena, 69.
49. Rodriguez 2010; Hoang and Yeoh 2015.
50. Lan in Ehrenreich and Hochschild 2003.
51. A *chawl* is a colonial housing typology in Mumbai, sometimes provided as worker housing, and architecturally identifiable by small tenements, large hallways that serve as communal balconies, and often shared bathrooms. Chawls are primarily occupied by lower-middle-class populations, and their redevelopment has come into sharp focus since the 1990s.

377

References

Aneesh, A. 2012. "Negotiating Globalization: Men and Women of India's Call Centers." *Journal of Social Issues* 68(3): 514–533. doi:10.1111/j.1540-4560.2012.01761.x.

Bajaj, Vikas. 2011. "Philippines Overtakes India as Hub of Call Centers." *New York Times*, November 25.

Bakker, Isabella, and Rachel Silvey, eds. 2012. *Beyond States and Markets: The Challenges of Social Reproduction*. New York, NY: Routledge.

Batt, Rosemary, Virginia Doellgast, Hyunji Kwon, Mudit Nopany, Priti Nopany, and Anil da Costa. 2005. *The Indian Call Centre Industry: National Benchmarking Report Strategy, HR Practices, & Performance*. CAHRS Working Paper Series, no. 7.

Bhabha, Homi. 1994. *The Location of Culture*. New York, NY: Routledge.

Clark, A. W., and T. V. Sekher. 2007. "Can career-minded young women reverse gender discrimination? A view from Bangalore's high-tech sector." *Gender Technology Development* 11(3): 285–319.

Chatterjee, Partha. 1986. *Nationalist Thought and the Colonial World: A Derivative Discourse?* London: Zed.

Dube, Dipa, Indrajit Dube, Bhagwan R. Gawali, and Subechhya Haldar. 2012. "Women in BPO Sector in India: A Study of Individual Aspirations and Environmental Challenges." *Asian Social Science* 8(7): 157.

Ehrenreich, Barbara, and Arlie Russell Hochschild. 2003. *Global Woman: Nannies, Maids, and Sex Workers in the New Economy*. New York: Macmillan.

Federici, Silvia. 2004. *Caliban and the Witch*. Brooklyn, NY: Autonomedia.

Freeman, Carla. 2000. *High Tech and High Heels in the Global Economy: Women, Work, and Pink-Collar Identities in the Caribbean*. Durham, NC: Duke University Press.

Ghosh, Mohul. 2015. "Govt Allocates Rs 498 Crore to Reignite BPO Revolution; 1.5L Jobs to Be Created." *Trak.in—Indian Business of Technology, Mobile & Startups*. http://trak.in/tags/business/2015/06/03/govt-funds-reignite-bpo-revolution-india-jobs-creation/, accessed on June 11.

Gupta, Amrita. 2012. "Health, Social and Psychological Problems of Women Employees in Business Process Outsourcing: A Study in India." www.pau2012. princeton.edu/ppers/121676/.

Harvey, David. 2001. "Globalization and the Spatial Fix." *Geographische Revue* 2(3): 23–31.

Hegde, Radha Sarma. 2011. *Circuits of Visibility: Gender and Transnational Media Cultures*. New York: New York University Press.

Hoang, L., and B. Yeoh. 2015. *Transnational Labour Migration, Remittances and the Changing Family in Asia*. New York: Palgrave Macmillan.

Katz, Cindi. 2001. "Vagabond Capitalism and the Necessity of Social Reproduction." *Antipode* 33(4): 709–728.

Kelkar, Govind, Girija Shrestha, and N. Veena. 2002. "IT Industry and Women's Agency: Explorations in Bangalore and Delhi, India." *Gender, Technology and Development* 6(1): 63–84. doi:10.1177/097185240200600104.

Laslett, Barbara, and Johanna Brenner. 1989. "Gender and Social Reproduction: Historical Perspectives." *Annual Review of Sociology*: 381–404.

Mirchandani, Kiran. 2005. "Gender Eclipsed? Racial Hierarchies in Transnational Call Center Work." *Social Justice* 32(4): 105–119.

Mitchell, Katharyne, Sallie A. Marston, and Cindi Katz. 2004. *Life's Work: Geographies of Social Reproduction*, Vol. 52. Malden, MA: Wiley-Blackwell.

Mountz, Alison, and Jennifer Hyndman. 2006. "Feminist Approaches to the Global Intimate." *Women's Studies Quarterly*, Vol 34(1/2): 446–463.

Narayan, Uma. 2013. *Dislocating Cultures: Identities, Traditions, and Third World Feminism*. New York: Routledge.

Ng, Cecilia, and Swasti Mitter. 2005. "Valuing Women's Voices Call Center Workers in Malaysia and India." *Gender, Technology and Development* 9(2): 209–233. doi:10.1177/097185240500900203.

Parikh, Aparna. 2013. "Jane in the Call Center: (In)securities From and Adaptations to Neoliberalization." *Critical Planning Journal* 1(20): 2013.

Patel, Reena. 2006. "Working the Night Shift: Gender and the Global Economy." *ACME: An International E-Journal for Critical Geographies* 5(1): 9–27.

Patel, Reena. 2010. *Working the Night Shift: Women in India's Call Center Industry*. Palo Alto, CA: Stanford University Press.

Picchio, Antonella. 1992. *Social Reproduction: The Political Economy of the Labour Market*. New York: Cambridge University Press.

Poddar, Suhita. 2010. "'Second Shift' Pressure High on Indian Working Women." *Wall Street Journal*, December 6. http://blogs.wsj.com/indiarealtime/2010/12/06/second-shift-pressure-high-on-indian-working-women/

Radhakrishnan, Smitha. 2009. "Professional Women, Good Families: Respectable Femininity and the Cultural Politics of a 'New' India." *Qualitative Sociology* 32(2): 195–212.

Rodriguez, Robyn Magalit. 2010. *Migrants for Export: How the Philippine State Brokers Labor to the World*. Minneapolis: University of Minnesota Press.

Sinha, Mrinalini. 2000. "Refashioning Mother India: Feminism and Nationalism in Late-colonial India." *Feminist Studies* 26(3): 623–644.

Sudan, R. 2010. *The Global Opportunity in IT-Based Services: Assessing and Enhancing Country Competitiveness*. World Bank.

Tara, Shelly, and P. Vigneswara Ilavarasan. 2009. "'I Would Not Have Been Working Here!' Parental Support to Unmarried Daughters as Call Center Agents in India." *Gender, Technology and Development* 13(3): 385–406. doi:10.1177/097185241001300304.

Tara, Shelly, and P. Vigneswara Ilavarasan. 2012. "Cabs, Male Drivers and Midnight Commuting: Manufacturing Respectability of the Unmarried Women Agents of Call Centers in India." *AI & Society* 27(1): 157–163.

Vora, Kalindi. 2010. "The Transmission of Care: Affective Economies and Indian Call Centers." In *Intimate Labours: Cultures, Technologies and the Politics of Care*, edited by Eileen Boris and Rhacel Salazar Parreñas, 33–48. Stanford, CA: Stanford University Press.

Xiang, Biao. 2007. *Global "Body Shopping": An Indian Labor System in the Information Technology Industry*. Princeton, NJ: Princeton University Press.

22

Reinterpreting Gender in Globalizing India

Afghan Sikh Refugees in Delhi City's Built Environment

Shelly Pandey

The discourse about gender and the built environment determines how cultural rules of gender are expressed through the use of space, and how the social relationship between men and women are contested in the built form[1]. The literature on the built environment has not, however, explored refugees' settings.

Whenever we discuss the gender concerns in the context of refugees, issues like safety, violence, and the harassment of women take priority. The focus remains on how the host countries' policies and social environment are conducive for refugees, and especially refugee women. Questions about how the built environment of the host country has an impact on the gender construction of refugee women remain, however, because refugees generally migrate to countries with better life chances, and there is a large possibility that the built environment of the host country will be more modern that of their country of origin.

The present chapter analyzes the impact of the changing built environment of Delhi city in a globalizing India post-1990. By taking up an ethnographic study of Afghan Sikh refugees in Delhi, the study explores how women of this particular refugee community have found changes in gendered experiences in their everyday life in Delhi city.

Afghan refugees began arriving in India in 1992, coinciding with a period of transition in Delhi city. The forces of globalization were bringing many service sectors into and around the city, and were making Delhi city into one of the places of aspiration for many young men and women seeking employment. Along with this, Delhi city witnessed remarkable changes in its built environment. From public transport to shopping venues to recreational opportunities, spaces became more gender friendly as the public-space access of women in the city increased. The physical changes in the city had major impacts on the lives of refugees from Afghanistan as well, especially Afghan women. These women had led a very restricted life in Afghanistan due to a situation of political and social upheaval. While emigrating to Delhi was a struggle for refugee families who were uprooted from their own spaces, refugee women found new meanings of femininities in Delhi city.

Afghan Refugees in India

Afghans constitute one of the world's largest refugee populations, with most having settled in Iran and Pakistan. In these countries, the issue of refugees has become a protracted situation, as it becomes clear many Afghans are not willing to move back to Afghanistan and that repatriation will thus not be the outcome of the refugee problem.[2]

For this reason, governments and other agencies have started discussions regarding the refugees' long-term requirements, and the implications of Afghans' permanent settlement in their host countries.[3] The attack on the World Trade Center in New York City on September 11, 2001 (the 9/11 terrorist attack), further added to the problems of Afghan refugees as well as the governments in the countries they settled in, as they were now seen as a potential national security threat.[4] Much of the literature about Afghan refugees indicates that they live in a state of limbo: unwilling to return to Afghanistan, yet faced with a situation in which their host country does not have any plans or policies to help them. Many thus continue living in their host countries in the hope that one day they might become citizens of their adopted home country.

The Afghan refugees in India fall under two categories: those who are registered with the United Nations High Commission for Refugees (UNHCR) and those who are not. There are 13,381 Afghan refugees registered with UNHCR;[5] the number not registered is difficult to estimate. The Afghan asylum seekers, refugees, and non-refugees are an ethno-linguistically and religiously heterogeneous group, and include people from the Hindu, Sikh, Muslim, and Christian religions. As per UNHCR's categorization of Afghan refugees in India, Muslims are called ethnic Afghans and others are described by their religion, as in Hindu or Sikh Afghans. Ethnic Afghans' identities are linguistically recognized as Pashtun, Hazara, Tajik, or Turk. Hindus and Sikh Afghans claim ethnoregional identities; these are Kabuli, Ghaznichi, Laghmani, Koshti, Kurmewal, and Chharakari—the names of regions where the migrants come from. Within Delhi, the group known as ethnic Afghans have largely settled in areas like Lajpat Nagar, Malviya Nagar, Bhogal, Saket in South Delhi, and Faridabad in Delhi National Capital Region, an area that includes Delhi and cities at its periphery, such as Gurgaon, NOIDA, Ghaziabad, and Faridabad. The Sikh Afghans have settled in Tilak Nagar, and Vikaspuri in West Delhi.

According to media reports, although the Afghan refugees live an undetermined life, they do not wish to return to Afghanistan; rather they hope to stay in India. Most of the Afghan refugees feel that their children are safe in Delhi city and they do not perceive such safety in Afghanistan, even in the post-Taliban regime.[6] Most media stories about the Afghan refugees focus on the hardships they face, as they do not have proper employment opportunities due to their refugee status.[7] Many refugees manage their livelihood by running small businesses or taking odd jobs.

How have the cities in which the Afghan refugees have made their new home influenced the gender reconstruction of this refugee group? Based on an ethnographic study of Afghan-Sikh refugees in Delhi city, the present chapter locates the experiences of Afghan-Sikh refugee women in different built environments of Delhi city, using as an example the Delhi metro rail and various shopping malls. A study of these spaces shows what kind of social milieu is created by the built environment of Delhi city, and how it contributes to gender practices.

Refugee Women and the Built Environment

There is very limited work on the built environment of refugees. A refugee's status demands that immediate necessities be fulfilled first, with the built environment taking a back seat in this context. Nevertheless, in recent work in the field of architecture, the focus has shifted to the built environment and how it affects refugees' lives. For example, studies on the architecture of refugee camps have indicated that they should be designed in keeping long term needs of refugees in mind.[8] Media reports on refugees' built environments have called attention to the unsafe nature of tent compounds for refugee women. Women in such environments are subjected to sexual violence as their vulnerable status of being refugee women becomes exacerbated due to the temporary and uncontrolled structure of refugee camps.[9] Concerns like proper lighting in the camps, or separate bathrooms, are suggested for the safety of women in the camp along with features that would increase safety while cooking and heating.[10] Largely in this area of refugees and the built environment, the focus has been on the idea that the refugee camp should not be seen as just a camp, but rather that it should be planned like a city. The life of a typical refugee camp varies from 7 to 17 years, making it necessary to plan for spaces apart from those that merely shelter, such as spaces for education, discussion, meeting, shopping, and performing other daily needs.[11] In planning refugee camps, organizers should keep in mind that a substantial proportion of the refugee population is women; nevertheless, plans for refugee camps do not normally reflect women's specific concerns.

This chapter examines the experiences of Afghan Sikh refugee women in various built environments of Delhi city. Delhi has witnessed a remarkable growth of modern infrastructure, including transportation, recreation, and shopping. The chapter examines what kind of social milieu is created by the built environment of Delhi city, and how it contributes to gender practices in the Afghan refugee population. The growth of this built environment in Delhi city stands in diametric opposition to the destruction that happened in Afghanistan during the same period, where the structures of leisure, education, and activities requiring any space that women could use were broken during the Taliban's reign in an attempt to assert greater control over women. Against this backdrop it is important to examine the experiences of Afghan (refugee) women in a place where the growth of modern infrastructure is taking place. This chapter thus explores how the modernity of a space impacts the (re)construction of gender in a refugee community, during a time when the refugees negotiated with their traumatic experiences of conflict.[12]

Fieldwork for this study was conducted in 2016 in various locations of West Delhi, where many Afghan Sikhs have settled. In the context of refugees, a random sampling technique could not be used to collect data, therefore, the respondents were either approached through local acquaintances at the site of the study or through the assistance of a non-governmental organization (NGO) called Khalsa Diwan Welfare Society.[13] The data was collected through open-ended interviews with 25 refugee families residing in the West Delhi area. The purpose for speaking with the whole family instead of only women was to understand the changes in the gender realities embedded in their settings. This allowed us to analyze the gender relations between men and women against the backdrop of their built environment, and also to locate the changes taking place in the younger generations, if any. Interviews conducted with the men of the families asked about their views regarding public space access of the women from their community in Delhi city.

The study also used participant observation to explore refugees' everyday life experiences in various settings that represent the modern built environment in Delhi city. The spaces mentioned by and frequently visited by refugee women were observed as part of the data collection. Participant observation was started with refugee women's experiences during travel and transportation in Delhi city at the metro stations in the West Delhi area. We accompanied the women respondents during various journeys originating from West Delhi stations such as Tilak Nagar and Janakpuri East/West to stations close to well-known market areas such as Karol Bagh and Connaught Place.

Another place we observed during participant observation was shopping malls around the West Delhi region, specifically Pacific Mall at Subhash Nagar and TDI Mall at Rajouri Garden, because respondents reported frequently visiting these malls. Participant observation became an important tool to understand the meaning of these spaces for Afghan women refugees. Women's comfort level at these places and their attire gave clues to the meaning of these spaces for the women. Participant observation enabled the researcher's "immersion" into the spaces frequented by the respondents, thereby generating empirical insights and a rich understanding of respondents' social practices that are normally hidden from the public gaze.[14]

We analyzed the ethnographic data we collected thematically, focusing on identifying and describing both implicit and explicit ideas, while identifying and categorizing the key issues that emerged. A rich interpretation of the data then allowed us to generate tentative theoretical explanations.

Built Environment, Public Space Access: Doing Gender in Afghanistan and India

Before discussing the reinterpretation of gender identities by the Afghan Sikh refugees in Delhi city, it is imperative to discuss their gender identities in Afghanistan. Afghanistan's different ethnicities had one thing in common; namely, that a community's honor depended on controlling the behavior of women. Women's mobility and access to public space were controlled by the men of each respective family. Consequently, Afghanistan's built environment did not make allowances for women's limited access to public spaces. Apart from certain schools and educational institutions for girls, there were not many places where women's mobility existed or was expected. Women had to have a male companion to use the public transport system. There are media reports that indicate that before the nation's political conflicts started in the 1980s, women used to drive in Afghanistan, but those women were from highly affluent families. Most women found that their presence in public space was regulated by male family members. This was so because "unprotected" women were considered to be alone, and women alone in public spaces were an affront to the honor of the whole family.[15] For this reason, too, houses had high walls to hide women from the outside world.[16]

In India, the majority of Afghan refugees are Afghan Sikhs. While still living in Afghanistan, the Sikhs usually controlled women's movements more strictly than other ethnic groups did, because they belonged to a minority community. For example, the men of this community were largely businessmen while the women took on the role of wife and mother. Girls' education was not encouraged in this community, as women were not supposed to work. Overall, women's participation in the Afghan labor force was very low; therefore, the architecture of the buildings and workplaces was not gender friendly.[17] Exacerbating the situation, 30 years of conflict and upheaval in Afghanistan had left the country devastated, with many buildings damaged or reduced to rubble. Many people focused on sheer survival and on obtaining life's basic necessities. Buildings and architecture were thus rarely of concern, aside from news stories pertaining to the destruction of various structures during the war and as a result of upheavals.

As people from Afghanistan migrated to India, India was opening its doors to globalization. One of the impacts of globalization was the growth of India's service sector, with a white-collar Indian labor force providing services in the information technology sector to clients in Western countries.[18] The number of women in these new employment sectors gradually started increasing until it reached 50%.[19] This led to demands for a more gender friendly built environment in and around Delhi city. In the last decade, Delhi has witnessed the expansion of metro rail services, and to respond to the demand for more gender-friendly services, they introduced a women's coach in 2010. Additionally, there has been ongoing construction of shopping malls, which have changed the experiences of shopping and leisure for middle-class women.

Our study indicates that the built environment of the host country creates distinct gender identities for refugee men and women who inhabit these spaces. Studies have found that identity processes have location implication and that place is part of identification.[20] In the early 2000s, the area where Afghan Sikhs reside in Delhi city was converted to express a modern outlook via drastic changes in the built environment. This area was connected to the rest of the city by Delhi metro rail's blue line in 2005. As of this writing, there are seven shopping malls in this area, along with the residential areas belonging to different income groups. The architecture and structure of both the Delhi metro and shopping malls represent a modern space setting in the mind of the viewer. The glass buildings and the high-tech and glossy interiors produce an atmosphere that replicates that of a Western city, and induces a more Western identity among people staying in and visiting the area. The architecture of newly constructed structures of transportation, recreation, and shopping in Delhi city presents a marked differentiation from the spatial layouts of Afghan cities, from where these refugees arrived in 1990. Even now, the reconstruction process in Afghanistan focuses more on building structures that will fulfill basic needs, such as educational institutions and administrative blocks. Within the reconstruction process of post-conflict Afghanistan, women have struggled to have their voices included, yet without much success.[21]

After coming to India, women's access to public space improved. India's current-day globalization brought changes in men's attitudes towards women's access to public space, as these men adjusted to the new sociocultural milieu of Delhi city. Women were now allowed to move out and about, and girls were allowed an education. In this new sociocultural milieu the built environment played a substantial role. Women's access to public space depends greatly on the transport system of that specific place. Delhi city's metro rail, constructed by the early years of the twenty-first century, made women's access to public space in Delhi city much easier.

The Afghan Sikh refugee community can be divided into two groups based on their economic condition. One group is made up of businessmen who had small businesses and shops in Afghanistan, and their families. When these families migrated to India, they had to leave everything behind and start their business from scratch in the new country. In this group, women had to take up employment after learning new skills, in order to augment the family's income. The other group was made up of businessmen who had their business in other countries, especially in Central Asia, as well as their families. While the men traveled for business, their families stayed in Afghanistan. This group's economic condition was not affected much after they migrated, as they were able to maintain their business links abroad. The women of this group remained housewives after emigrating to India, but their access to public space was not as controlled as it was in Afghanistan. For the purpose of this study, I will call women in the first group of immigrants "working" and women in the second group "affluent."

According to the women of both groups, those who left the house to work as well as those who left for shopping or leisure, the arrival of Delhi metro changed what it meant to be a woman traveler in the city. Women specifically mentioned the "women's coach" of Delhi metro rail, which provided them a kind of private space within the world of public transport. Such a space had been completely unimaginable for them in their previous gender constructions. While explaining their experiences in Afghanistan, the women mentioned that public space access had been correlated with the question of respectability. Women were expected to moderate their behavior in public to avoid being seen as unrespectable. The volume of their voice, their tone, and their body language were aspects of this moderation. Inside the women's coach of Delhi city metro rail, our observations attested to a different scenario, one that reflected the sense of space and freedom among women in many ways. Women could often be found as part of a group sitting on the floor of the train, chatting with each other. They seemingly felt less conscious of their actions in the women's coach than in the other coaches with men. Women passengers reported that they could talk, sit, and laugh without being conscious of the presence of men.

In the gender and space discourse, public space is the site for exchanging ideas and values as well as being a platform for men's leisure activities. For women, however, public spaces are often regarded as transit ways to other regions—from one private space to another.[22] Women's negotiation of public spaces is more likely to be governed by standards stipulated specifically for them, such as physical appearance, proper decorum, non-verbal communication, proper attire, and so on.[23]

Women's claim to the freedom of body language and choice of clothes reflects how space and spatial considerations contribute in the constitution of femininity.[24] Many geographers maintain that it is important to understand that there is a difference between the metaphorical (or cultural) space and material space. This understanding becomes particularly imperative if we consider how cultural ideas of space influence the bodily practices of women, conceptualizing and embodying a socio-spatial matrix.[25] The understanding of bodily practices in the women's metro coach emphasizes the spatial perspective of women's experiences, and shows how spatiality itself participates in the production of gendered bodies. The freedom of conduct provided by the women's coach reveals, first, how a private space is created for women in a public transport system that allows transit from one space to another; second, how gender is reproduced in a new environment; and third, how women conduct themselves to fit their own notion of expressivity.

For the Afghan refugee women, traveling was a concern while they were in Afghanistan, due to the constraints on their movements, which led to dependency on male family members if women wanted to take public transportation. In Delhi, for those refugee women who go out to work, the construction of the Delhi metro has made the men of their families less worried about women's travel. Women's physical interaction with men has been almost eliminated during travel in the Delhi metro. Many women reported that they hire a cycle rickshaw to travel from their home to the metro station, get themselves frisked at the women's security counter, and most of them use a smart card (a prepaid swipe card used by frequent metro travelers), so they do not even need to stand in line with men to buy a token. On the platform, they have a separate space to stand while waiting for the train's arrival, a space marked by pink banners, as well as stickers on the floors that read "women only."[26]

Many refugee women reported that they do not mind the crowded platforms, now that they have a separate space to stand. Even refugee men reported that when they travel with women family members on crowded routes, they ask the women to travel in the women's coach and meet them at their destination. Women traveling with men also prefer to travel in the women's coach, and on the platform they stand in the space reserved for women.

Even at night, women reported feeling safe in the women's coach. The metro trains run from 6:00 a.m. until approximately 11:00 p.m. Many women who travel to stations in the outskirts like NOIDA or Gurgaon (cities at the periphery of Delhi) have to travel by metro after dark. But these women reported that the women's coach provides them a secure space to travel, while a male from their family comes to pick them up at the metro station near their home. Many women can be seen waiting for a male family member outside the metro station during the day. However, during the night hours, women report that they prefer to wait at the women-only section of the platform, as they find this space safer than the space outside the metro station. Many women mention the women-only section of the platform as a waiting place. Sometimes, even in daytime, women can be seen waiting in the women-only section of the platform. Women report that the women's space is more secure than any other public space because women passengers keep on passing through the area.[27]

Apart from separating women from male passengers, the women's coach provides them a distinct space of actions and interactions in the public built environment. The segregation of women's from men's spaces is not a new phenomenon for Afghan women, but having such segregation during their travel through the city provides them with a distinct space to exercise agency, and this agency is an unprecedented construction for them. Women admitted that access to this kind of space provided by the modern built environment in Delhi city was not possible for women in Afghanistan. They explained that a rise in the demand for women as employees in the service sector brought changes in the public built environment to make them more woman-friendly. A demand for female employees did not exist in Afghanistan, and consequently, similar changes in the built environment were not achievable in Afghan cities.

Locating Femininities and Masculinities Through Shopping Malls

Shopping malls in West Delhi, an area where many refugees live, present a further modern built environment that plays an important role in Afghan refugee women's lives. These shopping malls are connected to the metro rail service and are thus easy to reach. Shopping malls are an example of a space that both groups of refugee women (working and affluent) reported accessing. In this way, both groups demonstrated that they have become modern enough in their outlook that they visit shopping malls for leisure. Further questioning, however, revealed that these shopping malls have supermarkets that offer daily goods at a discounted price. Working women's use of the shopping malls is largely dominated by use of these supermarkets, while women of the affluent class tend to visit the high-end boutiques.

Women of both groups reported that shopping malls provide them with a safe place to have a stroll, as going for a walk in public spaces in Afghanistan was not possible for women.[28] The glass buildings, with security at the gates and an air-conditioned environment, made the idea of a stroll very simple and easy for them. Many women reported than in such a place it is not necessary to be accompanied by male relatives, because the shopping mall is a closed public space where women without men can roam around. Feminist geographers have argued that the safety of women in public has long served as a litmus test of the maturity and progress of a particular nation.[29] In Afghanistan, women's public-space access was associated with danger, especially during the time of upheaval, and the notion of pleasure was not at all associated with such access. According to one respondent:

> We have always been expected to walk a straight line from home to school, or a relative's home. The idea of a pleasure or loitering in the public space was introduced to us with these shopping malls. Where we can walk looking at things at the display windows, look at people around us, eat and chat. For us, all these activities were for men to do.

Women were not expected to loiter in public space, as it was associated with questionable respectability. Afghanistan did not offer any public spaces where women could go just simply for pleasure. Even now, Kabul is the only city in Afghanistan that has a handful of sleek shopping malls.[30]

The social milieu of Afghan refugees in Delhi city has been studied as standing in stark contrast with their social environment in Afghanistan. We found that structures associated with a modern built environment also aid in establishing a place-related identity construction. For example, the images on billboards in and around the shopping malls show how images used as a marketing strategy in shopping malls are structured by the concept of femininity as represented through a modern, educated woman who spends for her own pleasure. These factors construct new discursive orders that promote the idea of a self-determined womanhood. The study found that apart from several markers of identity, such as age, sex, and ethnicity, spatial factors also contribute significantly to identity formation.[31] The study found that the modern structures surrounding the locations of refugees' residences sought to project an image of a liberated woman who makes her own autonomous choices, and who is free to pursue her own work and leisure.

Changes in identity that took place as a result of the migration from Afghanistan to India were most strongly represented in the second generation, that is young women who were born and raised in India of Afghan refugee parents. Although born in India, this generation continues to have refugee status and does not obtain Indian citizenship. These young women connect their identities with the women of India's new middle class, which is modern, educated and working. Our study found that even in affluent families, where women were expected to be full-time wives and mothers, women were willing to have some exposure before getting married. They learn English in the local language schools, and are willing to work in the service sectors to expand their horizons before getting married. When they were asked how the built environment adds to their desire to find affiliations with Indian middle-class women, they explained that the built environment provides them with the opportunity to observe other women. The new generation of refugee women finds that the overall image of women is changing around them in terms of clothing choices, appearance, and education. Young refugee women then want the same choices for themselves. Built environments thus serve as opportunities for individuals to be seen by others, allowing women to observe the diversity around them.[32] As this study shows, shopping malls and the women's coach of the metro provide opportunities for refugee women to observe other women more closely, as these spaces bring them together for a longer period of time.

In the feminist studies that examine the social construction of gender, gender itself is constituted through interactions.[33] Shopping malls and the women's coach of the Delhi metro provide women with spaces of action and interactions with other women in the public environment. The freedom to choose both conduct and clothing in the public spaces provided by the modern built environments reveals how spaces of recreation and entertainment can be created for women in public spaces. It also shows how such spaces provide women with opportunities to observe other women, and how this impacts the expression of their own feminine identity. The modern built environments described in this study can be seen as providing distinct kinds of sheltering spaces within the public sphere. The women's coach of the Delhi metro and the separate washrooms, fitting rooms, and feeding rooms for women in shopping malls are the latest example of such spaces.

A Host Country's Built Environment and Refugees' Gender Identities

Spaces created through the built environment can actively reproduce and transform social relations, as these spaces are used either to reinforce or resist relations of inequality and authority. This comes about as built environments are organized to facilitate the activities and movements of some individuals, while constraining those of others.[34] The changes in the built environments in Delhi city, which have created spaces for women to travel and pursue leisure activities, have their impact on the lives of refugees who originate from an extremely patriarchal society like Afghanistan. The built environment in Afghanistan was designed to facilitate the movements and activities of men. Women's movement outside the home was not of concern because women were not seen as individuals outside their homes, but rather as someone who represents the family's honor.

This is contrasted by the situation in India, where changes brought about by globalization, and the consequent expression of modernity through the built environment, have sought to project an image of a modern and liberated middle-class Indian woman who makes her own choices, and who is free to pursue her career and leisure activities. The built environment has a role in contributing to this image, and all these changes also contributed in the built environment's architecture to facilitate the movement of women instead of constraining them. The benefits of gender-inclusive changes in the built environment initially made for one group of women have benefited other women as well (e.g., refugee women) who, while they do not represent the new, modern middle-class Indian women, nevertheless share some of the same desires for work and leisure. The newly built environments have thus had an impact on gender relations for the Afghan refugee community. Men of the community no longer feel the need to control women's mobility, because women are not morally evaluated if they travel by metro or visit shopping malls.

The study also shows how the built environment, and its corresponding socioeconomic connotations, have affected the masculine nature of the Afghan refugee community. While in Afghanistan men were in control of women's mobility, in India, where various public spaces have been created for women's leisure, access to these spaces is indicative of a family's economic class. The paradigm of masculine concerns has shifted now. If women go to shopping malls, it is a sign of her husband's (or father's) good earnings. The built environment is also indicative of a society's economy. In Afghanistan, the economy of the Sikh community was based on trade, and the markers of prosperity were an upscale home, jewelry for women, and large expenditures on festivals and marriages. When the refugees arrived in India, the country was in the midst of constructing a new middle class, with new meanings of femininities and masculinities projected through various forms of conspicuous consumption. As a result, the meaning of masculinities began changing for Afghan men as well. In Afghanistan, men of a community had been providers, protectors, and women's controllers. In India, they became the provider and facilitator for women's activities that represented men's identities as belonging to an affluent class. Men's affluence was indicated by activities such as having their families visit places like shopping malls.

It has been argued that gendered identities are being constantly reconstructed in different contexts.[35] The analysis of Afghan refugees' built environment puts forward two important concepts. First, the place-related identification with the place of settlement (which includes the presence of various forms of built environments) contributes to the renegotiation of gender identities towards a more modern femininity and masculinity. Second, the spaces inside these built environments expose women to new leisure activities that are constantly restructuring their concept of femininity, for example through freeing their mobility from the presence of men.

Globalization and the subsequent rise of modernity in India have brought Indian women unprecedented experiences with their built environments. This is especially true for Afghan refugee women, whose spatial experiences were quite limited in the past. A variety of spaces have been introduced into women's everyday life experiences. These spaces represent gender-integrated built environments and an amalgamation of "glocalized" culture, providing novel experiences to women by making new types of recreational and socialization spaces available to them. The study establishes how the built environment and place-related identification are creating a space for these women, in which they negotiate with new meanings of femininity for themselves by creating an identity within their inhabited space.

Notes

1. Desai 2007.
2. Tober 2007; Ghufran 2008.
3. Edwards 1986.
4. Noor 2006.
5. UNHCR 2016.
6. Baweja 1992.
7. Stillwagon 2011.
8. Allen 2013.
9. Jacobs 2017.
10. Slater 2014.
11. Babos 2016.
12. To understand the everyday realities of refugee women in complex setting of different built environment, the study this chapter is based on follows an ethnographic approach. The central aim of ethnography is to provide rich, holistic insight into people's views and actions as well as the location they inhabit, enabling the researcher to study the impact and meaning of a space on people's identities. The study uses methodological triangulation, a technique designed to compare and contrast different types of methods to provide more comprehensive insights into the phenomenon under study. This type of triangulation allowed validation of the findings because sometimes, what people self-report can contrast with their actual behavior (see Reeves, Albert, Kuper, and Hodges 2008).
13. Khalsa Diwan Welfare Society is an NGO established by Afghan Sikhs in West Delhi that works for the welfare of this community in India.
14. Reeves, Albert, Kuper, and Hodges 2008.
15. Barnabe 2013.
16. Carabelli 2009.
17. See Barnabé 2013.
18. See also the chapter by Aparna Parikh in this volume.
19. Singh, Pandey 2005; McMillin 2006.

20. Twigger-Ross and Uzzell 1996.
21. Grenfell 2004.
22. Gardner 1990.
23. Paul 2011.
24. Niranjana 2001.
25. Soja 1989.
26. Tara 2011.
27. Tara 2011.
28. Barnabe 2013.
29. Phadke, Khan, and Ranade 2011.
30. Tylor 2014.
31. Macdowell 1999.
32. Holland, Clark, Katz, and Peace 2007.
33. West and Zimmerman 1987.
34. Rotman and Nassaney 1997.
35. Messner 1993.

References

Allen, Katherine. 2013. "Beyond the Tent: Why Refugee Camps Need Architects." October 14. www.archdaily.com/435492/beyond-the-tent-why-refugee-camps-need-architects-now-more-than-ever.

Babos, Annamaria. 2016. "Why Isn't the Profession Seeing Refugee Camps as Architectural Projects?" October 11. http://architectureforrefugees.com/why-isnt-the-profession-seeing-refugee-camps-as-architectural-projects/.

Barnabé, Mònica. 2013. "In Afghanistan, Streets Are Spaces for Men and Only for Men." www.publicspace.org/en/post/in-afghanistan-streets-are-spaces-for-men-and-only-for-men.

Baweja, Harinder. 1992. "The Horror of Home." July 31. http://indiatoday.intoday.in/story/most-afghans-living-in-delhi-detest-leaving-indias-democratic-and-open-society/1/307382.html.

Carabelli, Gulia, 2009. "Cities: Urban Built Environments: Afghanistan." In *Encyclopaedia of Women & Islamic Cultures*, edited by Suad Joseph, 152. Davis: University of California Press.

Desai, Madavi. 2007. *Gender and the Built Environment in India*. Delhi: Zubaan.

Edwards, David Busby. 1986. "Marginality and Migration: Cultural Dimensions of the Afghan Refugee Problem." *International Migration Review* (July): 313–325.

Gardner, Carol Brooks. 1990. "Safe Conduct: Women Crime and Self in Public Places." *Social Problems* 37(3): 311–328.

Ghufran, Nasreen. 2008 "Afghans in Pakistan: A 'Protracted Refugee Situation.'" *Policy Perspectives* (April): 117–129.

Grenfell, Laura. 2004. "The Participation of Afghan Women in the Reconstruction Process." *Human Rights Brief* 12(1): 22–25.

Holland, Caroline, Andrew Clark, Jeanne Katz, and Sheila Peace. 2007. *Social Interactions in Urban Public Places*. London: Policy Press.

Jacobs, Karrie. 2017. "Rethinking the Refugee Camp." January 25. www.architectmagazine.com/design/rethinking-the-refugee-camp_o.

Macdowell, Linda. 1999. *Gender, Identity and Place: Understanding Feminist Geographies*. Minneapolis: University of Minnesota Press.

McMillin, Divya C. 2006. "Outsourcing Identities: Call Centres and Cultural Transformation in India." *Economic and Political Weekly* 41(3): 235–241.

Messner, Michael A. 1993 "'Changing Men' and Feminist Politics in the United States." *Theory and Society* 22(5): 723–737.

Niranjana, Seemanthini. 2001. *Gender and Space: Femininity, Sexualization and the Female Body*. New Delhi: Sage.

Noor, Sanam. 2006. "Afghan Refugees After 9/11." *Pakistan Horizon* 59(1): 59–78.

Paul, Tanushree. 2011. "Public Spaces and Everyday Lives: Gendered Encounters in the metro City of Kolkata." In *Doing Gender Doing Geography: Emerging Research in India*, edited by Saraswati Raju and Lahiri-Dutt Kuntala, 248–267. New Delhi: Routledge.

Phadke, Shilpa, Sameera Khan, and Shilpa Ranade. 2011. *Why Loiter? Women and Risk on Mumbai Streets*. New Delhi: Penguin Books.

Reeves, Scott, Mathieu Albert, Ayelet Kuper, and Brian David Hodges. 2008. "Why Use Theories in Qualitative Research." *British Medical Journal* 337(7670): 631–634.

Rotman, Deborah L., and Michael S. Nassaney. 1997. "Class, Gender, and the Built Environment: Deriving Social Relations From Cultural Landscapes in Southwest Michigan." *Historical Archaeology* 31(2): 42–62.

Singh, Preeti, and Anu Pandey. 2005. "Women in Call Centres." *Economic and Political Weekly* 40(7): 684–688.

Slater, Julia. 2014. *Urban Systems of the Refugee Camp*. Architecture Thesis Prep. Paper, no. 272. http://surface.syr.edu/architecture_tpreps/272.

Stillwagon, Ryan. 2011. "The Afghan Diaspora in New Delhi." June 1. www.gatewayhouse.in/afghan-diaspora-delhi/.

Soja, Edward. 1989. *Postmodern Geographies: The Reassertion of Space in Critical Social Theory*. London: Verso.

Tara, Shelly. 2011. "Private Space in Public Transport: Locating Gender in the Delhi Metro." *Economic and Political Weekly* 46(51): 71–74.

Tober, Diane. 2007. "Introduction: Afghan Refugees and Returnees." *Iranian Studies* 40(2): 133–135.

Twigger-Ross, Clare L., and L. David Uzzell. 1996. "Place and Identity Processes." *Journal of Environmental Psychology* 16(3): 205–220.

Tylor, Alan. 2014. "The Modern Face of Kabul." March 31. www.theatlantic.com/photo/2014/03/the-modern-face-of-kabul/100707/.

UNHCR. 2016. "India: Fact Sheet." www.unhcr.org/protection/operations/50001ec69/india-fact-sheet.html.

West, Candace, and Don H. Zimmerman. 1987. "Doing Gender." *Gender & Society* 1(2): 125–151.

Index

Note: Italicized page numbers indicate a figure on the corresponding page. Page numbers in bold indicate a table on the corresponding page.

24/7: Late Capitalism and the Ends of Sleep (Crary) 133

abject 238, 240, 244, 245, 246, 247, 248
Academy of Social Sciences, German Democratic Republic 189
Adjdari, Abbas 257
aesthetic discernment in Khrushchev era 171–173
Afghan Sikh refugees in India: built environment 383–385; femininities and masculinities 385–387; introduction to 380; overview of 380–381; refugee women 381–382
African American women in the workplace 94
Agrest, Diana 107
Ahmet Hamdi Akseki Mosque 279–283, *280, 281, 283*
AKP (Turkey), *see* Justice and Development Party, Turkey
Alberti, Leon Battista 107
Alexander, Christopher 121
alienation 241, 242
All Union Congress, Soviet Union 188
Amandahaus, Rostock 208–211, 214–215
amateur needlework in Khrushchev era 173–174, *174*
Anglophonic missionary schools for girls in Iran 254
Anti-Dühring (Engels, Marx) 290
anti-home modernity 44
Arab-Israeli War (1967) 272
ARAVA system 50
Architect and his Office, The report 135
architectural modernity 3, 111
Architecture, Ethics and Globalization (Owen) 141
Aries, Phillippe 70
Aristotle 144
Art Deco in India 360–361, *361*
Association 9 (*Yhdistys 9*) 57
Association of Iranian Architect-Diplom (AIAD) 253
Atatürk, Mustafa Kemal 255
Athens Charter 120, 127
Attfield, Judy 165
Aufbau journal, Austria 15, 18–19
automobile industry in the United States 100
Autonomous Women's Association, Germany 208

avant-garde in architecture 3, 4
avant-garde Russian artists 158

bacteriological city 45
baroque buildings in Rostock 207
Bassenatratsch (sink gossip) 15
bathroom design in the US 71–72
Baudelaire, Charles 5
Beginenhof, the 211–214
Benjamin, Walter 5, 153, 156
Berlin Wall 208
Berman, Marshall 3, 5, 44
big business and globalization 140–141
Bildt, Carl 32
binary spatial theory 29–30
Birth of Biopolitics, The (Foucault) 133
Blaisse, Petra 142
Blue Monday 71
body, the: in *Fresh Air* (film) 238–249, *240, 241, 242, 243, 244, 245, 247, 248*
Bolshevik Revolution 154
Boorstin, Daniel 101
boundaries: in *Fresh Air* 238–249, *240, 241, 242, 243, 244, 245, 247, 248*; of kin-related elder care in Russia 229–233, *231*
bourgeois domesticity in the Soviet Union 154, 166
Boyer, Kate 93
Braunfels, Wolfgang 165
Braverman, Harry 88
Breuer, Marcel 264
Brodskii, Boris 166
Buchli, Victor 167–169
building boom and gender in East Germany 205–208
Building Information File, Finland 48
built environment in India 1, 383–385, 387–388
bungalow modernity in Gujarat, India: Art Deco influence 360–361, *361*; in cantonments 356–357; feminism and 352; introduction to 350–352, *351*; as middle-class home 358–359; modernist houses 361–362, *363*; nationalist ideology 359–360; as new concept 356; pre-colonial dwellings 354–355,

391

Index

355; summary of 363–364; as villa 357–358; women and domestic realm 354; women and society in 353

canned foods in US households 72
cantonment modernity in Gujarat, India 356–357
capitalism: feminism and 134; housing industry and 67, 100, 108–109; Iranian modernization process 260, 266; suburban communities 106
Cardiff Bay Opera House 136
caregiver life in Russia 227–229
cars, women as consumers in US 102–106, *103*, *105*
central business district (CBD) 88
centralized heating in the US 72
chadour covering, Iran 256
Cheap Road in Shanghai *see* migrant women on the Cheap Road in Shanghai
Chew, Matthew 322
Chicago School 88
childcare concerns in Austria 13, 15; in China 310, 341; in India 370, 375; in Russia 225; in Sweden 28–9; in the US 76
children's play in suburban homes 53
China *see* gendered spatial features in Chinese workplace; gender role in Chinese migrant households; migrant women on the Cheap Road in Shanghai
China Labor Watch 347
China Labour Bulletin 345
city of short distances 126
Civil Rights Movement in the US 94
cleaning chores by housewives 76–77, *105*
clerical work *see* office/working women
Clerkenwell Penthouse *132*, *136*, 137–140, *138–139*
Cohen, William A. 246
cohousing 59
cold-hearted mothers (*Rabenmütter*) 206
cold-modern caregiving model 222
Cold War era 153–154, 158, 176, 260, 272–273
Colomina, Beatriz 4
color symbolism in film 239
communicative aspects of care work 231
communist comfort 153–154
Communist Manifesto 172
Communist Party of Germany (KDP) 188
Comprehensive Plan for Tehran 263–264
conflicts of kin-related elder care in Russia 229–233, *231*
Confucian ideology 307
constructivism 3, 161
consumerism 106
counter-home spaces 229–233, *231*
couple migration in China 309
Crary, Jonathan 133, 142
creation narratives 107
creative class 134, 135–137, *136*
crisis-focused organizations 213
Cullen, Gorden 121
cultural discernment in Khrushchev era 171–173

cultural dynamics of workplaces 90
cultural relativism 33
curative dwelling, Finland 45

Dalokay, Vedat 271
Da Roit, Barbara 233
Davis, Michael 140
de Beauvoir, Simone 134
de Certeau, Michel 176
Decorative Art of Today, The (Le Corbusier) 137
Dekorativnoe iskusstvo SSSR (Decorative Art of the USSR) journal 166, 173
Democrat Party in Turkey 271
demographic characteristics of new construction in the German Democratic Republic 194–195
Deng Xiaoping 320
Dennis, Richard 87
Department for Cultural Affairs, Vienna 19
Derrida, Jacques 5
desire 239, 240, 241, 246, desiring subject 239, 246, 248, desiring identity 247, desiring subjectivity 248
de-Stalinization 159
Deutsche, Rosalyn 4
dichotomous citizenship 53
Di Giorgio, Francesco 107
DIN codes, Germany 198
Doctor Zhivago (Pasternak) 156
domestic culture in Iran 254–257, *256*
domesticity in Khrushchev era 156–159, *157*
domestic violence 44, 217
Domosh, Mona 87
domovodstvo (domestic science) 162
dormitory-factory regime in China 347
dormitory towns in Finland 55
Dostrovsky, Nadine 109
Dresden Frauenkirche 206
Dunham, Vera 158
Dunham-Jones, Ellen 141

earth mother 134
Eastern Bloc state socialism 186
East Germany (GDR) *see* feminist restorations in East Germany; women as "socialist" dwellers in GDR
East India Company 350
economic goods 76
economic rationalism 133–134
economic stratification 100
educational training centers in East Germany 214
Edwards, Beth Yarnelle *112*
Ekbatan housing project, Tehran 264–265, *265*
elder care *see* kin-related elder care in Russia
electrification in US households 71
emotional aspects of care work 231
emotionalization of housework 81
Engels, Friedrich 4
English-language texts 3
Enquiry by Design 124
environmentalism in Turkey 288–291
environmental planning in Finland 59

392

Equality Act in the UK (2010) 122
Era of Baroque and Present Time in Hetzendorf, The (Harnisch) *20*, 22
Erdemli, Kadriye 274
Ergene River pollution 288, 291, 293, 295–296
Eurocentric liberalism 352
European Union 213, 293
everyday routines in urbanism 123

Fadillioglu, Zeynep 275
familial co-residence 222–226, **223**, **224**
family-free labor 133
family-friendly planning ideology 23, 28
farm women in Turkey 292
Federal Republic of Germany (FRG) 188
Felski, Rita 2, 5, 44, 86
female abuse in film 246–247
female-led prayer in Turkey 273–274
femina domestica 134
Feminine Mystique, The (Friedan) 106
femininity concerns 338, 385–388
feminism: bungalow modernity in India 352; cultural conceptions of 44; geo-historical context of 370; introduction to 2, 5; neoliberal workplace 132, 133–134; Second Wave feminism 119–121; Swedish research on 31
Feminism and Geography (Rose) 2
feminist restorations in East Germany: Amandahaus 208–211, 214–215; the Beginenhof 211–214; building boom 205–208; introduction to 202–205, *203–204*; summary of 214–215
fenjia practice in China 309
fetishization 290
Filarete 107
filth 245, 246, 247
Findhorn in Scotland 59
Finland *see* modern home environment in Finland
Finnish Association of Architects 48
Finnish Association of Women Architects 58
floating population in China 305
Ford, Henry 92, 101, 104–105
Fortune magazine 91
Foucault, Michel 133
Fourier, Charles 58
Foxconn Technology Group 338–339, 341–347, *342*, *343*
Frampton, Kenneth 48
Francophonic missionary schools for girls in Iran 254
Fraser, Nancy 134
Fresh Air (film) 238–249, *240*, *241*, *242*, *243*, *244*, *245*, *247*, *248*
Friedan, Betty 82, 106
Friedman, Alice T. 4
functionalism 45, 47–50, *48*, *50*, 69–70

Gandhi, Mahatma 353
Garden City 120
Gartman, David 3
Geddes, Patrick 58

Gehry, Frank 136
Gemütlichkeit 155
gender and social housing in Vienna: interwar era 12–14; introduction to 2, 3, 11–12; post–World War II policies 14–22, *16–17*, *18*, *20–21*; summary of 22–23
gender-based violence 206, 211, 213–214
gendered household expectations in Mumbai, India *see* outsourced call centers in India
gendered spatial features in Chinese workplace: Foxconn Technology Group 338–339, 341–347, *342*, *343*; introduction to 338–339; work unit 338, 345–347; work unit as urban form 339–341, *340*, *341*
gendered suburban criticism 55–58, *56*
gendered urban design: introduction to 119; mainstreaming 121–123; neoliberalism in UK 123–127, *124*, *125*; Second Wave feminism 119–121; summary of 127; *see also* urbanization/urban planning
gender equality in Sweden: intersectionality as reality 35–36; introduction to 26–27; male view of women's place 27–32, *29*; Million Program 9, 26, 27–28, *28*, 32–37; racialization and neoliberalization 32–33, 36; socio-spatial stigmatization 33–35, *34*; summary of 36–37
gender globalization in India *see* Afghan Sikh refugees
gender identities 32
gender-neutral class inequality 4
gender politics in Islam 272–274, 284–285
gender relations of rural modernity in Turkey: contradictions of 290–292; historical tour of 292–296, *294*, *295*; introduction to 288–290, *289*; summary of 297–298; women's activism in Turkey 296–297
gender role in Chinese migrant households: household strategy 305–307; gender division of labor 307–309; intergenerational division of labor 309–310, *310*; introduction to 305; left-behind wives 307–309, *308*, 314–315; left-behind children 309; summary of 314–315; transactional marriages 310–314, *312*, *313*, *314*
gender-segregated residential patterns in Sweden 36
gender segregation 90, 217, 273, 359, 362–363, 385
gender-specific apartments in the German Democratic Republic 195, *196*
General Motors 101–102, *103*, 104–105
generational co-residence in Russia 226–227
gentrification in Sweden 35–36
geographic mobility in Russia 217
geo-historical context of feminism 370
Gerchuk, Iurii 161
German Democratic Republic (GDR) *see* feminist restorations in East Germany; women as "socialist" dwellers in GDR
Gharb-zadegi (West-intoxication) 266
Giles, Judy 43
Glidden, Carlos 90

393

Index

globalization: big business and 140–141; femininity and 329; introduction to 303; laissez-faire globalization 132; *see also* Afghan Sikh refugees
Goethe, Johann Wolfgang von 5
Golzar, Rahman 264
Gorbachev, Mikhail 188
Gothic buildings in Rostock 207
Gray, Francine du Plessix 154–156, 159, 166
Great Transmigration in Khrushchev era 159–161, *160*
green widow 60–61
Gregson, Nicky 165
Grihvidhan (Mehta) 359
Grosz, Elizabeth 238, 240, 245
Gruen, Victor 263
Grundmann, Siegried 189
Gujarat, India *see* bungalow modernity in Gujarat, India
Gullestad, Marianne 165
Guo, Terry 341, 343–344
Gurske, Kirsten 192

Hadid, Zaha 131–144, *132*, *136*, *138–139*; *see also* neoliberal workplace
handicraft in Khrushchev era 173–174, *174*
Happy Housewarming 162
Harnisch, Walter *20*, 22
Harris, Richard 109
Harvey, David 4, 87
Hausgemeinschaft (households in same building) 187
hayat (yard) in Iran 262
Hayden, Dolores 104, 106
Heidegger, Martin 153
Helsingin Sanomat newspaper 55
Hochschild, Arlie Russell 221–222
Holub, Dagmar 139
Home Insurance Building, Chicago 89
"home–is–my–castle" mentality 166
homelessness in Khrushchev era 159
homemakers in Khrushchev era 163–164
homemaking and elder care in Russia 227–229
home mothers (*kotiäiti*) in Finland 57
homo oeconomicus 67, 132, 133–134, 143
household germ 76–77
housewife-ization phenomenon in Iran 255
housewives: in Finland 55–57; introduction to 17–18; post–World War I *73–74*, 73–80, *78–79*
housing: bathroom design 71–72; curative dwelling 45; discrimination concerns 36; industrial revolution in the home 69–82, *74–75*, *78–79*; privatization of public life in designs 108; shortages in 33; standardization of 11; *see also* gender and social housing in Vienna; housing estates; modern home environment in Finland; women as housing consumers in US
housing estates: in the German Democratic Republic 196–197; in Hungary 238, 240, 242
Hovanesian, Vartan 257
Howard, Ebenezer 120

hukou system in China 305–306, 321
Human Settlement Network in Finland 59
hygienic dwellings 45–47
hypergamy in China 311

ideal modernism in Iran 257–260, *258*, *259*
identity crisis in elderly 227
ideology of social equality 189–192, *191*, *193–194*
Ikhwanul Musliminn, Turkey, *see* Muslim Brotherhood, Turkey
illustrations of post-war women's chores *73–74*, 73–76
Image of the Architect, The (Saint) 135
independent woman 133
India *see* Afghan Sikh refugees; bungalow modernity in Gujarat, India
Indian Cement Company 359
indoor plumbing in the US 72
industrial, standardized construction in the Soviet Union 164–165
industrial-era clerical workers in the US 94
industrialization: China 314; Finland 2; introduction to 2; in Khrushchev era 161, 171; Marxism and 188; Turkey 292, 297
industrial revolution in the home 69–82, *74–75*, *78–79*
inside and outside spheres 307
interface 238, 240
intergenerational division of labor in China 309–310, *310*
intergenerational mobility in Russia 217
intergenerational residential attachment in Russia 225
interior splendor *111*, 111–114, *112*
intermediary level 58–59
international architectural modernism 45
internationalization in Iran 264
International Monetary Fund (IMF) 293
International Style 121
interrelationships of gender 60–61
intersectionality as reality 35–36
Iran *see* middle-class housing in Iran
Iranian Revolution (1978–9) 253, 266
Irish Men's Sheds Association (IMSA) 122
Islamic gender politics 272–274
isomorphism 238, 244, 246, 248
IT (information technology) sector in India 367, 370–371
Izvestiia newspaper 162

jacks-of-all-trades 82
Jacka, Tamara 307
Jacobs, Jane 121
James, Jason 206
jane-of-all-trades 82
Jeffries, Stuart 142
Jena-Lobeda case study 192, 194
Journal of Bank-e-Sakhtemani 260
Justice and Development Party (AKP), Turkey 270, 273, 284, 290

394

Kaika, Maria 44, 290
KALAD concrete system 258–259, *259*
Kantor, Karl 164
Karelian refugees in Finland 41
Kennedy, Margaret 58
Kennedy Doctrine 255, 260
Keynes, John Maynard 154
Keynesian Social Democratic regime 32
khoziaika (housekeeper) 156
khrushchevki architecture in Russia 161
kibbutzim in Israel 59
Kim Swoo Geun 264
kin-related elder care in Russia: boundaries and conflicts of 229–233, *231*; familial co-residence 222–226, **223**, **224**; generational co-residence 226–227; homemaking and 227–229; introduction to 217–218; localization of 221–222; research data/methodology 218, *219–221*; summary of 234
kitchen standards in Finland 49
Klein, Viola 57
Kocatepe Mosque project 271
Kocsis, Ágnes 238–249, *240, 241, 242, 243, 244, 245, 247, 248*
kommunalka (shared apartment) 233
Komsomol (Party Youth League) 167
Koolhaas, Rem 132, 142
Kröpeliner-Tor-Vorstadt case study *see* feminist restorations in East Germany
Kristeva, Julia 240
Kuy-e Farah housing development *261*, 261–263

Labor and Monopoly Capital (Braverman) 88
labor divisions in China 307–310, *308, 310*
labor force participation by women in the US 80, 88
Ladies' Home Journal 71, 72
laissez-faire globalization 132
Land Acquisition Act in Finland (1945) 47
Land Use and Building Act in Finland 59
Last Train Home (film) 305
Le Corbusier 3, 4, 101, 119, 137, 264, 362
Le Doeff, Michèle 4
Lefebvre, Henri 176
Leffingwell, William H. 92
left-behind children in China 309–310
left-behind elders in China 310
left-behind wives in China 307–309, *308*, 314–315
Leftist Party in Iran 266
leitmotif of housing planning 51
Lenin, Vladimir 166
Levinson, Nancy 135
Levittowns 108
LGBTQ sexual identities 32, 35
liberal values 67
lifestyle quality 114
Lindroos, Katja 51
living quarters (*shenhuo qu*) in China 339
Loos, Adolf 4, 171
Low, Setha 108

low-income women 120
Lynch, Kevin 121

macrospaces 249
Mahmood, Saba 273
mainstreaming in gendered urban design 121–123
Male Figure (Schmidt) *21*, 22
male view of women's place 27–32
Mannes-Abbott, Guy 141
Mao's "half the sky" intervention 315
Marefat, Mina 260
market economy 5, 100
marketing household appliances in the US 104, *105*
marketization in China 346
market-oriented urban development 58
marriage market in China 315
Marx, Karl 4, 159
Marxism-Leninism 188
Marxist modernism 156, 164
Marzahn case study 194–195
masculinity concerns 31, 44, 385–387
Massey, Doreen 4
mass-line doctrine 343
materialist ambition 144
materiality and elder care in Russia 227–229
materiality of modern in Shanghai 323–325
May, Ernest 5
McCracken, Grant 156, 175
media stigmatization in Sweden 34–35
Mehta, Virendraray C. 359
memory objects 172
meritocracy 102
metro 238, 243, 244, 384–385
Metropolitan Life building *89*, 89–90
microspaces 249
middle-class bungalow modernity in India 358–359
middle-class housing in Iran: domestic culture and 254–257, *256*; ideal and popular modernism 257–260, *258, 259*; introduction to 2, 3, 253–254; mass housing and modern taste 260–263, *261*; modernity and 254; summary of 266; as transnational model 263–265, *265*
middle-class nonrural American families 81
middle-class women in the US 70–71, 87, 93–94, 101
migrant women on the Cheap Road in Shanghai: introduction to 320–321; materiality of modern 323–325; spatiality of modern 331–334; study methodology 322–323; summary of 333–334; unfashionability of 321–322; visualization of modern 325–331, *326, 327, 328, 329, 330*
migration policy in Sweden 33
Mill, John Stuart 131
Miller, Daniel 165
Million Program in Sweden 9, 26, 27–28, *28*, 32–37, *34*
Mills, Charles Wright 92
Ministry of Housing and Urban-Rural Development (MOHURD) in China 321

Index

misogynistic modernism 153
mixed-use neighborhoods 122
modern, defined 43–45
modern home environment in Finland: gendered suburban criticism 55–58, *56*; interrelationships of gender 60–61; introduction to 41–43, *42*; New Everyday Life group 58–59, *60*; overview of 43–45; pleasure of *53*, 53–54; practical hygienic dwellings 45–47; rural functionalism 47–50, *48, 50*; suburban environments 50–53, *51, 52*
modernism *vs.* traditional values 251
modernist houses in Gujarat, India 361–362, *363*
modernist ideology 255
modernist minimalism 175
modernity: anti-home modernity 44; architectural modernity 3; as aspiration 101–102; cantonment modernity in Gujarat, India 356–357; cities and working women 86–90, **88**, *89*; defined 1–2, 41–43; gender and neoliberalism 143–145; gender and space 93–95; interior splendor *111*, 111–114, *112*; introduction to 1; Iran and 254; middle-class bungalow modernity in India 358–359; middle-class housing in Iran 254; neoliberal workplace 143–145; office/working women 86–90, **88**, *89*; Second Wave feminism 119–121; social welfare modernity 9; spatial expression of 2–4; through gender lens 4–5; wide view of 5–7; *see also* bungalow modernity in Gujarat, India; gender relations of rural modernity in Turkey; spatial modernity
modernization 1–2, 41–43
Modern Movement in India 350, 361–362
modern welfare state 26–27
monostructures 198
Mosaddegh, Mohammad 254
mosque architecture in Turkey: gender politics in Islam 272–274; gender politics of mosques 284–285; introduction to 270–271; pious bourgeoisie and 274–278, *275, 276*; in Republican Turkey 271, *272*; state mosque design 279–283, *277, 280, 281, 283*
motherhood responsibilities in Germany 206
Muschamp, Herbert 136
Muslim Brotherhood 273
Myrdal, Alva 57

Narmak, project in Iran 257–259, *258, 259*
national advertising campaigns in the US 81
Nationale Front 187
National New-Type Urbanization Plan (2014–2020) 321
National Socialism 14–15
National Socialist German Workers' Party (NSDAP) 15
nation-states 2, 3, 292
Nazi rule 22
Nehru, Jawaharlal 361
neo-Gothic buildings in Rostock 207
neoliberalism in UK gendered urban design 123–127, *124, 125*

neoliberalization 32–33, 36
neoliberal values 67
neoliberal workplace: Clerkenwell Penthouse *132, 136*, 137–140, *138–139*; creative class 134, 135–137, *136*; feminism and 132, 133–134; globalization and big business 140–141; *homo oeconomicus* 132, 133–134, 143; India 370; modernity and gender 143–145; in 1970s 131–133, *132*; wellbeing and the self 141–143
neo-Nazi activity 208–209
neo-Ottoman mosque form 271, 274, 284–285
New Everyday Life 58–59, *60*, 122
new ideologies 73
Newman, Janet 134
new urban woman in the US 95
Nicomachean Ethics, The (Aristotle) 144
nomadic mobility in the Soviet Union 159
non-European immigrants in Sweden 36
nongmingong, defined 321
non-governmental organizations (NGOs) 59, 224, 345, 382
nonrural American families 81
Novyi mir journal 166
nuclear family 26, 52, 189
nüshen (goddess) 331

office/working women: introduction to 86; labor force participation by women 80; modernity, gender and space 93–95; modernity and cities 86–90, **88**, *89*; summary of 95–96; technology and 90–93, *92*; *see also* outsourced call centers in India
One Day in the Life of Ivan Denisovich (Solzhenitsyn) 167
On Liberty (Mill) 131
open communal spaces in Germany 212
Open Door Policy in China 320
open kitchens in Finland 55
open spaces in India 355
O'Shea, Alan 45
Ottoman mosques *see* mosque architecture in Turkey
outsourced call centers in India: adaptation networks 374–376; continued household responsibility 373–374; crisis as justification 372–373; emerging themes 371–372; introduction to 367; overview of 367–370, *368, 369*; summary of 376; theoretical framework 370–371
Owen, Graham 141
Owen, Robert 58

Pahlavi, Mohammad Reza 251, 253, 254
Palme, Olof 32
Pang Yuan 324
Pasternak, Boris 156
patriarchal urban planning 27–32, *29*
patriarchy in China 307–309, *308*
patrilocal exogamy tradition in China 312
Peiss, Kathy 95
"People's Home" in Finland 9, 42
People's Houses in Turkey 293

396

People's Republic of China (PRC) 320–321
performativity of femininity 134
perheenäiti (family mother) 57
perheenemäntä (family household manager) 57
Pfau-Effinger, Birgit 12
physical exhaustion of caregivers 232
pious bourgeoisie in Turkey 274–278, *275, 276*
Platte, defined 186, 188
Plattenbau, defined 202, *204*, 204–205, 207–209, 215
Playboy magazine 137
playgrounds in the German Democratic Republic 197
Politburo of the Central Committee of the SED in the German Democratic Republic 192
popular modernism in Iran 257–260, *258, 259*
Post, Emily 76
post-communist *see* post-socialist
post-socialist 151, 205, 222, 238–239, 240, 248
post–World War I *73–74*, 73–80, *78–79*, 88
post–World War II era: gender and social housing in Vienna 14–22, *16–17, 18, 20–21*; housing in Finland 41–43; introduction to 9, 11–12; Soviet Union expansion 151; suburban communities 108; urban planning in Sweden 26, 32, 37
power 239, 243, 244
practical dwellings 45–47
practicality and elder care in Russia 227–229
pre-colonial dwellings in India 354–355, *355*
pre-war Functionalist ideal 53
Pringle, Rosemary 90
prisoner-of-war (POW) camps 19
privacy concerns of caregivers 233
privatization of public life 101, 107–108
professional femininity 134
psychological burnout of caregivers 232
public space 5, 30, 43, 59, 87-88, 101, 114, 121–122, 244, 246, 256–257, 270, 274, 303, 362, 369, 380–387 *see also* privatization of public life
public toilet in film 244–245

qipao (fashionable) 322
Qipulu Clothing Wholesale Market 325, 331–332

racialization in Sweden 32–33, 36; in the US 93
Rapoport, Amos 352
Reagan, Ronald 131, 133
Realsozialismus, defined 207
reconstruction process 19
Red Vienna policies 12–13
refugee women in India 381–382
Reichert, Dagmar 30
Remington typewriter advertising 91
remittances 309, 315
Rendell, Jane 5
renoviction 35
reproductive arrangement 12
residential segregation 26, 32, 156
Rose, Gillian 2, 4, 30
Rostock Women's Initiatives 211

Royal Institute of British Architects (RIBA) 135
Ruble, Blair 165
rural English families 70
rural functionalism 47–50, *48, 50*
rural-urban migration in China 306
Russia *see* kin-related elder care in Russia
Russian avant-garde artists 158
Russian peasant society 151
Russian Revolution 120, 153

Sabarmati Ashram in Ahmedabad 353
Saint, Andrew 135
Sakirin Mosque, Turkey 274–278, *275, 276, 277*, 284
Sant'Elia, Antonio 3
Schmidt, Rudolf *21*, 22
Schumacher, Patrik 135
Scientific Office Management 92
Second Sex, The (de Beauvoir) 134
Second Wave feminism 119–121
segregation: gender segregation 90, 217, 273, 359, 362–363, 385; residential segregation 26, 32, 156; social segregation 27, 33–34, 306
self-actualization 159
self-built housing in Finland 59
self-fulfillment narratives 209
sensuality and elder care in Russia 227–229
separatism of marginalized groups 107
settler's movement in Austria 13
sex ratio in China 312
sexual identities 32
sexual self-determination 3
sexuality 238, 239, 240, 245, 246, 247
Sholes, Christopher Latham 90
Shvartberg, Manuel 135
signature landmarks 89
simulacrum in film 241–242
single-family homes in the US 106
"single-kitchen building" project in Vienna 13
skyscrapers 88–89, 95
Sloan, Alfred P., Jr. 102
social characteristics of new construction in the German Democratic Republic 194–195
Social Democratic Workers' Party (SDAP), Austria 12
social equality ideology 189–192, *191, 193–194*
social function of family 69
socialism 151, 153, 187, 206
social isolation in caregiving 232
socialist modernism in Khrushchev era: cultural and aesthetic discernment 171–173; domesticity in 156–159, *157*; Great Transmigration 159–161, *160*; handicraft 173–174, *174*; industrial, standardized construction 164–165; introduction to 153–156, *155*; practices of *uiut* 175–176; public meaning to apartments 161–164; summary of 176–177; *uiutno* 162, 163–165, 166–170, *168, 169, 170, 171*
Socialist Unity Party (SED), German Democratic Republic 187, 190
social reforms in Iran 255

Index

social reproduction 58, 256, 367, 370–371
social revolution 2
social segregation 27, 33–34, 306
social welfare modernity 9
socioeconomic status in the US 80
socio-spatial stigmatization 33–35, *34*
socio-spatial structures 44–45, 87, 198
Soja, Edward 4
Solzhenitsyn, Alexander 167
Soviet Union 2, 3, 41, 151; *see also* socialist modernism in Khrushchev era
sozialistische Lebensweise 187
Spain, Daphne 87, 107
spatial modernity: binary spatial theory 29–30; boundaries in *Fresh Air* 238–249, *240, 241, 242, 243, 244, 245, 247, 248*; built environment in India 383–385, 387–388; differentiation in 49; expression of 2–4; in Iran 257–258; migrant women in Shanghai 331–334; in Turkey 291, 293; in the US 87–88, 95, 111; women and 1, 95
Spencer, Douglas 137
split-household arrangements in China 308–309, 315
spouse's attributes (*tiaojian*) 311
Stalin, Joseph 156–160
state mosque design in Turkey 279–283, *277, 280, 281, 283*
state-sponsored clubs in the German Democratic Republic 197
Stratigakos, Despina 143
Strom, Sharon Hartman 94
subjectivity in *Fresh Air* (film) 238–249, *240, 241, 242, 243, 244, 245, 247, 248*
suburban environments: in Finland 50–53, *51, 52*; introduction to 27; women as housing consumers 108–109, *110*
supportive infrastructure of everyday life 59
survivors of violence 213
suzhi (quality) 321
Sweden *see* gender equality in Sweden
Swedish *Folkhem* 26–27
Swyngedouw, Erik 290

Tapiola Garden City 53
Taste War in the Soviet Union 159
Technical Aesthetics discipline 173
technical norms in Germany (FRG and GDR) 198, **199**
technology: IT (information technology) sector in India 367, 370–371; office/working women and 90–93, *92*; revolution in the home 69; telecommunications technologies 346; women as "socialist" dwellers in the GDR 188
Tekelioglu, Nehat 271
Tekhnicheskaia estetika (Technical Aesthetics) journal 160
telecommunications technologies 346
Ten Books on Architecture (Vitruvius) 107
Thatcher, Margaret 131–133, 141–142, 143

Theory of Shopping, A (Miller) 321
Third Way politics 123, 126
Thrace Region, Turkey 288, *289*
Tinggaarden, Denmark 59
Toll Brothers houses *110, 111*
top-down planning 61, 186
topographic town planning 51
Torshilova, Elena 175
traditional values 251
traffic separation principle 27
transactional marriages 310–314, *312, 313, 314*
Treaty of Amsterdam (1997) 121–122
Trud newspaper 162
Turkey *see* gender relations of rural modernity in Turkey; mosque architecture in Turkey
Turner, John 58
Turner, Magnusson 36

uiutno (cozy) 162, 163–165, 166–170, *168, 169, 170, 171,* 175–176
Unabhänginger Frauenverband (UFV) 208
UN-Habitat's New Urban Agenda 119
uncanny 238, 240
unique selling point (USP) 134
Unité d'Habitation (Le Corbusier) 264
United Kingdom (UK), gendered urban design 123–127, *124, 125*
United Nations High Commission for Refugees (UNHCR) 381
Upton, Northamptonshire *124,* 124–125, *125*
urbanization/urban planning: China 314; community resources and 106; Finland 43, 57; India 350; Iran 266; Russia 217; Sweden 26; Turkey 290, 292, 297; United Kingdom 123–127, *124, 125*; United States 87, 90; work unit as urban form in China 339–341, *340, 341*; *see also* gendered urban design
urban renaissance 123–124
US Department of Agriculture 77
US population demographics 87
utopian ideologues 159

Varga-Harris, Christine 166
Vers une architecture/Towards a New Architecture (Le Corbusier) 101
veterans' houses in Finland 47–50, *48, 50*
Vienna *see* gender and social housing in Vienna
Vienna Municipal Building Authority 15
Vienna's Association of Artists 19
village cooperative (*Köy-Koop*) 293–294, *294*
Village Cooperatives Union 294
Village Institutes 293
villa modernity in Gujarat, India 357–358
visualization of modern in Shanghai 325–331, *326, 327, 328, 329, 330*
Voeikova, Irina 169
Volksgemeinschaft (national community) 22
Vriesendorp, Madelon 142

Index

Wajcman, Judy 90
walkable neighborhoods 122, 127
warm-modern caregiving model 222
wartime shortages in the US 72–73
WBS 70 model, German Democratic Republic 189, 191, *191*, 198
welfare system in Russia 225
wellbeing and the self 141–143
Western European urbanism 121
White Collar (Mills) 92
White Revolution in Iran (1962) 266
White Walls, Designer Dresses (Wigley) 137
Wigley, Mark 137
Wilson, Elizabeth 44, 95–96
Wohnungsbaukombinate (building cooperatives) 188
Woman and Child (Schmidt) *21*, 22
women: agency of 60–61, 86, 95–96; home as realm of 17–18; labor force participation by 80; male view of women's place 27–32, *29*; managers of the private sphere 30, 156, 234, 357; roles in preindustrial families 69–70; spatial interpretation of modernity 1; *see also* bungalow modernity in Gujarat, India; migrant women on the Cheap Road in Shanghai; office/working women; outsourced call centers in India
Women and the Making of the Modern House (Friedman) 4
women as housing consumers in US: car and house 102–106, *103*, *105*; consumerism and 106; industry trends 108–109, *110*; interior splendor *111*, 111–114, *112*; introduction to 100–101;

modernity as aspiration 101–102; privatization of public life 107–108
women as "socialist" dwellers in GDR: gender-specific apartments 195, *196*; ideology of social equality 189–192, *191*, *193–194*; introduction to 186–187; in large housing estates 196–197; nuclear family and 189; social/demographic characteristics of new construction 194–195; technology and social progress 188; women's assessments of 198–199, **199**
women readers in Khrushchev era 167
women's activism in Turkey 296–297
women's labor assumptions 28–29
women's movements 13, 383
Working the Spaces of Power: Activism, Neoliberalism and Gendered Labour (Newman) 134
working women in China 346–347
work-life balance 225
work unit in China 338, 339–341, *340*, *341*, 345–347
World War I 11, 73, *73–74*, 73–80, *78–79*
World War II 11; *see also* post–World War II era
Wright, Frank Lloyd 76, 362

Xiaoping Li 322
Xi Jinping 320–321
xin nüxing (new woman) 322

Zaha Hadid Design 136
zero-hours contracts in the UK 126
Zheng Tiantian 325
zoning in Khrushchev era 170

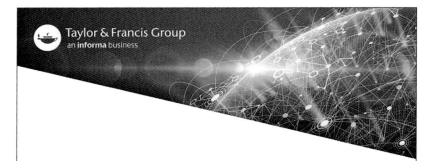